Global Law, Human Rights, and Intersections With Honor Killing

Somesh Dhamija
GLA University, India

Tarun Pratap Yadav
GLA University, India

Jae-Seung Lee
Miami University, USA

Harshita Singh
Amity University, India

Myunghoon Roh
Salve Regina University, USA

IGI Global
Scientific Publishing
Publishing Tomorrow's Research Today

Published in the United States of America by
IGI Global
701 E. Chocolate Avenue
Hershey PA, USA 17033
Tel: 717-533-8845
Fax: 717-533-8661
E-mail: cust@igi-global.com
Web site: https://www.igi-global.com

Copyright © 2025 by IGI Global. All rights reserved. No part of this publication may be reproduced, stored or distributed in any form or by any means, electronic or mechanical, including photocopying, without written permission from the publisher.
Product or company names used in this set are for identification purposes only. Inclusion of the names of the products or companies does not indicate a claim of ownership by IGI Global of the trademark or registered trademark.

Library of Congress Cataloging-in-Publication Data

CIP DATA PENDING

ISBN13: 9798369395967
EISBN13: 9798369395981

Vice President of Editorial: Melissa Wagner
Managing Editor of Acquisitions: Mikaela Felty
Managing Editor of Book Development: Jocelynn Hessler
Production Manager: Mike Brehm
Cover Design: Phillip Shickler

British Cataloguing in Publication Data
A Cataloguing in Publication record for this book is available from the British Library.

All work contributed to this book is new, previously-unpublished material.
The views expressed in this book are those of the authors, but not necessarily of the publisher.

For the late Shri Bhagirath Yadav
(30th June 1925 to 30th January 2002)

Editorial Advisory Board

Sinchul Back, *University of Scranton, USA*
Sung-hun Byun, *University of South Carolina, USA*
Kundaiah Jonnalagadda, *National Law University, India*
Jonathan Lee, *Penn State, USA*
Amar Pal Singh, *Ram Manohar Lohia National Law University, India*
Chandra Prakash Singh, *University of Lucknow, India*
Maheshwar Singh, *National Law University, India*
Sanjay Singh, *Ram Manohar Lohiya National Law University, India*
Yogesh Pratap Singh, *National Law University, India*
Manoj Kumar Sinha, *Dharmashastra National Law University, India*
Yogendra Srivastava, *Hidyatullah National Law University, India*
Anju Vali Tikoo, *University of Delhi, India*
Cassio Eduardo Zen, *Faculdade de Pinhais, Brazil*

Table of Contents

Preface xxi

Acknowledgment xxvi

Introduction xxviii

Chapter 1
Honor-Based Violence: A Brutal Abuse Against Civil Liberties 1
    Chunrye Kim, Saint Joseph's University, USA
    Siddhi Agrawal, GLA University, India

Chapter 2
Khap Panchayats and Their Misogynistic Approach: The Dishonor Behind
Honor Killing 17
    Heeuk D. Lee, Weber State University, USA
    Aranya Agrawal, GLA University, India

Chapter 3
Patriarchal Enmity in the Guise of Honor: An Indian Enigma 35
    Somesh Dhamija, GLA University, India
    Nikita Singh, GLA University, India

Chapter 4
Dishonor, Death, and Coercion in the Arena of Justice 53
    Myunghoon Roh, Salve Regina University, USA
    Muskan Gautam, GLA University, India

Chapter 5
Evolution of Moralistic and Ethical Dimensions of Honour Killing 73
    Megha Singh, GLA University, India
    Jae Seung Lee, College of Liberal Arts and Applied Science, Miami
        University, USA

Chapter 6
Effect of Culture-Based Violence on Human Psychology 93
    Aruna Dhamija, GLA University, India
    Mugdha Garg, GLA University, India

Chapter 7
Honor Killing: Defining the Undefined 113
   Tarun Pratap Yadav, GLA University, India
   Tanisha Jain, GLA University, India

Chapter 8
Honor Killing: An Infringement of Right to Life With Dignity 129
   Avinash Dadhich, Manipal Law School, India
   Aditya Raj, GLA University, India

Chapter 9
Honor Killing in the Indian Context: Law Ought to Be..................................... 147
   Harshita Singh, Amity University, Noida, India
   Tulsi Gupta, GLA University, India

Chapter 10
The Legal Framework for Murder on Provocation in the Egyptian Penal Code
as a Type of Honor Killing 165
   Ramy El-Kady, Police Academy, Egypt

Chapter 11
Honor's Cost: Lives Lost, Justice Frost 193
   Indra Kumar Singh, Amity University, Haryana, India
   Sudiksha Dhungel, GLA University, India

Chapter 12
Honor Crimes vs. Constitutional Rights: A Comparative Constitutional
Conundrum 213
   Govind Singh Rajpal, MIT-ADT University, India
   Aditya Lohani, GLA University, India

Chapter 13
Understanding the Impact of Immigration on Honor Killing: Instances From
Various Countries 231
   Myunghoon Roh, Salve Regina University, USA
   Prestha Chhaparia, GLA University, India

Chapter 14
Camouflaged Tenets of Peace Makers on Account of Honor Killing 247
   Avinash Dadhich, Manipal Law School, India
   Himanshi Dixit, GLA University, India

Chapter 15
Media Trial and Honor Killing: Media as an Agent in Shaping Perception
and Laws Around the World 277
    *Sudhir Kumar, School of Legal Studies, Babu Banarsi Das University,
      India*
    Barkha Agrawal, Amity University, Noida, India

Chapter 16
Honor Killing: A Social-Legal Position in India in the Last Decade 295
    Heeuk D. Lee, Weber State University, USA
    Chanchal Garg, GLA University, India
    Shweta Tyagi, Hemaadri International, India

Chapter 17
Consanguinity of Caste Prejudices With Honor Killing 313
    Govind Singh Rajpal, MIT-ADT University, India
    Raunak Upmanyu, GLA University, India

Chapter 18
Role of Class Conflict in Honor Killings 331
    Deepika Pandoi, GLA University, India
    Somendra Ashok Singh, GLA University, India

Chapter 19
Cognitive Strands of Honor Killing 351
    Praveen Kumar Mall, Teerthanker Mahaveer University, India
    Anusha Kulshrestha, GLA University, India

Chapter 20
Honor Killing in Pakistan and Women Standing Under Islamic Law 369
    *Pratibha Singh, B.M.S. College of Law, Karnataka State Law
      University, India*
    Ishika Raghuvanshi, GLA University, India

Chapter 21
Honor Killing in International Law: A Critical Study of Honor-Based
Violence Under UNCEDAW 391
    *Bhavana Tushar Kadu, MIT-Art Design and Technology University,
      India*
    Aayushi Singh, Amity Law School, Amity University, Noida, India
    Aditya Tomer, Amity Law School, Amity University, Noida, India

Chapter 22
An Analysis of Multiculturalism and Racism in the UK and USA 413
  Nupur Kumari, Bennett University, India
  Radhika Garg, GLA University, India

Compilation of References 433

About the Contributors 465

Index 477

Detailed Table of Contents

Preface xxi

Acknowledgment xxvi

Introduction xxviii

Chapter 1
Honor-Based Violence: A Brutal Abuse Against Civil Liberties 1
   Chunrye Kim, Saint Joseph's University, USA
   Siddhi Agrawal, GLA University, India

The chapter provides an overview of the issues surrounding honour killings, particularly in the context of India, and the challenges they pose to human rights and gender equality. It highlights the persistence of traditional gender norms and patriarchal structures that underpin these crimes, leading to the denial of women's autonomy and rights. The abstract discusses the reasons behind honour killings, such as perceived threats to family honour and fear of losing control or power. It also delves into the legal and societal responses to honour killings, including the role of religious and customary laws, as well as the obligations of states under international conventions like CEDAW. The abstract concludes by emphasizing the need for comprehensive legal frameworks, effective law enforcement, and societal awareness to combat honour killings and uphold human rights.

Chapter 2
Khap Panchayats and Their Misogynistic Approach: The Dishonor Behind Honor Killing 17
    Heeuk D. Lee, Weber State University, USA
    Aranya Agrawal, GLA University, India

Khap Panchayats have historically played a significant role in administering justice at local level, criticism arises due to their male-dominated, patriarchal nature, often resulting in anti-women biases. Their members often include in barbaric practices of killing on the name of safeguarding honor which violate the fundamental and democratic rights of people. An honor killing is a murder carried out to reclaim or preserve the family's honor, often perceived as damaged by the actions of the victim. Honor Killings, viewed as a form of punishment, highlight the manifestation of patriarchal ideologies. This chapter examines the role of Khap Panchayats behind honor killings and explores their dominance in society, influencing even prominent politicians. The chapter further delves into the phenomenon of Khap Panchayats, the self-proclaimed Kangaroo Courts lacking constitutional legitimacy yet enjoying authority within specific caste segments as guardians of honor. The study seeks to understand the reasons for the continued existence of Khaps in India and analyzes their source of strength.

Chapter 3
Patriarchal Enmity in the Guise of Honor: An Indian Enigma 35
    Somesh Dhamija, GLA University, India
    Nikita Singh, GLA University, India

The title of the chapter emphasizes the constructivist approach of patriarchy which eventually results into honor killing and frequently mirrors the violent patriarchy committed in the name of honor. Since izzat, or the ideology of honor, is a gendered concept in India, men and women represent it in very different ways. As a daughter, wife, and mother, a woman holds the family honor, which a man controls. The UNFPA estimates a very shocking number of 5000 females including both women and girls are murdered by members of their own families. In India, 356 cases of honor killings and 65 cases of culpable homicide were registered, according to a recent National Crime Record Bureau report. It is evident that a broad spectrum of moderation in an effective manner is required to combat masculinist violence and women's sovereignty in India. The statement "The Freedom of Belief doesn't mean Freedom to Kill" is appropriate to highlight in this situation. Everybody has the right to lead an equitable, honorable, and dignified life.

Chapter 4

Dishonor, Death, and Coercion in the Arena of Justice 53

Myunghoon Roh, Salve Regina University, USA
Muskan Gautam, GLA University, India

The term "honor killings" refers to severe forms of domestic violence in which a woman is killed with the help of her family or network. But in non-secular and ethnic societies, spousal violence is sometimes motivated by a sense of "honor." In this chapter, we contend that a discursive collision occurs between ethicized women. As victims of honor murders, women are hidden behind the non-public/public divide that defined the domestic violence narrative and the cultural relativism of British multicultural discourse. Ethicized women have become more visible after September 11th, but because of the discourse of fear and threat posed by the presence of the Muslim foreign "other," they are now restricted and shaped in the public consciousness. By adopting a robust human rights stance to respect homicides, it would be feasible to overcome the 'gender trap' of cultural relativism in the liberal democratic debate on diversity.

Chapter 5

Evolution of Moralistic and Ethical Dimensions of Honour Killing 73

Megha Singh, GLA University, India
Jae Seung Lee, College of Liberal Arts and Applied Science, Miami University, USA

Every human has a right to live their life according to their own will. No one should be compelled to live for others or to live to guard someone else's honour. In the context of Honour Killing, a person or especially a woman is forced to live according to the morals of the society, norms or principles made for them. If they go against any of these principles, norms or morals, they are considered as characterless or impure and is said to have shamed their family or the community and brought dishonour to the family. Honour Killing is the murder of a women or young girl by the male family members, community, tribe or people related to clan for being accused of bringing dishonour to the family. The present chapter contains a brief overview about honour killing and the reasons for its prevalence in the ancient as well as in the modern world. In what context religion and sexism is related or affects honour killing and in what way honour killing evolved and is still prevalent in this modern world of developed nations are further points of discussion in the chapter.

Chapter 6
Effect of Culture-Based Violence on Human Psychology 93
    Aruna Dhamija, GLA University, India
    Mugdha Garg, GLA University, India

In the 21st century, modernization, employment, literacy, and technological advancements have led to acceptance of inter-caste and inter-religion marriages. However, the caste system persists, leading to discrimination and "Honor Killing" or culture-based violence. This chapter explores cultural and psychological factors that motivate such violence, the historical background of this issue, and the influence of "Khap Panchayats" on people. It highlights the impact of this violence on society, its psychological effects, and suggests preventive measures and strategies to help victims.

Chapter 7
Honor Killing: Defining the Undefined 113
    Tarun Pratap Yadav, GLA University, India
    Tanisha Jain, GLA University, India

Honor Killing is an issue which needs to have a solution which is more or less universally accepted but before that it is important to understand what is Honor Killing, a definition which defines this heinous crime. Various states and its government bodies, organizations and jurists have tried to define the aforesaid crime but the definition still remains blurred. Different definitions have covered different aspects. This chapter basically deals with how various important organizations and others have defined or have given its stance on Honor Killing. This chapter also contains issues regarding the nomenclature, namely, gender biases. Almost everywhere the crime is considered to be a violence or abuse or crime in respect of women. It is not wrong to consider it as a violence against women because women were really subjected to it for a long time and it may not be wrong to say that the situation has become worse. But there is another side of the coin too. This crime can no longer be considered an offence related only to women.

Chapter 8
Honor Killing: An Infringement of Right to Life With Dignity 129
   Avinash Dadhich, Manipal Law School, India
   Aditya Raj, GLA University, India

Honor Killings involves unlawful killing of blood relations which is done by their own family member when they felt that the act involves immoral behaviour. The Hon'ble Supreme Court of India has also condemned this type of atrocious act. In a country like India which runs on the thread of rule of law, such atrocious act must be dealt with hardship. This doctrinal research provides an analysis of honor killing as infringement life with dignity which is guaranteed at national as well as international level. It focuses on positive obligations which are imposed on states by international law and International Human Rights law. It also focused on Indian legal framework on honor killing and Judicial Response to protection of women from honor killing. In this chapter, it is also argued that why honor killing is human right issue with certain examples of other states where the same offences have been committed in the name of so-called honor.

Chapter 9
Honor Killing in the Indian Context: Law Ought to Be..................................... 147
   Harshita Singh, Amity University, Noida, India
   Tulsi Gupta, GLA University, India

The value of Honor is highly regarded by all individuals, being a crucial part of human life. It is not acceptable for anyone to justify taking a life in the name of culture. Whether it is for personal or collective reasons, taking someone's life is always considered morally and legally wrong. It goes against the constitution, which guarantees every citizen the right to life and dignity. The Indian constitution ensures that every individual is protected from any harm to their life. Society and culture cannot override the right to live with dignity in society. Committing murder in the name of protecting family Honor does not restore or replace any perceived lost Honor. This chapter aims to examine the concept of Honor and Honor killings in India through a legal lens. It also looks at key court decisions to understand how the law is interpreted, ways to prevent Honor Killing effectively, and why India has not adequately addressed this issue within its legal system.

Chapter 10
The Legal Framework for Murder on Provocation in the Egyptian Penal Code
as a Type of Honor Killing 165
Ramy El-Kady, Police Academy, Egypt

The chapter explores the legal provisions regarding murder on provocation in the Egyptian penal code, specifically in relation to honor killings, a form of violence against women. It provides a legal justification for reducing punishment for murder committed by a husband who witnesses his wife engaging in adultery and kills her. Honor killings are characterized by premeditation and intent, as specified in the legal statutes. The chapter uses a comparative descriptive-analytical method to understand the concept of honor killings, its definitions, and variations in Arab legislation. It also examines the correlation between honor killings and religion and the act of murder based on provocation as outlined in the Egyptian penal code. The chapter also explores the lenient treatment of honor crimes in Egypt through the application of judges' clemency as stipulated in Article 17 of the Egyptian penal code.

Chapter 11
Honor's Cost: Lives Lost, Justice Frost 193
Indra Kumar Singh, Amity University, Haryana, India
Sudiksha Dhungel, GLA University, India

Honor killings are serious human rights crimes that affect the victims, their families, and the communities where they take place for a very long time. This chapter delves into the motivations behind honor killings and their intricate aftermath, demonstrating how the families are forced to commit these crimes by social pressure and humiliation. Chronic mental health issues including anxiety, sadness, and PTSD (post-traumatic stress disorder) can be brought on by this emotional upheaval. Honor killings put a pall over societies, creating an atmosphere of mistrust and apprehension. Honor killings put a pall over societies, creating an atmosphere of mistrust and apprehension. The victim's family may face hostility and ostracism. This horrifying crime be dealt with in a multifaceted manner, involving strong networks of care for the survivors and changes in the law. When we are aware of the entire extent of the aftermath, we may be better equipped to understand the urgent need for comprehensive solutions to put an end to honor killings and build a more just and equitable society.

Chapter 12
Honor Crimes vs. Constitutional Rights: A Comparative Constitutional
Conundrum 213
    Govind Singh Rajpal, MIT-ADT University, India
    Aditya Lohani, GLA University, India

In this chapter, cultural norms, human rights, and constitutional principles vis-à-vis Honour Crimes are thoroughly examined. It begins with a perceptive introduction that highlights the importance of addressing honour crimes on a global scale and highlights how they continue to pose a threat to the fundamental principles of equality and human rights. The chapter explores the origins of honour crimes in cultural norms and critically examines how they violate fundamental human rights from a jurisprudential standpoint. It reviews constitutional responses to honour crimes globally, examining how well various legal systems protect individual rights while taking cultural factors into account. The comparative jurisprudential analysis at the chapter's heart aims to highlight the problems that honour crimes present and offer creative constitutional remedies.

Chapter 13
Understanding the Impact of Immigration on Honor Killing: Instances From
Various Countries 231
    Myunghoon Roh, Salve Regina University, USA
    Prestha Chhaparia, GLA University, India

In recent years, various discussions and debates are taking place in western countries which tries to explain the role of immigrant communities in honor related crime. Immigrant communities, although not an only factor but plays a major role in explaining honor related crimes. Various scholars and professors have analyzed honor killings in different countries and presented their ideas about the factors driving the crime of honor killing. This chapter discusses in detail the impact of immigration on honor killing along with the instances from countries namely, Canada, Sweden, Germany, Britain, United States and Netherlands.

Chapter 14
Camouflaged Tenets of Peace Makers on Account of Honor Killing 247
    Avinash Dadhich, Manipal Law School, India
    Himanshi Dixit, GLA University, India

The issue of honor killings is a deeply rooted problem with cultural, societal, and legal implications, necessitating comprehensive efforts from peacemakers to address and eradicate this form of violence. This study explores the background and rationale for addressing honor killings, highlighting the role of peacemakers in challenging cultural norms and promoting societal change. The research problem focuses on the challenges faced by peacemakers in addressing honor killings and the strategies employed to foster lasting change. The aim is to examine the impact of peacemaking initiatives on societal attitudes and legal reforms related to honor-based violence. The methodology involves a qualitative analysis of peacemaking efforts, including legal advocacy, education, community engagement, and international collaboration. Participants include global figures such as Malala Yousafzai, local activists, religious leaders, and governmental and non-governmental organizations.

Chapter 15
Media Trial and Honor Killing: Media as an Agent in Shaping Perception and Laws Around the World 277
    Sudhir Kumar, School of Legal Studies, Babu Banarsi Das University, India
    Barkha Agrawal, Amity University, Noida, India

The power of the media lies in its omnipresence. However, the advantage of being closely related to the happening is that the media has the potential to paint a real and authentic picture. In the case of honor killing, this power of the media can potentially be used to reduce violence and crime through honest information in real time. Though there are worries about skewed and prejudiced coverage in the media, media reports have been vital in helping to understand this issue. The way the media portrays these social crimes helps to both bolster public opinion and convey about the backward social customs connected to them. The chapter focuses on the ability of the media to influence public opinion, which can play a key role in ending honor killings around the world. Media can contribute to the development of a fairer society for women by criticizing media portrayals of honor killings and examining the causes of this violence. The purpose of this chapter is to examine the quality of media coverage of honor killing and the relationship between them Media and Popular Culture.

Chapter 16
Honor Killing: A Social-Legal Position in India in the Last Decade 295
    Heeuk D. Lee, Weber State University, USA
    Chanchal Garg, GLA University, India
    Shweta Tyagi, Hemaadri International, India

Honor Killing is the evil that makes its present felt not only in India but also a global phenomenon or threat that requires serious consideration. In Indian families, honor is given the supreme position and bringing the dishonor on the family is the prime cause that makes one to kill or harm their own loved ones. It paves its way through similar patterns of thinking among people and based on their faith, to follow the old tradition passing from generation to generation. These killings are not restricted by gender and affect the perpetrators as they are only losing their loved ones instead of getting any gain. this chapter is focused on how India is getting affected by this barbaric crime in the last decade and what is its socio-legal position and how the act done in the name of honor is only motivating the people to attempt dishonored actions or can say crimes. This chapter has specifically tried to cover every aspect of social trigger of this shameful act that has contributed in affecting the people in last decade along with the legal provisions.

Chapter 17
Consanguinity of Caste Prejudices With Honor Killing 313
    Govind Singh Rajpal, MIT-ADT University, India
    Raunak Upmanyu, GLA University, India

The chapter will deliberate on the unnoticed and dangerous issue that is rooted in society i.e. Honor killing. Honor Killing is a wrongful act with the false idea of protecting the pride of the family. It happens because of the uneducated at the grassroots level, patriarchal mentality, casteism, economic angle, and religious issues. This study aims to understand the root cause of the problem of Honor Killing i.e. caste. The study would contain the problems of caste-based marriage and why there is a social barrier to inter-caste marriage. The chapter will also focus on the causes of honor killing due to inter-caste marriage and what is the mentality of Indian parents in the rural area. In this study, Ground field Research has been conducted in the town of Raya Mathura, India in which some questions have been asked to the people on what their reasoning on inter-caste marriage and honor is killing. The chapter would also aim to analyze the Supreme Court judgment around honor killing, the right to marry your life partner, the scope of Article 21, and different marriage acts.

Chapter 18
Role of Class Conflict in Honor Killings 331
    Deepika Pandoi, GLA University, India
    Somendra Ashok Singh, GLA University, India

In India, a sizable population is frequently the victim of terrorism, famine, torture, humiliation, mutilation, and murder. Among these is the complicated phenomena known as "honor killing," which reflects a startling social crime, a moral conundrum facing the civilizations, and an obstacle across cultural boundaries. Generally speaking, intentional killing is murder, even when inadvertent killing is possible. According to this perspective, honor killing is defined as murder, typically committed by a member of the victim's own family or friends in order to exact revenge or shame for any disloyalty or other actions deemed inappropriate by the culture. In light of this, the purpose of the article is to investigate societal perspectives and attitudes about women's rights to life, equality, dignity, and self-determination in all spheres of life, as well as related theoretical issues. The theoretical implications of honor killing in connection to the accuser and victim are covered in this work.

Chapter 19
Cognitive Strands of Honor Killing 351
    Praveen Kumar Mall, Teerthanker Mahaveer University, India
    Anusha Kulshrestha, GLA University, India

This chapter deems to highlight the misguided views of honor and the marginalization of those who deemed to be violators of this heinous crime. These thought processes are further cemented by social pressures and the fear of rejection. In order to question and alter the deeply held beliefs that support honor killings it is essential to comprehend the cognitive component of these crimes which are dealt with substantially in the chapter. Cultural traditions that have been entrenched over many generations can lead to a skewed sense of responsibility and honor, which results in people willing to go to great lengths to defend their perceived family honor. Furthermore, the chapter will highlight how humans justify violent behaviors as a way to restore honor by balancing their personal convictions with societal standards which can lead to cognitive dissonance. The cognitive strand is sustained by deeply ingrained gender norms that reinforce the idea that women are responsible for maintaining family honor.

Chapter 20
Honor Killing in Pakistan and Women Standing Under Islamic Law 369
    Pratibha Singh, B.M.S. College of Law, Karnataka State Law
       University, India
    Ishika Raghuvanshi, GLA University, India

Because of the rise in crimes against women, including honor killing and other forms of violence related to honor, the Islamic Republic of Pakistan is regarded as one of the world's most risky and hazardous places for women. Using general sayings of the Prophet Muhammad, peace be upon him, a number of researchers and Islamic scholars have tried to defend the practice of honor killing. Unquestionably, women around the world are vulnerable to arbitrary cultural norms and outdated ideas. Throughout history, women have experienced marginalization in various civilizations due to their minimal involvement in decision-making within both public and private domains. Sadly, physical assault against women is sometimes mistakenly identified as a sign of masculine dominance. The fear of abuse and social pressures forced the women from different backgrounds to remain silent on such intrusive matters. It is important to note that all faiths condemn honour killing as a socio-cultural evil

Chapter 21
Honor Killing in International Law: A Critical Study of Honor-Based
Violence Under UNCEDAW 391
    Bhavana Tushar Kadu, MIT-Art Design and Technology University,
       India
    Aayushi Singh, Amity Law School, Amity University, Noida, India
    Aditya Tomer, Amity Law School, Amity University, Noida, India

The concept of 'honor' is intertwined with the conscious of any civilisation, act of any family member or an individual who is a part of the society can have a cascading effect on the other members. This 'honor' is threatened or is diminished when a girl marries outside her community or religion which leads to her subsequent murder. The United Nations General Assembly adopted the "United Nations Convention on the Elimination of all Forms of Discrimination against Women" (UNCEDAW). It was brought in on 3rd September, 1981 and ratified by 189 nation States. India was among the first of countries to having signed and ratified the convention. The various provisions of the UNCEDAW highlight the menace of homicide committed for saving the "honor" of the family, which in most of the cases is associated with the social status of a family in the society. This paper attempts to analyse the status of Honor Based Violence as defined under UNCEDAW.

Chapter 22
An Analysis of Multiculturalism and Racism in the UK and USA 413
Nupur Kumari, Bennett University, India
Radhika Garg, GLA University, India

The phenomenon of honor killings in the multicultural settings of the US and the UK is examined in this chapter. Honor killings, which are defined as horrific acts of violence against women who are believed to have brought embarrassment to their families, undermine multiculturalism's tenets by drawing attention to the conflicts between human rights and cultural norms. To demonstrate the intricate dynamics at work, the chapter examines case studies and the horrific events of Michelle Rai & Shafilea Ahmed. The chapter explores the connections between sexism, racism, and gender-based violence in honor killings and emphasizes the stigma minority women experience. The need to treat honor killings with cultural sensitivity, while criticizing violence and protecting human rights, is noted in the conclusion. To prevent honor-based violence, it is essential to promote open communication, provide support services, & actively oppose racism and xenophobia to build inclusive societies where everybody is valued and protected.

Compilation of References 433

About the Contributors 465

Index 477

Preface

In recent years, the pervasive issue of honor killing has gained heightened international attention, yet it continues to go unnoticed in many regions due to cultural, social, and political factors. This form of violence, predominantly targeting women, is rooted in complex family dynamics and rigid patriarchal norms, making it a profound human rights violation that transcends geographic boundaries. From South Asia to the Middle East and Arab countries, and even among migrant communities in Western Europe and North America, honor killings persist, raising urgent questions about global law, human rights, and societal structures that allow such practices to endure.

Our book, *Global Law, Human Rights, and Intersections with Honor Killing*, represents a critical contribution to the academic and policy-oriented discourse on this subject. With few comprehensive studies available on honor-based crimes, this work fills a glaring gap in the literature, providing a nuanced and in-depth analysis of the ideological, cultural, and legal factors that underpin honor killings globally. By bringing together diverse perspectives from law, sociology, psychology, and human rights advocacy, this book seeks to shed light on an issue often hidden in plain sight.

The phenomenon of honor killing is more than an act of violence; it is deeply embedded in societal structures that value familial reputation and patriarchal dominance over individual rights. This book examines the patriarchal ideologies that not only perpetuate honor killings but also inhibit justice for victims. We explore how these ideologies intersect with socio-economic class conflicts, migration patterns, and gender inequality, revealing the intricate layers of discrimination and violence that honor killings encapsulate.

A central theme of this book is the urgent need for a coherent and coordinated global response to honor killings. While there have been advancements in data collection, risk assessment, and legal frameworks, the reality remains that many legal systems are fraught with bias, unresponsiveness, and inefficacy in addressing such crimes. In this context, we propose that the solution goes beyond mere legal reforms—it requires proactive community engagement, resource allocation for support systems, and a parallel system of justice that operates within the very communities where these crimes occur. We emphasize the necessity of specialized agencies and measures that can protect vulnerable women and other marginalized groups, including the transgender community, from honor-based violence.

Chapter 1 delves into the deep-seated patriarchal structures that fuel honor killings, with a particular focus on India. It examines the traditional gender norms that deny women autonomy, highlighting the role of family honor in these crimes. The chapter also discusses legal and societal responses to honor killings and calls for comprehensive legal reforms to uphold human rights and gender equality.

Khap Panchayats, despite lacking constitutional legitimacy, wield significant influence in parts of India. Chapter 2 explores their patriarchal nature and how they perpetuate honor killings under the guise of safeguarding honor. The chapter critically examines the socio-political power these self-proclaimed courts hold and how their authority contributes to the persistence of honor killings in India.

Chapter 3 highlights how the gendered notion of honor places the responsibility of family honor on women, subjecting them to violent control by male relatives. The UNFPA statistics and the National Crime Record Bureau reports show the prevalence of honor killings, underscoring the need for social and legal moderation to counter patriarchal violence and protect women's rights to live with dignity.

Focusing on honor killings in Western multicultural contexts, chapter 4 discusses how ethicized women are caught in a "gender trap" of cultural relativism. It critiques how the public and private spheres intersect in narratives of domestic violence, and calls for a stronger human rights approach to overcome the biases entrenched in liberal democratic discourses.

Chapter 5 presents an overview of how religion and sexism intertwine to perpetuate honor killings across time, even in modern societies. It reflects on the persistence of these crimes, tracing their historical and religious roots, while calling for more comprehensive solutions to eradicate such violence against women and ensure gender justice.

While modernization has brought increased acceptance of inter-caste and inter-religion marriages, the caste system continues to fuel violence in the name of honor. Chapter 6 examines the cultural and psychological factors behind honor killings and explores strategies for addressing this form of violence, with a focus on the role of Khap Panchayats and societal attitudes.

Chapter 7 highlights the challenges of defining honor killings, with a focus on gender bias. While traditionally viewed as a crime against women, the chapter explores the broader implications of honor-related violence. It critically examines how various organizations and legal frameworks address the issue and calls for more inclusive approaches to tackling honor crimes.

Chapter 8 focuses on honor killings as a violation of human rights, with specific attention to the Indian legal framework and international human rights obligations. It explores how such acts infringe on the right to life and dignity, discussing legal responses and judicial interventions that aim to protect women from honor-based violence.

Chapter 9 examines honor killings from a legal perspective, emphasizing how the Indian constitution protects the right to life and dignity. It reviews court decisions on honor crimes and discusses the limitations of the Indian legal system in effectively addressing these crimes, offering suggestions for more robust legal interventions.

Chapter 10 explores the legal provisions in Egypt that reduce punishments for honor killings, specifically in cases of adultery. It uses a comparative approach to examine how Arab legislation treats honor killings and highlights the problematic leniency applied to such cases, calling for more stringent legal reforms.

Honor killings have long-lasting effects on victims' families and communities, often leading to mental health issues such as PTSD, anxiety, and depression. Chapter 11 discusses the social and psychological toll of these crimes and emphasizes the importance of building strong care networks and legal reforms to prevent further violence.

Chapter 12 provides an in-depth analysis of how honor crimes violate fundamental human rights. It offers a comparative review of global constitutional responses to honor crimes, examining legal systems that prioritize human rights while considering cultural factors, and proposes constitutional remedies to address these violations.

Chapter 13 discusses how immigration influences honor-related crimes in Western countries, focusing on case studies from Canada, Sweden, Germany, Britain, and the United States. It explores the factors driving these crimes within immigrant communities and highlights the importance of addressing cultural and social integration to prevent honor-based violence.

Chapter 14 explores the role of peacemakers in challenging the cultural norms that sustain honor killings. It examines peacemaking initiatives, including legal advocacy, community engagement, and education, and discusses how these efforts contribute to societal change and the promotion of human rights.

Chapter 15 critically examines how the media portrays honor killings and its influence on public opinion. It highlights the potential for media to contribute to reducing violence through accurate and unbiased reporting, and explores the role of media in challenging harmful social customs and promoting a fairer society for women.

Chapter 16 discusses the socio-legal dimensions of honor killings in India, focusing on how the concept of honor has led to a pattern of violence within families. It examines the legal provisions addressing honor killings and the societal triggers that perpetuate this crime, offering insights into the challenges of combating it.

Chapter 17 investigates the root causes of honor killings, particularly in relation to inter-caste marriages. Through ground-field research conducted in rural India, the chapter explores societal attitudes towards inter-caste marriage, casteism, and the patriarchal mindset that fuels honor-based violence.

Chapter 18 explores the theoretical implications of honor killings, focusing on societal perspectives regarding women's rights to life, equality, and dignity. It provides an analysis of the cultural and moral dilemmas associated with honor killings, highlighting the complex interplay between accusers and victims in these crimes.

Chapter 19 examines how social pressures and misguided views of honor contribute to the marginalization of those involved in honor killings. It calls for a reexamination of societal norms and advocates for a shift in attitudes to prevent the perpetuation of honor-based violence.

Chapter 20 deliberated on how honor killing is justified on the name of religion in some countries. The miserable situation of women in ancient Islamic times offers terrible historical proof of this evil custom. The chapter further discusses on how honor killing is practiced in Pakistan and ways to mitigate it.

Chapter 21 attempts to analyze the status of Honor Based Violence as defined under UNCEDAW. The various provisions of the UNCEDAW, as discussed in the chapter, highlight the menace of homicide committed for saving the "honor" of the family, which in most of the cases is associated with the social status of a family in the society.

Chapter 22 explores the connections between sexism, racism, and gender-based violence in honor killings and emphasizes the stigma minority women experience. The chapter further discusses the social and legal structures which multicultural societies have put in place to deal with honor killings. It analyses the effectiveness of the laws in place and the role played by authorities in deterring and combating these offenses.

In addressing honor killings, the book also draws connections between this form of violence and broader discussions of gender equality. The intersection of culture, law, and human rights is critically examined, with special attention to the evolution of global legal frameworks and the need for more stringent laws. We delve into international legal instruments, particularly the Convention on the Elimination of All Forms of Discrimination Against Women (CEDAW), and analyze their relevance and limitations in addressing honor-based crimes. Additionally, the book provides a comparative analysis of the legal responses to honor killings in various countries, offering insights into both progress and challenges.

Through a multidisciplinary lens, this book explores the socio-psychological dimensions of honor killings, providing a comprehensive understanding of the criminology behind these crimes. We delve into the family dynamics, societal pressures, and psychological drivers that facilitate honor-based violence. By doing so, we aim to present honor killing as not just a legal issue but a deeply ingrained social problem that requires a multifaceted approach to solve.

As editors, we have curated this collection to provoke thought, challenge assumptions, and inspire action. We believe that this book will serve as a vital resource for policymakers, legal professionals, researchers, students, and activists who are committed to addressing honor-based crimes and advocating for gender justice. Our hope is that the insights offered here will contribute to the global fight against honor killings and pave the way for more effective legal and social reforms.

In conclusion, *Global Law, Human Rights, and Intersections With Honor Killing* seeks to bring honor killings out of the shadows and into the spotlight of international human rights discourse. It is a call to action for national and international bodies to develop strategies that not only punish perpetrators but also protect and empower victims. The road to justice for victims of honor killings is long, but it is one that must be traveled with urgency, compassion, and unwavering commitment to human dignity.

Somesh Dhamija
GLA University, India

Tarun Pratap Yadav
GLA University, India

Jae Seung Lee
Miami University, USA

Harshita Singh
Amity University, India

Myunghoon Roh
Salve Regina University, USA

Acknowledgment

First of all, we would like to thank the Almighty God with whose help everything becomes possible.

We owe our sincere thanks and profound gratitude to all the contributors of the book for their invaluable guidance and encouraging attitude in completing this manuscript. They gave all encouragement and help as a guide. A special thanks to the student editors namely Tanisha Jain and Aayushi Singh without whose support this book would not have been possible.

The book offers an in-depth analysis of Honor based crimes around the globe. Few books are available on this topic and a dire need is felt to have an academic discussion so as to make this crime visible in the eyes of public. The book reflects the ideology behind Honor Killing as well as the role of Patriarchal societies in enhancing the crime. It further elucidates the concept of Gender Equality in totality and the views of various thinkers on it, in addition to, covering socio-culture based factors and demystifying the evolution of global legal framework vis-à-vis honor killing. Hence, we are obliged to various Governments around the world, Civil Society Groups, NGOs, Self Help Groups for providing data, reports and surveys vis-a-vis associated factors causing Honor Killing around the world.

We are also indebted to the staff members of the Library of Salve Regina University, USA, Library of Miami University, USA, Indian Law Institute, India, Library of University of Delhi, India, Library of Jawaharlal Nehru University, India, Library of Manipal Academy of Higher Education, India, Library of Amity University, India, Library of GLA University, India and Library of Chaudhary Charan Singh University, Meerut, India for their generous help.

Our heartfelt thanks to our better halves, who always supported us, taken full interest in our topic from the starting point of this book and co-operated us till the end. A sweet thanks to our parents and elders for their blessing and good wishes.

We are thankful to the learned teachers, scholars, friends and relatives who have assisted us in completing this book. This work would not have been possible without their valuable support and assistance. We are grateful to various legal luminaries whose scholarly and celebrated works have been helpful in completing the book.

Last but not the least we would like to thank all persons directly or indirectly related to the book.

Introduction

In the lack of a coherent strategy, honor killings are mostly seen as a societal problem rather than a crime requiring global solutions. Why is the honor killing threat so pervasive? How can we examine or concentrate on the social and legal strategies used by nations to stop honor killing? How much direction have court authorities given in establishing criteria for the avoidance and management of honor killings? How much has the presence or absence of honor killings have been influenced by social, moral, religious, and ethical values? This book explores variants of the phenomenon and makes an effort to provide answers to the requisite queries.

Hono killing perpetrators, who are not limited to any one nation or social group, desire complete immunity from punishment. Honor killing is not regarded as a crime or recognized as such in some nations. This crime now qualifies as one of the rarest cases, according to the judiciary, in some nations, including India, meriting sever penalties. Because honor killings are rarely reported, it is impossible to determine the severity and scope of he crime. This book's qualitative methodology is really adapted to reach the soio-legal reality of honor killings. Only by conversing with people in their own circumstances and posing open-ended questions about the subject during conversation was it possible to get a sense of how honor killings are viewed and upheld in social, legal, moral, and religious contexts.

To provide a comprehensive theory of family honor violence, execution by family takes patriarchy, culture, and kindship into account as well as extending them. This book examines the "honor belt," a collection of nations spanning from North Africa to southeast Asia, where comparable types of inequality, patriarchy, group authority, and gerontocracy are common. It also examines how honor killing thrives within the boundaries of this inequality. The book further analyzes the future of honor-based violence by reviewing poll data and pointing to a multifaceted international social movement. Execution by family will be of interest to anyone interested in family dispute, violence, crime, and popular morality given the increased awareness of family honor violence.

I want to express my appreciation for the editorial team in addressing this delicate subject which needs to be studied in the context of violence against women as a whole and should be handled appropriately. Additionally, this book will be invaluable reading for professors, academicians, and students working in the fields of criminology, criminal justice, sociology, social psychology, and anthropology.

Somesh Dhamija
GLA University, India

Tarun Pratap Yadav
GLA University, India

Jae-Seung Lee
Miami University, USA

Harshita Singh
Amity University, India

Myunghoon Roh
Salve Regina University, USA

Chapter 1
Honor–Based Violence:
A Brutal Abuse Against Civil Liberties

Chunrye Kim
Saint Joseph's University, USA

Siddhi Agrawal
https://orcid.org/0009-0009-1883-2378
GLA University, India

ABSTRACT

The chapter provides an overview of the issues surrounding honour killings, particularly in the context of India, and the challenges they pose to human rights and gender equality. It highlights the persistence of traditional gender norms and patriarchal structures that underpin these crimes, leading to the denial of women's autonomy and rights. The abstract discusses the reasons behind honour killings, such as perceived threats to family honour and fear of losing control or power. It also delves into the legal and societal responses to honour killings, including the role of religious and customary laws, as well as the obligations of states under international conventions like CEDAW. The abstract concludes by emphasizing the need for comprehensive legal frameworks, effective law enforcement, and societal awareness to combat honour killings and uphold human rights.

BACKGROUND

Honor killings remain a significant challenge to human rights and gender equality, particularly in India, where traditional gender norms and patriarchal structures continue to underpin these crimes. According to the National Crime

DOI: 10.4018/979-8-3693-9596-7.ch001

Records Bureau (NCRB), 24 cases of Honor killings were reported in India in 2020, though the true number is likely higher due to underreporting. Globally, the United Nations estimates around 5,000 such killings annually, with some reports suggesting the figure could be as high as 20,000. Women constitute around 93% of the victims, reflecting the focus on controlling female autonomy, particularly in matters of marriage and sexuality (Bhopal, 2019). In India, the majority of Honor killings stem from inter-caste marriages, accounting for 72% of cases, with other factors such as love marriages (10%) and inter-religious unions (18%) contributing as well. Victims are typically young women aged 16-25, caught between their personal choices and family expectations (Elakkary et, 2014). India's obligations under international conventions like the Convention on the Elimination of All Forms of Discrimination Against Women (CEDAW) further underscore the need for robust action against such crimes. Despite some high-profile court cases resulting in strict penalties, including the death sentence for perpetrators, the societal acceptance of Honor killings remains a significant barrier to eliminating these practices. Public awareness campaigns and the efforts of civil society organizations are gradually making inroads, but deep-rooted cultural factors continue to perpetuate violence in the name of Honor (Dasgupta, 2000). Comprehensive legal reform, effective law enforcement, and greater societal awareness are crucial to addressing this issue and upholding human rights and gender equality in India.

Methodology

The research for this study involves a multi-pronged approach combining both qualitative and quantitative methods. Primary data is collected through the analysis of legal case studies, judicial verdicts, and reports from governmental agencies such as the National Crime Records Bureau (NCRB). This allows for an understanding of the frequency, regional distribution, and legal outcomes of Honor killings. Secondary data is gathered from scholarly articles, sociological studies, and reports by non-governmental organizations (NGOs) working in the field of gender rights and social justice. These sources provide insight into the cultural, social, and economic factors that perpetuate Honor-based violence. To examine the legal framework, this study analyzes existing laws under the Indian Penal Code, alongside international obligations under conventions like CEDAW. Furthermore, qualitative interviews with legal experts, human rights activists, and community leaders help shed light on the challenges of enforcing laws in regions where patriarchal norms are deeply rooted (Abu-Lughod, 2011). The research also involves a comparative analysis, looking at similar practices in other countries like Pakistan and Middle Eastern nations, to contextualize India's situation in a global framework. Through this mixed-method approach, the study aims to identify gaps in the legal and societal responses to

Honor killings and propose solutions for more effective intervention and policy reform (Abu-Lughod, 2011).

Key Terms

Fundamental terms include "Honor rights" and "Honor killing" in the arena of Honor Based Violence a brutal Abuse Against Civil Liberties. Broader terms like "violence"(Bhui, 2003) and "collectivistic cultures"(Caffaro, 2014) and "criminal justice"(Singh, 2014) and "Social Distress"(Dasgupta, 2000) and " Homicide" (Droga, 2014). An Honor Killings Research Paper on its Dark Face and Hidden Atrocity requires careful consideration of inclusion/exclusion and article research, as well as the selection of appropriate publications. Publications with an emphasis on international law, gender studies, human rights, and related interdisciplinary topics were chosen for publishing in the journal selection process.

Relevance was a key component of the inclusion criteria, which made sure that only papers that directly addressed honor-based violence against civil liberties, or related legal and cultural issues and norms are taken into account. Current viewpoints and data were included as a result of prioritizing recent articles, ideally those that were published within the last ten years. The foundation of our research, in order to uphold academic rigor, consisted of government and recognized NGOs reports as well as peer-reviewed literature.

Literature Review

The primary role of Honor Based Violence consistently frames it as a severe violation of civil liberties and human rights, particularly against women and marginalized individuals within patriarchal societies. Studies have shown that such violence is not confined to a particular region but is present across cultures, especially in South Asia, the Middle East, and among diaspora communities in Western nations (Gill, 2009). Sociologists argue that Honor-based violence is a direct challenge to individual autonomy and civil liberties, as it punishes individuals—predominantly women—for exercising personal freedoms, such as choosing their partners or rejecting family-imposed marital arrangements. These crimes are embedded in societal structures that prioritize community Honor over personal rights, often justified through cultural or religious norms.

International human rights frameworks, including the Convention on the Elimination of All Forms of Discrimination Against Women, have been instrumental in calling for stronger legal measures against Honor Based Violence (Abu-Lughod, 2011). However, as the persistent lack of accountability and awareness at both societal and governmental levels hampers progress in effectively combating this form of violence (Sperry,2012). Honor-based violence remains a brutal abuse of civil liberties, demanding comprehensive legal reform, societal education, and international pressure to eradicate this deeply entrenched practice.

Research Gap

This chapter highlights the unique context of Civil Liberties, where honor killings are intricately linked to caste and religious norms, and contrasts with broader global studies by focusing on this specific region. The chapter employs a comprehensive approach, utilizing case studies, content evaluation techniques, and an observational-analytical framework to investigate honor killings, with a focus on Fundamental rights in India (Lewisohn Ludwig,1909). The research examines how honor-based crimes are triggered by familial intolerance towards premarital relationships and marriages outside caste or religion, often resulting in passionate, impulsive violence by family members or hired perpetrators (Khan, Khatija Bibi, 2014).

Initiatives taken against Honor killing is entrused in this chapter that Encourage the implementation of constitutional educational initiatives for all genders so that they may learn about their specific privileges legal purposes help for women should be provided (Sulatan, 2011). Safeguard women who are at risk of Honor killings. Those who are in danger must be given safe housing and protection. Encourage extensive education for the public programs (in Europeans and in Third nations) To break the taboo around murder of honor and change the way that both men and women view it, extensive public education campaigns should be launched via all available channels, which include the conventional media, the Internet, schools, non-profit organizations, and community organisations. The chapter underscores the urgent need for both legal reform and cultural change to address these entrenched practices and protect women's rights in the face of enduring patriarchal values.

INTRODUCTION

Concept of Honor Killings

Even after many years of independence in neoliberal India, which prides itself on freedom, most marriages are still arranged by family, through marriage brokers, newspapers advertisements, web-based marriage portals or long-term marriage. Creating an oral tradition: word of mouth. If it does not work, marriage is forced to save Honor, and the woman may be killed for refusing to marry the partner of her choice, which the daughter of the house cannot accept. Killings in the name of honor amounts to an utter denial of "equality," an essential principle of the constitutional framework of India, and demonstrates how the values of "feudalism" and male-dominated society are ingrained in our social systems. Honor crimes are the illegal orders by caste/community local governments that cancel or restrict relationships. Societal prohibitions and even killings of couples have finally brought the matter to the notice of the State. Khaps doesn't appear to be any different from Afghan ruling families who administer fairness in a distinctive manner.

Despite our advanced proficiency in computers, the message that we remain in the gloomy periods appears all over the globe. It is pointless to celebrate our Chandrayan's findings of liquid on the moon's surface in addition to technological advancements.

Murders based on honor are a type of intra-family assault in which women are frequently murdered by masculine closest to them (typically dads or siblings) on the grounds that the women have slandered the entire family. Women are supposed to remain virgins and chaste because they are viewed as the protectors of men's honor and that of their households. If she doesn't, it will be assumed that she has betrayed the family's Honor and in order to restore it, she must be slain. (Rana & Mishra, 2013) Each civilization has its own definition of what constitutes an affront to honor. It was thought that once India gained its autonomy, it would transform into contemporary countries have free from tyranny and servitude on the basis of race, class, faith, or dialect. Equality values will usurp the traditions of past generations. Only with the freely given and well-informed permission of both spouses may the union be called off. The family unit has a right to protection from both the state and its peers since it is a fundamental and natural social group. However, alarming reports of violence against teenage men and women in inter-caste and interreligious weddings are emerging from around the nation. The greatest thing a boy or girl's parents can do if they disapprove of a between castes or inter-religious marriage is to cut off social connections with their offspring; nevertheless, they are not allowed to coerce or encourage such a union violent deed. Additionally, ladies who wed the males of their choosing have further legal options. Because of how they behave in public, they defame their parents and force them to use assault in an attempt to win them back. Marital relationships require a delicate and balancing act. It is believed that any disruption of this balance on the part of the woman who refuses to choose her father affects the father's status in society.

Honor killings have been taking place for an extended period. They have been occurring globally for centuries. Crimes of honor involve violent actions, often leading to murder, committed by family members against male or female relatives thought to have brought shame upon the family. Simply the belief that a woman has acted in a manner that brings shame upon her family can lead to violence against her. A woman might be singled out by her family for various reasons, such as declining to participate in an arranged marriage, experiencing sexual assault, wanting a divorce from an abusive spouse, or (supposedly) engaging in adultery. The choice to murder the daughter in order to preserve the family's honor could be based on various factors. The reason why this practice continues to happen quickly and frequently is primarily due to the rural areas of India sticking to their traditional views on marriage. They argue that if a girl goes against her parents' desire for marriage and chooses to marry someone from a different gotra or caste, it would disgrace the family honor, thus leading to the decision of giving her the death penalty. Sociologists argue that the unchanging rigidity of the caste system is responsible for the prevalence of honor killings. Here, they engage in this despicable action because they are afraid of losing their social status, which provides them with numerous advantages. Illegal activity. The mindset of the people has not progressed to the point where they can comprehend that marriage can take place within the same gotra or outside of one's caste, leading to honor killings.

In collective civilizations, the concept of honor is essential since the actions of one member of the family or society can have an influence on the rest. Younger generations have been constantly exposed to liberal ideas through the global media, which has led them to start pondering the rigidly enacted ideals of the previous society. Honor killing is without a doubt the most horrific of all the various crimes of honor that take place. Even though some of the elements required for murder under a nation's legal systems may also apply to honor killing, there are a few specific features that make honor killing even more horrible than murder. An honor killing usually targets a friend or relative who is a member of the victim's own social network. Often, the person who is responsible is a sibling, father, mother, or other family member whose job it was traditionally to keep the victim safe. Honor killings are inherently murders of individuals. All murders of individuals that are prosecuted if they fall within the ambit of sections 299 and section 300 of the IPC.. Globally, both murder and non-murderous homicides are included under the CEDAW's rules. The treaty's provisions, which broadly prohibit any level of physical or psychological suffering experienced by women, directly address all aspects and perspectives of honor killings committed against women. The executive must use every reasonable effort to ensure that the member states of the CEDAW take preventive measures to safeguard women and forbid any kind of discrimination against them.

Reasons for Honor killings

> <u>Patriarchal and traditional gender norms</u>: In some societies, patriarchal social structures and traditional gender norms place a high value on a woman's virginity, chastity, and obedience to male authority. When a woman's actions or behaviour are perceived as bringing shame or dishonor upon the family, some individuals may resort to violence to restore the family's reputation.

<u>Family and community pressure</u>: Family and community expectations and pressures can play a significant role in Honor killings. The fear of social stigma and the desire to maintain the family's reputation within the community may lead to extreme actions in order to preserve perceived Honor.

<u>Perceived threats to family honor</u>: Honor killings are often associated with situations such as alleged adultery, premarital relationships, interfaith or inter-caste marriages, or acts that challenge societal norms. In these cases, some individuals may believe that taking a life is necessary to restore the perceived Honor of the family.

<u>Fear of losing control or power</u>: Honor killings may also occur when certain individuals within a family fear losing control or power over their family members. This can be particularly true when it comes to women who challenge traditional gender roles or attempt to assert their independence.

The notion of honor and the name of honor are some of the main reasons that disfavor women. The belongings of the men in the immediate family, no matter what race, socioeconomic status, or religious group is how women are viewed. Owners of real estate are entitled to determine its future. Even in the current era, many civilizations and cultures are greatly impacted by these perceptions of women. For instance, crimes against honor are rife in nations like Pakistan and Syria. Secondly, there seems to be a strong foundation of traditional values in the understanding of what honor is, which is widely interpreted as being related to men's control that extends not only to women's bodies but also to all actions, including gestures, language, and actions (Bhopal, 2000). Women's disobedience in any field damages men's Honor and ultimately damages the Honor of the family and society. Thirdly, sociologists believe that the reason why Honor killings become popular is because of the fear of losing caste status, which gives them a lot of advantages, which leads them to commit this heinous crime. Another reason is that people's mindset has not changed, and they simply cannot accept the fact that marriage can take place "within the same gotra" or outside the caste. The fundamental reason for the increase in Honor killings is that public power does not reach rural areas, and Honor killings that should have been abolished continues another reason is the imperfection of the formal judicial system.

The Infringement of Women's Civil Privileges

"The concept of honor murder" is a type of domestic assault in which women are frequently slain by men's family who feel they have betrayed their reputation. In this kind of violence, women are viewed as the protectors of their husbands' or families' honor and must so preserve their sexual purity and celibacy and ought

Honor to be spared from certain death? "Honor murders" are rooted in antiquated customs that are observed across numerous societies.

According to the traditions of this tribe, the head of the family is a woman. In Pakistan, for example, women are seen as representing the respect of "the men to whom they belong." If they are found to be in an "illegal" relationship or behaving "inappropriately", they will be deemed to have violated the respect of their guardian and family. A person's ability to maintain his reputation is judged by his family and neighbours. Therefore, he must reveal his power to the public, protect his Honor by restoring it, and return it by killing those who speak ill of him. This is why most Honor killings like Samia Sarwar and Lal Jamila Mandokur are committed in public. Another motivation for killing people is to cover up embarrassing situations such as divorce, rape, incest and other sexual crimes. For example, according to the group's principles of Palestinian society, such "scandals" should be concealed or reduced by forcing each other to buy or eventually kill the women involved, in accordance with the principles of the Bible and Dapdabeh (Bond, 2012). In some societies, the understanding of what constitutes blasphemy differs and becomes blurred. Sometimes one belief or opinion is enough to damage a person's reputation. "Honor killings" are often used when women are believed to have had sexual intercourse outside of marriage. Rape victims will be killed in the name of Honor. Consent is considered irrelevant to the issue of reputational damage. Women are killed in the name of honor because they express their opinions in choosing a spouse, marry against their family, or want to divorce their husbands. In some parts of Pakistan, the karikaro system offers people who have lost their culture and dignity an opportunity to make money or cover up other crimes. Some even talk about "work." Some argue that "killing" inverts the law of honor and points to its negative aspects. Honor crimes are a broad category that also includes other forms of violence against women in the name of Honor, such as beatings, acid attacks and rape. The following cases may be examples of dangerous crimes in Pakistan. The 18-year-old girl was kidnapped by four men, including a member of the village council (panchyat). The girl's 11-year-old brother ordered it to punish the girl's family after she was caught walking with an adult member of the girl group. This is because it is an affront to the collective dignity of the girls of the caste. Four men then allegedly dragged her into her home and attacked her as hundreds of men stood outside. He then had to walk home naked in front of hundreds of spectators. It has been claimed that the functioning of honor crimes has also changed with changes in society, changes in ideas about respect and disrespectful behavior, and changes in sexuality. There are reports that "genocide" is still ongoing in Pakistan. There is no doubt that, with the increase in the number of criminals, "murder" news in the media has also increased in recent years. At the same time, the actual crime rate increased. There was clearly a sense of justice in the fact that the murder was committed in public and in broad daylight. There are many reasons for this growth. Many men dislikes women's influence on the outside world and their self-confidence. At the same time, young women in particular are becoming more aware of their rights. Basically, leaders of the Palestinian people reported seeing women participating in work outside the home and their independence and economic power increasing through morality, as these led to social changes that departed from Arab and Islamic traditions. The group's leaders said returning men and women to traditional roles, banning women from working outside the home, and banning children, marriage, and marriage are the best ways to prevent murder. Therefore, "closing" may be considered a bad idea, otherwise known as "culture". Another dimension of the problem is that "murders" occur frequently in immigrant communities, the societies where murders are not common. In these situations, accusing the victim of infidelity is a disservice in most cultures and is unacceptable to the woman's family. It has been researched that some immigrants in the West have a higher risk of becoming victims of genocide than in their own countries.

Honor Killing in India

In India, Honor killings are found in some developed states. These incidents are committed under the pretext of 'Honor' of society, class, and family. Acts of violence include killing of men or women, public lynching of couples, murder disguised as suicide, public beatings, humiliation, slander, social boycotts, and imposition of fines. Punjab, Haryana and Uttar Pradesh have reported the highest number of cases. (Rana & Mishra, 2013). One of the reasons why such crimes are becoming more and more visible is the pattern of more girls entering educational institutions, meeting people from different walks of life and classes, and forming relationships that transcend class and community boundaries. No one dares to break down class and community barriers because such people, whether boys or girls, are persecuted. It is noteworthy that in most cases, it is the socially and economically majority classes that organize, instigate and encourage such acts of revenge.

In 2003, there were at least 13 murders in the Muzaffarnagar district of western Uttar Pradesh over a nine-month period. In 2002, 10 murders were reported but 35 pairs were missing. Haryana and Punjab alone account for nearly 10% of all murders in the country. Of course, these crimes are not in the state's records. (Bui, H.N., 2003) There is very little information about these cases and most of them may be considered illegal. Additionally, most such cases go unreported, and even if they are, often initial information is not provided, and no decision is made. Caste panchayats play an important role in Haryana and elsewhere, especially with political support. Central to the theme of Dignity and Crime is the work of girls and women from all groups and communities. Female chastity is a social "respect", and women have no control over their bodies at any point in their lives. Her revenge will be swift and cruel, especially if she crosses the boundaries of her race and class and chooses a lesser man as her husband.

There are two major evils in India. As Swami Vivekananda phrased it, "trampling on the women and grinding the poor through caste restrictions" describes Indian womanhood. In India, gods used to admire women. He (Indra) met Uma, the Himmvat (Himalaya) daughter, a breathtakingly beautiful woman dressed in gold, in that very sky. "Who is this adorable being?" he inquired. Compared to men, women are twice as hungry, four times as bashful, six times as courageous, and eight times more compassionate and loving. The ancient Indian belief that "mother is goddess" is known as Matri Devo Bhava. Since the immemorial, women have been considered as goddess but in contrast, more goddess are being killed in womb, burnt alive, harassed, raped, abducted, exploited and discriminated. Indians venerate and salute India as Janani or mother. One the other hand, they disregard their sisters, mothers and wife.

It was an old saying, 'Where women are Honored, Gods reside there'. She was known as 'Ardhangani'—one half of the husband's body. As a mother, wife and sister, she occupied an Honored place. She is the epitome of courage and boldness, love and affection, sacrifice and suffering. Traditions such as Sati, Jauhar and Devadasi among some communities have been banned in modern India. However, some instances of these practices are still found in remote parts of India. The purdah is still followed by Indian women in some communities. Child marriage remains common in rural areas, although it is illegal under the current Indian law. In spite of these conditions, women often became prominent in the fields of politics, literature, education and religion. But still, India ranked as the fourth worst country in terms of women's safety. The reason behind this is increase in the rate of crime against women.

A challenge that pops up when addressing "Honor crimes" in relation to the global rights-based agenda is whether they should be classified as "correctional crimes" in the West or as infringements of human rights only in the East. Is it anything worth thinking about? Does it come along with it too? (Caffaro et al., 2014) The main consideration when analyzing acts of assault made by people as an offense of human rights is whether the state encourages such conduct or if it fails to protect fundamental human rights. Victims of abuse of such a nature. Nevertheless, it's essential to keep in mind that honorable killings and murders inspired by passion are not exactly the same. Understanding these differences helps the reader understand the rationale behind the actions of criminals and police officers. Judges and lawmakers are members of the society in which they live. Moreover, most cases of exoneration appear to be genuinely motivated by considerations of Honor rather than passion.

It is also worth noting that there is some opposition to the use of the word "honor" in the murder, with some suggesting that the term "femicide" is a better choice. Others spoke of "honor killings" or "shame killings" practices favored by United

Nations Secretary-General Kofi Annan. This quote seems to indicate a desire to separate the word "Honor" from violence and murder. However, as noted above, "respect" is a very complex concept and respect pervades many types of behaviour; in extreme cases, this includes killing people in the name of honor rather than shame or "just so. "This is called respect." (Dogan R., 2014)

Laws on Honor Killing

The concept of honor-based murders is a complex lawful issue. Defendants in Western criminal courts tend to justify their actions on the grounds of customary law and moral compliance (for women). They want to lessen the punishment by arguing that the family's honor was preserved or upheld when the murder was carried out. There is little doubt that Islamic societies do not adhere to the habeas corpus doctrine. As a result, women's freedom is not assured. The penal codes of nations like Pakistan, Jordan, and Turkey—which accept or tolerate such crimes—do not expressly mention Honor crimes. Honor killings are not expressly mentioned in Sharia law, and Islam opposes the death penalty for crimes pertaining to honor. However, while Sharia law provides for severe punishment for zina (extramarital sex). In some countries (such as the North Nigeria), the death penalty is still recommended as Premarital sex. (Can, M., & Edirne, T., 2011) The punishment should be less than 100 lashes, and adultery should be punished by stoning, but it is not considered an 'Honor killing' in itself. Islamic courts tend to be very lenient when it comes to bail applications. For example, Pakistani courts tend to look for "mitigating circumstances" for Honor killings, setting the bar for provocation very low. The defense of provocation is usually successful, and the woman in question was "assaulted." If the facts can be proven, the defendant is acquitted. The manliness of the family. The Senate of Pakistan passed a bill in December 2004 that strengthened the prohibition on Honor killings. (Dasgupta, S., 2000). According to the bill, the highest punishment for offenses in which the victim is found to have embarrassed their family is the death penalty. Jobaida Jalal, Pakistan's only female president at that time, claimed that the bill did not go far enough to protect women from violence, and that protection against violence would also apply to male mothers who were considered to harm their families. Jordanian law clearly states that the group must be "cleansed" of injustice. Murder is rarely attempted, and when attempted the average sentence is six months (usually after the victim's death). Despite Queen Rania of Jordan protesting the murders in the country, the Jordanian parliament passed a bill banning the murders in October 2004. On June 23, 2005, judges in Turkey sentenced a small number of murderers have the right to remove it. Who was caught? However, since the new Turkish law, based on EU law, came into force, honor killings have been classified as murder and punishable by life imprisonment. On the other hand, criminals seek protection and removal from culture. As a result, law enforcement agencies in Western Europe have little awareness of how to deal with problems arising on their territory. Honor killings are tolerated in Muslim-dominated countries. Such crimes fall under the criminal code governing murder and other serious crimes against persons.

Since 2000, there have been 12 documented occurrences of honor killings in the UK, however the offenders are hardly ever prosecuted. A special task team was formed by London police in 2003 to look into Honor killings. Honor crimes are admissible in the event of "extreme provocation." In the event that it is successful, the defendant will either go free or get a light sentence. Turkish penal code states that if an illegitimate child is murdered shortly after birth, Article 453 provides for a reduced term; whether murder is committed just before, during, or after delivery, the sentence is lowered by one-eighth. suspicions of infidelity. or promiscuity.

One of the most famous murders was the murder of Heshu Yones, the 16-year-old child of a Kurdish family in London. In 2002, Hersh's father, Abdullah, decided to kill his daughter in the bathroom and became so enraged that he attacked her with a kitchen knife and stabbed her 11 times, leaving her blood on the floor. During the hearing, Abdullah Yunus said in his defense that Hersh attacked her western clothes and her Christian boyfriend. Another defense argument was that he was "willing to kill" Heshu because he had "tarnished" his family's reputation and put his father in an "impossible situation."

The rights to life, liberty, and personal security, as well as the freedom from torture and cruel, inhuman, or humiliating treatment or punishment, as well as the right to equality within the family, are all violated by gender-based violence, sometimes known as "Honor crimes." Additionally, you are entitled to the best possible level of mental and physical well-being. India, as a State party, has an obligation to eradicate all forms of discrimination against women in matters pertaining to marriage and family relations by affording them equal rights to these matters within the broader framework of patriarchal ideas that give rise to "Honor crimes." You can freely choose your spouse and marry only with his free and full consent. This includes refraining from imposing dictatorship on informal customary decision-making bodies such as khap panchayats and interfering with women's right to choose a spouse.

Article 2(c) of CEDAW states that India, as a State Party, is legally obligated to eliminate discrimination against women by any person, organization, or enterprise. The 25 States Parties are required to take the necessary actions to end discrimination against women. Anyone, any group, or any business can do it. Prejudice and customs such as "crimes against Honor" that are "based on the inferiority or superiority of one sex". (Version, 2017) It is necessary to create laws to criminalize various acts that constitute Honor crimes, but it is not sufficient unless the laws are systematically enforced. Sturdy prosecution is one way to make sure that States parties carry out their duty to "take all appropriate measures to eliminate discrimination against women" and to successfully execute the removal of discriminatory concepts like "Honor crimes."

The Indian Constitution holds many clauses that support and allow a citizen to do as and what they choose as long as they do not infringe upon the rights of others. To enable Indian people and individuals to make their own judgments, several fundamental rights and civil liberties have been interpreted broadly. However, fundamental rights and guiding principles of public policy must be construed to permit the application of these liberties and freedoms into ever-more-pervasive spheres of life instead of constantly explicitly addressing issues and freedoms. Honor killings are by definition personal murders. Honor crimes are clearly against both national and international law, which India is required to respect. Thus, the necessary legislative framework is in place to guarantee that the police forces take the appropriate action to guarantee that honor killings do not occur in the nation. Repeated enforcement of these regulations is necessary to guarantee an adequate decrease in the frequency of their violations.

CONCLUSION

Although crime is increasingly occurring in society, the situation is often worsened by the unknown and lack of recognition by the authorities or the courts. Although Honor killings have become cultural and legal in countries such as India, Turkey, Jordan and Pakistan, this does not mean that the murders will be terrible, they should be approached with compassion.

Honor crimes are obviously against both national and international law, which India is required to observe. Therefore, the appropriate legislative structure is in place to ensure that the police forces take the necessary steps to establish that honor killings are prevented in the nation. Repeated enforcement of these regulations is necessary to guarantee a substantial drop in the frequency of their violations. The 1993 "Declaration on the Elimination of Violence against Women" and the 2003 "Working towards the Elimination of Crimes against Women Committed in the Name of Honor" are two UN documents that specifically address crimes of honor killings. In these documents, it is stated clearly that "violence against women is one of the crucial social mechanisms by which women are forced into a subordinate position compared with men, and that violence against women is a manifestation of historically unequal power relations between men and women, which have led to discrimination over and against women by men and to the prevention of women's full advancement." But the issue is not with the legislation itself, or even with its enforcement to a certain extent. The wider problem at hand is that the communities that reside in the places where Honor crimes are most prone to happen actively encourage criminal activity of this kind. The single biggest barrier facing the force created to stop honor crimes is this.

Criminals who appear in court often try to defend their actions for many reasons. Therefore, when considering crimes, the court should evaluate them as "aggravating (not mitigating)"; Under no circumstances should a judge provide some form of "legal" or "religious" defence. Lawyers should adopt a "zero tolerance" attitude and religion or culture should not become legal or judicial defences of violence or murder.

In addition to the problem of domestic violence, the police need to receive the necessary training to be able to demonstrate their work to women Honor killers from different cultures. Crime enforcement agencies must ensure that crime is investigated effectively and efficiently. Courts should not accept "honorary" sentence reductions or qualifications for crimes. Most importantly, the whole society needs to work together to raise public awareness in praise of violence against women. It should be accepted, at the very least, that behavioural crime is challenging and that spotting early warning indicators can be the first step toward saving lives. The only way to end this extremely dishonest conduct will be through strict criminal penalties and aggressive law enforcement.

REFERENCES

Abu-Lughod, L. (2011). Honor and the Sentiments of Loss in the Global Discourse on Muslim Women. In *Violence and Belonging: The Quest for Identity in Post-Colonial Africa* (pp. 16–37). Routledge.

Bhopal, K. (2000). South Asian Women in East London. *European Journal of Women's Studies*, 7(1), 35–52. DOI: 10.1177/135050680000700103

Bhopal, K. (2019). *Gender,'race'and patriarchy: a study of South Asian women*. Routledge. DOI: 10.4324/9780429456305

Bond, J. E. (2012). *HONOR AS PROPERTY - WestlawNext. 202.*

Bui, H. N. (2003). Help-seeking behaviour among abused immigrant women: A case of Vietnamese American women. Violence Against Women, vol. 9, issue(2), pp207-239. https://doi.org/DOI: 10.1177/10778012022390006

Caffaro, F., Ferraris, F., & Schmidt, S. (2014). Gender Differences in the Perception of Honor Killing in Individualist Versus Collectivistic Cultures: Comparison Between Italy and Turkey. *Sex Roles*, 71(9–10), 296–318. DOI: 10.1007/s11199-014-0413-5

Can, M., & Edirne, T. (2011). Beliefs and Attitudes of Final-year Nursing Students on Honor Crimes: A Cross-Sectional Study. *Journal of Psychiatric and Mental Health Nursing*, 18(8), 736–774. DOI: 10.1111/j.1365-2850.2011.01732.x PMID: 21896117

Dasgupta, S. (2000). Charting the course: An overview of domestic violence in the South Asian community in the United States. *Journal of Social Distress and the Homeless, vol9, issue*(3), pp173-185.

Dasgupta, S. D. (2000). Charting the course: An overview of domestic violence in the South Asian community in the U.S. *Journal of Social Distress and the Homeless*, 9(3), 173–185. DOI: 10.1023/A:1009403917198

Deol, Singh Satnam. 2014. "Honor Killings in Haryana State, India: A Content

Dogan, R. (2014). Different cultural understandings of Honor that inspire killing. Homicide Studies, vol18, issue(4),pp 363-388. DOI: 10.1177/1088767914526717

Khan, K. B. (2014). Versions and Subversions of Islamic Cultures in the Film. The Stoning of Soraya M. *Journal of Literary Studies*, 30(3), 149–167. DOI: 10.1080/02564718.2014.949415

Lewisohn, L. "The Modern Novel." *The Sewanee Review*, vol. 17, issue 4, 1909, pp. 458–474. *JSTOR*, www.jstor.org/stable/27532320

Perry, A. (2012). *Honor Killings in Pakistan: An Everyday Matter.* TIME Magazine.

Rana, P. K., & Mishra, B. P. (2013). Honor Killings-A gross violation of Human rights & Its Challenges. *International Journal of Humanities and Social Science Invention*, 2(6), 24–29. www.ijhssi.org

Version, A. U. (2017). General Recommendation No. 35 on Gender-Based Violence against Women, Updating General Recommendation No. 19: Committee on the Elimination of Discrimination against Women. *International Human Rights Law Review*, 6(2), 279–305. DOI: 10.1163/22131035-00602003

Chapter 2
Khap Panchayats and Their Misogynistic Approach:
The Dishonor Behind Honor Killing

Heeuk D. Lee
Weber State University, USA

Aranya Agrawal
GLA University, India

ABSTRACT

Khap Panchayats have historically played a significant role in administering justice at local level, criticism arises due to their male-dominated, patriarchal nature, often resulting in anti-women biases. Their members often include in barbaric practices of killing on the name of safeguarding honor which violate the fundamental and democratic rights of people. An honor killing is a murder carried out to reclaim or preserve the family's honor, often perceived as damaged by the actions of the victim. Honor Killings, viewed as a form of punishment, highlight the manifestation of patriarchal ideologies. This chapter examines the role of Khap Panchayats behind honor killings and explores their dominance in society, influencing even prominent politicians. The chapter further delves into the phenomenon of Khap Panchayats, the self-proclaimed Kangaroo Courts lacking constitutional legitimacy yet enjoying authority within specific caste segments as guardians of honor. The study seeks to understand the reasons for the continued existence of Khaps in India and analyzes their source of strength.

DOI: 10.4018/979-8-3693-9596-7.ch002

BACKGROUND

Sexual praxis has changed with the change of time, but there stands one retrogressive institution in the village community that rigidly refuses to accept modernity. These are the omnipotent Khap Panchayats, perpetuating a patriarchal order. Khap Panchayats are the gathering of upper castes, having muscle & land power, and are influential in a particular village belt. These self-titled guardians profess orthodox morality and distribute justice at will. Khap Panchayats' obsolete faith of the same-gotra marriage is a misdemeanor which makes the guilty to be socially boycotted, exile from the village, drink urine, paraded naked, beaten up or, in predominance, killed, hence become the victim of the infamous honor killing (Mulick, 2007). In their strange belief, falling in love of a man and woman belonging to a same gotra is a worst form of social violation and such a crime attracts an immediate punishment. In cases of honor killings, the target victim is usually a member of the perpetrator's own family or social circle, and more specifically, it is the female member of the family. Khap Panchayats significantly influence honor crimes in rural regions, while such incidents are less prevalent in urban areas.

Key Terms

The central idea of this chapter revolves around the term "Khap Panchayats" and the term "Misogynistic Approach" associates the subject matter of the chapter with "Honor Killing". The terms such as "Intra-gotra marriage", "Inter-caste marriage", "Inter-religious marriage", and "Intra-village marriage" vouch for this approach. Deeper understanding of the terms "Community Governance" And "Public Dispute Redressal Mechanism" provides the basis for the subject matter. Real and substantial terms such as "Regional Dominance", "Political Mileage", Police Ineffectiveness" and "Vote-bank Politics" reveal the social backing behind the adversities of Honor Killing as adjudicated by the Khap Panchayats.

Research Methodology

This study employed a qualitative research method to explore the Khap Panchayats and their Misogynistic Approach as a dishonor behind Honor Killings in India. The process of Data Collection was done in two steps:

1. Keyword identification: Key terms and main headings were identified to guide the data collection process.

2. Literature search: A comprehensive search of written materials was conducted, including research articles, Journals, Newspaper reports and articles, Survey reports and the Interviews with victims (conducted by various news reporters).

Another step was the Data Analysis. Relevant and appropriate data were selected based on the precision of the data to the concept of the chapter and retained for further analysis. Codes were assigned to the selected data to identify patterns and themes forming the chapter headlines. New arguments were framed using the coded data forming the subject matter of the chapter. A comprehensive study of the contemporary concepts of Political Mileage, Vote-bank Politics, Regional Dominance, Police Ineffectiveness and Kangaroo Courts, which shape the accountability and persistence of the Khap Panchayats in the present times was done to trace out the current social standing of the Khap Panchayats. Moving further was forming the Chapter Structure. The data analyzed were integrated to form the overall structure of the chapter.

Literature Review

The Khap Panchayats have a long history, with their origins tracing back to approximately 600 AD, though the exact timeframe is unclear. Dr. Birpal Singh Thenua, Assistant Professor, Sociology, Dayalbagh Educational Institute, Agra, India, in his research article "Khap Panchayats among the Jats of North-West: A Socio-Historical Interpretation of Medieval Period" specifically mentions that the Khap Panchayats gained scholarly attention primarily when media coverage highlighted some of their decisions that infringed upon individual human rights. These controversial decisions often pertained to marriages that contravened traditional moral conduct, particularly those related to village, clan, or Khap brotherhood, which are fundamental to community harmony in northern Indian villages. According to him, Khap Panchayats are believed to have originated as social systems to maintain order in agrarian societies, evolving from tribal councils designed to resolve intra-tribal disputes and facilitate inter-tribal interactions.

According to local lore, the Sarv-Khap Panchayat was first established by Emperor Harsha at Prayagraj (modern-day Allahabad) in the 7th century. Historical records indicate that the Sarv-Khap Panchayat meeting took place on the 10th Ashad, Samvat 1256 (1191 AD) in Tikri Village, Meerut, with 60,000 attendees from various Khap Panchayats. Furthermore, a brief history of the Sarv-Khap Panchayat comes from the Pothi, the unpublished handwritten accounts by Pandit KanhaRam, a resident of Shauram village in Muzaffarnagar district. In his Pothi, Pandit KanhaRam details various historical incidents related to the Khap Panchayats. The Pothi contains 16 handwritten pages, which describe the locations and dates of Khap Panchayat assemblies. Pothi suggests that the first Sarv-Khap Panchayat meeting occurred in the forest of Baraut in 1195 AD, where it was decided to form defense volunteers against Muhammad Ghori's attacks. Another meeting in Samvat 1254 (1197 AD) addressed the imposition of Jazia and restrictions on Panchayats by Qutubuddin Aibak.

Dr. Shereen Sadiq, Department of Sociology, A.M.U., Aligarh, India and Asif Khan, Department of Social Work, A.M.U., Aligarh, India, in their research article "Khap Panchayats In India: Precepts And Practices" have explained how the judicial vacuum in India had led to the evolution of the Khap Panchayats and highlighted that Khap Panchayats served two main purposes before the judicial system was set up and developed in India. First, they provided a platform for resolving conflicts through direct negotiation between the parties involved, which saved time and money compared to more formal legal proceedings. Second, they enforced traditional moral codes of conduct within the community, ensuring that social norms and values were upheld.

The authors Ratika Thakur, A. K. Sinha and R. K. Pathak, Department of Anthropology, Panjab University, Chandigarh, in their research article "Khap Panchayats in Transition with Contemporary Times: An Anthropological Evaluation" draws attention to the fact that while many Indians today are embracing modern perspectives, there is still a segment of the population that clings to old societal practices and resists any change. Tensions rose in June 2010, when a Public Interest Litigation (PIL) was filled by the members of the Khap Panchayats seeking to amend the Hindu Marriage Act, 1955, to prohibit marriages within the same gotra (clan). This unrest was not spontaneous but rather a well-organized effort of the Khap Panchayats.

Shakti Vahini, a women's right NGO, in collaboration with the National Women's Commission carried out a survey for the year 2008–2009, based on data from First Information Reports (FIRs) related to honor killings. 354 cases of violence were analyzed. The survey found that 72 percent of these honor killing cases were related to inter-caste marriages, 3 percent to same-gotra marriages, and 15 percent to the non-consent of parents. Consequently, only 2.4 percent of cases fell under the category of gotra marriage. Notably, most of these so-called 'crimes' were instigated by Khap Panchayats, which often lack legal or constitutional authority. These panchayats typically claim legitimacy based on historical traditions or social conventions.

Research Gap

Khap Panchayats are indeed a significant aspect of rural governance in certain parts of India, particularly in Haryana, Uttar Pradesh, and Rajasthan. Despite their importance, there is a scarcity of written material and academic research on this topic. Much of the existing information about Khap Panchayats comes from news reports, which often focus on controversial and sensational cases, such as illegal diktats imposing harsh punishments like honor killings or forced marriages, caste-based discrimination and violence, restrictions on women's rights and freedoms, opposition to inter-caste marriages and love marriages, support for regressive social practices, etc. To fill the knowledge gap and promote a deeper understanding of Khap Panchayats, contributions from academicians, researchers, and practitioners are essential. They have a crucial role to play in shedding light on the complexities of Khap Panchayats and their impact on society.

INTRODUCTION

To fully comprehend the phenomenon of honor killings in India, it is essential to examine the historical roots and evolution of the social systems that enable and encourage honor killings. Although there is ambiguity regarding the origin of Khaps, the expert's opinion holds it to have originated from the term "khatrap" of Saka language, which implies clan-specific region, and to have dated back to around 600 AD (Amardeep, 2021). Khap Panchayats are the local groups at the village level, representing a North-Indian caste-group or clan(gotra). They are mostly found among the Jats and Gujjars of Northen States like Haryana, Western Uttar Pradesh, but also in Rajasthan and Madhya Pradesh, and some parts of Punjab. The Khaps are more powerful in the Rohtak, Jhajjar, Bhiwari, Sonipat, Jind, Kaithal, Karnal and Hisar districts of Haryana ("What are Khap Panchayats?", 2010). The Jats are divided into numerous gotras (clans), more than any other community. Ancient literature about the Hindu caste system emphasizes the crucial role of gotras. The common belief is that gotras are named after a shared ancestor, creating a sense of brotherhood among members of the same gotra. This is why Khap Panchayats oppose intra-gotra marriages and are now seeking an amendment to the Hindu Marriage Act (Bharadwaj, 2012).

Historical Evolution of Khap Panchayats

The Khaps were an integral part of social structure and were renowned as the social institution resolving disputes until the judicial system was developed and established in India. Khap Panchayats have played a major role as the public dispute redressal forums at the local levels where the parties could negotiate differences and advance to settlements without wasting money and time. These panchayats provided a platform to settle disputes by mutual agreement and under the guidance of the village elder men who would have found the way out without going against the ethos of the village. Khap Panchayats, established centuries ago, were originally intended to unify and safeguard local communities and traditions. Khap Panchayats, as headed by the elderly, acted as the guardian of social conduct, an agency to decide the moral code of conduct and to enforce the measure of the social control. Decisions made by these assemblies were binding for both parties. If a party ever wished to challenge a decision, they could seek recourse with the Sarv-khap, a higher assembly composed of representatives from neighboring Khaps in the region. The quick and efficient mechanism of justice-delivery, coupled with the strong sense of unity and community backing provided by villagers, solidified the Khaps' respected position in society (Khan & Sadiq, 2018).

Recently, the influence and importance of Khap Panchayats have decreased because they are traditional and as per the Constitution, elected Panchayats have come ("What are Khap Panchayats?", 2010). Khap Panchayats have been subjected to criticism for delivering numerous judgements which majorly hinders basic freedom of people. Khap leaders have ordered intentional killing of young couples many times since they hold a prejudice of inter-caste, inter-religious and intra-village marriages as against the ethos. As a result, it is needed to examine its functioning.

Geographical Context for the Persistence of Khap Panchayats in North-West India

Khap Panchayats are thought to have been established by the upper caste 'Jats' to strengthen their authority and status within the community. The first Khap Panchayat was of Jats. The Jats & Khaps draw a parallel with each other. Gotra is the third parallel to them. These three elements are the agency of authority & power among the rural communities of the North-Indian States, where the Jat community exists. Khap Panchayats are predominantly found in North India due to many historical, social, and cultural reasons. Especially in rural areas of Punjab-Haryana, Jats have vast lands, they have significant influence in administration and politics, and their population is also very high. Apparently, they are influential in these states and hence Khap Panchayats are dominated in North-West Indian states (Sangar, 2009). North India has a predominantly agrarian economy, and Khap Panchayats have traditionally played a role in resolving disputes related to land, agriculture, and social norms within these rural communities. In many rural areas of North India, formal legal and governance structures were less accessible or trusted by the local population. Khap panchayats had filled this gap by providing a localized and culturally resonant mechanism for dispute resolution and community governance.

The Khap Panchayats have a long history dating back to the 14th century, but their significant influence is largely a result of the trust and dependence people had on them during the British colonial era. Khap Panchayats were not only custodians of social norms and values but also played a crucial role in providing both external and internal security to their communities, especially against invaders. These councils ensured that social order was maintained and that the community was protected from external threats (Thenua, 2016). Local lore suggests that Khaps from the Jat community, known for their warrior spirit, resisted both Mughal invaders and the Britishers (Makkar, 2013). In general, the Jats, who were often part of these Khaps, exhibited a strong democratic inclination in their behavior. This democratic ethos was reflected in the functioning of the Khap Panchayats, where decisions were made collectively, and the opinions of various representatives were considered before arriving at a consensus. This democratic approach helped maintain a sense of unity and order within the community.

Khap Panchayats were particularly influential during the Delhi Sultanate and Mughal periods. These local councils held considerable military power and played a significant role in maintaining order within their jurisdictions. Notably, several Delhi rulers, such as Ibrahim Lodi and Muhammad Shah, sought military assistance from the Wazirs (leaders) of prominent Khap Panchayats, like the Balian Khap, to quell revolts and expel rebels from their territories. However, this support was contingent on the approval of the Sarv Khap Panchayat, a larger assembly representing various Khaps. The conditions for providing military aid were thoroughly discussed and agreed upon by the representatives of these Khaps, ensuring that the assistance aligned with the collective interests of the communities involved (Thenua, 2016).

Given that the Khap Panchayats are typically composed of members from various Jat gotras, which explains why their primary activities are concentrated in regions like Haryana, Western Uttar Pradesh, and the rural areas surrounding the National Capital of Delhi (Bharadwaj, 2012).

Adjudication of Khap Panchayats

The functions of Khap Panchayat can be categorized as adjudicative, legislative, and executive. The legislative functions, though, have got limited now as they have no legal authority as they enjoyed earlier. However, Khap Panchayats function only as adjudicative bodies now to decide the cases of flouting social norms (Pradhan, n.d.).

One single gotra or all the gotras of a community together form a Khap Panchayat. Since independence, there has been a change in the pattern of population in an area. A village that initially consisted of 5 gotras is now composed of 15–20 gotras. Consequently, the restrictions that were imposed on making relations between castes, clans or gotras within a particular village have now become difficult to follow. For example, if earlier there was a ban on marriage within five gotras, now the ban has been extended to 20 gotras. Such a widening of the restrictions has increased the limitations on choosing a partner for marriage. Moreover, when the population of girls is already lower in the Northern States as compared to that of boys, there is a lot of pressure on the institution of marriage. On the other hand, as the children are getting more educated, the opportunities for boys & girls to meet each other are also increasing. When you go out of village limits, you do not care which caste or clan the person you meet belongs (Sangar, 2009).

Issuing fatwas for declaring marriage as void, making husband and wife as brother and sister, ordering abortions has been the method of the Khap Panchayats to order honor killing. These fatwas are so bizarre and frequent that a series of writ petitions against these diktats have been filed in many High Courts. If the Khap Panchayat has any objection to the marriage, then they decide to separate the boy and the girl, cancel the marriage, socially boycott the family, or expel them from the village, and in exceptional cases, even kill the boy and the girl. This practice has long been followed and as the villages got settled, such traditions started developing (Sangar, 2009).

Whenever there arises a discussion on violence and murder that occurs in the name of safeguarding honor by a caste or family group, it is conventional for the Khap Panchayat to enter the discussion. In cases of marriages against the social order, even if a family prefers to resolve the matter peacefully, they are pressured by Khap Panchayats to treat it as a grave issue of honor. They remain ready to intervene if the family does not conform, effectively forcing them to make sacrifices of their sons and daughters in the name of preserving honor. Consequently, the concept of honor often overrides human emotions and values (Khan & Sadiq, 2018). Honor crimes can stem from various actions such as same-gotra marriages, inter-religious marriages, inter-caste marriages, inter-class marriages, having pre-marital relationships, or any marriage that defies the wishes of one's parents or the ethos of society.

As speaking of now, they have become oppressive and contradicting the law of the land. It must be acknowledged that the cases of honor killing have increased a lot in recent times (Sangar, 2009). While a process of metamorphosis characterized by the withering of old customs & traditions is occurring in India, society and people are catching up to modernity. Khap Panchayat sticks to and resists any change in age-old practices. This disturbance increased when the Khap Panchayat filed a PIL which sought to ban same-gotra marriages by amending the Hindu Marriage Act, 1955 (Thakur et al., 2015).

Honor Killing: A Result of Khap's Misogynistic Approach

Khap Panchayats adjudicate purely on patriarchal and caste-ridden lines, as they are the assembly of village elder men who are all male. Women are neither included nor represented in them. Khap Panchayats function as the custodians of honors. In Indian patriarchal families, honor is a deeply cherished value that transcends caste, regional, and religious boundaries. This concept of honor is inherently gender notioned in India, with distinct meaning of honor assigned to men and women. Women are seen as the bearers of family honor in the roles of daughters, wives, and mothers, while men are viewed as the guardians of this honor. They believe that the term honor always relates to the women of the family, and the men are considered to protect it and prevent women from abusing it. Honor is intricately linked to women, with men holding the authority to ensure that women do not compromise it. The control is exercised over women through mechanisms such as arranged marriages, child marriages, the prohibition of divorce, strict enforcement of monogamy, bans on widow remarriage, and the severe isolation of widows. Consequently, being a woman involves being simultaneously protected and subjected to violence (Khan & Sadiq, 2018).

Such a patriarchal mindset is predominantly preached by the Khaps of the North-Western States. Khaps, being male-dominated, attempt to regulate marriages in accordance with patriarchal social norms. The intense fear of losing honor drives men to rationalize and justify acts of aggression and violence towards women. Such attempts ultimately and unfortunately end with the gruesome act of honor killing, predominantly of which the females fall as victims (Khan & Sadiq, 2018).

Khap Panchayats have been in the news due to their anti-women decisions and interference in people's personal matters. These male dominated bodies are infamous across the world for ordering harassment and even murder in the name of honor (Sinha, 2014). There are instances in which the staunch misogynist approach of these Khap Panchayats came clearly evident in many public gatherings where the leaders or the members of the various Khap Panchayats have made strong male-centric comments.

Balwan Singh Nain, an old farmer and a member of Sarva Jaateeya Venain Khap of Damoda Kalan Village, Haryana, said in an interview that the family's honor is in the hands of women, not men. If she cannot keep the honor, she is solely at fault. He explained that the Khap Panchayats work on a formula of social pressure. If a man's honor is transgressed due to his daughter's or sister's or wife's overstepping the social boundaries, he cannot live with his head high. In order to save himself from such insult, he might decide to kill the concerned female. This view appears to directly comes from the heels of the misogynist approach behind honor killing which leads such patriarchal Khaps to order killing a couple who had married against the social norms (Kumar, 2012). Naresh Tikait, head of the Balyan Khap of Haryana, criticised love marriages by precepting marriages as a union of two consenting families, not just two individuals, so the families have a direct say in that. Tikait furthered to make a staunch Chauvinist remark that it is not acceptable to the parents that the girls whom they raise, educate, and invest in for their upbringing marry by their own choice. In more than one instance, Naresh Tikait made such misogynistic statements. In February 2018, he reacted to the Supreme Court's verdict regarding

Khap Panchayat's opposition to marriage and honor killing practices as illegal and a violation of the Indian Constitution. To this, he threatened to promote the female feticide or to stop educating girls if such orders were passed by the Supreme Court (Rai, 2019). Ram Swaroop Singh, leader of Sheoran Khap of Bhiwani District in Haryana, unapologetically showcased his intolerance to the same-gotra marriages and held that it is a crime which is to be published (Rohit Mulick, 2007).

Police forces are often criticized for their ineffectiveness in safeguarding those at risk of honor crimes, frequently showing reluctance to register complaints or conduct thorough investigations. This can be attributed to the traditional patriarchal attitudes many officers hold. According to Shakti Vahini's interviews with 300 police officers in northern India, 85% opposed same-gotra marriages, 70% were against inter-caste marriages, and 62% admitted they would react strongly if an inter-caste marriage occurred in their own family.

Not only undemocratic, but also anti-women have always been the approach of these Khaps. The strong hold of patriarchy to the Khap Panchayats had never led women to take part in Khap deliberations. So, the male gets away, but the female never does from the retribution of these Kangaroo Courts (Thakur et al., 2015).

Khap Panchayats' Transformation into Kangaroo Courts

Courts play a crucial role in democratic society. In addition to the official Indian Courts, many communal Courts are recognized by the local residents to settle numerous concerns within their community. One such body dispensing the functioning of unauthorized Courts is Khap Panchayat. These extra constitutional units of judgement delivery give verdicts that hold unconstitutional status and at most instances, contradictory of the Constitution. These non-democratic entities believe themselves to adjudicate in the matters of societal norms and practices, and punish the rule breakers (Amardeep, 2021). In North-Western states, these bodies operate largely retrogressive and unofficially correspond to official law-enforcement agencies, thereby literally transforming into Kangaroo Courts. Even though the Khap Panchayats are illegal entities, their word prevails as a de-facto law in many North-Western states (Rohit Mulick, 2007). Because these are not officially recognized panchayats, hence, in modern India if any class is feeling insecure or is worried about its decreasing influence, then it is the Khap Panchayat. That is why Khap Panchayats raise sensitive and emotional issues so that they can get the support of common people (Sangar, 2009).

The most oppressive and challenging decisions given by Khaps limit the choice of life partner. Khaps have long been in terms of limiting the persons who chose their life partners beyond social etiquette and social structure. The wedding provides sanctity in lineage; anyone who contracts it in contravention of social norms is considered to have introduced shame on the honor of the lineage. Therefore, Khaps hold that, being the leaders of the culture, they are under a duty to preserve the cultural norms and practices. Democracy places everyone equal. In this situation, if a boy or girl takes their own decision regarding marriage then they have legal sanction, but not social because of these self-titled Kangaroo Courts. The AIDWA (All India Democratic Women's Association) in its report of investigation of the various decisions of the Khap Panchayats, alleged Khaps to have triggered the threat of murder and violence to couples, who marry outside of the circle (Rajalakshmi, 2004).

Some time ago, the Punjab-Haryana High Court has talked about bringing these Caste Panchayats under the ambit of the 'Unlawful Activities Prevention Act' to control those who defy the laws provided by the Constitution. After the strictness of the Haryana High Court, the administration also had to be strict. It suspended some of the revenue officers of Rohtak who had participated in a panchayat that declared a man and a woman performing endogamy as the brother and sister (Pradhan, n.d.). Khap Panchayats do not even adhere to the provisions of the Hindu Marriage Act, 1955, according to which sagotra and intercaste marriages are not barred but operate on their own laws. The traditional Khap Panchayat governs mainly in four spheres of rural life: unity (Aikya), community (Biradari), honor (Izzat), and brotherhood (Bhaichara). They hold the bhaichara as included in gotra, caste, and territory. The principle of bhaichara considers the males and females of the same gotra and village as brothers and sisters. Therefore, Khaps insist on gotra exogamy but caste endogamy. Territory exogamy prohibits marriages within the same villages or the neighbouring villages (Thakur et al., 2015).

One of the instances which hit the headlines for the Khap's inhumane verdict against the choice of life partner was in 2004 when the Rathi Khap of Asanda village located in the Jhajjar district of Haryana. Sonia and Ram Pal, who had been married for a year then and were expecting their first child were ordered to annul their marriage and terminate the pregnancy. In accordance to the most usual method of Khap Panchayats, Sonia was forced treat her husband as a brother to remain in the village. This drastic decision was due to the couple sharing the same gotra, despite such marriages being recognized under the Hindu Marriage Act. It was only after the High Court intervened and instructed the Haryana government to provide protection that Sonia and Ram Pal could live together again (Rohit Mulick, 2007).

Politics and Khap

The Khap Panchayat's unparalleled dictatorship and undemocratic court system have been stalled numerous times. But even the Supreme Court's decisions were rendered ineffective due to the political support these Khap Panchayats enjoy. But why cannot such irrational organizations be outlawed? The complicated political system of India is the answer to this issue. Khap Panchayats are regioned in Jats and Gujjars dominated areas, where these two communities have both a majority population and power. This implies a larger political force and a large voting bank, which would result in a larger electoral loss for the ruling party. Consequently, society's harmony is being destroyed by the political tactics. For two or three decades, these Khaps have been mobilized for political mileage in the cloak of safeguarding traditions. The politicians deal with them with the utmost care and as fragile bodies for fear of losing their vote banks. Packed with such solid support, it is evident that the Khap Panchayats are not hesitant to hail their unjust instant justice. To substantiate this, some politicians have given their assent to the Khaps and regard them as playing a vital role in society (Rohit Mulick, 2007).

Monohar Lal Khattu, the current CM of Haryana defended Khap Panchayats in an interview. He compared them with the guardian of a child and regarded Khaps to function as a court system at the grass-root level which prevents a matter from going into the official judiciary for years. He added that as the Khap Panchayats consist of the elder male members of the society, thus, they are respectable. Bhupinder Singh Hooda, the former CM of Haryana, strongly favoring Khaps put forward that Khaps are welfare units like NGOs and are right in limiting same gotra marriages as such marriages are against our culture. Therefore, the country, whose leaders openly support institutions behind honor killing would have fate only in the hands of injustice (Rohit Mulick, 2007). At a public gathering in Rohtak, Haryana, the natives narrated the incidents in which the Khap Panchayats have made life difficult for the young couples who marry outside social parameters. Organised by the All-India Democratic Women's Association, its president highlighted the particular trend that the local administration observes in village belts. The administration is never keen on taking action on its own in such cases. Rather, it greatly functions reluctantly, even when it is under pressure to do it. The influence of these Khaps, being the traditional institutions is so big and alike among villages and urban class that the administration fails to act on time to their diktats (Rajalakshmi, 2004).

The Panchayati Raj Singh System in many villages has been overshadowed by these Khap Panchayats. Khap Panchayats take over the elected Sarpanches of the official Panchayats and do not allow them to function. In some cases, the constitutionally elected Sarpanches also side with them, as without their support, it is difficult for them to get elected. Thereby the idea of decentralization has failed in many North-Western states (Makkar, 2013). The Khap system has been corrupted in the past few decades due to some vested interests: To begin with, the Khap Panchayats enjoy faith as these are the non-economic entities, contrary to the elected panchayats, sarpanches of which are often accused of misappropriation of funds. In addition, Khap Panchayats act as the instant redressal forums at the community level to settle social disputes.

Honor Killing Decisions of Khap Panchayats

Mehrana Honor Killing Case: The Khap Panchayats of Mehrana Village of Mathura District of Uttar Pradesh has decreed the honor killing of a dalit boy, who had eloped with his girlfriend, a higher caste Jaat, and also of the boy's cousin who had helped the couple to run away to marry. The killing took place in 1991 (India 'honour killers' face death for 1991 murders, 2011).

Smt Laxmi Kachhwaha V/S State of Rajasthan, 1993: A petition highlighted the atrocities as being committed by the Khap Panchayats against women and how these bodies act as the autocratic and male-centric Kangaroo Courts. The guidelines were issued by the Rajasthan High Court to the state authorities restricting the functioning of these Khaps and ordering the arrest of its members in case they are found acting as the infringer of basic human rights (Smt_Laxmi_Kachhawaha_vs_The_State_And_Ors_on_15_March_1999, n.d.).

Manoj-Babli Case, 2007: The story of Manoj and Babli is the one which could very probably be the story of many couples who fell victim to honor killing as ordered by the Khap Panchayats. On an assumption that since the couple belong to the banwala gotra of the Jat community, they are related as siblings and thus, their marriage is incestuous, the Khap Panchayats of Karora village of Kaithal district of Haryana decreed to murder them for bringing shame to the honor of the village (Rajalakshmi, 2004). So much so was the dominance of these Khap Panchayats that even the local police administration was reluctant to arrest the leaders of the Karora Khap Panchayat. The Khap Panchayats around Haryana were issuing warnings against the arrest of leaders. A senior police officer cited in the court that the arrest of the Khap leader would create a law-and-order situation (Dashing hopes, Emboldening Khaps- The High Court verdict on the Manoj Babli Case, 2011).

The Manoj Babli case was the classic example of the age-old tradition of oppression against women. As observed by Judge Vani Gopal Sharma, this honor killing case reflected the most inhumane and ruthless behaviour of Khap Panchayats towards women, as guarded by their misogynistic approach. These so-called Kangaroo Courts had extended their autocracy to the extent that their fear not only stalked the couple that married out of the circle, but they also started the alarming judiciary of Haranya. The judge who gave a death sentence to five convicts in the Manoj and Babli case sought transfer after being threatened by the Khap members. Most of the honor killing are women centric and very rarely targeted on men, leading to gender-based violence (Rajalakshmi, 2004).

Ved Pal-Sonia Case, 2007: This case is yet another identical case where the Khap Panchayats have attempted to control the destiny of a young couple. The Khap Panchayats of Jind district of Haryana had ordered the killing of a young couple Vedpal & Sonia who performed the love marriage within the adjoining village. Thus, the Khap rules says they had brought dishonor to their respective village and must be killed for preserving honor (Nandal, 2009).

Jharkhand Journalist Honor Killing Case, 2010: In the yet another case of honor killing as ordered by the Khap Panchayats of Jharkhand, a women journalist Nirupama was murdered by her parents for performing an inter-caste marriage with her alleged boyfriend Priyabhasu (Journalist's mother arrested for alleged honour killing, 2010).

Arumugan Servai V/S State of Tamil Nadu, 2011: The Supreme Court stated the acts of honor killings as institutionalized by the Khap Panchayats as illegal and regarded these bodies as corresponding to Kangaroo Courts. The Court gave strict guidelines for the arrest, prosecution, and earliest conviction of those who were involved in such barbaric crimes.

Sivakumar-Megala Case, 2018: This case is the manifestation of the patriarchal Khap's total intolerance towards women marrying the life partner of their own choice. It is evident from this case that the area of influence of the Khap Panchayats has not only remained in the Norther-Western States, but these Khaps have spread their tentacles all over India. The present case is of a similar type where a young couple was brutally killed to death by a village member in Chennai, Tamil Nadu, for bringing dishonor to the community by performing a love marriage (Umachandran, 2010).

Shakti Vahini V. Union of India and Others, 2018: In this landmark judgement, a bench of the Supreme Court consisting of Chief Justice Dipak Misra, Justice AM Khanwilkar, and Justice DY Chandrachud held that it is illegal for these self-styled Kangaroo Courts or any such assemblies to pass diktats or punish the couples in the name of honor for exercising the right to choose their life partners. Khap Panchayat cannot take law into their own hands and also doesn't have any authority to determine the validity of the marriage. The Court further directed the administration and issued guidelines to tackle the Khap Panchayats strictly (Dahiya, 2019).

Any police officer or District Administration officer who comes to know about the Khap Panchayat gathering must immediately inform the jurisdictional Deputy Superintendent of Police and Superintendent of Police. The DSP must inform the Khap Panchayat members that holding a meeting is against the law. Despite the information, if the meeting commences, the DSP must personally attend it and make it clear to the group that no decisions should be made that could harm the couple or their family members; otherwise, everyone present at the meeting would be personally responsible for any criminal offences committed (Singh, 2023). Regardless of the preventive measures taken by the state police, Khap Panchayats have passed any diktat to take action against a couple or family of an inter-caste or inter-religious marriage or any other marriage that is against their ethos. The jurisdictional police official shall immediately lodge an FIR under the appropriate provisions of the Indian Penal Code.

CONCLUSION

In conclusion, this chapter has explored the intricate dynamics surrounding Khap Panchayats and their misogynistic approach, particularly in the context of honor killings. Despite lacking constitutional legitimacy, these self-proclaimed courts wield significant influence, perpetuating a patriarchal order that disproportionately impacts women's rights. The study has highlighted the transformation of Khap Panchayats into unofficial Kangaroo Courts, challenging the principles of democracy and posing obstacles to societal progress. The analysis of specific honor killing cases has brought to light the harsh consequences faced by individuals who defy the norms imposed by Khap Panchayats. The paper underscores the urgency of addressing the deep-seated patriarchal ideologies within these institutions, which not only disregard legal frameworks like the Hindu Marriage Act but also operate in contravention of basic human rights.

Furthermore, the examination of political support for Khap Panchayats reveals a complex landscape where these entities often enjoy protection due to their influence on vote banks, creating a challenge for the effective implementation of legal measures against them. The reluctance of the administration to counteract Khap decisions in certain regions underscores the pervasiveness of their impact, even in the face of legal opposition. In moving forward, it is imperative for society, legal institutions, and policymakers to collectively challenge and dismantle the regressive practices of Khap Panchayats. Efforts should be directed towards raising awareness, fostering gender equality, and reinforcing the rule of law to eradicate honor killings and ensure the protection of fundamental rights. The transformation of social attitudes and the empowerment of women within these communities are vital steps towards dismantling the misogynistic foundations that sustain Khap Panchayats.

REFERENCES

Amardeep. (2021, August 7th). *Honour Killings in India and Role of Khap Panchayats*. Retrieved from Legal Services India E-Journal: https://www.legalserviceindia.com/legal/article-7542-honour-killings-in-india-and-role-of-khap-panchayats.html

Bharadwaj, S. B. (2012). Myth and Reality of the Khap Panchayats: A Historical Analysis of the Panchayat and Khap Panchayat. *Studies in History*, 28(1), 43–67. DOI: 10.1177/0257643013477250

Dahiya, K. (2019). Role of Khap Panchayat in Honour Killings. In *International Journal of All Research Education and Scientific Methods (IJARESM)* (Vol. 7, Issue 2).

Dashing hopes, Emboldening Khaps- The High Court verdict on the Manoj Babli Case. (2011, March 18th). Retrieved from Nwes Click: https://www.newsclick.in/dashing-hopes-emboldening-khaps-high-court-verdict-manoj-babli-case

India 'honour killers' face death for 1991 murders. (2011, November 16th). Retrieved from BBC News: https://www.bbc.com/news/world-south-asia-15759470

Journalist's mother arrested for alleged honour killing. (2010, May 4th). Retrieved from NDTV: https://www.ndtv.com/india-news/youth-beaten-to-death-for-marrying-398516/amp/1

Khan, A., & Sadiq, S. (2018). KHAP PANCHAYATS IN INDIA: PRECEPTS AND PRACTICES. In *Article in International Journal of Current Research*. https://www.researchgate.net/publication/329311612

Kumar, R. (2012, October 12th). *In Rural Haryana, Women Blamed for Rape Where Men Make Rules*. Retrieved from India Ink, The New York Times: https://archive.nytimes.com/india.blogs.nytimes.com/2012/10/12/in-rural-haryana-women-blamed-for-rape-where-men-make-the-rules/

Makkar, S. (2013, May 1st). *Panchayats under the shadow of Khaps*. Retrieved from mint: https://www.livemint.com/Politics/nW03eT80k8lmHDfAUGh33J/Panchayats-under-the-shadow-of-the-khaps.html

Nandal, R. S. (2009, July 23rd). *Youth beaten to death for marrying*. Retrieved from NDTV: https://www.ndtv.com/india-news/youth-beaten-to-death-for-marrying-398516/amp/1

Pradhan, M. (n.d.). *The Jats of Nother India and their Traditional Political System*. Retrieved from The Economic Weekly: http://www.epw.in/system/files/pdf/1965_17/51/the_jats_of_northern_indiatheir_traditional_political_systemii.pdf

Rai, S. (2019, November 23rd). *Love Marriages not acceptable, we won't allow them: Balyan Khap leader*. Retrieved from The Times Of India: https://timesofindia.indiatimes.com/city/meerut/love-marriages-not-acceptable-we-wont-allow-them-khap-leader/articleshow/72190461.cms

Rajalakshmi, T. (2004). *Caste Terror*. Frontline.

Rohit Mulick, N. R. (2007, September 9th). *Panchayats turn into kangroo courts*. Retrieved from The Times of India: https://timesofindia.indiatimes.com/home/sunday-times/deep-focus/panchayats-turn-into-kangaroo-courts/articleshow/2351247.cms

Sangar, A. (2009, August 5th). *What are Khap Panchayats, why they have dominance?* Retrieved from BBC News: https://www.bbc.com/hindi/india/2009/08/090805_honorkill_expert_as

Singh, J. (2023, November 2). *Shakti Vahini vs. Union of India (2018): Case Analysis*. Retrieved from iPleaders: https://blog.ipleaders.in/shakti-vahini-vs-union-of-india-2018-case-analysis/#)

Sinha, A. (2014, April 26th). *Transformation of Khap Panchayats*. Retrieved from Sahara Samay Live: http://m.samaylive.com/editorial/262627/khap-deleted-conditional-ban-on-interracial-marriages.html

Smt_Laxmi_Kachhawaha_vs_The_State_And_Ors_on_15_March_1999. (n.d.).

Thakur, R., Sinha, A. K., & Pathak, R. K. (2015). Khap Panchayats in Transition with Contemporary Times: An Anthropological Evaluation. *South Asian Anthropologist*, 15(1), •••.

Thenua, B. S. (2016). Khap Panchayats among the Jats of North-West: A Socio-Historical Interpretation of Medieval Period. *IRA-International Journal of Management & Social Sciences (ISSN 2455-2267)*, 5(3), 402. DOI: 10.21013/jmss.v5.n3.p2

Umachandran, S. (2010, July 7th). *Now, honour killing rocks TN: Father attacks daughter*. Retrieved from The Times of India: https://m.timesofindia.com/india/now-honor-killing-rocks-tn-father-attacks-daughter/articleshow/6136096.cms

What are Khap Panchayats? (2010, May 12th). Retrieved from Hindustan Times: https://www.hindustantimes.com/india/what-are-khap-panchayats/story-aAx17V9V2eDeD4hMA4wb4N.htm

Chapter 3
Patriarchal Enmity in the Guise of Honor:
An Indian Enigma

Somesh Dhamija
GLA University, India

Nikita Singh
GLA University, India

ABSTRACT

The title of the chapter emphasizes the constructivist approach of patriarchy which eventually results into honor killing and frequently mirrors the violent patriarchy committed in the name of honor. Since izzat, or the ideology of honor, is a gendered concept in India, men and women represent it in very different ways. As a daughter, wife, and mother, a woman holds the family honor, which a man controls. The UNFPA estimates a very shocking number of 5000 females including both women and girls are murdered by members of their own families. In India, 356 cases of honor killings and 65 cases of culpable homicide were registered, according to a recent National Crime Record Bureau report. It is evident that a broad spectrum of moderation in an effective manner is required to combat masculinist violence and women's sovereignty in India. The statement "The Freedom of Belief doesn't mean Freedom to Kill" is appropriate to highlight in this situation. Everybody has the right to lead an equitable, honorable, and dignified life.

DOI: 10.4018/979-8-3693-9596-7.ch003

Copyright © 2025, IGI Global. Copying or distributing in print or electronic forms without written permission of IGI Global is prohibited.

INTRODUCTION

Thematic connections between patriarchy and honor killing in India are explicit as both are based in a culture that promotes male dominance and female subjugation. Honor killing, a violent murder carried out by family members aimed at a victim who is believed to have violated the honor of the family or community, and patriarchy, a social structure in which men are perceived as holding a higher position of power, are two closely connected characteristics. The correlation within patriarchy and honor killings is especially noticeable in India due to the country's lengthy history of patriarchal laws and customs and the prevalence of honor killings there.

'What is honor, and why is it pervasive in all cultures and civilizations? In a nutshell it is described as "a person's morally righteous deeds that can garner respect from the person, family, and society." Many people around the world base their lives, customs, and values on honor, which is a code of conduct, way of life, and social order. The identification becomes problematic when this moral ideal veers too close to individual autonomy. Any society or civilization has deeply rooted norms, ethics, values, and so on that revolve around honor, pride, respect, or izzat (Kaushal, 2020). It is common in everyone's behavior, whether eastern or western, caste or religious.

Honor killing is a brutal means of enforcing the rigid gender rules that patriarchy establishes and upholds. Promoting gender equality and women's rights as well as challenging and undermining patriarchal practices and attitudes are essential to ending this vicious cycle. It is a very severe kind of discipline applied to individuals, usually women who are believed to have embarrassed their family or community. Getting married outside of one's caste or religion, having sex before or after marriage, or even clothing in a way that is considered improper can all be causes of the perceived dishonor.

In India, patriarchy is firmly embedded and can take many different forms, including child marriage, dowries, discrimination against women, and domestic abuse. It is a system that tightly upholds gender roles and conventions, favors men, and subjugates women. Women are subject to stringent rules on their behavior, particularly with regard to their sexuality, as they are considered the stewards of family honor in this society. Any deviation from the accepted norms is perceived as a threat to the family's honor and reputation.

In layman's terms, "honor killing" is the murder of a female family member by multitudinous male members of the family. However, female family members are occasionally involved in this crime as well. The entire globe watches this horrific crime. It has received widespread coverage in Islamic Republic of Iran, Turkey, Afghanistan, Iraq, Saudi Arabia, Egypt, Palestine, Jordan, Bangladesh, Algeria, Brazil, Ecuador, Morocco, State of Israel, Ethiopia, Somalia, Uganda, the Balkans,

Sweden, Holland, Germany, Italian Republic, Yemen, Republic of India, and many other nations (D'Lima et al., 2020).

The United Nations Population Fund estimates a bold number of 5000 women and girls are slain by members of their family and/or kinsman each year in the sake of honor across globe (UNFPA, 2004). However, Robert Linier indicated in his study, 'Can Murders and Girls be stopped', that the number 5,000 is likely to be underestimated and that the amount is approximately 20,000 each year worldwide (Kaushal, 2020).

Research Methodology

This chapter aims to draw attention to the constructivist view of patriarchy, which frequently reflects the violent patriarchy carried out in India in the name of honor and ultimately leads to honor killings (Vishwanath & Palakonda, 2011). The qualitative approach to research has been used for the study's objectives. For research purposes, references have been made to surveys, interviews, research articles, government ministry reports, research papers, research articles, international journals, research papers, and reports from international organizations. The qualitative method was chosen since the sources are quite reliable and all kinds of elements, including social, cultural, conservative, and gender-related ones, could be discovered and subsequently developed upon (Kaushal, 2020). Men and women have both been victims, according to the findings. Patriarchy and conservative ideas, based on the research, tend to influence honor killings (Chowdhary, 2007).

Key Terms

Core term include "patriarchy" (Chowdhary, 2007) and "honor killing" (Kaushal, 2020) strongly related because historically, men have dominated women, which has contributed significantly to the continuation of these fierce acts. Male dominance and conventional ideas are viewed as being threatened by "inter-caste relationships" (Chakravarti, 2003). "Women's subjugation" is commensurate with the hierarchy of castes (Liddle & Joshi, 1986). In order to preserve social hierarchies and avoid inter-caste partnerships, which can result in honor killings when rejected, patriarchal civilizations frequently prohibit inter-caste unions and instead encourage "forced marriages" (D'Lima et al., 2020).

Literature Review

The concept of honor killings has been extensively explored in academic literature, with a growing body of research highlighting the role of patriarchal norms and gender-based violence in perpetuating these crimes. Patriarchal ideology has been identified as a key driver of honor killings, with men seeking to maintain their dominance over women and punish those who transgress societal norms (Vishwanath & Palakonda, 2011). The notion of "honor" is often used to justify violence against women, with men claiming to be protecting their family's reputation and social standing (Welchman & Hossain, 2005). The literature suggests that honor killings are a symptom of a broader patriarchal system that seeks to control and oppress women. Addressing these crimes requires a comprehensive approach that challenges patriarchal norms and promotes gender equality.

Future Research Directions

This chapter attempts to expose the brutal practice of killing a daughter or sister in order to oppose her marriage choices, as well as the ancient patriarchal norms that torment women and their lives. This chapter emphasizes the need to recognize "honor killing" as a distinct crime in order to deter those who would commit such killings, as there is a dearth of specific data on the subject due to underreporting and the fact that it is not recognized as such in almost all countries. The lack of government intervention in such crimes, sexism, and conservative ideologies are only a few of the variables that the author has thoroughly examined (Ramseshan, 2011). This chapter covers the following topics: how male dominance resulted in the murder of women; how it is considered honorable to maintain sexual purity prior to marriage and to view any violation as a betrayal of the family's honor; and how controlling behavior, particularly in social and sexual contexts, is seen as a mark of masculinity among female family members (Chowdhary, 2007). This chapter emphasizes how losing one's virginity before marriage is viewed as sinful and how a man is not considered manly if he is unable to regulate his female family members' sexual behavior (Chakravarti, 2003). Furthermore, the author highlights the grave problem that honor killing is perceived by those who do it as a noble deed rather than a criminal offense. This chapter emphasizes even more how urgent it is to spread awareness of human rights issues and promote the reporting of such crimes. Even though all of the contributing reasons have been covered in detail, the chapter is limited in that it doesn't discuss the actions that have been taken to lower these homicides. Therefore, these actions as well as the function of international organizations, NGOs, and education in reducing such deaths may be the subject of future research.

SUBORDINATION OF WOMEN IN INDIAN SOCIETY

Women's subjugation is commensurate with the hierarchy of castes. The more prestigious the caste in the hierarchy, the more restrictions she faced. Her libido is suppressed by forced marriage, child marriage, harsh divorce restrictions, strict monogamy, sati, the prohibition against widow remarriage, as well as the widow's strict seclusion. Males see their widows as their personal sexual property even after they pass away (Liddle & Joshi, 1986).

A woman is simultaneously protected and vulnerable to harm because she is the source of honor in her family and her caste. Males rationalize and justify their aggression and violence against her out of a fear of losing this honor. As a daughter, sister, wife, mother, and member of the patriarchal order, she faces violence inside the four walls of her home on a regular basis, which finally transcends caste boundaries. She is the target of public violence, which is always carried out in response to cultural norms within the greater community (Chowdhary, 2007). The community, which is prepared to step in if the family fails to comply, forces the family to relinquish their daughters in the name of the caste group. The family is not allowed to resolve the issue of intercaste marriages amicably, even if they so choose. Instead, the community treats it as an issue of honor. Therefore, human feelings and ideals are sacrificed in the service of the concept of honor.

The girl or woman who is assumed to be guilty must be retrieved, punished, and cannot be disowned in order to restore the honor of the family. Since it is typically impossible to reintegrate her into the conventional *biradari* network, her physical eradication seems to be the most morally just choice for her family. She is forced to accept the stigma, which can only be erased by putting an end to her, that is, by making her the target of disgrace. On the other hand, those who commit honor crimes are not stigmatized by society; they are cleared of all charges since it is believed that maintaining and reestablishing honor within the family is more important than protecting it.

Patriarchal Enmity Prioritizing 'Honor'

In Indian patriarchal society, honor is the most prized virtue. The three pillars of a family's honor are money, power, and inappropriate behavior by women. The Indian social framework places a strong emphasis on family honor since families continue to be highly powerful social forces (Chakravarti, 2003). Being able to exert such influence over his women is a major component of a man's honor. Due to their shared ancestry, the entire clan, caste, and society share this honor (Chowdhary, 2007). For the female, the social bond of marriage tames this powerful energy. As a restraining force, the male subjugates the female through marriage, making him distinguished (Dewan, 2000).

Indian communities such as the Jats and the Sikhs in the state of Punjab, the Jats in state of Haryana, and the Rajput's in the state of Rajasthan are strong patriarchal societies that are known for their honor-based society. In patrilineal communities, inheritance is customary. Furthermore, the fundamental social, economic, and political units are the family and kin group rather than the lone. Thus, it can be shown that community elders and, in particular, community congress (like the Khap Panchayat in the state of Haryana) support and shield the perpetrators of "Honor Killings" in all such cultures. Unexpectedly, these traditional patriarchal communities reject the role of the state and the law in stopping "Honor Killings," viewing it as an unwelcome intrusion into their family and familial dynamics, socio-cultural values, and customs (D'Lima et al., 2020).

Prohibiting marriages between people of different castes, religions, gotras, and regions is a sign that the male-dominated hierarchical patriarchy that rigidly divides all of humanity into competing factions has been imposed. The ideas of "shame" and "honor" serve to reinvent male control, which is thought to have been jeopardized by post-colonial Indian women's legal empowerment.

Honor killings had been incredibly vicious. They included physical and torture abuse and served as a warning about the kinds of infractions that would not be accepted. The families of the girls who were killed were crucial. Fathers and brothers were typically the main offenders in both nations. Another thing that both nations had in common was the especially heinous violence associated with honor killings brought on by unapproved marriages. In a particularly brutal Indian case, the victim's parents skinned her face to prevent identification after strangling her and chopping her body into eleven pieces (D'Lima et al., 2020).

Electrocution and hacking to death with various implements were practices exclusive to, or more common in, India. The death penalty comprised beheading, stabbing, burning, strangling, and stoning. When a male or couple is killed for honor, the assault and murder become a kind of public spectacle and humiliation. The victims may be paraded in their undies, forced to shave their heads, publicly beheaded, or set on fire.

Honor Killing in India

Indian culture possesses an extensive, varied, and age-old legacy. Thus, the unique culture in question was combined based on outside ideals. The external enforcement of power, particularly violent power shown through gender standards, is what honor is. Not only does it still exist in modern culture, but it was also present in medieval times. Akbar, the fabled Mughal emperor, was even responsible for the demise of his son's beloved Anarkali. As she performed in his courtroom also known as the *Darbar* and fell in love with his son Jahangir, he buried her alive in the wall. Caste and religion have a negative influence on modern culture, and murdering someone in the name of "honor" is becoming more and more commonplace than showing others love and affection.

The northern part of India has seen an increase in the number of honor killings, with Punjab and Haryana ranking first on the list. Women and girls are the target of these honor killings. Even in the twenty-first century, women still need to live lives that uphold "Honor." Certain Indian women may face violence at some point in their lives, and state-by-state variations exist in women's status. Though the statutory laws are the same across the nation, women's status and unwritten norms vary greatly from East to West, North to South, Tribal to Brahmin, and Hindu to Muslim. When a woman leaves the house, she frequently faces moral and psychological abuse, character assassination, and the most terrible one is murder committed in the name of "honor" (Kaushal, 2020). Since many cases go unreported, it is challenging to determine the exact number of "Honor Killings." As long as the offenders escape punishment, society will continue to accept the legitimacy of honor killing.

Various forms of antagonistic and diverse marriages, such as the ones that break the laws of gotra exogamy, widow remarriage, territorial exogamy, religious exogamy, and caste endogamy, are viewed as an attack on izzat (Welchman & Hossain, 2005). These marriages have primarily resulted in honor crimes, conflicts, and violence. In order to resolve marriages, the Indian agricultural caste groups adhere to caste endogamy, village, clan and territorial exogamy. The Hindus observe the gotra exogamy within the same caste. Since the superior castes in India do not acknowledge any honor held by the inferior caste groupings, they typically hijack the concept of caste honor (Chowdhary, 2007).

Marriage or a romantic relationship between a girl from a higher caste and a guy from a lower caste is usually disputed and illegal since intercaste weddings have the tendency to erode the distinctions between the various caste groups and upset the caste hierarchies. At times, even the judges and the police play the role of docile bystanders and unresponsive defenders of honor.

Breaking the endogamy and exogamy rules can result in ritualistic execution, expulsion, removal from the caste, and the murder of the mother and child (Chakravarti, 2003). The awful thing about the segregation laws is that they made it illegal for anyone to eat, drink, or conduct business with the outcaste; no barber would shave him; no Brahmins would perform sacred ceremonies for him; no man would marry his children; moreover funeral attendees would not follow the deceased's customs (Banerjee-Dube, 2008).

In Northern India, particularly in the region of Haryana, older male caste members defend caste and familial notions that young people are challenging by rejecting the idea of honor, rejecting hypergamy and village exogamy, and breaking sexual taboos and norms. When young couples who are in love decide to leave their families and caste-village norms and feelings behind, the male family members will directly harm them, especially the girl. When a woman violates family, kinship, and caste moral norms, she faces increased societal burden and disapproval since it is seen as a direct challenge to masculinist power and should be suppressed, managed, and channeled. The respectability of women influences the respectability of men, families, and entire castes. This kind of society thinking causes the woman to be killed or her family members to force her to take her own life. Frequently, she finds herself compelled to get into a highly precarious marriage where the spouse is either a widower, an elderly guy, a man having children, disabled, inebriated, or unfit for anything. The family cuts off all communication with her after that (Chowdhary, 2007).

Honor crimes are prevalent in North India and are gradually becoming more noticeable in other regions as well. Indian women are vulnerable to severe violence, terror, deprivation, discrimination, and devaluation. Their acquaintance with the person in question and their filial values have prevented them from adequately resisting the humiliation, abuse, and exploitation they have endured (Ahuja, 2011). Furthermore, there is rarely a cure for violence and crimes committed "behind closed doors" (Walker, 1987). Her safety, freedom of choice, and rights are compromised in the name of upholding family honor at any costs.

Moreover, the desire of a woman to marry a man of a lower caste or the desire of an unapproved couple to escape were the driving forces for honor killings in India, which led to incredible, prolonged torment that ultimately culminated in death. A group of 200 people, including some members of the girl's family, stoned a young couple to death in Uttar Pradesh, for instance. Before having their throats chopped, a couple in New Delhi endured a night of burning, electrocution, and torture. An under-caste girl received a love letter from a 15-year-old Bihari lad. He was taken hostage by the girl's male relatives, who tortured him and forced him to march through the city in only his underwear and a shaved head before dumping him beneath a train. These crimes were made possible by unspoken societal support, just like honor killings that were justified by an unapproved marriage (BBC, 2013).

Effects of Honor Killing: Indian Statistics

The past two decades has witnessed a dramatic rise in the honor-based violence against the women's but more often not the psychological aspect of such violence on the victim's is left unheated. The old conformist mindset of the victim's family members jovially defends the honor-based violence which creates a lasting impact on the women's psych. The most obvious impact of "honor" is the loss of life of thousands of women per year, however the impact doesn't last here victim may choose not to report the violence she has suffered a as it could be considered stain on the family's honor in the society which traumatizes the women and puts her mental position in the state of guilt and confusion. The after effect is not limited to suicide, the women are incarcerated to flee their home country and take shelter in another country where she faces many an issue ranging from living a basic life to a dignified life.

Women have been impacted by honor killings for a number of reasons, including as strict caste systems, prejudices, the absence of official government in rural areas, male chauvinism, religious influence, social control, fear of social rejection, and the need to maintain the alleged purity of their heritage. In the recent times, there has been an increase in honor killings across the Indian subcontinent . In the northern Indian states of Bihar, Haryana, Uttar Pradesh, and Punjab, women have occasionally been victims of honor killings due to reasons such as falling in love with someone else (Sarkar, 2015).

An estimated 1000 individuals are slain in India annually as a result of suspected honor killings. A significant number of honor killings occur in the Punjab. The Crime Report of Punjab, 2014, states that 34 Honor Killings were registered in the state between 2008 and 2010. Of those, 10 occurred in 2008, 20 in 2009, and 4 in 2010 (Crime Report of Punjab, 2014).

The Hindu woman, Geeta, who had an affair with a Muslim man, was brutally murdered in Gujarat during the height of the unrest, after being forced from her home and placed on the streets to serve as a warning to others about social mores (The Times of India, 2002). A few months later, right-wing thugs forced a Hindu girl married to a Christian to dissolve their union and abort her four-month pregnancy (The Asian Age, 2003). In regard to intercommunity marriages, this already violent situation is made worse by self-appointed police of community boundaries and morality police.

In 2016, V. Shankar, a 22-year-old Dalit man as Kausalya's husband, was brutally killed in broad daylight in an instance of honor killing. The disapproval of Kausalya's family forced her to elope with Shankar; she was from an Agamudaiyar family. The crime was planned by her parents, Annalakshmi and B. Chinnasamy. Hired men attacked them with sickles in March 2016, killing Shankar and injuring Kausalya. Listed as an "honor" killing, the case attracted interest from all throughout the state. Determined to find those responsible for her husband's death, Kausalya spearheaded operations that led to the arrest of 11 persons, including her parents. Six defendants, including her father, received death sentences from a Tiruppur Sessions Court in 2017. Through her efforts, Kausalya has become a well-known voice in Tamil Nadu opposing caste-based violence and a *Survivor* in case of honor killing (Frontline, 2024).

According to an analysis by the *NGO Shakti Vahini*, heinous instances of honor killings have been documented throughout the nation, and in 90% of the cases, the criminals were members of the girl's family. According to a survey conducted on behalf of the National Commission for Women, couples who married outside of their caste made up 72% of the 326 cases that were recorded between 2009 and 2010. A horrific incident that shocked the country in the recent past involved the murder of Manoj and Babli, a young couple from Kaithal, Haryana, in 2007. The couple was forced to sip poison by the girl's family after being dragged out of a bus, and their bodies were discovered in a canal with their hands and feet knotted. In addition, in Jharkhand, in June 2010, Nirupama Pathak, a journalist, was murdered by her mother due to her romantic feelings for her classmate Ranjan, who belonged to a different caste (Kumar, 2012).

The National Crime Records Bureau (NCRB) states that 25 honor killings were registered in India in 2019 and 2020, and 33 in 2021. However, because of underreporting, true figures might be higher. At least seven incidences of honor killings have been reported in Karnataka since October 2022, with Mandya, Kolar, Tumakuru, and North Karnataka seeing the greatest number of these cases. Senior counsel KBK Swamy points out that intercaste relationships are punishable by 'Yele Hoote,' a cruel kind of public death, and that honor killings have a long history in Karnataka, extending back to the 12th century (TNIE, 2023).

Status of Women: Evolution or Degradation?

Additionally, there has been ongoing violence against women for many years. The practice of honor killings, in particular, is one of the oldest forms of honor-based violence that has been practiced for generations in India. There appears to have been a near egalitarian Vedic society. It is asserted that women's status in society reached a level that surpassed that of ancient Greece and Rome during the Rig Vedic Period (1500–100 BC). In the Vedas, there is a ceremony to guarantee the birth of a girl who is intelligent. In addition to becoming well-known scholars and philosophers (such as Visvavara, Ghosala, and Apala), women also made their mark as seers or authors of Vedic hymns. Women were free to choose their husbands, took part in religious rites, and were married at the legal age of 16 or 17. It was uncommon to be polygamous. Girls had to go through the student phase of life and receive an education similar to that of boys. Religion viewed women as equals with men (Coward, 2005). Since 600 BCE, women have enjoyed more independence thanks to the opposing religions of Buddhism and Jainism. In Southern India Tamil culture, women have a superior status because to the predominance of the gynarchy system.

However, women's equivalent position was short-lived and gradually decreased starting from 1000 BCE in the Post-Vedic era (Coward, 2005). During the degrading time, women were also denied of all their rights by the priests, who declared the other castes incapable of studying the Vedas. If not, you will discover that throughout the Vedic or Upanishadic era, Maitreyi, Gargi, and other women of great recall replaced the Rishis with their knowledge of Brahmans. At a meeting of a thousand well-read Brahmans who knew a great deal about the Vedas, Gargi dared Yajnavalkya to debate Brahmans. Why shouldn't women now have the same advantage of spiritual knowing that these ideal ladies did? Indeed, a situation that has occurred before can occur again. History repeats itself. Because they treated women with respect, all nations have achieved greatness. Such a nation and that country, which do not value women, would never rise to greatness. That you show no regard for these live manifestations of Shakti is the main cause of your race's extreme degeneration.

In "The laws of Manu," where the wife's individuality is combined with her husband's, the uneven outcome is clearly visible. For women, strict isolation is advised; for widows, strict discipline is advised. "While praising motherhood and giving women complete control over running the home, (Manu) approved of child marriage and polygamy." "Where women are respected, God rejoices; and where they are not, all work and efforts are in vain," according to Manu. Where women are devalued and forced to live miserable lives, there is no chance for that family or nation to prosper. They must therefore be brought up first (Manusmriti V).

According to Hindu law codes, Puranas, Tantras, and epics like the Mahabharata and Ramayana, women are supposed to live their life for their husbands and children. Women were reborn, had oriented knowledge, and were familiar with the rituals because they were denied schooling during the time of the Brahmans (c. 1000–800 BCE). Hindu families hold chaste daughters in high regard and continue to revere them as virgin goddesses. Parents under stress arranged for their daughters' marriages to take place as soon as possible. The dearth of education for girls contributed to the trend of early marriage. Advancing the marriage to the period just fore-and-after puberty; relieving parents of the duty to safeguard the daughter's virginity (Coward, 2005). The concepts of auspiciousness and purity throughout classical Hinduism (c. 700 BCE to CE 1000) also significantly contributed to the subjugation of women. For a lay Hindu, life revolves around two axes: auspiciousness and inauspiciousness, which cross the first axis of purity and impurity.

Even greater attention was placed on the unjust status that women endured throughout the classical Hinduism era during the Muslim conquests and Mughal Empire (CE 1000–1750). The Mughal's isolation of women reinforced the Hindu's notion that women belonged in the house, subservient to the male family members—the husband, father, and, ultimately, the sons. India adopted the pardah, or head covering, habit brought by Muslims. Hindu ladies from upper caste homes took up the pardah custom. Palanquins with covers are used when they walk outside (Coward, 2005).

Protest initiatives within Buddhism, Jainism, Vaishnavism, Veer Shaivism, Arya Samaj, and Sikhism have been launched in an effort to change the social positioning of women within the Hindu community. Families prefer sons even before daughters are born as they must deal with the dread of honor. In his 1990 study titled "More than 100 Million Women are Missing in Asia", Nobel laureate Amartya Sen claimed that deliberate family carelessness in son-preference cultures resulted in the abortion of female foetuses and the killing of female infants.

There was an old proverb that said, "Where women are respected, gods dwell." Being recognized as "Ardhangani," she represented one half of her husband's body. She held a respected position in her roles as a wife, mother, and sister. She is the embodiment of bravery and audacity, affection and love, pain and sacrifice. In contemporary India, customs like Sati, Jauhar, and Devadasi, among others, are outlawed. In isolated areas of India, there are still few occurrences of these customs. In certain areas, Indian women continue to have the pardah. Even though it is against the law in India today, child marriage is nevertheless prevalent in rural regions. Women frequently rose to prominence in the domains of politics, writing, education, and religion despite these obstacles.

Nevertheless, India was found to be the fourth least safe nation for women. The rise in the number of crimes committed against women is the cause of this. India's police data indicate that crimes against women are quite common. In 1998, the National Crime Records Bureau stated that by 2010, the pace of increase in crimes against women would surpass the rate of population growth. The idea that women are property and that domestic violence is a matter for the family rather than the courts are reinforced by the community (Chaudhary, 2011).

Mother, sister, and cousins are among the female family members who usually do back attacks. According to Zaynab Nawaz, a program assistant for women's human rights at Amnesty International, "it's a community mentality" (Mayell, 2002).

No matter what class, ethnicity, or religion a woman belongs to, she is viewed as the male family member's property. The property's owner is entitled to choose the outcome. Women are now considered commodities that may be bought, sold, and traded due to the ownership notion (Khan T., 1999).

Thus, elopement offers a way to fulfill the "love" or "choice" marriage that families either truly or erroneously believe are forbidden. But elopements have also created a space where the "criminality" of a "love" marriage can flourish when it transcends religious boundaries. This is especially true when Hindu women marry Muslim men, as the taboo nature of their union necessitates elopement (Moody, 2002).

The deeply rooted notion that women are their communities' sexual property stirs up the family and the community as a whole, typically with violent outcomes. The political restrictions between the Hindu and Muslim religious communities began to solidify in the 1920s and 1930s, and since then, there has been talk of abduction and coercion surrounding these relationships (Datta, 1999). However, recent right-wing Hindu mobilization has stimulated both managerial and philosophical actions to counteract these relationships. First, these groups monitor announcements of upcoming marriages made public, as required by Sections 10-15 of the Special Marriage Act of 1954. They also let the woman's parents know that their daughter intends to get married in secret under court order. Due to these processes, young Hindu women are forced to convert to Islam before being married in accordance with Muslim law.

The traditional tribal ways of living simply, cheaply, patiently, perseveringly, and diligently were replaced by narrow-mindedness, aggression, exploitation, pride in one's race and tribe, and other restricted attitudes. As a result of violence and battle, Izzat (honor) came to imply greater wealth and women than it did respect for others. It also meant more Pardah, or the isolation of women from all outside activities and employment (Khan M., 1972). Nowadays, the new social ethics of shame (Sharam) meant that husbands and masters should feel ashamed if their wives and daughters were seen in public. This was because such behavior was seen as an affront to their Izzat (Honor), or social pride. Malicious outcomes, including mutilations or death, would ensue if a woman ventured to act freely due to impudence, ignorance, or perversity (Khan M., 1972).

Indian Law on Honor Killing

'The term "honor crimes" refers to a wide range of actions taken against women, such as "honor killings," assaults, incarceration, and meddling with the right to choose a spouse. Although "honor" isn't included in law, the idea of honor was conferred to justify violence in ways that benefit the victim or sufferer. Criminal courts in India take a protectionist stance, which tends to place the onus of proof on the prosecution and, by extension, on the survivor. It is still not acknowledged by the Indian court system that crimes of honor are acts of violence against women and cannot be excused as "crimes of passion," "fits of rage," or acts of so-called honor (Ramseshan, 2011).

The Indian Penal Code (IPC) classifies honor killings as serious offenses, which includes homicide. Section 300 of the IPC deals with murder, while Sections 299 and 301 deal with culpable homicide that is not the same as murder. Honor killings are similar to homicides in that the victims are slain with the intention of killing them because it is thought that they have brought dishonor to the family. In accordance with Section 302 of the IPC, those who promote suicide in defiance of the community's accepted standards risk facing repercussions from their family members, Khap panchayat, and fellow offenders. Sections 299 and 300 of the IPC Manual cover "honor killings," which are the killings of certain people, especially women. Additionally, honor killings violate Articles 14, 15(1) and (3), 17, 18, 19 and 21. Every person's right to equality before the law or equal protection under it is guaranteed by Article 14. According to the Indian Constitution, ordinary courts have jurisdiction over every individual, regardless of their circumstances.

A historic judgment by the Additional Session Court in Karnal in the *Manoj-Babli 'Honor Killing' case*, in which five suspects were sentenced to death, sent shock waves among caste panchayat leaders, reminding them that they were not above the constitution. The police presence in the Manoj-Babli case was acknowledged by the court. On the other hand, a caste panchayat conference comprising Jat communities in Rajasthan, Haryana, and in the state of Uttar Pradesh was called to Kurukshetra on April 13. It was decided that panchayats would fight for their legal standing in order to maintain social order in a legitimate manner. This Sarv-Khap panchayat was formed primarily to push for amendments to the Hindu Marriage Act of 1955 that would forbid sacred union between male and female within the same gotra. This statute already prohibits marriages between specific mother and paternal lineages.

The Supreme Court, in the case of *Arumugam Servai vs. State of Tamil Nadu (2011)*, harshly condemned the behavior of Katta panchayats enforcing laws on their own and engaging in offensive acts that jeopardize the private lives of individuals who choose to marry. While giving the ruling, Justice Markandey Katju made an observation:

"I've heard about Khap panchayats, also known as Katta panchayats in Tamil Nadu, in recent years. These groups have been known to order or support Honor Killings or other institutionalized atrocities against boys and girls from various castes and religions who aspire to or have already been married, as well as to meddle in people's private lives. We believe that this ought to be completely eradicated because it is prohibited. Honor killing and other crimes are nothing but savage and despicable murder; there is nothing honorable about them. Severe punishment is warranted for further atrocities against the personal lives of people committed by violent, feudalistic individuals. We can only eradicate such acts of brutality and feudal attitude in this manner. Furthermore, these actions amount to kangaroo courts, which are completely unlawful and take the law into their own hands".

The Supreme Court ruled that "Neither the family members nor the members of the collective have any right to assault the boy chosen by the girl" in the controversial Nitish Katara murder case of *Vikas Yadav v. State of U.P. (2016)*. Her own decision is her self-respect and damaging will undermine her honor. Furthermore, it is an extremely violent crime to eliminate her option in order to enforce so-called class, fatherly, or brotherly honor. The idea that these crimes are rooted in culture, customs, and traditions, however, is also concerning because society is resistant to change and the existence of Khap Panchayats (Community Councils) in the state of Haryana is a sign that these inflexible traditions are widely accepted. In India, honor killings are particularly common in marriages between members of different castes and religions.

Suggested Reforms to adhere upon

1. In a recent ruling of ***Shakti Vahini vs. Union of India (2018)***, the Supreme Court held that guardians or Khap Panchayats cannot intervene with an adult couple's decision to marry. The most recent ruling upholds the superlative court's 2010 directive to the Indian government to take action in relation to honor killing.
2. Equitable penalties for criminals and wrongdoers must be implemented by the enactment of a complete, unbiased law. The Indian Penal Code, 1860's stated provisions are insufficient to address honor killing in the context of the planning committee's commitment to protecting women's and children's rights during the 12th five-year plan. The agency has advised that anyone who publicly commends harassment or killing carried out in the name of honor would face consequences and a trial.
3. A crucial recommendation to modify the Indian Penal Code and impose limitations on Khap Panchayats.
4. The Hindu Marriage Act, 1955, which mandates the dissolution of same-gotra marriages, needs to be amended.
5. Death sentence if found guilty of honor killing, the accused shall receive a life sentence or be imprisoned for life, with a minimum punishment of Rs 7 lakhs. The punishment for major or serious grievous hurt is 14 years of life imprisonment and a fine of Rs 5 lakhs; in certain situations, the punishment is 4-5 years in jail and a fine of up to 4 lakhs for harm or injuries.
6. The regaining of equality of women in our society is a long war, however this fight of equality stands strong with idea of education as a key progression. The education system needs to be marched from teaching us to inherit the traditional values and social norms. The topic of honor killing being hesitant to approach, education can gradually start to change the minds which will progressively bring about the reformed outlook resulting in decreased number of unnecessary deaths.

CONCLUSION

When combined with restrictions on choosing a spouse, violence against women constitutes a serious violation of their rights. International conventions, declarations, and protocols forbid violence resulting from disagreements and stress the value of women's permission and choice in marriage-related concerns. The General Assembly addressed honor crimes against women on a global scale with Resolution 55/66, highlighting the duty of state parties to prevent, look into, and punish offenders as well as to protect victims (Vishwanath & Palakonda, 2011).

The Indian Constitution lists the fundamental obligation to uphold peace and fraternity among all people, regardless of differences in language, religion, geography, or social class. In India, intercaste unions have been legalized since 1949. The Hindu Marriage Act of 1955 abolishes the need to match prospective spouses based on caste and allows both sagotra and intercaste unions. The goal of the Protection of Women from Domestic Violence Act of 2005 is to do away with the right to the defense of honor in cases when a female family member is beaten or killed.

Women's rights are highly valued in Hindu Dharma, and women are expected to have the utmost respect and protection from their fathers, brothers, wives, and brothers-in-law, right through their life. It is essential every individual in the society, particularly women, have their rights respected in order to maintain Dharma.

The Anthropological Survey of India (ASI) of the Government of India has recognized 2,800 castes, including 450 Scheduled Castes, 461 Scheduled Tribes, and 766 Backward Castes, in an effort to reduce honor crimes in the country. In order to truly break caste, interfaith marriage is the solution, and relevant laws must be passed to limit the authority of caste panchayats (Rajshekar, 2007).

The general public and the common man should be made aware of the horrors of honor crimes, the significance of the female population, and the worth of life through massive campaigns, public discussions, media coverage, and public discourse. Strong and efficient criminal law procedures should be in place to deter, prosecute, and punish honor crimes. Judges, parents, society's elders, young men, the police, and legislators should all be considerate of gender roles.

To conclude, it is imperative to address the serious issues of violence against women and restrictions on marital choice. Harmony and societal advancement depend heavily on the defense of women's rights, equality, dignity, and non-exploitation. Quoting Manu, *"Where women are respected, God rejoices"* (Manusmriti V), consequently, a nation must strive towards the advancement of women and put an end to their devaluation to prosper.

REFERENCES

Ahuja, R. (2011). *Social Problems in India*. Rawat Publications.

Banerjee-Dube, I. (2008). *Caste in History*. Oxford University Press.

BBC. (2013). *India honor killings: Paying the price for falling in love*. BBC (British Broadcasting Corporation) News India. Retrieved from https://www.bbc.co.uk/news/world-asia-india-24170866

Chakravarti, U. (2003). *Gendering Caste: Through a Feminist Lens*. Stree.

Chaudhary, D. R. (2011). Khaps, shoudn't be allowed, to have their way. *The Tribune*.

Chowdhary, P. (2007). *Contentious Marriages, Eloping Couples: Gender, Caste and Patriarchy in Northern India*. Oxford University Press.

Coward, H. (2005). Human rights and world's major religions. *The Hindu tradition*, 4, 145-150.

Crime Report of Punjab (2014). Punjab Police. Retrieved from www.punjabpolice.gov.in

D'Lima, T., Solotaroff, J. L., & Pande, R. P. (2020). For the Sake of Family and Tradition: Honor Killings in India and Pakistan. *Indian Journal of Women and Social Change*, 5(1), 22–39. DOI: 10.1177/2455632719880852

Datta, P. (1999). *Carving blocs: Communal ideology in early twentieth-century*. No Title.

Dewan, V. K. (2000). *Law Relating to Offences against Women*. Orient Law House.

Frontline, T. H. (2024). *In Tamil Nadu, the survivor of an honor killing fights caste violence*. Frontline, The Hindu.

Kaushal, K. (2020). No Honor in Honor Killing: Comparative Analysis of Indian Traditional Social Structure vis-à-vis Gender Violence. *Indian Journal of Women and Social Change*, 5(1), 52–69. DOI: 10.1177/2455632719880870

Khan, M. (1972). Purdah and polygamy: A study in the social pathology of the Muslim society. *(No Title)*, 49.

Khan, T. (1999). Chained to custom. 9. The Review.

Kumar, A. (2012). Public policy imperatives for curbing Honor Killing in India. *Politics and Governance*, 1(1), 33–37.

Liddle, J., & Joshi, R. (1986). Daughters of Independence: Gender, Caste and Class in India. New Delhi: Kali for Women & London:Kali for Women & London: Zed Books.

Manusmriti. (n.d.). *V.*

Manusmriti V. (n.d.).

Mayell, H. (2002). *Thousands of women killed for family honor.* National Geographic News.

Moody, P. (2002). Love and the law: Love-marriage in Delhi. *Modern Asian Studies*, 36(1), 223–256. DOI: 10.1017/S0026749X02001075

Rajshekar, V. T. (2007). *Caste: A Nation within the Nation: A Recipe for a Bloodless Revolution.* Books for Change.

Ramseshan, G. (2011). The construction of honor in India criminal Law: An Indian Lawyer perspective, honor, violence, women and Isla . 114.

Sarkar, G. (2015). *Death sentence for daughter murder.* Bhagalpur: Times of India. Retrieved from www.timesofindis.indiatime.com/2015/1/30/archivelist/year/2015

Shakti Vahini v. Union of India, (2018) 7 SCC 192., 192 (Supreme Court 2018).

2003. *The Asian Age.* Retrieved from www.asianage.com

2002. *The Times of India.* Retrieved 19 April, from www.timesofindia.com

TNIE. (2023). *Killing honor in the name of 'honor killings.* The New Indian Express.

2004. *UNFPA.* Retrieved from https://www.unfpa.org

2004. *UNFPA.* Retrieved from https://www.unfpa.org

Vishwanath, J., & Palakonda, S. (2011). *Patriarchal Ideology of Honor and Honor Crimes in India* (Vol. 6(1/2)). Thirunelveli: International Journal of Criminal Justice Sciences.

Walker, A. (1987). *Woman physiologically considered as to Mind, Morals, Marriage, Matrimonial Slavery, Infidelity and Divorce.* Motilal Banarsidass Publishers.

Welchman, L., & Hossain, S. (2005). *Honor. Victoria: Spinifex Press.* Zed Books.

Chapter 4
Dishonor, Death, and Coercion in the Arena of Justice

Myunghoon Roh
https://orcid.org/0009-0001-4634-9457
Salve Regina University, USA

Muskan Gautam
GLA University, India

ABSTRACT

The term "honor killings" refers to severe forms of domestic violence in which a woman is killed with the help of her family or network. But in non-secular and ethnic societies, spousal violence is sometimes motivated by a sense of "honor." In this chapter, we contend that a discursive collision occurs between ethicized women. As victims of honor murders, women are hidden behind the non-public/public divide that defined the domestic violence narrative and the cultural relativism of British multicultural discourse. Ethicized women have become more visible after September 11th, but because of the discourse of fear and threat posed by the presence of the Muslim foreign "other," they are now restricted and shaped in the public consciousness. By adopting a robust human rights stance to respect homicides, it would be feasible to overcome the 'gender trap' of cultural relativism in the liberal democratic debate on diversity.

DOI: 10.4018/979-8-3693-9596-7.ch004

METHODOLOGY

The primary goal of the research is to put light towards the crime of honour killing against women in the arena of justice. The main aim of this chapter is to realize that conversations regarding the facts or interpretations that someone pushed were greatly influenced by their personal reputation, especially in intellectual and scientific institutions. The employment of weapons remained the final choice for a man whose honour or integrity was publicly questioned in these situations as well as other public places during the nineteenth century n these social frontiers, women pioneers often made the decision to become part of all-female organization groups. because they felt alienated from the purely masculine culture, language, and dispute resolution techniques of these groupings. As a result of the gender integration of public life, the male honor culture that formerly acted as the main protector of decency in public has gradually been undermined. This chapter contains highlighted studies of National, European and International effect of honour killing and various rules in that regard.

KEY TERMS

Fundamental terms include "Dishonour" and "honour killing" in the arena of justice related to the death or coercion done against women. Broader terms like "violence"(H.N. Bhui, 2003) and "collectivistic cultures"(Caffaro, F, 2014) and "criminal justice"(Singh Deol, 2014) and "Social Distress"(Dasgupta, 2000) and " Homicide" (Dogan, 2014) we used these keywords to select relevant articles from multiple online sources, for example, 'Library of Congress, Research Gate, Google Books, Springer, JSTOR, Sage, IJSSHR, Scopus, Web of Science, Taylor & Francis and Google Scholar'.

An Honor Killings Research Paper on its Dark Face and Hidden Atrocity requires careful consideration of inclusion/exclusion and article research, as well as the selection of appropriate publications. Publications with an emphasis on international law, gender studies, human rights, and related interdisciplinary topics were chosen for publishing in the journal selection process.

To further narrow down the research publications that are pertinent for this Chapter, we have established both inclusion and exclusion criteria. The following studies met our inclusion criteria: ones where "experience" was examined as a concept or a variable in the context of ecotourism; Research must be published in English and restricted to journal articles—that is, those having an impact factor of 1.0 or above in Journal Citation Reports and peer-reviewed papers, or those with a B grade or higher in the Journal Quality list.

LITERATURE REVIEW

All for one and one for all" was the motto that protected these groups' integrity, independence, and trade secrets. If men could adhere to a shared unwritten rule of open communication that honored unique sensitivities while allowing each man to express his freedom, then good intercorporate relations would be guaranteed. (Bhopal, 1998). Although women are not expressly targeted by the honor test, it has effectively kept them out of social, civic, and professional groups for decades even when they were otherwise perfectly qualified for them. (Bui, H. N., 2003). The codes of behaviour that governed women's clubs, labour unions, and gossip networks may have been very different from those that applied to similar groupings of men (Caffaro et al., 2014). According to cultural conventions and customs, honor relates to the designated duties that women have in the home and sexual spheres. These customs regarded rape, cheating, falling in love with a "wrong" person, suspected pregnancies without a marriage, sexual misconduct, and nonmarital or sexual relationships as abuses of the overall their family's reputation. (Elakkary et, 2014). Apart from the autonomous formation of honour societies, social mimesis lost its significance as an explanation for the rise in honor and shame among upwardly mobile aristocratic bourgeois, especially after the seventeenth century. In European culture, honor was associated with great bravery and heroic character. (Dasgupta, 2000).

RESEARCH GAP

This chapter highlights the unique concept of "Dishonor, death and coercion in the arena of justice". The idea of crimes against honor is fluid, changing according to time, place, and the modes of interpretation and representation in the community. Honour crimes might be characterized as patterns of behavior that span across groups, cultures, faiths, and nations and appear in a variety of forms of violence aimed, and in most cases, they cannot be relinquished for individual or community objectives. Killing someone is always immoral, criminal, and a severe violation of human rights. (Lewisohn Ludwig, 1909). This chapter mainly focused on the points that how honour and sociability differ from, each other and no cultural group or religion can defend the hideous act of honor killing. Belief in liberty does not equate to the ability to commit murder. The courts have proclaimed several crimes and offenders to be penalized. the dominating power of patriarchal societies over women and give it a name of customs and religion honour killing is ubiquitous that not only limited in Islamic countries but also found in east region like Canada and America. (sulatan abeda,2011). This research consist The purpose of honor killing is to uphold the dignity and grace of the family. However, killing someone is never honorable, especially if that person is someone you love deeply; it is not valuable it. The citation of "religious beliefs and " society " as justifications for the murder of women or other individuals is forbidden since both faith and law are inherently arbitrary and open to interpretation. Everybody is entitled to a fair and honorable life.

Worldwide and national governments, lawmakers, media, academic institutions, and a wide range of civil society organizations for women's empowerment and gender equality.Within this broader movement, the issue of violence against women (VAW), which includes honor killing, has progressively gained recognition as a significant human rights concern after being mostly addressed as a medical issue at first (Khan, Khatija Bibi 2014). The main perspective taken to control honour-based crimes is to in order to promote gender equality holistically, support efforts that combat honor murders. According to the European Parliament's resolution on the state of the fight against the European Parliament, in cooperation with national counterparts, promote and support a thorough and carefully planned strategy to combat crimes of honor within communities or societies where these crimes are accepted This movement is mainly driven by the frameworks established by the Millennium Development Goals, which were set at the World Social Summit in 2000, and the Beijing Declaration and Platform for Action (BFPA), which was issued as a follow-up to the Fourth World Conference on Women (FWCW) in Beijing in 1995. To protect prospective victims, report crimes, and guarantee that they are brought to justice, a comprehensive referral system including law enforcement, medical professionals, educators, non-governmental organizations, religious and community leaders, and others must be put in place(Bui, H. N. 2003).

Initiatives taken against honour killing is entrused in this chapter that Encourage the implementation of constitutional educational initiatives for all genders so that they may learn about their specific privileges legal purposes help for women should be provided. Safeguard women who are at risk of honour killings. Those who are in danger must be given safe housing and protection. Encourage extensive education for the public programs (in Europeans and in Third nations) To break the taboo around murder of honor and change the way that both men and women view it, extensive public education campaigns should be launched via all available channels, which include the conventional media, the Internet, schools, non-profit organizations, and community organisations.

HONOR AND SOCIABILITY

Today's dignity and humiliation took on more subdued shapes. Since the late Middle Ages, the liberal professions and artisan guilds have been united by a strong sense of corporate or communal honor. "All for one and one for all" was the motto that protected these groups' integrity, independence, and trade secrets. If men could adhere to a shared unwritten rule of open communication that honored unique sensitivities while allowing each man to express his freedom, then good intercorporate relations would be guaranteed. (Bhopal, 1998) There were occasions when disagreements among co-workers developed into full-fledged affairs of honor, which might be embarrassing for the parties involved as well as the group's image as a whole. Over time, etiquette progressively changed to allow guilds, professional associations, and eventually clubs and various volunteer organizations to regulate their members and ensure their reputation and good order. Since the seventeenth century, gentlemanly society has distributed intricate duelling handbooks, which served as the basis for the norms of etiquette or politeness that emerged to preserve good relations between men. Gradually, these structures delineated offence levels, methods of compromise and rapprochement, and, by the middle of the 1800s, "honor courts" that adjudicated disputes among participants. It is crucial to realize that conversations regarding the facts or interpretations that someone pushed were greatly influenced by their personal reputation, especially in intellectual and scientific institutions. If a guy had integrity, he could be confident that others would take his words seriously, even if they weren't true. However, if a man's integrity was questionable, he could anticipate opposition and challenges at every turn. The employment of weapons remained the final choice for a man whose honor or integrity was publicly questioned in these situations as well as other public places during the nineteenth century. (Bond, J,2012).

Club, professional, and political life remained mostly male domains far into the twentieth century. The societal, cultural, or spiritual exclusion of these groups have been greatly influenced by the endeavour to eliminate the "incorrect type of man," whether it be Jews, Catholics, or those from regional that were not seen to inherently possess the requisite attributes of honor. Although women are not expressly targeted by the honor test, it has effectively kept them out of social, civic, and professional groups for decades even when they were otherwise perfectly qualified for them. (Bui, H. N., 2003) Help-seeking behaviour among abused immigrant women, On these social frontiers, women pioneers often made the decision to become part of all-female organization groups. because they felt alienated from the purely masculine culture, language, and dispute resolution techniques of these groupings. As a result of the gender integration of public life, the male honor culture that formerly acted as the main protector of decency in public has gradually been undermined. It is unclear if historians will discover proof of female-specific kinds of honor or female sociability throughout the past several centuries that have governed and shaped social interaction. The codes of behaviour that governed women's clubs, labour unions, and gossip networks may have been very different from those that applied to similar groupings of men. (Caffaro, F., Ferraris, F., & Schmidt, S 2014). Gender differences in the perception of honor killing in individualist versus collectivistic cultures: Comparison between Italy and Turkey

Women who participated in resistance activities, especially in the 20th century, or who fought in national and civil conflicts may be considered similarly affected. Stated differently, it's possible that women drew inspiration from a uniquely feminine kind of honor that went beyond simply defending their sexual honor, which was their only obligation under the pretext of masculine honorability. The erosion of honor has coincided with the rapid female integration of previously all-male groups in the late 20th century, including the diplomatic corps, government agencies, clubs, sports teams, and the military. While it is still feasible to discuss the concept of a "man of honor" in public settings and for a former German chancellor to justify confidential financial transactions in accordance with a personal code of honor, these discourse patterns are becoming less common in contemporary society. (Can, M., & Edirne, T. 2011) In certain regions, there are still all-male bastions. In other places, women have colonized historically male-only vocations and hobbies, and they may employ traditionally masculine honorific titles and customs. In France, Germany, and other European nations, there are still laws that punish personal and corporate insults, but they are seldom upheld. These laws are based on affronts to honor.

Honor and Social Class

The differences between honor and shame cultures according to class are among the most intriguing and little-studied aspects of their evolutionary history. More than any other class, we comprehend the concept of honor inside the quality. As we've seen, honor societies' customs and traditions first appeared in aristocratic environments. However, there's reason to think that wherever individual land ownership arose, or where social building directives or military fellowships like the Knights of Malta had strong commercial ties, mechanisms arose where the application of mannish and family honor resembled the highest forms of noble honor. Apart from the autonomous formation of honor societies, social mimesis lost its significance as an explanation for the rise in honor and shame among upwardly mobile aristocratic bourgeois, especially after the seventeenth century. In European culture, honor was associated with great bravery and heroic character. (Dasgupta, S. 2000)

Social degradation for poltroonery or dodging military duty or evading attention on the pointed' honor, was harsh and corroded a man's assets and moral fiber at the same time. To question a man's honesty was enough to suspect that he was concealing something behind his woman's skirts, some deep-rooted religious or moral precept, or even a monarch's Banon whipping. A language culture that produced cuts, promises of fidelity, and other types of special allegiance offered an unstable basis for political action throughout the sixteenth and seventeenth centuries, influencing the public speeches of lords. When there were unclear contractual terms, the primary components of political speech were declarations, barrancas, and counterbluffs. (Dogan, R. 2014). The state-structure monarchs of England, Spain, and France employed a tactic to lessen the discord among the dishonor-deprived Lords: they curtailed their independence, bonded them more closely to court culture, and converted the sometimes violent and disruptive customs of shame evasion into remarkable, analogous courtier regimens. The final aim of honor was maintained while transforming displays of fury or weaponry expertise into guidelines of grace, style, and humour. In his seminal study of the development of civilization, Norbert Elias conjectured that the expression "embarrassment at his estate" stemmed from an opulent culture that had replaced the strict rules of elegance with the coarse methods of war. A strategy of living with the wealthy and obtaining titles and services revealed a widespread middle-class desire to comprehend the most seductive aspects of virtuous ethical behaviour, such as having the right to wear the moniker and participate in the pointd'honneur, in the back streets of western nations, where the growing economy brought about a corpulent as well as aspirational upper class. However, middle-class males had also created their own interpretations of honor and respect, especially via actions that had preserved or even brought about the survival of their forebears. Among these were the advantages of financial independence and providence, self-control over one's sexuality, and the capacity for productive labour, all of which were derived from lofty ideals. Similar to the noble qualities of bravery, loyalty, and military skill, which were seen as standards embedded in the noble man of honor, sexual "respectability" and the will to work and save money were inherent components of bourgeois honorability. A middle-class man swore to live a moral life in conformity with the ideals of his class after feeling humiliated by the prospect of financial collapse or accusations of sexual misbehaviour. (Singh, Raghu N et al., 2016).

It is often accepted that aristocratic and bourgeois characteristics blended to become the upper-class honors that appeared throughout Europe at the end of the eighteenth century. Aristocratic men proved that they could serve as directors or ambassadors in bourgeois administrations without bringing dishonor to themselves, and middle-class men assimilated the innate courage and readiness to stand up for a character for daring that had hitherto been considered a quite commendable quirk. Across European borders, fear of humiliation would determine whether men would act via artistic and social distinctions rather than class. Protestant lords in Ireland wholeheartedly embraced the dogfight's sacredness as a means of asserting their status as a class above both politics and religion. This evolution, with its chivalric querulousness, emphasized oneness while ignoring the customary divides between pleb and nobility. (Deol, Singh Satnam. 2014)Similarly, public divides had a greater impact on French, Italian, German, and Russian officers during the Napoleonic Wars and the ensuing service occupations than did class differences, creating a veritable epidemic of patriotic affairs of honor (Khan, Khatija Bibi. 2014). Academics have shown that throughout the ancient governance, there were significant forms of honorability and respect in both pastoral and civic contexts. Though there were differences in the ways that respect was exercised, it seems that shame and honor operated in comparable ways at all social classes. Offences against a man's honor in the pastoral southern Mediterranean area might range from physical conflict to insults or even attacks on his womenfolk to just being disagreeable. Certain original lights, like wealthy peasants and small-town businessmen, would feel compelled to take strong measures to protect their honor (Eisner M & Ghuneim K. 2013). For the lawbreaker or his family, for whom the refined customs of social disputes offered little solace, this was typically achieved by direct attack. On the other hand, similar issues of honor tended to matriculate every member of a clan, and enmity might last for decades. The reactions of distaste to reported cases of "honor killing" are understandable, but they do not offer a strong basis for addressing this sociologically projected issue. The act of a male relative killing a woman out of honor is a coordinated, planned, socially accepted, and philosophically predicted act of violence carried in the relevant family and culture. It is insufficient and unhelpful to respond by denouncing male aggression and offering safe havens to women who are in danger. The causes, effects, and background of honor killing are examined in this briefing chapter, along with a number of suggestions for the Europeans Parliament to take into account. It is acknowledged that prompt action against honor killings is necessary, but that the elimination of the underlying causes—which are primarily related to wider gender disparities in society—must also come first. "Crime of passion" and "honor killing" express the viewpoint of the one who committed the crime and provide justification for it. The topic is how honor killings differ from crimes of passion, which are usually given the same latitude because of the extreme provocation of the offender. Honor killings are often planned crimes as opposed to acts of passion. Often, a woman's parent, brother, or uncles carry out honor murders with understanding and approval of their entire family and community. Nonetheless, women typically commit "crimes of passion" against their partners, boyfriend, or lover, as well as maybe against the male that she feels has been violated. Crimes of passion are primarily about a person's right to private sex, not a group's possession of the capacity for reproduction. They are frequently committed by a single person against their sexual partner. Honor killings and other crimes motivated by passion are usually justified by the people who commit them as necessary to keep their honor from being brought into unbearable humiliation. It has been reported that in Sao Paolo alone in 1980, men murdered their lovers in 700 separate occurrences, all in the name of "the legitimate defence of honor." Because of this defence, many Brazilian men who killed their spouses were acquitted of all charges until 1991, when the Supreme Court ruled that murder was never a justifiable response to infidelity. State Responses to Crimes of Dignity (Simon, Roger I., and Claudia Eppert,1997)

Patriarchal Societies and Honor Killing

Because honor killing frequently takes place in places where Muslims predominate, it is frequently wrongly assumed that honor killing is an Islamic custom or that Islam supports it. Honor killing is really prohibited in Islam, and neither the Qur'an nor the Hadiths make any reference to it. In nations where Muslims predominate, like Indonesia or Malaysia, there is less evidence of the practice. Honor killings take place in strongly patriarchal civilizations, sometimes known as "honor-based" societies, which are mostly located in South Asia, the South Mediterranean, the region of the Balkans, and the Middle East. Families and kin groups are the primary economic, social, and political units of traditional patriarchal civilizations with patrilineal inheritance. The organization's existence and continuity depend on the women's capacity to give birth lawfully, which is why family control over women's sexual and reproductive abilities is so important. People's rights and positions are subservient to their families in these cultures. Typically, women in overtly patriarchal societies are treated as legally minors for the remainder of their life; they are only transfer as the possessions of their biological father's family to being part of their husband's family, never having the right to vote or have an independent voice in politics or the economy.

Patriarchal Societies' Codes of Honor

Codes of honor, which define what constitutes and does not constitute "honor," are prevalent in societies where honor murders have place. Honor is related to how other people see a person and may be gained or lost. As long as the code is observed and adhered to, the community has a duty to respect an individual. Given that the practice of honor killing embodies and is a reflection of the most fundamental, gender-neutral values of patriarchal societies, long-term, multifaceted solutions are required to address both the symptoms and the underlying causes of these incidents (Van Eck, Clementine,2003).

Violence exerted on non-western women during opposing codified occurrences, and, in the subsections that follow, an overview of the suffering experienced against women, especially within the context of crimes against honor. The representational method linguistics structuring trauma in worldwide discourses of identity and rights for everyone are examined, concluding that women's perspectives must be central to the conversation. Orientalist presenting and control over women as symbols of honor, as well as patriarchal standards, keep tensions between contemporary sensibilities and cultural relativism alive.

According to cultural conventions and customs, honor relates to the designated duties that women have in the home and sexual spheres. These customs regarded rape, cheating, falling in love with a "wrong" person, suspected pregnancies without a marriage, sexual misconduct, and nonmarital or sexual relationships as abuses of the overall their family's reputation (Elakkary et al., 2014). Numerous of examples, both known and unpublished, show how the antiquated patriarch ruling classes specifically target women. The primary obstacle preventing women from progressing and developing is patriarchal. The general principles—that is, that men are in charge—remain the same regardless of variations in levels of dominance. This control's behavior might be different. Therefore, in order to fight for women's growth in a methodical manner, it is vital to comprehend the framework that maintains women's dominance and subordination and to dissect its workings (sulatan abeda,2011).

EFFECT OF HONOR BASED KILLING AT INTERNATIONAL, EUROPEAN AND NATIONAL LEVELS

Worldwide and national governments, lawmakers, media, academic institutions, and a wide range of civil society organizations for women's empowerment and gender equality. Within this broader movement, the issue of violence against women (VAW), which includes honor killing, has progressively gained recognition as a significant human rights concern after being mostly addressed as a medical issue at first. A thorough overview of the global movement towards gender equality cannot be provided in the limited space of this brief paper. This movement is mainly driven by the frameworks established by the Millennium Development Goals, which were set at the World Social Summit in 2000, and the Beijing Declaration and Platform for Action (BFPA), which was issued as a follow-up to the Fourth World Conference on Women (FWCW) in Beijing in 1995.Two noteworthy developments can be briefly mentioned here, although the main focus in the paragraphs that follow will be on human rights laws and treaties. First, working with both male offenders and female victims of violence is becoming more and more important in Europe and developing nations in order to identify and address the underlying causes of violence. This field has been worked in by Sweden and other Scandinavian nations. UNICEF's work in underdeveloped nations, especially in relation to Female Genital Mutilation (FGM), offers significant expertise in collaborating with men and women to tackle this. Second, the Internet is being used more and more to advocate for legislative change as well as to follow and report on violent episodes and how they are handled.

NGOs and civil society organizations have been the main ones to acknowledge its potential thus far, but official authorities could fully utilize it.

International Human Right Legislation

It goes without saying that honor killing violates each victim's right to life. The 1948 Universal Declaration of Human Rights is only one of the major human rights treaties that guarantee this right, which is seen as the most fundamental of all rights. Furthermore, since family honor is viewed as a mitigating circumstance, it might be argued that honor killing discriminates against women by targeting them and offering a less severe punishment than murdering a man. The Universal Declaration of Human Rights and other significant human rights treaties, however, are widely recognized to be "gender neutral," based on the tenet that "the human condition is gender free." Their main worries are on how the state or its agencies treat each and every person, as well as about the rights of individuals in regards to the government. International human rights legislation frequently exempts non-state actors from accountability, and human rights abuses in this regulatory framework can only be done by governments or their agents. Individual instances of cruelty towards another person in their own residence or private sphere are not handled from this perspective, despite the fact that state-perpetrated brutality against any individual, such torture(Source Title,2020).

Achievements in Resolving Patriarchal Abuse of Women

Indian Supreme Court's views on Honor Killings:
A particular organization in India that has gained recognition for its generous contributions is the judiciary. Indians have great hopes and aspirations for the Palace of Justice. The almost 70-year journey has yielded a durable addition to the political structure. By encouraging harmony, balance, and collaboration between the government's many ministries, the judiciary served as a peacemaker. The court initially may have been strict, rendering decisions only from a legal perspective by interpreting statutes and regulations, but as time went on, it broadened its scope and produced precedent-setting rulings. In their capacity as the architects of justice, the judges drew their rulings using a scientific, procedural, technological, and methodical approach, broadening the scope of essential It issued various directives to protect the human rights and dignity of the people of India via a series of decisions, with a particular emphasis on women, children, bonded labour, the misery of imprisoned individuals educationally and socioeconomically disadvantaged people, the law of the environment, and so on. In a research published by the National Crime Records Bureau, at least 281 instances of this kind of violence were reported between 2014

and 2016. This startling statistic provided the impetus for a historic ruling that ruled honor-based violence to be both illegal and a violation of adults' basic right to exercise choice, as protected by the Constitution's Articles 21 and 19(1)(a), which safeguard the rights to a life of dignity and freedom of expression, respectively. As a result, choosing one's own spouse for a significant other has turned into a fundamental right.

Convention on the Elimination of All Forms of Discrimination Against Women (1979)

Approved in 1979, the Convention on the Elimination of All Forms of Discrimination Against Women (CEDAW), popularly known as the "international bill of rights for women," marked a significant turning point in addressing the acknowledged gender bias in human rights law. The recognition that equal treatment of people in unequal conditions perpetuates rather than confronts prejudice is one of the ways that CEDAW varies from previous agreements, which are similarly the principle of non-discrimination. States Parties to the CEDAW are required to control the conduct of other public and private organizations and persons in addition to abstaining from all forms of discrimination against women. With regard to different forms of Gender-based Violence (GBV) or Violence Against Women (VAW), this article imposes regulatory responsibility on the state on private sector acts. One of the more extreme examples of gender-based violence, or violence against women, is honor killing, as was previously described. In addition to recognizing the harmful consequences of social norms and cultural practices based on the false belief that one sex is innately superior to the other or on gender stereotypes, CEDAW explicitly recognizes that infringements of women's rights take place in a variety of settings. The Standing Committee on CEDAW (Bhugra & Bhanthia, 2015) has frequently brought up the subject of honor killing in its closing views on national reports. It is imperative that all states parties amend their national laws pertaining to honor killing as quickly as possible, nonetheless, given the lax enforcement measures and the cautious ratification (Taneja, 2018).

CEDAW Recommendation on Violence Against Women (1992)

Throughout the process of keeping an eye on how CEDAW is being implemented, it has been apparent that several provisions of the Convention need to be given greater attention or detailed consideration than is provided in the main text. In order to enhance important areas, some additional recommendations have been made. A Recommendation on Violence Against Women (Lindholm, Charles, 1981). is one of them, and it directs States Organizations should pay particular attention to incidents of gender-based or violence against women that are suggestive of prejudiced social conventions and attitudes. This suggestion urges parties to take "preventative maintenance regulations which includes education and outreach applications that modify attitudes regarding the positions and standing of men and women" and highlights the importance of "productive constitutional regulations such as penal penalties, lawsuits, and compensating the provisions that safeguard women towards every kind of violence, including among others assault and battery in the family. "Europeans level (a) The 1950 European regulations to stay the Promotion and Protection of the Declaration of Human Rights and Fundamental Freedoms, which states that everyone has the right to life, that slavery and torture are prohibited, that everyone has the right to liberty and safety, and that discrimination is prohibited (see Section 1, Articles 2 and 3, 5, and 14), is a significant turning point for Europe.

(B) The European Parliament's resolution on the state of the fight against violence against women today and any upcoming initiatives This issue's most recent statement dates back to June 2006. Honor killing is one of many kind of assault against women, and the Resolution acknowledges this, advocating for a zero tolerance approach and outlining certain collaborations and actions to be implemented (Welchman & Hossain, 2005)

National Level

Approximately 185 nations have accepted CEDAW and an additional 88 have ratified the Optional Protocol too far. In theory, states parties must align their national legal frameworks and statutes in relation to other global human rights legislation that includes CEDAW. Nevertheless, many nations that have ratified the CEDAW and other pertinent Conventions still have provisions in their penal codes that view the protection of "honor" as an extenuating circumstance that justifies a far lighter sentence than would be given to a murderer. It is important to amend these criminal statutes to comply with international human rights obligations. States that engage in honor killing may argue that the international community lacks the authority to scrutinize the legitimacy of their actions. In a similar vein, governments in nations where honor killings take place among minority communities could be reluctant to condemn human rights abuses committed there out of aspect for religious difference. The phrase "blind eye" refers to a variety of situations when someone may commit this offence, including when a judge or jury is called in to hear a case involving the police or emergency medical services. Honor killing is frequently excused on religious or cultural grounds in order to prevent it from being prosecuted as a serious offence. The debate over honor killing has actually been the subject of multiple debates among so-called "universalists," who hold that implementing someone's life is always unacceptable, and "relativists," who defend the rights of other cultures to view the killing of a woman for honor as a less serious offense. The concept of the "cultural" defense pertains to the accused's potential use of (foreign) cultural norms to minimize or reject accountability for an act. Honor murders are permitted in Jordan under the provisions of Article 340 of the Criminal Code, which states that "a spouse or another close family member whoever killed a woman into circumstances that are that is highly suspicious of promiscuity is going to be totally exempt from sentence." Following intense advocacy and pressure from women's organizations, the legislation was changed to ensure that women would have equal rights in the event that their spouse engages in adulterous behavior. The "more lightweight punishment for masculine homicides of female members who have carried out a crime that is considered improper in the perspective of the offender" is guaranteed under Article 98, however an honor slaying homicide is often punished with three to six months in prison. The law, as activists point out, is really a holdover from the French Criminal Code that the Ottomans inherited in the 1800s. The movement to treat honor killings the same as other murders is supported by a broad spectrum of people and organizations, despite the Lower House of Parliament's conservative members' persistent and unwavering resistance to changing the law. The Jordan Times' English-language journalist and award-winning writer Rana Husseini has been raising awareness of the problem's scope since 1994. Other royal family members, including King Abdullah II, have voiced their objections in a same manner. In addition to giving pro bono legal assistance to ensure women's access to justice, legal groups are educating women about their rights. During the 60th Commission on Human Rights meeting in 2004, the UN Special Rapporteur on the Freedom of Religion and Belief made a noteworthy statement that bears attention: "Some customs are worthwhile; others violate fundamental freedoms and should be abandoned." You have to be able to tell the difference between being oblivious to human rights violations and essential tolerance. For women's rights and religious freedom to coexist together, the former's intrinsic right to diversity cannot turn into a right to disregard for women's conditions.

CONCLUSIONS AND RECOMMENDATIONS

Suggestions for the European Parliament Concerning Ways to Respond Regarding the Honor Killings

In order to promote gender equality holistically, support efforts that combat honor murders. According to the European Parliament's resolution on the state of the fight against the European Parliament, in cooperation with national counterparts, promote and support a thorough and carefully planned strategy to combat crimes of honor within communities or societies where these crimes are accepted.

This is one of the recommendations for future action regarding violence against women. Research has demonstrated that honor homicide is a behaviour that results from deeply rooted patriarchal norms that affect men and women equally in some cultures. Therefore, ending this behaviour requires the effective promotion of gender equality. A strategic strategy calls for concerted political, economic, legal, and cultural initiatives to advance gender equality. This entails tackling cultural views and ideals around masculinity, individual vs. group rights, and elevating the status of women in every line of work.

Determine, Enlist and Assist the Internal Forces Driving Societal Change

It has been demonstrated that governmental intervention in cases of honor murders or other forms of gender-based violence (GBV), such as female genital mutilation (FGM), exacerbates the problem since established norms and authority may become even more ingrained in the face of opposition. The identification of entrance sites in national societies where a change-related momentum already exists and can be strengthened and supported is something that national authorities should be encouraged to do. While the process of changing such values is long-term, it may be accelerated by the state and members of civil society through a variety of practical short-, medium-, and long-term activities. Assist third-country legislative bodies in their capacity as lawmakers Honor killing is already forbidden by a number of international conventions and declarations. It is also well known that these international organizations are limited to making suggestions; laws cannot be enforced by them. States must approve and join important international agreements and guidelines, including the alternative protocol of the CEDAW for states. To ensure that they fulfil their responsibilities, the parties must pass new legislation and ensure that existing laws that condone honor killing are modified. This is also very important. Men's and women's killings must be treated equally. Clauses that discriminate against justifications, defenses, or explanations based on honor or passion must be removed.

Support to National NGOs

Assist the NGO community in order to enable it to submit an efficient "shadows analysis" to the Convention on the Rights Committee, which will include information about the frequency and handling of honor murders. Help non-governmental groups improve women's access to the judicial system, educate the public about honor killings, and raise the conversation about these crimes.

Support to the Judicial System

It is necessary to report, investigate, and punish every case of honor killing. When it is shown that law enforcement officials have concealed, covered up, or condoned instances of honor killing, they ought to be removed. Robust criminal sanctions must be imposed for those who commit the homicides as well as for family members or community members who lend any support or assistance in any way. Either before or after the act, reports of honor killing need to be accompanied by security. aid in the judicial system's capacity-building Respect killing is against the law and cannot be justified on the basis of "honor" or "passion." Therefore, the State must make sure that everyone involved—police, prosecutors, magistrates, and the judiciary—gets the necessary training to guarantee that the laws are applied correctly.

Backing for the Creation of an Extensive Recommendation Network

In order to protect prospective victims, report crimes, and guarantee that they are brought to justice, a comprehensive referral system including law enforcement, medical professionals, educators, non-governmental organizations, religious and community leaders, and others must be put in place. Encourage the implementation of constitutional educational initiatives for all genders so that they may learn about their specific privileges legal purposes help for women should be provided. Safeguard women who are at risk of honor killings. Those who are in danger must be given safe housing and protection.

Encourage Extensive Education for the Public Programs (in European Countries and Third World Nations)

In order to break the taboo around murder of honor and change the way that both men and women view it, extensive public education campaigns should be launched via all available channels, which include the conventional media, the Internet, schools, non-profit organizations, and community organizations. The efforts of non-governmental organizations, social the community, the media, religious institutions, both male and female categories, as well as other socialization facilitators have contributed significantly to the formation of a culture that condemns killings of honor and other forms of gender-based violence. It is imperative to prioritize the inclusion of men in the conversation and discuss "a substitute male identities," or alternate interpretations regarding what it implies to fall apart when a man, while also utilizing the wealth of existing research in this field.

Encourage Worldwide Initiatives Addressing Crimes Against Honor

Help the pertinent UN agencies (such as UNFEM, the United Nations Council on the Situation of Women, the UN Council on Human Rights, etc.) with their work.

Assist and encourage the UN Personal Rapporteur on Abuse Towards Women in gathering information on cases of assault on women, including honor killing, and provide recommendations for corrective actions.

REFERENCES

Bhopal, K. (1998). South Asian women in East London. Motherhood and social support. *Women's Studies International Forum, vol.21, issue*(5), pp.485-492. DOI: 10.1016/S0277-5395(98)00067-3

Bui, H. N. (2003). Help-seeking behaviour among abused immigrant women: A case of Vietnamese American women. *Violence Against Women*, 9(2), 22.

Caffaro, F., Ferraris, F., & Schmidt, S. (2014). Gender differences in the perception of honor killing in individualist versus collectivistic cultures: Comparison between Italy and Turkey. *Sex Roles: A Journal of Research, vol. 71, issue*(9-10), pp296- 318. https://doi.org/DOI: 10.1007/s11199-014-0413-5

Can, M., & Edirne, T. (2011). Beliefs and attitudes of final-year nursing students on honor crimes: A cross-sectional study. *Journal of Psychiatric and Mental Health Nursing, vol.18, issue*(2),pp 736-743. http://doi.org/DOI: 10.1111/j.1365-2850.2011.01732

Dasgupta, S. (2000). Charting the course: An overview of domestic violence in the South Asian community in the United States. *Journal of Social Distress and the Homeless, vol9, issue*(3), pp173-185. https://doi.org/DOI: 10.1023/A:10094039171983

Deol, S. S. (2014). Honor killings in haryana state, india: A content analysis. *International Journal of Criminal Justice Science.*, 9(2), 192.

Dogan, R. (2014). Different cultural understandings of honor that inspire killing. *Homicide Studies, vol18, issue*(4),pp 363-388. https://doi.org/DOI: 10.1177/1088767914526717

Eck, C. V. (2003). Purified by blood. Honour Killings amongst Turks in the Netherlands, Amsterdam. DOI: 10.1515/9789048505050

Eisner M, Ghuneim K. Honor killing attitudes amongst adolescents in Amman, Jordan. Aggr Behav 2013vol39, issue5, pp.405-17

Elakkary, S., Franke, B., Shokri, D., Hartwig, S., Tsokos, M., & Püschel, K. (2014). Honor crimes: Review and proposed definition. *Forensic Science, Medicine, and Pathology*, 10(1), 76–82. DOI: 10.1007/s12024-013-9455-1 PMID: 23771767

Khan, K. B. (2014). Versions and Subversions of Islamic Cultures in the Film. The Stoning of Soraya M. *Journal of Literary Studies*, 30(3), 149–167. DOI: 10.1080/02564718.2014.949415

Singh, R. N., & Dailey, D. J. (2016). Honor Killing. In *Encyclopedia Britannica.* https://www.britannica.com/topic/honor-killing

ADDITIONAL READINGS

Lewisohn, L. "The Modern Novel." *The Sewanee Review*, vol. 17, issue 4, 1909, pp. 458–474. *JSTOR*, www.jstor.org/stable/27532320

Lindholm, C. (1981). The structure of violence among the Swat Pukhtun. *Ethnology*, 20(2), 147–156.

Simon, R. I., & Eppert, C. "Remembering Obligation: Pedagogy and the Witnessing of Testimony of Historical Trauma." *Canadian Journal of Education / RevueCanadienne De L'éducation,* vol. 22, issue 2, 1997, pp. 175–191.*JSTOR,*ww.jstor.org/stable/1585906

Taneja, R. (2018). What Is Rafale Deal Controversy? All You Need to Know. *NDTV*, (February), 9.

Welchman, L., & Hossain, S. (2005). Introduction:'Honour', rights and wrongs.

Chapter 5
Evolution of Moralistic and Ethical Dimensions of Honour Killing

Megha Singh
GLA University, India

Jae Seung Lee
College of Liberal Arts and Applied Science, Miami University, USA

ABSTRACT

Every human has a right to live their life according to their own will. No one should be compelled to live for others or to live to guard someone else's honour. In the context of Honour Killing, a person or especially a woman is forced to live according to the morals of the society, norms or principles made for them. If they go against any of these principles, norms or morals, they are considered as characterless or impure and is said to have shamed their family or the community and brought dishonour to the family. Honour Killing is the murder of a women or young girl by the male family members, community, tribe or people related to clan for being accused of bringing dishonour to the family. The present chapter contains a brief overview about honour killing and the reasons for its prevalence in the ancient as well as in the modern world. In what context religion and sexism is related or affects honour killing and in what way honour killing evolved and is still prevalent in this modern world of developed nations are further points of discussion in the chapter.

DOI: 10.4018/979-8-3693-9596-7.ch005

BACKGROUND

The chapter begins with defining honour killing and tracing its history from ancient civilizations to contemporary societies. The chapter delves into the complex intersection of religion and honour killing and how sexism contributes in the continuation of honour killing. Data is examined on the prevalence of honour killings, with a special focus on SAARC nations where the incidence of such crimes is shockingly high. Case studies and statistical analysis from nations such as Pakistan and India demonstrate the enduring cultural influences that motivate this behaviour. The chapter extends to global prevalence, pointing out that although honour murders are more frequent in some areas, they also happen in Western diaspora populations. Analysis of the national and international legal framework on honour killing and the challenges of addressing honour killing through the law. Despite the fact that many nations have made these kinds of actions illegal, societal norms that are strongly embedded make enforcement challenging. In what way honour killing evolved and is still prevalent in this modern world of developed nations are further points of discussion in the chapter.

According to the latest data from the National Crime Records Bureau (NCRB), there were 25 honour killings in India in each of the years 2019 and 2020 and 33 in 2021. The Human Rights Commission of Pakistan reported 460 cases of honour killings in the year 2017. Pakistan has a population of 170 million and about three women are killed each day in the name of honour restoration (Ullah, 2010). Honour-based crimes are not exclusive to any one religion or faith; they occur all around the world. According to officials, at least twelve women in the United Kingdom (UK) fall victim to honour killings each year. Looking into criminal records for partner homicides from 1996 to 2005, the German Federal Criminal Police Office found that, out of an average of about 700 yearly homicides, there were about 12 cases of honour killings in Germany annually. The Afghanistan Independent Human Rights Commission states that from March 2011 to April 2013, 243 incidences of HK were reported in Afghanistan. Between 2000 and 2010, 50 HKs were reported in Jordan. 52 instances of HK occurred in Egypt in 1997, while 400 women in Yemen became victim in the same year. The Women's Centre for Legal Aid and Counselling in Palestine reported 27 cases in 2014 and 15 cases in 2015. These modest figures, nonetheless, could underestimate the severity of the issue (AlQahatani & Almutairi, 2022).

Research Methodology

The purpose of this chapter is to gain thorough understanding of honour killing, its fundamental causes and other factors. The information for this chapter was collected in the form of checking records from magazines/ libraries/ journals/ articles/ interview/ surveys/ websites/ books, etc. The study uses a qualitative research approach, combining the sociological aspects of honour killing with the legal perspective to understand multifaceted approach of honour killing. The research examines surveys from various countries where honour killing is most prevalent, along with religious texts and feminist theories (AlQahatani & Almutairi, 2022).

The study looks at the traits of honour murders, how they appear in various cultural contexts, and how they relate to gender norms, legal frameworks, and society ideals. This method, which focuses on nations like Pakistan, Jordan, and India where honour murders are still most common, enables a thorough examination of the historical, legal, and social settings of these crimes. It also explores how sexism and patriarchal institutions interact, framing women as the guardians of family honour and justifying violence against them (Prabhune, 2020).

A thorough examination of case studies, government reports, human rights group findings, legal documents, and case law on honour murders from different countries provides the key data for this study. The study includes a comprehensive analysis of scholarly works, feminist ideas, and sociological studies of gender roles, sexism, and women's legal standing in communities where honour murders take place (Kumar, 2023). To investigate the variations in legal systems and judicial reactions to honour murders among different jurisdictions, a comparative legal study is carried out.

Key Terms

Core terms include Honour Killing (Jha & Rai, 2023) and izzat (Tyagi, 2021) that directly depicts that these heinous crimes are committed and directly related to the honour of the family. If honour is harmed by the female member of the family, she is subjected to such honour based crimes, violence (Korteweg, 2011) and inter-caste marriage (Singh, 2017) that shows caste is a very prevalent and dominating factor in the society, nobody wants to marry their childrens into different caste and if they do so forcefully they are subjected to violence by their family which may also result into their death, khap panchayat (Prabhune, 2020) and murder (Raghu N Singh, n.d) khap panchayats are very prevalent in the villages and they are often very ruthless, if any case of inter-caste marriage, love marriage, extra-marital affair comes to this community, they decide it mercilessly and in many cases punishment of murder is given to the offenders or we can also say to the victims, patriarchal society (Dailey, n.d) it means a society that is living with ancient mentality of seeing womens as only house holders and cannot digest their freedom, human rights watch (Mishra, 2011) it defines the term honour killing, crime (Chaturvedi, 2021) killing someone just because he/she brought dishonour to the family is a crime and there should be separate provisions for its punishment, caste system (Mishra, 2011) it is very prevalent and is one of the fundamental reason for these crimes, dishonour (Heydari et al., 2021) the reason of these crimes, it is a very vague word and covers various actions majorly being committed by the female members of the family that often has same reaction of anger in the male members of the family and the result of which is the murder of the female members or the victims.

Literature Review

Honour killing is defined as the murder of a female member by the male members of the family and the killers justify themselves by claiming that the victim brought dishonour to the family's name (Raghu and Singh, 2016). Honour killing is a legal problem as the crime of honour killing is increasing fast due to complex socio-cultural difficulties; the basic reason of the crime is that most caste members oppose inter-caste partnerships under the pretext of defending the dignity of their caste or the social standing of their family and this is one of the fundamental cause of such crimes that are supported in this chapter (Kumar, 2023).

Women's sexuality is seen as an important object that controls the system of honour and that the women's sexuality belongs to the male members of the family or groups. (Christianson, 2020) supports the studies that suggests that women may be seen as having betrayed their female chastity norms when they lose their virginity before marriage, if they socialize with other mens in their society, or even if they dress up however they want (Heydari et al., 2021).

The author suggests honour killing as a killing for protecting so called izzat and what are the articles of Indian constitution that such honour-based crimes violate and that there is a need to take initiatives against Khap Panchayats and also says that it is the high time to change the mentality of society for women. (Ganguly, 2022) analysed the data of NCRB that gives the number of honour killing's cases in India (Tyagi, 2021). The national and international legal framework that is provided against these violent crimes are studied by the author (Khan, 2023).

Future Research Directions

This research is an attempt to provide a comprehensive understanding of the evolution of moralistic and ethical dimensions of Honour Killing by thoroughly examining the concept of honour of killing, its meaning and definition. There were various parameters through which research was conducted beginning with the thorough examination of the concept of honour killing, the reasons for the happening of such grave offence, followed by the relation of honour killing with religion and sexism. Although numerous studies have explored these aspects separately, this research goes further into the linkages between gender prejudices, religious interpretations, cultural norms, and legal responses, both domestically and worldwide. The research attempts to fill the vacuum in the literature by providing a thorough, statistically supported assessment of the practice in SAARC nations as well as a comparative analysis of the worldwide phenomena (Ganguly, 2022). Often, previous studies have failed to integrate these multiple aspects in a single cohesive structure.

Future Research Direction could focus on a number of important areas that still need to be developed or are understudied. The social development of honour killing in contemporary civilizations is one significant aspect. It would be beneficial to look at how communities that have historically carried out honour murders perceive them in light of globalization, change gender roles, and shifting social norms—especially in light of the growing public outcry against these practices (Heydari et al., 2021). Research on how the media, social movements, and outside pressure affect public perceptions of honour-related violence can be a part of this.

A more thorough investigation of the psychological drivers of honour murders is another potential direction of research. The background is provided by cultural, religious, and gendered standards; however, little is known about the exact psychological triggers, which might include personal humiliation, familial pressure, or a desire for societal conformity. Knowing the psychology of the person and the group that supports this violence's continuation may help develop more targeted interventions aimed at preventing it.

Future research may also concentrate on how well national and international judicial systems handle honour murders (Khan, 2023). Although the legal frameworks of many nations are covered in this research, a longitudinal analysis of the enforcement, weaknesses, and practical effects of these laws would be crucial to determine whether or not they are accomplishing the goals for which they were designed. Research comparing nations with comparable cultural norms but dissimilar legal systems may also provide important information about the best legal tactics.

Finally, given the changing nature of gender roles and the expanding worldwide feminist movements, it would be interesting to investigate how honour murders relate to other instances of gender-based violence like femicide or domestic abuse in the future. Examining the intersections between these problems and determining if the motivations behind honour killings are unique or coincide with other types of violence may offer a more thorough framework for comprehending and addressing gender-based violence in general (Dailey & Singh, 2016).

This chapter had not covered the psychological aspect of the offenders or the male family members that consider themselves in the dominating position in the family and how the evolution of modern society is accepting changes and women's freedom but still there are peoples who are not ready to accept women's freedom. How their psychology can be changed so that they can adopt the modern world. Scholars might build on the findings of this study by extending the research in these directions and providing more sophisticated and practical approaches to comprehending and eliminating honour murders.

INTRODUCTION

Honour killing is an evil practice in which women are killed by the male members of the family because they feel or identify that they have brought dishonour to the family. It is a little difficult to understand the word honour killing because from the beginning the whole society has been objecting to how the word honour killing can be related to honour i.e. respect. Honor killing is used for such murders which are done to protect the honour. Historically, there is no evidence of the origin of honour killing, but some studies suggest that it originated from the Balush people of Baluchistan, the main province in South Asia and as these people spread across the world, these crimes started spreading across the world. It is also possible that this crime, due to tradition, may have spread across the world from Pakistan and India.

According to Human Rights Watch, honour killing is an evil act in which women are killed by men in their families because the men feel or think that their family or their honour has been harmed (Mishra, 2011). Studies have revealed that many women are killed only based on belief or suspicion that a woman has an immoral relationship with a man or if she becomes pregnant due to such an immoral relationship or the woman has entered into an inter-caste marriage or has entered into a love marriage without the consent of the family. Many times, flatulence due to the tumour in the stomach or cessation of menstruation due to anemia also becomes a basis for suspicion and women are killed.

Research has also revealed that it is women who instigate men to commit murder. It would not be wrong to say that women are the instigators of honour killings and are often ignored.

The largest issue in punishing someone who has committed the crime of honour killing is that no one comes forward to testify, and even members of the public appear to be in favour of this crime. The disturbing thing is that the villagers don't stop there; they are also seen applauding these kinds of deeds. Talking about IPC, 1860, under it, criminal offences like honour killing have not been made punishable separately. Honour Killing in IPC comes under Sec 300 i.e. murder and Sec 299 i.e.

Culpable Homicide. Of which punishments are given under Sec 302 and 304, that means, the maximum sentence can be life imprisonment or death penalty.

Just as Sati Pratha has been abolished in India, there are some suggestions which should be implemented to eradicate honour killing or it seems that honour killing can be eliminated. Like Khap Panchayats should be settled and they should be properly informed about the law and what work they can do and what they cannot do. In 2012 or 2013 in West Bengal, one such Panchayat sentenced a girl to gang rape as a punishment that the villagers gang rape her and the girl's fault was only that she married someone out of her caste. This case has gained a lot of attention because Birbhum is the birthplace of former President of India Pranab Mukherjee or it is here that the Human Rights Commission, Women's Commission took all the actions or the members of the Panchayat who gave this punishment for rape were also got arrested and the case against them for abetment of crime is still under trial.

Panchayat or other Panchayat should be educated about which category is included in their work area, which category is not included, what should they do and what will be the punishment for doing so. Then women should be educated and work should be done towards making them self-reliant. One very important thing that can be done is promoting inter-caste marriage. If inter-caste marriages are promoted, I feel that crimes like honour killing will be decreased. Then the law or the administration will also have to be successful, they will have to take the right steps so that this crime can be stopped at the appropriate time.

In such cases of abduction, the court should also give a thorough trial and severe punishment should be given to the person who commits the crime or the abductor. Another important thing is that the media should not exaggerate such news which may inspire people to commit such crimes or think of committing such crimes. And I feel that by adopting such tips, crimes like Honour Killing can be reduced.

Honour Killing: Killing for Protecting So-Called Izzat

"Humare ghar ki izzat," I think this phrase is enough to explain the reasons behind such a heinous crime of Honour Killing. Honour Killing is a death, awarded to men or women by their family members especially by male members of the family for having an extra-marital relationship, pre-marital relationship, having a lesbian or gay relationship, marrying outside the caste by going against family members, marrying within the same gotra. There could be many other reasons for Honour Killing. The generation gap and mentality of people is the main cause of this as people are not ready to accept or believe the fact that their children can live according to themselves, they can marry outside the caste, within the same gotra or can have a lesbian or gay relationship or they can make their own choices. There are certain cases where girls of the family are murdered just because they have male friends.

The friendship of a male or female is also a taboo in most places and girls are not allowed to make male friends or talk with them or go with them and any girl doing any of such things is considered characterless and said to bring dishonour to their family. Families impose the burden of izzat on their daughter's shoulders. They are restricted from doing anything of their own choice in their life. They are not allowed to go out of their house except for school or education and even at some places they are not allowed to go to school as it will give them a chance to interact with males and they are told to do everything after marriage. Most of the families do not prioritize the choice or opinion of their daughters regarding their marriage.

Honour killing is not at all a new concept, it could be linked back to the time of partition of our country when several women were killed to preserve the honour and dignity of the country. Crimes like honour killing violate human rights, infringe Article 21 i.e., the right to live with dignity and also violate Articles 14,15,19 and 31 of the Indian Constitution. In today's world, crimes like honour killing are not only confined to rural areas but are also very common in metropolitan cities.

Reasons for the Predominance of Honour Killing

1. **Caste System:** The caste system is very prevalent in Indian Society. The rigidity of the caste system and the traditional mindset that is present in Indian society, have contributed to the presence of social evil that is Honour Killing. The caste is inherited from generations due to which they get some benefits or respect in society, they fear that due to inter-caste marriages in their families, they may lose respect and also have a fear of social ostracization which encourages male members of the family to commit such heinous crimes. In India, caste marriages are considered a taboo and any person doing so by going against their family is said to have brought dishonour to the family. Such crimes are committed to preserve the honour and respect of the family in society and to give lessons to other family members so that they do not engage in any kind of act that brings dishonour to the family. According to the National Commission of Women, a study shows that among 326 cases of conflict surveyed, 72% were due to inter-caste marriages and 3% due to inter-religious marriages. In the case of Latha Singh vs. State of Uttar Pradesh, the statement made by Justice Markandey Katju that "No honour involved in such killings and honour killings are nothing more than cold-blooded murder." The Supreme Court further noted that to reinforce society's social cohesion, inter-caste and inter-religious unions ought to be promoted.

Marriage within same gotra or inter-religious marriages: The present system that is prevalent in Indian society is caste andogamy and gotra exogamy. The mentality of the society is very awful such that they are not ready to accept marriages within the same gotra and inter-religious marriages. This also provokes violence against women. Not only inter-caste marriage but also inter-religious marriages lead to Honour Killing. A report says that "family members have no other socially acceptable option than to kill the women to remove the stain on their honour, but the regime of honour is unable to forgive a woman who has fallen under suspicion and has not allowed clarifying herself.

2. **Patriarchal Society:** In our society, the burden of the family's honour or dignity is on the women and men are considered to monitor the women's and prevent them from abusing the honour of the family. This shows the patriarchal mindset of the society. Women are not allowed to express their views and do anything according to their own will or of their choice. They exist in society only to follow the orders of the male members of the family and any woman going against it, is considered as an oppression against the social norms and traditions. And they are killed just because they did anything of their choice by going against the family. This mindset is still prevalent in today's modern world. People are very narrow-minded that they do not want to give free will to women, they want to control them according to themselves and do not want to give women equal positions in society.
3. **Khap Panchayat:** Khap Panchayat is a community or organization representing a clan or a group of related clans especially found in North India. The major reason behind Honour Killing is the caste punishment or the caste dictates that are announced by these extra-constitutionalized Khap Panchayats. They are persistent in Indian society despite their extra-constitutional status because of the weak legal system in rural areas. The absence of formal institutions such as Panchayat Samiti leads to the brutal governance of the illegal and extra-constitutionalized panchayats. The people present in the Khap panchayat or the people holding it are not well educated about the powers and boundaries within their scope. They take the law into their own hands and judge according to their will which endangers the life of the individuals that marry according to their own free will or against the will of the society. A landmark case against the decision of Khap Panchayat is Smt. Laxmi Kachhwaha vs. State of Rajasthan (1999). In this case, the unlawful operation of Khap Panchayats, which violates people's fundamental rights, has been the subject of a PIL filed in the Rajasthan High Court. In this case, the court directed state authorities to impose limitations on the Khap Panchayat's operations and to apprehend and penalize its members. Consequently, it ought to be eliminated (Prabhune, 2020).

4. **Illiteracy about the rights:** Most of the people who adhere to the traditional system, the people who are involved in Khap Panchayat the people who do not adhere the modern society and also the people who are victims of such crimes are illiterate. The larger section of society is not aware of the rights that are made to protect them from any kind of violence due to lack of education. In rural areas people especially women are not sent to school to get an education because of the so-called societal norms that they cannot get educated as they are only born to take care of the house. They are very less aware of the rights within the society, what the government says about their legal rights what the Supreme Court says regarding their legal rights or whether they can approach directly the Supreme Court or high court if they fear that they have been chased by the caste community. This factor contributes to the social evil of Honour Killing and leads women to become victims of such heinous crimes.

5. **Poor Judicial System**: The perpetrators who are involved in the crimes of Honour Killing are not punished due to the dominance of the caste. As killing for honour is accepted within society the criminal actions of the people doing so are justified and the people seeing such crimes may also not report it. Our Indian Judicial System is very lengthy and time-consuming justice discourages victims from reporting such criminal activities and gives a benefit to the perpetrators that they can roam free even after doing such a heinous act. When such an act is supported by the whole society it becomes more difficult to against it. This is one of the main reasons that the crime of Honour Killing is increasing even today.

Religion and Honour Killing

No culture or religion is exclusive to the ideas of honour and shame and how they are used to justify killing and other violent acts. Every religion has some dogmas, principles or rules that are to be obeyed by the people of the particular religion and anyone who breaks those principles can make himself/herself the victim of Honour Killing. Honour Killing is the planned assassination of a relative, generally a young woman because she has purportedly betrayed her family's honour. It usually predominates in civilizations where intolerant religious and tribal beliefs, patriarchal power systems, and communal solidarity limit individual liberties.

Although Honour Killing is not explicitly sanctioned by either religion i.e., Hindu or Muslim, they both contribute to its legalization in South Asian societies. Hindu religious law and custom prohibit getting married to someone from a different caste or engaging in sexual relations with them. Similarly, romantic relations with a member of the same sub-caste (gotra) are prohibited. Most Hindu honour killings are committed against young Indians who are thought to have broken one of these commandments. The Muslim community has set some standards for women's belonging to their community. Honour killing can result from refusing to wear burqas or from dressing in a way that is perceived as 'foreign' or 'Western'. Sex outside of marriage by men or women, or zina, is punishable by severe punishments according to traditional interpretations of Sharia, or Islamic law.

Honour killing can occur when someone disobeys religious principles, for example, changing or giving up their faith. Many Indians, from a variety of religious backgrounds, according to the survey, believe that "it is very important to stop people from marrying into other religious groups." According to the report's findings, around two-thirds of Hindus surveyed in India want to prevent Hindu women (67%) and Hindu men (65%) from getting married outside their religion. Muslims are more likely to agree, with 80% saying it is crucial to prevent Muslim women from getting married outside their faith and 76% saying it is crucial to prevent Muslim men from doing the same.

Sexism and Honour Killing

Sexism is based on the belief that the members of one sex are less able, intelligent, skillful, etc. than the other, especially women who are considered inferior to men. For a very long time, we have seen discrimination between the genders as women are not allowed to work outside of their home, interact with other male members or have any kind of relation with the male members of the society. In some places especially in rural places girls or women are not even allowed to go to school because of the traditional mindset that women are only meant to take care of the house and should not go outside their prescribed territory and because of the thinking that it will be only waste of money to get them educated as their family aims to get them married. On the other hand, men are considered superior to women as they take care of the house by bringing money or by working outside of the house. They want to have control over women and act as a caretaker of women's behaviour. Any misconduct by the women will be treated as a crime and then women become subject to severe punishments such as violence, assault, etc. Honour Killing is one such severe punishment that is given by the male members of the family or society to the female members who bring dishonour to the family by breaking the rules that are made for them. It is a particularly dangerous and unsettling method of controlling women's conduct. It has been done for thousands of years and continues to be practiced globally. Honor killings are regarded as masculine homicide where women are the primary victims. Because women have to submit to men, men have the authority to rule over them and take any action required to uphold or preserve the honour of their families. This viewpoint is essentially predicated on the notion that a woman is her family's property. Honour becomes an obsession and "a biased scale both men and women use to judge all women". A man's honour depends not only on his reputation for his virtues and his own moral integrity, but also on the preservation of the honour of the entire family in cultures where family honour is highly valued. This is strongly correlated with the chastity and morally righteous behaviour of the female family members. The basis of honour killing is the disapproved sexual behaviour by women which varies depending on the community and occasionally even the family; it usually encompasses a variety of behaviour, such as flirting, refusing an arranged marriage, having sex before marriage, and even being sexually assaulted or raped. When is woman is believed or proven to have violated sexual traditions of her family, community, or religion, it is viewed as disrespectful or dishonouring these traditions and bringing dishonour on the family or community. To regain their honour, they kill women in the name of honour killing. (Heydari et al., 2021).

HONOUR KILLING STATISTICS IN SAARC NATIONS

Honour Killing is a practice that has significantly and consistently occurred in South Asia and the Middle East. Honour Killing is very much seen in the SAARC Nations such as India, Bhutan, Afghanistan, Bangladesh, Nepal, Pakistan, etc.; with nearly half of its killing occurring in India and Pakistan.

Honour Killing in India

Honour has proven to be something that is valued beyond everything in Indian culture, where patriarchal families predominate. People would never hesitate to kill their loved ones to defend the "honour" of their family, tribe and community. Historically, women have always had to pay the price to uphold the family's honour because they were viewed as weak and dependent and were shouldered with the responsibility to maintain the purity and honour of the family. Honour Killing has become a common crime in India, a nation known for having the largest constitution and democracy in the world, human rights and the right to life as well. In India, it is now a customary practice. The Supreme Court's ruling on honour killing demonstrates that the practice is forbidden and subject to penalties. It is unlawful to kill or physically abuse a girl or woman who marries a male against the wishes of her family. In many parts of Northern India such as Punjab, Haryana, Uttar Pradesh and Rajasthan, there have been many cases of honour killing as a result of women getting married against their family or outside the caste or religion and these cases are increasing year by year. In Haryana, honour killings are horrifyingly common in the communities ruled by lawless "khap panchayats." In the case of Manoj and Babli, the court of Karnal district sentenced five perpetrators to life sentences who were involved in the murder. This is the first case of honour killing that has resulted in a historic ruling that gives the accused a life sentence. It was the first time when honour killing was seriously taken into account.

According to the latest data from the National Crime Records Bureau (NCRB), there were 25 honour killings in India in each of the years 2019 and 2020 and 33 in 2021. To address the issue of honour killings among particular ethnic groups in North India, the National Commission for Women established a legislative body in 1990. This body examined women's issues as well as laws, the constitution, and other rules. (Tanni Ganguly, 19 November 2022)

Honour Killing in Pakistan

In Pakistan, the practice of honour killing is referred to as "karo-kari." Karo refers to a black man, and Kari to a black lady, and it describes extramarital sex. Family members feel they have the right to kill any woman who is labelled as "kari," as well as the co-accused "karo." The word "karo kari" is frequently used interchangeably with "honour killing," particularly in Pakistan's Sindh province. In most of these cases, female victims are attacked by male family members or community members. "When wealth is lost, nothing is lost; when health is lost, something is lost; when honour is lost, everything is lost" (Amir Hamid Jafri, Oxford University Press 2008). is a traditional proverb from Pakistan that aptly captures the cultural significance of honour. Upholding honour is essential for both men and women; males preserve honour via masculinity and women via modesty.

In Pakistan, hundreds of women across all age groups and regions are reportedly killed each year in the name of honour. Numerous cases go unreported. Millions of women in Pakistan are bound by customs that compel them to live in severe seclusion and submit to men, many of whom use violence to exercise their nearly proprietorial authority over them. In 2015 nearly, 1100 women were murdered in honour killings. The Human Rights Commission of Pakistan reported 460 cases of honour killings in the year 2017. Pakistan has a population of 170 million and about three women are killed each day in the name of honour restoration (Muhammad Zia Ullah, 27-05-2010). Since releasing Pakistan: Violence against Women in the Name of honour2 in 1999, Amnesty International has discovered that although there have been some encouraging developments for women's rights, the Pakistani government still largely fails to protect women from abuses while under their custody, in the family, and in the community.

GLOBAL PREVALENCE OF HONOUR KILLING

Honour Killing is not a small concept, it exists in the whole world. The word honour means respect and it is not limited to a particular area or region or specific kind of people. It is a worldwide concept and everyone in the world wants to live with respect. In most countries or almost every country, the respect of the male members of the family, community or tribe is vested in the female members of the family or their sexuality. According to surveys conducted in Egypt, Palestine, Israel, and Tunisia, the core idea behind family honour is that women, in particular, must act in a way that upholds the family's honour. Honour-based violence is committed in every part of the world. Although the types of violence can vary by country; gender and socioeconomic disparities are the root causes of this worldwide issue. According to various studies, women may be seen as having betrayed female chastity norms when they lose their virginity before marriage, become unfaithful after marriage, or socialize with men outside of their family. They may also be perceived as acting independently when they pursue independent goals like obtaining an education, landing a job, leaving an abusive husband, or dressing however they want (Christianson, 2020).

Honour-based crimes are not exclusive to any one religion or faith; they occur all around the world. Nonetheless, honour killings have been quite common throughout the Middle East and South Asia, with India and Pakistan accounting for about half of all cases. Up to 5,000 women are estimated to be killed each year for honour-related reasons, according to estimates from the United Nations Population Fund; despite the widespread suspicion, many crimes go unreported. According to the Special Rapporteur's report on cultural practices in the family that are violent towards women, there have been reports of honour killings in Egypt, Jordan, Lebanon, Morocco, Palestine, Syrian Arab Republic, Turkey, and Yemen; other countries in the Mediterranean and Persian Gulf; Western and European countries such as France, Germany, U.K., Canada, USA; and Asian countries such as India, Pakistan, Bangladesh, Sri Lanka, etc. Human Rights Watch's advocacy director, Widney Brown, claims that honour killing is a tradition that is common to many cultures and religions (Xavier, 2015).

According to a survey conducted among teens in Amman, the capital of Jordan, nearly half of the males and one in five of the girls think it is justifiable to kill a daughter, sister, or wife who has "dishonoured" or shamed the family. Among the teenagers who took part in the study, one-third supported honour killing.

The Roman law 'Lex Julia de adulteries coerced', which was put into effect by Augustus Caesar, allowed for the execution of unfaithful wives' lovers by their husbands as well as the murder of daughters and their lovers who committed adultery at the hands of their fathers. According to officials, at least twelve women in the United

Kingdom (UK) fall victim to honour killings each year; these homicides primarily occur in Asian and Middle Eastern households. Looking into criminal records for partner homicides from 1996 to 2005, the German Federal Criminal Police Office found that, out of an average of about 700 yearly homicides, there were about 12 cases of honour killings in Germany annually. These cases included cases involving collective family honour and individual male honour. Honor killings have been more prevalent in Europe recently, and as a result, their prevalence needs to be addressed. In 2009, the European Parliamentary Assembly brought this up in Resolution 1681, emphasizing how urgently honour crimes need to be addressed (Pattanaik, 2020).

Therefore, crimes about honour are prevalent worldwide and always have the same result, not just in undeveloped or developing nations but even in the most developed nations.

Honour Killing: A Dark Phenomenon of Modernity

It is a little difficult to understand the word honour killing because at the mention of this word, our society reacts directly or indirectly or shows objection as to how the word killing can be related to honour or respect. The word honour itself has been made a cruel joke by associating it with killing. Honour killing is a wrong word, coward killing is the right word for such a crime. There are some such creatures who kill their own children and eat them, human beings are one of them, they kill their own children but they do not eat them and do so because of the fear of the society or the world; their stupid, illogical, conservative useless thinking, they kill their own children. In today's world, nations are economically getting modern and growing forward on daily basis but their mentality is still very traditional and orthodox. Their minds are still blocked with the complexities of ill practices of religion. Modern people are still not ready to accept women as their equal or to give them right to live according to their own free will. Being traditional and moralistic is not bad, it shows how much we believe and respect our traditions, morals and societal norms but not in all the ways. If we see the scenario of old times, women accepted themselves as the caretaker of the house surrendered to the male members or masculinity of the family or community and accepted all the decisions made for them regarding their marriage, education or their freedom. But now the times have changed, in a growing nation, people also grow mentally, physically and economically which has changed some old scenarios now women are not ready to surrender themselves to the masculinity of men, they want to live with free will and they have right to do so, which has created a situation of conflict between the genders. It is very sad that everyone wants to live in a modern society but doesn't want to change anything about the status of women.

The presence of such an ill practice shows the dark reality of modern and developed nations. Growing economically is not the only criterion of developed nations, treating every gender equally, giving fair chance to everyone and less or no violence against women due to such illogical reasoning, refers to how modern a nation is. And unfortunately, the road ahead is still very far away for women to get recognition from the nations. But the very high prevalence of crimes like Honour Killing shows that the nations should make strong laws against it so that such crimes can be reduced and everyone can live with free will as well as dignity.

Indian Legal Framework on Honour Killing

The body of laws that make up the criminal justice system is public laws, which includes the criminal laws. Since criminal activities have an impact on the public at large and the government is obligated to safeguard its citizens, activity that jeopardizes or threatens the public interest is prohibited under criminal law. Societal and cultural values inherently influence and form criminal jurisprudence due to its direct correlation with the well-being of society.

The **Indian Constitution** is the cornerstone of government, serving as a code of conduct for administrative coordination and the defense of citizens' rights. **Article 14** (the Right to Equality), **Articles 15 (1) and (3)** (Prohibition of Discrimination on Grounds of Religion, Race, Caste, Sex, or Place of Birth), **Article 17** (Abolition of Untouchability), **Article 19 (1)** (the Freedom to Speech and Expression), and **Article 21** (the Right to Life and Personal Liberty) are the constitutional provisions that offer protection against honour killing.

Even though they are optional, the **Directive Principles of State Policy (DPSP)** are used to evaluate a nation's capacity for successful governance. Therefore, the state is required by **Article 39(a)** to give everyone a suitable means of sustenance. Nonetheless, honour killing negates the woman's life in most cases, and **Article 39(e) and (f)** mandates that the state protects infants and young people against exploitation and increasing or increasing material abandonment. In contrast to this traditional practice of honour killing, many children, teenagers, and married couples face threats of murder and are put in perilous circumstances. Therefore, it is the duty of the state to protect these vulnerable peoples and their lives from this terrible behaviour.

Honour killing perpetrators are, as said before, regarded as murderers. Since homicides are usually covered up by the community, it might be challenging to identify the perpetrators, but it is possible. The offender may also assert, as a defense under **Section 300** of the **Indian Penal Code, 1860**, that nothing was planned or premeditated and that he acted in response to a grave and sudden provocation. The victim's deed was so profoundly moving that he lost all self-control and simply followed his instincts, which was an act of dishonouring the family. In addition, **Sections 300, 302** (murder and its penalty), **304, 307** (attempt to commit murder), **Sections 120A and 120B** (criminal conspiracy), and **Sections 34 and 35** (common intention) are examined in order to evaluate the act of murder from killing. Under the Indian Penal Code (IPC), honour killings are defined as cases of homicide (Section **304**) and murder (Section **302**), which are considered serious crimes.

Section 13 of the **Indian Evidence Act of 1872** empowers the judiciary and the administration to take legal action against anybody who seeks to conceal or alter evidence.

Apart from the aforementioned provisions, there exists human rights legislation, such as the **Protection of Human Rights (Amendment) Act, 2006**. It establishes a legal framework that shields Indian citizens from various acts and situations that could deny them access to basic necessities of life.

If a woman is harmed physically, psychologically, or publicly by her spouse and his family, she is protected against them by the Protection of Women in **Domestic Violence Act of 2005**.

International Legal Framework on Honour Killing

Through its numerous laws, treaties, and conventions, the United Nations is always striving to defend human rights across the globe. The United Nations General Assembly ratified the **Convention on the Elimination of All Forms of Discrimination Against Women (CEDAW) in 1979**. India is a signatory and has also ratified this convention. Women are protected as a class or category under the CEDAW, which forbids discrimination against them.

Apart from CEDAW, there is the **1948 UDHR, or "Universal Declaration of Human Rights."** The declaration defends against discrimination based on gender and class, and on those grounds, it shields the rights of both men and women against assailants who kill them in an effort to uphold the honour of the family.

Additionally, there is the **1976 "International Convention on Economic, Social, and Cultural Rights," or ICESCR**. According to Article 12 of ICESCR, it is the responsibility of State parties to make every effort possible to guarantee the right of all individuals to the highest standard of physical. and mental health.

REFERENCES

AlQahatani, S. M., Almutairi, D. S., BinAqeel, E. A., Al-Qahatani, R. D., & Menezes, R. G., (27 Dec 2022): *Honour Killings in the East Mediterranean Region: A Narrative Review*

BBC News, (April 2016): *Pakistan honour killings on the rise*

Chaturvedi, P., (4 Jan 2021): *Honour killings in India and need for urgent reforms and new laws*

Christianson, M., (20 Dec 2020): *A woman's honour tumbles down on all of us in the family, but a man's honour is only his": young women's experiences of patriarchal chastity norms*

Dailey, J. D. & Singh, R. N., (2016): *Honour Killing*

Ganguly, T. (19 November 2022) published by Social Legal Corporation- *Honour Killings in South Asia*

Heydari, A., Teymoori, A., & Trappes, R. (2021). Honor killing as a dark side of modernity: Prevalence, common discourses, and a critical view. *Social Sciences Information. Information Sur les Sciences Sociales*, 60(1), 86–106. DOI: 10.1177/0539018421994777

Honor-Killing-A-Feminist-Analysis (n.d)-C1F9653CC31408AA

Jafri, A. H. Oxford University Press (2008): *Honour Killing: dilemma, ritual and understanding*

Jha, K. & Rai, H., (2023): *A Socio-Legal Study on Honour Killing: A Menace to the Indian Society*

Kalnawat, Dr. A.M., (n.d): *Indian Legal Framework on Honour Killing*

Khan, Mr. S., (5 May 2023): *Honour Killing - Current National and International Legal Framework*

Korteweg, A. C., (March 2011): *Understanding Honour Killing and Honour Related Violence in the Immigration Context: Implications for the Legal Profession and Beyond*

Kumar, Mr. S., (March 2023): *Honour Killing in India- A Socio-Legal Problem*

Latha Singh vs. State of Uttar Pradesh 2006 5 SCC 475 (7 July, 2006)

Law Commission of India, (August 2012): *Prevention of Interference with the Freedom of Matrimonial Alliances (in the name of Honour and Tradition): A Suggested Legal Framework*

Mishra, A., (13 Dec 2011): *Honour Killings in India: The Law it is and Law it ought to be*

Pattanaik, S., (4 Sep 2020): *Analysis of Honour Killing: National and International Perspective with Relevant Legislations*

Prabhune, A. (2020) – *A Socio-Legal Study On Honour Killing As A Crime In India*

Report by- Amnesty International- (2001): *Human Rights*

Research By University of Cambridge; Published in Journal "Aggressive Behaviour" (n.d)

Singh, Dr. D. K., (June 2017): *Inter-Caste or Inter-Religious Marriages and Honour Related Violence in India*

Smt. Chandrapati vs. State of Haryana and Others on 27 May 2011

The Wire Staff (30 June 2021): *Majority of Indians Across Religions Oppose Inter-Religious Marriage*

Tyagi, M., (20 June 2021): *Honour Killing in India*

Ullah, M. Z., (27-05-2010): *Honour killings in Pakistan under Theoretical, Legal and Religious Perspectives*

Xavier, Dr. M. S., (March 2015): *Honour Killings: A Global Concern*

Chapter 6
Effect of Culture-Based Violence on Human Psychology

Aruna Dhamija
https://orcid.org/0000-0001-8825-7414
GLA University, India

Mugdha Garg
GLA University, India

ABSTRACT

In the 21st century, modernization, employment, literacy, and technological advancements have led to acceptance of inter-caste and inter-religion marriages. However, the caste system persists, leading to discrimination and "Honor Killing" or culture-based violence. This chapter explores cultural and psychological factors that motivate such violence, the historical background of this issue, and the influence of "Khap Panchayats" on people. It highlights the impact of this violence on society, its psychological effects, and suggests preventive measures and strategies to help victims.

BACKGROUND

We live in the 21st century and are progressing in terms of modernization, employment, literacy, technological inventions and innovations, which also includes accepting and acknowledging inter-caste and inter-religion marriages. Still, there are some factors or aspects due to which the caste system in India prevails that in turn lead to caste-based and religion-based discrimination. The caste system has been supported just to save the honour and prestige of a particular caste, whose deterioration leads to "Honour Killing". It can also be considered as Honour-based or Culture-based Violence. This chapter particularly deals with cultural aspects along with psychological factors that affect and motivate Honour Killing. It also focuses on the historical background of Honour-based Violence, the emergence and suppression of this violence in various parts of India and the influence of *"Khap Panchayats"* on people even after the existence of legal and Indian constitutional provisions relating to marriage and caste. Homicides are being committed in the name of honour, so this chapter also points out why culture, moral beliefs, honour etc. have more significance than someone's life and psychological concepts like feelings, humanity, emotions, sentiments etc. A special section in the chapter has contributed to the impact of "Honour Killing" on Indian society and to what extent cultural aspects create panic and havoc that eventually leads to an imbalance in people's social and psychological lives along with the deterioration of the nation's development and progress. Lastly, the preventive measures, strategies and suggestions to help victims of honour-based or culture-based violence in terms of psychological issues have been highlighted in this chapter.

Tamil Nadu and Bihar in India accounted for 41% (18 out of 44 instances) and 32.4% (22 out of 68 cases) of homicides caused by caste-related conflicts and class strife, respectively, according to NCRB region-wise estimates. Of the 28 cases of murders resulting from honour killings, 7 cases or 25% came from Madhya Pradesh, India. Uttar Pradesh in India also accounted for 23.0% (300 out of 1,307 incidents) of reported homicides resulting from extramarital affairs (Mahanty & Parmar, 2020). Uttar Pradesh, India holds the terrible distinction of being the state with the greatest number of murder cases related to love affairs and honour killings in 2015. Out of the 192 honour-killing instances reported nationwide, 131 were committed in Uttar Pradesh alone (Sagar, 2016).

Research Methodology

This chapter aims to draw attention to the psychological effects and influence of honour-based violence, which reflects that the victim has dishonoured the family name or prestige by breaching moral values and purity (Ahammed, 2019). The qualitative approach to research has been used for the study's objectives. For research purposes, references have been made to surveys, interviews, research articles, government ministry reports, research papers, research articles, international journals, and reports from international organizations. The qualitative method was chosen since the sources are reliable and all kinds of elements, including social, cultural, psychological, and gender-concerned, could be discovered and subsequently developed. A woman's social and sexual attitude plays a vital role in preserving the honour of a family that relies on the effectiveness of that woman to handle deeply embedded rules of society, according to the findings (Rekha Verma, 2023). This mentally constructed aspect of honour killing has become a part of our culture and is more prominent than the lives and well-being of individuals (Sule et al., 2015).

Key Terms

Core terms include "Honour Killing" (Kejriwal, 2018) and "Psychology" (Ahammed, 2019) directly linking the subject matter to the role of behaviour and attitude of individuals in maintaining status or honour in society. Broader themes like "Psycho-Social Aspects" (Rekha Verma, 2023), "Humanity" (Ahammed, 2019), "Gender-Based Violence" (Maz Idriss, 2018) and "Psychological Theories" (Moore, 2011) contextualise the issue. Analytical perspectives like "Delinquent Behaviour" (Moore, 2011) and "Collectivism" (Digvijay Kumar, 2016) allow for exploring the complexities of collectivist society and immoral behaviour triggered by social theories.

Inclusion criteria emphasized relevance, ensuring that only articles directly addressing honour killings, delinquent behaviours, or associated legal and cultural issues are considered. Exclusion criteria filtered out non-academic sources, such as blogs or opinion pieces, and articles with only tangential relevance to the topic. Conducted article research using academic databases like JSTOR, PubMed, and Google Scholar is crucial, employing targeted keywords such as "Honor Killing" (Kejriwal, 2018), "Psychology" (Ahammed, 2019), "Gender-Based Violence" (Maz Idriss, 2018) and "Humanity" (Ahammed, 2019) to identify the most pertinent studies for our paper.

Literature Review

Moore, 2011 talks about Psychological Theories that focus on individual differences leading to criminal behaviour, identifying correlational relationships between pathology and delinquent behaviour, and understanding contingencies responsible for non-conforming behaviour.

Rekha Verma, 2023 discusses that Honour killing and honour-based violence are influenced by various physical-social aspects such as purity, emotions, love, fear, attitude, religion, anxiety, roomer, and even parents.

Nisha (2018) focuses on Honour killing in Indian society, dating back to the fourteenth century, which has been a longstanding issue, with the Khap Panchayat responsible for numerous innocent lives and heinous verdicts.

Daryani & Hejazi (2023) talks about Honour killing which refers to the murder of females by male relatives for inappropriate behaviours like marital infidelity, premarital sex, contacting different faiths, initiating divorce, rape, and gossip.

Ahammed (2019) sees Honour as a perceived quality of worthiness and respectability that affects social standing and self-evaluation. It is assigned worth based on actions aligning with a specific code of honour and societal moral code, defining an individual's duties.

Future Research Directions

The authors' intention to denounce honour-based violence is evident in this study; they see it as a serious violation of human rights and point out how deeply embedded patriarchy contributes to this kind of violence against women (Rekha Verma, 2023). Psychology and honour killings interact when one understands the social dynamics, cultural influences, and psychological foundations of such severe behaviour (Heydari et al., 2021). Future research on honour killings and psychology will concentrate on comprehending the ingrained social, cultural, and psychological elements that motivate this behaviour (Rekha Verma, 2023). The writers examined how a sense of family honour, community identity, and shame maintains these behaviours. Honour killings can be better understood holistically by combining psychology, sociology, anthropology, and law through interdisciplinary approaches. The authors have also conducted additional studies on the effects of psychological theories and survivor support networks on the mental health of victims and perpetrators' families (Shojaee, 2012). In addition to highlighting the significance of culturally aware teaching and prevention strategies, authors have also emphasised the need to question the norms that support this kind of violence and advance alternate stories about honour and identity. In the study, there is still scope left for acknowledging some Psychological Interventions to prevent Honour Killing like Counselling Sessions, Community Awareness Programs etc. The impact of digital and social media on human psychology is also left to be researched and worked upon.

INTRODUCTION

Honour is one of the vital aspects that has an impact on the social status and the self-evaluation of an individual or corporate body, such as a family, school, or even the whole nation, because it presupposes a remarked trait of eminence and prestige. Certain actions and conduct of honour entrusted to individuals and corporate bodies ensure their worth and status in society (Ahammed, 2019). In addition, they are assigned responsibilities towards social groups and their respective families to guard them against degradation and defilement. For the sake of this protection and maintenance of reputation in the outer world, incidents of honour killings have increased. They are generally related to the murder of females because of certain objectionable and insupportable behaviours like marital infidelity or unfaithfulness, premarital sex, marrying outside a different caste, faith, or religion, initiating a separation or divorce, being a rape victim, and rumour or gossip about female transgression or misbehaviour (Daryani & Hejazi, 2023).

In the recent past, honour killing cases have become more rampant in a few North Indian states, like Uttar Pradesh, Rajasthan, Bihar, Jharkhand, Punjab and Haryana and now it is being increasingly reported and shown in the South Indian States too, including Karnataka. As per the recent data from the National Crime Records Bureau (NCRB), the number of honour killings traced and reported in India was 25 in 2019 as well as in 2020 and 33 in 2021. Although these figures can be estimations of the people who reported this and the actual numbers and figures could be more than those mentioned.

Honour killings have been prevalent in Karnataka, including Kolar, Tumakuru, Mandya and some parts of North Karnataka. From October 2022 until now, at least 7 dreadful cases have been reported in the state. Senior advocate KBK Swamy said that honour killing in Karnataka is not new rather it finds its origin in the 12th century when inter-caste marriages or relationships attracted a punishment called *"Yele Hoote"*, which is a ruthless act of tying the individuals engaged in the activities like inter-caste relationships to an elephant's leg and making the elephant roam around town, killing the unfortunate victims. Mostly, the women who have married men of a lower caste than their own, are punished for such acts.

Different cultures in our country lay a great emphasis on "honour" and due to the herding system, they have generated a "culture of honour". This culture became a valuable trait or characteristic that puts weight on the practice of enforcing one's will on others with the motive of protecting the former's reputation. This has been done by justifying honour-based abuse and related actions by claiming that the victim has dishonoured the family name or prestige by breaching moral values and purity. In Western nations, people are more open-minded and have higher education and they acknowledge purity norms and rituals connected with sexual behaviour as a matter of choice and liberalism. On the other hand, in many other nations, violations of purity are still considered breaches of a sacred code. This breach tarnishes not only the families but also their image, which eventually leads them to kill or punish those who have infringed on their sacred code to cleanse this defilement. Mostly, the breach of this honour relates to female infidelity which brings a loss of status to the husband, and they feel less masculine. This exercise is presumed to have brought dishonour upon the family. The use of the word 'honour' for such dishonourable acts is ill-fated as these acts are nothing but ferocious and disgraceful acts of murder committed by cruel and feudal-minded or narrow-minded people (Sule et al., 2015).

In the domain of psychological behaviours, emotions and feelings play a vital role in controlling the respective thought process and related physical actions to which our body also responds in a certain manner, and this leads to coping activities. When negative thoughts are generated in our minds, they lead to responses and actions that are vigorous and full of frustration. This frustration can be shown sometimes in other ways only to justify the responses. For example, a child who has been scolded for some mischief may punish and destroy his toys just because they cannot revert back to their parents. These emotion-related behaviours depend on the mood and one's ability to make decisions. Respect, reputation, prestige, and honour are also essential parts of the "emotions" that determine the attitude of a particular section of society. In addition to this, whenever a crime is committed, the ill motive or motivation behind committing that particular crime becomes crucial in understanding and revealing insights about the psychological state and thought process of the perpetrator. Given this, let us consider an example where 'A' person holds two conflicting opinions regarding the same issue i.e. *sex before marriage is a sin or a wrong* and on the other hand, he thinks that *sex is a physical or physiological need*. This disturbance is referred to as Cognitive Dissonance which is an internal conflict that results in psychological and emotional disturbances ultimately influencing people to take insignificant steps. Also, they commit extreme acts by making this dissonance a justification or reasoning for their violent acts.

In the field of psychology, attitude can be defined as a behaviour or belief towards a specific person, thing or event that depends on someone's past nurturing or upbringing. In terms of "honour", during old times, people were taught to give more prominence to their culture, values and norms rather than their opinions, feelings, choices, points of view etc. That's why honour has a powerful influence than psychological concepts like humanity, emotions, sentiments etc. Attitude is a psychological tendency that is expressed by estimating a particular unit with some degree of approval or disapproval (Ahammed, 2019).

A person's attitude depends on his or her experiences, whether direct or resulting from observations. Norms and rules of society have a strong impact and influence on attitudes that determine their behaviour in society in a particular role or context. Social values convey to us what actions are considered righteous, and they become a part of our culture. Sexual behaviour and actions done by a woman are surrounded and restricted by societal norms and boundaries. Disrespect for ethical and social rules has been considered a violation of family honour. This mentally constructed aspect has become a part of our culture and is more prominent than the lives and well-being of individuals or groups of individuals (Sule et al., 2015).

In concern with "honour killing", a question that should be contemplated is whether killing in the name of honour brings back the honour to the family or is in actuality adding more dishonour. Another important dynamic should also be resolved: whether the honour of any community, society, or family is so weighty and crucial that it is making people so blind and deaf that they are unable to acknowledge the feelings and emotions of their own family members (Kejriwal, 2018).

Historical Background of Honour-Based Violence and Legal Frameworks: An Indian Context

Honour killing or culture-based violence indicates too much male dominance and provides low status to females in society. The main reason behind these killings, abuse, and even female infanticide is that in many cultures and regions, women's life value is considered to be of no prominence and negligible in comparison to the male section of society. Violence has been done in the name of notions of honour and shame. Patriarchal mindsets and patriarchal families have prevailed since ancient Roman times when honour killings preserved the right to kill an unmarried but sexually active daughter or a disloyal wife.

Traces and origins of honour killing can be found in ancient ages when gender-based crimes were widespread. Females were killed to protect the honour of one's family and to conserve patriarchal rule or dominance in the community or society. Although men are also the victims of this evil practice, they do not remain untouched, but they have just formed forgotten voices because of certain reasons, like fear of being ridiculed or shamed. Barriers for men to report their abuse also exist in the form of concepts of masculinity, honour and shame. All these issues can prevent male victims from coming forward (Maz Idriss, 2018). Still, there are more and a plethora of cases where the female sect of the family is being killed just for some definite reasons like having an adulterous relationship, pre-marital sexual relations, marrying a man of her choice, etc. The mere perception is that a woman has disregarded the code of sexual behaviour that damages honour.

Particularly speaking, there is not even a single law, provision or statute that specifically targets the heinous crime of honour killing which is still not termed an "Offence" legally. In 2012, the Law Commission released its Report titled *"Prevention of Interference with the Freedom of Matrimonial Alliances (in the name of Honour and Tradition): A Suggested Legal Framework"* in which the Commission asserted that the acts of women that go against the patriarchal culture of the society is one of the major causes of honour-based violence. Inspired by the above-mentioned report, Rajasthan also passed the *Rajasthan Prohibition of Interference with the Freedom of Matrimonial Alliances in the Name of Honour and Tradition Bill* in 2019. In regards to this Bill, the DHRDNet report said that honour falls under the pre-existing legislation like Sections 300 and 302 of the Indian Penal Code, 1860 and the SCs and STs (Prevention of Atrocities) Act, 1989. Afterwards, it was observed that *"Since the crimes in the name of honour are committed specifically by parents and relatives belonging to dominant castes, there are specificities that need to be addressed by the law. These crimes cannot be treated as murders or attempt to murder as the impact is on entire communities and families."*

Role of Khap Panchayats and Their Legal Status

Traces of Khap Panchayats cannot be found but they are supposed to be developed in 600 AD and can be described as a group of villages that operate and govern in a particular geographical area and target a particular caste. In India, the Khap panchayat mostly exists in western Uttar Pradesh, Eastern Rajasthan, but it is mostly pervasive in Rohtak, Jhajjar, Sonipat, Bhiwani, Karnal, Jind, Kaithal and Hisar districts of Haryana. A long time ago, Khap Panchayats were represented by different upper castes, but nowadays, they are run merely as a *jat* institution. The work of these institutions is handled by powerful and dominant people who are elected by the people of the respective villages. Mostly, the senior citizens of a certain caste are entrusted with the duty of sustaining the values, norms, and morality of a specific religion.

The main role of Khap Panchayats was to maintain honour, cultural ideologies, religious values, and brotherhood in the particular region, but they achieved these values through brutal acts such as killing innocent people for the sake of honour. Such brutality done by them is a splotch on our law ("Khap Panchayats or Honour Killing: A Curse", 2018). *Khaps* are basically councils of tribes that were involved in inter and intra-tribal dispute resolution mechanisms (Ranbir, 2010). The Khap Panchayats exercise extra-constitutional powers. Moreover, due to the part of Khap Panchayats in affairs relating to inter-caste marriages, they have been the highlights in news channels (Kachhwaha & Manohar, 2011). The members of the Khap Panchayats believe that all boys and girls within a Khap are recognized as siblings ("Khap Panchayats Or Honour Killing: A Curse", 2018). If they marry each other, being of a different caste, then it would be considered an offence or wrongdoing, which, according to the Khap, ultimately reflects a bad custom in society. But in reality, for the protection of humanity and mankind, honour killing must be considered a prejudicial and ruthless custom in our society. The disgraceful practice of honour killing is exercised because of certain immoral behaviours that, according to these institutions, would bring "shame" and "dishonour" to the family, caste, or class.

Some of the acts that were considered to be unethical and immoral in the eyes of the Khap Panchayats were:

Adopting clothing or dressing, which is unacceptable to society/families;
Opposing to enter into an arranged marriage or desiring to marry at one's own will with a person of one's own choice;
Involving in sexual activities either with the opposite or same sex (Singhal, 2014).

Although Khap Panchayats were declared illegal in various Supreme Court pronouncements, they continue to exist in backward regions of our country, like Haryana, Uttar Pradesh, parts of Rajasthan, etc., because people there still recognize love marriages and inter-caste marriages as taboo. In the case of *Shakti Vahini v. Union of India*, research on *"honour killings in Haryana and western Uttar Pradesh"* was performed by the petitioners, the Shakti Vahini Organization who were authorized by the National Commission for Women and they concluded that there has been a pervasive rise in honour killing cases in the above-mentioned areas. In this particular judgement, the Apex Court held that after the study of the petitioners, they revealed the horrible truth and the unearthly action that was performed by the Khap Panchayats. These actions are unlawful and have to be discontinued as soon as possible. The honourable Supreme Court of India directed that, in any such circumstance, the state has to institute criminal proceedings against everyone guilty of such disclosed activities. They also have to be condemned for the same. The state government was instructed to suspend the district magistrate along with the SP of that specific district (*Shakti Vahini v. Union of India*, 2023).

Conclusively, various other case laws ascertained that it is illegal and unconstitutional to restrict two consenting adults from marrying each other. It otherwise clearly promotes caste discrimination and curbs the right to live with dignity and choice. Additionally, to preserve these fundamental rights, the court proposed and advocated separate legislation and preventive, remedial, and punitive actions to tackle and stop honour-based crime.

Ascendance of Culture and Belief Over Humanity and Mental Well-Being

Culture can be defined as a notion that embraces the social behaviour, associations, norms, and customs discovered in human societies, along with the knowledge, beliefs, arts, laws, traditions, abilities, capabilities, and habits of the individuals in these societies. It is generally derived from these particular regions and places and is also endorsed in that area. Culture gains more status as a result of the bifurcated beliefs of different groups and societies. In other words, culture, religion, values, and traditions depend on the beliefs of an individual in society.

Broadly, two bifurcations of emotion are love-based emotions and fear-based emotions. Stress, sadness, confusion, loneliness, guilt, anxiety etc. are fear-based emotions and on the other hand, happiness, trust, joy, mankind, truthfulness etc. are love-based emotions. The thoughts and behaviour of a person are a result of either love or fear and can also be conflicting sometimes, especially among the members of the family (Ahammed, 2019). The beliefs of family members and society are the outcome of the strength of the above-mentioned emotions. Majorly, negative emotions, i.e., fear-based emotions, have a dominant characteristic over sentiments and feelings related to 'love'. Caste, religion, and various communities have made such insubstantial rules and regulations that influence and guide individuals' acts to lead a good life, but at times these people devalue their emotional quotient by falling into the trap of false pride and honour. They follow these harmful beliefs due to fear and not love, which is known as cultural stigma and makes it harder for those tussling to talk openly.

It can also be implied that belief is the species and culture is its genus along with various other genera. Even after long efforts of modernization and safeguarding humanity and human rights, the practice of shielding and maintaining the culture in the society is more prevalent and for this, families are willing and ready to sacrifice any individual, material object, things etc. At this point, it is imperative to dissect that socially constructed and generated concepts get their meanings from the belief in society which eventually decides the socially deemed fitting behaviour of an individual (Poddar, 2020). Ultimately, if these behaviours of any individual are not in line with social practices, it would lead to disagreements, penalties, and disapprobation. It has not been concerned for the psychological conditions and mental well-being of the people because, in our society, the keywords "honour" and "dishonour" are more discussed and focal than humanity, emotions, and well-being. By this, it can be found that the liberty and room that love extends to humans are not attainable in fear. Fear is a fastened and restricted emotion that will not permit people to think realistically. It will hinder the lenient and optimistic thoughts of the human mind and persuade them to do dreadful things. As a result, the ascendency of fear over love helps shape attitudes and behaviours among individuals (Ahammed, 2019).

Specifically in concern with "honour killing", it has been legitimated and acknowledged by society and its people because of their social norms of honour, and it has been widely practised to eradicate the blemishes from the honour of a family. It is creating a vast downbeat impact on the mental health and well-being of individuals, the reason being that cultural norms and values are deeply embedded in the tradition on which "honour killing" is based and founded. The term "honour killing" can be ascertained as a result of negative beliefs or views of society that are proficient in affecting mental health on a large scale. If there are negative and misrepresented views of society, then it would surely lead to the generation of undesirable emotions like anxiety, depression, isolation, etc. that remain unaddressed due to the dominance of societal and cultural factors (Therapy Brands, 2022). To be more specific, it can be asserted that cultural factors develop our thought system which is eventually related to people's mental health and it can be impacted differently according to different cultures (Shojaee, 2012).

Psycho-Social Aspects Encouraging Honour-Based Violence

Numerous psycho-social aspects and facets are responsible for how an individual might act in a particular society or community. Some of them are discussed here together as one unit that leads to honour killing.

Purity

Any quality that is free from any kind of contamination, guilt or sin is considered purity. It relates to the maintenance of the body and sexual behaviour following societal customs and norms. If impurity is rooted in any caste or community, then it is considered a crime, especially in Indian culture. For instance, losing virginity before marriage, immodesty, immoral behaviour etc.

Belief

It can be understood as some values and customs that a certain section of the population believes and follows according to their religion and culture. Most families believe in a "culture of honour" where they are trying to preserve their culture so badly that they can sacrifice anything for the latter. Clashes of belief can also be seen within the families i.e. between two generations regarding various social aspects like education, dressing sense, sexual behaviour, expectations of the family and community etc.

Religion

Due to the diverse nature of our society, people have different beliefs following their different religions and consequentially it is not permitted to marry in different religions or with the members of *sapindas*. This conduct could lead to moral outrage, hatred and vengeance which is enough to justify harsh homicide (Rekha Verma, 2023).

Psychological Theories and Delinquent Behaviour

The term, "Delinquent Behaviour" is used to denote a young person who is involved in immoral or illegal activities regularly such as school misconduct, drugs, smoking, maladaptive attitude etc. Such behaviour is influenced or triggered by various factors of society and psychological theories of crime help us to understand and focus on those contributing factors that often stimulate such kind of behaviour or attitude. There are two sides to a coin, one is individual differences and psychological variables and the other is societal and environmental influences that lead to criminal behaviour (Moore, 2011). A few psychological theories to understand this deviant behaviour are described below in brief.

1. Learning Theory

Some Psychological Theorists believe that the frequency of an individual's behaviour is influenced and determined by environmental consequences and circumstances. On the other hand, the process of shaping behaviour by experiences and people interactions was also observed. Some theorists believe that this theory concentrates on the use of operant conditioning in learning criminal behaviour. Operant conditioning is the process by which an environmental stimulus produces a voluntary response, and the response is either positively or negatively reinforced, which affects its extension or non-existence.

2. Intelligence Theory

Individuals' normal or delinquent behaviour is largely dependent on the intelligence level, common sense and IQ of that particular being. Most of the thinkers and theorists analysed that there is a link between delinquency and IQ, considering school performance as a mediating factor. Feeble school performance leads to the young generation getting into more problems which ultimately results in the emergence of delinquent behaviours. Another study found that low IQ in combination with high anxiety and depression because of low school performance contributes to delinquent behaviours. Therefore, it is concluded that the relationship or connection between IQ and delinquency is most likely indirect as it needs some mediating factor to establish that link.

3. Personality Trait Theory

The trait theory of personality infers that people have certain basic traits or characteristics and the strength and intensity of those traits account for personality differences. One of the renowned theorists is Sigmund Freud who postulated three components of personality: Id, Ego and Superego. The Id represents the impulsive actions that are driven by pleasure, the Superego is the learned moral reasoning of the personality and the Ego represents the conscious part of the personality that maintains a balance between the Id and the Superego to make rational decisions. The internal tussle that leads to delinquency, usually rooted in a conflict between the Id and societal values acknowledged by the ego, is very painful to the person, so that person pushes them into the unconscious. Then, that person grows coping methods called defence mechanisms to tackle these conflicts that can lead to problematic personality traits and problematic behaviours, like delinquency.

Collectivism Over Individualism

Collectivism can be referred to as giving more value to the opinions of society at large, unlike individualism, where individuals' opinions and points of view are respected. The ideas of collectivism and individualism are dependent on the cultures, standards, and values set by different societies. Western and Eastern societies are different in terms of dealing with culture, setting up rules and regulations, etc. For example, in the former, individualism is considered a main aspect of setting people's living strategy, whereas the latter places more value and prominence on collectivism. Individualism and collectivism are united by a common concept: "positive relationships with each other". It can be understood that maintaining social teamwork and coordination is crucial because the more collectivist a society is, the more supportive its members become.

However, this trait can be proved to be a failure because certain individualistic characteristics and values highly value "self-expression" and "self-importance" and in this race, societal factors remain behind. In our country, the expression of emotions that are betrothed in social interactions such as pride and shame are more appreciated in comparison to the individualistic countries. Therefore, it can be ascertained that cultural values and norms have a major impact on people's expression of emotions (Shojaee, 2012).

Another important cultural issue is the parenting style in which Eastern countries are very discriminating because of the factor that males are still given more autonomy and freedom than females. After all, the latter is considered as the pride and honour of the family. In the name of honour only, they are restricted from fulfilling their desires and wishes that portray a cultural difference or dissimilarity in society. It also sets an unhealthy example for upcoming generations that women are considered as honour of one's family and in the name of that honour only, they are being killed by their family members because of some acts that are considered to be socially inappropriate and unacceptable.

A Shift in Social Paradigm

The conduct of individuals and their practices are directly linked to society and the cultural values and norms formulated in that society. Various societal notions help its people take a proper shape and space, eventually preserving societal aspects like pride, honour, and values. To accomplish this, these notions started putting restrictions on the freedom of vulnerable sections of society who are supposed to live within cultural boundaries, and any encroachment of these norms and values by them was seen as lowering the honour of the family and the society, which were controlled through ruthless sanctions (Digvijay Kumar, 2016). It can also be seen as any change in the conduct of the individuals which is unacceptable to the society will have a great impact on the society and its norms leading to a downfall in the honour and prestige of the community.

The idea of honour and the practice of honour killing find their roots in the view that the honour of a man and society lies in their women and damsels, and to protect this honour, they started putting limitations on the acts and conduct of the women, which eventually became part of the socialization process. Preservation of women's bodies and sexuality has become so crucial that it is now seen as a dynamic of personal honour and dishonour. This concept diminishes the balance between the saving of honour and the freedom to live with one's choice. Every act done by a woman concerning her sexuality created a lot of problems because their acts were supposed to be within the strict behavioral patterns and codes of conduct that were formulated by society itself.

The idea of honour is not only limited to the preservation of women's sexuality but also related to the caste system and the concepts of clan and gotra that boldly resist inter-caste marriages and marriages solemnized within the same gotra. Marriage provides future expectations of good kinship and respectable caste that can only be achieved by keeping in mind certain factors like caste purity, caste status, power, and hierarchy. Even after various judgements regarding the right to marry of one's choice and the right to live freely, the act of choosing a partner on their own by anyone, especially a woman, is still regarded as an act that causes dishonour to the family and society. So, it can be seen that society has been impacted in various forms because of honour and values.

As a leading source of moral value and social standing, honour acts as an authorization for social membership in honour-based cultures. In other words, "It is through the embracing of honour that individuals find a room in the community". A disreputable act, such as not swearing at one's words or not replying to insults, is one that is seen to disrupt the value system of the social group. Dishonourable acts create defame or indignity along with injury to one's reputation or moral worth in society and consequently curb involvement in various facets of public life (Heydari et al., 2021).

Impact of Societal Pressure on Psychological Lives

The social group and their way of perceiving and estimating certain actions play a decisive role in individuals' social connections and lives in honour-based communities, which in turn shapes the proficiency and capability of individuals to join the group, taking into consideration that group acceptance is fundamental and necessary to honour. In addition to this, honour codes become a unifying component of the culture and ethnicity that are embedded in individuals' social lives. As a result, honour codes inflicted on individuals are not an issue of personal choice but of community standards and cooperatively shared values and morals in these communities that have been discussed above in collectivism (Digvijay Kumar, 2016).

These honour codes not only affect the individuals' social lives but also their psychological and mental lives because they eventually impact their feelings and emotions. The behaviour of every individual is majorly influenced by their emotions and ability to understand certain things. Every so often, these individuals have to regulate their behaviours following societal rules and regulations because, in the end, they have to be a part and parcel of the society and their respective communities. For instance, women in our society are still punished and even killed for putting a black mark on the "honour" of the family by their act of falling in love with any person or marrying any person who might not get approved by the former's family (Hanan Parvez, 2020). So, in this kind of situation, women are expected to behave in a sexually proper way by suppressing their choices and requirements, concerning their lives only.

In terms of culture, a woman's social and sexual attitude plays a vital role in preserving the honour of a family that relies on the effectiveness of that woman to handle deeply embedded rules of society (Rekha Verma, 2023). It sends a clear message to the rest of the community to behave and act in a particular manner that should be acceptable and appropriate to society, implying that societal factors and pressures influence people's emotions and behaviours to a certain level that ultimately affects their psychological lives. Other societal aspects are patriarchal thought processes and strict parenting styles that support honour killings in a way that these aspects results in the aggressive behaviour of individuals and the application of these behaviours later in their life decisions. For instance, patriarchal thinking could increase the possibility that the male section of society starts to treat women as a means to safeguard the honour of the family. To be more precise and accurate, a shift in attitude towards violence can be brought about by managing any childhood distress and mistreatment efficiently, as well as by desensitisation after exposure to violence (Hanan Parvez, 2020).

SUGGESTIONS AND RECOMMENDATIONS

Honour killings mostly remain unreported and unidentified because of a lack of awareness of people regarding the same. Also, there is no legislation to tackle this grave situation which is severely affecting people's mental lives. This social evil can be eradicated from society if every community of the society contributes to abrogating it. Some suggestions can be considered (Kejriwal, 2018):

1. **Caste System:** Although there are different castes and religions but discrimination among them should be removed so as to allow acceptance and acknowledgement of inter-caste and inter-religious marriages in society. It would also broaden the narrow thinking of the individuals.
2. **Mentality:** Our society is dynamic as it changes with time and people but some ideologies still prevail because of their past cultural prevalence and most importantly, the honour. As an example of this, till now, various parts of our society do not acknowledge inter-caste marriages and even consider it as a bane to their families. Such mentality should be changed so that the paths of these social evils must be restricted and also to make people more aware of morals and humanity.
3. **Education and Media:** These two are the most effective tools or pillars in spreading awareness about any cause or matter that is either in debate or has been continuing for past years. Indian mentality is so narrow that they respect their so-called honour over an individual precious life. A change in attitude and behaviour especially towards women can end this social cycle of believing women to be a dependent entity. On one hand, education can help upcoming generations to make their mindsets concerning these social evils and not to consider these a taboo. On the other hand, media and the internet can aware individuals of victims' rights and laws to change their mentality.
4. **Proper Legislation:** There is not a single law that penalizes or discusses honour killing which shows the failure of legislators to acknowledge this serious issue. Laws should made strict and clear that can act deterrent to people in committing such heinous crimes. (Kejriwal, 2018) Since crimes in the name of honour are committed specifically by parents and relatives belonging to dominant castes, some specificities need to be addressed by the law. These crimes cannot be

treated as murders or attempt to murder as the impact is on entire communities and families.

CONCLUSION

Honour killing is one of the nastiest social evils predominant in society and has taken many guiltless and innocent lives of girls and boys for ages as a matter of honour for the family or society. It has been obeyed by the members of the society, and as a concern for Izzat, or dignity, the members think that by honour killing they can clean up the sins being committed by other members who have gone against the social norms.

Despite scientific developments and modernization, ancient views and theories exist in many different parts of the world. Societies tend to stick to malicious opinions and beliefs with the view that by doing so, they are maintaining their culture, origin, and ethnicity. Honour killing and honour-based violence originate from such wrongly held belief systems. The problem may be seen as primarily social but is definitely in a flowing union with cultural and biological aspects, yet it is scattered with genetic and personality-factor-based undercurrents. Mental well-being professionals, lawmakers, political parties, and social workers need to work in unity and collaboration if they aim to abrogate the crisis. The job at hand is not an easy one, but steps forward on a firm footing may help future generations benefit from the fruits of the efforts put in by the present generation.

REFERENCES

Ahammed, H. (2019). *"Honour" killing in India: A Psychological analysis Sub Theme:-Psychology for Social Justice and Equality Presentation mode:-Poster.*

Daryani, Y., & Hejazi, E. (2023). *Perception of honor killing: The role of culture, gender, and moral beliefs.*

Digvijay Kumar. (2016, March 28). *Honor Killing and its Impact on Society.* Racolb Legal.

Hanan Parvez. (2020, November 8). *Psychology of Honor Killings.* PsychMechanics.

Heydari, A., Teymoori, A., & Trappes, R. (2021). Honor killing as a dark side of modernity: Prevalence, common discourses, and a critical view. *Social Sciences Information. Information Sur les Sciences Sociales*, 60(1), 86–106. DOI: 10.1177/0539018421994777

Kachhwaha, K., & Manohar, R. (2011). All rights reserved. Under a creative commons Attribution-Noncommercial-Share Alike 2.5 India License Criminal Justice Sciences (IJCJS). In *Official Journal of the South Asian Society of Criminology and Victimology* (Vol. 6, Issue 2).

Kejriwal, -Neelam. (2018). *HONOUR KILLING IN NORTH INDIA.*

KHAP PANCHAYATS OR HONOUR KILLING: A CURSE. (2018).

Mahanty, J., & Parmar, M. N. (2020). VIOLENCE AGAINST WOMEN: NO HONOUR IN HONOUR KILLINGS. In *International Journal of Creative Research Thoughts* (Vol. 8). www.ijcrt.org

Maz Idriss. (2018, May 23). *The forgotten male victims of honor-based violence.* The Conversation.

Moore, M. (2011). Psychological theories of crime and delinquency. In *Journal of Human Behavior in the Social Environment* (Vol. 21, Issue 3, pp. 226–239). DOI: 10.1080/10911359.2011.564552

Poddar, A. (2020). *Reprehensible Behaviour: The Social Meaning Behind Honour Killings in India.* 'Ranbir, S. (2010). The Need to Tame the Khap Panchayats. *Economic and Political Weekly*, 45(21), 17–18.

Rekha Verma, D. (2023). PSYCHO-SOCIO FACETS OF HONOUR KILLING. In *RUSSIAN LAW JOURNAL: Vol. XI.*

Sagar, A. (2016). HIGHEST NUMBER OF HONOUR KILLINGS IN UTTAR PRADESH-A CRITICAL REVIEW. In *International Journal of Management and Applied Science* (Issue 2).

Shakti Vahini v. Union of India (September 23, 2023).

Shojaee, M. (2012). *The influence of some cultural factors on mental health.* https://www.researchgate.net/publication/340815848

Singhal, V. K. (2014). *Honour Killing in India : An Assessment.* https://ssrn.com/abstract=2406031 DOI: 10.2139/ssrn.2406031

Sule, R., Acharya, A., & De Sousa, A. (2015). Psychosocial Aspects of Honour Killings. *Indian Journal of Mental Health*, 2(2), 132. DOI: 10.30877/IJMH.2.2.2015.132-143

Therapy Brands. (2022, September 5). *The Relationship Between Culture and Mental Health.* Therapy Brands.

Chapter 7
Honor Killing:
Defining the Undefined

Tarun Pratap Yadav
https://orcid.org/0009-0005-4262-0683
GLA University, India

Tanisha Jain
https://orcid.org/0009-0008-5553-7098
GLA University, India

ABSTRACT

Honor Killing is an issue which needs to have a solution which is more or less universally accepted but before that it is important to understand what is Honor Killing, a definition which defines this heinous crime. Various states and its government bodies, organizations and jurists have tried to define the aforesaid crime but the definition still remains blurred. Different definitions have covered different aspects. This chapter basically deals with how various important organizations and others have defined or have given its stance on Honor Killing. This chapter also contains issues regarding the nomenclature, namely, gender biases. Almost everywhere the crime is considered to be a violence or abuse or crime in respect of women. It is not wrong to consider it as a violence against women because women were really subjected to it for a long time and it may not be wrong to say that the situation has become worse. But there is another side of the coin too. This crime can no longer be considered an offence related only to women.

BACKGROUND

While defining it is important to keep in mind that this offense is gender neutral as there are instances where a man or a transgender has been guillotined. As of year 2023, there were 2,905 honor-based abuse recorded by the police in England and Wales. There is a change of 1% from 2020 to 2021 (Crown Prosecution Service, 2023). The United Nations Population Fund estimates that 5,000 women are executed by members of their family every year in the name of honor killing. In Mexico and Central America killing of women have been increased. Estimately, 740 'femicides' occurred between 1993 and 2009 in Mexico (United Nations Human Rights, 2013). Some NGOs estimate that 20,000 honor killings are committed worldwide annually. (Solotaroff J. & Prabha R., 2020)

Research Methodology

The main objective of the chapter is to compile the definitions and approaches upheld or propounded by global organizations as well as conferences oh 'Honor Killing'. The chapter also incorporates the different conventions and conferences and also addresses the concerned problem as a heinous offence with the angle of gender biasedness. The information regarding the chapter is taken from Reports/ Articles/ Surveys/ Records etc. Therefore, qualitative research is adopted. (Uzoma, 2020) The primary and secondary research carried out resulted in several observations such as need of an international and national legislation for honor killing, how it has a gender biased offence existing in society, need of a universal definition etc. There are several organizations which has not considered honor killing as a gender biased offence (Crown Prosecution Service, 2023). The chapter gives the clear understanding of the approaches of global organizations on honor killing. However, from the information collected for the purpose of honor killing shows kind of failure on the part of these global organization, that objective is to maintain peace and secure environment with human rights, on handling this global issue of honor killing.

Key Terms

Core terms include 'Honor Killing' (Lari,2011) directly linking the subject matter that is defining the honor killing by important organizations. Broader themes like 'defining the undefined' attempts to highlight or provide the definition, different important organization of the world has given. Organization such as 'United Nation Population Fund' (Report of UNFA/UNDP, 2005) and 'Crown Prosecution Service' and 'Human Rights Watch' and 'CEDAW'. 'International Research and Training Institute for the Advancement of Women (INSTRAW)' and 'United Nations Development Fund for Women (UNIFEM)' are some organizations related to woman whose standing on honor killing has been incorporated. Some other key terms are 'femicide' (Welchman, 2007), 'woman suffering' (Lynch 2007), 'violence related to honor' (Reddy, 2018).

Conducted Article research using academic database like Google Scholar, JSTOR, Google Advance Search employing targeted keywords such as 'Honor Killing', 'Global organizations' 'United Nation', 'Human Rights Watch', 'World level Conferences' to identify the most pertinent studies of our paper.

Literature Review

Ajula and Gill, 2014 talks about how these killing falls under the broad concept of Domestic Violence. They appropiately pointed out how these murders are not treated separately and has become a gender biased offence, as gender played an important role in these crimes.

Chesler P., & Bloom N. (2012) talks about honor killing in respect to two controversial religious communities that is Hindus and Muslims. They had incorporated the similarities and difference between both. According to them Indian Hindus abandon this horrifying activity when they move towards west, however Pakistani Muslims do not. They further observed that almost ever honor killing revloves around the myth that patriarchal and tribal values are under attack.

Reddy, R. (2014) talks about the relevance of debate that honor related violence which includes honor killing is a part of so-called gender based violence. According to him honor killing has been a hot topic to discuss in last decade of Britain.

Welcham, L. (2007) examines the position of women's rights and consider Chief Islamic Justice of Palestinian Authority who had public intervention against the 'murder as revenge or in defense of honor' in West Bank and Gaza Strip, in the light of jurisprudence, legislative and social arguments.

Future Research Directions

The authors clearly abandon this practice of killing people for so called 'Honor'. It violates human rights. Authors intends to compile and provide with the definition propounded by Global Organizations. It shall also include various organizations related to woman and various conferences held on the same and what has been propounded and how the steps have been taken by these organizations to prevent Honor Killing. Chapter title clearly states that an attempt to define the undefined Honor killing has been made by authors. It is clearly shown that there is no universal definition to define the same because the factors behind every honor killing may depend on different factors such as Religion, Marriages, doing anything against the rules of case or religion, patriarchy etc. But most of the time victim is woman, as many a times honor is related to woman (Article12, 1949). Authors contends the reasons for which a definition, which is needed to determine the penal actions which may be applicable universally, and law that is international as well as customary shall be enacted to successfully disintegrate this practice from each and every society. However, there still may be a scope for further research there still may be some questions and research which may not be addressed in future research.

According to structure, a "good woman" is someone who can perform the duties of mother, wife, and daughter that are socially acceptable. 'Good' women are generally discouraged from expressing their own wants or taking charge of their lives, and are encouraged not to explicitly express their sexuality (Solotaroff & Pande, 2014). A "good" woman is only valued to the point that she serves the purposes of reproduction and productive labor contribution to the household; they are additionally required to stick to certain modesty norms (Lynch, 2007) that define how they dress, where they go, with whom they involve and their body language, particularly in public (Mishra, 2013).

As a result, the standards of honor and the possibility of violent enforcement function as a social control mechanism that directs the behavior of women. Under this system, girls and women must be safeguarded; but they are only entitled to protection from violence if they carry out their responsibilities and functions in the household's private area (Jafri 2008; Mayeda &Vijaykumar, 2016).

Women also use the word "honor" to defend themselves against perceived personal or familial transgressions of any kind. This covers a variety of topics, like settling property disputes, settling family conflicts (Lari, 2011), and prohibiting women from selecting a spouse or sexual partner without permission from their family.

There isn't a widely acknowledged standard for honor killing. There are several different stances that exist regarding the concerned offense. Also, it has become a social issue or has been existing as a social issue for a longer period of time. Many countries, organizations, jurists, or thinkers have defined honor killing in their own ways, but there are several points on which they have a similar view, as discussed below. Honor killings are said to have originated from tribal traditions and are common throughout the world, particularly in immigrant communities in countries where honor killings are not otherwise encouraged by societal norms. These countries include the MENA region, the Philippines, the Indian subcontinent, and other regions. Although they can also exist in metropolitan areas, they are frequently linked to rural and tribal regions.

> Three fundamental components should be included in any definition of honor-based violence:

1. The ability or desire to control a woman's behavior;
2. The humiliation a man feels over his perceived or actual lack of control over her behavior;

The role that family or the community play in fostering and treating this shame. There are several myths that exist in society, one of which pertains to the offender and victim of honor killing. According to several thinkers, it is often believed that honor killings are only committed by men, but there are cases where women are also involved in execution. Further, it is highly believed that honor killing is a crime done against women, which is not true. Men are also executed by their families and communities in the name of honor just like women.

This chapter tries to define honor killing, or honor-based violence, or honor-based crime. In several places, these interchanging phrases are used by the concerned organizations, jurists, or bodies of the respective bodies of a country.

Regarding nomenclature, there is disagreement over what honor crimes are called. Aujla and Gill provide an example in which the terms "honor killing" and "honor crimes' are frequently used interchangeably. (Ajula & Gill, 2014) Some academicians like the phrase "violence related to honor" instead (Reddy, 2018) of honor-based violence (Idriss, 2017) to avoid supporting the implication that violence is, in fact, motivated by honor, as this could provide a defense or serve

as a justification, by not using the phrase "honor-based violence". 'Honor-based violence' is a word used in official papers (including those from the United Nations, the Home Office, the Crown Prosecution Service, and the Police). In a similar vein, honor-based violence additionally occurs in direct quotes from sources that utilize this phrase in this chapter. The terms "honor killing" and "honor crime" are problematic, according to Welchman, not only because they seem to adopt the perpetrator's point of view but also because they can mask the true reasons for the violence, which may have for only financial gain. She goes on to explain that because of this, the definitions are very difficult to interpret and that some women's organizations would prefer to interpret these terms more as "femicide." (Welcham, 2007)

But according to Shalhoub- Kevorkian, merely outlining the definition of the assassination of a female is insufficient to reveal "the torturous process following up to her death." Accordingly, she defines "femicide" as "any violent acts that induce an eternal apprehension in women or girls." of being executed with the pretext of honor. (Jerusalem: Women's Centre for Legal Aid and Counseling, 2004)

All harmful activities, regardless of the cause, greatly endanger the general health, and women's reproductive and sexual health. Human rights organizations have also called on nations to shield teenagers from any harmful behaviors and stated that harmful practices violate women's rights as human beings. Deadly practices that are types of aggression against women are largely influenced by age, sex, gender, and various types of prejudice.

UNITED NATIONS

"Honor killing" was not specifically mentioned by the UN in the 1975 documents from the inaugural World Conference on Women, which was held in Mexico. Nonetheless, the UN did start talking about discrimination against women in that year, emphasizing how important it is for families to provide stability, equality, and dignity for all of their members. Therefore, the UN and its several organizations considered honor killing as a gender biased crime where the victim shall always be a woman. The identification of violence against women as a significant barrier to development, equality, and peace, as well as the designation of battered women, women trafficking, and women in custody as areas of particular concern, did not occur until the Nairobi World Conference in 1985. The UN General Assembly passed the initial resolution on domestic assault in 1985.

The Conference and the United Nations Decade for Women (1976–1985), which was proclaimed by the General Assembly five months after the Conference's conclusion, marked the beginning of a new era in efforts to improve women's advancement by igniting a global dialogue on gender equality. At this summit, the three objectives for the decade development, equality, and peace were set.:

1. Complete gender parity and the abolition of discrimination based on gender;
2. The inclusion and active involvement of women in development;
3. Greater contribution by women in promoting global peace.

The Declaration on the Elimination of Violence against Women was adopted in 1993 and emphasized violence against women as *"any act of gender-based violence that causes or is likely to cause women to suffer from bodily, sexual, psychological harm including threats of such actions, coercion or arbitrarily denying them their freedom rather than public and private."* Honor killings were deemed to be an integral part of this definition.

The Conference also requested that nations create national strategies, objectives, and priorities. It led to the establishment of the International Research and Training Institute for the Advancement of Women (INSTRAW) and the United Nations Development Fund for Women (UNIFEM), both of which merged with two other UN agencies to become UN Women in 2010. In the 1975 conference, women were prominently featured. "National level initiatives and approaches for putting this plan into action should take into account the requirements and issues for various age groups and categories of women", the Conference's Final Report declared. Nonetheless, governments ought to focus particularly on enhancing the status of women in various areas where they have experienced the greatest disadvantage, especially for women who live in both urban and rural locations.

According to High Commissioner for Human Rights Navi Pillay, " The reality for the majority of victims, including those who have been the victims of honor assassination is that state institutions have failed them. Additionally, the majority of abusers of domestic violence can count on a culture of impunity for the actions they commit, which are frequently regarded as offenses and punished accordingly (UN Office, 2010). "The majority of the 5,000 honor killings that are allegedly committed annually in the world go unreported, as do the numerous other acts of violence committed against women and girls by spouses, fathers, sons, siblings, uncles, and other male - and occasionally even female - family members.

"Women and girls are horribly regularly shot, stoned, burned, buried alive, strangled, smothered, and knifed to death in the name of upholding family 'honor."

The UN human rights chief on the occasion of International Women's Day, notes that the issue is made worse by the fact that people who commit honor killings are still either completely or partially immune from punishment under the domestic legal systems of a number of nations, including through discriminatory laws. In these communities, those who commit crimes can even receive special recognition and be regarded with admiration. But honor killings are not something that can be written off as a strange, archaic crime that occurs in the past, the speaker continues. "They are a severe symptom of discrimination against women, which is a global problem that includes various types of domestic abuse.'

Violence against women is experienced by almost two thirds of them at some point in their lives, usually at the hands of an intimate partner. "We occasionally hear that these kinds of behaviors are cultural in nature, but that is erroneous."

Change in Approach of United Nations

Violence was not specifically mentioned in the 1975 World Plan of Action, which was approved at the First World Conference on Women in Mexico. The 1980s Copenhagen Conference mentioned domestic abuse in its final report and passed a resolution on "devastated women and families." At the parallel, non-governmental platform of the 1985 Nairobi World Conference, violence against women became a major global concern. Violence against women became a significant global topic at the parallel non-governmental forum of the Nairobi World Conference in 1985. The conference approved forward-looking strategies that connected the abolition of gender-based violence in public as well as private places to the promotion and maintenance of peace. According to Connor, "although not specifically directed at women, the Nairobi Conference resulted in the first General Assembly resolution on domestic violence, which formed the background to the 1986 UN Expert Group Meeting on Violence against women in the family and to the 1989 study of the same name."

This 1989 article discussed the ways in which violence against women manifests itself and demonstrated how the community or state may accept and even condone abuse.

The UN's stance on the matter shifted as knowledge of the link between gender and violence increased- first, violence against women was no longer only considered to occur in the family. All of these activities brought attention to the concern about assaults related to women and allowed it to come to light. Second, violence against women is classified as a human rights issue because of its gendered aspect and connections to discrimination, inequality between men and women, and subordination.

UNFPA- United Nation Population Fund

The United Nations Population Fund, or UNFPA, does not define honor killings in any particular way. Nonetheless, the group acknowledges that honor killings are a type of gender-based violence and endeavors to eradicate such detrimental customs by tackling the underlying reasons of gender-based violence and advocating for gender parity. With the goal of ending these destructive customs by 2030, UNFPA co-leads the Global Program to End Child Marriage and the Joint Program on the Elimination of FGM (Female Genital Mutilation). In nations where honor killings are frequent, UNFPA supports women's shelters and offers medical and psychological support to victims of gender-based violence, such as honor killings.

According to the report, the state needs to implement a zero-tolerance policy in order to destroy the mindset that accepts "honor" killings. All social institutions— including government workers, educators, law enforcement officials, representatives from religious organizations, legislators, prosecutors, judges, and others—should fully embrace this approach. NGOs, local authorities, family, judges and media should all support it. (Report of UNFA/UNDP, 2005)

The United Nations Population Fund, or UNFPA, addresses the underlying causes of gender-based violence and advances gender equality in an effort to prevent destructive traditions like honor killings. In its strategic plan, UNFPA reiterates its goal to assist in the elimination of female genital mutilation (FGM) and child marriage, two detrimental traditions that can result in honor killings. The overall goals of UNFPA's efforts to combat harmful customs like honor murders are to empower women and girls, advance gender equality, and fortify the laws and regulations that defend women's rights and stop gender-based violence.

Crown Prosecution Service (United Kingdom)

The main government organization in charge of carrying out criminal prosecutions is the Crown Prosecution Service. As an act of violence involving threats of violence, extortion, intimidation or abuse (including financial, emotional, psychological, sexual abuse), *the Crown Prosecution Service (CPS) in the United Kingdom defines "honor-based" violence as one who has or may have pledged to uphold the dignity of a person, family, and/or community in the event of alleged or perceived transgressions of the code of conduct for the family, community, and/or individual* (Crown Prosecution Service). Threatening behavior, assault, or abuse are all considered as criminal offenses by the CPS and are classified as "honor crimes" by both the named offender and the CMS, Case Management System.

Unlike the UN and its organizations, CPS does not consider honor killing or honor-based violence as a gender biased crime. CPS states that men and boys, including heterosexual men as well as gay, bi, and transgender men, may also be impacted by this type of crime. Men and boys may find it difficult to ask for assistance. When a male victim of honor-based abuse is in an intimate relationship with a woman, they are frequently singled out or held accountable for the actions of the woman, who is thought to be a disgrace to her family, society, or culture. It's possible that the woman in question experienced injury due to familial control. A male may come under attack if he attempts to stand up for a woman who is being treated unfairly since it will be assumed that he does not adhere to cultural norms around what constitutes acceptable masculinity.

Similar to women and girls, men may be coerced into marriage in order to meet the expectations and responsibilities of their families, obtain visas, or simply to maintain their family's reputation and rein in undesirable behavior. For reasons related to sexuality, the family and community may also support forced marriage. Because their families are aware of or think that the male victims are gay or bisexual, the victims may be compelled to marry women.

Human Rights Watch and Other Organizations

Human Rights Watch is an international NGO related to human rights. This organization includes several issues and regions such as the Middle-east, Asia, Africa and America. According to Human Rights Watch, "honor crimes" are described as *"Violent, typically murderous acts by male family members against female family members who are seen to have brought shame upon the family".* This idea was based on their research and advocacy on human rights, particularly in relation to violence against women. Human Rights Watch has pushed for states to outlaw and prohibit every kind of violence directed at women. The organization has worked on this problem in a number of overseas regions, including the Americas, Asia, the Middle East, and North Africa. Additionally, they demand that states guarantee compensation to women who have been sufferers of aggression and put a stop to prejudice directed towards women in both legislation and practice.

Human Rights Watch (2016) has tirelessly advocated for changes in legal systems, urging the governments of Pakistan, India, and Jordan to look into and prosecute honor crime perpetrators and to impose a "zero tolerance" attitude on the violence. Law improvements alone, however, won't stop the violence; in cases where the legal system is corrupt, police forces must withstand pressure from the local village council, the political establishment, and religious organizations to stop looking into homicides of this nature (Human Rights Watch, Pakistan, 2016). It is important to take into account the organization's scope while examining these global sources of law and agreements, such as the United Nations, or regional sources like the African Charter on Human and People's Rights or the European Convention on Human Rights. The question whether human rights are actually a global set of rights or if they can vary based on geographical, cultural, and religious differences is reflected in the division between universal and regional international human rights law.

International Covenant on Economics, Social and Cultural Rights (ICESCR) is a multinational agreement ratified by the UN General Assembly in 1966. To address the issue concerning assault against women, including honor killings, the provisions require State parties to take action to both prevent and punish such actions as well as to defend the rights of women and girls. In addition, they provide a platform for advocacy and action by people and civil society groups committed to ending honor killings and other forms of abuse against women.

The Universal Declaration of human rights is an international document that upholds the freedoms and rights of all people, which the United Nations General Assembly endorsed. According to the UDHR, state parties must take action to stop, penalize, and defend these kinds of crimes against women and girls. The Universal Declaration of Human Rights (UDHR) is a non-binding proclamation that upholds everyone's rights, such as the entitlements to life, liberty,

and privacy, as well as the restriction on any kind of suffering whether cruel, brutal, or humiliating (UN Report, 1985)

Convention on the Elimination of all Forms of Discrimination against Women- Acts of honor-related violence have been discussed in relation to rights of humanity and violence against women breaches from the viewpoint of international law. CEDAW is an international agreement signed by the UN General Assembly in 1979. While not specifically mentioned, honor-related violence is included in the Convention on the Elimination of all the two primary globally approved texts that aim to advance gender equality and classify domestic abuse as a violation of women's human rights: the Forms of Discrimination against Women (1979) (CE-

DAW) and the UN Declaration on the Elimination of Abuse Against women (1993). Furthermore, the Convention and Declaration reject any rationalization of such violence against women on the grounds of tradition, custom, or culture. CEDAW is often mentioned as an international women's charter of rights. (UN Report, 1985) The Committee on Violence Against Women published a broad recommendation in 1989, suggesting that states submit reports on incidents of violence involving women to the Committee. A general proposal addressing the excision of females and other customs detrimental to women's health was made in 1990. Furthermore, in a number of concluding observations, the CEDAW Committee advised that state parties should deal with honor crimes and honor killings.

While state parties are required by international human rights legislation to safeguard the rights and freedoms of their inhabitants, Johnson and Shalhoub-Kevorkian point out that in certain occupied regions, where the indigenous population is present, there is uncertainty about who holds political authority since it is transnational, non-sovereign, divided, under threat, or shared by other governments (Johnson, 2008). It is unclear in such circumstances who is applying international human rights law and in whose best interest. In addition, this kind of circumstance might actually make patriarchal violence more common. It also leads into the idea that "women's social issues are weighed against a political concern and are considered a secondary concern" (Johnson, 2008).

One of the first international agreements to specifically mention the word honor (Article 12, 1949) was the 1949 Geneva Convention (also known as the Fourth Geneva Convention), which states in Article 27 that - Women are to have special protection against every attack on their honor, including indecent assault, forced prostitution, and rape.

The literal phrase "honor and dignity" appears in Article 27 of the Stockholm draft convention, which is where paragraph 2 of Article 27 gets its start. Nevertheless, the Geneva Convention proposal did not include the Stockholm draft. But since the Fourth Geneva Convention's prohibitions describe rape as an offence against honor rather than as a clearly violent and sexual offence against women, the specific reference to "honor" under Article 27 has sparked scholarly discussion. Since men and women associate honor differently—men define honor as bravery, fortitude, and independence, whereas women define honor as continence, humility, fragility, as well as dependence. It is unclear how gender classifications of honor are applied when every sexual assault is viewed as an attack on a person's honor rather than their dignity. This sparks a discussion on the claim that by focusing on how men see rape and other sexual misdeeds rather than how women experience them, the gendering of the pardon principle itself conforms to ideas associated with masculinity.

It is argued that sexual offence such as rape ought to be viewed as crimes against a woman's personality rather than the honor her family's society has conferred upon her. Such language disregards women's sexual autonomy and instead perpetuates the subjugation of women under international human rights legislation.

The European Court of Human Rights (ECHR) first recognized in the 2009 decision of *Opuz v Turkey* that a gender-based discrimination occurs when the state fails to handle honor-related domestic abuse. The incident of Opuz, the first instance of honor-related domestic abuse brought before the European Court of Human Rights, demonstrated that Turkey had transgressed its responsibility to keep women safe from abuse at home under the ECHR. Turkey was held accountable in this case for failing to shield Nahide Opuz and her mother from her abusive ex-husband. Following the husband's vicious attack between 1995 and 2008, Nahide filed multiple police complaints and started the divorce process.

In these situations, the criminal courts preferred to punish the offenders for these offenses with either very light sentences or no penalties at all. According to the European Court of Human Rights, the opening line of Article 2 (Securing the ECHR's Right to Life) requires the state to take adequate action to safeguard the lives of those under its control in addition to abstaining from the deliberate and illegal taking of life. The State is primarily responsible for protecting the right to life by enacting strong criminal law regulations.

Need of the Hour

Firstly, there is a need to provide or set the factors on which such heinous actions and activities are performed as it may differ in places, religions, castes, race and genders and shall fall under the category of Honor killing. It can be done by providing a universal definition which is subjective to inclusion and liberal interpretation.

Secondly, the need is to address the issue in a global manner, that is to say, all countries shall have specific laws and punishments regarding this offense. The laws and stance may vary from region to region but it can never be negative. International law shall also refine their measures for imposing duty on states to protect the human rights of their citizens.

And it is to be pointed out separately that the definition or punishing such offence shall not be gender biased. It shall include male, female and transgender as well.

CONCLUSION

To conclude, Honor killings are a severe kind of biased domestic violence with particular characteristics connected to the social and cultural standards of tribal, patriarchal societies. The assassinations are done in an effort to mend the damage that the victim's violation of highly rigid standards limiting female sexuality caused to the family's status as a whole. The assailants believe that the killings are a fair retribution that is often approved by the local populace as well as by governmental bodies. While the classic honor killing involves the death of a young woman by her male relatives, descriptions of the crime usually include occurrences including male victims as well as homicides committed in intimate partnerships. Men and women alike are more likely to be killed in honor killings in Hindu communities in India if they are involved in forbidden love relationships (Chesler & Bloom, 2012). Data from India indicates that male honor killings were particularly violent and infused with a performance element. Moreover, honour killings motivated by a woman's desire to marry a lower-caste man or an unapproved couple seeking to flee often resulted in spectacular, drawn-out torture sessions that ended in death. In one such instance, a young couple in Uttar Pradesh were stoned to death by an enormous crowd of 200 individuals, involving a few of the girl's relatives. (BBC News India, 2013).

Since, this chapter attempts to cover all the aspects in which honor killing can be defined or is defined, it is important to notice that many at times honor killing are also treated as a type of 'Mob lynching'. Mob lynching is a form of violence in which a group of people without following principle of natural justice and in the name of justice, execute the so called offender. Thus, resemblance of these often made the honor killing a part of Mob lynching

Honor killings are grave human rights violations, according to Human Rights Watch, especially for women in the Muslim and Mediterranean regions. Male family members frequently conduct these crimes against female relatives who they believe have brought shame or dishonor to the family. For instance, in Jordan, women who do "immoral or shameful" activities run the possibility of being killed by male relatives, who may do so with the support of their families and the wider community. Courts frequently show mercy towards the murderers, and police seldom ever look into these cases. For their own safety, women who are threatened by family members frequently wind up behind bars, and there aren't enough shelters or other safe havens for them. Human Rights Watch has demanded that those responsible for crimes take responsibility, that women and girls who are in danger be protected, and that sections of the criminal code that have spared "honor" murders from harsh penalties be changed or eliminated.

While various strategies have been put to an ending on aggression against women in the name of "honor," one strategy is unmistakable: community discussion of the problem is essential if attitudes towards women are to change in society. Similar conditions exist for human rights in India, where very few laws provide protection to females. Nonetheless, *the Shakti Vahini v. Union of India* [(2018) 7 SCC 192] .The ruling from the Indian Supreme Court in 2018 is recognized as a historic victory. The decision is noteworthy because it declares honor-based violence to be illegal and a violation of one's constitutional rights, including the freedom of speech and the right to life and dignity, according to the nation's top court. It is frowned upon for women to tell their own stories of sexual agency (Siddiqi et al., 2012, p. 164). This is usually occupied by older males who accuse young women of being raped or abducted if they have made decisions with their partners in a mutual manner. (Solotaroff & Pande, 2014).

REFERENCES

Ajula, W., & Gill, A.K. (2014). "Honour" Killings in Canada: An Extreme Form of Domestic Violence. *International Journal of Criminal Justice Sciences 154*.

Article 12. (1949). In *Universal Declaration of Human Rights, 1949*.

BBC News India. (2013). India Honour Killing: Paying the price for falling in love.

Chesler, P., & Bloom, N. (2012). Hindu vs. Muslim honor killings. *Middle East Quarterly*, 19(3), 43–52.

Crown Prosecution Service (2023): *Statistics on so called Honour- based abuse offenses, England and Wales, 2022 to 2023 Defending Human Rights Worldwide*. (n.d.). Human Rights Watch.

Crown Prosecution Service-. *So Called Honor Based Abuse*.

Human Rights Watch, Pakistan. (2016). *Prosecute Rampant 'Honor killing'*.

Idriss, M. (2017). 'Not Domestic Violence or Cultural Tradition: Is Honour-based Violence Distinct from Domestic Violence? *Journal of Social Welfare and Family Law*, 39(1), 1–19. DOI: 10.1080/09649069.2016.1272755

Jerusalem: Women's Centre for Legal Aid and Counselling. (2004). Mapping and Analyzing the Landscape of Femicide in Palestine Society.

Johnson, P. (2008). Violence All Around Us. 120-121.

Lari, M. Z. (2011). *A pilot study on 'honor killings' in Pakistan and compliance of law*. The Aurat Foundation.

Mayeda, R., & Vijaykumar, D. (2016). A review of the literature on honor-based violence. *Sociology Compass*, 10(5), 353–363. DOI: 10.1111/soc4.12367

Mishra, P. (2013). Sex ratios, cross-region marriages and the challenge to caste endogamy in Haryana. *Economic and Political Weekly*, 48(35), 70–78.

UN Office. (2010). *Impunity for Domestic Violence, 'Honour Killing' cannot continue*.

Reddy, R. (2014). Domestic Violence or Cultural Tradition? Approches to Honour Killing as Species and Subspecies in English legal Practisce.

UN Report. (1985). *Declaration of Basic Principles of Justice for Victims of Crime and Abuse of Power*.

Report of UNFA/UNDP. (2005). *Zero Tolerance Crucial to Confronting "Honour" Killings in Türkiye.*

Siddiqi, D. M., Manisha, G., Awasthi, R., & Chickerur, S. (2012). Blurred boundaries: Sexuality and seduction narratives in selected 'forced marriage' cases from Bangladesh. In Gupte, M., Awasthi, R., & Chickerur, S. (Eds.), *Honour and women's rights: South Asian perspectives* (pp. 155–184).

Solotaroff, J. L., & Pande, R. P. (2014). *Violence against women and girls: Lessons from South Asia.* World Bank Publications. DOI: 10.1596/978-1-4648-0171-6

Solotaroff J. L., & Prabha R.P. (2020). *For the Sake of Family and Tradition: Honour Killings in Pakistan and India. Volume 5, Issue 1.*

United Nations. (2013). *Human Rights.* Gender- Related Killings of Women and Girls.

Uzoma. (2020). Introduction to Legal Research Method and Legal Writing.

Welcham, L. (2007). 'Honour and Violence in a Modern Shar`i Discourse'

Chapter 8
Honor Killing:
An Infringement of Right to Life With Dignity

Avinash Dadhich
Manipal Law School, India

Aditya Raj
GLA University, India

ABSTRACT

Honor Killings involves unlawful killing of blood relations which is done by their own family member when they felt that the act involves immoral behaviour. The Hon'ble Supreme Court of India has also condemned this type of atrocious act. In a country like India which runs on the thread of rule of law, such atrocious act must be dealt with hardship. This doctrinal research provides an analysis of honor killing as infringement life with dignity which is guaranteed at national as well as international level. It focuses on positive obligations which are imposed on states by international law and International Human Rights law. It also focused on Indian legal framework on honor killing and Judicial Response to protection of women from honor killing. In this chapter, it is also argued that why honor killing is human right issue with certain examples of other states where the same offences have been committed in the name of so-called honor.

BACKGROUND

Honor Killings involves unlawful killing of blood relations which is done by their own family member when they felt that the act involves immoral behaviour. The literal meaning of 'Honor Killing' is Killing of someone to save honor. The

DOI: 10.4018/979-8-3693-9596-7.ch008

so-called honor is false notion due to which many young people especially women in India have been the victims of this crime. In most cases it happened just because they want to live life on his/her condition, expressed their choice. Every Individual has the right to express opinion and live on his/her own condition. Even after so many years of Independence in the newly so-called modern India, which is proud of her democracy, our ill mindset are still not broadened enough to accept these changes.

Crime of honor killing has always been the matter of controversy and it is criticized not only in India but globally. The Hon'ble Supreme Court of India has also condemned this type of atrocious act and also made observation in many cases which proved to be significant to deal with this. The Supreme Court has even formed a law commission to draft new legislation to deal with such crimes, but no concrete decision has been taken by the legislature due to lack of political will. In a country like India which runs on the thread of rule of law, such atrocious act must be dealt with hardship. This doctrinal research provides an analysis of honor killing as infringement life with dignity which is guaranteed at national as well as international level. 'Right to life is recognized as most sacrosanct right at national and international level and should not be infringed at any cost. Right to life with dignity must not be curbed in the lieu of any cultural pressure nor from societal pressure. It focuses on positive obligation which is imposed on states by international law and International Human Rights law. It also focused on Indian legal framework on honor killing and Judicial Response to protection of women from honor killing. In this chapter it is also argued that why honor killing is human right issue with certain examples of other states where the same offences have been committed in the name of so-called honor.

According to the World Health Organization (WHO) in 2012, it was estimated that around 5000 murders occur each year worldwide in the name of honor. (World Health Organization, 2012) The report says that some commonly used methods in honor crimes include strangulation, burning, stabbing, buried alive, Fire burning, acid burning, stone pelting, and forcing a female to take poison . Instances of Honor Killing cases go underreported throughout the world this can be assessed that even though there are not many studies on this issue reported in Saudi Arabia, however researcher found that rate of domestic violence in Saudi Arabia is 58% when compared to worldwide rate, which lies between 10 – 52%. These reasons compelled to see honor killing as global human right issue and lay down an internation instruments on this. (Eid J.A, 2020)

Research Methodology

The purpose of this chapter is to gain an understanding of honor killings. The information for this topic wax collected in the form of checking records from libraries/Newspaper/Magazines/Interviews/Sample/Surveterviews/Sample/Survey/Internet etc. Therefore, qualitative research strategy had been adopted for this study in order to address its objective covering both primary and secondary sources. Certain characteristics such as the participant's ethnicity, age, and gender need to be observed using qualitative methods to avoid biasness. From the primary and secondary research carried out, it became clear that honor killing not only infringed the fundamental right to life with dignity but also human right issue at global level. After doing intensive research work it is clear that honor killing is not restricted to any geographical entity but takes place across the world, it's phenomenon which has been around for many centuries. The problem has been undermined not only at national level but remained ignored even by International Institutes such as UN. The chapter gives a clear understanding of honor killing in context with fundamental right, that is right to life with dignity. However, from all the information that was collected on perception of honor killings, it is considered as infringement of right to life with dignity and also a global human right issue.

Key Terms

Core terms include "Honor Killing" (Ruane, 2000) and "Human Right law" (Cook, 1994) directly linking the subject matter and interconnectedness of honor killing as global concern and urges global player to combat this issue globally by laying out rule and guidelines regarding this. Broader themes like "Right to life with dignity" (Maneka Gandhi vs UOI, 1978), "Gender Based Violence" (Shripad, 2024) and "Intra-Family Violence"(Husseini, 2002) contextualize the issue and exploring the complexities of gender-based crime in the society and infringement of basic right guaranteed by every domestic and international legal instrument across the world due to immoral behaviour triggered by social theories.

Inclusion criteria emphasized relevance, ensuring that only articles directly addressing honor killings, right to life with dignity, Intra-Family violence, Gender Based violence and Human Right law are considered. Exclusion criteria filtered out non-academic sources, such as blogs or opinion and articles with only tangential relevance to the topic. Conducted research article using academic databases like JSTOR, PubMed and Google Scholar is crucial, employing targeted keywords "Honor Killing" (Ruane, 2000), "Gender Based violence" (Shripad, 2024) and "Human Right law" (Cook, 1994) to identify the most pertinent studies for our paper.

Literature Review

Intra-Family violence involves killing of Men or Women when they seen to have defiled the family's honor and the author discussed that it occurred due to changed phase of cultural tolerance and in order to restore the so-called lost honor (Husseini, 2002). The author highlights the honor killing as human right issue to protect individuals against abuses perpetrated by the state and its officials as well as abuses committed by private actors which have traditionally been excluded from the ambit of International human rights law (Cook, 1994). The focus of author on Honor Killing with respect to right to life with dignity which is guaranteed in every civilized state which is considered as supreme right and sees the idea of honor and lost honor are based on notion of justification of collective injury (Abu-Odeh, 1997).

The author discuss over Honor killing and honor based violence which are influenced by various physical-social aspects such as vitim of a sexual assault, committing adultery, refusion to enter family's choice of marriage, seeking a divorce, the victims in some cases also belong to LGBTQ community (Ruane, 2000). These authors discussed that the reason for discussing Honor Killings as gross violation of International Human Rights law and conventions and justified by giving examples of incidents of this type of social crime in countries like Pakistan, Middle east and south Asian countries (Yamani, 1996), (Husseini, 2002) , (Sing, 1999).

Future Research Directions

This research is an attempt by the authors correlating honor killing with infringement of right to life with dignity and also highlight the human right perspective involving in this social crime. This research viewed honor killing as cultural crime and blows to the fundamental right, i.e., right to life with dignity. The author in this chapter analyses this issue which doesn't receive the required attention in earlier research as mentioned even though the apex court have so many times reiterated the need of legislation on this matter but it remains in complete mundane condition due to lack of political will from the side of legislative and non-committal toward this sensitive issue.(Grewal, 2012) This issue has also not gained support from public which paved it difficult for the law enforcement agencies to show concern towards the prevention or prosecution of guilty. There are research studies/guides mentioned here on this topic highlighting the interlinkage of honor killing with Right to life, but through this chapter the author has worked upon interlinkage of honor killing with right to life with dignity as well as with global human right perspective. (Baker et al., n.d.) The main aim of the research is to focus on the very important aspects of human being, that is protection of life with dignity which is considered as essential aspect in international sphere, and the express provision given in International legal instruments.

The author has also lay emphasis on provision entrusted by Indian legal framework on honor killing, though there is no specific legislation to deal with this issue but can be traced from different legislation such as IPC, CRPC, IEA, Protection of Human Rights Act. In addition to this, the author conducted additional study on judicial response, the contribution of judiciary which expanded its horizon and delivered landmark judgement giving protection of women from honor killing. In future research on honor killing, a multi-faceted study is crucial to deepen the understanding and enhancing the legislative efforts to combat this issue and eradicate this practice from all spheres of life.

INTRODUCTION

The criminal laws come under the arena of public laws. It is the duty of the government to provide security and protection to the public when any misdemeanor practices are being followed which shook the conscience of public interest. It also affects the value of society and culture which result in change in the dynamics of criminal jurisprudence. Not only India but whole world has witnessed the political upheavals and societal change and change in law and these changes taught people to accommodate each other by corresponding each other's need.

Our journey from conservative society to Neo Modernism, we have witnessed many cultural changes which have revamped up our cultural ethos, law like Love Marriage concept instead of Traditional Arranged Marriage, now one more adds up to list is Live-In Relationship, but these changes are not appealable to all. There are many people who are not prone or we can say keep themselves associated with such changed phase of cultural tolerance that's where the cultural crimes like Honor Killing comes into picture. This crime comes under the purview of Cultural crimes because it took place within the context of Culture.

Honor Killing is a form of Intra-family violence which involves killing of Men or Women, but mostly happened with women, by their family when they seem to have defiled the family's honor. From the time immemorial, women are considered as repositories of the man's or family's honor and they killed in order to restore it. Defiling of Honor varies from society to society, but usually the reason for an honor killing is the suspicion of Illicit relationship outside marriage. More Often mere rumours or insinuation are enough for people to feel their family's honor has been defiled. (Ruane, 2000)The other reasons for targeting are being a victim of a sexual assault, committing adultery, refusion to enter family's choice of marriage, and seeking a divorce. The victims in some cases also belong to LGBTQ community.

Although, these cases are more prevalent in a few North Indian states, like Uttar Pradesh, Bihar, Rajasthan, Haryana, Jharkhand and Punjab, but it is seen to be more significantly in the south too, including Karnataka. As per the latest data from National Crime Records Bureau (NCRB), the number of honor killings reported in India was 25 each in 2019 and 2020, and 33 in 2021.but these figures are based on reported but several cases go unreported, and the number could be much higher than mentioned. (Shripad, 2024)

This chapter is divided into four parts. The first part briefly deals with the compelling reasons to consider Honor killing as human right issue and should not be discussed at national level but at international level. Further in second part, the author had discussed the honor killing with the context of right to life with dignity and conceivable idea of 'right to life' given by Indian Judiciary and by Internationalal Judicial functionaries. The third part deals with Indian legal Framework which include legal point from the constitutional point of view and other criminal laws (IPC, CRPC, IEA) and some other acts involved in these types of instances. The fourth and last part discussed the judicial protection of women from honor killing in which the apex court also made observations and sought recommendation on this sensitive issue of honor killing.

Why are Honor Killings a Human Rights Issue?

The purpose of human right law is to protect individuals against abuses perpetrated by the state and its officials as well as abuses committed by private actors which have traditionally been excluded from the ambit of international human rights law. (Cook, 1994) The notion of state's responsibility at international level has expanded its horizon in recent years.

In the words of the Inter-American Court of Human Rights:

"An illegal act which violates human rights and is not ... imputable to a State (for example, because it is the act of a private person...) can lead to the international responsibility of the State, not because of the act itself, but because of the lack of due diligence to prevent the violation or to respond to it." (Velasquez Rodriguez case, 1988)

In other words, apart from the positive obligation to respect every individual's human right, it is the positive obligations of the state to make sure that no one get deprived of his fundamental freedoms and jeopardize their human rights. The dialogue and discussion on honor killings should takes place at international level and should be the part of agenda in the organisation that deals with the international human rights agenda because it is the failure on the part of states to introduce any preventive measure and remedials even though these crimes come under the domestic laws. There are numerous reasons which justify the reason for discussing Honor

Killings as gross violations of International Human Rights law and conventions, some of the prominent reasons are discussed thereunder:

- In today modern era, many cases of honor killings go unreported, and even if reported then no investigation takes place, just because of the simple reason, that is, gender-based attitude of the police, lack of resource and corruption.
- At International level, there are presently various states, particularly Middle eastern States, which shows clearly discriminatory provocation defenses in their criminal codes. These provisions provide for either exemption or reduction of penalty for a man who kills his wife for reasons of adultery or reduction of penalty if a man kills his sister other family relative for "Illicit sexual relations". (Yamani, 1996) The similar provision can be seen in Pakistan, where the qisas and diyat provision of Islamic law provide for another codified mean of reduction of exception of penalty of person, who is considered to be the perpetrator of an honor killing. (Quraishi, 1996)
- Many states follow discriminatory application of general provocation, sometimes they deodorize circumstance provision. A notorious example can be seen is the application of Article 98 of Jordanian Penal code which states that "A perpetrator will be exempted from the punishment for murder if his criminal act was due to a state of extreme anger in response to a wrongful and serious act on the part of the victim". (article 98 of Jordanian penal code,1960) In many cases of honor killings, the sentences of imprisonment were reduced where brother or father had killed his daughter or sister for the illegitimate pregnancy or some other reasons associated with honor killing. (Husseini, 2002)
- In some countries like Pakistan where a parallel judiciary system runs to deals with the honor killing cases. A system of tribal justice operates alongside the official courts which deals with a considerable number of cases of honor crimes and killings, they are running without having consideration of official laws or guarantee for a fair trial. (Amnesty International, 2002) Outside the Middle East and South Asia, the so-called cultural defence has been invoked to reduce defendant's responsibility for certain crimes, including honor killings. (Sing, 1999)

The above-mentioned examples which provide sufficient reason and basis for considering honor killings as violation of International Human Rights Law and International conventions.

Honor Killing Within the Context of Right to Life with Dignity

"Life is a Divine gift. To preserve it is commendable. To destroy it is condemnable," (Jan, 2012)

The term "Honor Killing" seems to be a new word in the contemporary world, but the offence has been continuing from very early period. If we extract the literal meaning of this term, then it suggests killing for the sake of so-called honor. So, it is the behaviour of others on which person's behaviour is dependent and if the code if breached, the person (and his family) loses his self-conceived honor. The word honor killing was first coined by a Dutch Scholar Ana Nauta in 1978, basically it was coined to make a distinction between Honor Killing and blood feuds. Societies where Honor killing are characterized by the existence of codes of honor and that honor depends upon the outside world's view of a person. (Rana & Mishra, n.d.)

So, it is the behaviour of others on which person's behaviour is dependent and if the code if breached, the person (and his family) loses his self-conceived honor. We can say that the ideas of honor and lost honor are based on a notion of justification of collective injury. (Abu-Odeh, 1997) It is when the so-called lost honor becomes public then it becomes a reality. Thus, honor killings are highly unlikely unless the transgression becomes known in the community (Baker et al., n.d.).

According to National commission for Women, when any existing code is challenged or breached by the young people then it becomes a breeding ground for honor killing. Honor Killing in the name of violence infringes the inalienable right, that is 'right to life'. Honor killing not only deprive the right to life from someone but also curtails liberty and threatened the security of that individuals. The right to life also includes right to be free from inhuman treatment or degrading treatment. As India is one of the signatories to international convention which deals with human rights, so India is obliged to protect international commitments. 'Right to life' is guaranteed in every civilized state, this right is the supreme right and no right is above this right. It is considered as most sacrosanct of all right.

John Locke was of the view that one cannot take one's life and cannot also permit others to take it. (Locke, 1980) Thomas Hobbes also expressed a similar view. The Plato and Aristotle also objected on Killing or taking life for whatsoever reason as the state loses a citizen. Kant also stated that the human being is the supreme personality on this earth. According to him, all the worldly thing is secondary to the value of life. He himself believed that it is the worldly institution which should be used to raise the human being, which he portrays as 'the supreme creation'. It is the society who goes against the civilized state of human being which is the natural state to preserve ridiculous customary practice which has no significance.

Everyone as a human being has inherently good and bad qualities inside himself. It should be in the conscience of every individual that they let prevail their inherent good part rather than bad part and for that everyone should strive to do in such manner. The cost of human being's life is much precious than the tradition so no such tradition should be defended which is against the humanistic values. We should not forget that 'He' who gives life reserves the absolute and undivided right to take it and this is also the divine command "thou shall not kill". Thus, honor killing goes against the divine command of preserving the life against all odds.

The right to life runs like a sacred thread in every civil society, no other values have that much of weightage which can shift down this fundamental value. This basic right is available even in those jurisdictions which do not expressly guarantee it. Some of the express provisions which guarantee right to life at the international spheres are:

- **European Convention for Protection of Human Rights and Fundamental Freedoms:**

    "Every one's right to life shall be protected by law"
    "Everyone has a right to liberty and security of person [...] save in accordance with the procedure established by law". (Article 5 and Article 21 of European Convention of Human Rights and Fundamental Freedoms,1950)

- **Universal Declaration of Human Rights:**

    "Whereas the recognition of inherent dignity and of equal and inalienable right of all the members of human family is the foundation of justice, peace in the world [....] everyone has a right to life, liberty, security of the persons."(Preamble of Universal Declaration on Human Right, 1948)

- **Article 6 of the International Covenant on civil and Political Rights 1966:**

    "Every human being has an inherent right to life. This right shall be protected by the law and no one shall be arbitrarily deprived of such a right". (Article 6 of ICCPR,1966)

There must be consideration of Right from the jurisprudential Perspective before placing any right in any legal system. Some rights are considered as basic and inalienable right and these rights are enjoyed by person from the birth of human being. The term 'life' has been given a very wide meaning by interpretation of the court. Here are some of the following observations of the meaning 'right to life' on different cases:

Justice Field in the Case of *Munn vs Illions*:

[...] by the term life, something more is meant than mere existence. The inhibition against its deprivation extends to all those limbs and faculties by which the life is enjoyed.(Munn vs Illions,1877)

Justice Bhagwati in the Case of *Francis Carolie V. Union Territory, Delhi*:

We think that right to life means right to live with human dignity and all that whish goes along with it namely the bare necessities such as adequate food, clothing and shelter, and facilities for reading and writing and expressing oneself in diverse forms, freely moving about mixing, with fellow human beings further pointing out that inhibition would extend to all those faculties by which life is enjoyed. (Francis Carolie V. Union territory, Delhi,1981)

The Hon'ble Supreme Court from time to time has made clear stance on this subject and has interpreted the right to life and it embodies all the elements which requires it to maintain life with dignity. Article 21 of the constitution of India also embodies the principle of sanctity of life. Article 21 of Constitution of India guarantees each person the right to life and liberty. Article 21 of Constitution of India, 1950) The Hon'ble Supreme Court gave a new dimension to Article 21. The Court held that the right to live is not merely a physical right, but also includes within its ambit the right to live with human dignity. (Maneka Gandhi v Union of India, 1978)

The apex court have expanded the dimension of 'right to life' which is enshrined in Article 21 of the constitution of India that include any positive element which entails not merely a physical life but a dignified life. Right to life is considered as quintessential element of rule of law.

Honor Killing amount to gross violation of Fundamental Right and rule of law. Though our human life today has been regulated by legal codes, the concept of honor has remained intact despite the fact that it deprives the right to life of the persons. In most of the jurisdictions, several cases go underreported and barely addressed. The young couples who go against the wishes of their family and set of codes set by the community or society face various atrocities in the form of persistent harassment, wrongful confinement, mental torture, infliction of threat. Generally, the close relative or member of that community is involved in inflicting harms and cause of death. Sometimes the person faces the brunt of social boycott because the act of that individual doesn't match with the standard of that community and believed to be bring dishonor to the family.

These above-mentioned tortures prove to be clear violation of the fundamental right to life and liberty which demands to be halted as soon as possible. This right is guaranteed at the national as well as international level. If we truly analyze honor killings within the context of 'life', it shows that honor killings are in antithesis to the right to life.

Indian Legal Framework on Honor Killing

The Indian Constitution

The Indian Constitution which is considered as ground norm for administrative networking and which ensures the protection of right of every citizen indiscriminately. There are many following provisions available which ensure the protection against Honor Killing:

i. Article 14 [Right to Equality],
ii. Article 15 (1) and (3) [which prohibits discrimination on grounds of religion, race, caste, sex or place of birth],
iii. Article 17 [Abolition of Untouchability],
iv. Article 19(1) [The freedom of speech and expressions],
v. Article 21 [The right to life and personal liberty]. (Fundamental Rights of Constitution of India,1950)

In most of the case of honor killing, women are the primary target which becomes a nasty form of gender violence. Mere expressing the choice of women and men about their life decision results into violation of fundamental rights and sometimes death. This is clearly inconsistent with the Constitution of India. The Directive Principles of State Policy (DPSP), though not enforceable by law which guide the country to rule effectively by assessing the ability of the country. Article 39(a) talks about the mandate of state to provide all people with the appropriate means of subsistence. Article 39 (e) and (f) which obligates the state to ensure safeguard of Infancy and youth from exploitation and rising or growing material desertion Honor not only negate the women's life but also the provision of DPSP. (Article 39(a), (e) and (f) of Indian Constitution) It is the positive obligation of state to protect and empower every vulnerable individual and their lives from these types of atrocities and heinous crime. In India however there is no specific legislation to deal with honor crime and generally they are recorded under Indian Penal Code (IPC) offences.

The Indian Penal Code,1860 and Code of Criminal Procedure, 1973

Honor killing is considered as murder according to Indian Penal code (IPC),1860. Even though it is difficult to identify the perpetrators sometimes because this act of homicide is perpetrated and supported by society or community. In many cases it is seen that accused has taken the defence under section 300 of the Indian Penal Code and justifies the reason of his response taken due to grave and sudden provocation. In many cases, no FIR is filed which makes it difficult for the law enforcement to find the real culprit. Even after filling FIR and if the case is pursued further then conviction will be nearly zero. Due to the exercise of Khap panchayat as quasi-judicial body in the northern states like U.P, Haryana, etc. which follow the regressive measure to the modern thinking, there remains no choice of registering FIR which is prescribed in the criminal procedure.

Indian Evidence Act, 1872

The main object of this act is that court can come to conclusion about the facts of the case and pronounce judgement based on evidence. Indian Evidence Act, 1872 punishes individual who is involved in the concealing the facts either before, during or after the commission of crime. To understand the legal aspect of honor killing, there must be mentioned about section 13 of the act. - The following facts are relevant when determining the existence of any right or custom: (a) Any transaction by which the right or custom in question was created, claimed modified, recognized, asserted or denied, or which was inconsistent with its existence; (b) Specific instances in which the right or custom was claimed, recognized, or exercised, or in which its exercise was disputed. (Sec- 13 of Indian Evidence Act, 1872) The main object of this act is to ensure justice to the victims who suffered torture and atrocities due to the unjustified punishment given by the Khap Panchayat.

Special Marriage Act, 1956

The sole intention of the lawmaker of this act was to legally empowered and support the special form of marriages which include citizens from two different caste, class, religion in India. In our country, there exist thread of rigid caste system, this is more prominently seen is rural areas than urban areas. The above-mentioned statement is the reason for registering a greater number of inter caste marriage in urban areas than rural area. The act clearly states that marriage can be solemnized on the condition that tradition which govern any of the parties authorizes marriage between them.

Protection of Human Rights (Amendment) Act, 2006

This act was made for the protection of human rights of every individual. It also introduces the courts and the commissions to ensure the goals. However, honor killings continue to take place even after introducing such regulations which result in violation of human rights. (Puneet Kaur Grewal, 2012) If we critically analyse the framework of this act, no specific law is available to deal with the legal aspect of honor killings. This act doesn't provide any legal definition, any provision for preventive measure and legal protection just because most of the death are generally considered to be murder or culpable homicide. This is the main reason for missing the organized data for these types of crime.

Judicial Response: Protection of Women from Honor Killing

"Law without Justice is blind, Justice without law is lame, law geared to Justice is order" ...... *Justice V R Krishna Iyer*

The contribution of Judiciary as independent justice system is magnanimous and has also earned a lot of respect from the people of this country through its way forward delivery of judgements. Judiciary is considered to be as the temple of Justice and generally people of India have very high expectation and glaring hopes from this institution. The judiciary not worked as independent judicial institution but seen as a promoter of peace which foster harmony, balance and cooperation among three tier system of state. The Judiciary in numerous occasions has expanded its horizon and delivered landmark judgement on numerous issues like, expanded the ambit of fundamental rights and protection by interpreting the laws and regulations. There are numerous cases in which Judiciary gave numerous instructions for safeguarding the human dignity of individual and human rights, specially focussing on the issue of socially disadvantageous people like women, Children, bonded labour, Socially and educationally backward people. The apex court also made observations and sought recommendation on this sensitive issue of honor killing. Some of the landmark judgment discussed on honor killing are following:

In ***Lata Singh vs State of Uttar Pradesh*** and others, a bench of Supreme Court headed by Justice Markandey Katju had said "Honor Killings are nothing but barbaric cold-blooded murder and no honor is involved in such killings.... moreover, these acts take the law into their own hands, and amount to kangaroo courts, which are wholly illegal." (Lata Singh vs State of Uttar Pradesh, 2006). The Supreme Court in a case i.e., ***Shakthi Vahini Vs Union of India*** and others comprising of Chief justice Dipak Mishra, Justice A.M. Khanwilkar and Justice D.Y Chandrachud had made observation "that cases relating to honor killing should be tried in fast track court to get speedy justice and also made observation that the Khap Panchayat has no right to take law in their hands and cannot assume to be the law implementation agency." The judgement came in favour of Shakti Vahini a Non-governmental Organisation(NGO). (Shakthi Vahini Vs Union of India,2018)

In the case of ***Shafin Jahan vs Asokan K.M*** which is popularly known as ***"Hadiya case"*** also proved to be a landmark judgement for women's right to marry the person of her choice. Three judge bench of Supreme Court upholding Hadiyas marriage to Shafin Jahan and delivered its verdict in favour of Hadiya. (Shafin Jahan Vs Asokan,2018)A women name Hadiya who married to a Muslim guy name Shafin Jahan and after the marriage, she converted her faith in Muslim and changed her name. The parents of Hadiya successfully opposed her marriage in court, the high court maintained her father's claim to custody even though she was 25 years old. At that time the term "love jihad" was popularised by Indian Media as case highlighted and became part of debates and discussions. The apex held that "any individual have the freedom to choose religion and life partner of his choice as her basic and fundamental right" and granted her marriage valid and this is how the parental pressure was removed the garb of honor of the family. (Shafin Jahan vs Asokan K.M, 2018) The apex court as always tried to protect the life and the rights of individuals especially youngsters by their judgements which act as preventive action and shows light on this matter to deal with it strictly. Here the judge also plays an important role because he is considered as the architect of justice by adopting scientific, technical, procedural, methodological approach and expanded the horizon of fundamental rights and provide independent platform for redressing the grievances.

CONCLUSION

Honor related crimes have been common phenomenon in India in the past decade which become a social evil for many. It is very unfortunate that so many young people have lost their lives in the name of so-called honor in the contemporary world. The above-mentioned analysis of right to life with respect to honor killing clearly justifies that the honor killing violate the basic fundamental right which is considered as inalienable right. If we look out the instances of honor killing and analyze then it finds out that such crimes do not receive the required attention, and it is completely in mundane condition. The Court has many times condemned such actions and casual approaches taken by the government. However there has been a lack of political will from the side of legislative and non-committal toward this sensitive issue. In addition, caste hierarchies of society and social structure which overtly supported the caste-based structure have paved the difficult path to curb the menace of those cultural crimes. Since the crime has been ignored by the legislature, neither support came from public, in such condition it really become difficult for the law enforcement agencies to show concern towards the prevention or prosecution of the guilty. It is the need of the hour to have separate legislation for the honor killing to combat this socio legal issue before it takes an ugly turn, and the legislation should include the following:

- Special cells in each district have to be established which can provide safety to the young couples.
- There must be sufficient punishment which can deter the crime.
- Latches in Procedural law provision and leniency to grant bails should be eliminated. 'Religion' and 'Culture' cannot and must not be invoked as excuse for killing of women just because they express their desire or choice to the family members. The freedom of belief doesn't entail the freedom to kill. Only active laws can be the antidote to such dishonorable practices. There is no honor in honor killing.

REFERENCES

Abu Odeh, L. (1997). Comparatively speaking: The "honor" of the "East" and the "passion" of the "West.". *Utah Law Review*, 2, 287, 292–293.

Amnesty International, P. (2002). The tribal Justice system. Amnesty 2002, 33(24).

Ashwini, M. Shripad. (2024, January 27). killing honor in the name of honor killings. The New Indian Express. http://newindianexpress.com

Baker, N. V., Gregware, P. R., & Cassidy, M. A. (n.d.). Family killings fields: Honor rationales in the murder of women. *Violence Against Women*, 5(2), 164, 165, 171. DOI: 10.1177/107780129952005

Constitution of India,1950.

Rebecca Cook. (1994). State responsibility for violations of women's human rights. Harvard Human Rights Journal, 7, 125,127.

Eid J.A. (2020). A Qualitative Study of the Impact of Domestic Violence by Male Relatives on Saudi Female Students in the United States.

European Convention for Protection of Human Rights and Fundamental Freedoms, 1950.

Francis Carolie V. Union territory, Delhi, A.I.R 1981 S.C 746, 753.

Rana Husseini. (2002, June 12). Murder charge reduced to misdemeanour in Azraq crime of honor case. Jordan Times.

ICCPR,1966.

Indian Evidence Act, 1872

James J. Sing. (1999). Culture as sameness: toward a synthetic view of provocation and culture in criminal law. Yales Law Journal, 108(1845).

Jan, A. (2012). Socio-Legal Perspectives of Euthanasia, Jammu & Kashmir. Jay Kay Publisher, 50.

Jordanian Penal Code, 1960.

Kumar Rana, D., & Prasad Mishra, B. (n.d.). Honour Killings-A gross violation of Human rights & Its Challenges. www.ijhssi.org

Lata Singh vs State of Uttar Pradesh A.I.R. 2006 S.C. 2522.

Locke, J. (1980). *Second treatise of Government (C.B. Macpherson)*. Hackett.

Maneka Gandhi v Union of India. AIR 1978 SC.

Munn vs Illions,1877 94 U.S 113.

Puneet Kaur Grewal. (2012). Honor Killings and Law in India. IOSR Journal of Humanities and Social Sciences, 5.

Quraishi, A. (1996). Her honor: A critique of the rape laws of Pakistan from a women sensitive perspective. *Michigan Journal of International Law*, 18, 287.

Rachel, A. (1531). Ruane. (2000). Murder in the name of honor: Violence against women in Jordan and Pakistan. *Emory International Review*, 14, 1523.

Shafin Jahan vs Asokan K.M AIR 2018 SC 1933.

Shakthi Vahini Vs Union of India (2018) 7 SCC 192.

Universal Declaration on Human Right, 1948.

Velasquez Rodriguez case, Inter-American Court of Human Rights, judgment 27 July 1988, (Ser. C, No. 4), para. 172–4.

World Health Organisation. (2012). Femicide.

Yamani, M. (1996). Feminism and Islam: Legal and literary perspectives. New York University Press, 141–194.

Chapter 9
Honor Killing in the Indian Context:
Law Ought to Be

Harshita Singh
Amity University, Noida, India

Tulsi Gupta
GLA University, India

ABSTRACT

The value of Honor is highly regarded by all individuals, being a crucial part of human life. It is not acceptable for anyone to justify taking a life in the name of culture. Whether it is for personal or collective reasons, taking someone's life is always considered morally and legally wrong. It goes against the constitution, which guarantees every citizen the right to life and dignity. The Indian constitution ensures that every individual is protected from any harm to their life. Society and culture cannot override the right to live with dignity in society. Committing murder in the name of protecting family Honor does not restore or replace any perceived lost Honor. This chapter aims to examine the concept of Honor and Honor killings in India through a legal lens. It also looks at key court decisions to understand how the law is interpreted, ways to prevent Honor Killing effectively, and why India has not adequately addressed this issue within its legal system.

DOI: 10.4018/979-8-3693-9596-7.ch009

BACKGROUND

Every individual values Honor, which is an essential aspect of human existence. It is not acceptable for anyone to take away a precious human life in the name of culture or traditions. Regardless of individual or collective interests, killing someone is always morally and legally wrong, as it violates human rights. There is no legitimate reason to take someone's life without justification. Such an act is unconstitutional and against the law as the constitution guarantees the right to life and dignity to every citizen. This fundamental right is protected by the Indian constitution, ensuring that every person is safeguarded from any harm to their life. Every individual also has the right to make choices and express their opinions, including the right to marry and choose a partner freely. Societal and cultural pressures cannot infringe upon the right to live with dignity in society. Legislation has been enacted to address these unlawful practices of Honor killings. Killing someone under the guise of protecting family Honor will never restore or replace the so-called lost Honor; it amounts to murder. This chapter aims to analyze the concept of Honor and Honor killings in India within the framework of the law. It also discusses significant judgments made by the apex court to gain insights into the judicial interpretation of the law, effective measures to prevent Honor Killing and why India has failed to acknowledge and address the issue of Honor Killing within its legal system.

The most recent report from the National Crime Records Bureau (NCRB) for 2020 indicates that only 23 murders in the country were classified as honor killings. However, unofficial organizations like Evidence, which combat honor crimes, report that Tamil Nadu alone has seen 180 honor killings in the past five years. In 2022, there were 300 reported cases has seen in Uttar Pradesh. India holds the terrible distinction of being the state with the greatest number of murder cases related to honor killing. (Sripad, 2023), The NCRB has previously pointed out that crimes like honor killings are often seen as 'vague' and 'unreliable' in part because of unclear definitions, which results in their omission from final reports. Therefore, it is necessary to formalize the definitions and context of honor crimes for them to be properly acknowledged.

Research Methodology

The purpose of this chapter is to gain an understanding of honor killings. The information for this topic wax collected in the form of checking records from libraries/Newspaper/Magazines/Interviews/Sample/Surveterviews/Sample/Survey/Internet etc. Therefore, qualitative research strategies have been adopted for this study in order to address its objective covering both primary and secondary sources. Certain characteristics such as the participant's ethnicity, age, and gender need to be observed using qualitative methods to avoid biasness. From the primary and secondary research highlighting the need for a robust legal framework to address the issue in India. (Navratan Singh Fateh, 2012) After doing intensive research work honor killing are a grave infringement of the fundamental right to life with dignity and a significant human rights issue globally and the existing laws in India are inadequate to address honor killing. The chapter gives a clear understanding of honor killing in context with legal framework, that is law ought to be.

Key Terms

Core term include "honor killing" (Kishun, 2023) and "Gender bases violence" (Kaushal, 2020) established the direct connection between the issue of honor killings and its global relevance emphasizes the need for internationally cooperation. It calls on global actors to address this problem collectively by implementing laws and regulations to combat it. Broder theme like "legal action" (Dr.Pandey.J.N.,2015) and "legal obligation" (Shah, 2018) address the existing legal gap in preventing and addressing honor killing. "Blatant violation of human rights" (Rashika Bajpai,2016) and "gender violence" (Kaushal, 2020) contextualize the issue and exploring the complexities of gender-based crime in the society and infringement of basic right guaranteed by every domestic and international legal instrument across the world due to immoral behaviour triggered by social theories.

Inclusion criteria emphasized relevance, ensuring that only articles directly addressing honor killings, delinquent behaviours, or associated legal and cultural issues are considered. Exclusion criteria filtered out non-academic sources, such as blogs or opinion pieces, and articles with only tangential relevance to the topic. Conducted article research using academic databases like JSTOR, PubMed, and Google Scholar is crucial, employing targeted keywords such as "Honor Killing" (Anand Mishra,2010), "Gender-Based Violence" (Kaushal, K., 2020).and "legal action" (Pandey, 2015) and legal obligation (Shah, 2018) to identify the most pertinent studies for our paper.

Literature Review

Sneha Singh (2017) addresses the issue of honor killings, exploring their origins as a social issue in India and presenting various case studies that highlight the seriousness of these acts. She emphasizes the need for specific legislation in India and discusses the measures taken by the government and various commissions to combat such honor-related crimes. Keerthana R. Shenoi and Dr. S. Pandiaraj (2018), investigate the different factors contributing to honor killings in India, questioning the necessity for a codified legal framework addressing these crimes. They analyze the influence of a patriarchal society on honor killings and outline its underlying reasons. Singhal (2014) advocates for codified laws addressing honor killings in India in his paper, discussing how gender discrimination contributes to these crimes. He explains that the caste system serves as a fundamental cause of this societal issue, where individuals adhere to established codes of conduct, and those who deviate from these norms face ostracism.

R. Preethi and Dr. A. Sreelatha (2018) provide insights into the concept of honor killings, stressing the need to recognize the gravity of the crime and educate society about its implications while analyzing the triggers that lead to these incidents. They describe honor killings as actions undertaken by family members to restore familial purity, wherein a male family member may murder a female who allegedly dishonored the family. Such killings are often premeditated acts driven by external pressure from relatives, society, or neighbors, wherein the accused feels a sense of disgrace that incites them to act.

Future Research Directions

This chapter aims to critically examine the issue of honor killings, a significant concern in India and worldwide, by reviewing current legal frameworks and suggesting comprehensive reforms to combat this serious violation of human rights. Through this chapter the author focusses and emphasizes on the implementation of legislation on the grassroot level to combat this crime. It would be combat by implementing strong panchayat raj system because these matters generally happen in the rural areas and those areas still governed by khap panchayat (Kachhwaha, 2011). Also, it is important to implement strong legislation to uncover those crimes that never come in the eye of people. One thing that were lacking in research papers published earlier were that they do not give any suggestion regarding punitive measures and other effective measures to prevent honor killing but this chapter aims to provide various punitive measures and also suggests about the separate legislation to govern the matters of Honor Killing so that this social crime can be dealt with in more effective way so that the offenders will get appropriate punishment. (Singh, 2017)

The author is also emphasis on provision entrusted by Indian legal framework on honor killings through there is no specifically categorized as a distinct crime within its legal system. Perpetrators are usually charged under general provisions of the Indian Penal Code (IPC), such as Section 302 for murder, Section 307 for attempted murder, and Section 120B for conspiracy. The Criminal Procedure Code (CrPC) and the Indian Evidence Act offer frameworks for prosecuting these crimes, but they often overlook the socio-cultural motivations behind honor killings, treating them as regular homicides. This lack of specific legal focus diminishes recognition of the unique circumstances that fuel honor killings, which are frequently accepted or even encouraged by community or family norms.

Future inquiries should investigate why India's legal framework has not fully acknowledged honor killings as a specific crime. Thus, legal reforms in India should include establishing a dedicated law to address honor killings, acknowledging the social and cultural factors that motivate these acts and enforcing strict penalties for offenders, including families and community figures involved. Moreover, cases of honor killings should be prioritized, with special investigation teams created to ensure fair processes and safeguard witnesses, who are frequently threatened or pressured by the offenders. Research should also highlight the importance of gender-sensitive training for law enforcement, prosecutors, and the judiciary, as entrenched patriarchal attitudes in these institutions may lead to leniency in prosecution and sentencing. (Vishwanath & Palakonda, 2011) Subsequent research should explore how international human rights standards and responsibilities might impact domestic laws in India, prompting a recognition of honor killings as violations of fundamental rights, particularly the right to life, personal liberty, and dignity outlined in the Indian Constitution. Lastly, the chapter recommends creating a national registry to track and analyze honor killings for better data collection, along with victim compensation programs that offer financial, psychological, and legal support for survivors or the families of victims. By implementing these legal and preventive measures, honor killings can be effectively tackled, ensuring justice for victims and promoting greater gender equality and respect for individual freedoms in society. In future research on honor killing it is important to do a heterogeneous study to intensify the understanding and also amplifying the legislative efforts to combat with the issue of honor killing and eliminate this ill-practice from all spheres from our society (Mitra, 2018).

INTRODUCTION

Criminal law falls under public laws, which form the foundation of the justice system. These laws aim to provide security and protection to the public by prohibiting conduct that threatens public interests. They are closely connected to societal well-being and cultural values, shaping criminal jurisprudence. In India, cultural changes have influenced laws, such as the acceptance of love marriages and live-in relationships. The question that arises is whether the senior member of a family or clan should have the power to pass a judgment based on their emotions and put the lives of young individuals at risk simply because they chose to marry against their elders' wishes or against the traditions of the clan. The answer to this question unequivocally must be "No". This is because our society values personal freedom and dignity, and such treatment contradicts these values, especially when it is based on outdated beliefs. The concept of family Honor, regardless of how it is perceived, should not be given priority over an individual's right to choose, which is protected by our compassionate Constitution. This right to personal freedom deserves to be protected and nurtured so that it can thrive and flourish. It is also important to acknowledge that old customs must give way to new ones, and feudal perspectives should be forgotten to allow for the smooth passage of personal liberty. However, not all individuals are accepting of these changes, leading to cultural crimes like Honor killings. Honor crimes are complex and have been misunderstood for centuries. They occur across communities, cultures, religions, and nations, violating human rights and constitutional laws. A Research Study on "Honor Killings in Haryana, Punjab and Western Uttar Pradesh" was ordered by the National Commission for Women on December 22, 2009. It is also claimed that there has been a rampant increase in honor killings in Haryana, Punjab, and Western Uttar Pradesh, which has led to a sense of quail among young people who want to get married but are afraid to do so. The pressure from society and the inhumane treatment by certain groups who believe they are the lawmakers and impose cruel punishments create a climate of fear that drives victims to either commit suicide or endure severe suffering. These groups are supported by similar forces and behave as if they are above the law. They violate human rights and destroy fundamental rights under the guise of protecting class honor or group rights based on their distorted perception of honor. These individuals believe their actions are justified by following socially accepted norms and the ethical beliefs of their community, which leads to vigilantism. The group defines honor according to its own understanding and cleverly justifies its actions as normative.

A woman's existence in such a society is completely dependent on the male perspective of her family, community, and social circle. Sometimes, this perspective is based on inherited local values that are not easily understood. If a person chooses a life partner outside of the community's norms, it is seen as dishonorable and could ultimately result in their death by the hands of the community. A woman's reputation is determined by her behavior, and her family is put under pressure as a result. Sometimes, the family members become passive spectators or even active participants in the mistreatment, either because of their own determined behavior or an unwanted desire to redeem family pride.

The concept of Honor that we are discussing has many aspects. Sometimes, a young man can suffer from Honor killings or ruthless treatment at the hands of the girl's family if he falls in love with her or marries her. The community acts as a patriarchal monarch, treating wives, sisters, and daughters as subordinates without autonomy, desires, or identities of their own. The male members of the community emphasize the concept of status, only the presence of male dominance controls how Honor is perceived.

Honor-based crimes are actions that are associated with dishonorable behavior according to certain cultural norms. These actions include engaging in sexual activity outside of marriage, getting pregnant before marriage, being unfaithful, having relationships that are not approved by family or community, refuse the marriage as per the parents wish seeking divorce or custody of children subsequent to divorce, leaving the family home against the wish of family, causing scandal or gossip in the community, and even becoming a victim of rape. These crimes are particularly heinous as they often involve public acts of violence and humiliation, demonstrating a complete disregard for the law and the well-being of the victims. The perpetrators view their Honor as paramount, placing little value on the lives and feelings of others. Tragic examples of these crimes include murder in broad daylight, brutal attacks in front of witnesses, and acts of torture such as shaving heads or setting victims on fire. These incidents have been widely reported, causing outrage and disbelief among those who cannot fathom such abhorrent acts. A group called the parallel law enforcement agency, consisting of influential individuals from the same lineage or caste, gathers periodically to address issues affecting their community. They refer to themselves as Panchayats and possess the authority to mete out punishments for crimes and enforce social boycotts or mob killings. These Panchayats, sometimes known as Khap Panchayats, firmly believe in the righteousness of their duties and consider their actions unquestionable. The intensity of their meetings and discussions reflects their strong determination. These extra constitutional bodies, engaging in feudatory activities, do not hesitate to commit the crimes that are punishable under Indian law. This is primarily because the police do not take proper action against their violent acts, and the administration fails to question their functioning. In their collective actions, they disregard constitutional provisions and show no regard for human dignity. Article 21, which guarantees protection to life, liberty, and basic human rights, is ignored by these groups who, without any remorse, engage in Honor killings.

The right to life and dignity are guaranteed to every citizen, and societal and cultural pressures cannot infringe upon these rights. Legislation has been put in place to address Honor killings. The current focus is on understanding the true meaning of Honor killings, the causes behind them, evaluating existing laws, and studying past Supreme Court judgments to determine if new legislation is necessary. (Ram Kishan Kumar,2023)

Killed in the Name of Honor

The recent data from the United Nation Population Fund [UNFPA] reveals that approximately 5,000 women worldwide were murdered in the year 2000 in the name of Honor. However, the actual numbers are likely higher as many cases went unreported or were falsely labeled as suicides. This issue is prevalent in South Asia, the Middle East, and even some Western countries like the UK, USA, and Canada, particularly within immigrant communities. (Solberg & Kristin Elisabeth,2024) Honor killings are a global problem, but they are especially widespread in countries with deeply patriarchal societies, low literacy rates, and corrupt judicial systems. Women across the world face various forms of violence and abuse, ranging from dowry disputes to restrictions on marriage choices and property rights. Shockingly, studies indicate that up to 90% of women suffer from domestic violence at the hands of their husbands and in-laws, with many women unaware that their fundamental rights are being violated. The research also highlights that 9 out of 10 victims were killed due to allegations of extramarital relations, and the perpetrators were predominantly husbands, brothers, uncles, and grandparents. From these findings, it becomes apparent that Honor killings are more rooted in cultural factors rather than solely religious beliefs

Gender-Based Violence

Violence committed on the pretext of Honor has a significant impact on women and girls, but it should also be recognized that men can also be victims of such violence in certain situations. This is why Honor violence is categorized as a form of violence based on gender. Although it shares similarities with violence commits with women and girls, closely fitting to classify it as violence based on gender because it is driven by societal expectations of women's behavior in various aspects of their lives, while also affecting men who are gay, bisexual, or who choose to marry outside of their clan. Labeling violence on the pretext of Honor as domestic violence may suggest that it solely occurs within the family but separating it from violence commits in domestic relationships may lead to the marginalization of specific communities and create concerns about potential racism. Therefore, it is important to view Honor- related violence as a subset of violence based on gender.

The terms "gender-based violence" and "violence against women" are often used interchangeably, as most instances of violence based on gender are perpetrated by men against women. However, it is crucial to maintain that the concept should be viewed in the context of gender in order to highlight that violence committed against women is a manifestation of power inequality between genders. (Anand Mishra.2010) Treating violence related with Honor as violence based on gender also exposes the structural inequality of the Honor system. While a man can exert power and control over another man, such as a father forcing his son to solemnize marriage as per his wish, the son consequently exerts his own power and control over his wife. In this hierarchical structure, a woman who is already victimized by marriage against her wish is victimized once again. This reveals the unequal distribution of power and Honor within the family and society, with women and girls consistently being at the bottom. Amnesty International supports this viewpoint, stating that "so-called Honor killings [crimes] are based on a deeply rooted belief that women are objects and commodities, not people entitled to the same human dignity and rights as men."

The Legal System in India Regarding Honor Killings

The Indian Constitution serves as a guiding principle for governance and protection of citizens' rights. It includes provisions such as the Right to Equality, Prohibition of Discrimination, Abolition of Untouchability, Right to Freedom of Speech and Expression, Right to Life and Personal Liberty. Honor killings, primarily targeting women, are the form of gender violence that stifles individuals' ability to exercise their choices and violates their fundamental rights. Based on religion or caste, these killings cannot be justified and are completely incompatible with the Constitution. The Directive Principles of State Policy further emphasize the state's responsibility to provide means of subsistence and protect vulnerable individuals from exploitation and abandonment. Honor killings go against these principles as they endanger the lives of young people, teenagers, and married couples. Therefore, it is the state's duty to safeguard these individuals and their lives from such heinous acts.

The Indian Penal Code, 1860 and Criminal Procedure Code, 1973

Honor killing offenders are considered murderers, as mentioned previously. Identifying the culprits may be challenging as these acts of homicide often go undetected or protected by the community. However, it is still possible. The perpetrator may use Section 300 of the Indian Penal Code as a defense, arguing that their actions were a result of grave provocation and not premeditated. They claim to have acted purely on the emotional response to the victim's dishonorable actions towards their family. Other sections, such as 304 and 307, are also considered in assessing the act of murder. These killings are categorized under murder (Section 302) and culpable homicide (Section 304). In northern states, Khap Panchayats, who have authority over the judicial system, often order death sentences against their own family members, making it challenging for law enforcement to identify the true perpetrators. Due to the failure of the law to identify and gather evidence, police rarely file FIRs (First Information Reports), and even when cases are pursued, the conviction rate is practically non-existent. Khap Panchayats seem to disregard the legal formalities prescribed in the criminal procedural code for registering FIRs.

The Indian Evidence Act of 1872

The Indian Evidence Act of 1872 serves as the foundation for establishing proof in court cases, aiming to punish those involved in the concealment of facts before, during, or after a crime. Section 13 of the Act is particularly relevant in understanding Honor killings as it outlines the relevant facts when determining the existence of any right or custom. This Act aims to provide justice to individuals who suffer due to judgments made by Khap panchayats. These organizations have their own approach to handling situations, which may not always align with legal regulations.

The Indian Majority Act, 1857 addresses the issue of a person's legal age for various purposes. According to section 3, individuals domiciled in India are considered to have reached the age of majority when they turn 18, unless their personal laws state otherwise. However, if a guardian is assigned to a child, the age of majority is extended to 21. This Act becomes relevant in cases of Honor killings, particularly when Khap panchayats forcibly separate married couples who are eligible for marriage based on age or other factors. In such cases, the Act helps establish the disregard for the law exhibited by Khap panchayat members, who violate the provisions outlined in this Act.

The Hindu Marriage Act, 1955

The Hindu Marriage Act, 1955 lays down the fundamental requirements for a legally recognized marriage. Section 5 specifies that there are certain degrees of forbidden relationships that must be maintained for a marriage to be considered valid. Both civil and criminal laws aim to protect marital relationships by providing appropriate remedies in civil law and imposing severe penalties in criminal law. The Act does not impose restrictions on the choice of marriage partner, thereby permitting inter-caste marriages among Hindus.

Special Marriage Act, 1956

The Special Marriage Act, 1956 is designed to facilitate marriages without considering the caste, class, or religion of Indian citizens. It allows for the recognition and registration of inter-caste marriages. Due to the rigid caste system prevalent in Indian society, inter-caste marriages are more common in urban areas than in rural areas. The Act states that the parties involved must not be in prohibited relationships, but if a tradition followed by at least one of the parties allows for their marriage despite being in a prohibited relationship, it may be solemnized.

The Scheduled Castes and Scheduled Tribes (Prevention of Atrocities) Act, 1989

The Indian Parliament passed this Act with the intention of preventing acts of cruelty against the Scheduled Castes and Scheduled Tribes. The main objective of the Act was to facilitate the integration of Dalits into mainstream Indian society. Examples of atrocities covered by the Act include assaulting, dishonoring, and violating the modesty of a SC/ST woman, as well as exploiting them sexually and forcing them to disconnect from their families or communities. The Act acknowledges that Honor killings are connected to caste and religion and has been enacted to address this issue.

Protection of Women from Domestic Violence Act, 2005

Although there are various laws in place to protect women's rights, such as the Protection of Women from Domestic Violence Act, 2005, Honor killings remain prevalent, leading to severe human rights violations.

The Protection of Human Rights (Amendment) Act, 2006

The Protection of Human Rights (Amendment) Act, 2006 aims to safeguard the rights of all individuals and establishes commissions and courts to achieve this objective. Despite these measures, Honor killings persist, indicating a failure in the legal system to fully comprehend and address this issue. There is currently no specific law specifically addressing Honor killings, resulting in a lack of legal definition and recognition of the crime, inadequate protection for couples who choose their own partners, insufficient prevention measures, accountability, and penalties. Because many of these deaths are classified as either murder or culpable homicide, the true extent of Honor killings remains unknown, with no accurate data or organized record-keeping by the government.

Honor Killing Deserve Legal Attention

The Indian government's Department of home should step forward and collaborate with State Governments to promote knowledge within law enforcement agencies and engage all relevant parties in developing strategies to prevent violence, ensuring social justice and adherence to the rule of law. To Combat such violence, it is important to create an institutional mechanism that promotes coordination among all parties involved. This includes the collaboration between state government and the central government to raise awareness and enforce social initiatives among law enforcement agencies, in case where Khap Panchayat gatherings persist, the supreme court has established guidelines for the police forces to implement corrective actions.

1. **Remedial Measures:**
   a) In the event that the local authorities are informed about a Khap Panchayat happening and enforcing measures against a couple or family engaged in a marriage that goes against caste religion, they should promptly lodge a First information report under Indian penal code specifically section 141,143,503 in conjunction with 506of IPC.
   b) Once the First information report lodge, it is essential to immediately notify the Superintendent of police/Deputy Superintendent of police, who must ensure that the investigation into the crime is conducted promptly and effectively until its final resolution.
   c) Furthermore, it is important to take prompt action in order to ensure the safety of the couple or family and, if required, move them to a secure location within the same district or another area. This should be done while taking into consideration their safety and any potential threats they may face. The State Government could consider setting up safe houses in each District Headquarter to address this issue.
   d) Special cells should be established in all districts, consisting of the Superintendent of police and the district social welfare officer.

These cellular structures will be responsible for addressing the complaints of harassment and danger towards inter caste couples. Furthermore, the cells must establish a helpline that operates 24/7 to receive and record complaints, as well as offer the required support and advice for the protection of couples. Failure to adhere to these guidelines by the Supreme Court, or lack of adequate action from law enforcement officials to prevent or investigate incidents related to Honor-based crimes, will result in the following measures being implemented. (Keesari Rajitha and Another vs The State of Telangana, 2022)

2. **Punitive Measures:**
   (a) Failure by police or district officers to comply with the mentioned instructions will be seen as intentional neglect or misconduct. In such instances, departmental action must be taken in accordance with the service regulations. The departmental action needs to be initiated and finalized within six months by primary authority.

(b) In line with the ruling in Arumugam Servai, the States are directed to take disciplinary measures against officials who were aware of an incident but failed to prevent it or did not promptly apprehend and initiate legal proceedings against the offenders after the incident occurred.

Proposed Effective Methods to Prevent "Honor Killing"

The persistence of honor killing is rooted in the belief that it represents the loss of honor, which is primarily seen as a right to be respected. However, it is crucial to recognize that honor is not just about earning respect, but also about deserving respect.

1) The evident need for a major shift in attitudes towards women is urgent. It is necessary to consistently voice our concerns and confront practices and cultural aspects in both Muslim and non-Muslim nations that undermine the dignity and respect of all individuals, regardless of their gender.
2) To end the nightmare of violence and murder, we must find the inner strength to continue the struggle. Only by changing and upholding the concept of Honor to value and preserve lives instead of claiming them, can we achieve this.
3) Creating a distinct offence for honor killings would provide law enforcement agencies with greater clarity. One suggestion is to modify the Indian Evidence Act so that the burden of proof rests on the accused, making the Khap panchayat or the family members responsible for proving their innocence. Under the proposed law, both the Khap panchayat and the individual carrying out the killing would be held jointly liable for punishment.
4) At present, the definition and clarity regarding Honor Killing/ crime is lacking. The new law aims to address this and provide protection to couples through various measures. This includes giving special powers to magistrates at the district level and establishing a special police cell in each district. The new law also emphasizes on coordination among all stakeholders and sensitizing law enforcement agencies. It will also focus on social initiatives and awareness to prevent such violence. The scope of honor crimes should include all crimes against women that are committed by the community, such as branding women as witches, parading them naked, and subjecting them to public torture. These heinous offenses need to be addressed with a special law that includes stringent punishments, which can act as a deterrent.
5) The main idea is that Community Action Grants aim to assist local communities in their efforts to decrease violence against women and to implement zero tolerance programs in local sports clubs.

6) Community Action Grants aim to facilitate the efforts of local communities in combatting violence against women, as well as foster the establishment of zero tolerance initiatives within local sporting clubs.

Some Legal Suggestions

1. There should be a specific law implemented to address Honor killings, with stringent punishment measures put in place.
2. Public awareness needs to be raised about the crime of Honor killings and the remedies available to victims for seeking justice against their perpetrators. People should be educated about the complaints process and the legal options that victims can rely on.
3. Society needs to change its mindset and give importance to the choices made by individuals, whether they are men or women, regarding marriage.
4. The significance attributed to the caste system should be relaxed.
5. Khap panchayats, which have no legal recognition, should be completely abolished and declared illegal.
6. Education plays a crucial role in preventing Honor killings. Since a majority of illiterate individuals reside in rural areas and belong to economically and socially disadvantaged communities, women in particular are often marginalized and more susceptible to becoming victims of Honor killings.

Why India has Failed to Acknowledge and Address the Issue of Honor Killings Within its Legal System

Dr. B. R Ambedkar once stated that challenging societal norms as a reformer requires more bravery than challenging the government as a politician. However, despite the rising number of Honor-based crimes and the outrage expressed in Indian courts, successive governments have failed to address this issue. There are no legal definitions or protections for Honor killings, no safeguards for couples who choose their own partners, no preventative measures for these crimes, and no accountability or punishment for the offenders. Moreover, due to the lack of legal recognition, there is no available data on Honor crimes in the National Crime Records Bureau. In 2009, a motion was introduced to establish a separate law to address Honor crimes, with the support of members from various political parties. However, the Home Minister at the time argued against the need for a separate law, as Honor killings are already considered murder. A comprehensive bill titled "The Prevention of Crime in the name of Honor and Tradition Bill" was drafted by the legal branch of the All-Indian Women's Democratic Association in 2010 and submitted to the government. This bill outlines the definition of Honor crimes, identifies various related offenses, proposes preventative measures, and suggests punishments. It also encompasses the accountability of law enforcement and administration, as well as the involvement of caste or community-based bodies like Khap panchayats. Regrettably, the government did not advance the bill, despite its endorsement by the National Commission of Women. Two years later, in 2012, the Law Commission of India presented its own version of the bill, titled the "Prohibition of Unlawful Assembly (Interference with the Freedom of Matrimonial Alliance) Bill, 2011". However, this bill primarily focuses on unlawful assemblies formed by caste panchayats to prevent self-choice marriages and fails to comprehensively address the overarching issue.

The Stance of Indian Judiciary Against Honor Killing

In the matter of Lata Singh v/s State of Uttar Pradesh and Another (Lata Singh V State of Uttar Pradesh & Anr.,2006) it was established that consensual relationship between two consenting adults is not a crime. The court declared that a women is free to marry or cohabitate with whomever she desires. The petitioner in this case was a woman who married a man from a different caste and began living with him. Her brother filed a criminal complaint against her husband, but the court quashed the trial, stating that no offense was committed and the case was an abuse of the court's process.

In S. Khushboo V Kanniammal & Another (S. Khushbhoo Vs Kanniammal & Anr, 2010) the Supreme Court affirmed that while society generally expects sexual relations to occur only within marriage, there is no legal offense committed when adults willingly engage in sexual relations outside of marriage, except for adultery. The court referred to its previous decision in the case Lata Singh, which stated that a consensual relationship between adults is not a crime, despite being perceived as immoral. It emphasized that a woman is free to marry or live with anyone she chooses.

In the case of Bhagwan Dass v/s State of Delhi, the Court deemed Honor killings to be the most severe category of cases deserving of the death penalty. It called for the eradication of these savage and feudal practices, which reflect poorly on the nation. The court declared that the death penalty should serve as a deterrent for such outrageous and uncivilized behavior, warning potential perpetrators of Honor killings that they will face execution.

In Ashish Sharma and Another v. State of UP and others, the court recognized the various factors that impact the lives and security of married couples in India. Casteism, religious prejudice, Honor killings, and forced separation of couples by their families or parents all violate the right to life and personal liberty enshrined under Article 21 of the Indian Constitution. The court emphasized that such actions are not disguised, but rather clear violations of Article 21. Although Western culture has not been widely accepted in Indian society, it does not mean that the right of adult men and women to choose their life partners should be interfered with in all circumstances. (Grewal, 2012)

CONCLUSION

The act of Honor killing is done to protect the reputation and honor of a family, but taking someone's life, especially someone close to one's heart, cannot be justified in any way. It is not worth it and goes against the principles of dignity and fairness that everyone deserves. Religion and laws can be interpreted differently by different individuals, but they should never be used as excuses to harm or kill others, especially women. Aggressive legislation is necessary to combat such cruel acts, as there is no faith or culture that can justify Honor killing. However, even with laws in place, some offenders manage to escape punishment due to loopholes in the legal system. One such loophole is the lack of a specific law against Honor killing in India. By properly implementing the existing laws and legal standards, we can make progress in saving lives. However, relying solely on laws is not enough to eliminate the threat of Honor killings. It is important to reform people's mindsets and mentalities to truly eradicate this crime.

REFERENCES

Ashwini M Sripad,(2023),killing honor in the name of honor killings, Indian Express

Bajpai, R. (2016) Killing in the name of Honor: Blatant violation of humanrights, Journal on Contemporary Issues of Law, Vol.2, Issue 6.

Code of Criminal Procedure. (1973).

Dr. Pandey. J.N.,(2015) Constitutional Law of India Allahabad: Central Law Agency,

Grewal, P. K. (2012). Honor killings and Law in India, *IOSR. Journal of the Humanities and Social Sciences*, 5(6).

Jyothi Vishwanath and Srinivas.C Palakonda, (2011) Patriarchal Ideology of Honorand Honor Crimes in India, International Journal of Criminal JusticeSciences, Vol. 6

Jyothi Vishwanath and Srinivas.C Palakonda,(2011) Patriarchal Ideology of Honour and Honour Crimes in India, International Journal of Criminal Justice Sciences, Vol. 6 Issue 1,2,

Kavitha Kachhwaha,(2011) Khap Adjudication in India: Honouring the Culture with Crimes, International Journal of Criminal Justice Sciences, Vol.6, Issue 1&2,

Kaushal, K. (2020). No Honor in Honor Killing: Comparative Analysis of Indian Traditional Social Structure vis-à-vis Gender Violence. *ANTYAJAA: Indian Journal of Women and Social Change*, 5(1), 52–69.

Keesari Rajitha And Another vs The State Of Telangana . (2022). 27117.

Lata Singh V State of Uttar Pradesh & Anr. (2006)... *SCC*, 5, 475.

Mishra, A. (n.d.). *Honor Killing : The law It Is and The Law Ought To Be*. Manupatra.

Mitra, N. (2018). Routine unrecognized sexual violence in India. *New Feminist Perspectives on Embodiment*, 183-200.

Navratan Singh Fateh,2012 honor killing

Puneet Kaur Grewal. (2012) Honor Killings and Law in India, IOSR Journal ofHumanities and Social Science, Vol.5, Issue 6.

Ram Kishun Kumar. (2023). Honor killing: Challenges Indian Judicial System. *IJCRT.*, 2320–2882.

S. Khushboo vs Kanniammal & Anr (2010). *SCC, 5, 600*

Section 302. (1860). *Indian Penal Code*. Retrieved June 3, 2024, from https://lddashboard.legislative.gov.in/sites/default/files/A1860-45.pdf

Section 304. (1860). *Indian Penal Code*. Retrieved June 3, 2024, from https://lddashboard.legislative.gov.in/sites/default/files/A1860-45.pdf

Singhal, V. (2014). Honour killing in India: An assessment. *Available at SSRN 2406031*.

Sneha singh,(2017) Honour Killings in India: Need for composite and strict legal framework, International Journal of Interdisciplinary and multidisciplinary studies, Vol.4, Issue 3,

Solberg, & Kristin Elisabeth. (2024). Killed in the Name of Honor. *The Lancet, London, 373*(9679). from https://www.proquest.com/docview/199045895?sourcetype=Scholarly%20Journals

Vesvikar, M., & Agarwal, M. (2022). HONOR KILLING IN INDIA. *Perspectives in Social Work*, 31(1), 48–62.

Chapter 10
The Legal Framework for Murder on Provocation in the Egyptian Penal Code as a Type of Honor Killing

Ramy El-Kady
https://orcid.org/0000-0003-2208-7576
Police Academy, Egypt

ABSTRACT

The chapter explores the legal provisions regarding murder on provocation in the Egyptian penal code, specifically in relation to honor killings, a form of violence against women. It provides a legal justification for reducing punishment for murder committed by a husband who witnesses his wife engaging in adultery and kills her. Honor killings are characterized by premeditation and intent, as specified in the legal statutes. The chapter uses a comparative descriptive-analytical method to understand the concept of honor killings, its definitions, and variations in Arab legislation. It also examines the correlation between honor killings and religion and the act of murder based on provocation as outlined in the Egyptian penal code. The chapter also explores the lenient treatment of honor crimes in Egypt through the application of judges' clemency as stipulated in Article 17 of the Egyptian penal code.

INTRODUCTION

Some societies know the phenomenon of honor killing. Despite its conflict with divine laws and international conventions that prohibit the killing of a human being, regardless of the justifications or motives for it, it exists in some societies

DOI: 10.4018/979-8-3693-9596-7.ch010

according to the prevailing social customs. Although honor killings are illegal, they still occur every year.

It is shameful that some people resort to extreme measures such as killing their family members, and it is essential to realize that this behavior is unacceptable and that those responsible must be held accountable for their actions. Although divine laws, especially Islamic law, criminalize honor killing, the Egyptian legislature has considered it a legal excuse that reduces the punishment of the perpetrator.

Significance of the Study

The significance of this study is highlighted in its dealing with comparative legislation that takes a unique approach to dealing with the crime of honor killing by reviewing the Egyptian legislative approach, which is followed by several legislations in many Arab countries; this is a legislative trend that is worth highlighting. Additionally, the importance of the study appears with the literature on this topic, which varies based on the philosophy implemented in the legislation of different countries and claims that most Arab legislation allegedly includes provisions that grant partial or complete immunity to individuals who commit honor killings (Zaid, 2015). Hence, this study aims to focus on the trend of Egyptian legislation in dealing with honor killing from the perspective of criminal law.

Objectives of the Study

This chapter aims to shed light on the legal framework for Murder on Provocation in the Egyptian penal Code as a type of Honor Killing, which provides a legal excuse mitigating the penalty for the crime of murder if it is committed by a husband who sees his wife red-handed in adultery and kills her immediately. This is a form of murder with passion stipulated in the law.

Methodology

This study will use a comparative descriptive-analytical method, which addresses the phenomenon in all aspects, with a review the comparative experiences organized for this topic. The descriptive-analytical method is defined as *"the study of the phenomenon as it exists in reality, describing it closely and expressing it qualitatively or quantitatively to reach conclusions that contribute to understanding and developing this reality"* (Crootof, 2019); this approach aims to research and analyze the phenomenon of Honor Killing and the excuse of Murder on Provocation in the Egyptian penal code from its criminal legal aspects.

Chapter Plan

This chapter's topic will be explained in two parts: the first will introduce Honor Killing, its definitions, and the differences in trends in Arab legislation regarding honor killing. The nexus between Honor Killing and Religion will also be studied. The second will explain murder based on Provocation in the Egyptian Penal Code as a form of murder by passion and the application of the clemency of judges by Article 17 of the Egyptian Penal Code as a lenient treatment of honor crimes in Egypt.

PART ONE: INTRODUCTION OF HONOR KILLING

Definition of Honor Killing

There are several definitions of honor killing, which is known as shame killing and can be defined as *"a form of killing in which a person is killed by their family or relatives, usually for allegedly bringing shame to the family. This type of killing is most common in countries with conservative cultural norms. Honor killings often occur when someone commits a perceived crime, such as adultery or refusing an arranged marriage"* (Oberwittler & Kasselt, 2014).

Honor killing is murder directed against women and girls and is also a gender-motivated murder, or it is a form of violence against women. Hence, the crime of honor killing can be considered from this perspective as *"a murder that a male member of a family or a male relative of the same family against a female or a group of females in the same family often commits,"* where the perpetrator murders for reasons that are most often speculatively related to suspicions about the female (woman, girl, etc.) committing an immoral act in the eyes of the perpetrator, and the perpetrators of such crimes claim that their crime occurred to *"preserve the honor of the family,"* or what is described in Tribal circles with the process of *"washing shame."* Honor killing is the act of male family members murdering a woman or girl because they believe she has brought dishonor or humiliation to the family's name, reputation, or prestige (Oberwittler & Kasselt, 2014).

Main Reasons for Honor Killing

Therefore, honor killing, or shame killing, is *"murder often committed by a male member of a family or a male relative of the same family against a female or a group of females in the same family"* because the perpetrators believe that the victim has brought shame and humiliation on the family, or violated the principles of society or religion, and usually killing for reasons such as Divorce or separation from spouse, refusing to consent to an arranged marriage, being in a relationship that is not satisfactory to the family, having sex before marriage or outside marriage, being a victim of sexual rape or sexual assault, wearing clothes considered inappropriate (scandalous- indecent), engaging in sexual relations that are not a male-to-female relationship (heterosexual is the opposite of the concept of homosexuality), and apostasy from religion (Ragini, 2021).

Current Statistics of Honor Killing

A report prepared by the United Nations in 2020 indicated that approximately 5,000 people are victims of "honor killings," most of whom are females, annually in conservative societies, where they are killed by suffocation, burning, stoning, or stabbing. Honor killings have become common in many countries, which prompts human rights and international organizations to demand stricter penalties for this type of crime.

In Egypt, statistics from the National Center for Social and Criminological Research revealed family crimes, most of which fall under the name "honor crimes." These crimes are committed by spouses, parents, or siblings out of jealousy for "honor and washing away shame." The report confirmed that 70% of honor killings were committed by husbands against their wives, and 20% were committed by brothers against their sisters. While fathers committed only 7% of these crimes against their daughters, the remaining 3% were honor crimes. Sons committed it against their mothers at a time when the number of victims of honor crimes ranged from 900 to 2,000 crimes annually.

The independent research institute, Daftar Ahwal, monitored 371 patients who died or experienced injury. Under the pretext of "honor," it took place in Egypt during the period extending from January 1, 2015, until December 31, 2019. "Suspicion of behavior" was the cause of the most significant number of deaths, with a total of 231 deaths (4 males, 227 females). This was followed by the motive of "leaving home," with a total of 41 cases (all females), while "doubt about the child's lineage" claimed the most significant number of male deaths (13 males and 12 females, for a total of 25 deaths). The most common method used to carry out these crimes was stabbing, with a total of 104 cases. This method was followed by the "suffocation/drowning" method, with a total of 75 cases.

Areas Where Honor Killing is Widespread

Studies indicate that the phenomenon of honor killing is predominantly linked to the Greater Middle East and the Indian subcontinent. However, they also have historical roots in other civilizations, including the Philippines, Northern Caucasus, and Mediterranean Europe. They are also common among immigrant communities in nations where there are no other societal norms that promote honor killings. Honor killings are commonly linked to rural and tribal regions. However, they also occur in urban settings (De Guzman & Jamias, 2016).

Differences in Trends in Arab Legislation Regarding Honor Killing

The literature has shown some discrepancies between the trends of Arab legislation in dealing with honor crimes, including the exemption from sanctions, which varies in terms of its applicability, the specific act to which the exemption applies, and the intended beneficiaries of such exemption. The scope of applicability of honor crime laws differs depending on whether they provide complete immunity from punishment or decrease offender penalties. In Jordan, for example, the legal code offers a total exemption from penalty for husbands who catch their wives committing adultery. On the other hand, in Egypt, the legal code grants husbands a partial exemption from punishment in such cases but not a complete exemption as in Jordan.

The type of act to which the exemption applies differs depending on the specific act. For instance, the Egyptian legal code restricts acts that qualify for partial exemption to only cases of adultery. In contrast, the Jordanian legal code broadens the exemption to encompass various scenarios beyond adultery or ambiguous behaviors. Consequently, the exemption is occasionally broadened to encompass more scenarios beyond adultery (Odeh, 2010).

Regarding the beneficiaries of the exemption, the codes vary in terms of who qualifies for the exemption. According to Egyptian law, only husbands are excluded from punishment in cases of sexual misconduct, while Jordanian law includes all male relatives of the woman, not just husbands. This means that anyone unable to marry the woman due to blood relations, nursing, or existing marriages is also protected under the law (Zaid, 2015).

Is There a Nexus Between Honor Killing and Religion?

The answer to this question is critical from a practical standpoint. Honor killing is linked to many cultural factors, social customs, and traditions, and religion does not affect accepting this form of killing. Contrary to this opinion, some believe religion is related to this criminal phenomenon, so some say the practice transcends cultural and religious boundaries (Mayell, 2002).

The European Union adopted the first view that honor killing is due to cultural, not religious, reasons. Resolution 1327 (2003) of the Council of Europe acknowledges that "honor crimes" are not based on religious beliefs but rather on cultural traditions and are committed globally, particularly in patriarchal societies or communities. However, the majority of reported cases in Europe have been observed within Muslim or migrant Muslim communities, even though Islam does not endorse capital punishment for honor-related offenses.

A multitude of Muslim commentators and groups denounce honor killings as a cultural phenomenon that is not based on Islamic principles (Esposito, 2011). The Qur'an does not mention honor killing, which refers to the extrajudicial assassination of a woman by her own family. It is important to note that this practice contradicts Islamic law (Malik et al., 2019; Muhammad & BCPsych, 2013).

There is no prominent Muslim scholar, whether from the medieval or modern era, who has approved of a man murdering his wife or sister as a means of preserving her or the family's honor. For a woman or man to be subject to the death penalty for engaging in sexual intercourse outside of marriage, the evidence necessary by the Koran must be provided. This evidence can be in the form of a confession or the testimony of four male witnesses who are considered reputable by the court and who personally witnessed the act of penetration (Brown, 2014).

In addition, whereas honor killings are prevalent in Muslim nations such as Pakistan, they are virtually unheard of in other Muslim countries such as Indonesia, Bangladesh, and Senegal. These data corroborate the notion that honor killing is influenced primarily by societal culture rather than religion (Malik et al., 2019; Muhammad & BCPsych, 2013).

Murder on Provocation as a Type of Honor Killing

Honor killing encompasses a wide range of tactics used to commit murder, such as stoning, stabbing, beating, burning, beheading, hanging, throat slicing, lethal acid attacks, shooting, and strangulation. Occasionally, communities carry out public homicides as a means of cautioning other community members about the potential repercussions of participating in activities that are perceived as unlawful (Domazetoska et al., 2014).

PART TWO: MURDER ON PROVOCATION IN THE EGYPTIAN PENAL CODE

Many societies suffer from the phenomenon of honor killing; in Egypt, honor crimes are not explicitly defined in legislation. Despite the lack of explicit mention, certain scholars argue that Egypt effectively includes honor crimes in its legal system. They point to Article 17, which grants courts the authority to show leniency in sentencing for crimes based on the specific circumstances, and Article 237, which provides a reduced punishment for husbands who kill their adulterous wives (Leonard, 2020; Zaid, 2015; Odeh, 2010; Welchman & Hossain, 2005; Khafagy, 2005; Abu-Odeh, 1997).

In this section, we shed light on the legal analysis of the texts of the Egyptian penal code regarding killing motivated by provocation as a form of honor killing that takes a broader concept that includes other forms of violence against women. Intentional murder in the Egyptian Penal Code is a criminal act punishable by aggravated imprisonment, life imprisonment, or death, depending on the availability of aggravating circumstances.

Notably, the Egyptian legislature punishes the crime of honor killing in its general sense. However, the law, as an exception, has created a mitigating circumstance for the punishment for this crime if there is a specific case governing this crime, which is killing motivated by provocation. The legal framework for criminalizing murder motivated by provocation in Egyptian law was organized by the Egyptian legislature, which set special regulations and conditions so that the number of sentences imposed on the killer could be reduced.

The general rule is that the killer is subject to the legal provisions stipulated for the penalty of murder in Articles 234 and 236 of the Egyptian penal Code. At the same time, the legislature provided an exception that included mitigating the punishment for the husband who murders out of provocation according to specific circumstances stipulated by the legislature to regulate the provisions of this circumstance that reduce the punishment, which represents an exception to the general penalty prescribed for the crime of murder.

The general rule in the Egyptian penal Code is to punish murderers with aggravated imprisonment or life imprisonment, as Article (234/1) stipulates that (*whoever intentionally kills a person shall be punished with life imprisonment or aggravated imprisonment without prejudice to the reduced penalties specified in Article 17 of the Penal Code*). Article 17 of the Penal Code concerns implementing the rules of judges' clemency in applying punishment by the legislator's discretionary authority.

According to certain circumstances and conditions specified by the legislature, the Egyptian legislature has provided one exception that reduces the punishment of the murderer if the perpetrator of the murder is the husband. Suppose the mitigating circumstance of the punishment is met. In that case, the general text of the sentence is applied, which may lead to aggravated imprisonment or life imprisonment, according to specific considerations. The legislator estimated it to reduce the punishment for the perpetrator of the crime of murder, as Article 237 of the Penal Code stipulates that (*whoever surprises his wife in the act of adultery and kills her on the spot and whoever commits adultery with her shall be punished with imprisonment instead of the penalties stipulated in Articles 234 and 236 of the Penal Code*).

Some believe that this form of murder is a form of murder with passion (Srour, 2019), and the reason for reducing the sentence is the state of provocation to which the perpetrator is exposed when he surprises his wife committing adultery. This ruling adopted by the Egyptian legislature is not intended to authorize murder but rather to take into account the circumstances that occurred during the crime and require mitigation.

The criminalization of murder in criminal legislation is in fulfillment of international conventions that establish the human right to life, most notably Article 3 of the Universal Declaration of Human Rights, which stipulates that "every human being has the right to life" as well as what was specified in the International Covenant on Civil and Political Rights issued in 1966. (*every human being has the right to life inherent in him, protected by law, and no one is deprived of it arbitrarily*) (Srour, 2019).

Murder Motivated by Provocation as a Form of Murder by Passion

Some believe that honor killing is a form of murder by passion, which the author supports, as murder by passion is one of the topics concerned with criminal jurisprudence, and murder by passion is defined as *murder committed under intense emotional feelings such as anger or extreme provocation* (Srour, 2019). There is no dispute in jurisprudence about the availability of criminal intent in the case of murder with passion. There is no contradiction between the intention to kill, the loss of life, and a state of anger or provocation. However, this situation may negate the possibility of premeditation as an aggravating circumstance of punishment in murder if it is proven that it has prevented sufficient time for adequate and balanced thinking. The absence of a premeditated circumstance does not negate the criminal intent that constitutes the moral element of the crime (Srour, 2019).

A question has arisen in jurisprudence about the nature of the circumstance of provocation for the husband in the crime of murder and whether murder under the influence of provocation is suitable for mitigating judicial circumstances or mitigating legislative excuses. A part of criminal jurisprudence believes that passion for killing, no matter how severe, should not be considered an excuse that prevents punishment to protect the right to life from being tampered with. Some legislation, such as the Swiss Penal Code, has attempted to address this situation by making it a mitigating excuse for punishment under certain conditions, according to Article 133, which stipulates punishment—attenuated (if the killing was under the influence of intense emotion) (Srour, 2019).

A part of criminal jurisprudence believes that it is not sufficient to say that the killing was under the influence of intense emotion and that it was motivated by the vile grudges of the perpetrator, his selfish feelings, or his moral weakness. Instead, external circumstances must arouse the perpetrator. This indication undoubtedly depends on the psychological and moral makeup of the perpetrator, which is why it is necessary to examine the character of the criminal on the hill with emotion, as it may become apparent that although the motive for the killing was extreme excitement or provocation, the criminal is extremely dangerous. In this case, it is not helpful to punish him lightly. Instead, he must be treated punitively and appropriately, which may be necessary to impose precautionary measures on him (Srour, 2019).

As previously mentioned, Egyptian law does not define murder for passion except in one case, which is murder for provocation in the case of the wife's adultery. The Egyptian legislature considered this provocation a mitigating excuse for punishment by Article 237 of the Egyptian penal Code. Instances of other provocation or arousal are subject to general rules. Lenient punishment and its discretion are left to the trial judge according to what the court determines of the circumstances of the case and the accused (Srour, 2019).

Historical and Global Context

Several scholars argue that legal regimes can incentivize honor killings. These laws exhibit leniency toward murderers while simultaneously criminalizing certain behaviors, such as extramarital sex, "indecent" dressing in public places, or homosexual sexual acts. These laws serve to reassure perpetrators of honor killings that individuals engaging in these behaviors should be punished (Cusack & Cook, 2007; Welchman & Hossain, 2005; Abu-Odeh, 2004; Sonbol, 2003).

The murder on provocation is not a unique crime to Egyptian legislation but rather a crime known from time immemorial in many ancient and comparative legislations, and it is also known to several Arab legislations. Historically, during the Roman Empire, Augustus Caesar introduced the Lex Julia de adulteries coerced legislation that allowed fathers to kill their daughters and their lovers if they were found guilty of adultery. Additionally, the law permitted husbands to kill their wife's lovers if she was found guilty of adultery (Woolf, 2005).

Provocation in English law and related laws on adultery in English law, along with Article 324 of the French penal code of 1810, were legal principles that permitted less punishment for a husband who murdered his wife and her lover if he caught them in the act of adultery. Law no. 617/75 Article 17, enacted on 7 November 1975, abolished Article 324 of the French penal code from 1810 (Almusleh, 2021).

The Middle Eastern Arab countries replicated the 1810 penal code Article 324, which Napoleon enacted. Jordan's Article 340, which was inspired by this incident, initially allowed for the killing of a wife and her lover if they were caught in the act by the husband. However, the article has since been modified to include specific factors that may reduce the severity of punishment (Almusleh, 2021).

France's penal code Article 324 from 1810 inspired the Ottoman penal code Article 188 in 1858. French Article 324 and Ottoman Article 188 were references to create Jordan's Article 340. Despite a 1944 revision of Jordan's laws that did not affect public conduct and family law, Article 340 has remained in effect today, albeit in a modified form (Almusleh, 2021).

The French-imposed penal code was implemented during France's Mandate over Lebanon in 1943-1944. This included a Lebanese law on adultery, which treated women accused of adultery more severely than men did. Women could be sentenced to a maximum of two years in prison based solely on an accusation, while men had to be caught in the act and faced a maximum punishment of one year in jail.

France's Article 324 served as a model for legislation in several Arab nations, including Algeria's 1991 Penal Code (Article 279); The Penal Code of Egypt in 1937, specifically (Article 237) of Code no. 58; the Penal Code of Iraq in 1966, specifically (Article 409); and the Penal Code of Jordan in 1960, specifically (Article 340) of Code no. 16; Kuwait's Penal Code (Article 153); Lebanon's Penal Code encompasses (Articles 193, 252, 253, and 562); The amendments to these were made in 1983, 1994, 1995, 1996, and 1999, and the Lebanese Parliament ultimately revoked them on 4 August 2011; Libya's Penal Code (Article 375); The modified Penal Code of Morocco in 1963 includes (Article 418); and Oman's Penal Code includes (Article 252) (Almusleh, 2021).

In Palestine, there are two codes: Jordan's 1960 Penal Code in the West Bank and the British Mandate Criminal Code (Article 18 in the Gaza Strip); Article 1 and Article 2 of the 2011 Law No. 71, signed by President Mahmoud Abbas on 5 May 2011 and published in the 10 October 2011 Official Gazette no. 91, repealed these laws. The repeal applied to the Criminal Code of Palestine's Northern and Southern Governorates. The Penal Code (Article 548) in Syria was updated in 1953 based on the original version in 1949. In Tunisia, the Penal Code (Article 207), later repealed, was established in 1991; the United Arab Emirate's law no. 3/1978 (Article 334); and Yemen's law no. 12/1994 (Article 232) (Almusleh, 2021).

The legal framework in Pakistan was established by the 1860 Indian Penal Code (IPC), enacted by the colonial administration in British India. This code permitted the reduction of penalties for offenses involving assault or criminal force in situations of significant and unexpected provocation. The legal status of honor killing in Pakistan was justified using this clause even though it is not included in the IPC.

In 1990, the Pakistani government revised this law to align it with the principles of Shari'a, and the Pakistani Federal Shariat Court proclaimed that "under the teachings of Islam, the act of provocation, regardless of its severity or suddenness, does not diminish the gravity of the crime of murder." Nevertheless, Pakistani judges occasionally provide milder penalties for honor killings, rationalized by referencing the IPC's inclusion of a "grave and sudden provocation." (Idzikowski, 2017; Welchman & Hossain, 2005).

Murder Motivated by Provocation in the Anglo-American System

In both English and American legal systems, jurists commonly consider adultery as a prime example of sufficient provocation for honor killings. The act of being sexually provoked upon seeing one's wife's adultery is seen as a valid kind of provocation that can mitigate the severity of a murder offense (Coker, 1992). In numerous legal systems, sexual provocation is employed as a means of cultural self-defense (Cohan, 2009; Madek, 2005). Abusive men often justify their violent behavior by claiming that they were "out of control" due to the victim's provocation, which caused them to lose control (Coker, 1992).

Provocation is deemed acceptable within specific boundaries. The restrictions vary depending on the applicable legal system. The four elements that govern the doctrine of voluntary manslaughter under common law are as follows: a. A reasonable person experiencing provocation that leads to a state of intense emotion, b. The provocation is a direct result of this intense emotional state; c. There was insufficient time for a reasonable person to regain composure; d. The perpetrator did not regain composure before committing the crime (Coker, 1992; Donovan & Wildman, 1980).

Common law jurisdictions embrace the notion of provocation, provided that it meets the criteria of being sufficient provocation. The establishment of such sufficiency, commonly referred to as standard law classifications of sufficient provocation, is precise and can be defined by the occurrence of severe physical assault, aggravated assault, the perpetration of a crime against a close family member, and the observation of a husband witnessing his wife engaging in adultery (Abu-Odeh, 1997).

The primary inquiry about honor crimes performed within the American legal framework revolves around whether the offender was incited by the deceased and then acted impulsively and under the influence of intense emotions, causing them to act without exercising sound judgment. The resolution to that inquiry hinges upon whether the sufficiency standards are fulfilled. The questions would be formulated as follows: Was the provocation sufficient to generate an intense emotional response? Did the accused have enough time to regain composure? Did the accused commit the crime due to the intense emotional response triggered by witnessing the deceased engaging in adultery? (MDG., 1958) In all situations, the determination of appropriateness is entrusted to the courts (Abu-Odeh, 1997).

The Current State of Arab Legislation on Honor Crimes

Some scholars argue that Arab legislation varies in its approach to two primary issues. The primary concern lies in restricting the defense of provocation to cases of adultery and implementing a decrease in a penalty rather than a complete exemption. This can be most effectively demonstrated by examining the penal codes in Egypt, Tunisia, Libya, and Kuwait. Other codes encompass a broader range of situations that are considered provocative, including criminal sexual acts that cover all other sexual practices, except only adultery, as defined by the Jordanian penal code (Leonard, 2020; Abu-Odeh, 1997).

The second Arab legislative matter pertains to determining the beneficiaries of the justification of honor crimes. Due to the adoption of French terminology in the Syrian and Lebanese penal laws, individuals who profit from the justification are specifically the deceased's fathers, brothers, and sons, as they are considered female ascendants and descendants. The Jordanian penal code broadens the scope of justification to cover additional sexual actions that fall short of adultery (Zaid, 2015).

Egypt's stance on honor crimes might be characterized as a moderate attitude between two extremes. Article 237 of the Egyptian penal Code grants the husband, not the wife, the exclusive privilege of receiving a reduced punishment as a valid justification. Both the Egyptian and Algerian legal codes exclude males who are unable to establish a sexual connection with females through the extension of the application of reduction in punishment. While Article 247 of the penal code in Egypt only allows for a decrease in sanctions for husbands, it is commonly assumed in the literature on honor crimes in Egypt that Egyptian justice applies this same benefit to husbands as well. They assert that Egyptian justice evades the restriction outlined in Article 237 of the penal code and extends the same treatment to paternal relatives, aside from the husband, by utilizing Article 17 of the Egyptian penal code for those responsible for honor crimes (Zaid, 2015).

Is Killing Motivated by Provocation a Reflection of the Concept of Emotion or a Response to the Concept of Honor?

A question has arisen in jurisprudence as to whether killing motivated by provocation is a reflection of the concept of passion or a response to the concept of honor. Some scholars went on to analyze the trend of Arab legislation regarding honor killings, as the previous opinion noted the variation in the position of these legislations between two trends: the first reflects the concept of emotion; in Algerian law, both the husband and the wife are entitled to a reduction in punishment if they catch their partner engaging in adultery. The Algerian code demonstrates greater acceptance of the idea of passion rather than honor by allowing both husbands and wives to benefit equally from a reduction in penalty. In contrast, many other Arab codes, such as the Jordanian code, exclude female family members from receiving such benefits. According to Article 340 of the Jordanian penal Code, a husband who is provoked and catches his wife in the act of committing adultery is entirely immune to any penalties. It also allows for a decrease in punishment for individuals who harm or cause the death of their female ancestors and descendants due to engaging in an illicit sexual relationship. The Jordanian legal system prioritizes honor over emotion. (Leonard, 2020; Abu-Odeh, 1997).

Hence, Arab legislation is between two extremes, with the Algerian code representing one end and the Jordanian code representing the other. The first provision, which allows spouses to receive the same reduction in penalty, demonstrates the principle of passion. The second provision, which grants exemption from penalty to men who catch their wives committing adultery and reduces the penalty for men who catch their female family members in bed with someone else committing adultery, aligns with the concept of honor (Zaid, 2015).

Conditions for Mitigating the Crime of Murder Motivated by Provocation

The Egyptian legislature used three conditions to implement a provocation that mitigated the penalty for honor killing. These conditions constitute a specific framework for applying this mitigating circumstance, which the Egyptian legislature defines as an exception. These three conditions are the character of the perpetrator as the husband of the adulterous woman, the excuse of provocation by surprising the wife if she is caught in the act of adultery, and the condition. The third is immediate killing (Srour, 2019; Hosny, 2012; Hassanein, 2005), which we review as follows:

1st Condition: Characteristics of the Husband

Only the husband benefits from this mitigating legal excuse in the Egyptian Penal Code, and the point in determining the extent to which this characteristic is available is due to the personal status rules that regulate the provisions of marriage in Egyptian legislation. Therefore, a revocable divorce does not end the marital relationship by the provisions of Islamic Sharia law, while an irrevocable divorce ends it. Other people related to the adulterous woman, such as the father, brother, uncle, grandfather, and son, do not benefit from this excuse, no matter how great his relationship with the adulterous woman is. He is liable for the felony of premeditated murder without this excuse (Srour, 2019; Hosny, 2012; Hassanein, 2005).

The reason for deciding this mitigating excuse for the husband and not anyone else from the point of view of jurisprudence is due to the state of provocation that the husband suffers when he is surprised to see his wife engaged in adultery. This is a provocation due to his feeling of the severity of the violation that has befallen his honor and the honor of his family, and the result of this is that he experiences a psychological revolution that causes him loss. He cannot control himself, so he rushes into action without appreciating its risks because he would have appreciated them if he were in his usual state (Srour, 2019; Hosny, 2012; Hassanein, 2005).

Hence, this excuse does not benefit the relatives of the adulterous wife, whether ascendants, descendants, or brothers, despite the availability of the excuse of provocation and psychological upheaval for them when they see one of their relatives committing adultery. It is worth noting that the wife herself does not benefit from the excuse of provocation in mitigating the punishment if she sees the husband committing adultery because the rule of law is limited to the one who surprises his wife and who does not go to anyone other than the husband. This is without prejudice to applying the rule of law to mitigate judicial circumstances when necessary.

Jurisprudence believes the legislature's plan to limit the scope of benefiting from the husband's excuse is flawed. Suppose the reason for mitigation is provocation due to the insult and dishonor felt by the deceived husband. This reason is also available to the wife if she encounters the same circumstances; therefore, the logic of the legislation requires equality. There is no objection to that because the wife's adultery is more dangerous to the family than the husband's adultery (Srour, 2019; Hosny, 2012; Hassanein, 2005).

This consideration may explain the difference in punishment between their two crimes. However, it does not justify their distinction regarding benefiting from the excuse as long as its cause is available to them to the same extent. Instead, it is logical for the scope of the excuse to expand. Those closest to the wife's family, such as her ascendants, descendants, and siblings, have an excuse when they are surprised that the wife is caught in the act of adultery.

Hence, there were some attempts in one of the drafts of the Egyptian penal Code to include an article in the law that allows ascendants, branches, and siblings to benefit from this mitigating excuse, as Article 394/2 of the draft of the Egyptian penal Code of 1966 stipulates that (this provision applies to whoever surprises one of his ascendants, descendants, or sisters) Red-handed in the crime of adultery) (Srour, 2019).

Although the wife does not benefit from this legal excuse if she surprises her husband while she is committing adultery with another woman, she is not stripped of the right to legitimate self-defense if her husband intends to kill her while she is committing adultery with her lover. The excuse that the husband has does not negate the quality of his act as an assault.

Some jurists have called for amending the law to achieve equality between husbands and wives, who suffer from the same feelings if they are in the same situation. Establishing the principle of equality between spouses in applying this excuse requires us to scrutinize this issue. The basic principle is that according to the rules of personal status in Egypt, a person may marry another woman, unlike the wife, who is not permitted to marry two spouses. Therefore, when implementing these two assumptions, the husband who witnesses his wife committing adultery is, in this case, red-handedly committing the crime of adultery. In contrast, in the second case, the husband may be married to another woman. Then, his act is permissible and does not constitute a crime, as in the case of the wife, taking into account the assumption that the woman who was with the husband is not his wife, which constitutes the crime of adultery by the husband in this case (Hosny, 2012; Hassanein, 2005).

The husband may commit the crime of murder alone, and others may participate with him in committing it. Therefore, a distinction must be made in this case according to the husband's position in committing the crime. If the husband is the original perpetrator of this crime, he benefits from the availability of this excuse, which reduces the punishment. Some jurists believe that excuse provocation, in this case, would change the nature and description of the crime from a felony murder to a misdemeanor (Srour, 2019; Hosny, 2012).

Hence, jurisprudence believes that a third party considered an accomplice of the husband will benefit from this excuse if he or she knows about the factors provoking the husband. However, suppose he is ignorant of this and believes that he has contributed to an ordinary murder. In that case, he does not benefit from mitigation in applying the general rules of Article 41 of the Penal Code. Jurisprudence indicates that the husband's excuse is psychological, requiring the partner to be aware of the factors he deserves, given the diminished seriousness of his personality and reduced punishment.

However, if the murder was committed by a third party and the husband was an accomplice, this third party must be held accountable for the crime of premeditated murder, as the murder committed by each of them carries a degree of danger to society that is determined according to whether the mitigating conditions are available. In this case, the husband is liable as an accomplice to this third party in killing his adulterous wife if he contributed to its commission by any means of association because his criminality as an accomplice derives from the nature of the act committed by the original perpetrator, who is the third party (Srour, 2019; Hosny, 2012; Hassanein, 2005).

2nd Condition: Provoking the Husband by Surprising the Wife in the Act of Adultery

Two elements are required for this condition to be met: being caught in the act of adultery and being provoked by surprise. Being caught in the act of adultery does not mean that the husband is watching his wife during sexual intercourse with her lover. If the confusion were understood in this sense, the scope of the confusion would be unacceptably narrow. In addition, the husband's revolt is not limited to this case (Srour, 2019; Hosny, 2012; Hassanein, 2005).

It is not necessary to assess the situation of flagrante delicto by referring to the traditional circumstances of flagrante delicto as defined by the Code of Criminal Procedure in Article 30. Rather, flagrante delicto is understood in the meaning implied by Article 276 of the Penal Code, which considers it among the evidence of adultery. The unity of the meaning in the two texts is based on the fact that the situation is evidence of adultery, which makes it natural. That the husband's soul becomes aroused when he sees him and that he is provoked to do it, and then this meaning is ambiguous, in addition to watching the wife during sexual intercourse, every situation that leaves no room for rational doubt that adultery has taken place.

In this regard, the Egyptian Court of Cassation says that (*in flagrante delicto indicating adultery, it is not required that the adulterer be seen at the time of committing the act or shortly after it was committed. Instead, it is sufficient for flagrante delicto to be established that the adulterer and her accomplice are seen in circumstances that leave no room for reasonable doubt that the crime was committed* (Srour, 2019; Hosny, 2012; Hassanein, 2005).

Some judicial rulings have referred to such situations, such as if the husband sees his wife naked or covered only by a nightgown. At the same time, the partner is hidden under the partner, and if the husband sees them without pants, their underwear is placed next to each other. Alternatively, if the husband entered the house and noticed movement under the bed and by lifting the sheet, he found the accused with his lower half naked while holding his clothes. The mere presence of the partner in the place designated for the harem in a Muslim house is not considered flagrant delicto. However, this is considered acceptable evidence of adultery according to Article 286 of the penal code (Abuhattab, 2020).

The husband must witness the situation in the act himself (Srour, 2019; Hosny, 2012; Hassanein, 2005). It is not enough for someone else to tell him that he saw the wife in this situation because the provocation that justifies the excuse is only available under this condition. For provocation for surprise, Egyptian law does not consider provocation a mitigating element except in the case of a husband who surprises his wife in the act of committing adultery and kills her and the person he is committing adultery with. For this mitigating excuse to be available, the husband must be surprised by what he saw in a way that fulfills the meaning of provocation. This condition is linked to the reason for mitigation, so the husband is surprised. His wife, in the act of adultery, is the one who provokes him and creates the provocation in him that makes him lose control of himself and makes him rush into action (Srour, 2019; Hosny, 2012; Hassanein, 2005).

Surprise refers to the difference between what the husband believed regarding his wife's behavior and what happened to him when he saw her committing adultery. Surprise is a difference between belief and reality. Surprise is achieved in its complete form if the husband is confident in his wife's fidelity and then sees her committing adultery. Surprisingly, if the husband doubted his wife's behavior and then saw her committing adultery, whether he saw her casually, that is, the circumstances made it possible for him to do so, or he observed her and worked hard, even by trickery, to verify her behavior and become confident in her infidelity. There is a difference between what the husband believed and what she thought, which is suspicion of her behavior. His wife and what he saw were the certainty of betrayal, and with this difference, surprise was achieved (Hosny, 2012).

However, if the husband is aware of his wife's behavior or if he is more than satisfied with it, then his apology is not accepted for his revolt when he sees her red-handed in adultery and kills her. The Egyptian Court of Cassation decided that there was no excuse if the motive for the killing was merely a suspicion of the wife's behavior. Therefore, the conditions for mitigation were not met, as specified in Article 237 of the Penal Code. This excuse is also not available if the husband was confident of his wife's infidelity and decided to kill her the first time he caught her committing adultery. In this case, the element of provocation by surprise is not achieved.

The situation is different if the husband is not sure of the betrayal. However, he doubts his wife's fidelity, so he wants to determine the truth of the matter and lies in wait in the house so that when the lover comes and is alone with his wife, caressing her, caressing her, and then being alone with her, he emerges from his hiding place and kills him. In this case, the husband benefits from an excuse due to the availability of provocation. At the same time, there is no excuse if the motive for the killing was merely a suspicion of the wife's behavior (Srour, 2019; Hosny, 2012; Hassanein, 2005).

3rd Condition - Killing on the Spot

This condition refers to the temporal contemporaneity between the surprise of adultery and the resulting provocation and the commission of the murder, and this condition is closely related to the reason for mitigation, which is the commission of the murder under the influence of the psychological revolution (Hosny, 2012).

The husband must commit his crime when surprised, for which he is excused given the state of provocation he went through and the psychological revolution that engulfed him. However, if he waits until another time and then commits his crime, his act is stripped of justifications for mitigation. It becomes merely quiet revenge and not impulsiveness under the influence of the psychological revolution. In this case, the killing is subject to the general rules of intentional murder (Srour, 2019; Hosny, 2012; Hassanein, 2005).

Hence, this condition is temporary due to the estimation of the time that separated the surprise from the act, and its estimation is left to the judge of the matter. This condition does not mean that the murder is committed at the exact moment the wife is seen committing adultery. Saying that you lied narrows the scope of the excuse and leads to its denial despite the existence of its reason. If the murder was committed shortly after the wife was surprised but the husband had not yet calmed down, such as if he killed her after spending some time searching for turtles in an adjacent room, then he benefited from a reduced punishment. However, if a relatively long period passes between the surprise and the killing, during which he hesitates, turns things around, or refrains from killing and then decides to do so, he does not benefit from the excuse (Srour, 2019; Hosny, 2012; Hassanein, 2005).

A question has arisen in jurisprudence as to whether the excuse of provocation negates the circumstance of premeditation in the crime of murder, given that the presence of this circumstance requires calm thinking that takes time on the part of the killer to carry out his crime, as some argue that there is no premeditation in the outburst of provocation due to what may come to mind. There is a contradiction between the availability of the excuse of provocation and the claim that the husband premeditated killing his wife. However, another opinion is the opposite: if premeditation negates surprise, then in this case, there is no excuse (Srour, 2019; Hosny, 2012; Hassanein, 2005).

However, if this was not premeditated, the excuse remained available. The previous opinion distinguishes between two situations: First, if the husband doubts his wife's behavior, he thinks calmly and then insists on killing her if he realizes that she is cheating on her, and when he sees her red-handed in adultery, he kills her, then he benefits from the excuse. The surprise came when he realized the difference between his thoughts and what happened to him. However, if he was confident that she was cheating on him, he insisted on killing her when he saw her red-handed in adultery, and he did that. He does not benefit from the excuse since he is not surprised by anything, so what he believes is what comes true (Srour, 2019; Hosny, 2012; Hassanein, 2005).

The Effect of Reducing the Penalty

The availability of this circumstance results in the mandatory reduction of the penalty for premeditated murder to imprisonment (i.e., for a period ranging between 24 hours and three years). Although the law stipulates that the husband benefits from mitigation if he commits intentional murder or a battery that leads to death according to articles 234 and 236 of the penal code, he benefits from a fortiori if he commits a felony assault that leads to permanent disability. The law applies this excuse equally if the husband kills his wife and her lover together, which is the situation assumed by the text, or if he kills only one of them.

Egyptian jurisprudence and judiciaries believe that killing to provoke a husband is a killing accompanied by a legal excuse. Hence, reducing the penalty for murder was obligatory for the judge, meaning that the law had ordered that the penalty prescribed for the crime be reduced to imprisonment, and since that was the case and the basis for dividing crimes depended on the type of penalty prescribed for them, then if the law stipulated a penalty of imprisonment in this case, it would have considered. This crime is a misdemeanor, not a felony (Srour, 2019; Hosny, 2012).

In this regard, the Egyptian Court of Cassation says that (*the crime stipulated in Article 237 is a misdemeanor by law because imprisonment was imposed for it as an original penalty, and the judge did not have the right to reduce the penalty, as is the case in judicial mitigating circumstances in the excuses that allow the judge to rule on a felony penalty or a misdemeanor penalty*). It follows that if the perpetrator attempts to kill his adulterous wife or her partner, there is no point in punishing him or her as long as there is no punishment for attempting a misdemeanor except by a stipulation, unless this attempt results in injury to one of them, in which case he or she is punished for a misdemeanor by battery (Srour, 2019; Hosny, 2012).

Application of the Clemency of Judges by Article 17 of the Egyptian Penal Code

Article 17 stipulates mitigating judicial circumstances, a system that allows the judge not to impose the original penalty prescribed for the incident on the perpetrator but instead to impose a lighter penalty. Judicial circumstances are not exclusively specified, and mitigating them is permissible. Their discretion is left to the judges' discretion according to what appears to them of the circumstances of the case. Therefore, they are called mitigating judicial circumstances.

Fixed punishments such as the death penalty and life imprisonment are essential because they allow the judge to reconcile the specific rules of law with the realistic circumstances in which crimes are committed. In other words, determining mitigating judicial circumstances is an application of the principle of individualizing punishment, especially when that punishment is, at its minimum, disproportionate to the physical incident (El-Kady, 2024).

Applying Article 17 of the penal code is subject to certain restrictions, including a. It applies specifically to felonies. b. It is applicable within the boundaries defined by the law. c. The judge has the authority to use discretion in its application (Abdul-muteleb, 2011).

According to Article 17 of the Egyptian penal code, judges can exercise leniency in serious offenses whenever they deem appropriate. The leniency of the judiciary is based on its discretionary authority to decrease penalties as needed, taking into account the specific circumstances of the crime or act committed. A judge has the authority to substitute the punishment of capital punishment with the penalty of life imprisonment involving rigorous physical labor. Similarly, the penalty of permanent hard labor can be replaced with temporary hard labor or imprisonment. Temporary hard labor can also be substituted with imprisonment or confinement for at least six months. Last, an imprisonment sentence can be replaced with a confinement penalty of no less than three months (El-Kady, 2024).

Therefore, the requirement for applying Article 17 is that the penalties in felony cases may be replaced with lighter, custodial-restricting penalties if the circumstances of the crime for which the public lawsuit is brought require the judges' clemency. Then, the judge may lower the penalty by one or two degrees, as stated in the text of Article 17. Among the most prominent examples that the judiciary considered mitigating circumstances were the following: 1- The case of the offender's young age, even if he exceeded the limit in which young age was considered a legal excuse. 2- A state of provocation and anger (El-Kady, 2024).

The Court of Cassation ruled in one of its recent rulings that a state of provocation and anger are mitigating judicial excuses. It ruled that: *"The appellant's defense concluded that he was in a state of excitement, provocation, and anger that possessed him after he learned of his wife's misbehavior toward her, so the defense—in this form—does not support the plea of insanity or mental defect, and since the cases of excitement or provocation were or anger are merely mitigating judicial excuses, the matter being decided by the trial court without any comment from the Court of Cassation. These excuses were later refuted by the amendments to the Penal Code by Law No. 71 of 2009 in Article 62 of the Penal Code, considering psychological or mental disorder as a mitigating circumstance when determining the duration of punishment"*.

Applying Article 17 is within the trial court's discretion, and assessing mitigating circumstances is left to the court's discretion. That is, evaluating the reasons for clemency is one of the objective matters within the jurisdiction of the trial court, so it is free to apply Article 17 and not to use it according to what its belief dictates regarding the availability or nonavailability of these circumstances, without commenting on it and without asking for an account. Regarding the reasons for which the punishment was imposed to the extent it saw fit, note that if the court sees that the accused should be given clemency and treated by Article 17, then it must not punish except on the basis stated in this article, considering that it has replaced the punishment stipulated in it by the text of the law for the crime (El-Kady, 2024).

The assessment of mitigating circumstances is about each accused individual. Then, the judge is wrong if he determines that they are present about the crime in general because the circumstances that require judges' clemency, which were mentioned in Article 17, are not focused only on the facts of the case but are dealt with without. There is no doubt about everything related to the materiality of the criminal act insofar as it is associated with the person of the criminal who committed the act and the person on whom the crime occurred, as well as everything that surrounds the act, its perpetrator, and the victim in terms of circumstances and circumstances without exception, that is, the material circumstances and personal circumstances, and this group consists of those circumstances and circumstances. It is impossible to explain or quantify those left to the judge's discretion to take what he or she deems worthy of clemency from them (El-Kady, 2024).

Although the assessment of mitigating circumstances is for each accused individually, the Court of Cassation has deemed that the court must impose the same punishment for all defendants involved in the same criminal circumstances and one criminal project, as the difference in punishment for these defendants harms justice.

One of its rulings ruled *"the trial court's implementation of Article 17 and imposing the penalty on the convict. However, not the appellants, despite the unity of the facts, the criminal project and the circumstances are considered an error that requires it to be imposed on them"*. The Court of Cassation also ruled that "the *assessment of the punishment and the assessment of the reasons for clemency or its failure to do so are objective matters within the trial court's jurisdiction"* (El-Kady, 2024).

According to experts, Article 17 of the penal code ensures that those who commit honor crimes and are not eligible for reduced punishment, as outlined in Article 237, will face less severe legal consequences. The proposal suggests that both husbands and male paternal relatives can benefit from a reduction identical to the one specified in Article 237 of the penal code. They observe that Article 17 of the penal law indirectly extends the range of protection to include other male relatives, not only husbands. Some scholars contend that this premise is called into question when considering the analysis of the appeals presented to the Egyptian Court of Cassation on implementing Article 17 of the penal code (Zaid, 2015).

They presuppose that courts comprehensively apply mercy, often extending beyond crimes related to honor. Court leniency is granted for other extra offenses, such as murder unrelated to honor, illegal drug use, and bribery. Article 17 does not necessarily serve as a supplementary provision to Article 237 of the penal code, which ensures that offenders of less severe crimes against honor receive lenient prosecution. Leniency is only sometimes granted in every instance when it is presented to the courts (Zaid, 2015).

Can it be Said That Egyptian Legislation is Lenient About Honor Killings?

To answer this question, a study analyzing Article 237, which mitigates the punishment for a husband who kills his wife for committing adultery, and Article 17, which grants courts the authority to exercise leniency in felony cases when deemed suitable, was conducted. Article 237 of the Egyptian penal law restricts the decrease in penalties to spouses only while excluding other male paternal relatives. Moreover, article 17 of the penal code implicitly establishes the extent of protection to encompass further male relations beyond just husbands. Psychologically, this ensures that individuals who commit honor crimes receive lenient penalties, which allows them to avoid severe legal consequences (Zaid, 2015).

The study analyzes almost 1,550 cases presented to the Egyptian Court of Cassation between 1934 and 2014, which pertain to the implementation of Article 17 of the penal code and questions these assumptions. This demonstrates that the mercy of judges needs to be consistently applied in cases involving honor crimes. When examining appeals before the Egyptian Court of Cassation, it is understood that honor crimes are not necessarily the most frequently pardoned crimes by the judiciary. Leniency is typically presumed to be extended to various other offenses, including non-honor-related killings, unlawful possession of narcotics and weapons, bribery, and several other crimes. This study finds that leniency is frequently granted for a broad spectrum of offenses, including those related to honor (Zaid, 2015). Hence, the author's opinion is that Egyptian legislation and judiciaries do not tolerate honor killing crimes but rather apply the legal rules and provisions that regulate this issue in the texts of current laws.

To say that Article 17 of the Egyptian Penal Code grants judicial leniency to judges toward male perpetrators of honor crimes in Egypt is, from the author's point of view, an inaccurate statement in light of the following considerations: The application of Article 17 is intended to give judges discretionary power to single out the punishment for the perpetrator of the crime, whether male or female, without discrimination based on gender, to achieve the judicial function of choosing the appropriate punishment for the perpetrator in light of the material circumstances of the crime and the personality of the perpetrator (El-Kady, 2024).

The issue is not leniency toward perpetrators of honor crimes, from a narrow perspective, but from a broader perspective, the judge is given a measure of authority to determine the appropriate punishment for the offender to achieve justice and equality before the law. As the Supreme Constitutional Court in Egypt says, *legislative interference that prevents a judge from exercising his authority to determine the appropriate punishment constitutes interference in the work of the judicial authority, which is not permissible because it conflicts with the principle of separation of powers.*

The existence of Article 17 of the penal code allows the judge to properly apply the law by individualizing the punishment and choosing the appropriate punishment for the personality of the offender if the judge finds that the punishment prescribed by the legislator is not proportional to the seriousness of the crime and the circumstances of his commission of the crime without taking from a narrow perspective that the application of this article constitutes authority for the judge to be lenient with a particular category of crimes, which are honor killings (El-Kady, 2024).

This is what the Supreme Constitutional Court in Egypt emphasized in its rulings, saying: *"The defendants may not be treated as a fixed pattern or viewed as a single image that unites them to fit them into a mold, meaning that the principle of punishment is to individualize it, not generalize it."* Therefore, the individualization of punishment requires the discretionary authority of the judge to choose the appropriate punishment for the convict. While exercising his discretion in imposing the punishment, the judge must implement an individualization of the punishment that is consistent with the gravity of the crime and the seriousness of the offender, which are two objective standards accepted as a basis for the individualization of the punishment (El-Kady, 2024).

The judge's discretionary power in determining the penalty refers to his or her ability to match the realistic circumstances of the case with the penalty he or she decides therein. The controls determining how a judge uses his discretionary power can be summarized into two types. Objective controls, related to the materiality of the crime, when the judge uses his discretionary power toward an accused person of a crime, must make the amount of illegality that lies in its materiality one of the bases for determining his punishment, which, among the controls for measuring it are the seriousness of the violation of the right, the method of carrying out the criminal act, and the relationship between the accused and the victim.

Additionally, Controls related to the person of the accused, such as the amount of guilt involved in the moral element, the accused's share of eligibility for responsibility, and the degree of criminal danger of the accused, by taking into account his criminal past, the degree of his insistence on carrying out the crime, social circumstances, and his potential impact on the severity of the punishment, and there is no doubt that the proper use of this power the judge must cooperate with the devices for a technical examination of the accused's personality to identify it and determine the appropriate punishment in terms of type and amount (El-Kady, 2024).

The Supreme Constitutional Court was keen to emphasize the principle of judicial individualization as a means of the judiciary's work. It considered *"estimating the punishment that suits the crime to be a constitutional requirement to preserve the objectivity of its application, meaning that there is an inevitable relationship between the judge's power to individualize the punishment and its proportionality and their connection to the exercise of the judicial function"* (El-Kady, 2024).

Scholars widely accept that Egypt explicitly includes honor crimes in its penal code, specifically under Articles 17 and 237. According to scholars, Article 17 of the penal code provides less severe legal consequences for perpetrators of honor crimes not covered by the reduced punishment outlined in Article 237 (Zaid, 2015). They suggest that the reduction in sanctions specified under Article 237 benefits not just spouses but also male paternal relatives who often experience a similar reduction (Zaid, 2015). Examining appeals involving the application of Article 17 of the penal code before the Egyptian Court of Cassation requires considering another assumption. This assumption suggests that the extent to which courts apply leniency is so broad that it is difficult to conclude that the Egyptian judiciary has a lenient approach toward honor crimes. A study uncovers the actualities of court proceedings, suggesting that judges often use leniency in a wide-ranging manner, extending beyond crimes related to honor (Zaid, 2015). Courts often grant mercy for a variety of crimes, including but not limited to murder committed for motives unrelated to honor, illegal drug possession, bribery, and several other offenses. Article 17 of the penal code, which grants leniency, does not necessarily supplement Article 237, which ensures that perpetrators of less serious honor crimes are prosecuted less severely (Zaid, 2015).

CONCLUSION

This chapter examines the legal provisions regarding murder on provocation in the Egyptian penal code, specifically in the context of honor killings, which are widely recognized as acts of violence against women in various countries. The chapter elucidates the legal structure around murder on provocation, which offers a legal justification that reduces the punishment for the murder if it is done by a husband who witnesses his wife engaging in adultery and promptly kills her. This is a form of homicide characterized by premeditation and intent, as specified in the legal statutes.

This chapter employed a comparative descriptive-analytical method to elucidate the concept of honor killing, its definitions, and the variations in trends within Arab legislation about honor killings. Additionally, the correlation between Honor Killing and Religion will be examined, and murder will be explained based on

Provocation, as outlined in the Egyptian penal code, which constitutes a form of impassioned killing. Furthermore, this chapter will explore the lenient treatment of honor crimes in Egypt by applying for judges' clemency, as stipulated in Article 17 of the Egyptian penal Code.

The chapter determined that honor crimes are not clearly defined in Egyptian statutes. In the Egyptian legal system, murder committed in response to provocation is classified as a crime of passion. This classification is also followed by many other legal systems that consider the emotional turmoil experienced by a husband upon witnessing his wife engage in adultery.

REFERENCES

Abdul-muteleb, E. (2011). *Explanation of penal code*. National Center for Legal Publications.

Abu-Odeh, L. (1997). Comparatively speaking: The honor of the East and the passion of the West. *Utah L. Rev.*, 287.

Abu-Odeh, L. (2004). *Women of Jordan: Islam*. Labor, and the Law.

Abuhattab, A. (2020). Criminal Protection of Women's Rights against Violence in Palestine. https://core.ac.uk/download/373377011.pdf

Almusleh, N. N. (2021). *Honor Crimes: A Question of Honor*. Culture, and Humanity.

Brown, J. A. (2014). *Misquoting Muhammad: the challenge and choices of interpreting the Prophet's legacy*. Oneworld.

Cohan, J. A. (2009). Honor killings and the cultural defense. *Cal. W. Int'l LJ*, 40, 177.

Coker, D. K. (1992). Heat of passion and wife killing: Men who batter/men who kill. *SSRN*, 2, 71. DOI: 10.2139/ssrn.2669196

Crootof, R. (2019). The internet of torts: Expanding civil liability standards to address corporate remote interference. *Duke Law Journal*, 69, 583.

Cusack, S., & Cook, R. J. (2007). Honor": Crimes, Paradigms, and Violence against. *Women*.

De Guzman, J. T., & Jamias, J. K. V. (2016). The daughter clause: A study of Article 247 of the Revised Penal Code of the Philippines.

Domazetoska, S., Platzer, M., & Plaku, G. (2014). *Femicide: A global issue that demands action. (PDF). Genevadeclaration.org*. Academic Council on the United Nations System.

Donovan, D. A., & Wildman, S. M. (1980). Is the reasonable man obsolete: A critical perspective on self-defense and provocation. *Loy. LAL Rev.*, 14, 435.

El-Kady, R. (2024). *General Section-Penal Code*. Dar Al-Nahda Al-Arabiya.

Esposito, J. L. (2011). *What everyone needs to know about Islam*. Oxford University Press. DOI: 10.1093/wentk/9780199794133.001.0001

Hassanein, O. (2005). *Private Section-Penal Code*. Dar Al-Nahda Al-Arabiya.

Hosny, M. N. (2012). *Private Section-Penal Code*. Dar Al-Nahda Al-Arabiya.

Idzikowski, L. (Ed.). (2017). *Honor Killings*. Greenhaven Publishing LLC.

Khafagy, F. (2005, May). Honor killing in Egypt. In *an expert group meeting organized by the UN Division for the Advancement of Women* (pp. 17-20).

Leonard, M. M. (2020). *Honor violence, crimes d'honneur, Ehrenmorde: improving the identification, risk assessment, and estimation of honor crimes internationally* (Doctoral dissertation, Universitaet Mannheim (Germany)).

Madek, C. A. (2005). Killing dishonor: Effective eradication of honor killing. *Suffolk Transnational Law Review*, 29, 53.

Malik, R., Malik, F., & Imtiaz, A. K. (2019). Honor killings of women in Punjab: A sociopolitical context. *South Asian Studies*, 34(02), 401–418.

Mayell, H. (2002). Thousands of women were killed for family honor. *National Geographic News*, 12, 15.

MDG. (1958). Manslaughter and the Adequacy of Provocation: The Reasonableness of the Reasonable Man. *University of Pennsylvania Law Review*, •••, 1021–1040.

Muhammad, A. A., & BCPsych, D. P. M. (2013). *Preliminary Examination of So-called" Honor Killings" in Canada*. Department of Justice Canada= Ministère de la justice Canada.

Oberwittler, D., & Kasselt, J. (2014). Honor killings. In Gartner, R., & McCarthy, B. (Eds.), *The Oxford Handbook of Gender*. Sex, and Crime., DOI: 10.1093/oxfordhb/9780199838707.013.0033

Odeh, L. A. (2010). Honor killings and the construction of gender in Arab societies. *The American Journal of Comparative Law*, 58(4), 911–952. DOI: 10.5131/ajcl.2010.0007

Ragini, R. (2021). Honor Killing. *Issue 4 Int'l JL Mgmt. &. Human.*, 4, 1591.

Sonbol, A. E. A. (2003). *Women of Jordan: Islam, labor, and the law*. Syracuse University Press.

Srour, A. F. (2019). *Private Section-Penal Code, Crimes Prejudicial to The Public Interest – Crimes of Individuals – Funds Crimes*. Dar Al-Nahda Al-Arabiya.

Welchman, L., & Hossain, S. (Eds.). (2005). *Honor": Crimes, Paradigms, and Violence Against Women*. Spinifex Press. DOI: 10.5040/9781350220621

Woolf, G. D. (2005). *Ancient Civilizations. The Illustrated Guide to Belief, Mythology and Art*. Duncan Baird Publications.

Zaid, M. (2015). *The lenient treatment of honor crimes in Egypt* [Master's Thesis, the American University in Cairo]. AUC Knowledge Fountain. https://fount.aucegypt.edu/etds/169

Chapter 11
Honor's Cost:
Lives Lost, Justice Frost

Indra Kumar Singh
Amity University, Haryana, India

Sudiksha Dhungel
https://orcid.org/0009-0004-5412-1833
GLA University, India

ABSTRACT

Honor killings are serious human rights crimes that affect the victims, their families, and the communities where they take place for a very long time. This chapter delves into the motivations behind honor killings and their intricate aftermath, demonstrating how the families are forced to commit these crimes by social pressure and humiliation. Chronic mental health issues including anxiety, sadness, and PTSD (post-traumatic stress disorder) can be brought on by this emotional upheaval. Honor killings put a pall over societies, creating an atmosphere of mistrust and apprehension. Honor killings put a pall over societies, creating an atmosphere of mistrust and apprehension. The victim's family may face hostility and ostracism. This horrifying crime be dealt with in a multifaceted manner, involving strong networks of care for the survivors and changes in the law. When we are aware of the entire extent of the aftermath, we may be better equipped to understand the urgent need for comprehensive solutions to put an end to honor killings and build a more just and equitable society.

DOI: 10.4018/979-8-3693-9596-7.ch011

Copyright © 2025, IGI Global. Copying or distributing in print or electronic forms without written permission of IGI Global is prohibited.

BACKGROUND

Honor killings, rooted in deeply ingrained cultural standards, grave violation of human rights, and have a catastrophic and enduring effect on victims, families, and entire communities. This chapter delves into the motivations behind honor killings and their intricate aftermath, demonstrating how these crimes family honor than on individual rights. Families are forced to commit these crimes by social pressure and humiliation. The perpetuation of violence is facilitated by legal impunity and a lack of knowledge, as numerous countries impose light punishments or clear offenders. This chapter looks at the terrible fallout from honor killings, showing how the effects go well beyond the initial violent act. Close relatives of the victim may endure the most severe emotional and psychological distress. The majority of survivors are women who experience intense stress, guilt, and a deep feeling of loss. This chapter discusses the psychological trauma that these people go through, emphasizing the emotions of betrayal and terror that can persist long after the violent event. Families may be destroyed, and members' conflicting feelings of shame and grief may be made worse by society's need to uphold cultural norms that may have justified the crime. Chronic mental health issues including anxiety, sadness, and PTSD (post-traumatic stress disorder) can be brought on by this emotional upheaval. Honor killings put a pall over societies, creating an atmosphere of mistrust and apprehension. The chapter examines how knowledge of such horrible acts fuels social shame and marginalization in a community. The victim's family may face hostility, ostracism, and social marginalization. Members of the community may excuse or subtly support the crime due to deeply ingrained cultural norms, which would worsen their isolation. The shame associated with honor killings not only damages the immediate family but also encourages a cycle of violence and repression across the community, undermining efforts to promote social cohesion and growth. Due to societal pressures and cultural conventions that justify honor killings, efforts to end them confront formidable obstacles. This chapter looks at the ways that conventional ideas of family honor and gender standards lead to this kind of violence. With their strongholds, Khap Panchayats frequently serve as the guardians of these harsh standards, opposing judicial changes and sustaining cycles of oppression and alarm. Prevention measures are hampered by the absence of social pressure on offenders to take responsibility. Legal systems that are shaped by patriarchal ideals frequently grant light penalties or acquittals, and the families of victims are discouraged from pursuing justice out of fear of reprisals. Many women are forced to hide due to constant threats against them, which are made worse by a lack of resources and support. Honor killings uphold gender inequity and unfavorable views about women's roles and rights. In summary, this chapter explains the complex and wide-ranging consequences of honor killings which have far-reaching effects that extend well beyond the initial violent act. It is estimated that approximately 5,000 honor killings occur worldwide each year, with the true figure possibly far higher owing to underreporting. In India alone, nearly 1,000 honor killings occur each year, highlighting the critical need for structural change and more stringent legal frameworks to safeguard potential victims. It requires that this horrifying crime be dealt with in a multifaceted manner, involving strong networks of care for the survivors, changes in culture, and changes in the law. When we are aware of the entire extent of the aftermath, we may be better equipped to understand the urgent need for comprehensive solutions to put an end to honor killings and build a more just and equitable society.

Research Methodology

This chapter uses a primarily qualitative research style to reflect the complex and deeply established cultural and psychological dimensions of honor killings. The goal is to gain a thorough understanding of honor killings using a combination of qualitative and quantitative research methodologies. Information was acquired from a variety of sources, including library records, newspapers, magazines, interviews, polls, and websites. This technique enabled a full examination of the topic from both primary and secondary viewpoints. While quantitative data, such as statistics studies on the prevalence of honor killings globally and within specific locations, give important context, the center of this research is a qualitative investigation into the motivations, repercussions, and societal impact of these crimes.

To capture the complex and individualized experiences of people and communities impacted by honor killings, a qualitative approach was selected. This study makes use of in-depth case studies that look closely at particular honor killing instances in order to understand the underlying motives, the psychological damage that survivors endure, and the wider social ramifications. These case studies provide detailed accounts that go beyond the numbers, exploring the psychological and emotional anguish, including guilt, fear, and betrayal, that victims and their families experience. Research also includes testimony and interviews with survivors, relatives, and community members to offer firsthand perspectives on the social pressures, cultural norms, and legal issues related to honor killings. To reduce bias, important demographic factors like the participants' age, gender, and ethnicity were carefully taken into account.

Understanding the lived experiences of individuals affected and exposing the systemic reasons that support these crimes depend heavily on this qualitative data. The research intends to give a thorough and compassionate knowledge of honor killings by concentrating on these qualitative aspects, highlighting the necessity of multimodal solutions that address the legal and cultural aspects of this serious human rights violation.

Key Terms

This chapter's core concepts include "Honor Killings," which directly tackles the chapter's fundamental theme, and "Human Rights Violations," which connects the subject to broader human rights frameworks. This mindset is common in patriarchal civilizations around the world, emphasizing the worldwide breadth of the problem and the urgent need for societal and legislative changes to protect people's rights and lives (XAVIER, 2015). Broader themes such as "Cultural Norms," "Gender-Based Violence," and "Psychological Trauma" provide context for the issue. This interpretation of the term justifies violence against women and all socially enforced standards of suitable behavior (Smita Satapathy, 2023). Legal and policy words such as "Legal Impunity," "Criminal Justice System," and "Legislative Reforms" refer to practical answers and interventions. To successfully implement legal reforms, these barriers must be addressed via dogged campaigning, outreach, and international pressure to uphold human rights values (Kanchan et al. 2016). Analytical viewpoints such as "Socio-Cultural Dynamics," "Intersectionality," and "Community Impact" provide a more in-depth investigation of the complexity surrounding honor killings. Females are expected to follow their parents' directions regarding their dress sense, choices, and life decisions (https://upscsociology.in/explain-the-thematic-linkages-between-patriarchy-and-honor-killing-in-india-citing-some).

To ensure relevance and rigor, a variety of sources were used, including academic journals, books, and credible web databases. Journals such as "International Journal of Human Rights," "Gender & Society," and "Journal of Interpersonal Violence" were chosen for their emphasis on human rights, gender studies, and other multidisciplinary subjects. JSTOR, Google Scholar, and Scopus were important resources for identifying peer-reviewed articles and reliable reports.

The inclusion criteria stressed the relevance of honor killings and their impact, with a concentration on recent publications and peer-reviewed studies to incorporate current perspectives and data. But now the issue arises: are those murders satisfied? Did they all regain their honour? (Santhi, 2013). Exclusion criteria excluded non-academic sources such as blogs and opinion pieces, ensuring that the research was based on trustworthy, scholarly sources. The research technique sought to provide a thorough and sympathetic knowledge of honor killings, emphasizing the critical need for institutional and cultural changes to solve this serious human rights issue.

Literature Review

Xavier (2015) draws attention to the ways that patriarchal mindsets are global in nature and reinforce the pervasiveness of gender-based oppression. This widespread occurrence highlights how deeply ingrained patriarchal ideals are, and how they show up in different legal and cultural contexts, sustaining inequality and violence against women. In order to destroy these deeply ingrained systems, Xavier's study highlights the urgent necessity for both societal changes and legislative reforms. The argument highlights the need for a diverse strategy in order to achieve meaningful development, with legislation protecting people's rights and lives as important as changing societal views. The problem's worldwide reach also means that solutions must be based on a shared commitment to gender equality and human rights while being adapted to various cultural contexts.

According to Smita Satapathy (2023), socially imposed standards are reinforced by cultural interpretations of honor and behavior, which frequently justify violence against women. This viewpoint clarifies how deeply rooted cultural norms can support patriarchal control, in which women's behavior is observed and penalized in order to uphold the honor of their families and communities. These interpretations support gender norms that restrict women's autonomy and justify violence as a kind of discipline. According to Satapathy's perspective, it can be difficult to terminate the cycle of oppression and achieve gender equality because of the subtle ways in which cultural excuses for violence are normalized.

Singhal (n.d.) highlights how important it is for communities to change by accepting the basic right to self-governance and categorically rejecting violence. This viewpoint draws attention to a twofold challenge: promoting respect for personal autonomy and challenging cultural norms that support or even glorify the use of violence as a tool of social control. Communities are being urged to adapt as part of a larger movement for societal change, in which an outspoken condemnation of violence must coexist with the acceptance of individual liberties. Singhal makes a compelling case for the necessity of cultural changes that put human rights first and reject the use of violence as a means of upholding social order. This evolution is necessary to establish settings in which people can make independent decisions without worrying about the consequences, opening the door to more just and equal societies.

Patel (2015) underlines that three essential elements are needed for legislative reforms against honor killings to be effective. Stricter penalties, similar to those in the UK and Turkey, serve as a deterrence by emphasizing how serious honor-based violence is. Law enforcement personnel that receive specialized training, as is the case in countries like Sweden and Canada, are better able to handle these cases because of their increased comprehension of cultural dynamics and prejudices.

Ensuring survivors' safety and assisting them in their recovery require comprehensive victim support services, which include legal assistance and counseling. When combined, these extensive steps improve victim assistance and the overall efficacy of legal remedies to honor killings.

Research Gap

Despite widespread attention, the exact magnitude of honor killings is concealed by imprecise data and significant underreporting, leaving a fundamental gap in our understanding of this global epidemic. This hidden dimension must be addressed in research, using novel approaches to uncover the entire scope and subtleties of honor-based violence. Specifically, among orthodox families, being constrained is frequently recognized as a good standard, promoting the belief that "this is how the home should perform" (Kirti et al., 2011). Equally pressing is the need to understand how deeply rooted societal norms enable these crimes. Children frequently take up the same morals and ideas as their parents because they think they are giving them the best moral guidance and education possible to help them survive in society. (Case et al., 2017). The sad truth is that people frequently lose sight of who they really are because society has shaped their perceptions. (Singh, 2019). Current research falls short of investigating how specific cultural beliefs justify and maintain honor killings, leaving open a critical field of investigation that could yield revolutionary insights for cultural and societal change. Legal frameworks created to curb honor killings are frequently criticized for being useless, but the reasons for their success or failure remain unknown. Stricter sanctions for perpetrators, specialized training for court and law enforcement personnel, and the introduction of victim support services are examples of legislative reforms that could ensure survivors receive the assistance they require to rebuild their lives (Patel, 2015).

Investigating which legal approaches succeed and why may reshape strategies for developing and enforcing effective laws. Furthermore, the function of traditional organizations like as Khap Panchayats in propagating honor killings warrants additional investigation. Understanding how these institutions maintain their oppressive power may lead to solutions for countering and altering their impact. (Singhal, n.d.). Support services for survivors of honor killings also show severe shortcomings. Research studying the efficacy and breadth of these support mechanisms is critical for designing comprehensive care and reintegration plans.

Finally, the long-term psychological and social effects on survivors are significantly understudied. Exploring the long-term trauma and societal consequences may provide insights into more effective therapies. Furthermore, a critical examination of international human rights frameworks is required to assess their effectiveness in addressing honor killings and to recommend improvements that could strengthen global efforts to combat this heinous violation of human rights.

INTRODUCTION

Imagine, your partner being killed by your own family members just for the sake of saving the honour of your family because you married a person who was not of your caste. Strange? Well, this still happens across the globe and is considered as an act of saving the honour, dignity and reputation of the family.

Basically, honour killings are the murders of an individual in a family in all probability by a relative for the act of dishonouring and tarnishing the so-called PRESTIGE or HONOUR of the family.

But now a question arises, whether those murders are satisfied? Did they all get their honour back? (Santhi, 2013) Are they all happy to see that family disintegrating and falling into pieces?

The honour that they had maintained for years, will that honour be lost if someone gets married by their own choice?

"My choice made me die but which of your choices kept me alive,
The echo inside my brain is ripping apart my silent pain.
Got tired of begging for my life and died with a thought that at least I tried,
Whispers of - Sorry, for breaking my vow lingers but lastly,
The incomplete tale of my life weaves a melodious tapestry of melancholy."
-Sudiksha

Honor killings are caused by a confluence of several legal, social, and cultural causes. These are the main five reasons:

1. Cultural and Traditional Beliefs

Culture and customs have a big part in keeping honor killings alive in many different communities around the world. These ideas are based on the idea that a family's honor is closely related to the actions, especially the sexual behaviour, of its female members. Many cultures, including but not limited to Indian, Middle Eastern, African, and certain Latin American communities, hold this concept to be common. In these communities, honor is regarded as a quality shared by the entire family that needs to be preserved at all costs.

Since women are frequently seen as the carriers of this honor, it might be considered dishonourable for them to take certain activities, including picking their own spouse or filing for divorce, or even just acting too freely.

Social conventions that place a high importance on women's chastity and obedience exacerbate this pressure. According to conventional wisdom, any perceived infraction by a woman shames her family as a whole in addition to her. Families may turn to drastic methods, like honor killings, in an attempt to regain this lost honor. This is especially clear in the function that Khap Panchayats perform in Indian regions like Western Uttar Pradesh and Haryana. These predominantly male local councils frequently serve as the guardians of customary values, giving commands that force families to carry out honor killings in order to preserve or regain their perceived honor. In these villages, Khap Panchayats hold great sway over marriage laws and the punishment of individuals who disobey their decrees. Their choices are usually made with little regard for the law and are grounded in patriarchal interpretations of honor, which contributes to the continuation of a culture of violence and impunity.

The wider community frequently encourages or at least tacitly condones these behaviours, which feeds the cycle of violence. Khap Panchayat rulings provide a clear illustration of how deeply ingrained patriarchal norms justify and support violence against women in the name of upholding honor. In the past, these councils have opposed same-gotra and intercaste marriages, which frequently resulted in honor killings. Because of the community's backing, victims and their families find it difficult to pursue justice because of the constant fear of social rejection or even more violence.

Saroj Virath was a driven young lady who, in order to become independent and wed the man she loved, Hemant Mohanpuriya, chose to become a law enforcement officer. Saroj's Meghwal position elevated her over Hemant's Reigar group in the strict caste order, even though both came from Scheduled Caste communities. Because of this discrepancy, she faced strong resistance from her family, who forced her to wed a guy they had selected when she was still a young girl, subjecting her to the deeply rooted patriarchal tradition of child marriage.

It is normal in Rajasthan for a girl to get a visit from her child-marriage fiancé, who spends one night with her to confirm her virginity, once she has finished her schooling (usually up to the 12th grade or a basic degree). In addition to enduring this degrading practice, Saroj made an effort to buck it, which resulted in serious domestic violence. In 2018, Saroj filed for legal protection following years of abuse, threats, and an attempt on her life. She was later discovered dead under dubious circumstances, although her relatives had abducted her as a result of her disobedience. Hemant thinks Saroj was the victim of an honor killing because he is distraught and feels guilty. He keeps going to court to get justice, but it's still elusive as of right now. Saroj's story illustrates how community leaders and councils, such as Khap Panchayats, frequently uphold cultural and traditional ideas, pressuring families to follow antiquated customs that have disastrous results. The pursuit of justice is further complicated by local authorities' reluctance to intervene against such influential entities. Her tragic story serves as a stark reminder of the damaging effects that deeply ingrained cultural and traditional beliefs can have on a person's life. It also serves as a reflection of the persistence of patriarchal practices in society. (Pandey, 2022)

In Non-Western countries, women's behavior is highly valued in maintaining family honor due to long-standing cultural and traditional norms. The interplay of legal difficulties and cultural traditions is shown by the way organizations like Khap Panchayats enforce these rules. These councils, which frequently function outside of established legal frameworks, are essential to upholding and upholding these patriarchal ideals and perpetuating the oppressive and violent cycle. This is a reflection of the deeply ingrained mindsets that contribute to these catastrophes. This mentality is prevalent in patriarchal societies all over the world, underscoring the global scope of the problem and the pressing need for societal shifts as well as legislative changes to safeguard people's rights and life. (XAVIER, 2015)

2. Gender Norms and Patriarchy

Patriarchy and gender norms have a major role in the global persistence of honor killings. Strict gender roles in patriarchal countries govern how people should behave, particularly women, who are expected to adhere to customs of modesty, submission, and subservience. Conversely, men are typically perceived as the defenders of family honor and the ones who uphold these standards.

These gender norms are reinforced by a variety of institutional and cultural processes and are ingrained in the social fabric. Women who don't follow the rules like picking their own partners, going to school, or dressing in an improper way are frequently perceived as disrespecting their families and defying male authority. The patriarchal system is threatened by this disobedience, which leads to violent reactions to regain authority and restore perceived honor. Even if the caste system and patriarchal control have been formally overturned, oppressive practices such as these still exist in modern culture. It is expected of men to preserve these norms and values and to prevent disloyalty to the family and to the masculine honor. Women are expected to behave honorably at all times. This reading of the concept justifies violence against women and all socially imposed expectations about appropriate behavior. (Smita Satapathy, 2023)

In many places, patriarchal ideals also serve as the foundation for the legal and judicial systems, which leaves women with little protection and honor-based assault offenders with light sentences. The fact that criminals are rarely held accountable for their actions contributes to the cycle of violence. Furthermore, it is challenging to question and alter deeply ingrained views since society tolerates male dominance and control over women, which perpetuates these destructive practices.

3. Social Pressure and Stigma

Shame and social pressure are two strong factors that, in many cultures, continue honor killings. In many countries, upholding family honor is a communally enforced public requirement as well as a private one. There is a lot of pressure on families to fit in because they worry about being the target of rumors, being shunned, and losing their social status if they are seen as unworthy. Families may feel pressured to carry out drastic measures, including honor killings, in an effort to repair their reputation.

It is important to recognize the community's responsibility in upholding these standards. Families are forced to take extreme measures because of gossip and criticism from neighbors and other family members. The moral and ethical ramifications of taking a life can sometimes be eclipsed by the fear of social rejection and the need to fit in.

Is killing morally acceptable in order to preserve one's status in society? This query calls into question the basic basis of violence motivated by honor. Does social acceptability make murder acceptable? Should the sanctity of human life be subordinated to fear of stigma? Solving these problems is essential to ending the cycle of violence.

Social standards need to change so that human rights and dignity take precedence over destructive and inflexible ideas of honor. Communities must change to embrace people's right to self-governance while categorically denouncing violence (Singhal, n.d.). Only then would it be possible to adequately address the ingrained problems of stigma and social pressure.

4. Legal and Judicial Impunity

Honor killings are a serious problem since many legal systems around the world do not sufficiently confront and prosecute these crimes, which creates legal and judicial impunity. Due to the complexity of addressing honor-based violence, many jurisdictions lack or are reluctant to construct the complicated and culturally sensitive legal frameworks that are necessary.

Legal systems throughout various regions are shaped by patriarchal values that put the honor of the family before the rights of the individual. Honor killing criminals frequently receive light sentences or are completely exonerated as a result of this bias. Furthermore, because of the complex social and cultural issues involved, legislators can be reluctant to pass comprehensive laws. Effective lawmaking necessitates a thorough comprehension of gender dynamics, cultural norms, and human rights principles - a task that takes time, effort, and skill.

Strong legal protections are not often enacted because of larger systemic issues like political opposition, bureaucratic delay, and societal divides. In order to successfully implement legal reforms, these challenges must be overcome by tenacious campaigning, outreach, and international pressure to respect human rights norms. (Kanchan et al., 2016)

In addition, relatives of victims may encounter severe obstacles in their pursuit of justice, such as lack of access to legal resources, social stigma, and fear of retaliation. The absence of consequences in this situation feeds the vicious cycle of violence and impedes efforts to end honor killings.

Strengthening legislative frameworks, educating communities about human rights and gender equality, and training judges and law enforcement personnel are all necessary steps in the fight against legal and judicial impunity. It necessitates a dedication to justice as well as an understanding that no custom or cultural belief can excuse murder or acts of violence. Societies cannot effectively eliminate honor-based violence and secure justice for victims and their families without substantial legislative change and enforcement.

5. Lack of Education and Awareness

Honor killings are made more common by a lack of knowledge and understanding of them, which also makes it more difficult to successfully stop them. Traditional beliefs and practices are frequently accepted without question in many countries, especially those with high rates of illiteracy or restricted access to formal education. Generations of people maintain misconceptions about gender roles, family honor, and honor, which helps to justify violence against women under the pretext of upholding honor.

It is imperative that honor killings be included in college and school curricula in order to increase student knowledge and foster critical thinking. Students can learn about the legal ramifications of honor-based violence, the consequences for gender inequity, and the implications for human rights by incorporating it into textbooks and educational activities. This kind of education can help people become more understanding, empathic, and determined to stop damaging behaviors in their communities.

Furthermore, education is essential for enabling people women in particular to understand their rights and fight against social forces that support or tolerate violence. Additionally, it can give educators and community leaders the know-how and resources they need to support survivors of honor-based violence and push for legislative changes.

Through a comprehensive approach to education and awareness, civilizations can undermine the cultural and social norms that perpetuate honor killings. In order to develop empathy, advance gender equality, and eventually stop acts of violence committed in the name of honor in the future, education must be prioritized.

AFTERMATH

What a society's inane vogue that they think, their gone honour will take the lives of individuals to come back without thinking of the illations that will definitely come clinging to their ruthless acts.

Some of the major illations are as follows: -

1. Social Consequences
2. Psychological Consequences
3. Legal Consequences

Now let's understand these illations in detail.

1. Social Consequences

"Faith" is the bedrock that every member of a family has for one another and is the only idea on which a person relies without any surmise whether it's on a trusted family member, a friend, neighbour or even God! But stories and incidents of honour killings are typically based on the fact of "breaking one's faith," which makes society reconsider whether their faith is pertinent or not. Having faith is a normal human tendency, which even leads to a successful marriage, but what if that faith shatters and shows up with acts of brutality?

Eventually this chronic fact of faith will convert in fear which will cast its shadow across generations.

- **Fear of Losing Trust:** Trust is the foundation upon which all relationships are built. Seeing your very own family react positively to cases of honour killing may build the same thought in your mind and convincingly make you think accordingly that "when you do it, you will face the same." The realm of this thought is boundless and may create feelings of isolation and jeopardy, which culminate in losing trust in the family.
- **Fear of Being Killed:** Honour killings occur when a family member violates the perceived code of conduct, societal or cultural norms. This notion ties

the fear of getting killed for breaking such rules and values. Additionally, it dwindles the fact of getting married from your own free will. Fear of being killed is a legitimate worry in honour killing which may also cause a person reticent.

- **Fear of Getting Dishonoured:** It applies mostly in the case of females because the stigma of being a girl child curtails half of their rights at the very moment when they are born. Specifically in an orthodox family where the idea of being restricted is sound and taken positively as a fact that "This is how the home should perform" (Kirti et al., 2011). Females are made to follow the instructions given by their parents on their dressing sense, choices and life decisions. Even normal decisions in their lives depend on their parents' consent. So, how can she even think of getting married of her own choice, and even if her family allows for marriage, then they also have a condition to marry a boy of their own caste? There are bare-minimum families that encourage marriage within any caste. People know how to prattle about equality, discrimination, and all corresponding stuff, but they have never brought this notion into their own lives because they are living in the same realm of old societal norms, which makes females feel dishonoured so effortlessly.

- **Fear of Losing Support:** If trust is gone then support (as a good companion) will go as well. So, where will a person find support?

In family? In friends? In social groups? In therapist or counsellors?

Well, while understanding this fact, we need to see the hierarchy of the support system. After listening to SUPPORT, the very first word that comes to everyone's mind is family. Now, keeping their opinions in mind, families with traditional beliefs will show a red flag for the decision and ostracize them from being members of their family, and lastly, who knows, they might kill them. Now comes society's turn. Society has made such futile norms that have been followed for decades, and it won't even take a few minutes before they will swiftly start treating you as a taint of society. (Here, society includes friends, therapists, consultants, social groups, and all similar groups.) Now there will be no support except the support of each other, and that won't be enough to live a happy life together because, lastly, you have to survive in the same society, and if not, then where else will you go?

- **Fear of an Unknown Situation:** Nothing is constant, not even your own family. The family which praises you for being so righteous, diligent and obedient can kill you the very next moment for marrying out of your caste or doing such acts that may harm their reputation. Bizarre! but this is the truth of orthodox families who still believe that honour can be regained by killing an individual. Future uncertainties cannot be foreseen with naked eyes, which creates apprehension of getting killed and therefore can influence and shape lives of individuals over time.

- **Fear of Reprisal:** This refers to facing negative consequences in lieu of getting married. Marriage is a sacred bond that connects two individuals by heart and soul, but it may be perceived as a demeaning action for one's family or society. This creates the anxiety of facing retaliation in their minds, which leads them to end up severing their bond and living life according to societal norms. Here, feelings and being independent (taking your own decisions) are killed by society, including their family.
- **Fear of Trauma:** Trauma is something that shakes you up from head to toe after thinking. Half of the trauma in the victim's life is due to what has been written above. Thinking about what society will do and how our parents will treat us, will one or both of us be killed? These all give birth to the infant named Trauma, because trauma is something really dreadful that provokes emotions in a person that are very awful, terrible, atrocious, and remote. It prompts the consideration of not marrying based on personal likings and induces the decision to discontinue the relationship. Now, when you are not with your beloved person, won't you feel trauma? Will that intense emotional strain be any less than trauma? Indeed, no matter how far you run or what you do, trauma will not go away from you. This can cause emotional turmoil that might result in long-term mental health problems like PTSD, depression, and anxiety. Deep trauma is experienced by survivors and their families; enduring fear, grief, and humiliation exacerbates these conditions, leading to long-term psychological distress and impaired mental health.

2. Psychological Consequences

A child's brain is nurtured with the nutrients and water their parents and society provide. It's like a raw earthen pot that bends in the same direction you want it to, and if it doesn't, then it will become unserviceable. Now what is the use of society and that family who are stuck to the same pattern of making that pot and not being pervasive according to the exigency of time? Well, a child will have the same values and notions that their parents provide, and according to the parents, they are providing the best ethics and knowledge to grow their child and teach them the lessons of surviving in a community (Case et al., 2017). They are adhering to the same traditions and customs that they have been taught by society. This way of thinking is a bit foggy. You have a life; you make your own decisions; the child is yours; you make money to give shelter to the child; but still, you allow society to dictate your choices and beliefs. Isn't your life and your decisions ultimately yours to make and break? The tragic reality is that a person cannot be true to themselves because their perception has changed according to society (Singh, 2019). They are running away from themselves and secretly obeying societal norms.

Some psychological effects have a potent impact on altering and reshaping a person's cognitive outlook and understanding.

- **Social Seclusion:** As this rule of "every action has an equal and opposite reaction" is accepted worldwide, while applying it here too, we should comprehend that when a family murder one of their own in order to uphold their dignity due to the fabricated rules of society, which cannot be fragmented at any cost, So, they act knowingly unknown about the murder and start pretending that regardless of what she has done, after all, she was my daughter or sister. Then start isolating themselves and remain silent because they are afraid, they might be caught lying.
- **Identity Ambiguity:** The survivors of honour killings, whether the victim itself or their partner, this incident shakes the senses of their identity and security. Only a mere number of victims survive honour killings and cannot get off the horrific experience of touching death because for them, it's hard as hell to forget the same. Most honour killings are women centric, and if they succeed in surviving, and even if she doesn't, so will her partner, who will have the trepidation of getting killed any moment as long as they are alive. No matter whether he or she is immersed in any shell dug from the ground, fear will not let them live alone.
- **Intricate Grief:** The sudden death of loved one's may grapple with feelings of guilt and helplessness. It may seem insignificant to watch them cry, but do you know that witnessing the unexpected loss causes anxiety and can be so traumatic because they go through a significant loss, grief, and sorrow inside. The term "intricate grief" describes a loss and mourning process that is intricate and intricately entwined; involving a range of feelings, ideas, and behaviours. It generally includes difficulties adjusting to life without the lost person, as well as emotions of sadness, rage, guilt, and perplexity. This kind of mourning can be very difficult to handle because emerging from that zone is challenging and looks fairly difficult to come out of as it is not a simple undertaking.
- **Feeling of Rage and Bitterness:** Honour killings are the stories of murders happening with profound mystery, anger and resentment. Likewise, it is a frequent result of twisted sense of family or community honour, where people feel they have to defend ideals at all costs, even if it involves using violence (Singh, 2019). This distorts the reason for the anger and resentment. People who are involved could feel threatened by

perceived threats to their honour, resentful of society norms, or furious at the alleged transgressor. But it's important to understand that honour killings are violent crimes that cannot be justified, and the feelings that drive such atrocities do not validate or excuse them.

- **Remorse and Accountability:** A sense of self-blame and guilt is extremely common and obvious in the sufferer. Oftentimes, victims of honour killings are unfairly held responsible for deeds or situations that are thought to have embarrassed the family. If the victims absorb the idea that they are the wrongdoers and this is the fault that infringes on their circumstances, it can result in severe feelings of guilt and self-loathing. It's important to stress, nevertheless, that victims of honour killings are not responsible for their own deaths. The people who commit these acts of violence and the institutions of society that support or enable them are solely to blame. Regret and responsibility are frequently overwhelmed in the context of honour killings by deeply rooted cultural beliefs, flaws in the law, and societal attitudes that support violence and injustice. In order to combat honour killings, institutional problems must be challenged and changed, and vulnerable people who are in danger of violence must be supported and shielded.

- **Dysregulation of Emotions:** a condition in which an individual struggles to control and communicate their feelings, frequently leading to irrational or severe reactions to emotional cues. Emotional dysregulation can be a major factor in honour killings, both for the individuals who commit the crimes and for the larger social dynamics that support these crimes. A cycle of violence and dysfunction may be perpetuated by children raised in such situations by teaching them unhealthy coping strategies for handling their emotions, such as anger, denial, or repression. To tackle the emotional dysregulation that leads to honour killings, a comprehensive strategy encompassing individual, familial, and societal intervention levels is necessary. This could entail addressing detrimental gender norms and stereotypes, supporting education and awareness campaigns to counter the societal acceptance of honour killings, and offering mental health support and counselling to both offenders and survivors of honour-based violence. Honor-based violence can be avoided in the future by treating the underlying emotional dysregulation and cultural issues that contribute to these crimes, as well as by protecting the rights and dignity of every individual.

Accountability in honour killings is often elusive due to several factors. Firstly, perpetrators may not face legal consequences for their actions due to legal loopholes, lenient laws, or corruption within the judicial system. Lastly, fear of retaliation or social ostracization may deter witnesses or victims' relatives from seeking justice, further undermining accountability.

3. Legal Consequences

Legal consequences of honour killings revolve around legal ramifications that include filing criminal charges against those who commit them, enforcing suitable penalties, dismissing religious or cultural arguments as defences, handling issues with prosecution, and pushing for changes to the law that would make it stronger against gender-based violence and better protect survivors. The legal ramifications of honour killings differ based on the laws of the nation in which the crime is committed, as well as how successfully the legal and law enforcement institutions handle these kinds of situations. However, accountability in honour killings is often elusive due to several factors like perpetrators may not face legal consequences for their actions due to legal loopholes, lenient laws, or corruption within the judicial system because there is no specific law dedicated solely to honour killings. Generally, honour killings are punished under current criminal laws that deal with murder, manslaughter, or similar offences, as well as provisions that handle domestic abuse and gender-based violence.

Let's examine honour killings' legal ramifications in greater detail:
- **Criminal Charges:** Depending on the particulars of the case and the local laws, honour killings are classified as criminal offences and usually come under the headings of murder, manslaughter, or homicide. If the killing was premeditated, the perpetrators may be charged with first-degree murder; if not, they may be charged with second-degree murder. Manslaughter charges may be brought against those responsible in situations where the death was accidental or happened in the heat of the moment. The potential legal consequences that the offenders may face are determined by the seriousness of the charges.
- **Punishments:** Serious punishments including incarceration, life in jail, or, in certain cases, the death penalty are the legal repercussions for honour killings. The severity of the crime, aggravating circumstances (such premeditation or cruelty), the jurisdiction's legal system, and the judiciary's discretion, all play a role in determining the duration of a prison sentence or if the death penalty is applied. Depending on how in-

volved and how guilty each offender is, various penalties may be given to them in specific situations.
- **Legal Protection:** Honour killing perpetrators may try to utilize religious or cultural grounds, saying that the murder was required to preserve customs or preserve family honour. These defences, however, are typically rejected by juries and do not release defendants from criminal responsibility. Legal systems should respect the fundamental rights of all people and ensure that everyone is treated equally under the law, regardless of their cultural or religious beliefs. To guarantee that justice is done, jurors and judges must consider all available information and apply the law in an unbiased manner.
- **Prosecution Hurdles:** There are a number of reasons why honour killing prosecutions can be difficult, such as weak legal systems, corruption in the courts and law enforcement, cultural prejudices, and social pressures. The family of the offenders may intimidate or take revenge on victims and witnesses, making it challenging to obtain information and get convictions. Furthermore, because of deeply ingrained patriarchal views or cultural traditions that place a premium on family honour over individual rights, honour killings may occasionally be ignored or tacitly approved by authorities. Mamta, a young woman from Jaipur (India), is a moving illustration of how these obstacles actually appear in daily life. In what is commonly known as an honor killing, her husband was brutally slain after marrying Amit, a Keralan Nair, against the desires of her parents. Jeewanram Chaudhary and Bhagwani Devi, Mamta's parents, are accused of planning Amit's murder in May 2017. According to the police, they and an accomplice broke into Mamta's Jaipur home and shot Amit at close range as another accomplice waited in a car outside. Mamta's mother was recently given bail, demonstrating the justice system's compassion towards the defendants despite abundant evidence of this horrible conspiracy. Mamta, a mother and widow now, navigates a system that frequently fails to protect victims of honor crimes in her pursuit of justice. (The Indian Express, 2021)
- **Advocacy and Legislative Reforms:** Strengthening legislation against gender-based violence, enhancing victim protection protocols, and facilitating survivors' access to justice are all part of the fight against honour killings. Human rights organizations, grassroots advocacy movements, and international organizations are essential in bringing attention to honour killings, enlisting public support, and applying pressure on governments to act. Stricter punishments for offenders, specialized training for court and law enforcement staff, and the establishment of victim

support services are examples of legal reforms that might be implemented to guarantee that survivors get the help they need to start over (Patel, 2015).

Not just honouring the sadly tragic deaths but also bringing to light the immense pain that these senseless acts of violence have caused countless people. Every number conceals a real tale, a long life snatched and made short, and a bereaved family split apart. The cries of abandoned children, the tears of grieving mothers for their daughters, and the silent agony of those who live in constant fear of being the next victim cannot be disregarded. Honour killings are an insult to all of mankind and a clear illustration of the pervasiveness of cultural intolerance and patriarchal oppression.

Let us not give up in the face of the terrible reality of honour killings; instead, let us encourage our shared desire to condemn injustice and defend the inherent value and dignity of every person who offers us courage. We can only aspire to build a world where honour killings are relegated to the past because every life is valued and cherished by activism, education, and steadfast dedication. India has to pass a draft law that targets honour killings particularly in order to address this widespread problem. A separate legal structure for honor killings is essential, much as the Nirbhaya case sparked extensive legal reforms for rape in India. Honor killings should be clearly defined in this proposed law so that they are distinguished from other types of murder. It should impose harsher punishments on criminals, create specific training programs for judges and law police, and offer extensive support services to victims. The inclusion of a specific section on honour killings in the Bharatiya Nyaya Sanhita (BNS) would serve to highlight the gravity of these offences and enable more efficient legal proceedings.

Alternatively, in the event that creating a distinct section is impractical, honor killings should be expressly included in the definition of murder in the IPC to make sure that these crimes are recognized and dealt with by the law. Such legislative actions will demonstrate India's dedication to preserving justice and human rights while also being in line with international best practices. Legislative reform aimed at addressing honor killings will open the door to a more just and equitable society in which each person's right to life and dignity is upheld. Moving forward, we have to question ourselves: Can we as a society really call ourselves progressive while putting up with such cruel and antiquated practices? Justice necessitates not only legislative change but also a deep shift in societal perceptions, which starts with each of us facing the hard realities of our reality. Will we accept this challenge and work toward a time where respect and equality, rather than violence, are used to celebrate every life?

REFERENCES

Case, S., Johnson, P., Manlow, D., Smith, R., & Williams, K. S. (Eds.). (2017). *Criminology*. Oxford University Press. DOI: 10.1093/he/9780198736752.001.0001

Kanchan, T., Tandon, A., & Krishan, K. (2016). Honor Killing: Where Pride Defeats Reason. *Science and Engineering Ethics*, 22(6), 1861–1862. DOI: 10.1007/s11948-015-9694-5 PMID: 26293131

Kirti, A., Kumar, P., & Yadav, R. (2011). The face of honour based crimes: Global concerns and solutions. *International Journal of Criminal Justice Sciences*, 6(1/2), 343–357.

Pandey, T. (2022). Stolen glances to stolen lives: Stories behind the 'honour killings' of Rajasthan, Haryana. *ThePrint*. https://theprint.in/feature/stolen-glances-to-stolen-lives-stories-behind-the-honour-killings-of-rajasthan-haryana/893651/

Patel, V. (2015). *Smart cities have to be safe cities*. Retrieved from https://www.researchgate.net/publication/291514771

Santhi, J. V. (2013). *Honour killing: A national outcry*. Retrieved from https://www.researchgate.net/publication/301350397

Satapathy, S. D. R. (2023). Honour killing as a crime in India. *International Journal of Law Management & Humanities*, 6. Advance online publication. DOI: 10.10000/IJLMH.114514

Singh, A. K. (2019). *Social psychology* (2nd ed.). PHI Learning Pvt. Ltd.

Singhal, V. K. (n.d.). *Honour Killing in India: An Assessment*. Retrieved from https://ssrn.com/abstract=2406031 DOI: 10.2139/ssrn.2406031

The Indian Express. (2021). Honour killing: Accused should have waited for conclusion of trial before taking bail, says SC. *The Indian Express*. https://www.newindianexpress.com/nation/2021/Jul/09/honour-killing-accused-should-have-waited-for-conclusion-of-trial-before-takingbail-says-sc-2327797.html#:~:text=Mamta%2C%20Jaipur%2Dbased%20girl%2C,Amit%20Nair%27s%20murder%20in%20Jaipur

XAVIER, M. S. (2015). Honour Killings: A Global Concern. *PARIPEX - INDIAN JOURNAL OF RESEARCH, 4*(3).

Chapter 12
Honor Crimes vs. Constitutional Rights:
A Comparative Constitutional Conundrum

Govind Singh Rajpal
https://orcid.org/0000-0002-3078-311X
MIT-ADT University, India

Aditya Lohani
GLA University, India

ABSTRACT

In this chapter, cultural norms, human rights, and constitutional principles vis-à-vis Honour Crimes are thoroughly examined. It begins with a perceptive introduction that highlights the importance of addressing honour crimes on a global scale and highlights how they continue to pose a threat to the fundamental principles of equality and human rights. The chapter explores the origins of honour crimes in cultural norms and critically examines how they violate fundamental human rights from a jurisprudential standpoint. It reviews constitutional responses to honour crimes globally, examining how well various legal systems protect individual rights while taking cultural factors into account. The comparative jurisprudential analysis at the chapter's heart aims to highlight the problems that honour crimes present and offer creative constitutional remedies.

BACKGROUND

The chapter looks into the legal options available to victims of honor crimes and examines how constitutional rights can serve as protection. It also illustrates effective constitutional responses, sketches of technological developments influencing future legislation against honor crimes, and provides case studies and an analysis of emerging trends.

Embarking on legal doctrine's, cultural norms and constitutional solutions exploration, unravelling the convoluted threads binding the constitutional rights and honor crimes in a compelling narrative. The adjacency of honor crimes against the backdrop of constitutional principles sets the stage for a nuanced examination of potential solutions to one of the most challenging dilemmas facing the societies today.

In the past few years, honor killings have turned into a big problem. Many international investigations reveal that there's a growing trend of awful acts over the last twenty years. A United Nations report back in 2021 said that around 81,100 women lost their lives each year. But, when we look at the most recent report from the United Nations Office on Drugs and Crime, it a shocking number: 89,000 women were killed around the world in 2022! (U.N. Women, 2022). The report points out that roughly 50,000 of those women were killed by their husbands or family. It's heartbreaking to think about how many were hurt by people who should love them—like husbands, ex-husbands, fathers, brothers, uncles, cousins, & other close relatives. The reasons behind these tragic events often stem from jealousy, suspicion, or sometimes even a woman wanting a divorce. It's really sad to see this happen.

Key Terms

Core terms include "Honor Crimes" AND "Constitutional Rights". Broader themes like "Cultural Norms" AND "Human Rights", "Femicide/Feminicide" AND "Gender-based Violence", "Cultural Traditions" AND "Human Rights Violations" contextualize the issue. Legal and policy related terms such as "International Conventions" AND "Jurisprudential Perspective", "Enforcement Challenges" AND "Right to Equality", "Right to Dignity and Security" AND "Legal Challenges" connects to the practical application. Analytical perspectives like "Legal Systems" AND "Comparative Analysis", "Victim-Centered Approach" AND "Legal Rigor" allow for exploring the complexities of honor killings across different cultural and legal contexts.

Selecting the right journals and carefully conducting inclusion/exclusion and article research is essential for a Research Paper on Honor Crimes vs Constitutional Rights. The journal selection process focused on publications specializing in human rights, gender studies, international law, and related interdisciplinary fields. The author opted for journals like *Amnesty International*, *Paripex-Indian Journal of Research*, *UNODC* etc. which align with the subject matter and provide a platform for scholarly discussions on these topics.

Inclusion criteria emphasized relevance, ensuring that only articles directly addressing honor killings, Constitutional Rights, or associated legal and cultural issues like Human Rights are considered. Recent publications, preferably within the last decade, were prioritized which led to the incorporation of current perspectives and data.

Exclusion criteria filtered out articles with only tangential relevance to the topic. Conducted article research using academic databases like JSTOR and Google Scholar is crucial, employing targeted keywords such as "Honor Killing," "Gender-Based Violence," and "Human Rights Law" to identify the most pertinent studies for our paper. Non-credible online sources and news articles were excluded to avoid any discrepancies.

Literature Review

Gender-related killings of women & girls (Femicide/Feminicide). (2022). UNODC This brief from UNODC points out how important it is to have plans. Plans to fight against gender-based violence. The world is facing a crisis with femicide. To tackle this issue everywhere, the report talks about how we really need better data and stronger laws. The authors stress the importance of getting communities involved and changing laws to protect women & girls from such violence (U.N. Women, 2023) This new report builds on the one from 2022. It shares updated information and fresh views on the rates of femicide. To really deal with this problem, the authors point out that we still have a tough time reporting & understanding femicide cases and they highlight the need for better teamwork globally. Amnesty International. (2001). Broken bodies, shattered minds: Torture and ill-treatment of women Amnesty International digs deep into violence against women—especially torture & mistreatment. The writers argue that this violence isn't just a human rights issue, it shows a deep-rooted inequality between genders. The report calls for more global action to end these terrible practices and to protect women's rights. (Xavier, 2015) This article talks about "honor killings." It's when family members murder women to keep "family honor." To fight against this problem around the world, the authors push for changes in laws & educational programs, focusing on cultural and social reasons behind it. Martha Nussbaum and Amartya Sen discuss that to really tackle gender-based violence, social justice must include both protecting people's rights and creating chances for them to succeed. Aharon Barak emphasizes that proportionality is key for upholding human rights like security & life—super important in fighting femicide (Barak, 2012). Reeves (2017) shows how Dworkin's ideas can help support women's rights & stop gender-based violence. Human rights law in Magna Carta, Constitution of India, and International Conventions This article reviews how international conventions, India's Constitution, & the Magna Carta shape human rights law. The author looks at how these legal systems have impacted protecting women's rights and battling violence against women.

Future Research Directions

The research looks closely at a big problem around the world: honor. These issues come from old cultural beliefs & they lead to many serious violations of human rights. It gives a detailed look at different legal solutions that could help fix this issue, stressing the need for better laws. It explores how honor crimes really go against basic human rights, especially the right to life & safety. Plus, it digs into cultural norms and the way society thinks that help keep these crimes alive. We get a peek into why these things happen in the first place. The research also checks out how effective different laws have been in stopping honor crimes. It brings in lots of reports, court cases, and articles written by experts to support its points. This way, readers can get a clear picture of the whole situation.

Future research could look into how different countries respond to honor crimes. There have been some studies about laws, but we really need to dig deeper into how well these laws work at actually cutting down honor crimes. This kind of research can tell us which legal methods are super effective – & maybe even why that is. Another interesting area to explore is how education & awareness programs can help stop honor crimes. Sure, some studies show that learning can reduce gender-based violence, but not much has been done on honor crimes in particular. This new study could really focus on those crimes and see if these programs work in the long run. Also, it's important to check how different countries put their policies into action & make sure those laws are enforced. A lot of research talks about making policies, but less looks at how they're put into practice. This study would look at the challenges & successes in enforcing laws against honor crimes.

INTRODUCTION

"Honor of our home" or we can say "Ghar ki izzat" encapsulates the main reason behind this dreadful crime. Honor crimes represent a tenacious global challenge that violates the principles of equality and human rights. It is deeply rooted in cultural norms, transcending various legal systems and borders. Honor crimes are not incarcerated to any specific or particular region, they are manifested worldwide. The Clash between human rights which are universal and cultural traditions is very apparent in honor crimes. So, it becomes very important to know the approach of different legal systems across the world in dealing with honor crimes, and also how constitutional rights play a prominent role in promoting gender equality and human rights. While doing so there arises mainly two questions: First, do they uphold individual rights? Second, how do different legal systems balance cultural norms and constitutional principles? For getting answers to these questions, we have to firstly identify that what are the persistent challenges of honor crimes globally, then urgency of solutions and how constitutional frameworks respond to it.

Global Challenge

In a world where cultures are diverse, honor crimes continue to be a major global problem that calls for a thorough investigation of their causes and effects, and because honor crimes are so deeply rooted in cultural norms, they affect people everywhere, regardless of their social or economic background. Men are the sources, active producers, or agents of honor in many societies where it is highly valued, and women can only have a destructive effect on honor. In order to save face in the community, the family must exact instant retribution to restore honor once it has been destroyed by the woman. As stated in a statement by Amnesty International, "The regime of honour is unforgiving: family members have no socially acceptable option but to attack the woman to remove the stain on their honour after suspicion has been placed on her." (Amnesty International., 2001) Women who are the subject of suspicion are not given the chance to defend themselves.

According to the Special Rapporteur's report on violent cultural practices against women, honor killings have been documented in Yemen, Jordan, Lebanon, Egypt, Morocco, Syrian Arab Republic, Palestine, Turkey, and other countries in the Mediterranean and Persian Gulf. Asian nations like Sri Lanka, India, Bangladesh, Pakistan, etc.; and European nations like France, Germany, the United Kingdom, Canada, and the USA. Human Rights Watch's advocacy director, Widney Brown, claims that honour killing is a practice that is common to all cultures and religions. (Xavier, 2015)

For Example, from 2003 to 2008, there were over 1000 honor killings in Istanbul, with one honor killing occurring each week. In 2009, there were reports of a horrific honor killing involving a 2-year-old boy born outside of marriage. Researchers Sujay Patel and Dr. Amin Mohammad of Memorial University in Canada looked into how the custom of honor killings came to be in the country in 2007. According to their report, individuals can impose their traditions on others when they relocate to Canada. Honor killings are carried out in Pakistan according to the Kari-karo tradition. Reports of fictitious honor killings from Pakistan are numerous. (Xavier, 2015) Case such as Muhammad Siddique v State, 2002 involves A murder conviction for the father's honor killing of his daughter, son-in-law, and grandchild was upheld on the grounds that an honor killing constitutes murder. The Court determined that "No tradition is sacred, no convention is indispensable, and no precedent is worth emulating unless it meets the fundamental principles of civil society." (Muhammad Siddique v. State, 2002)

Family members or other individuals may choose to kill the daughters for a variety of reasons, including upholding the honor of their family. The most apparent and obvious reasons why this practice persists in many nations, and in India specifically, albeit much more quickly and almost daily, are: the fear of losing their caste and community standing; the rigidity of caste/Gotra/clan/tribe; fear of stigmatization; the obsession with maintaining the "purity" of lineage; the unwillingness of people to change their views on marriage; the lack of fear of formal governance or the law; the cultural practices in the family; the display of male chauvinism; the mindless adherence to traditional or family values; patriarchal, patrilocal, and patrilineal family structures; misperceptions of honor, repute, status, respect, etc.

Challenging Equality and Human Rights: The Need for Constitutional Solutions

"Everyone has the right to life, liberty, and security of person," according to Article 3 of the Universal Declaration of Human Rights, highlighting the fundamental significance of individual rights.(Universal Declaration Of Human Rights, art. III) Honor crimes, on the other hand, directly violate this fundamental right by continuing to commit acts of violence against people, especially women, on the grounds of alleged cultural norm violations. Laws have often had difficulty providing a sufficient response to crimes involving honor. Given the intersectionality of gender and the fact that women are disproportionately the victims of these crimes, the need for constitutional solutions becomes even more urgent. Honor crimes are one type of gender-based violence that the Convention on the Elimination of All Forms of Discrimination Against Women (CEDAW) highlights the need to combat with legal measures.

An examination of the legal systems of particular nations offers context for understanding the seriousness of the situation. For example, the Anti-Honor Killing Laws that were introduced in 2016 were a major step in the right direction towards addressing the issue of honor killings, which have been concerningly common in Pakistan (Chen & Saifi, 2016). The efficacy of these laws is still being examined, though, which highlights the complex difficulties in converting legal provisions into real change. Constitutional remedies differ around the world. While some countries have explicit legal provisions shielding citizens from honor crimes, others may not. Comprehending the variety of methods is essential to creating a comparative analysis that looks for practical solutions rather than just admitting the issue. By situating honor crimes within the larger context of human rights and equality, we lay the groundwork for a thorough examination of constitutional responses that seek to reconcile cultural traditions with universal principles.

INVESTIGATING HONOR CRIMES: A JURISPRUDENTIAL APPROACH

Cultural Norms as Legal Dilemmas

Honor crimes put us in conflict between deeply rooted cultural norms and universal human rights because they are frequently linked to maintaining family or community reputation. The principles of non-discrimination are highlighted in Articles 2 and 3 of the Universal Declaration of Human Rights (UDHR), which affirm that all individuals are entitled to the freedoms and rights outlined in the Declaration, without any form of discrimination.(Universal Declaration Of Human Rights, art. III, II) In this light, it becomes essential to look at particular instances where cultural norms conflict with these core values. A legal viewpoint that balances cultural customs and human rights is desperately needed, as demonstrated by the sad case of Pakistan's Qandeel Baloch, whose murder in the name of family honor shocked the entire world. (Saifi et al., 2022). Renowned legal scholars such as Martha Nussbaum contend that cultural relativism is insufficient justification for the infringement of fundamental human rights. Nussbaum, in her groundbreaking work, argues in favour of a capabilities approach, stating that regardless of cultural norms, a just society should allow people to attain certain essential capabilities. ("The Capability Approach," 2011)

Violation of Fundamental Human Rights

Honor crimes necessitate a careful examination of the fundamental human rights violations they cause in order to be examined jurisprudentially. In honor killing cases, the right to life, as guaranteed by Article 3 of the UDHR, is flagrantly violated. Furthermore, when people—mainly women—fall prey to heinous acts of honor-related violence, Article 5, which forbids cruel and torture, degrading or inhuman treatment or punishment, is frequently broken. (Universal Declaration Of Human Rights. art. V) The enforcement of national laws is essential in addressing these violations. For instance, changes have been made to Pakistan's Hudood Ordinances to better align them with constitutional guarantees. ("The Hudood Ordinances," 2011) These ordinances were previously criticized for making women more vulnerable. Nonetheless, difficulties still exist in putting these reforms into practice, which reflects the intricate relationship that exists between legal requirements and cultural norms.

A startling amount of honor crimes are still being reported worldwide. The United Nations Office on Drugs and Crime (UNODC) reports that every year, thousands of women become victims of honor killings. (UNITED NATIONS OFFICE ON DRUGS AND CRIME, 2019) The figures highlight how urgent it is to create a legal framework that effectively uses constitutional rights to both denounce and prevent these actions. The necessity of a strong legal response to honor crimes is stressed by jurists such as Aharon Barak, a former president of the Israeli Supreme Court. Barak's proportionality doctrine, which balances the public interest against the seriousness of a right violation, offers a jurisprudential tool for assessing the legitimacy and legality of legal actions intended to eradicate honor crimes. (Barak, 2012). A theoretical framework for comprehending the seriousness of human rights violations in the context of honor crimes is provided by eminent jurists like Ronald Dworkin and his "rights as trumps" theory. (Reeves, 2017) The idea put forth by Dworkin that some rights should take precedence over cultural customs serves as a road map for finding a jurisprudential solution. Also, Human rights must be given priority in legal systems, as demonstrated by the court's struggle in various cases to strike a balance between cultural customs and constitutional rights. These cases shed important light on the intricacies of honor crimes as legal conundrums.

Global Constitutional Framework

Upholding cultural norms or Individual rights? It is necessary to conduct a legal investigation in the intricate area where constitutional principles and cultural traditions converge. Many countries struggle to protect individual liberties while honoring deeply ingrained cultural norms. First, we focus on the constitutional protections that are ingrained in legal systems all around the world. All members of the human family have equal rights and inherent dignity, which are stated in the foundational document known as the Universal Declaration of Human Rights (UDHR). Particularly, Articles 2, 3, and 7 of the UDHR (Universal Declaration Of Human Rights, art. II, III, VII) emphasize the non-discrimination principle and the idea that all people have the right to the freedoms and rights outlined in the Declaration.

Legal Pluralism: A Jurisprudential Conundrum

An additional layer of complexity is introduced by legal pluralism, which is the coexistence of several legal systems within a society. Jurisprudential conundrums arise when culturally traditional customary laws clash with constitutional mandates. Nations such as India, whose legal system is so diverse, are good examples of this problem. Article 13 (Constitution Of India, art. XIII) of the Indian Constitution aims to guarantee the nullity of laws that contradict or violate fundamental rights. Nonetheless, the constitutional fabric is frequently put to the test by the existence of customary laws and personal laws. Legal scholar Upendra Baxi contends that constitutionalism must serve as a corrective mechanism, guaranteeing that no cultural norm can violate the fundamental values of equality and justice, after analysing well-known jurisprudential perspectives on legal pluralism. He highlights the idea that customary practices should yield to constitutional norms as the ultimate law.

Global Jurisprudential Trends: Striking Balance

A global analysis of legal systems reveals a variety of strategies for striking a balance between cultural norms and individual rights. European nations, for example, prioritize human rights and frequently step in when cultural practices infringe upon these rights. One important tool in this respect is the European Convention on Human Rights (ECHR), which forbids torture and other cruel, inhuman, or degrading treatment in Article 3 and guarantees the right to life in Article 2. (European Convention on Human Rights (ECHR), art. II, III) Case such as Opuz v Turkey, 2009 involves domestic abuse and honor-related violence in Turkey. (Opuz v. Turkey, 2009) The European Court of Human Rights ruled that Turkey violated Articles 2 and 3 of the European Convention on Human Rights by failing to safeguard the applicant and her mother, highlighting state responsibility to prevent honor crimes.

The problem of protecting cultural legacy while upholding international human rights norms is one that many legal systems face. The right to cultural, religious, and linguistic communities, for example, is recognized by the South African Constitution in Section 31(1), but it is not unqualified and must be in accordance with Sections 10 and 9, which deal with equality and dignity, respectively. On the other hand, some jurisdictions take a more cautious stance, especially those that place a lot of emphasis on cultural relativism. The notion of "reasonable accommodation" is frequently at the center of the jurisprudential reasoning in these kinds of situations. This idea, which has been expressed in Canadian jurisprudence, permits a complex interpretation of cultural customs as long as they do not violate the fundamental tenets of the Constitution. (Bribosia et al., 2013)

Legal Challenges

Honor crimes continue in spite of these constitutional protections, casting doubt on the effectiveness of existing legal systems. Notwithstanding constitutional guarantees, statistics from a number of nations, including Pakistan, Turkey, and India, highlight the prevalence of honor crimes. The Hudood Ordinances in Pakistan, which were infamous for their discriminatory treatment of women, were changed to conform to constitutional values. But honor crimes continue, which begs the question of how effective legal changes are in the absence of corresponding societal changes.

Jurisprudential Perspective on Enforcement

One of the biggest jurisprudential challenges is enforcing constitutional guarantees. Legal experts such as Martha Nussbaum argue that in addition to addressing legal formalities, we also need to address the cultural norms that support honor crimes. Nussbaum's capability approach places a strong emphasis on the necessity of educating people and changing society in order to guarantee that constitutional rights are actually realized.

Comparative Constitutional Solutions

A thorough analysis of the various jurisdictions' successful constitutional responses is necessary to comprehend the complexities of honor crimes. A prime example is Sweden, where the prevalence of honor crimes has dramatically decreased as a result of legislative changes and an unwavering commitment to human rights. Article 4 of the Swedish Penal Code, which emphasizes the protection of individual rights while criminalizing acts done to uphold family honor, serves as a beacon. The development of Turkish law is another important case study. The legal system in the nation has undergone a paradigm shift as a result of changes to the Turkish Penal Code that specifically address honor crimes. Today, violators face harsh penalties under Article 82 (Turkish Penal Code, art. LXXXII), demonstrating a commitment to preserving the equality and justice enshrined in the constitution. Innovation in jurisprudence is essential to meeting the changing challenges that Honor Crimes present. In this context, the fusion of technology and legal frameworks is becoming a potent weapon. To protect potential victims, for example, nations like the United Kingdom have implemented creative legal measures like protective orders and electronic monitoring. Furthermore, there is growing momentum for the application of restorative justice principles within constitutional frameworks. A precedent has been set by the South African Constitutional Court's acceptance of restorative justice in cases involving honor crimes. This strategy seeks to promote healing and reconciliation within impacted communities in addition to punishing offenders.

Role of International Convention and Treaties

For a considerable amount of time, eminent legal experts have maintained that international agreements and treaties play a crucial role in influencing constitutional reactions to human rights breaches. In the context of honor crimes, the United Nations Convention on the Elimination of All Forms of Discrimination Against Women (CEDAW) is especially relevant. In order to uphold family honor, gender-based violence is explicitly condemned in Article 16 of CEDAW, which also asserts the right to equality in family life and marriage. (Convention on the Elimination of All Forms of Discrimination Against Women CEDAW, art. XVI) Likewise, comprehensive legal frameworks are provided by regional treaties, such as the Istanbul Convention of the Council of Europe on Preventing and Combating Violence Against Women and Domestic Violence. Through emphasizing the significance of prophylactic actions, safeguarding measures for victims, and the outlawing of aggression, the convention establishes a benchmark for constitutional reactions to honor crimes throughout Europe.

Challenges and Controversies

Although there has been progress in creating constitutional solutions, problems and disagreements still exist. The conflict between deeply ingrained cultural norms and constitutional principles is one prominent challenge. Some contend that imposing legal frameworks that are Western-centric may not be appropriate everywhere and may unintentionally encourage cultural insensitivity. Judicial scholars are increasingly promoting culturally aware legal pluralism as a way to overcome these obstacles. This entails appreciating and honoring various legal systems inside a framework established by the Constitution. As an illustration, consider the Canadian Multiculturalism Act, which upholds the primacy of the Canadian Charter of Rights and Freedoms while valuing cultural diversity.

On the other hand, disagreements occur when religious beliefs appear to conflict with constitutional values. It is still very difficult to strike a balance between individual rights protection and religious freedom. The Indian Supreme Court's consideration of cases involving "honor killings" highlights how difficult it is to find constitutional remedies in a pluralistic and diverse society. The Court usually tries to balance different things, like protecting life and personal freedom, with respecting religious & cultural beliefs in India. Some people say this balancing act sometimes means that basic rights are not given enough importance because cultural and religious ideas are put first.

In places where the legal system isn't strong, enforcing constitutional rights can be hard. For example, in Pakistan, even though the law says it should protect life and dignity, crimes against honor still happen because laws aren't enforced well and old-fashioned ideas still exist. This shows a big difference between what the constitution says and what actually happens. The courts play a big role, but they often can't do much because society resists change and there are limits to what they can do. Looking at it from a different angle, the European Court of Human Rights (ECHR) sees honor crimes through a constitutional lens. They always stress the importance of protecting people from harm no matter what cultural reasons there may be for it. While this is good, some people criticize it for not considering why honor crimes happen in the first place due to culture.

Victim Centered Approach

In the pursuit of human rights and justice, victim centered approach is paramount. The clear acknowledgment of victims' rights within constitutional frameworks is one of the core tenets of victim-centered jurisprudence. The protection of people from violence and discrimination is emphasized in a number of international human rights instruments, including the Universal Declaration of Human Rights and the Convention on the Elimination of All Forms of Discrimination Against Women, which serves as a strong basis for constitutional protections. A fundamental component of creating constitutional protections is Article 3 of the UDHR, which upholds the rights to liberty, life, and security. Recognizing the gender-specific nature of many honor crimes, CEDAW's Article 5 calls on states to alter social and cultural norms in order to eradicate biases and practices that support violence against women. Analyzing national legal systems is essential to comprehending how constitutional protections are actually put into practice. Nations with particular laws addressing honor-based violence include Sweden, Canada, and the United Kingdom. For example, encouraging or advocating genocide is expressly prohibited by Canada's Criminal Code (Section 318), which is a crucial step in stopping honor crimes.

In Sweden, laws aim to stop honor-related violence by understanding the special reasons and motives for these bad acts. The Swedish Penal Code has rules that see honor as a serious part of crimes, making the punishments tougher and giving more security to victims. Likewise, the United Kingdom made laws to protect people from honor-based violence. The Forced Marriage (Civil Protection) Act 2007 lets victims and potential victims of forced marriages get legal help. Helping survivors is important, so they need good support like legal advice, therapy, and safe places to stay. Having access to these services is key helping victims heal and start over. Also, it's important to have campaigns and programs that teach the public about honor crimes and try to change the cultural beliefs that keep these crimes happening.

CONSTITUTIONAL RIGHTS AS SHIELD OR VULNERABLE

Right to Equality

Protecting victims is largely dependent on constitutional provisions guaranteeing equality before the law and non-discrimination. Article 15 of the Indian Constitution forbids discrimination on the basis of caste, religion, sex, race, or place of birth. This constitution's ethos is consistent with the views of prominent jurists such as Dr. B.R. Ambedkar, who emphasized the need to eradicate social inequality. However, using constitutional rights to protect against honor crimes can be tricky. These may sound strong in theory, but their actual implementation often faces challenges due to societal beliefs, legal complexities, and institutional limitations. Honor crimes mainly occur in communities that value tradition more than following constitutional rules, creating a conflict between what the law says and what happens in reality. This divide is further widened when local authorities give in to societal pressures and don't fully enforce constitutional protections.

Different countries have different levels of protection against honor crimes within their constitutional frameworks. Some nations have strict laws and effective enforcement mechanisms, while others struggle to incorporate constitutional principles into daily legal and administrative procedures. The effectiveness of using constitutional rights to shield against honor crimes depends on various factors such as the strength of legal institutions, societal views on equality, and the authorities' willingness to challenge established cultural norms. Analyzing how different jurisdictions handle honor crimes through their constitutions reveals that just having constitutional rules isn't enough. There needs to be a collective effort to bridge the gap between constitutional ideals and practical application. This involves not only having strong legal structures but also educating the public, making societal changes, and showing unwavering political determination to uphold equality and justice principles. In essence, while constitutional rights play a crucial role in protecting against honor crimes, their impact is limited without continuous efforts to enforce and embody these rights throughout society.

Right to Dignity and Security

The defense of individual security and dignity under the constitution is essential to the fight against honor crimes. For example, Section 10 of the South African Constitution guarantees the right to human dignity, and Section 12 guarantees the right to freedom and security. The fundamental principles of these constitutional protections are reflected in Nelson Mandela's statement that "to deny people their human rights are to challenge their very humanity." (Bose, 2021). The fundamental or basic rules of these protections in the constitution are shown clearly in what Nelson Mandela said, that "If you take away people's human rights, you take away their humanity." This saying reminds us how crucial it is to protect human rights as the foundation of a fair society. However, making sure these protections actually work can be tough, especially in places where honor crimes are common.

When we think about honor crimes compared to constitutional rights, it's like a tug-of-war. Constitutions act as both shields and weak spots. They protect victims of honor crimes by giving them legal help and keeping them safe. They make sure the authorities step in, stop these crimes, and punish the people responsible. This is clear in countries with strong laws that actively fight honor crimes through strict rules and enforcement. But sometimes, things get complicated. Cultural beliefs, social pushback, and not following the rules can weaken these protections. In some cases, traditions and community practices matter more than what the constitution says. This clash shows a big difference between what the law says on paper and what happens in real life.

Also, having different legal systems can be tricky. Traditional laws and religious rules may not always match up with formal constitutional laws that protect human rights. To solve this problem, we need constitutions that not only talk about protecting rights but also make sure they're enforced well to keep people safe and respected. That means trying different approaches like changing laws, teaching the public, and talking about cultural values to fit human rights standards. In the end, keeping people safe from honor crimes using constitutional rights is an ongoing challenge. It needs lawmakers, courts, and society as a whole to keep working hard to make sure everyone's dignity and safety are more than just words on a page—it needs to happen in real life too.

Challenges and Areas for Improvement

There are still obstacles in the way of laws being implemented effectively, even with constitutional protections. Significant gaps in the worldwide reporting and prosecution of honor crimes have been noted by the United Nations Office on Drugs and Crime (UNODC). Bridging this implementation gap and ensuring that victims receive real protections from the constitution are the jurisprudential challenges.

Legal Rigor vs Cultural Sensitivity

A common theme in legal jurisprudential discussions is finding a balance between cultural sensitivity and legal strictness. The International Covenant on Civil and Political Rights (ICCPR), which emphasizes the value of respecting cultural diversity, recognizes right to conscience, the right to freedom of thought, and religion in Article 18. (International Covenant on Civil and Political Rights (ICCPR), art. XVIII) But it begs the question of how far cultural relativism should go when faced with actions that violate basic human rights. Honor crimes are a serious problem for legal systems worldwide. These crimes, which often involve violence or murder to protect family or community honor, violate human rights. Balancing human rights with cultural diversity is challenging. One major issue is the different legal systems and how they handle honor crimes. Some places don't enforce laws well, or cultural reasons lessen punishments. This makes it unfair under the law and leads to more violence.

Another problem is that victims of honor crimes don't always get enough help from the legal system. They might not have good options for justice, and social pressure stops them from seeking help. Victims need better support to stay safe and get justice. Having multiple legal systems in some places makes things even more complicated. When customary law and statutory law exist together, it's hard to make sure they follow the constitution. This can let honor crimes keep happening. To fix these issues, strong laws against honor crimes that also respect culture are needed. Education and awareness are important to change harmful beliefs in society. International cooperation can also help share ideas that work well.

CONCLUSION

To sum up, we have explored the complex intersection of cultural traditions and fundamental human rights through the course of "Honor Crimes vs. Constitutional Rights: A Comparative Constitutional Solutions". Upon contemplating the jurisprudential elements expounded in this chapter, several significant insights become apparent. First, a jurisprudential lens has helped us better understand honor crimes by removing the layers of cultural norms and recognizing the serious human rights violations that frequently go hand in hand with them. The worldwide jurisprudential analysis of constitutional responses to honor crimes exposes a convoluted legal environment in which various legal systems struggle to protect individual liberties while negotiating the complexities of cultural norms. The foundation for our investigation of comparative constitutional remedies is laid by this analysis. Not content to just point out issues, this chapter is a call to action for jurisprudence. Through cross-national constitutional approaches, we hope to better understand problems and come up with novel solutions. We examine the legal remedies available within the framework of constitutional rights and highlight the need to protect those impacted by honor crimes with our focus on victim-centered constitutional safeguards. As the problem of legal pluralism is examined in the context of jurisprudence, it makes us think about how constitutionalism can reconcile various cultural norms with fundamental rights. The jurisprudential analysis of case studies and new developments offers insightful information about effective constitutional responses and the changing environment brought about by technological developments. The jurisprudential focus emphasizes how crucial it is to continuously modify constitutional frameworks in order to address the changing obstacles presented by honor crimes and guarantee that human rights supersede deeply ingrained cultural customs.

"Honor Crimes vs. Constitutional Rights: A Comparative Constitutional Solutions" is essentially a call to action based on jurisprudential investigation rather than just the title of a chapter. Through comprehending, contrasting, and creating within constitutional frameworks, the authors aim to make a positive impact in a world where cultural traditions are subordinated to human rights.

REFERENCES

Amnesty International. (2001). *Broken bodies, shattered minds : torture and ill-treatment of women*. Amnesty International.

Barak, A. (2012). *Proportionality: Constitutional Rights and their Limitations*. https://doi.org/DOI: 10.1017/CBO9781139035293

Bose, A. (2021, May 17). *Human rights law in Magna Carta, Constitution of India and International Conventions - IPleaders*. iPleaders. https://blog.ipleaders.in/human-rights-law-magna-carta-constitution-india-international-conventions/#:~:text=%E2%80%9CTo%20deny%20people%20their%20human,become%20operational%20since%20their%20birth

Bribosia, E., Rorive, I., European Network of Legal Experts in the Non-discrimination field, European Commission, Human European Consultancy, & Migration Policy Group. (2013). *Reasonable Accommodation beyond Disability in Europe?* Office for Official Publications of the European Union.

Chen, K., & Saifi, S. (2016, October 8). *Pakistan passes legislation against 'honor killings.'* CNN. Retrieved from https://edition.cnn.com/2016/10/06/asia/pakistan-anti-honor-killing-law/index.html

Constitution Of India, art. XIII.

Convention on the Elimination of All Forms of Discrimination Against Women CEDAW, art. XVI.

European Convention on Human Rights (ECHR), art. II, III.

International Covenant on Civil and Political Rights (ICCPR), art. XVIII.

Muhammad Siddique v. State 54 PLD (2002).

Universal Declaration Of Human Rights, art. III

Universal Declaration Of Human Rights, art. III, II .

Opuz v. Turkey App No 33401/02 ECHR (2009).

Reeves, A. R. (2017). Ronald Dworkin's Theory of Rights. In *Encyclopedia of the Philosophy of Law and Social Philosophy*. https://doi.org/DOI: 10.1007/978-94-007-6730-0_4-1

Saifi, S., Syed, A., & Mogul, R. (2022, February 15). *Court frees brother who confessed to killing social media star Qandeel Baloch.* CNN. https://edition.cnn.com/2022/02/15/asia/pakistan-qandeel-baloch-brother-acquittal-intl-hnk/index.html

The Capability Approach. (2011). In *Stanford Encyclopedia of Philosophy*. Retrieved January 3, 2024, from https://plato.stanford.edu/entries/capability-approach/#pagetopright

The Hudood Ordinances. (2011, May 7). *DAWN*. Retrieved January 3, 2024, from https://www.dawn.com/news/626858/the-hudood-ordinances

. Turkish Penal Code, art. LXXXII.

UNITED NATIONS OFFICE ON DRUGS AND CRIME. (2019). GLOBAL STUDY ON HOMICIDE. In *GLOBAL STUDY ON HOMICIDE*. United Nations. https://www.unodc.org/documents/data-and-analysis/gsh/Booklet_5.pdf

Universal Declaration Of Human Rights, art. II, III, VII.

Universal Declaration Of Human Rights. art. V .

U. N. Women. (2022). Gender-related killings of women and girls (femicide/feminicide).

Women, U. N. (2023). Gender-related killings of women and girls (femicide/feminicide). Retrieved from https://www.unwomen.org/sites/default/files/2023-11/gender-related-killings-of-women-and-girls-femicide-feminicide-global-estimates-2022-en.pdf

Xavier, S. (2015). Honour killings: A global concern. *Paripex-Indian Journal of Research*, 4(3), 6–9.

Chapter 13
Understanding the Impact of Immigration on Honor Killing:
Instances From Various Countries

Myunghoon Roh
https://orcid.org/0009-0001-4634-9457
Salve Regina University, USA

Prestha Chhaparia
GLA University, India

ABSTRACT

In recent years, various discussions and debates are taking place in western countries which tries to explain the role of immigrant communities in honor related crime. Immigrant communities, although not an only factor but plays a major role in explaining honor related crimes. Various scholars and professors have analyzed honor killings in different countries and presented their ideas about the factors driving the crime of honor killing. This chapter discusses in detail the impact of immigration on honor killing along with the instances from countries namely, Canada, Sweden, Germany, Britain, United States and Netherlands.

BACKGROUND

Murdering some other person cannot be justified on any ground, be it to protect the honor of the family. In modern day scenario, where human rights are discussed on a global level, every individual has a right to live on their own terms and conditions.

DOI: 10.4018/979-8-3693-9596-7.ch013

It needs to be strongly learnt that killing someone cannot protect the honor of the family. There are various cultural and religious explanations behind these killings, but at the end murder means murder. In recent years, various discussions and debates are taking place in western countries which tries to explain the role of immigrant communities in honor related crime. Immigrant communities, although not an only factor but plays a major role in explaining honor related crimes. Various scholars and professors have analyzed honor killings in different countries and presented their ideas about the factors driving the crime of honor killing. Although various scholars define honor killing as the crime against women, but it is not correct to enclose this heinous crime in such a watertight compartment. This chapter discusses in detail the impact of immigration on honor killing along with the instances from countries namely, Canada, Sweden, Germany, Britain, United States and Netherlands.

Many research and media reports suggest that 12 cases of honor killing has taken place since 2002 in Canada. Although we do not have a specific data as many of the cases might be unreported, but the reality is that this crime does exist in Canadian society. Five honour killings are anticipated to occur in Sweden annually, however many cases go unreported since there is insufficient evidence to classify them as accidents or suicides (Gapf, 2020). According to data, within the past twelve years, there have been roughly 10–12 honour killings every year in Great Britain, 12 in Germany, 11–14 in the Netherlands, and 5 in Belgium (Sadowa, 2015). At the same time, several scholars stress that these figures may be far lower than the true magnitude because of the widespread tendency to conceal such acts and/or make them appear like accidents or suicides, as well as the complexity of the problem.

Research Methodology

The aim of this chapter is to gain an understanding of the impact of immigration on honor related violence. For the research purpose, qualitative method of research (Kothari, 2004) has been adopted. International journals, research articles, reports from government ministries, research paper & reports from international organizations, surveys, interviews etc. have been referred to for the research purpose. The research indicates that although immigration plays a role in honor-based violence but at the same time it is not the only reason due to which honor-based violence occurs. The data collected points on the fact that in certain communities, honor is a life and death situation and when these communities immigrate to another country, they are unable to adapt themselves and hence such crime occurs. The research further includes instances from various countries around the world where honor killing happened pertaining to the change in cultural beliefs and values as a result of immigration.

Key Terms

Core Terms include "Honor Killing" and "Immigration" (Korteweg & Yurdakul, 2010) highlighting the fact that immigration is also one of the reasons for honor-based violence around the world. Instances surrounding the main theme of the chapter are taken from various countries around the world which includes "Canada" (Shier & Shor, 2016), "Sweden" (Darvishpour & Lahdenpera, n.d.), "Germany" (Korteweg & Yurdakul, 2010), "Britain" (Dyer, 2015), "United States" and "Netherlands".

Inclusion criteria emphasized relevance, ensuring that only articles directly addressing honour killings and immigration are considered. Exclusion criteria filtered out non-academic sources, such as blogs or opinion pieces, and articles with only tangential relevance to the topic. Conducted article research using academic databases like JSTOR and Google Scholar is crucial, employing targeted keywords such as "Honor Killing" and "Immigration" (Korteweg & Yurdakul, 2010).

Literature Review

Korteweg & Yurdakul (2010) proposed that gender equality is being used as a tool in the political and media discourse on forced marriages and honour killings, which might create a clear social divide between the immigrant community and the majority culture.

Hellgren and Hobson in 2008 examined three recent incidents of honor killings that occurred in Sweden, focusing on how the media shapes conversations about culture and contended that these cases have deep cultural significance and struck a chord with Swedish society.

Shier & Shor (2016) talk about the Canadian news media's fabrication of a racial identity through the usage of the term "honor killing" and how it dehumanises and discriminates against South Asians, Muslims, and immigrants in Western society.

According to Darvishpour and Lahdenpera (n.d.) one of the most prominent figures on honor killings in Sweden, refers to the monitoring of women's sexuality and the male family member's need to uphold the family's dignity as "honor culture."

Manisha Gupta, 2015 talks about the problems encountered by the people belonging to a particular community when they migrate to a different country and how difference in culture and values leads to honor based violence.

Future Research Directions

It is evident from the chapter that author tries to establish a relation between immigration and honor killing and also elaborated the instances from various countries around the world where such killings took place as a result of immigration. As a result, author came to a conclusion that there is insufficient data on honor-based violence taking place in different countries and the reason for this is that majority of such instances go unreported and are often given the name of suicides and accidents. Further there is no specific law in any country which exclusively deals with honor killing and is often included in crimes such as murder, assault etc. Most of the research papers concludes honor killing as a gender-based violence against women (Shier & Shor, 2016) but the author elaborates that in today's scenario, victims are not only women but also men and people belonging to LGBTQ+ communities.

Honor killings should be treated as a distinct crime and there is a need to inculcate the same in every judicial system across the world. There is a future scope of improvement in the present paper as the author fails to present the accurate data of honor killing as a result of immigration.

INTRODUCTION

Honor killing, in its literal sense, can be defined as a killing or murder in the name of honor. Various people define honor killing as a crime against women. It is due to the reason because traditionally it has been well established that a woman is the honor of any family. If she does anything which is against the societal norms or traditional family values, then the honor of a man, be it her husband or father, is at stake. Honor killing is often associated with culture and religion and due to this immigration becomes a prominent factor in determining honor-based killings in any country. Tracing its origin, violence in relation to honor has been prevalent in Latin America, South Asia, North Africa, the Middle East, and Southern Europe, with varying patterns of violence in each of these areas. Western nations that attract immigrants have had to deal with honor killing and other types of violence in relation to honor throughout the last few years. The deaths of, Fadime Sahindal in Sweden, Mrs. Gul, Zarife, and Schijman Kuashi in the Netherlands, Hatun Surucu in Germany, Amandeep Atwal, Aqsa Parvez, and the Shafia sisters and their aunt in Canada, Heshu Yones and Banaz Mahmod in Britain are among the well-known murders that have been openly referred to as honor killings in the context of migration. (Korteweg, n.d.)

Various scholars and professors have analyzed honor killings in different countries and presented their ideas about the factors driving the crime of honor killing. Meetoo and Mirza in 2007 contend that honor killings in the UK have been considered cultural crimes due to their ethnicization within the British multicultural framework, resulting in a collision of discourses that affect immigrant women. Terman argues that immigrant populations experience disproportionately high rates of domestic violence, according to Western media. The media unfairly blames Muslims and other immigrant populations for rape and sexual assault, while ignoring the full scope of violence against women. This is true even if same crimes are often committed in the West. (Vatandoost, 2012)

Hellgren and Hobson in 2008 examined three recent incidents of honor killings that occurred in Sweden, focusing on how the media shapes conversations about culture. They contend that these cases have deep cultural significance and struck a chord with Swedish society. The murders in Sweden also sparked discussions among feminist organizations and the perspectives of immigrant women in society. The discourse on immigrant integration has been significantly impacted by the public debate on violence against women among Muslim immigrants, they explained, given that conversations about politics and policy in Sweden revolve around the idea of a "good society." As a result, distinct lines have been established separating immigrants from the mainstream community. (Hellgren & Hobson, n.d.)

Impact of Immigration on Honor Killing

Honor-related crimes are a very reflection of the mindset of the people living in a particular society. Every society has its own norms, rules and regulations and the people living in that particular society has to abide by it. If they fail to do so, they are considered to bring shame to the society and are not accepted. Families form a part of society and head of the family takes the responsibility that every member of his family will abide by the set norms of the society. If any member tries to oppose these norms, they are brutally killed in the name of family respect and honor.

It is contended that honor-based violence is a type of gendered violence, and that in the context of immigration, it must be understood in relation to the history of immigration to the new nation, the ethnic and religious backgrounds of each individual immigrant community, as well as the integration policies, conceptions of gendered violence, and responses to domestic violence of the immigrant-receiving nation.

Immigration largely affects honor killing as immigrant communities who come to a new country or society are often influenced by encountering new value system and culture. This diversion from their own culture is often unacceptable by their families which ultimately results in honor related crimes. Honor killing is discussed in the context of a wider discussion about perceived gender inequality in immigrant communities in nations that receive immigrants. Western society is portrayed in public discussions as if it offers the promise of equality and justice, if not in actuality. Muslim immigrants are perceived as having a culture derived from their religion. This logic concludes that in order to address their (gender-related) issues, Muslim immigrants in Western nations must renounce their religion and/or cultural customs and embrace Western ones. Though these conversations about honor killing highlight the issue of violence against women, they frequently condemn entire immigrant communities by accusing them of participating in illegal activities that have their roots in uneven gender relations. (Korteweg & Yurdakul, 2010)

For instance, children of immigrants encounter many contradictory emotions as they grow up in the United States. A large number of them acquire the ability to live with contrast both inside and outside of their dwellings. They may dress, speak, or act entirely differently depending on whether they are in South Asian or mainstream American settings. When opposing worldviews collide over issues like dating, staying out late, sexual activity, getting pregnant before marriage, marrying outside of caste, religion, or race, or coming out with non-traditional gender and sexual preferences, these differences of opinion become a matter of family honor. In more traditional households, there may be grave violations of family honor if one interacts with "foreigners," wears makeup, leaves a violent marriage, or is thought to have "bad character." (Gupta, 2015)

Over the last few years, discussions surrounding honor related crime and its relationship with immigration communities have been taking rounds in various countries either through media or newspapers. Various research scholars and professors presented detailed research in regard to honor killing and immigration communities. Two such professors namely, Korteweg and Yurdakul in 2009 examined newspaper conversations on well-known honor killing cases in Germany and the Netherlands. They discovered that a large portion of newspaper coverage in both nations frequently serves to further draw lines between immigrant and majority populations by characterizing honor killings as a type of gender-based violence with roots in Islam, ethnicity, and national origin. These stories frequently characterized Islam and ethnic traditions as unitary, uniform, and ahistorical. In 2010, they extended their analysis to the newspaper coverage in two more nations: Canada and the United Kingdom. They listed the main discourses in the media and public on honor killings, including those that condemn immigrant groups. (Korteweg & Yurdakul, 2010)

This chapter further discusses the various instances from different countries that establish a relation between honor related violence and immigration.

Canada

So far, it has been discussed that religion, ethnicity or culture plays a prominent role in honor related crime. Honor killings in Canada have been a burning topic of discussion over the last few years. Among various factors involved, the role of immigrant communities, their hesitancy to adopt western culture and discrimination against South Asians and Muslims forms a major reason for honor killing in Canada. This emphasis upholds the stereotype that people from particular cultures, ethnicities, and faiths are innately sexist and motivated by ideas of honor and shame that do not apply to people in Western nations. The Canadian news media's fabrication of a racial identity through the usage of the term "honor killing" dehumanises and discriminates against South Asians, Muslims, and immigrants in Western society. (Shier & Shor, 2016) Some killings in Canada in the name of honor have gained recognition at international level due to its brutal nature and how a diversion from own culture can lead to fatal consequences. Once such case is of the murder of a sixteen-year-old Aqsa Parvez by her own father and brother. At the age of eleven, Aqsa, the youngest of eight children, rebelled against her parents' firm instructions about what to wear and how to behave with her peers in social situations after her family migrated from Pakistan to Canada. Aqsa was frustrated due to the various restrictions imposed on her by her family and often tried to revolt against it. She often tried to run away from home and few weeks before her brutal murder, her father sworn on Quran that he would kill her if she again tries to run away. After few weeks of this incident, she was strangulated to death by her father and brother. Numerous characteristics of honor killings in the context of modern immigration are present in the murder of Aqsa, most notably the contradictions and multiplicities in the processes of meaning-making that occur both inside and between families as well as between families, the larger community, and institutions of higher learning and social services. (Korteweg, n.d.,)

Another case involves the murder of Shafia women. The assailants of the Shafia sisters, an "honor killing" case that has garnered a lot of media attention, are another example of how immigration from South Asia or the Middle East and Western culture and civilization are incongruous. Mohammad Shafia, an Afghan Canadian, his son Hamed Mohammad, and his second wife Tooba Yahya, killed Mohammad's three daughters, Geeti, 13, Sahar, 17, and Zainab, 19, on June 30, 2009, in addition to his first wife, 50-year-old Rona Amir Mohammed. Many articles in Canadian press regarded this murder as the case of honor killing as they were someone who were against the traditional rules and regulations and often revolted against it. It was believed that their behaviour brought humiliation to the family. Immigration status, culture, and religious background were frequently cited as the main causes of the murder. (Shier & Shor, 2016).

Talking about the laws in Canada in order to prevent such crime, it is to be noted that there is no specific legislation regarding the same. Such types of cases are dealt within the ambit of murder and assault under the criminal code of Canada.

Sweden

Mehrdad Darvishpour, one of the most prominent figures on honor killings in Sweden, refers to the monitoring of women's sexuality and the male family member's need to uphold the family's dignity as "honor culture." According to him, honor killings are a severe and brutal manifestation of men's presumptive collective right to dominate women. Honor killings fall within the larger category of honor-related violence (HRV), which also covers practices like forced marriage and female genital mutilation (FGM). Women in families and communities are also capable of enforcing these norms and customs, in addition to men. (Hellgren & Hobson, n.d.)

Since the beginning of 21st century, the concepts of honor-related violence, honor-related killings, and honor-related problems have been used in discussions surrounding "immigrants," "migration," and "integration." In the Swedish language, the terms "immigrant" and "integration" are typically associated with "problems and tension," which is highlighted in the use of the terms "us and them." As a result, people from ethnic backgrounds other than Swedish are frequently interpreted as having come from an honor culture, and/or honor-related problems are frequently associated with "immigrants" and how "immigrants" are to be integrated into Swedish society. (Darvishpour & Lahdenpera, n.d.)

Although there had been deaths that could have been classified as honor killings prior to Sara, Pela, and Fadime, the concept of honor killings was not widely discussed in Sweden until the 1990s because of these three high-profile incidents. In all three cases, there were Kurdish families and girls, and the families thought that the daughters had abandoned their homeland culture and adopted Swedish standards of gender, sexuality, and individualization, and that they were no longer abiding by chastity and familial authority. In each of the three instances, the media was crucial in identifying and defining the problems related to honor killings.

After the case of Pela who was killed by her own father and uncle in the name of family honor, the assumption that immigrant families, regardless of length of stay in Sweden, are cultural bearers became stronger. The murder of Fadime, whose family had been residing in Sweden for more than 20 years, served as a catalyst for this idea. The case of Fadime gained a lot of recognition as she was the lady who took a stand for her choice not only in front of her family but demanded her rights in public. She refused to marry her cousin chosen by her father and instead demanded to marry a Swedish man with whom she was in a relationship. As her father refused, she ran away from home and took the help of media and police and claimed her right to marry in public. Later in 2002, when she went to visit her mother, she was brutally killed by her own father. The killing has also had a significant effect on the Swedish authorities' efforts to protect girls who are the children of migrants. Protecting and assisting migrant girls who are facing abuse and threats in their homes has become a top priority for both government agencies and non-governmental organizations.

After this case, media, NGOs and scholars tried to give various explanations for honor killings in Sweden and one of the reasons among it was immigration. Although many of them also refused to consider immigration as the possible explanation for honor killings in Sweden. For instance, a Swedish NGO (ROKS), issued a statement in media after the murder of Fadime that honor is unrelated to any other murders. It refers to a Swedish man's pursuit or murder of his ex-wife as a "jealousy-drama." There is a "family tragedy" when he murders his ex-wife and their kids. In the women's movements, the issue is one of anti-woman sentiment. The patriarchal culture that permeates all civilizations, including Swedish society, is the issue, not immigration. (Hellgren & Hobson, n.d.)

Germany

In Germany, honor killing is mostly associated with forced marriages. The issue of honor killing or its relation to immigration was widely discussed in Germany after the murder of Hatun Aynur Sürücü, a Kurdish-Turkish women, in 2005. She was 23-year-old women who used to live in Germany She was forced to marry her cousin at the age of 16 and later she divorced him. After this, she was brutally killed by her own brother in the name of family honor. Her case is a typical example of a helpless women who are not allowed to live their life on their own terms and rather their life is guided by the harsh customs backed by old traditional family values. Her murder spurred a public discussion on family violence, particularly honor killing, among Muslim immigrant groups in Germany. According to newspapers, this was Berlin's sixth murder of the type in a single year. The controversial book Die Fremde Braut by Turkish-German sociologist Necla Kelek was published at the same time as Hatun Sürücü's murder. This book and several other studies established a connection between specific types of gendered violence and the low socioeconomic involvement of Muslim immigrants in Germany. The murder of Hatun Sürücü and the book by Necla Kelek sparked heated discussions in the media about honor killing and the uneven treatment of women among Turkish immigrants. (Korteweg & Yurdakul, 2010)

In various public discussions, some people supported the idea that honor related killing or forced marriage do not belong to a particular community and that the idea that Turkish are unable to adjust to the values of Germany is irrelevant. Rather, it was all about the universal human rights. However, the discussion on universal human rights did not sit well with news reporters, and condemning discussions about the conflict between German and immigrant values persisted in news reports. Honor killings in Germany and its relation to immigration was highly politicized by political leaders in Germany.

Britain

Like Germany, honor killing in Britain was mostly linked with marriages by force. Although most of the victims are women, in some cases men are also the victim of honor killing. In terms of comprehending the issue, immigrants from nations with sizable Muslim populations were portrayed in newspapers and parliamentary debates as engaging in forced marriages and honor killings, in contrast to other regions like Latin America or Southern Europe where honor-based violence is prevalent but rarely discussed in the media. The bulk of South Asian individuals targeted in the UK's most publicized "honor" killings and attempted killings are of Pakistani ethnicity. London, Bradford, and Birmingham are the three UK cities with the largest populations of Pakistani descent. They also happen to be the three locations with the biggest number of "honor" killings or attempted killings that have been publicized in the media in recent years. Honor-based violence was once thought to be an alien phenomenon that would disappear with first-generation immigration. However, second and third generation immigrants who were born and raised in the UK are also perpetrators of honor-based violence. (Dyer, 2015)

The prominent murder of Banaz Mahmod in 2007 sparked a debate in relation to honor killing and its relation to Muslim immigrants. Banaz was a 20-year-old British national with Kurdish ancestry from Iraq who was forced into marriage at the age of 16 and later went through a divorce. After her divorce, she started dating someone else. Her relation was not accepted by her father or uncle, who gave the order to have her killed. After her murder, some other facts also came forward which also included that even after seeking multiple help from police authorities, they didn't take her seriously. The murder of Banaz was reported in two different ways. First, Muslim immigrant men in particular as well as immigrant groups in general were criticized by the media. Secondly, the media held the police's inability to portray Banaz accountable, linking British diversity to their concern about coming across as racist when addressing issues unique to a certain culture. In response, newspaper reporting made the case that immigrants need to be accepted as full members of British society. This made it possible to consider honor-related violence in immigrant communities as a problem that is unique to their environment. (Korteweg & Yurdakul, 2010)

The murder of Shafilea Ahmed is another example of how an exposure to different culture and values can give rise to conflict within families which ultimately leads to killing in the name of honor. Shafilea Ahmed, the oldest of five children, was born in Bradford on July 14, 1986, not long after her parents left Pakistan. Shafilea went at Warrington's Great Sankey High School until her father took her out of the classroom in February 2003 so she could travel to Pakistan. That year, she was killed later. The year before Shafilea passed away, her parents, Iftikhar and Farzana, and Shafilea became more tense due to differences in "Western" and "traditional" values.

The Ahmed family resided in a "third space," as defined by Homi Bhabha (1994), which was both British and Pakistani at the same time. Though in various ways, this is applicable to both generations. Shafilea's social location was influenced by her parents' migration from a rural Pakistani area and the fact that she was born in postcolonial Britain in the 1980s. Shafilea was enmeshed in a patriarchal gender structure that resulted from more than just the Ahmeds' "backward" rural upbringing and antagonism to the progressive British society outside of their home. Rather, Shafilea's life was shaped by the patriarchal beliefs of her parents' rural Pakistani upbringing as well as the British patriarchal norms to which all women in Britain are subject.

United States

In United States, almost all of these "honor-killing" cases—including the one involving Noor Faleh Almaleki—involve people who are immigrants and belongs to Muslim, Middle Eastern, or South Asian groups. These immigrants have been ruled out for special discrimination ever since the 9/11 terrorist attacks took place. Furthermore, the fathers and husbands of the migrant women who were the victims of these "honor-killing" murders are migrant males, and it is these same migrant men who are the main targets of an increasingly anti-Islamic atmosphere.

Faleh Hassan Almaleki drives his Jeep Grand Cherokee into a parking lot in Phoenix, Arizona on October 20, 2009, and runs over two women: Noor Faleh Almaleki, his daughter, and Amal Khalaf, the mother of her boyfriend. Following the disaster, Faleh Hassan Almaleki, 49, takes out for Mexico and boards a plane bound for London. Faleh is detained by British officials in London on October 29, 2009, and he is extradited to the US, where he is accused of two charges of aggravated assault. Amal, 43, escapes the attack; but, Noor, 20, passes away from her wounds on November 2, 2009, following back surgery. Following his immigration to the country in the middle of the 1990s, Faleh, her father and a citizen of the United States, is charged with one count of first-degree murder. This charge and his prosecution mark one of the first times that a murder is categorized as a "honor killing" in the history of the American legal system. Faleh is tried over the course of the following year and a half, found guilty of second-degree murder, aggravated assault, and fleeing the scene of the accident, and given a 34 ½ year jail sentence. The bulk of the media coverage characterizes Noor's death by her father, an Iraqi Muslim, as an instance of a "honor killing," explaining in the news articles that it happened because she chose a Western/American lifestyle over an Iraqi/Muslim one.

Netherlands

The bulk of immigrants to the Netherlands during the 1960s have come from four non-Western nations: Turkey and Morocco, the Dutch protectorate of the Antilles, and the former colony of Surinam. Currently, 11% of Dutch people are descendants of non-Western immigrants.

The public first learned about honour killing in the Netherlands in 1999 when news outlets covered two incidents: Kezban Vural's murder by her husband in broad daylight and a school shooting in Veghel where a young man of Turkish descent tried shooting the boy who was dating his sister. Although certain initiatives were taken in response to these incidents but neither widespread media coverage nor the formal policy-making stage were attained by these initiatives. Two further killings in 2003 and 2004 thrust the problem into the official policy-making process. Zarife was a high school student who ran away from home after having arguments with her father. She lived in a refuge for fugitive girls until her father convinced her to go back to her family's house. Then, while on a family holiday in Turkey, he murdered her. In a different occasion, Mrs. Gül was hiding in front of the women's refuge when her husband shot and killed her. In response, a five-year policy plan covering 2005–2010 was created by the government and immigrant organizations to combat honor-based violence in the Netherlands. The strategy focused on three areas: prosecution, protection, and prevention.

Local immigrant organizations created and carried out initiatives to educate service providers about the unique circumstances surrounding domestic violence, violence against women, and honor-based violence as well as to provide resources to victims of honor-based violence. Additionally, a range of immigrant groups held conversations on gendered violence and gender equality through the development of general programs by immigrant organizations. In order to address what they perceived as problematic disparities within immigrant communities and to mobilize immigrants' own understandings of desirable gender relations and familial interactions, immigrant organizations leveraged the policy discussion on honour killing and honor-related violence. Prevention-focused organizations contended that immigrants have to be seen as both the cause of issues and their source of remedies. Using the honour killing arguments, they argued that the focus should be on transforming the mindset of immigrant communities, enhancing individuals' ability to take care of themselves through the use of various social services, creating behavioral alternatives, and working with professional parties.

Hence, from the above discussion, it can be concluded that immigrant organizations in Netherlands played a major role in combating the problem of honor-based violence.

Laws and Policies Around the World

Legal sanction plays a crucial role in regulating crimes and acts as a deterrent. Identifying the gravity of crime and its impact on the society determines the amount of punishment which should be given for a particular crime. In most of the countries around the world, there is no exclusive legislation which deals with honor-based violence. It does not mean that they are not punishable under any law. For example, Honor-based crimes are tried under existing criminal laws of Sweden, even if "honor-based violence" is not specifically mentioned in any distinct law in Sweden. Honor-based violence is now clearly classified as a serious crime according to changes made to the Swedish Criminal Code in 2022. This involves acts of coercion driven by ingrained ideas of family honour, such as threats and violence. It is a major development that took place in order to combat such types of crime. The German example demonstrates how conversations that associate honour killing with Islam and/or the "backwardness" of immigrant groups can stigmatize whole immigrant populations and influence restrictive immigration laws. These includes enhancing the age of marriage for immigrants from nations like Turkey to get married, making it necessary to speak German fluently in order to receive an entry visa, and mandating protracted integration programs after they arrive. The issue of forced marriages and honour killings serves as justification for these rules. German politicians choose to confront entire immigrant populations as potential threats to German society, instead of creating focused measures to handle this as a kind of domestic abuse. In the British and Dutch situations, however, a different pattern emerges, with media debates approaching culture more in line with this article's suggestions. They somewhat sidestep conversations about honor-related violence that essentialize the customs and culture of those communities as a whole by characterizing it as a contextually informed type of violence against women that happens within certain immigrant communities. Compared to the German situation, this results in significantly more focused policies in the legislative and policymaking spheres.

In the opinion of author, a separate legislation on honor killing should be introduced in every judicial system. To properly comprehend and handle cases involving honor-based violence, law enforcement officers, prosecutors, and judges should undergo additional training. Acknowledging the distinct cultural and psychological facets of honor-based oppression and reacting suitably are part of this training. The significance of sensitive and in-depth investigations should be emphasized by the new requirements. When conducting an investigation into honor-based violence, law enforcement authorities must adhere to certain rules in order to guarantee that victims receive compassionate and respectful treatment and that all pertinent elements are taken into account.

CONCLUSION

The impact of immigration on honor killings is a complex and multifaceted issue that involves sociocultural, legal, and economic dimensions. While honor killings are often rooted in deeply ingrained cultural practices, immigration can influence these practices in various ways. Immigrant communities may strive to preserve their cultural traditions, including practices related to honor and family reputation. In some cases, this preservation can include harmful practices such as honor killings. Immigrants, particularly in tightly knit communities, might adhere to these customs more strictly as a means of maintaining cultural identity in a foreign environment. Over time, exposure to the legal and cultural norms of the host country can lead to a gradual decline in the practice of honor killings. The process of integration and assimilation can challenge and change traditional views on gender roles, family honor, and individual rights. Education, social services, and community outreach programs in the host country play crucial roles in this transformation.

Honor killing is a violation of human right to live with dignity and the right to choose. Based on above analysis of honor killing and its relation to immigration, it can be concluded that most of the debates in various countries discussed widely the role of particular communities where honor killing is most prevalent. These communities, when they migrate to a different country, are encountered with new culture and values. Unable, to adjust in the new society provokes them to commit a murder in the name of honor killing. Sometimes it has been argued that honor killing belongs to a particular religion, namely, Muslim but it should be taken into account that it is not only restricted to it as it is also a part of Hindu and Christian. Hence, although it is not restricted to religion but it surely has a connection with culture.

Gökçe Yurdakul, a professor, whose one of the interest areas is immigration has also argued that in general, immigrant populations adapt and expand upon native customs while also redefining them in their new nation. According to this viewpoint, it is important to understand the history of immigration to the new nation, the ethnic and religious backgrounds of each individual immigrant community, as well as the integration policies, perceptions of gendered violence, and responses to domestic violence of the nation receiving the immigrants. (Korteweg, n.d.,)

It is possible that there are dominant immigrant community in different countries which contributes to the majority of cases of honor killing in a particular country. For instance, in UK, most of the cases of honor killing is related to Pakistani population while in Netherlands it relates to Turkish values. Every country has its own perspective. Furthermore, the public's perception of honor-based violence in Canada has been formed and characterized by the coverage of the Shafia trial in 2012. Instead of examining the wider spectrum of violence, the Canadian media frequently frames honor killing as a focus on immigrants' abuse of women and girls, particularly domestic violence, which affects people of all demographics, sociocultural values, and customs. Western countries often try to escape the blame in contributing to honor killing by blaming that it is a practice of eastern countries.

Things discussed so far signifies that although immigration do play an important role in honor related killings, but it is not the only factor which leads to a brutal killing of an individual. For instance, patriarchy also play an important role in honor related killing as majority of the time, honor related crimes are often linked to gender-based violence. Majority of the victims all over the world are women. Hence, honor killing is a crime that is deeply rooted in the minds of people in the name of tradition or culture.

The impact of immigration on honor killings is a dynamic interplay of cultural preservation, legal frameworks, economic factors, and community dynamics. While immigration can initially reinforce traditional practices due to cultural preservation, it also offers opportunities for integration and change. Effective legal protection, economic empowerment, education, and community advocacy are key factors in reducing the incidence of honor killings among immigrant communities. Empowering immigrant communities to take a stand against honor killings through awareness campaigns and community-driven initiatives can lead to more sustainable change. As immigrant populations continue to grow and diversify, ongoing efforts to address and prevent honor-based violence must be adaptive and culturally sensitive, ensuring that the rights and safety of all individuals are upheld.

REFERENCES

Darvishpour, M., & Lahdenpera, P. (n.d.). Honor-Related Problems in School Contexts in Sweden – theoretical perspective and prevention. *Mälardalen Studies in Educational Sciences*, 10, 13.

Dyer, E. (2015). 'Honor' Killing in UK. *The Henry Jackson Society*, 21.

Gupta, M. (2015). The Role of 'Honor' in Violence against South Asian Women in the United States. *Manavi Occasional Paper No. 11*, 2.

Hellgren, Z., & Hobson, B. (2008, September). Cultural conflict and cultural dialogues in the good society: The case of honor killings in Sweden. *Ethnicities*, 8(3), 385–404. Advance online publication. DOI: 10.1177/1468796808092449

Korteweg, A. C. (n.d.). Understanding Honor Killing and Honor Related Violence in the Immigration Context: Implications for the Legal Profession and Beyond. *Canadian Criminal Law Review*, ●●●, 136.

Korteweg, A. C., & Yurdakul, G. (2010). Religion, Culture and the Politicization of Honor-Related Violence: A Critical Analysis of Media and Policy Debates in Western Europe and North America. *Gender and Development Programme Paper Number 12*, 4.

Kothari, C. R. (2004). *Research Methodology: Methods and Techniques* (illustrated, reprint, revised ed.). New Age International.

Riksorganisationen GAPF- Glöm Aldrig Pela och Fadime. (2020). Available at: https://gapf.se/rapporter-och-statistik/

Sadowa, K. (2015). "Honour" killings in Europe as an effect of migration process: Perspective for Poland. *International Letters of Social and Humanistic Sciences*, 58, 83–90. . DOI: 10.18052/www.scipress.com/ILSHS.58.83

Shier, A., & Shor, E. (2016). "Shades of Foreign Evil": "Honor Killings" and "Family Murders" in the Canadian Press. *Violence Against Women*, 22(10), 1164. DOI: 10.1177/1077801215621176 PMID: 26712236

Vatandoost, N. (2012). *The News Coverage of Honor Killings in Canadian Newspapers*. University of Ontario Institute of Technology.

Chapter 14
Camouflaged Tenets of Peace Makers on Account of Honor Killing

Avinash Dadhich
Manipal Law School, India

Himanshi Dixit
GLA University, India

ABSTRACT

The issue of honor killings is a deeply rooted problem with cultural, societal, and legal implications, necessitating comprehensive efforts from peacemakers to address and eradicate this form of violence. This study explores the background and rationale for addressing honor killings, highlighting the role of peacemakers in challenging cultural norms and promoting societal change. The research problem focuses on the challenges faced by peacemakers in addressing honor killings and the strategies employed to foster lasting change. The aim is to examine the impact of peacemaking initiatives on societal attitudes and legal reforms related to honor-based violence. The methodology involves a qualitative analysis of peacemaking efforts, including legal advocacy, education, community engagement, and international collaboration. Participants include global figures such as Malala Yousafzai, local activists, religious leaders, and governmental and non-governmental organizations.

DOI: 10.4018/979-8-3693-9596-7.ch014

BACKGROUND

The context of the study encompasses regions affected by honor killings, with a specific focus on the Indian context and the challenges faced by law enforcement and policymakers. The findings highlight the multifaceted challenges faced by peacemakers, including cultural resistance, legal gaps, limited awareness, threats to activists, and religious misinterpretations. Karma Nirvana, a UK-based charity founded by Jasvinder Sanghera, receives over 800 calls monthly from victims of honor-based violence and forced marriages. Sanghera's work has led to policy changes in the UK, including the creation of the Forced Marriage Unit in 2005, a government body tasked with addressing forced marriages and honor-related violence (*About Us: KarmaNirvana*, 2005).

"Law without justice is blind, justice without law is lame, law geared to justice is order."
.... Justice VR Krishna Iyer

Research Methodology

The research methodology for this study will utilize a qualitative approach, focusing on interviews, case studies, and content analysis to examine the role of peacemakers in combating honor killings (Mark Van Hoecke, 2013). Data will be collected through semi-structured interviews with activists, religious leaders, legal professionals, and survivors of honor-based violence across countries like Pakistan, India, Afghanistan, and Canada. This will help explore the cultural, legal, and religious dynamics surrounding honor killings. The study will also include an examination of religious texts and their interpretations to uncover the role of misinterpretation in justifying honor killings, along with efforts to challenge these views. This research aims to explore the underlying ideologies and societal narratives that contribute to the justification of violent acts committed in the name of maintaining family honor and social peace. It will investigate how cultural, religious, and socio-political frameworks often conceal or rationalize these actions, focusing on the role of community leaders, religious authorities, and legal institutions in either perpetuating or challenging such violence. The study will employ a qualitative approach, analyzing case studies, interviews, and literature to uncover how these actors navigate the tension between upholding tradition and addressing human rights violations, and how their interventions are often framed as efforts to preserve societal harmony while overlooking individual rights and justice (Saha, 2010).

Key Terms

Honor killings refer to violent acts, often murder, committed to restore perceived family honor, usually due to a family member's actions deemed dishonorable. Peacemakers, including individuals and organizations, work to prevent these killings by promoting "gender equality" (Wynn, 2021), challenging "patriarchal systems" (Quealy-Gainer, 2019), and addressing "religious misinterpretations" used to justify such violence. "Legal reforms" and "education" are critical tools for dismantling the cultural norms that perpetuate honor killings, while "community engagement" (Singh & Bhandari, 2021) fosters open dialogue to shift societal attitudes. Through advocacy, "religious leaders" also play a key role in promoting non-violence and respect for human dignity.

Literature Review

The author's view is that the newly developed 17-item scale effectively measures attitudes toward honor killing in Pakistan, providing a valid tool for understanding public perceptions. The scale's two identified factors, affirmation and deterrents, offer insights into how different attitudes might influence views on honor killing. (Huda & Kamal, 2020a)

The author highlights how patriarchal societies often view women as bearers of family honor, punishing those who defy traditional norms to prevent further rebellions and preserve cultural values. The documentaries provide perspectives from both victims and perpetrators, revealing how societal rejection of progressive ideas, especially regarding women's emancipation, fuels honor-based violence. (Singh & Bhandari, 2021)

The author suggests that societal rejection of progressive ideas, particularly those related to women's emancipation, drives this violence. By examining both the perspectives of victims and perpetrators in documentary films, the author emphasizes how cultural pressures and fear of dishonor fuel these extreme actions. (Roberts et al., 2013)

Future Research Directions

Future research on honor killings should focus on a multidimensional approach, addressing both cultural and legal aspects. Studies could explore the effectiveness of education and awareness programs in changing societal attitudes toward gender equality and reducing honor-based violence. (Wynn, 2021) Investigating the role of religious leaders in debunking misinterpretations of religious texts that justify violence is another important direction. Additionally, research could examine the implementation and impact of legal reforms, including the effectiveness of specific laws against honor killings and the challenges law enforcement faces in prosecuting these crimes. (Shendurnikar, 2011) A comparative analysis of successful interventions in different regions could also offer valuable insights for developing culturally sensitive, comprehensive strategies to eradicate honor killings globally.

INTRODUCTION

Education is an efficient tool for peacemakers to demolish honor killing. By addressing gender equality and fighting discriminatory practices in educational institutions, educators contribute to changing society's perception. Religious leaders also play a vital role as peacemakers in honor killing situations. Throughout all the distorted interpretations of religious teachings, many honor killings are justified. Addressing these misinterpretations and promoting a more just and inclusive understanding of their faith, the dialogue of religious leaders contributes to peacemaking. Some organizations, such as the UN, provide platforms for engaging best practices, coordinating efforts across borders, and putting diplomatic pressure on countries where honor killings are practiced. Peacemakers have made a substantial impact on society in the fight against honor killings. Their efforts have led to an increase in awareness, legal reforms, community empowerment, and educational changes. While challenges preserve, the cumulative effect of these peace-making initiatives is gradually converting the norms and attitudes of society, creating a more just environment that does not accept violence in the name of honor. In different particular cultures, while both men and women are usually involved in heinous crimes, which are honor-related cases, various expectations exist for each gender. In several South Asian cultures, men are taught that their honor lies in their family's reputation, the modesty of women, sexual purity, and the virginity of women. Men are deemed to have a sense of control over women's social and sexual behaviour, with an inherent responsibility towards restoring their pride and honor whenever it has been challenged by their woman (Huda & Kamal, 2020b). Whereas women often face distinct standards regarding chastity, on the other side, men may be tasked with committing violent acts to uphold honor.

Human rights such as the right to live with dignity (Article 21 of the Indian Constitution) should not be compromised by societal and cultural pressure. Despite the legality of committing murder in the name of family honor, it is mandated to emphasize that taking a life does not rectify lost honor; rather, it constitutes a criminal act. Further, this explores the intricate concept of honor killings in an Indian context, binding them into a legal framework, and examining the apex court decision to comprehend the judicial interpretations surrounding this issue. This mainly explores the challenges law enforcement faces in addressing the diverse forms of violence against women in India, which also include domestic, family, and intimate partner violence. Additionally, it places emphasis on the ongoing need for improvements in order to respond to this heinous crime, underscoring the importance of considering how legislation and policymakers affect police perceptions. The professional's duty as a police officer is to protect victims as well as identify perpetrators, but these duties require more refined understanding, intervention, support, and exact and appropriate knowledge to approach violence in a family context.

Frontline practitioners may not be fully equipped to deal with cases of honor killing in India, and the effectiveness of training techniques in many regions may not be examined. In Indian society, a rising number of honor killings have been reported in the last few months. But the number of cases that are not reported is relatively high. There have been various efforts to decrease honor killing incidences, including the work of international organizations (e.g., World Health Organisation [WHO] and the Convention on the Elimination of All Forms of Discrimination against Women [CEDAW]), local activism, and organizations (Wynn, 2021). Honor killings are most common in south India and western Indian states such as Maharashtra and Gujarat. Though there are many laws for the prevention of such heinous crimes, there are no specific codified laws governing similar types of killing by family members. In parliament, protection from the lynching bill was introduced for a reduction in the number of such cases, but in the current situation, it is in a dormant position. Still, the station of bar, supernatant, and council in similar cases can be analyzed with the support of judicial precedents and other codified laws that hold on to similar practices and inferiors.

Local authorities, such as the judiciary and police, fight against honor killings through law enactment, legal measures, awareness campaigns, community engagement, and support services. The work done by local authorities on this issue is crucial for creating a just society. By seeing this issue in multiple ways, it has been shown that peacemakers want to create long-lasting change and promote a society that values human life and individual rights over harmful cultural traditions. Honor killings, a deeply troubling and pervasive form of violence, continue to be a grave human rights violation in many parts of the world. These killings, often carried out by family members, are intended to protect or restore the family's honor, usually after a perceived affront to cultural or religious norms. Despite international condemnation, the practice persists, claiming thousands of lives each year. In this context, the role of peacemakers—individuals and organizations working to prevent honor killings and promote peace and reconciliation—becomes crucial. This article explores the unique and vital contributions of peacemakers in the fight against honor killings, emphasizing their strategies, challenges, and the transformative impact they can have on communities.

Honor killings are rooted in patriarchal systems and traditional beliefs that place a disproportionate value on female chastity and family reputation. The victims are often women and girls accused of tarnishing their family's honor through behaviour such as refusing an arranged marriage, seeking a divorce, being a victim of sexual assault, or even dressing in ways deemed inappropriate by their community. Men, though less frequently, can also be victims in cases involving sexual orientation or other perceived dishonorable acts.

The perpetrators, typically male family members, believe that restoring honor justifies the most extreme measures, including murder. This belief is perpetuated by societal norms that condone or even encourage such actions, coupled with legal systems that often fail to prosecute offenders adequately.

Honor killings speak to one of the most guileful shapes of savagery against people, transcendently ladies, sustained beneath the pretense of securing family honor. These shocking acts are profoundly established in social, social, and now and then devout convictions that have been camouflaged to legitimize extraordinary savagery. Understanding these covered up precepts is pivotal in disassembling the structures that back honor killings and cultivating a more fair and sympathetic society.

The Cloak of Social Norms

At the heart of honor killings lies a complex web of social standards that direct satisfactory behaviour, especially for ladies. These standards regularly emphasize the control of female sexuality and independence as central to keeping up family honor. The fundamentals that support these convictions are profoundly inserted in the collective mind of communities where honor killings happen, making them troublesome to challenge.

Patriarchal Control: One of the most critical camouflaged principles is the conviction in the outright specialist of men over ladies. In numerous social orders, this patriarchal control is displayed as a characteristic and fundamental arrange, where men are seen as the defenders of family honor and ladies as its bearers. Any deviation by a lady from endorsed parts or behaviour is seen as a coordinate risk to this honor, justifying serious punishment.

Female Chastity: The idea of female chastity being synonymous with family honor is another profoundly imbued precept. Women's bodies and their sexual behaviour are closely observed and controlled, with any seen transgression—real or imagined—considered a recolour on the family's notoriety. This control amplifies choices around marriage, dress, social intelligent, and indeed instruction and employment.

Collective Duty: In communities where honor killings are predominant, there is regularly a conviction in collective obligation. The activities of a person are seen as reflecting on the whole family or community. This conviction can weigh on family individuals to uphold extraordinary measures to 'cleanse' seen dishonor and reestablish communal standing.

Religious Justifications

While honor killings are not endorsed by any major religion, culprits regularly camouflage their activities with devout legitimization. These vocations are ordinarily based on specific elucidations or through and through mutilations of devout teachings.

Distortion of Writings: In numerous cases, devout writings are confused or taken out of setting to bolster the idea of honor killings. For illustration, verses that emphasize humility, family values, or submission are turned to legitimate extraordinary control and viciousness. These elucidations are once in a while scrutinized inside the community, permitting them to sustain unchallenged.

Clerical Supports: In a few occurrences, neighbourhood devout pioneers may underwrite or implicitly back honor killings, encourage legitimizing the hone. Their specialism and impact can make it troublesome for disagreeing voices to be listened, and their translations are frequently acknowledged without address by the community.

Honor killings are a severe form of violence that occurs within certain cultural and social contexts, often justified by perceived notions of honor and shame. Religious leaders, wielding significant moral authority and influence within their communities, can play a crucial role in preventing and addressing honor killings. Their contributions as peacemakers involve a range of activities from advocacy and education to direct intervention and support for victims. Here's an in-depth look at how religious leaders contribute to addressing honor killings:

1. Education
    a. Promoting Human Rights and Gender Equality: Religious leaders can advocate for human rights and gender equality from a moral and ethical standpoint. By emphasizing the inherent dignity and worth of every individual, they can challenge cultural norms that justify honor-based violence. This advocacy includes:

    - Preaching and Sermons: Religious leaders can use sermons and public addresses to condemn honor killings and promote the values of compassion, justice, and equality. By framing these issues within a religious context, they can influence followers' beliefs and attitudes.

- Educational Programs: Many religious leaders organize educational programs and workshops that address the harmful effects of honor-based violence. These programs often include discussions on the importance of gender equality and respect for individual autonomy, drawing on religious teachings to support these messages.

   b. Engaging in Community Dialogues: Religious leaders can facilitate dialogues within their communities to address cultural practices that perpetuate honor killings. By creating safe spaces for discussion, they can help shift societal attitudes and encourage more progressive views on honor and family dynamics.
2. Intervening in Specific Cases
   a. Mediating Conflicts: When disputes arise that could potentially lead to honor-based violence, religious leaders can act as mediators. Their role involves:

   - Conflict Resolution: Religious leaders can mediate conflicts between family members or between individuals and their communities. They use their authority to negotiate peaceful resolutions and discourage acts of violence.
   - Counseling and Support: They offer counseling to individuals who are at risk of honor-based violence, providing emotional and spiritual support while working to address underlying issues within families or communities.

   b. Protecting Vulnerable Individuals: Religious leaders can intervene directly to protect individuals at risk of honor killings. This may involve:

   - Providing Safe Havens: Some religious leaders have established shelters or safe houses for individuals fleeing situations of honor-based violence. These sanctuaries offer protection and support until the person can find a more permanent solution.
   - Liaising with Authorities: Religious leaders often act as intermediaries between at-risk individuals and law enforcement, helping to ensure that threats are taken seriously and that appropriate protective measures are implemented.

3. Promoting Legal and Social Reforms
   a. Supporting Legislative Changes: Religious leaders can advocate for legal reforms that address honor-based violence. Their contributions include:

- Lobbying for Change: They work with policymakers and advocacy groups to push for stronger laws and regulations that protect individuals from honor-based violence and ensure that perpetrators are held accountable.
- Public Campaigns: By leading or supporting public campaigns, religious leaders can raise awareness about the need for legal reforms and mobilize community support for these changes.

  b. Building Partnerships: Religious leaders often collaborate with non-governmental organizations, human rights groups, and community activists to promote broader social and legal reforms. These partnerships help create a more comprehensive approach to combating honor-based violence.
4. Providing Long-Term Support
   a. Counseling and Rehabilitation: Beyond immediate interventions, religious leaders play a role in the long-term support and rehabilitation of survivors. This includes:

   - Mental Health Support: Offering counseling and spiritual guidance to help survivors cope with trauma and rebuild their lives.
   - Reintegration Programs: Assisting survivors in reintegrating into society, which may involve helping them find employment, housing, and social support networks.

   b. Building Community Resilience: Religious leaders contribute to building community resilience by:

   - Fostering Inclusive Communities: Promoting inclusive values and fostering environments where individuals feel safe and respected, thereby reducing the risk of honor-based violence.
   - Supporting Victim Advocacy: Encouraging and supporting the formation of advocacy groups that focus on protecting and empowering individuals affected by honor-based violence.

In Pakistan, where honor killings have been a significant issue, religious leaders have played a pivotal role in addressing this violence. For instance:

- Fatwas Against Honor Killings: Some Islamic scholars have issued fatwas (religious edicts) condemning honor killings, arguing that they are incompatible with Islamic teachings on justice and human dignity.

- Community Outreach: Religious organizations have conducted outreach programs to educate communities about the Islamic principles of gender equality and non-violence.
- Support Networks: In some areas, religious leaders have established support networks for victims of honor-based violence, offering both practical assistance and emotional support.

WHO ARE PEACEMAKERS?

The issue of honor killings is a deeply entrenched problem rooted in cultural norms, patriarchal structures, and misguided interpretations of honor. While resolving this issue requires comprehensive societal changes, several individuals and organizations have been actively working towards dismantling the structures that perpetuate honor killings.

Malala Yousafzai, a Nobel laureate and global advocate for girls' education, has been a prominent voice against honor killings. Born in Pakistan, Malala survived a Taliban assassination attempt for her advocacy of education for girls. Her courage and dedication to promoting education as a means of empowerment contribute to challenging traditional beliefs that underpin honor-based violence. In addition to Malala, the Honor Based Violence Awareness Network (HBVAN) plays a pivotal role in addressing honor killings (Quealy-Gainer, 2019). The network, founded by activist Jasvinder Sanghera, aims to raise awareness, provide support to victims, and work towards policy changes to combat honor-based violence. Jasvinder herself is a survivor of a forced marriage and has been instrumental in shedding light on the hidden struggles faced by many. Local activists within affected communities are also at the forefront of peace-making efforts. These individuals often face immense personal risks as they challenge deeply ingrained traditions and work towards shifting societal attitudes. By fostering dialogue and promoting understanding, these activists contribute to the gradual erosion of harmful practices.

Governments and legal institutions are crucial players in fostering peace in the context of honor killings. Legislation that explicitly condemns honor-based violence and ensures stringent punishment for perpetrators is essential. Moreover, effective implementation of these laws, along with the provision of support services for victims, is vital for bringing about lasting change.

Religious leaders who advocate for a more inclusive interpretation of religious texts contribute significantly to peace making in honor killings. By challenging misinterpretations that may be used to justify violence, these leaders promote a more compassionate understanding of faith, emphasizing the values of love, tolerance, and respect for human life (Singh & Bhandari, 2021). Community-based initiatives that focus on education and awareness play a critical role in challenging stereotypes and dismantling the culture of silence surrounding honor killings. These initiatives engage with communities to foster open discussions, dispel myths, and promote alternative narratives that reject violence in the name of honor.

Media can also act as a peacemaker by responsibly reporting on honor-based violence, bringing attention to the issue without sensationalizing or perpetuating harmful stereotypes. Media campaigns can contribute to changing public perceptions and challenging the social acceptance of honor killings (Shendurnikar, 2011). International organizations and diplomatic efforts are essential for addressing honor killings on a global scale. The United Nations, through its various agencies, works towards promoting gender equality and ending violence against women. By fostering collaboration between nations, sharing best practices, and advocating for policy changes, these organizations contribute to a more coordinated and effective response to honor-based violence. Peacemakers in the context of honor killings come from diverse backgrounds and work on multiple fronts. From global figures like Malala Yousafzai to grassroots activists within affected communities, each plays a crucial role in challenging the deep-rooted structures that perpetuate honor-based violence. Through education, awareness, legal reforms, religious advocacy, community engagement, and international cooperation, these peacemakers strive to bring about lasting change and create a world where honor is associated with respect for human dignity rather than violence.

Trials and Triumphs in the Pacifier's Journey

Peacemakers working against honor killings encounter a myriad of challenges that stem from deeply ingrained cultural norms, systemic issues, and resistance to change. Understanding these challenges is essential for developing effective strategies to address and eradicate honor-based violence.

> 1.Cultural Resistance and Tradition: One of the primary challenges faced by peacemakers is the resistance embedded in cultural norms and traditions that perpetuate honor killings. These deeply rooted beliefs often view any deviation from prescribed gender roles as a threat to family honor, making it challenging to challenge these practices without facing backlash.
>
> 2.Lack of Legal Frameworks: In many regions, there is a lack of specific legislation addressing honor killings. Even when laws exist, they might not be adequately enforced or carry sufficient penalties to deter potential perpetrators. Peacemakers face the challenge of advocating for and implementing comprehensive legal frameworks that condemn honor-based violence and hold offenders accountable.

3.Limited Awareness and Education: Peacemakers often grapple with the challenge of limited awareness and education, particularly in conservative societies where information about human rights, gender equality, and alternative interpretations of cultural norms may be restricted. Initiatives focusing on education and awareness are crucial but can face resistance due to societal resistance to change.

4.Threats to Activists: Those actively working against honor killings often face personal risks and threats to their safety. Activists challenging deeply entrenched practices may become targets of violence themselves, making it challenging to sustain advocacy efforts. The fear of reprisals can hinder the mobilization of individuals to speak out against these crimes.

5. Gender Inequality: The root cause of honor killings often lies in deeply ingrained gender inequality. Peacemakers must confront societal structures that perpetuate unequal power dynamics, limiting the agency and autonomy of women. Achieving meaningful change requires challenging these structural inequalities, which is a complex and long-term endeavour.

6.Religious Misinterpretations: Honor killings are sometimes justified through misinterpretations of religious texts. Peacemakers face the challenge of engaging with religious leaders and communities to promote a more inclusive and accurate interpretation of faith that rejects violence. This task requires navigating delicate religious sensitivities and debunking harmful interpretations.

7. Lack of Support Systems: Victims of honor-based violence often face isolation due to societal and familial pressures. Peacemakers encounter the challenge of establishing effective support systems for victims, including shelters, counselling, and legal assistance. The absence of robust support networks can make it difficult for victims to break free from oppressive situations.

8. Media Sensationalism: The media can play a significant role in shaping public perception, but sensationalism and misrepresentation of honor killings can pose challenges. Peacemakers need to work towards responsible media reporting that sheds light on the issue without perpetuating harmful stereotypes or sensationalizing tragic events.

9. Government Indifference: Some governments may lack the political will to address honor killings, either due to cultural conservatism or other priorities. Peacemakers must navigate the challenge of convincing authorities to prioritize legislative reforms, allocate resources, and actively work towards eradicating honor-based violence.

10. Stigma and Shame: Victims of honor-based violence often face stigma and shame, both within their families and communities. Peacemakers struggle against societal attitudes that blame victims rather than perpetrators, making it challenging to encourage victims to come forward and seek assistance.
11. Cultural-Socio-Legal Diplomacy: In the intricate realm of diplomacy, the peacemaker faces a myriad of challenges when addressing the deeply rooted issue of honor killings. This diplomatic tightrope requires finesse, cultural acumen, and an unwavering commitment to transforming entrenched societal norms. This exploration delves into the complexities encountered by the peacemaker in navigating the delicate landscape of honor killings within the diplomatic arena.

One of the primary diplomatic challenges faced by the peacemaker lies in respecting the autonomy of different cultures while advocating for change. Honor killings are often deeply ingrained in cultural traditions, making it imperative for the peacemaker to strike a delicate balance between promoting human rights universally and recognizing the diversity of cultural perspectives. Navigating this fine line requires a nuanced understanding of cultural contexts to avoid imposing external values and fostering resentment. Legal diplomacy presents another formidable challenge. Honor killings are frequently perpetuated in societies where legal frameworks may be inadequate or lenient, contributing to a culture of impunity. The peacemaker must engage in diplomatic efforts to encourage nations to strengthen and enforce laws that unequivocally condemn honor-based violence. This involves navigating the intricacies of international legal collaboration, urging for the implementation of measures that hold perpetrators accountable on a global scale.

12. Media Diplomacy: It becomes a crucial avenue for the peacemaker to address honor killings, but it comes with its own set of challenges. The portrayal of honor killings in the media often perpetuates harmful stereotypes and sensationalizes incidents, making it challenging to create a nuanced understanding of the issue. The peacemaker must engage with media outlets diplomatically, advocating for responsible reporting that contributes to awareness without reinforcing damaging narratives.

International collaboration in diplomatic initiatives faces challenges due to varying levels of commitment and cultural differences. Bridging these gaps requires sustained efforts to build trust, share best practices, and establish a collective front against honor-based violence. The peacemaker must navigate diverse geopolitical landscapes, fostering collaboration that transcends political and cultural boundaries. In conclusion, peacemakers tackling honor killings confront a complex web of challenges deeply embedded in cultural, legal, religious, and societal structures. Overcoming these obstacles requires a multifaceted approach that combines legal reforms, education, advocacy, and cultural change initiatives. While progress is possible, it demands persistent efforts and collaboration on local, national, and international levels to create a world where honor is no longer associated with violence.

Psychological Effects on Survivors

Survivors of honor killings, which may include those who narrowly escape such violence, family members who lose loved ones, and others in the immediate aftermath, face an array of severe psychological challenges.

1. Trauma and PTSD: Survivors often experience acute trauma, which can manifest as Post-Traumatic Stress Disorder (PTSD). Symptoms may include flashbacks, nightmares, severe anxiety, and emotional numbness. The trauma is compounded by the brutal nature of violence and the betrayal of trust from close family members or community members.
2. Grief and Loss: The loss of a loved one through an honor killing leads to profound grief. Survivors may grapple with complicated mourning processes, including feelings of guilt, anger, and disbelief. This grief is often exacerbated by the stigma and isolation that follow such killings.
3. Fear and Hypervigilance: Survivors, particularly those who escape an attempted honor killing, live in constant fear for their own safety. This fear can lead to heightened states of hypervigilance and anxiety, making it difficult to lead a normal life.
4. Identity and Self-Esteem Issues: The stigma associated with honor killings can lead to identity crises and severe self-esteem issues. Survivors may internalize societal judgments or feel disconnected from their cultural heritage, leading to an ongoing struggle with self-worth and identity.

Impact on Communities

Communities affected by honor killings experience a range of psychological and social impacts:

1. Erosion of Trust and Social Cohesion: Honor killings can erode trust within communities. The violent act and the secrecy often surrounding such cases lead to a breakdown in social cohesion, as fear and suspicion become prevalent. The sense of safety and communal support is undermined, leading to a fractured social fabric.

2. Normalization of Violence: Repeated instances of honor killings can contribute to the normalization of violence within a community. When such acts are not adequately addressed, they can perpetuate cycles of violence, where similar acts become viewed as acceptable or justified responses to perceived dishonor.
3. Stigmatization and Social Isolation: Communities may react to honor killings with stigmatization of the victims and their families. This isolation can manifest as social exclusion, economic disadvantage, and limited access to support services. Victims' families may face backlash, further compounding their distress and isolating them from potential sources of help.
4. Cultural and Societal Shifts: Honor killings can prompt broader cultural and societal shifts. On one hand, they may galvanize movements for change and reform, fostering greater awareness and advocacy for gender equality and human rights. On the other hand, they can entrench regressive attitudes if left unchallenged, reinforcing harmful traditional practices.

Addressing the Psychological Impact

Addressing the psychological impact of honor killings requires a multifaceted approach:

1. Trauma-Informed Support: Providing trauma-informed care to survivors is crucial. This involves understanding and responding to the complex effects of trauma with sensitivity, ensuring survivors receive appropriate mental health support and counseling.
2. Community Education and Advocacy: Raising awareness about the psychological and social consequences of honor killings can help shift cultural norms and attitudes. Advocacy efforts should focus on educating communities about human rights, gender equality, and the need for legal reforms.
3. Legal and Social Reforms: Strengthening legal frameworks and ensuring the effective implementation of laws against honor killings are essential for protecting potential victims and holding perpetrators accountable. Social reforms should aim to create supportive environments for survivors and challenge discriminatory practices.
4. Support Networks: Developing support networks and resources for survivors and affected families can aid in their recovery. Community organizations, mental health professionals, and advocacy groups play a vital role in providing both immediate assistance and long-term support.

Unveiling Task of Harmonizer

Peacemakers addressing honor killings navigate a complex landscape, acknowledging the deep-rooted cultural and societal norms that contribute to such incidents. Their approach involves a blend of legal, educational, and community-based initiatives to foster lasting change.

Legal avenues play a crucial role, with peacemakers advocating for stringent laws against honor killings, ensuring that perpetrators are held accountable. Simultaneously, efforts are made to educate law enforcement officials and judicial bodies about the cultural nuances surrounding honor, fostering a more empathetic and informed approach to handling cases. This we can observe from the judgement of Supreme Court, in which Justice VS Sirpurkar and Justice Deepak Verma said it wasn't a rarest of rare case. "The murders were the outcome of a social issue like a marriage with a person of so-called lower caste. Such killings do not fall in the category of the rarest as the family of the girl has to face lot of taunts and humiliation in the society for the acts of the girl. However, time has come when we have to consider these social issues relevant while considering death sentence in such circumstances (Mishra, n.d.).

Education emerges as a key tool in peacemaking, aiming to challenge traditional norms and stereotypes that perpetuate honor killings. Initiatives include promoting gender equality in schools, raising awareness about the consequences of honor crimes, and engaging communities in dialogue to shift perceptions. Community involvement is paramount, as peacemakers collaborate with local leaders, religious figures, and influencers to dismantle harmful cultural practices. Empowering women and providing them with support networks are essential components, fostering resilience against oppressive norms and creating avenues for them to seek help.

Honor killings represent a grave human rights violation, deeply entrenched in cultural and patriarchal norms that undermine the dignity and safety of individuals, particularly women. Addressing this form of violence requires a multifaceted approach, with community-based interventions playing a crucial role. Peacemakers, who work at the grassroots level, are pivotal in implementing strategies that respect cultural contexts while promoting significant and sustainable change. This article highlights key community-based intentions of peacemakers in combating honor killings.

Fostering Dialogue and Understanding

One of the primary intentions of community-based peacemakers is to foster open dialogue within communities about honor killings. Peacemakers organize forums, workshops, and discussion groups where community members can engage in conversations about the cultural and social factors contributing to honor-based violence. These dialogues serve multiple purposes: they challenge harmful cultural norms, promote understanding and empathy, and educate participants about the broader implications of honor killings. By creating safe spaces for these discussions, peacemakers help to deconstruct the myths and justifications surrounding honor-based violence, paving the way for cultural transformation.

Building Coalitions and Alliances

Peacemakers recognize the power of collective action and work to build coalitions of community leaders, religious figures, activists, and local organizations. These alliances are instrumental in addressing honor killings from multiple angles. By collaborating with influential individuals and groups, peacemakers can leverage their authority to advocate for change. These coalitions facilitate the development of culturally sensitive initiatives that challenge honor-based violence while respecting local traditions. Building strong, supportive networks helps to create a unified front against honor killings and fosters a collaborative approach to finding solutions.

Empowering Local Leaders and Advocates

Empowering local leaders and advocates is another critical intention of peacemakers. They provide training and resources to community leaders, religious figures, and activists to help them effectively address honor killings and advocate for gender equality. Empowered leaders can use their influence to promote non-violence, support survivors, and mobilize community members. Training programs often focus on raising awareness about human rights, legal protections, and the social impacts of honor killings. By strengthening the capacity of local leaders, peacemakers enhance the community's ability to address and prevent honor-based violence.

Supporting Survivors and At-Risk Individuals

Providing support services for survivors of honor killings and individuals at risk is a vital aspect of community-based interventions. Peacemakers facilitate the establishment of safe houses, counseling services, and legal aid tailored to the needs of survivors. These services are designed to offer refuge, psychological support, and practical assistance to those affected by honor-based violence. By ensuring that survivors have access to the resources they need to escape abusive situations and rebuild their lives, peacemakers help to mitigate the immediate impact of violence and support long-term recovery.

Promoting Educational Initiatives

Education plays a crucial role in preventing honor killings, and peacemakers work to integrate educational initiatives into community programs. They collaborate with schools, community centers, and local organizations to implement curricula that address gender equality, human rights, and the harmful effects of honor-based violence. Educational programs aim to raise awareness from an early age, instilling values of respect and equality. By targeting youth and the broader community, these initiatives contribute to long-term cultural change and challenge the norms that perpetuate honor killings.

Advocating for Legal and Policy Reforms

Peacemakers are also involved in advocating for legal and policy reforms at the local level. They work to raise awareness about existing legal protections and push for stronger laws against honor killings. This advocacy includes supporting the development of new legislation, ensuring effective implementation of laws, and holding authorities accountable for enforcing justice. Peacemakers may organize campaigns, engage with policymakers, and collaborate with legal experts to advocate for reforms that address honor-based violence and protect victims.

Creating Safe Spaces for Women and Youth

Creating safe spaces for women and youth is an essential aspect of community-based peacemaking. These spaces offer a supportive environment where individuals can seek refuge, access resources, and engage in activities that promote empowerment and personal development. Safe spaces can include women's groups, youth clubs, and community centers focused on building resilience and providing support. By fostering environments where individuals feel safe and valued, peacemakers help to reduce the risk of honor-based violence and promote positive social change.

Encouraging Positive Role Models

Highlighting and promoting positive role models is a strategy used by peacemakers to inspire change within communities. Role models who defy traditional gender norms and advocate for human rights serve as powerful examples of positive transformation. By showcasing individuals who have successfully resisted harmful practices and promoted gender equality, peacemakers provide tangible examples of alternative pathways and encourage others to follow suit. These role models can influence cultural attitudes and inspire a shift towards more progressive and non-violent practices.

Addressing Socioeconomic Inequalities

Peacemakers also address socioeconomic inequalities that exacerbate the risk of honor killings. They work to improve access to education, economic opportunities, and healthcare, which can help reduce vulnerabilities and empower marginalized groups. By addressing these inequalities, peacemakers contribute to creating a more equitable society where individuals have greater agency and are less susceptible to violence. Economic and social support can play a crucial role in reducing the factors that contribute to honor-based violence.

Monitoring and Evaluating Impact

Finally, peacemakers focus on monitoring and evaluating the impact of their interventions. This involves gathering feedback from community members, assessing the outcomes of various initiatives, and making necessary adjustments to strategies. Continuous evaluation helps to ensure that community-based efforts are achieving the desired results and making a meaningful difference in preventing honor killings. By analyzing the effectiveness of their work, peacemakers can refine their approaches and enhance their impact over time.

Furthermore, peacemakers strive to create safe spaces for dialogue within communities, facilitating conversations that challenge ingrained beliefs while respecting cultural diversity. These discussions often involve religious leaders who can play a pivotal role in interpreting religious texts in a way that promotes gender equality and condemns violence in the name of honor. International collaboration is also crucial, with peacemakers working to create a global understanding of honor-based violence. This involves sharing best practices, conducting research, and leveraging diplomatic channels to exert pressure on regions where honor killings persist. Ultimately, the peacemaking process is a multifaceted endeavour that recognizes the interconnectedness of legal, educational, and community-driven solutions. By addressing the root causes and fostering cultural shifts, peacemakers strive to eradicate the deeply ingrained practice of honor killings, creating a safer and more just society for all.

CASE STUDY: THE HONOR KILLING OF NOOR ALMALEKI

Background

Noor Almaleki, a young Iraqi-American woman, was murdered by her father, Faleh Hassan Almaleki, in a case that highlighted the tragic consequences of honor-based violence within immigrant communities. The case garnered significant attention, emphasizing the complex interplay of cultural traditions, family dynamics, and legal challenges faced by survivors of such violence(Rubin, 2010).

Early Life and Migration

Noor Almaleki was born in Iraq and moved to the United States with her family when she was four years old. The family settled in the Phoenix area of Arizona in the mid-1990s, living first in Glendale and later in the Paradise Views subdivision of Phoenix. Faleh Hassan Almaleki, Noor's father, was originally from Basra, Iraq. Noor attended Dysart High School in El Mirage and later graduated from high school. She enrolled at Glendale Community College, aiming to build a future for herself.

Conflict and Cultural Tensions

As Noor reached adulthood, tensions with her family intensified due to cultural and lifestyle differences. Her father and family were deeply rooted in traditional Iraqi values, which clashed with Noor's more modern and independent lifestyle. Specific issues included:

1. Arranged Marriage: Noor's father attempted to arrange a marriage between her and an older cousin in Iraq. Noor resisted this arrangement and, instead, pursued a relationship of her own choosing. She returned to the U.S. in 2008 after initially being sent to Iraq for the marriage.
2. Lifestyle Disputes: Noor's choice of clothing, dating preferences, and desire for independence were at odds with her family's expectations. Her father, in particular, was displeased with her refusal to adhere to traditional norms.
3. Living Independently: In 2009, Noor attempted to assert her independence by moving into her own apartment. However, her family members frequently confronted her at her places of employment, leading to financial instability and forcing her to move back into her family's home. By June 2009, she had relocated to the household of other Iraqi Americans, where she began a relationship with the son of the family. This romance further alienated her from her relatives.

4. **Legal and Protective Measures:** Noor sought legal protection from her family. She filed for a restraining order, but according to reports, she did not complete the process. This failure to finalize the paperwork left her vulnerable and unprotected.

The Murder

On October 20, 2009, Faleh Almaleki deliberately struck Noor with his vehicle in a parking lot in Peoria, Arizona. Noor suffered severe injuries and died on October 30, 2009, as a result of the attack. The murder was a calculated act of honor violence, motivated by Faleh's belief that Noor had dishonored the family.

Legal Proceedings and Consequences

1. **Arrest and Trial:** Faleh Hassan Almaleki was arrested and charged with first-degree murder. During the trial, it became evident that the crime was premeditated, with Faleh admitting to the intent to kill his daughter as punishment for her defiance. He was convicted of murder and sentenced to life in prison.
2. **Impact on the Community:** The case prompted widespread media coverage and community reaction. It brought to light the issue of honor-based violence within immigrant communities and sparked debates on the need for legal reforms and better support systems for women facing similar threats.

Peacemakers' Involvement

Peacemakers played a crucial role in addressing the aftermath of Noor's murder and working towards preventing future incidents. Their involvement can be categorized into several key areas:

Mediation and Conflict Resolution:
Initial Response: After Noor's murder, local peacemakers, including community leaders, activists, and mediators, stepped in to manage the immediate aftermath. They facilitated dialogues between the grieving family and the broader community, seeking to address the underlying tensions and prevent further violence.
Mediation Efforts: Peacemakers worked to mediate between the family and community members who were outraged by the act. They organized meetings to address grievances and foster mutual understanding, aiming to reduce the potential for retaliatory violence.
Advocacy and Awareness:

Raising Awareness: Peacemakers, in collaboration with human rights organizations, launched awareness campaigns about honor killings and their devastating impact on individuals and communities. They used Noor's case as a focal point to educate the public about gender equality and the need for legal reforms.

Community Engagement: They organized workshops and seminars in schools, religious institutions, and community centers to challenge traditional norms that condone honor-based violence and promote alternative conflict resolution methods.

Legal and Institutional Support:

Legal Advocacy: Peacemakers lobbied for legal reforms to strengthen protections against honor killings. They worked with lawmakers to ensure that Noor's case highlighted the need for more stringent laws and effective enforcement to prevent such crimes.

Support Services: They helped establish support services for survivors of honor-based violence, including counseling, legal aid, and safe shelters. These services aimed to provide immediate support to those at risk and offer long-term assistance for their recovery.

Cultural and Social Change:

Challenging Norms: Peacemakers engaged in cultural and social change initiatives to challenge and transform harmful practices and beliefs. They worked to redefine notions of honor and shame in their communities, promoting values of respect and human dignity.

Empowerment Programs: They implemented programs to empower women and marginalized groups, providing them with tools, education, and resources to advocate for their rights and challenge oppressive practices.

Operative Measures of Peacemakers

Addressing the issue of honor killings requires a comprehensive approach by peacemakers that combines cultural sensitivity, community engagement, legal reforms, education, and advocacy for human rights. In this detailed discussion, we'll explore how peacemakers navigate the complexities surrounding honor killings to create lasting change.

1. **Understanding the Cultural Context:**

Peacemakers recognize the importance of understanding the cultural context in which honor killings occur. They engage with local communities, establishing relationships built on trust and respect. Cultural sensitivity is crucial to avoid imposing external values and to ensure that interventions are tailored to the specific needs and beliefs of the community.

2. **Community Engagement and Empowerment:**

Engaging with communities is a cornerstone of peacemaking efforts. Peacemakers work collaboratively with local leaders, religious figures, and influencers to promote dialogue and challenge harmful norms. By involving the community in the process, peacemakers empower individuals to take ownership of the issue, fostering a sense of collective responsibility for change.

3. **Education Programs:**

Peacemakers implement targeted education programs to challenge traditional beliefs that perpetuate honor killings. These programs focus on promoting gender equality, human rights, and non-violent conflict resolution. Schools, community centres, and religious institutions become platforms for educating individuals, especially the younger generation, on alternative perspectives that reject violence based on honor.

4. **Legal Reforms and Accountability:**

Advocacy for legal reforms is a crucial aspect of addressing honor killings. Peacemakers collaborate with lawmakers and governmental bodies to strengthen legislation related to honor crimes. The judges as the architect of justice crafted the pronouncements by adopting scientific, procedural, technical, methodological approach and expanded the ambit of fundamental rights and protected and provided platforms for all the laws (Kumar, 2023). This includes advocating for stricter penalties for perpetrators, improved law enforcement response, and legal protections for victims. By holding perpetrators accountable through the legal system, peacemakers aim to deter future incidents.

5. **Counselling and Support Services:**

Peacemakers recognize the importance of providing support services to potential victims and their families. Counselling services address the complex psychological and emotional factors involved, aiming to break the cycle of violence. Peacemakers work to create safe spaces where victims can seek help without fear of retribution, emphasizing the importance of mental health in the overall well-being of individuals affected by honor-related violence.

6. **Dialogue and Mediation:**

Facilitating dialogue between conflicting parties is a delicate yet crucial component of peacemaking efforts. Peacemakers bring together community leaders, religious figures, and family members to engage in constructive conversations. Mediation processes aim to find non-violent resolutions, fostering understanding and reconciliation within families and communities. The goal is to break down the barriers that contribute to the acceptance of honor killings.

7. **Advocacy for Women's Rights:**

Peacemakers play a vital role in advocating for women's rights within societies where honor killings persist. This involves challenging discriminatory practices and promoting the empowerment of women. By highlighting the importance of autonomy, equality, and freedom from violence, peacemakers contribute to shifting societal attitudes towards gender roles and expectations.

8. **International Collaboration:**

Recognizing the global nature of human rights issues, peacemakers engage in international collaboration. They work with organizations and institutions on a global scale to share best practices, resources, and support. By fostering a unified, cross-cultural effort against honor killings, peacemakers contribute to a broader movement that transcends geographical boundaries.

Despite their crucial role, peacemakers face numerous challenges in their efforts to combat honor killings. These challenges include:

1. **Cultural Resistance:** Deeply ingrained cultural and religious beliefs can be significant barriers to change. Peacemakers often encounter resistance from communities that view their efforts as an attack on their traditions and values.
2. **Safety Risks:** The work of peacemakers can be dangerous, as they often confront individuals and groups who are willing to resort to violence to maintain their control. Protecting themselves and those they assist is a constant concern.
3. **Limited Resources:** Many peace-making organizations operate with limited funding and resources, which can hinder their ability to provide comprehensive support and reach a broader audience.
4. **Legal Obstacles:** In some regions, weak legal frameworks and corruption can undermine efforts to hold perpetrators accountable and protect victims.

CONCLUSION

The exploration of honor killings as a manifestation of cultural norms and societal expectations reveals a complex and deeply rooted issue. The research on peacemaking in the context of honor killings underscores the necessity for a multi-faceted approach that addresses cultural, legal, and educational aspects to bring about lasting change. Understanding the cultural context is crucial in designing effective interventions. Peacemaking initiatives should engage with local communities, fostering open dialogue and challenging harmful traditions without imposing external values. This approach aims to promote a sense of ownership among community members, encouraging them to reevaluate and reshape cultural norms in a way that respects human rights. Addressing economic factors can be integral to peacemaking. Empowering women economically can provide them with alternatives to traditional roles, reducing dependency on familial structures that may perpetuate honor-based violence. Economic independence can act as a catalyst for social change, breaking the cycle of violence and promoting gender equality. The conclusion drawn from this somber exploration emphasizes the critical role of legal interventions in the fight against honor killings. The graveyard of the peacemaker underscores the urgency for robust legal frameworks that not only condemn such acts but also ensure swift and stringent consequences for perpetrators. Closing the legal loopholes and fostering collaboration between legal authorities and community leaders is imperative to break the cycle of impunity. In the critical analysis of the peacemaker within the public sphere concerning honor killings, it is evident that addressing this deeply rooted issue requires a nuanced understanding of the dynamics at play. The research underscores the complex interplay between cultural norms, legal frameworks, and the role of the public sphere in shaping perceptions and driving change. In the critical analysis of the peacemaker within the public sphere concerning honor killings, it is evident that addressing this deeply rooted issue requires a nuanced understanding of the dynamics at play. The research underscores the complex interplay between cultural norms, legal frameworks, and the role of the public sphere in shaping perceptions and driving change. The research underscores the public sphere as a battlefield of ideas and values. Peacemaking in this context demands a strategic dissemination of information through media, education, and various platforms. By challenging stereotypes, promoting gender equality, and raising awareness, the peacemaker within the public sphere becomes an agent of change, shaping societal attitudes and perceptions. In summary, the diplomatic approach of the peacemaker in the context of honor killings is a multifaceted strategy that demands cultural sensitivity, legal advocacy, and international collaboration. Through diplomatic channels, the peacemaker becomes a catalyst for change, fostering understanding, encouraging legal reforms, and promoting a global consensus against honor-based violence. In the diplomatic pursuit of peace, the research concludes that strategic engagement and persistent dialogue can pave the way for a world where honor killings are unequivocally condemned, and human rights prevail. Honor killings are a tragic manifestation of deep-seated cultural and patriarchal norms that devalue the lives and rights of individuals, particularly women. Peacemakers play an indispensable role in addressing this form of violence, employing strategies that range from education and advocacy to direct intervention and community engagement. Their work is not without challenges, but their efforts can lead to transformative changes that protect lives and promote justice and equality. Robust legal frameworks are fundamental in the fight against honor killings. Establishing and enforcing laws specifically addressing honor-based violence is crucial for ensuring justice and accountability. Legal reforms must focus on closing existing loopholes that allow perpetrators to evade punishment. This includes defining honor killings explicitly in the legal system, ensuring that laws are comprehensive and clear, and removing any provisions that may allow for leniency based on cultural justifications. Moreover, effective implementation of these laws requires collaboration between legal authorities, community leaders, and advocacy groups. Training law enforcement and judicial personnel to handle cases of honor-based violence with sensitivity and expertise is also vital. By creating a legal environment that unequivocally condemns honor killings and holds perpetrators accountable, we can work towards eradicating this violence.

As we continue to confront the issue of honor killings, it is imperative to support and amplify the work of peacemakers. Their dedication and courage are crucial in the fight against this egregious violation of human rights, and their impact extends far beyond individual cases, contributing to the broader movement for peace, equality, and justice worldwide. Honor killings are a manifestation of deeply entrenched beliefs and norms that have been camouflaged under various guises. To effectively combat this practice, it is essential to uncover and challenge these hidden tenets. Through cultural change, religious reinterpretation, economic empowerment, and legal reforms, we can begin to dismantle the structures that support honor killings and move towards a society that values and protects the dignity and rights of all individuals. Tackling honor killings demands a multifaceted and integrated approach that addresses cultural, legal, economic, and societal dimensions. Understanding cultural contexts and engaging with communities in a respectful manner is essential for fostering internal change. Economic empowerment provides women with alternatives to traditional roles, reducing their vulnerability to violence. Robust legal reforms and effective implementation are crucial for ensuring justice and accountability. Public advocacy and media campaigns play a significant role in shaping societal attitudes and promoting gender equality. On a global scale, diplomatic efforts are vital for building consensus and supporting best practices. By combining these strategies, we can work towards a society where honor killings are eradicated, human rights are upheld, and all individuals are valued and protected. The ongoing commitment to these efforts will be crucial in driving transformative change and ensuring a future free from the scourge of honor-based violence. Community-based interventions by peacemakers are essential in the fight against honor killings. By fostering dialogue, building coalitions, empowering local leaders, supporting survivors, promoting education, advocating for legal reforms, creating safe spaces, encouraging positive role models, addressing socioeconomic inequalities, and monitoring impact, peacemakers work to transform cultural attitudes, strengthen community resilience, and create a safer, more just society. Their efforts are vital in addressing the complex issue of honor killings and driving meaningful change within communities.

REFERENCES

Huda, S., & Kamal, A. (2020a). Development and validation of attitude towards honour killing scale. *Pakistan Journal of Psychological Research*, 35(35), 227–251. DOI: 10.33824/PJPR.2020.35.2.13

Huda, S., & Kamal, A. (2020b). Development and Validation of Attitude Towards Honour Killing Scale. *2020, VOL. 35, NO. 2, 35*(35), 227–251. https://doi.org/DOI: 10.33824/PJPR.2020.35.2.13

Kumar, R. K. (2023). Honour Killing: Challenges Indian Judicial System. In *International Journal of Creative Research Thoughts* (Vol. 11). www.ijcrt.org

Mark Van Hoecke. (2013). *METHODOLOGIES OF LEGAL RESEARCH which kind of method for what kind of discipline?which kind of method for what kind of discipline?* Mishra, A. (n.d.). *HONOUR KILLINGS: THE LAW IT IS AND THE LAW IT OUGHT TO BE.* https://www.hrw.org/press/2001/04/un

Nirvana, K. (2005). https://karmanirvana.org.uk/about/about-us/

Quealy-Gainer, K. (2019). Malala: My Story of Standing Up for Girls' Rights by Malala Yousafzai. *Bulletin of the Center for Children's Books*, 72(5), 229–230. DOI: 10.1353/bcc.2019.0070

Roberts, K. A., Campbell, G., & Lloyd, G. (2013). Honor-based violence: Policing and prevention. *Honor-Based Violence: Policing and Prevention*, 1–197. DOI: 10.1201/b16114

Rubin, P. (2010). How a Muslim Woman Was "Honor-Killed" by Her Father Because He Believed She Was Too Americanized. *Phoenix New Times*. https://www.phoenixnewtimes.com/news/how-a-muslim-woman-was-honor-killed-by-her-father-because-he-believed-she-was-too-americanized-6445842

Saha, T. K. (2010). *Textbook on Legal Methods, Legal Systems & Research*. 243.

Shendurnikar, D. N. (2011). HONOUR IN THE NEWS: MEDIA REPRESENTATION OF HONOUR KILLINGS. *HONOUR IN THE NEWS: MEDIA REPRESENTATION OF HONOUR KILLINGS*. https://www.academia.edu/3237160/HONOUR_IN_THE_NEWS_MEDIA_REPRESENTATION_OF_HONOUR_KILLINGS

Singh, D., & Bhandari, D. S. (2021). Legacy of Honor and Violence: An Analysis of Factors Responsible for Honor Killings in Afghanistan, Canada, India, and Pakistan as Discussed in Selected Documentaries on Real Cases. *SAGE Open*, 11(2), 21582440211022323. Advance online publication. DOI: 10.1177/21582440211022323

Wynn, L. L. (2021). 7. "Honor Killing": On Anthropological Writing in an International Political Economy of Representations. *Love, Sex, and Desire in Modern Egypt*, 137–155. https://doi.org/DOI: 10.7560/317044-008/XML

Chapter 15
Media Trial and Honor Killing:
Media as an Agent in Shaping Perception and Laws Around the World

Sudhir Kumar
School of Legal Studies, Babu Banarsi Das University, India

Barkha Agrawal
Amity University, Noida, India

ABSTRACT

The power of the media lies in its omnipresence. However, the advantage of being closely related to the happening is that the media has the potential to paint a real and authentic picture. In the case of honor killing, this power of the media can potentially be used to reduce violence and crime through honest information in real time. Though there are worries about skewed and prejudiced coverage in the media, media reports have been vital in helping to understand this issue. The way the media portrays these social crimes helps to both bolster public opinion and convey about the backward social customs connected to them. The chapter focuses on the ability of the media to influence public opinion, which can play a key role in ending honor killings around the world. Media can contribute to the development of a fairer society for women by criticizing media portrayals of honor killings and examining the causes of this violence. The purpose of this chapter is to examine the quality of media coverage of honor killing and the relationship between them Media and Popular Culture.

DOI: 10.4018/979-8-3693-9596-7.ch015

BACKGROUND

The power of the media lies in its omnipresence. We find it in all areas of our lives, regardless of what is private and what is public. However, the advantage of being closely related to the happening is that the media has the potential to paint a very real and authentic picture. In the case of honor killings, this power of the media can potentially be used to reduce violence and crime through honest information in real time. Honor killings have a long history in our country. Though there are worries about skewed and prejudiced coverage in the media that has affected the situation as a whole, media reports have been vital in helping to understand this issue. Culture is significantly influenced by the mass media, and vice versa. The way the media portrays these social crimes helps to both bolster public opinion and convey to the general public about the backward social customs that are connected to them. While the media can raise awareness of social issues, it can also promote misconceptions or problematic portrayals of an issue. The chapter focuses on the role of media and other social media platform's ability to influence public opinion, which can play a key role in ending honor killings in India. The media can contribute to the development of a fairer and more equal society for women by criticizing media portrayals of honor killings and examining the causes of this violence. The purpose of this chapter is to examine the quality of media coverage of honor killing and the relationship between them Media and Popular Culture.

Statistical Data

In 2000, a survey conducted by the United Nations estimated that approximately 5,000 honor killings occur globally each year (UN, 2009). In India, a study from 2010 suggests that about 900 honor killings were reported in the states of Haryana, Punjab, and Uttar Pradesh, with an additional 100 to 300 cases reported in other parts of the country. (Annavarapu, 2013) Several prominent cases have gained national attention due to the media coverage, including the infamous case of 2010 murder of Ankit Saxena in Delhi and the 2018 killing of Loveleen Kaur in Punjab.

Home Office data reveals that there were 2,905 honor-based abuse offenses in the UK in 2022-23, marking a 1% increase from the previous year and a 10% rise since 2020-21. (Bhanbhro, 2023) The Human Rights Commission of Pakistan (HRCP) reports that approximately 1,000 honor killings occur each year. In 2019, there were 1,119 reported cases of honor killings involving women. Whereas 384 instances of Honor Killing were reported in 2022. Notable cases, such as the 2016 murder of social media personality Qandeel Baloch, have significantly raised media awareness about the issue. Honor killings are relatively uncommon in the U.S., with estimates indicating that approximately 23 to 27 cases have occurred over the past decade. This figure is derived from data gathered by various reports, law enforcement agencies, and advocacy groups. In countries with fewer honor killings, any incidents that occur are less likely to go unreported. Such cases often attract significant attention, which has contributed to increasing public awareness about honor killings.

In the past decade, media coverage of honor killings has significantly increased, especially in Western countries, reflecting a growing awareness of these crimes. Both print and digital media have reported on these cases more frequently. This heightened coverage has contributed to greater public discourse, spurred legal reforms in some countries, and intensified international pressure on governments to tackle the issue.

Research Methodology

The purpose of this chapter is to explore the influence of media trials on honor killings and their impact on legal reforms and public perceptions worldwide. The research methodology involved a thorough review of various sources, including research papers, academic journals, articles, and official reports. This approach integrated both primary and secondary data to offer an in-depth analysis of the topic. Primary research focused on examining media coverage, while secondary research included a review of academic literature, journals, research papers, and online sources. A qualitative research strategy was used to explore how media coverage portrays honor killings, often highlighting sensationalism and bias, and to assess the broader societal impact. The study considered factors such as ethnicity, age, and gender to provide a nuanced and unbiased perspective. The chapter details the relationship between media portrayal and honor killings, emphasizing how media framing, sensationalism, and narrative techniques impact societal understanding and response. The findings highlight the critical need for thoughtful media analysis to better grasp the implications of honor killings coverage and to advocate for more responsible and nuanced reporting to effectively address this human rights issue.

Key Terms

To thoroughly research Media Trials and Honor Killings, the author employed a methodical approach to selecting relevant articles from a range of respected online sources, including the Library of Congress, ResearchGate, Google Books, Springer, JSTOR, Sage, IJSSHR, Scopus, Web of Science, and Google Scholar. Key terms such as "Media Trial," "Honor Killing," (Santhi, 2013) "Media," (Dalvi, 2022)

"Culture," "Social practice," "Public opinion" (Shendurnikar, 2020) "Voluntary killings" (Santhi, 2013) were used to pinpoint the most pertinent scholarly articles.

The selection process concentrated on journals specializing in media studies, criminal justice, human rights, and cultural studies to ensure a well-rounded perspective. Journals like Media, Culture & Society, Journal of Criminal Justice, Human Rights Quarterly, and Gender & Society were selected for their relevance to the topic, offering a platform for detailed analysis and academic discussion on the influence of media on public perception and the cultural aspects of honor killings. Additionally, primary sources including national laws, court decisions, journalism ethics guidelines, and international human rights reports were crucial for providing authoritative insights into the legal and ethical contexts of these issues.

Inclusion criteria for this research focused on articles that specifically addressed media trials, honor killings, or related legal and cultural issues. Recent publications from the past decade were prioritized to ensure current perspectives and data. Peer-reviewed articles and official government publications were included to maintain academic rigor and credibility. Exclusion criteria aimed to ensure research quality and relevance. Non-academic sources, such as opinion pieces, and articles with only peripheral relevance were excluded.

Literature Review

Honor-based violence is prevalent across different cultures and communities (Faqir, 2001). Although honor killings are the most extreme form, such violence exists regardless of cultural or religious backgrounds. However, these incidents have often been overlooked by the media, only gaining attention when the frequency of killings became too significant to ignore (Shendurnikar, 2020).

Honor killing can be defined as the act of taking another person's life to defend the perceived honor of the perpetrator or their community. This so-called 'honor' might be tied to societal image, which could be influenced by differences in caste, religion, or economic status between parties. Even when these factors are equal, personal satisfaction within a community might still drive the act, all in the name of protecting pride and prestige (Dalvi, 2022). Honor killings often involve family members, with global data showing that two-thirds of the victims are killed by their own relatives (Santhi, 2013).

The media plays a significant role in shaping culture, and its portrayal of social crimes like honor killings influences public opinion and educates the public about harmful social practices. However, the coverage of such crimes often prioritizes sensationalism, driven by the desire to increase ratings and readership, under the guise of catering to audience interest (Shendurnikar, 2020).

In recent years, the term 'honor'-based violence (HBV) has gained more recognition among the British public and policymakers, a stark contrast to the past when it was seldom used or understood. Significant strides have been made in raising awareness about HBV, with reports of 'honor' killing victims frequently making headlines (Dyer, 2015). However, in cases of trial by media, justice is often not only denied but derailed, reducing tragedies to sensational dramas (Lidhoo, 2020). While media can help raise awareness of social issues, it also has the potential to promote misleading ideas or problematic portrayals of cases. The pursuit of a 'newsworthy' narrative often results in altered news coverage aimed at higher TRP ratings and readership. This obsession with newsworthiness can degrade the quality of coverage, unfairly targeting and scrutinizing women. This phenomenon, known as the 'media circus,' can lead to 'trial by media' and/or 'media activism' (Babuji, 2023).

Future Research Directions

This research critically examines how media shapes laws and public views on honor killings, emphasizing the significant impact media trials have on both legal outcomes and societal perceptions. By framing these acts in a sensationalist manner, media coverage can significantly influence public perception and legal outcomes. The paper also explores how media trials can affect legislative reforms and public policies, either by pressuring governments to act or by deepening existing biases.

The authors critically assess how media coverage interacts with legal frameworks aimed at addressing honor killings. The chapter offers a comprehensive exploration of how media covers honor killings, delving into the nuances of media portrayal, its potential negative impacts, and the broader societal consequences. This chapter delves into the significant yet underexplored role of the media in portraying honor killings and shaping public perceptions. While previous research has centred on media activism, particularly examining how the media strives to render honor killings newsworthy, these studies have generally overlooked the comparative analysis of media coverage across different countries. (Shendurnikar, 2020) Unlike the current chapter, which focuses on media coverage in the UK, USA, Canada, and India, studies often focus on honor killings within a particular country and how the media of the country report on such honor killings. (Dalvi, 2022) There are research that shows a comparative analysis of honor killings in two countries or multiple countries, however lack an in-depth exploration of how the media in these countries portrays honor killings. (D'Lima et al., 2020) While approaches focusing on socio-cultural contexts and international human rights perspectives are crucial, it is also essential to consider the views of the general public. (Faqir, 2001) Understanding public opinion is important because it impacts ground-level efforts and interventions addressing the issue of honor killings. This chapter offers a comparative international perspective on media practices.

Future research should investigate the complex ways media influences legal and cultural responses to honor killings. This includes assessing the effectiveness of media watchdogs, the impact of media literacy programs on public perception, and the role of media in advocating for legal reforms. Additionally, comparing media practices across different countries and their effect on honor killing legislation could reveal best practices and highlight areas needing improvement. Examining how international media campaigns and local media coverage interact with legal systems to address honor killings will provide valuable insights into the intricate relationship between media, law, and societal change.

INTRODUCTION

Media has been covering several incidences of violence against women which can be read or found in several newspapers, television channels. Numerous cases of violence against women are reported in the media and can be read or found in various newspapers and television channels. However, these are only severe types of violence that are meant for the sake of protecting honor. The press coverage of honor-based violence was rare. It was only when murder cases became too frequent that the media decided to give the topic space to be published and disseminated. The United Nations Population Fund (UNFPA) estimates shows that over 5,000 women and girls worldwide are killed for the sake of honor every year, although the number is probably higher. (D'Lima et al., 2020) According to Human Rights Watch, nearly 15-20 honor killings happen in Jordan every year, while many cases go unreported. Without a doubt, the COVID-19 epidemic has contributed to a rise in gender-based violence in all of its manifestations; the UN has called this rising reality a "shadow pandemic."

Some examples of violence committed in the name of honor includes forced marriages, lack of education and freedom, lack of freedom of one's ability to pursue goals and to choose a partner, caving in to demands of dowry, trafficking women into enslavement, etc. Honor killings are carried out by men who believe that a female relative has committed something to humiliate them. Numerous so-called honor killings are driven from the perception of sexually explicit behavior by a woman. Having an affair, spending time alone with a man who isn't your spouse or parent, or even just posting on social media can be considered as indecency. Some men think that clearing their family of all disgrace is the only way to regain their supposed honor. Only now is the media speaking freely about issues that they should have addressed much earlier. However, it cannot be denied that the young company only became aware of these events through active media reporting. These murder cases would have remained unknown forever without the media. As a result, media focus on such substantial issues raises awareness and help mobilize public opinion against such regressive practices.

Mass media has a deep impact on culture and vice versa. The manner in which media talks about such social crimes builds public opinion as also educates masses about regressive social practices around them.

Practice of Honor Killing

The history of honor crimes in India was first documented in its most heinous form during the 1947–1950 national divide. At that time, many women were slain by force in order to protect the family's honor. Multicultural and customary practices also gave rise to several inhumane practices that became so ingrained in society that a large part of the population began to view them as something to be proud of. For example, the practice of Sati used to be considered pious and a matter of pride, but no one thought of the suffering that women go through. However, thanks to the constant efforts of leaders like Raja Ram Mohan Roy, the practice was made a punishable offense. Although this practice has been associated with religion and customs, there is also an evil practice of honor killing that is not directly related to any religion but is simply based on self-proclaimed prestige, pride, and social image in the society. (Dalvi, 2022) That's why it says "KILL" from the start. Honor killings are sometimes associated with religious beliefs. But in reality, they are not necessarily the result of religious beliefs. They are considered an ancient custom in the Middle East and Southwest Asia.(Santhi, 2013) Honor killings were considered a tradition in ancient Rome. They are strongly supported by the patriarchal social structure. Honor killings are a family collaboration. Globally, two-thirds of victims were killed by their own family members. History teaches us that child marriage and love marriage with a stranger, especially a child from a low caste or community, is due to family wealth remaining in the family. Parents played an active role in most of the murders. All female victims were tortured to an unexpected extent by their male family members; and the men who loved her were killed.

Therefore, an honor killing can be described as the killing of a human being by a human being to protect the honor of the perpetrator or the perpetrator's community. This supposed "honor" can serve to protect the self-proclaimed image in society, which is sometimes based on the fact that the caste of one party/community is different from the other, sometimes the religion of one party/community is even different from that of the other the economic status of one family/community becomes a problem with that of another, even in some cases, all things being equal, the personal happiness of a community also becomes a problem and all of these, whether collectively or individually, becomes the cause. to commit this honor killing in the name of saving pride and prestige.

Portrayal of Honor Killing by the Media

Before we delve into the way media platforms handle the affair of honor killings, it is crucial to consider the portrayal of honor killings in the media in a broader perspective. The representation of honor killings in the media can vary greatly depending on the cultural context, the specific media company, and the goals of the reporting. Some media outlets may sensationalize honor killings, focusing on graphic details and dramatic narratives to attract attention. Others strive for objectivity and present facts and context without unnecessary dramatization. Documentaries and reports offer the opportunity to explore honor killings in more depth. They can delve into the historical, cultural and social factors that contribute to these actions, providing a nuanced perspective. Media that emphasizes cultural sensitivity avoids perpetuating stereotypes or generalizations about communities or religions. They recognize that honor killings are not part of a specific culture but are often associated with distorted interpretations of cultural norms. Global media can provide a comparative analysis of honor killings in different countries, highlighting differences in prevalence, cultural context and legal responses. This approach promotes a more nuanced understanding of the problem. Media coverage may feature activists who challenge traditional norms and work to end honor killings. This throws light on the resilience and courage of those driving change despite significant challenges. The approach that the media should take should also be to use investigative journalism, to expose problems such as failures in the legal systems, corruption or complicity. In-depth investigations can highlight causes and obstacles to justice.

How Does Indian Media Address Honor Killing?

If a person has the right to live his life with dignity as provided under Article 21 and the right to choose his partner as provided under Articles 19(1)(a) and 21 of the Constitution of India, communication agencies also have the means to protect these rights within their scope by raising people's awareness of these rights. There are several other ways to raise awareness and motivate the public to protect their rights, but one of the most important and influential is the media. Justice Patanjli Shastri in the case *Romesh Thapper v. The State of Madras (1950)* stated that *"Freedom of speech and that of the press is the foundation of organizations, for without free political discussion no public education, so essential for the proper functioning of the process of popular Government, is possible."* We can do this associated with the freedom of choice of a group of people who have the right to marry of their own choice. However, these opinions of the judges remain valid today.

Indian media has played a crucial role on issues that serve the welfare of society. On the other hand, it led to several results that were unacceptable. Therefore, it is very important for the media to adopt a balanced approach, especially with respect to the Indian society as the Indian population mainly depends on the media and learns various things through the media.

Making News Newsworthy

Undoubtedly, the media is obsessed with news of young couples who fled to avoid the pressure and violence from their communities for getting married outside caste boundaries. While they share news about India's GDP growth, they are by no means enthralled with the idea of educating their audience about the persistent social violence committed in the name of caste and religion. The idea is that crime makes news and news makes money. These posts get solid TRP and viewership.

The example of the media circus in the murder case of Aarushi Talwar in Noida demonstrates that the media is not concerned in carrying out investigations that can lead to the truth. Instead, it's about presenting your own truth and filling information spaces. More than a decade ago, SMS did the same job. While the investigation into the Aarushi-Hemraj double murder case was underway, media channels were busy asking viewers to guess who the murderer was via SMS. On May 15, 2008, Aarushi Talwar's body was found along with domestic help Hemraj. Three teams (one from the UP Police and two from the CBI) investigated the murders, but the investigation ended with insufficient evidence being cited in the CBI's final report. The Talwars, who were accused by the media of Aarushi's murder, were later acquitted in 2017. In this case too, the media viciously played up various aspects like honor killing, her father's alleged extramarital affair, fabrication of news that Aarushi was an adopted child and the Talwars' supposed lack of crying on TV. Some channels even showed her 17-year-old friend's phone number live on the screen. (Lidhoo, 2020) Cases of honor killings were not treated differently.

Striving for a "newsworthy" model of news reporting increases the likelihood that information will be edited to achieve higher TRPs and reader ratings. The fascination with the value of information can lead to low-quality informational messages that can be unfairly targeted and analyzed by women. This phenomenon, often referred to as a "media circus," can also lead to a "media trial" and/or "media activism." (Nidhi Shendurnikar, 2020) As we look at trends in sensationalism and sexist portrayals in the media, a question arises: Does media coverage "create awareness" or "desensitize" the individual's mind to violence?

While ideally the media is responsible for ensuring that news does not lead to further violence, there is also another form of violence, the so-called "media violence", which points to the effects of media violence on the psyche of the individual. (Babuji, 2023) In this case, the "language" used to portray violence plays an important role in the formation of perception. Multimedia content influences audiences in different ways and at different levels. Violence is fascinating – it is almost always "extraordinary". Whether it's news, movies or video games, violence can arouse curiosity. However, the intensity and frequency of viewing violence can also lead to a person's desensitization. One way to desensitize your audience is the language you use. The vocabulary used to describe violence and honor killings can determine how women are portrayed and treated. When people become depersonalized, violence is more likely to continue. So how can we ensure that public debate about violence does not further desensitize people? How can one speak publicly about this private intimacy between people of different castes?

Portrayal of Honor Killings in Social-Media and Indian Cinema

Social media platforms provide real-time information on honor killings. News, images and personal stories can spread quickly and ensure that incidents receive attention quickly and are not easily ignored. Social networks facilitate the global exchange of information. Awareness campaigns, hashtags and movements can transcend geographical borders and promote international solidarity and support against honor killings. Various campaigns and initiatives against honor crimes find a platform on the social networks. Using hashtags, viral challenges, and multimedia content can attract widespread attention and engagement. Platforms like Facebook, Instagram and others have various pages where they raise awareness about various social issues. In some cases, these platforms have even been viewed as disseminators or distributors of news. People share posts from these sites, which leads to this mass distribution in multiple areas that normal media may not have a focus on or ability to reach. This is possible because commonly known people are connected to each other on every social media platform, and this facilitates the spread of the news not only in one area or street but even in small houses. Therefore, social media is used to raise awareness about evil practice of honor killing. These media platforms can bring people into a modern and reflective environment that then makes these practices a sin and not a matter of pride.

The English media uses several clichés when describing these killings as a widespread rural incident. They mislead the general public to think that honor killings are exclusive to rural and backward areas. This leads to a completely wrong perception of the rural population among city dwellers. Indian cinema, known worldwide as Bollywood, has contributed significantly to social challenges and the formation of public impressions. While honor killings have featured in some Indian films, it is important to understand that Bollywood as a whole neither condones nor supports such violent crimes. Indian cinema, on the other hand, has typically taken a progressive stance when it comes to addressing social issues and promoting change. The film "Gulaal (2009)", which explores a number of social and political issues in India, including honor killings, is a case in point. (Dalvi, 2022) These films help raise awareness on the issue, but they do not speak for the entire Indian film industry. It is important to distinguish how honor killings are portrayed in Indian cinema and how common they are in real life.

Concepts of Trial by Media and Media Activism

Crime reporters interpret the killings as regular crime stories, with no intention of reveal an incident that is not an ordinary crime but a social turmoil. Like in some normal crime beat, the journalist's first objective is to figure out the reason and manner in which the crime was committed in order to present it with a headline that catches attention. (Nidhi Shendurnikar, 2020) The story of *Rizwanur Rehman's Death* in Calcutta in 2007 was initially lost on the inside pages of newspapers as a typical crime story. The Telegraph, a satirical editorial from Calcutta, decided that the police had chosen to look into a lawfully registered marriage instead of pursuing robbers and murderers. It was only later that the media discovered that it was an honor killing because Rizwanur married his student Priyanka, a daughter of the renowned Todi business family. (Sengputa, 2007) The media revealed the truth about many incidents, such as the murders of Jessica Lal and Priyadarshini Mattoo, and increased pressure on the authorities to bring those responsible to justice. The rich and powerful could influence the country's legal system even without the media's efforts. But there is more to this story than meets the eye, as the role of the media in such situations is linked to ethical and moral questions. Opponents argue that the media should not judge and instead simply report the facts.

The Indian media has taken several initiatives to help reduce honor killings in India and to put an end to honor killings in India. An example of this is the launch of a campaign by News publisher "The Times of India" in 2017 entitled "Stop Honor Killings". The campaign called for an end to the practice and included testimonies from people who had suffered honor killings. These efforts succeeded in drawing attention to the problem and putting pressure on the administration to act upon it and take action. In 2018, NDTV, a news channel, aired a documentary titled "Honor Killings: The Hidden Truth" the film dealt with the issue of honor killings in India and the impact of this practice on human lives. (Dalvi, 2022)

Instances of Presentation of Honor Killing by International Media

It is important and very relevant that honor killings are not just limited within India but is an international issue which the international media has been covering for a while. However, it is pertinent to note that not all cases of honor killings make it to the press while the majority of it pass unreported. (Nidhi Shendurnikar, 2020) According to Phyllis Chesler, the author of "Woman's Inhumanity to Woman," honor killings of Hindu couples in India have been reported and covered by the New York Times, Washington Post and Los Angeles Times, but have never brought up honor killings in Muslim countries like Afghanistan, Iran, Pakistan, Jordan etc. (Chesler, 2010) So, it is the media that decides which story should be made public and which not. When reporting these stories, the media often uses cover-up tactics and pursues their own agenda. The most important thing to remember is that honor killings have attracted media attention both at home and abroad. Media must reject prejudice based on religion, caste, community etc. and examine these incidents from the perspective of human.

United States of America

Honor killings are very rare in the United States, but when they occur, they are widely reported in the media. When honor killings occur in the United States, the media reports on them and informs the public. This reporting can help raise awareness of the problem and educate readers about the details of individual cases, such as the circumstances, legal history, and solutions. This information is usually reported by local media. The amount of insurance coverage can depend on factors such as the seriousness of the crime, the surrounding circumstances and the involvement of law enforcement. The American media generally approaches honor killings with cultural sensitivity. (Friedersdorf, 2010) They aim to avoid reinforcing stereotypes or generalizations about specific communities, recognizing that these events are not representative of any particular cultural or religious group. Media coverage can victimize honor killings and communities that impact people. The media can help people affected by Honor-based violence by sharing their stories and giving a voice to the victims and their families. This promotes empathy, understanding and support.

Please be informed that there are a number of factors that might affect how much and what kind of media coverage honor killings receive in the US, such as the crime's seriousness, the area, and the news cycle at the time. The media also has its own editorial freedom in choosing the topics covered and the way in which they report on them.

United Kingdom

It should be remembered that the functioning of the media is not without difficulties. Concerns about sensationalism, cultural bias and the possibility of perpetuating stereotypes must be taken into account. The most reported honor killings of women in UK have been of South Asian women or women of Pakistan ethnic origin. (Dyer, 2015) Ethical journalistic practices, compassion and a commitment to accurate representation are essential to responsible media coverage of honor killings. Overall, the British media has the opportunity to inform, educate and influence public perceptions of honor killings. The media can help combat honor violence and advance social reform by raising awareness, dispelling myths, and supporting debate. Trials in honor killing cases are frequently discussed in the media, including updates and analysis. Through this offering, the public can better understand the difficulties associated with such situations, the legal system surrounding them and the consequences of legal action. The media provides a forum for victims of honor killings and their families to tell their stories and express their voices. Survivors and advocates can challenge social norms and demand change through interviews, articles, and personal stories.

Canada

In Canada, the media can be an effective tool in the fight against honor killings. The media can support victims and their families, advocate for changes that can help prevent honor killings, and raise awareness of the problem by honestly and accurately reporting the facts. In 2014, media reports about the killing of Aqsa Parvez contributed to the national dialogue on honor killings. (Dalvi, 2022) Aqsa Parvez, a 16-year-old Canadian of Pakistani origin, was murdered by her father and brother because she did not want to marry the man, they had chosen for her. The case's media coverage contributed to recognition of the problem of honor killings and the demand for care for victims and their respective families.

Negative Impact of Media Coverage of Honor Killing

Although the media plays a key role in shaping perception of the society and raising public awareness of important issues, including honor killings, in some cases their media coverage can have negative effects. (Dalvi, 2022)

> **Negative Impact**: High-profile reporting tends to focus on the shocking and horrific aspects of honor killings, often at the expense of a detailed understanding of the underlying issues. This can have a negative impact on public perception as the focus may be on sensationalism rather than information.

Perpetuating Stereotypes: Media coverage that does not place honor killings in a broader cultural and social context can perpetuate harmful stereotypes about certain communities or religions. This can contribute to the marginalization and stereotyping of certain groups.

Victim Blaming: Some media may inadvertently contribute to victim blaming by unduly emphasizing the victim's actions or behavior. This could distract from the root causes of honor killings, such as deep-rooted cultural norms and gender inequality.

Imitative Behavior: In rare cases, videos of honor killings may inadvertently encourage people to imitate or repeat behavior observed on television. To minimize potential negative impacts, it is important to approach sensitive topics with caution. This phenomenon, known as "copy behavior," has been observed in a variety of circumstances

Misinterpretation and Misrepresentation: Viewers' perception and interpretation of the video content may vary. Instead of interpreting a film as a criticism, viewers sometimes misunderstand its meaning and believe it is an endorsement or justification of honor killings. Misinformation and harmful beliefs can be perpetuated by misrepresentations or misinterpretations of a topic.

Ethical Violations: In some cases, the media can cross ethical boundaries by violating the privacy of victims and their families. This can lead to further trauma for those affected and make it more difficult to cope with the consequences of such events.

Ignoring the Root Causes: When media coverage does not address the root causes of honor killings, such as: Such as gender inequality, patriarchal norms and cultural expectations, there is a risk of missing the opportunity to contribute to long-term solutions. Superficial reports may focus on symptoms rather than systemic problems.

Impact on Trials and Preventive Litigation: Media reports that sensationalize or bias the case have the potential to influence trial proceedings. The fairness of legal proceedings can be compromised if public opinion is formed before all evidence has been presented in court, which could impact the pursuit of justice.

Selective Reporting: Selective reporting that focuses disproportionately on some cases and neglects others can lead to a distorted perception of the frequency and nature of honor killings. This can lead to misinformation and an incomplete understanding of the overall problem.

Alarm and Panic: Media reports that exaggerate the frequency of honor killings can create a sense of panic and fear, which can lead to overgeneralization and unwarranted distrust within communities.

Comparison to Incidents Around the World: Media coverage may include comparisons to honor killings in other parts of the world. This comparative analysis can provide context and highlight differences in cultural, legal, and social responses to such events.

Impact of Honor Killing Coverage on the Society

The ongoing honor killings in India are largely due to the media. The belief that honor killings are acceptable and that the families of women killed in this way have been dishonored by their actions is often reinforced by media reports of honor killings. Such a guarantee can make it more difficult for women to leave an abusive relationship and can also lead to more violence against women. The media supports honor killings in various ways. First, these killings often result in media sensationalism, which can influence the public's perception that they are acceptable. For example, the media may highlight details of a murder, such as the technique used, or the number of people involved. Women may find it more difficult to leave an abusive relationship if they believe that honor killings are common and acceptable because of this type of relationship. Secondly, the image often presented in the media is that women killed in honor killings have brought shame on their families.

Third, the media often ignores the causes of honor killings. Patriarchal ideas about family honor and social honor are often the basis for honor killings. By focusing on the root causes of honor killings, such as gender imbalance and discrimination against women in India, the media can help debunk these views.

CONCLUSION

The media can influence public opinion and play a key role in ending honor killings in India. The media can contribute to the development of a fairer and more equal society for women by criticizing media portrayals of honor killings and examining the causes of this violence. The media can support efforts to end honor killings in several ways. First, the media should stop covering these murders on the front page. The media should focus on the human cost of this brutality rather than the details of the murder. The media can also report on the testimony of survivors of honor killings and the efforts of groups fighting to end this brutality. Second, the media has the power to dispel the myths that promote honor killings. Women can be portrayed in the media as confident, self-assured and free to live their lives as they see fit. The media can also refute the idea that women killed in honor killings humiliated their families. Third, the public can learn about the honor killings through the media. The media can inform people about the factors that contribute to this violence and the consequences it has on victims of crime. Information on how honor killings can be stopped and how victims of this violence can be helped can also be found in the media. (Dalvi, 2022)

The ongoing honor killings in India are largely due to the media. The belief that honor killings are acceptable and that the families of women killed in this way have been discredited by their actions is often reinforced by media reports of honor killings. Such a guarantee can make it more difficult for women to leave an abusive relationship and can also lead to more violence against women.

In conclusion, media coverage of honor killings can have both positive and negative effects, and the way these incidents are portrayed plays a key role in shaping public perceptions and influencing public attitudes. While responsible media coverage can help increase awareness, empathy and support, there are also potential pitfalls that can have damaging effects. The negative impact of media messages often results from sensationalism, perpetuation of stereotypes, victim blaming, simplification of complex issues, cultural insensitivity, and ethical violations. These factors can hinder a different understanding of honor killings, fuel xenophobia and contribute to a climate of fear and mistrust within communities.

For the media to play a constructive role, it is important that reporting on honor killings is approached with cultural sensitivity, ethical journalistic practices, and a commitment to addressing the root causes. Balanced and informed reporting can contribute to a more comprehensive understanding of the problem, promote empathy, support advocacy, and promote meaningful social change. Ultimately, it is the responsibility of the media to carefully examine the complexities of honor killings, acknowledge the human impact of these incidents, and contribute to a public discourse that promotes understanding, tolerance, and justice.

REFERENCES

Annavarapu, S. (2013). Human rights, honour killings and the Indian law: Scope for a 'right to have rights'. *Economic and Political Weekly*, 48(50), 45–54.

Babuji, N. (2023). Private Love, Public Eyes: Media, Family, and Honour Killings in India. Shuddhashar Magazine. Retrieved June 29, 2024, from https://shuddhashar.com/private-love-public-eyes-media-family-and-honor-killings-in-india-nandhitha-babuji/

Bhanbhro, S. (2023, November 29). Reports of 'honour-based' abuse increased following lockdowns and change to police recording rules. *The Conversation*. Retrieved August 8, 2024, 2024 https://theconversation.com/reports-of-honour-based-abuse-increased-following-lockdowns-and-change-to-police-recording-rules-214512#:~:text=Home%20Office%20figures%20show%202%2C905,honour%2Dbased%E2%80%9D%20since%202019

Chesler, P. (2010, July 12). Are some honor killings more equal than others? Fox News. Retrieved June 03, 2024, from https://www.foxnews.com/opinion/are-some-honor-killings-more-equal-than-others

D'Lima, T., Solotaroff, J. L., & Pande, R. P. (2020). For the Sake of Family and Tradition: Honour Killings in India and Pakistan. *ANTYAJAA: Indian Journal of Women and Social Change*, 5(1), 22–39. DOI: 10.1177/2455632719880852

. Dalvi, A.P. (2022). Addressing 'Honour Killings' in India: Role of Media, social platforms, and film in depicting cases of honour killings in India. UGC Care Group 1 Journal, 52(4(I)), 1268-1270. ISSN: 0378 – 4568.

Dyer, E. (2015). 'Honour' killings in the UK. The Henry Jackson Society. Retrieved June 10, 2024, from https://henryjacksonsociety.org/wp-content/uploads/2015/01/Honour-Killings-in-the-UK.pdf

Faqir, F. (2001). Intra family femicide in defence of honour: The Case of Jordan. *Third World Quarterly*, 22(1), 165–182. DOI: 10.1080/713701138

Friedersdorf, C. (2010). American newspapers and honour killings (Updated). The Atlantic. Retrieved June 10, 2024, from, https://www.theatlantic.com/projects/ideas-2010/archive/2010/06/american-newspapers-and-Honour-killings-updated/58292/

. Jeyasanthi, V., Mayeleswari, S., & Abiram, R. (2014). Honour Killing: A National Outcry. COLLEGE SADHANA - Journal for Bloomers of Research, 6(2), February 2014.

Lidhoo, P. (2020, September 1). Aarushi Talwar to Rhea Chakraborty: A tale of two media trials and zero lessons learnt. *The Wire*. Retrieved June 05, 2024, from https://thewire.in/media/rhea-chakraborty-sushant-singh-rajput-aarushi-talwar-media-trial

Romesh Thapper v. The State of Madras, AIR 1950 SC 124

Shendurnikar, N. (2020). Honour in the News: Media Representation of Honour Killings. University of East London. Unpublished manuscript, Transnational Organised Crime (CR7003).

Chapter 16
Honor Killing:
A Social-Legal Position in India in the Last Decade

Heeuk D. Lee
Weber State University, USA

Chanchal Garg
GLA University, India

Shweta Tyagi
Hemaadri International, India

ABSTRACT

Honor Killing is the evil that makes its present felt not only in India but also a global phenomenon or threat that requires serious consideration. In Indian families, honor is given the supreme position and bringing the dishonor on the family is the prime cause that makes one to kill or harm their own loved ones. It paves its way through similar patterns of thinking among people and based on their faith, to follow the old tradition passing from generation to generation. These killings are not restricted by gender and affect the perpetrators as they are only losing their loved ones instead of getting any gain. this chapter is focused on how India is getting affected by this barbaric crime in the last decade and what is its socio-legal position and how the act done in the name of honor is only motivating the people to attempt dishonored actions or can say crimes. This chapter has specifically tried to cover every aspect of social trigger of this shameful act that has contributed in affecting the people in last decade along with the legal provisions.

DOI: 10.4018/979-8-3693-9596-7.ch016

BACKGROUND

Honor Killing is the evil that makes its present felt not only in India but also a global phenomenon or threat that requires serious consideration and needed to be taken care of. In Indian families, honor is given the supreme position and bringing the dishonor on the family is passing from generations to generations even if in any case, they become abusive to them. These killings are not restricted by gender and other than its nature to abuse the victim; it also affects the perpetrators because they are only losing their loved ones instead of getting any gain. Here, this chapter is mainly focused on how India is getting affected by this barbaric crime in the last decade and what is its socio-legal position and how the act done in the name of honor is only motivating the people to attempt dishonored actions or can say crimes. This chapter has specifically tried to cover every aspect of social trigger that could result into this shameful act or be the instigating factor of the same and have also described on how these points of factors have contributed in affecting the people in last decade along with the legal provisions applied or steps taken by the Government of India in the same tenure in the direction of reducing these harmful attempts against the innocents.

Data analyses of various research papers have been studied and the most suitable data or reports of cases within standard time period have been opted for research. Although, it's very difficult to identify the cases of such crimes as they are mostly registered as death of natural cause, suicide and various other factors but the reports that has tried to include most of the genuine cases of these honor based violence are opted like the data of National Crime Records Bureau of 2014 to 2016 has also been considered where they mentioned that 281 cases of honor killing were reported in India which is a great number in itself and further as per the survey reports done by AIDWA (All India Democratic Women's Association) that highlighted the specific part of India where most of the cases are reported like Western Uttar Pradesh has been the place where over 30% of the cases from the country has been reported. (Kalnawat, 2021) This data has its significance as it's clearly describing about the status of the reported cases of the crime in India and also specifying the red area of such crimes in order to clearly understand the position of the country within that tenure and could also be helpful to research about how different causes of such crimes were successful in instigating the violence in different areas and if there were different prime triggers of honor based violence in different regions.

Moreover, a detailed media content analysis of 101 cases was conducted in India from 2005 to 2017 where most cases were included were from 2010 that showed how 79 out of 100 cases were women that states that they were more prone to become victim of such crimes at that time but also showed women were not the only victim of honor crimes and included other social groups also. (Solotaroff et al., 2020). This data gives clarity on women being the prime target victim of these killings but also leaves scopes of other social groups being victims and facing the consequences of the crime.

Key Terms

Most appropriate term for the content analysis are *"Honor Killing"* and *"Socio-Legal Position"* that direct the reader towards the subject matter regarding the socio-legal position in India. Other Broader term for the content includes *"Customary Killings"* and *"Social Impact"*, *"Honor Killings"* and *"Socio-Legal Position in India"*, *"Social-Triggers"* that leads to the various causes of Honor Killings included in the subject-matter effecting India in last decade. Other terms that could relate to the content analysis could be, *"Honor"*, *"Honor and Homicide"*, *"Khap Panchayat"*, *"Patriarchal Society"* and *"Honor Crimes"*, *"Liberal Conduct"* and *"Honor Based Violence"*.

In line with *International Indexed & Referred Research Journal* (Bhatia, 2012), *Lexforti Legal journal* (Raizada) , *and Multi-Disciplinary Journal* (Arora, 2023), we used these Key words to select various relevant articles and research papers from multiple online sources like, Sage, Taylor & Francis and Google Scholar, Research Gate, ISSN, JETIR (Newme, 2018), *Antyajaa: Indian Journal of Women and Social Change* (Solotaroff et al., 2020) , *International Journal of Pure and Applied Mathematics* (Sehnoi & Pandiaraj, 2018) *and Indian Journal of Integrated Research in Law* (Manhas).

As there is an essential requirement of selecting the research article for conducting inclusion/ exclusion of the articles for the subject matter of this chapter, publications specializing in socio-legal impacts of honor killing, triggers of honor crimes and data analysis of recent incidents has been included for journal selection. Author relied on primary sources like *AIDWA* (Kalnawat, 2021) whereas the journal opted by the author are *Indian Journal of Integrated Research in law* (Manhas), and *Lexforti Legal Journal* (Raizada).

Inclusion Criteria on ensuring the articles directly addressing the concept of Honor Killing, the effects of honor-based violence within the last decade and the patterns of the triggers affecting the crime. Data Analysis of those reports including the cases from the tenure of past decade and their result, Government and Recognized NGOs reports are the crucial part of the research in order to include the recent position or stats for better analysis.

Exclusion Criteria filtered out all the non-academic posts, blogs, opinions or views on unverified websites. Non credible online sources were not taken into consideration along with Non-Peer Reviewed Research articles. Editorials or news articles from non-credible sources were also excluded for removing any discrepancies.

Literature Review

Kejriwal, Neelam gives insights of the possible outcomes that resulted into acts of Honor killing and their consequences specifically in the area of North India. This chapter has highlighted the cases of victims of such act in North India and discussed different reasons for the killing by analyzing the Delhi based survey report of Indian Population Statistics Survey (IPSS) and have given the recommendations accordingly.

Newme, Widonlule (2018) has briefly talked about the causes of honor killing following with the major roles of women in these crimes and comparing such customary killings with other forms of crimes. This chapter has further included some international instruments on the crimes along with the legal frameworks of India.

Dr. Kalnawat, Aarti Mohan (2021) has analyzed the concept of Honor Killing in India under basic legal framework and has included the demographics of the killings and Supreme Court's View on the killings by referring landmark judgments and need of disagreement against the new law on this crime.

D'Lima, T; Solotaroff, J L; Pande, R P (2020) have conducted a descriptive analysis of media reported cases of honor killings in India and Pakistan in order to compare their similarities and differences with regards to motivation, characteristics, risk factors and other protective measures of the crime.

Poddar, A. has analyzed the newspaper articles from time span 2000-2019 from two of leading publications of India regarding the honor killing and demonstrated that these acts of customary killings include social groups beyond women and is far reaching than expected and there is also a major role of women perpetrators and male victims in such acts. This paper also talked about collective social institutions' contribution like Khap Panchayats.

Raizada S, has addressed the critical problem of cultural crimes and how they are becoming an uncontrollable demon in the chapter Socio-Legal Analysis of honour killing in India. This chapter has briefly talked about the special triggers like inter and intra caste marriages that most often are the cause of honor killing while explaining other triggers and their effects.

Future Directions

This research is an attempt by the author to let the readers know about how this barbaric crime of honor-based violence has been affecting the society of India in last decade. Author has followed a pattern while doing the research and drafting the subject matter that starts with basic meaning of honor followed by the interpretation of honor killing by adjoining it with the historical context of India on how honor is considered as a supreme ornament by Indians and how insights of honor killing can be seen in ancient times also. (Kalnawat, 2021)

Afterwards, the author has taken data analysis of various reports like AIDWA (Kalnawat, 2021) and credible news articles like *The Hindustan Times* (Sunny, 2017) etc that are of past decade only in order to analyze the recent social impacts of different triggers of honor killings. Author has also mentioned the smallest details of issue that could instigate or become the reason of these violent acts to also know the cause roots of crimes like patriarchy has formed the major role in such crimes and showing cruelty to female victims, but Honor Killing is a crime that has much broader range of only women being victims of such crimes and also include other social groups as its victims also. Author has also tried to supply with evidence of recent reports in order to support the arguments used in the research which are taken from various research papers like *For the Sake of Family Tradition: Honour Killings in India and Pakistan* (Solotaroff et al, 2020)

This chapter has also included the nature of honor killing to clearly understand the concept of honor killing and what are its social and legal effects on society. Author has mentioned the judicial approach of honor crimes along with the actions taken by the govt. specifically in the last decade for it. (Sehnoi & Pandiaraj, 2018) Although research has been done on this point, but this chapter can be considered as the updated version of those research as author has considered those research articles like (Prabhune) that have included the arguments related to the issue and have further explained it.

Although there are a few research papers similar to the topic but this chapter marks its significance from other chapters through giving specific research of socio-legal position in India in Last Decade. Other research articles are slightly similar to the chapter's topic that the author have considered for the research and taken help to draw an updated version from are (Avraj, 2023) and many more. The research has been conducted by taking the duration of time period as supreme priority and analyzes how the specific Country, India is getting affected in the given time in social and legal positions through these customary Killings and what are the development actions that have been taken regarding the same which certainly gives the systematic idea and a brief view on the past situations through which new action can be taken for future directions.

Another potential area of study could be the comparative analysis of situation of India regarding such crimes with a different country having same time zone for future research.

INTRODUCTION

India is highlighted through its rich heritage and diverse cultures professing different religions and following various customs from generations; still existing together in same dimension by having the sense of brotherhood and abided by the laws of land. There is one thing that Indians consider as one of their supreme ornaments i.e. Honor. Here, the question arises that what is honor? It has a subjective meaning as it could differ for different personalities but mostly, it is considered as respect or dignity of an individual in the society due to his morally correct deeds, ideals or values. Women are considered as the bearer of honor of their respective family and thus also called as 'Devi' in ancient texts of India that makes them responsible for protecting the honor and hold them accountable if any harm is received to the same. This responsibility of protecting honor makes other family members to take brutal action that even includes killing against their own family mostly women as they are only considered as property of male dominance. This cruelty on victim by their own loved ones is termed as 'Honor Killing'.

This practice of killing based on honor is not a new idea but its roots can even be traced from the sacred times of Ramayana and Mahabharata and its origin mainly arise from the dignity, pride or honor of female characters. (Aarti & Kalnawat, 2021) Like in Ramayana, when Lord Rama rescued Sita, due to the question of her chastity being separated from her husband, she had to live separately in the forests. Even in Mahabharat, war happened between brothers because five husbands of Devi Draupadi lost her honor in a game of gambling and she had to face the embarrassment, disgrace, demeaning behavior of whom her husband's lost her pride in front of whole community. These acts laid the foundation of great wars fought cause of honor.

This cruel practice of honor killings is a disgrace for society. Mostly Women become the victim of this cruelty due to many reasons like inter-caste marriages, questions and doubts arising on their chastity, any act like wearing western clothes that are not acceptable as decent in the society. Most of the reasons for these customary killings are no more than truffles but still result into taking the life of an innocent just because they took decisions on their own. Although these killings have been there for a long time and could even be included as one of the custom; still there are on such specific laws for victims as remedy and this presence of no such specific laws encourages the local people to perform such activities and gives freedom for the same somewhere.

This felony is not just exercised in India but existence of this felony is found in many different countries also like Jordan, Canada, Iran, Iraq, Lebanon, Palestine etc. and mostly in all countries, reasons for these customary killings made women their prey. This chapter is focused on what are the actions taken legally and what was the social position of India in last decade in regards of such honor-based violence.

Triggers of Honor Killing

Both male and female could become the object of these customary killings where death is rewarded to them by their own family members that are supposed to love and support them rather become rivals because of their mentality to protect their pride. Thus, it could be said that the prime trigger to this heinous crime is mentality of people to protect their 'Ghar ki Izzat'. (Tyagi, 2021) There are other triggers too that were mainly arisen due to the prime trigger and how they are changed or have affected the society in last decades are as:

Patriarchal Society: India consists of families that have been following the patriarchal form of society where male is dominant than female members. Being the head of the family, they indulge more in executing this cruel practice considering that it's their duty to preserve the honor and presupposes that it's harmed by any action of women. A detailed media content analysis of 101 cases of honor killing was conducted in India from 2005-2017 in which most of the cases that were used were from 2010 where it was observed that among victims of these practices, 79 out of 100 were women. (Solotaroff et al., 2020) They rather than feeling guilty instead justify their actions of killing out of anger through veil of honor and pride.

They are of the mindset that just when women refuse to be obedient or doesn't follow the orders of them, honor of their clan is at stake. So, in order to protect it, they act as if they have to do this foul practice and even name it as a sacrifice or suicide. For e.g. In Sati practices, widows are in extreme societal pressure along with pressure from their family to do sacrifice their life by burning themselves in the cremation of their dead husbands. It could be considered as an example of honor killing as it was supposed earlier that it's a shame for widows to live after the death of their husbands. Although this practice was held illegal and abolished by Governor – General Lord William Bentick in 1829 and prevention of Sati act, 1987 also came into force that resulted that it's almost extinct now yet some widows had to go through this and at least four such cases were recorded between 2000 and 2015. (Jain, 2023)

Caste Hierarchy: In India, caste system is at its peak and the cast which is at dominance over an area tends to wield political and domestic power over other castes. This caste system leads to customary killings of members belonging to lowers castes and the members of upper dominant castes who are found indulging with lower clans as it's considered as humiliation for upper castes to even talk with the people of lower clan people. They don't even like get touched by mistake with lower castes as it was supposed that they would get impure by doing so.

These types of fallacy could be seen from many instances of past times and is even mentioned in Manu Smriti like there was a law that if any body part of Brahmin gets touched by Sudras or lower class, then that limb of his body must be removed or cut off. Once, Mahatma Gandhi was also not allowed to draw and drink water from well by servants of Rajendra prasad because they thought him to be a peasant of lower castes and claimed that even few drops from the bucket, he would drink from cold pollute the whole well. If we look at the recent example, then in Mysore village, there are nineteenth Jati groups or castes, but Okkalinga were the biggest landowner and consists of nearly half of the population. (Kejriwal) They have dominance in political power, economic strength, rituals or traditions and even settle disputes between their own and other clans. So, in order to retain their dominance, honor-based violence or crimes come into existence.

Endogamy: It is more like a tradition in our society for everyone to marry in the same clan as them. As love marriages are starting to get accepted by the parents nowadays but still people prefer to marry within their own clan and if some refuse to do so, they became victim of such honor crimes. This system was followed to ensure and preserve the richness and culture of one clan within themselves but soon, it became a triggering cause of such crimes making the orthodox mindset of people.

This orthodox mindset sows seeds of revenge and vengeance in people deep down as if one has committed certain act, then even when a decent time has passed, they can't be escaped from the misfortunes they have to face due to these acts of killings. This can be ascertained through a case happened in Madhya Pradesh in 2012 where Deepa and Rajkumar decided to marry each other even when Deepa was Thakur and the boy was a Dalit. As they knew about what the consequences of their marriage could be, so they fled and settles in Ludhiana. Even after a long time passed, family of girl's side could not accept their marriage even when the couple had two children and were living happily. So, in order to take revenge of hurting their family's pride, they faked to reestablish their relations with the couple and then one fine day, males of Deepa's family stabbed her husband and slit his throat just because of him being Dalit on a railway station. (Avraj, 2023)

Relationships and Marriage: This is one of the most noticed triggers of honor-based crimes. It includes both inter-caste marriage as well as marriage within the same gotra. Although, endogamy is preferred here but still to be married under same gotra is not allowed and considered as an attack against Honor. Nowadays, although due to the start of Love marriages, in some modern families, exogamy is accepted and youths are somewhat allowed to have exogamy love marriages in the last decade even though such marriages are still very less to be seen but to marry someone in the same gotra is strictly prohibited and are guided by sapinda system or consanguinity. This gotra reason is mainly present in Hindus that provides more way for these crimes to grow their roots in society. Even under Hindu Law, it's prohibited, and such marriages are void as they come under the region of sapinda relations or prohibited relations per section 5 but just because it's prohibited, to kill someone out of protection of honour is just paving way for another crime.

As per research conducted based on making 21st century as time frame, caste being the motivation for disapproval of relationship in both inter-caste marriage and marriages under same gotra has the highest percentage of 25.13% among the reported cases in North India that shows how this caste system is affecting the society and depriving the people to freely choose their partner for life. (Poddar, 2020)

This factor also includes refusal to have an arranged marriage or if someone refuses to marry the person family suggests. Also, dissolution of marriage becomes base for making women victim of murder under this fallacy. As per Manu Smriti, A women can never have a second husband and ties of marriage could never be severed in any circumstances. So, she could never dissolve her marriage even by sale or abandonment and if she does so, it's supposed to harm the honor of the whole clan. These all are specific triggers of causing such heinous crimes related to marriage.

Liberal Conduct: It is considered that if a person is not doing what the one is pre-supposed to do as decent codes of conduct by society, then that person is putting the honor of their family a stake by being too liberal. It could be affected by various reasons like in some families, even if a girl is found talking on the phone with a boy, then that girl has committed a heinous action and in order to maintain their respect in the society, her own family uses the way of honor-based violence against her. Girls are even required to wear those clothes only that are considered as decent by the society. (Chauhan, 2020) Her own family members haven't given her the minimum freedom to choose the clothes as per her comfort. She would be alleged with the allegations that she has taken down the family's honor only through her dress sense. According to an instance, victim's family was angry on her being too liberal that was hurting their honor which resulted into them chopping off victim's head and hands and they didn't even try to hide their crime as it was right according to them. (Sunny, 2017) In one case of Uttar Pradesh, a minor girl was killed by her own father for being furious over her just when she returned home due to her decision of spending the night with her friends. (Poddar, 2020)

Homosexuality is also one of the factors that are included under too liberal way of living life. If a person comes out to be homosexual where that person likes same sex person as themselves or if they indulge in homo sexual acts like men acts or talks in a more feminine way or wear feminine clothes and vice versa for females also, then they're harming the pride of families according to orthodox mindsets that makes them victim even when they are innocent. (Raizada) Their right to life and personal liberty as per article 21 of Indian Constitution is derived from them.

If a person is indulged under any sexual activities out of their marriage or when they are single, then it also leads to honor-based crimes. (Manhas) There was a case of 2014 where a father after he found her daughter (Sarita Devi) with her lover (Dinesh Kumar), killed her in Nurankhera District of Sonipat village of Haryana when both students were undergraduate although both father and grandfather of the girl went to jail for this act. (Kejriwal) There was a case of New Delhi in 2015 where Sagar, a 20-year boy, had an illicit relation with a sixteen-year-old minor girl, so he was mercilessly beaten and cruelly killed by relatives of girl after they took him to an isolated place. (Kejriwal) Although, when the case was reported, all the accused were arrested but still the boy had to face the consequences by being the prey of such honor-based crimes.

Society also believes that women are supposed to preserve their virginity until marriage and if that is lost before marriage by whatsoever reason, then she has brought disgrace to the whole family and have brought the nose of male members of family down. So, if such things happen, she gets boycotted by the whole family. This also includes those women that were the rape victims. They also had to face all the same consequences and society even treats them as if they are untouchable and leaves them with no choice other than suicide. (Manhas) Women also fall as prey to such killing if they undergo pre-marital pregnancies and they are also supposed to be chaste even after marriage. Murti Devi, 32 years old villager of Kansala village, Rohtak District, Haryana was killed by her own brother in 2014. She was married and had two children but later on she fell in love with her husband's relative and was indulged in sexual relations with him and even started living with him. (Siwach, 2014) So, by being enraged with all these acts, her brother shot her for the sake of honor. Later, he was charged with accusations of murder.

Khap Panchayat: These types of panchayats are mostly present in rural parts of Northern India like in some parts of Haryana, Uttar Pradesh, Around Delhi and adjoining areas. This can be understood as quasi-judicial body but they have unwritten laws and don't give their decisions based on any constitutional laws while pronounce cruel punishments based on their own desire and impose self-created rules on local communities in the veil of preserving moral values and decency in society. Their decisions results into crimes based on honor killing sometimes like when they impose their self-centric laws related to marriage and if a particular marriage is not following those provisions, then they give verdicts like annulling the marriage, boycotting the couple from society, ordering killing or declaring the couple as sibling after dissolving their marriage, corporal punishments etc.

There is a very dark and brutal side of these Khap panchayats. Although there are instances where these Khap has also shown that they could also deviate from their old tradition like in a recent case where inter-caste marriage was allowed by amending the 600 year old norm at Satrol Khap Panchayat in Narnid Village of

Haryana but, still there are more cases where Khap have shown their villainous image and implies that their verdicts could go to any extent even if it's illegal in the eyes of law just to satisfy their own ago and to make one caste supreme over another. (Khap Panchayat allows inte-caste marriages, 2014) This could be emphasized more through the landmark case of Manoj-Babli of 2007 where the couples belonged to the Jat community and decided to marry, but they were of same Banwala gotra due to which Khap panchayat of their Karora village of Haryana ordered to kill them as one can't marry in the same gotra according to their tradition and they have violated their social norm. (St. Chandrapati Vs State of Haryana and Others, 2007) But the couple refused to dissolve or annul their marriage instead they preceded it, so they were abducted and killed by family of Babli. First, they were kidnapped by her relative when they were in a bus near Raipur Jatan village, and then beaten followed by her being forced to consume pesticide by her own brother. Both the couples were packed by them in a sack and were thrown in Barwala link Canal of Hisar District. (Sehnoi & Pandiaraj, 2018) This shows how one wrong decision of Khap could influence and affect not the family but the whole society to attempt such a heinous crime.

Nature of Honor Killing

Honor killing could be of both public and private in nature. Killings that are categorized as private are those that are executed when no-one is present to be a witness when the crime happened while public ones are those that are attempted in front of whole public view in order to set as an example for the whole community that these would be the consequences to whoever would do the same acts as done by victim that resulted into the honor to be at stake. These public killings are mostly influenced by Society leaders of dominant castes to highlight that the particular family is surrendering before them and abided by the orders given to them just like in Khap panchayats. In such kind of honor killing, people show that they could go to any extent to protect their pride in the society but they are just pressurized by old set expectations of some abusive traditions getting followed in the community. In order to cope with fear that their whole family will be boycotted by the society, will get corporal punishments or have to do acts like putting nose on the ground in front of everyone because of the victim's acts that are considered as too liberal by the society, they blame everything on victim and commit crimes like customary killings.

There is an instance of a case where such public honor killings reached to its extreme peak in which a man out of suspicion that his daughter was having multiple affairs killed her. He first beheaded her in private at home, and then wandered in the village by flaunting the cut off head of the girl. (Poddar, 2020) In such nature of committing crime, people even take pleasure and pride that they executed such acts in front of their clans. For instance, there was a case of 2007 where accused Jai Bhagvan himself informed the police and disclosed that he is the killer. (DH News Service, 2007) He didn't even show a single penny of remorse while waited near the corpse until police came to arrest him. After, he was investigated; he even boasts about his crime that he was so proud that he was able to save the honor of his family by doing this. These honor killings are such a disgrace for the society and doesn't only question the morality or humanity but also makes a question on public conscience.

On the other hand, one should not confuse the private honor killings as those violent acts that are performed in a secret location or where no one could be informed about it but instead they comprise of those crimes that are covered and misrepresented into other forms as suicide, heart attack, death by natural causes etc. by hiding the truth by lying to community, destroying the evidences and body through cremation or burial ceremony as soon as possible. For instance, father and his son together killed the daughter and later buried her body in the field and also ran a tractor over the field to destroy any trace of evidence that could be found there. (Poddar, 2020) In this kind of honor killing, it is very difficult to determine that the case falls under honor killing or not as there are no traces of evidence; victim's family makes everyone believe that it's either suicide or cause of natural circumstances.

This suggests that although family is convinced by societal determinants to execute such course of actions against their own family members but still, they somewhere have guilt or remorse deep down out of loyalty and love towards the victim that they don't want to be highlighted in front of the society or can say, they don't want to publicly show or accept the reality that they are the ones who have committed such heinous acts out of their ego and rage. So, if someone is influenced by powers or dominants like Khap panchayats or if someone wants to regain their position in the society that was taken away due to loss of honor, then Public Honor Killings are the factor that could help them to achieve it easily rather than private killings.

Honor Killing vs Homicide

There is no particular section mentioned in the Indian law that deals with Honor killing and it's mainly included under sec 300 IPC as murder or treated as homicide. But if their nature, procedure, outcomes or other related things are looked upon, they have a keen difference in them. Like, the first difference could be considered as the men's area where offenders under honor killing have delusional thinking and their mind is so much installed with traditional norms that out of their thinking and societal pressure, they commit crime just to protect their honor as aforesaid while on the other hand, offenders of homicide get their motivation to commit the crime out of any personal benefit or monetary gains.

Homicide could be committed by a complete stranger, third party or someone victim barely know if he's having profit out of that act but honor killing is mostly committed by own family members who once were in a role of caretaker of victim who later became perpetrators. Accused under homicide tries to hide their act and sometimes they could even show grievance after the crime committed but in honor killing, accused instead of being in remorse even openly admit that they have committed customary killing and even boast about it that makes this crime more heinous than any other cruel crime that could be executed in the society. These behaviors of offenders of honor killing are so horrible that it doesn't just sows seeds of terror, panic and trauma in the society but also questions the general consciousness of society.

If we look deep into it, then it can also be observed that perpetrators of such killings can't be blamed solely for their acts as they are influenced by societal norms set by others and the orders given by dominants of community like in Khap panchayats and as long as the honor is not at stake, then no such hurtful acts could even be in the thought of the accused. They are also a victim through a different angle as they are not getting any benefit out of it but even, they are losing their own loved ones out of the manipulation of protecting imaginary or abstract honor. So, it could be said that the responsibility should also be on every other person that were included under incitement and provocation of trigger puller equally. Although it's difficult to identify each and every person who was a participant in such acts but these crimes should not simply be included under murder or homicide as they are different in their essence with each other and a different sub-section should be there in the law and tries to trace other accused of crimes too so that range of these crimes could be minimized.

But if we look into the position of India regarding this cruel practice, then the proposal to amend section 300 of IPC of murder to include honor killing as a sub-section and add clauses to the definition of murder has been rejected by the Law Commission as they are of the view that existing laws are enough to attend these acts of crimes so there is no need to add any other clause and doing so would only cause more confusion and unnecessary doubts or issues would be raised. (Newme, 2018) But a new bill was proposed by the Commission named as, The Prohibition of Unlawful Assembly Bill(Interference with the freedom of matrimonial alliances) in 2011 where it checked honor killings and stated that no one is allowed to gather with the intention of condemning a marriage that is although not prohibited by the law but is putting the honor of a particular community at stake according to some old traditional societal norms. (Newme, 2018)

Legal and Judicial Approach

It has already been stated that honor killing doesn't have a separate section in the law of India but these cruel acts violates many other laws under which the accused can be punished like Constitutional law of India provides individuals certain rights to enjoy and is independent with any discrimination based on caste, gender, race, color, class or residence etc. and the articles of it that gets violated due to barbaric act of killing are article 14 that talks about right to equality, article 15 giving rights of not getting any ill treatment based on discrimination, article 17, 18 that talks about abolition of untouchable and titles respectively and mainly the article 21 that gives right to life and personal liberty, article 19 that gives right to freedom and freedom of speech and expression. Individuals can also directly approach Supreme Court if the above, mentioned articles are violated as per the writs given under article 32 of Indian Constitution.

Supreme Court have also directed under the case of Lata Singh Vs Union of India that one has freedom to marry whosoever they like and if their parents are against their marriage, then they are not allowed to give any kind of threat or to commit any violence or harmful acts in order to harass the couples. (Lata Singh Vs. Union Of India, 2006) The only extent they could go to is that they can break social ties with the couple who has committed a marriage not prohibited by the law. The court has also ordered to take stern action against anyone who is found to harass any such couples in order to stamp out such offences. Practice of Khap Panchayat to take law in their hand and to give bias decisions based on their societal norms of caste has been strongly deprecated by the Supreme Court in the case of Arumugam Servai Vs State of Tamil Nadu. (Arumugam Servai Vs State of Tamil Nadu, 2011)

The other acts that get violated by such shameful offences are Indian Penal Code, 1860 and Indian Evidence Act, 1872 specifically the sections related with murder, homicide, criminal conspiracy and their punishments. A person has freedom to marry anyone irrespective of religion, caste or faith under special marriage act, 1954 that gets offended by the torments of such violence. There are many more acts or laws that could include this crime in its purview like Protection of women from Domestic Violence act, 2006 or Protection of Human Rights Act, 2006 etc. (Arora, 2023) So, it could be observed that this torment crime is solely affecting such a large section of acts and laws but still this is difficult to stamp away from the society as most of the cases are buried in the walls of house as they were not reported and even if some are reported, then it's difficult to make offender pay with punishment due to lack of evidence being destroyed by the family members of victim themselves. National Crime Records Bureau data represented that 281 Honor killings were reported in India during the time frame of 2014-2016 where this count was considered as an undercount due to many cases going unreported and some were misreported to general murders or suicide etc. (Kalnawat, 2021)

If the initiatives are looked upon that are taken by India during recent times regarding such barbaric crimes, then it was first brought up, discussed and debated upon in Rajya Sabha in 2009 where it was also discussed that a separate law should also come on this. (Prabhune) Then, in August 2010, A bill called,' Prevention of Crimes in the name of honor and Tradition Bill' was submitted to the government by a legal cell of All India Democratic Women's Association (AIDWA) in which variety of crimes and violence in addition of murder happened due to honor killing was included and preventive measures along with range of penalty levels were proposed. (Kalnawat, 2021) This bill filled the gaps and corrected the loopholes that were left in former law that was sent to law ministry named as, ' Indian Penal Code and Certain Other Amendment Bill 2010' in which recommendations regarding crimes due to honor were proposed where only murder was included as crime and other torments, harassment, torture was excluded from it. (Kalnawat, 2021) Afterwards, Prohibition of Unlawful Assembly Bill, 2011 was presented by Law Commission in its 242nd report where unlawful assemblies like Khap panchayats are its main focus although this proposal is still in line of waiting. This bill proposed that it is not allowed to gather with the intention to deliberate on, or condemn any such intended or proposed marriage that is not prohibited by the law but is has been affecting the respect of family member, member of assembly or any local of the case of couples by dishonoring the caste relations, their traditions or culture of the community (Bhatia, 2012)

CONCLUSION

It is clearly observed until now that there is no honor in taking life of someone innocent because it's not worth it to murder our own loved ones out of rage or ego. Domains of Religion, customs, culture and tradition are always a subjective topic to discuss and interpret and should not become a pretext or a justification to do harassment and cruel violent acts against another. Everyone is free to live their life with dignified means and according to his own terms and conditions. If there is anything that the parents or old generation is not finding apt or decent or they are against with their descendants or with anyone, then rather than accepting the cruel way and tries to torment the other, they should just make their distances with them and should not be in contact with them by breaking the social relations with them as it'll be beneficial for both of them and could save both parties to be a victim of something that should not have happened in the first place cause although everyone has right to freely profess and practice any custom and religion as per Indian Constitution still a mere belief on an old tradition doesn't give the right to murder. So, people need to be more aware and should avoid being manipulated or influenced by any unlawful authority and focus more on reforming their mentalities, only then can this barbaric course of actions could be eradicated out of the society.

REFERENCES

Arora, R. K. (2023). *Honour Killing: Legal Framework in India*. Multi-Disciplinary Journal.

Arumugam Servai Vs State of Tamil Nadu (The Supreme Court 2011).

Avraj, A. (2023, 9 19). *A socio-legal reading of honour-based killings in India*. Retrieved 1 24, 2024, from The Leaflet: https://theleaflet.in/a-socio-legal-reading-of-honour-based-killings-in-india/

Bhatia, A. (2012). *Honour Killing- A Study of the Causes and Remedies in its Socio Legal Aspect*. International Indexed & Referred Research Journal.

Chauhan, S. S. (2020). *A Socio-Legal Study on Honour Killing: Manslaughter in Name of Family's Honour*. MyLawman Socio Legal Review.

DH News Service. (2007, June 28). Retrieved january 2024, from The Deccan Herald: https://www.deccanherald.com/

Jain, R. (2023, 12 27). *The History Behind Sati, a Banned Funeral Custom in India*. Retrieved 2023, from Culture Trip: https://theculturetrip.com/asia/india/articles/the-dark-history-behind-sati-a-banned-funeral-custom-in-india

Kalnawat, A. M. (2021). Indian Legal Framework on Honour Killing. *SLS Nagpur*, 1-25.

Kejriwal, N. (n.d.). *Honour Killing in North India*. Retrieved January 2024, from Probono India: http://probono-india.in/Indian-Society/Paper/92_honor%20killing%20by%20Neelam.pdf

Khap Panchayat allows inte-caste marriages. (2014, 4 21). *The Economic Times*.

Lata Singh Vs. (2006). *Union Of India*. The Supreme Court.

Manhas, D. A. (n.d.). HonourKillings: Socio-Legal Aspects. *Indian Journal of Integrated Research in Law* .

Newme, W. (2018). Honour Killings in India. *JETIR*, 1-6.

Poddar, A. (2020). Reprehensible Behaviour: The Social Meaning Behind Honour Killing in India. *Brown University*, 1-74.

Prabhune, A. (n.d.). *A Socio-Legal Study of Honour Killing as a Crime in India*. Retrieved january 2024, from Legal Service India E Journal: https://www.legalserviceindia.com/legal/article-2425-a-socio-legal-study-on-honour-killing-as-a-crime-in-india.html

Raizada, S. (n.d.). SOCIO-LEGAL ANALYSIS ON HONOUR KILLING IN INDIA. *Lexforti Legal Journal* .

Sehnoi, K. r., & Pandiaraj, D. S. (2018). Honour Killing in India- A Socio-Legal Study. *International Journal of Pure and Applied Mathematics.*

Siwach, S. (2014, 5 16). 2 cases of Honour Killing in Haryana. *The Times of India.*

Solotaroff, J. L., D'Lima, T., & Pande, R. P. (2020). For the Sake of Family and Tradition: Honour Killings in India and Pakistan. *ANTYAJAA: Indian Journal of Women and Social Change*, 22-39.

St. Chandrapati Vs State of Haryana and Others. (2007). *Crl. Misc. No. M-42311 of 2007 (O&M)*. The Supreme Court.

Sunny, S. (2017, 8 26). Delhi: Man kills sister-in-law for 'honour', beheads body, chops her arms. *The Hindustan Times.*

Tyagi, M. (2021). Honour Killing in India. *The Times of India.*

Chapter 17
Consanguinity of Caste Prejudices With Honor Killing

Govind Singh Rajpal
https://orcid.org/0000-0002-3078-311X
MIT-ADT University, India

Raunak Upmanyu
GLA University, India

ABSTRACT

The chapter will deliberate on the unnoticed and dangerous issue that is rooted in society i.e. Honor killing. Honor Killing is a wrongful act with the false idea of protecting the pride of the family. It happens because of the uneducated at the grassroots level, patriarchal mentality, casteism, economic angle, and religious issues. This study aims to understand the root cause of the problem of Honor Killing i.e. caste. The study would contain the problems of caste-based marriage and why there is a social barrier to inter-caste marriage. The chapter will also focus on the causes of honor killing due to inter-caste marriage and what is the mentality of Indian parents in the rural area. In this study, Ground field Research has been conducted in the town of Raya Mathura, India in which some questions have been asked to the people on what their reasoning on inter-caste marriage and honor is killing. The chapter would also aim to analyze the Supreme Court judgment around honor killing, the right to marry your life partner, the scope of Article 21, and different marriage acts.

DOI: 10.4018/979-8-3693-9596-7.ch017

Copyright © 2025, IGI Global. Copying or distributing in print or electronic forms without written permission of IGI Global is prohibited.

STATISTICAL DATA

From records provided by the National Crime Records Bureau (NCRB) regarding honor killings it can be seen that it has been a constant and burning problem in India. As pointed in Rajya Sabha Unstarred Question No. 2449, the NCRB has start building record on honor killing from the year 2014 under IPC Sections 302 and 304. For the record, Uttar Pradesh – the state always on the headlines of programs relating to violent crimes recorded 168 honor killing cases in the year under consideration. (Ministry of Home Affairs, 2016)

Source Rajya Sabha unstarred question and answer no 3734 of 2023 also show that there are year to year variation in honor killing cases in different states. Jharkhand tops the honor killing list registering 41 cases in 2017 and came down to nine cases in 2018. The details showed that Punjab had the highest number of honor killing cases in Pakistan in 2019 and that was 6. The cases pointed to highlight temporal and geographical differences in the honor killings and portray how the social and family honor impacted on the honor crimes (Ministry of Home Affairs, 2023).

From the details of the statistics compiled, it can be deduced that even though there has been a gradual decrease in honor killing related deaths in the past few years the states of Haryana and Punjab continue to be amongst the most notorious in this regard. An analysis of the trends and numbers of murders across India for a period of 2017-2021(Ministry of Home Affairs, 2023). Presented by the NCRB gives a picture that though there was variation in the numbers in each year, the overall rate marginally dipped. The murder rates oscillated between 28000 and 29000 each year and the crime rate being constant at approximately 2. 2 per 100,000 population.

Concerning the communal violence, the data reveals that the number of murders due to the communal violence reached its highest level in 2020, when the number was standing at 62. The states where extravagant instances of such murders were reported include Bihar and Uttar Pradesh. Despite such high crime rates, the Ministry of Home Affairs says that these are predicates of other societal problems and not inefficiency of the police.

RESEARCH METHODOLOGY

This chapter's methodology follows a basic approach, incorporating research done in the Indian town of Raya, Mathura. For the purpose to comprehend how the community views on intercaste marriages, honor killings, and related societal and regulatory issues, such an approach involved accumulating of primary data through surveys and interviews. Ninety respondents representing various castes and religions were asked questions with the objective of soliciting their opinions on substantial issues on inter-caste and inter-religious marriages, the existence of laws prohibiting honor killings, and the function of traditional authorities such as the Khap Panchayats.

The majority of respondents (81%) to the research study stated the significant opposition to inter-caste ceremonies such as weddings citing constraints from society and the notion that same-caste marriages guarantee a better relationship. The results showed an obvious disparity in different points of view. The fact that 95% of respondents were ignorant of any legal framework addressing honor killings was a significant result, demonstrating the absence of legal knowledge and education in rural geographical areas. It's fascinating to note that 66% of attendees agreed with Khap Panchayat decisions, demonstrating the continued influence of traditional authority.

For the purpose to accurately represent the attitudes and mentalities that are prevalent throughout rural India concerning caste-based marriages and honor-related violence, this methodology depends on direct interviews in combination with quantitative and qualitative data collecting (Ihugba U,2020) The knowledge accumulated gives the research more comprehensive exploration vis a vis honor killings, constitutional lapses, and caste skepticism--- an empirical framework. Considering this data, the chapter makes compelling arguments that to successfully solve honor killings, additional legal education and changes are required.

KEY TERMS

Core terms including 'Honor Killing' 'Caste' and 'Prejudice', (Bethany A. Corbin, 2014) directly linking the essence of research that is the relation between caste prejudice and honor killing or how caste becomes the reason of honor killing. Broader themes like 'Caste based marriage' (Caffaro et al., 2014) and 'Inter- caste marriages' and 'Inter- religious marriage' (Olwan, 2013) contextualize the problems with these marriages in India and 'Khap Panchayat' role in Honor Killing. 'Caste and Patriarchy' (Mukherjee, 2023) examines patriarchy and honor killing and 'Gender based violence' (Chesler, 2021) refers to violence against individuals especially those considered to be of the wrong gender in the eyes of the society.

LITERATURE REVIEW

Dr. Sulakshana Banerjee Mukherjee's in **'The Crime of Honor Killing'** presents a socio-criminal overview of honor killings with focus on cultural, gender and criminality. She goes deeper on the reasons for this crime on basis of patriarchy where norms hinder ladies against revenge as a type of honor. With regards to theories, her utilization of the principle of feminism, coupled with the views held in criminology offers a strong theoretical framework with which to explain this phenomenon. The book also contains evidential information, case studies, and appraisal of different legal systems' failure to safeguard the victims, which makes it helpful resource in understanding the genesis as well as possible reform for honor killings.

Rao Arif Ali khan's work **The Crime of Honor Killing** is a melodrama that covers the aspects of history and the present world to cater to the issue of honor killing. Tracing a history of the killings from Middle Ages to the modern days, as well as including religious and legal sources, the book reveals the functions, by which the patriarchal culture and communal values justified those murders. Through the discussion Khan also describes how the custom of honor killings, commonly targeting women are practiced even in the contemporary world to punish dishonorable behaviour. The strength of khan's work is in the fact that it combines both archival evidence and modern analysis of honor-based violence. It compiles a comprehensive historical account and is of use to scholars, activists, researchers and advocates for change in the legal systems.

Mukherjee, (2023) examines patriarchy and honor killings, although he does not analyze caste aspects, which are central to honor killings in India. Your study, however, presents the linear causality between caste structures and honor killings in rural region especially in Uttar Pradesh, categorizing data on how prejudices do prevail of castes when dealing with honor killing of daughters who eloped or married against caste system. This addition to the discourse is necessary because, in Mukherjee's work, caste is not categorised as a motivation for these crimes.

Caffaro et al., (2014) speak about difference in the cultural perceptions of honor killings across different countries, but they do not elaborate the study on caste violence. This research fills this gap by showing that honor killings are more likely to be inflicted on poor women of lower castes and revealing how factors of prejudice based on caste entwine with the gendered superiority of patriarchal power. This link, omitted in Caffaro's comparative integration, enhance the knowledge about gendered violence in the societies with caste system influence.

Tandon et al., (2016) reveal the impact of socio-economic factors as factors that cause honor killings but fail to explain the extent of organized caste-based group involvement in these killings. This is where your study is simply help sought since it explains the way that caste organizations and especially those of rural India are involved in the perpetuation of violence on social norms while Tandon's socio-economic analysis seems to overlook this given aspect. Thus, this focus on the socio-political systems that are peculiar to caste systems enriches the discourse on the 'drivers' of honor killings.

FUTURE RESEARCH DIRECTIONS

In this chapter, the author explores existing research by identifying key shortcomings in knowledge surrounding honor killings and strategically situate the presented research within caste and regional perspectives. They are the problems with the failure of the international legal regimes in eradicating honor killings; however, they do not target Indian laws exclusively. In this Chapter, the author has endeavoured to fill out all the gaps left by the previous research regarding honor killing by presenting the exhaustive understanding of honor killings in relation to caste system, regional rapport, legal sensitization, and socio-political-economic frameworks (Tandon et al., 2016). However, prior studies have provided a lot of research findings, author attempts to bring new empirical evidence and broad and penetrated outlooks that were not considered in earlier research. Although authors have tried to cover all the aspects of this research but there may be researches in future which can deal with this topic in a more elaborative and exhaustive way.

INTRODUCTION

Purity is a hidden illusion. Honor killings in the country are a tragic testimony to the strange and complex interplay of cultural norms, stereotypes, and deep-rooted casteism. Deep in the heart of India lies the dark side of cultural practices and prevailing social norms, the connection between honor killing and caste requires an examination of the ancient context. Social attitudes play a decisive role here and influence character and life. India and the caste system date back thousands of years to Hindu historiography, which classifies the concept of untouchability as a social hierarchical structure where positive communities deemed impure were marginalized and discriminated against.(Kanchan et al., 2016) A strong and concrete legal system with proper legislation and proper education is needed to break the stereotypes of the people and make them understand the current scenario that honor killings are blessings of the society which should be given great attention and care. There is no separate law or law for honor killings in India. There is no mention of such murder provisions, and the main provisions of the IPC, such as Sections 299-304 of the IPC, punish the perpetrators as murderers, which are not murderers. Several articles of the Constitution of India deal with the rights of individuals, especially Articles 14, 15 (1), 19 (3) and 21 of the Constitution of India. Honor killings violate the right to free movement, the right to equality, and the right to security. According to the Constitution of India. The Constitution of India prohibits untouchability and discrimination based on caste or religion. Caste, on the other hand, is very important among Indians. The Indian social system is dominated by the Hindu caste system.

Although we live in the 21st century, we still use the caste system. Each caste had its rituals, customs, and values. Such crimes are initiated to instill fear in the people of the society and ensure adherence to patriarchal norms. The victims of honor killings are mostly women and the perpetrators are men. Such acts of violence against women are punished in the community because it is believed that women bring shame to the community (Olwan, 2013).

Historical Context

The historical context of honor killings in India is deeply intertwined with the social and cultural fabric of the nation. India has historically struggled with complex social hierarchies, deeply entrenched patriarchal structures, and religious dogmatism, all of which have contributed to the prevalence of honor killings. The concept of honor, often associated with family reputation and community status, was a prevalent ideology in Indian society and used to control and subjugate women. In traditional Indian society, the concept of honor is deeply rooted in religious teachings and texts. For example, the ancient Hindu legal text Manu Smriti contains codes and principles that continue to subjugate women and support the idea of women as property, thus creating an environment where honor killings are justified as a means of preservation. these traditional ways. beliefs Certain interpretations of Islamic Sharia have also been used to justify honor killings, further highlighting the intersection of religious dogmatism and gender-based violence. In addition, India's historical economic and educational inequality contributed to the continuation of honor killings and number 39. Poverty and lack of education reinforced existing patriarchal norms, making women more vulnerable to violence and discrimination. The intersection of religious dogmatism, patriarchal norms, and socioeconomic factors has created a complex web in which honor killings flourish. State institutions and legal frameworks have helped address honor killings in India. The effectiveness and limitations of existing laws and policies have been carefully studied because they form the backbone of society in this matter. In addition, government initiatives and popular movements have become important actors in the fight against religious dogmatism and the promotion of gender equality. These efforts helped challenge deeply entrenched patriarchal norms and religious dogmatism that perpetuate honor killings. To understand the phenomenon of honor killings in India, it is important to delve into the complex interplay of religious dogmatism, social norms, and historical context. Only by understanding these multidimensional factors can comprehensive interventions be designed to effectively combat this widespread gender-based violence. Despite the importance of social norms in honor killings in South Asia, there is little research on socioeconomic risk factors, motives, and patterns at the individual or household level. This article aims to address these gaps through a content analysis that examines the main motives, perpetrators, and victims of honor killings in Pakistan and India in recent years. One of the central motives behind honor killings in India is the desire to preserve the honor of the family or community. This motivation is deeply rooted in cultural and social norms that value family honor and reputation. Religious dogmatism, especially in the context of certain conservative interpretations of Islam and Hinduism, exacerbates the problem by maintaining patriarchal norms and justifying violence against women who have violated social norms. (Jarrar S. M, 2019) In addition, the dynamics of honor killings in India have also been influenced by social changes brought about by factors such as urbanization, globalization, and economic development. Religious dogmatism in India has historically played an important role in shaping social attitudes towards honor killings. It is important to note that although honor killings can occur in any religious community, the link to Islam is highly emphasized in media and academic discourse. This emphasis led to a heated debate about the role of religion in honor killings. Some argue that honor killings are primarily the result of oppressive practices associated with the undisputed authority of patriarchal figures, placing women in subordinate positions in the family and society.

Present Situation of Honor Killing

Honor killing is a harmful practice that has constantly plagued Indian society and is fueled by deep-rooted religious dogmatism. It is a form of violence directed against individuals, usually women, who are believed to have brought shame or dishonor to their families or communities. The purpose of this chapter is to examine the phenomenon of honor killings in India, with special attention to the role of religious dogmatism in perpetuating that violence. In India, honor killing is considered a crime against religious belief under Section 309 of the Indian Penal Code. (Singh & Bhandari, 2021) Honor killings are not limited to one particular religion, but occur in many different cultures and societies around the world. However, in the Indian context, religious dogmatism plays a significant role in justifying and perpetuating honor killings. Indian religious dogmatism is deeply rooted in social norms and practices that strongly emphasize the so-called anduoite; glory and quot; family and community, often at the expense of individual rights and freedoms. This chapter examines the historical and cultural roots of religious dogmatism in India and how this affects the prevalence of honor killings. The chapter also discusses how religious dogmatism influences social attitudes and perceptions of honor killings, shapes patriarchal power structures, and reinforces gender inequality. Shakti Vahini Vs. In Union of India (2018), petitioner Shakti Vahini Organization approached the Supreme Court of India under Article 32 (right to constitutional remedies) of the Constitution of India. The National Commission for Women directed the petitioner organization to conduct an inquiry into honor killings in Haryana and West Uttar Pradesh with an order on December 22, 2009. In Haryana, Uttar Pradesh, and Punjab, cases of people not marrying for fear of increasing honor killings have been observed. The petitioner sought directions from the respondents (State and Central Government) under the Constitution of India to take initiatives and preventive measures to combat honor killings and other honor killing-like crimes and a national and state action plan to reduce and control them. against the said crimes and direct the state governments to establish or set up special cells for the safety and welfare of couples. (Vesvikar & Agarwal, 2022) State governments have also been asked to prosecute all such honor killings and take necessary steps to deal with such honor crimes and the ill feelings of some members of society. In addition, this chapter critically analyzes the role of religious texts such as the Manu Smriti in Hinduism and some interpretations of Sharia in Islam in maintaining patriarchal norms and justifying violence against women in the name of honor. In addition, this chapter examines how religious leaders and institutions promote the perpetuation of honor killings through their teachings and ideologies. This chapter also examines the impact of socioeconomic factors on honor killings in India, as poverty and lack of education often exacerbate existing patriarchal norms and religious dogmatism, leading to the prevalence of honor killings. In addition, this chapter sheds light on the role of national institutions and legal frameworks in dealing with honor killings in India. It critically analyzes the effectiveness and limitations of existing laws and policies in combating the practice and examines the role of government initiatives and grassroots movements in challenging religious dogmatism and promoting gender equality. That chapter concludes with an emphasis on the importance of treating religious dogmatism as a major cause of honor killings in India. The chapter argues that religious dogmatism perpetuates patriarchal power structures and contributes to the prevalence of honor killings in India. In her work on honor killings in the American and Indian media, Inderpal Grewal argues that many different management techniques have emerged in response to honor killings and quot; These management methods include not only legal initiatives and law enforcement but also social and cultural interventions aimed at challenging and changing patriarchal norms based on religious dogmatism. Addressing religious dogmatism and its impact on society's attitudes and behavior toward women is therefore crucial to combating honor killings and promoting gender equality. As Korte Weg and Yurdakul have shown, there is a huge debate in the scientific literature about the role of religion in society. the origins of honor killings. In particular, it is debated whether honor killings are more to be explained by the religion of Islam or by oppressive practices associated with the undisputed authority of the patriarch, which places women in a subordinate position within and within the family. for society This debate raises important questions about religious beliefs, patriarchal power dynamics, and the subjugation of women in both the family and social structures. To understand the complexity of honor killings in India, it is necessary to analyze the deep-rooted patriarchy that underlies these acts and the ways in which religious dogmatism reinforces and perpetuates that patriarchal power.

CASTE MARRIAGES IN INDIA

Marriage in India has always been a sacred institution. Mate selection in this process depends upon several contributing factors. Some of the most important ones are caste, religion, mother tongue, economic conditions, etc. Among these, belonging to the same caste is the foremost consideration when it comes to marriage.

History of Caste-Based Marriages in India

During the British era, Hindu marriage was widely considered to be a sacrament. The only prohibitions were based on caste, religion, gotra, and blood relations. However, these restrictions of caste were not dominant in the Vedic Era. In the Vedic era, two types of marriages used to be followed, anuloma marriages and pratiloma marriages, and in both, belonging to the same caste was not necessary. But after the Vedic era, Hindu sages started to approve of sa-varna marriages and disapprove of inter-varna marriages. As the concept of caste(jati) emerged, this prohibition extended to inter-caste marriages too. Looking upon the Indian human development survey data (2011-12), which examined 42,512 households, reveals 3 different periods of marriages in India, 1951-1978, 1978-1994 and 1994-2012. This data shows that since, 1951, inter-caste marriages have started to increase rapidly in society, breaking the bonds created by the orthodox society. (Caffaro et al., 2014)

Problems with Inter- Caste Marriages in India

Inter-caste marriage, which is a type of marriage between two people belonging to different castes, has always struggled to take its place in Indian society. Inter-caste marriages face several challenges, which make it difficult for these couples to enter into the sacred institution of marriage. The major issues faced by inter-caste marriages are:

Although the Indian constitution gives equal rights to every citizen of India, still inter-caste couples struggle to obtain the right of marriage. The legislation which is there for these marriages is the Hindu Marriage Act, of 1955 and the Special Marriage Act, 1954. Although the Hindu Marriage Act approves the validity of inter-caste marriages, it is difficult for inter-caste couples to perform marriage according to the saptapati ritual, which is a necessity of a valid marriage under this law. This is because of social negligence and also the disapproval from the families. Hence the only legislation left for inter-caste marriages to take place is the Special Marriage Act, of 1954. However, the 30-day registration period in this law is a major problem for inter-caste couples. During this period, these couples face a lot of challenges, and hence legal issues are faced by Intercultural couples. Family issues (honor killing etc) The most dangerous problem faced by Intercultural couples is honor killing. Honor killing is a heinous act of crime committed by a family member towards the girl of that family. This crime is generally committed when a girl of a family is involved in a relationship with a member outside of the family's religion or caste. This extreme form of violence is practiced majorly in the rural areas of our country. The report of the Dalit human rights defender network stands as testament to the act of honor killing faced by lower caste individuals. Looking upon the issues faced by Inter-caste marriages in India, it becomes important for us to eradicate this social stigma of same-caste marriage. Hence appropriate actions should be taken to give space to these types of marriages in the country.

Problems with Inter-Religious Marriages in India

In India, generally, marriages are arranged by families. Hence, these families prefer marriage between the same faith or religion. Now, Interfaith couples in India face a number of issues. Major issues faced by these couples are:

There are several social issues faced by inter-faith couples. First and foremost is the family issue. In most cases, families expel these couples and do not provide any support to them. This becomes a major obstacle in inter-faith marriages in the country. Second is the stereotype in the society, that these types of marriages happen for forced conversion to take place. And sadly, government policies are supporting this argument. As per Muslim law, to get married to a non-Muslim, conversion to the religion is the only way. But the principles still stand here, that where is the space for inter-faith marriage?

Hence, the only legislation left is the Special Marriage Act, of 1954. But this act only is not sufficient as some provisions of this legislation also make it difficult for inter-faith marriages to happen (Olwan, 2013). Moreover, the anti-conversion laws in the country, make it much more difficult. The common title given to inter-faith marriages is "love jihad" because of these laws. There are many provisions that make it difficult for inter-faith couples to marry in these laws. For example, section 3 and section 6 of Uttar Pradesh, prohibition of unlawful conversion or act,2021. Here, conversion for marriage is prohibited. So, despite the equal rights provided by the constitution, Interfaith couples struggle to get these rights, with the help of the law too.

Methodology

We conducted an on-ground survey in the village of Raya, Mathura. The survey involved 90 people from different castes and religions. The survey was question-based and involved people giving their views on honor killing and the caste-based system in India. The questions were:

1. What is your name?
2. What is your address?
3. Which caste do you belong to?
4. Whether you believe in inter-caste marriages?
5. Whether you believe in inter-religious marriages?
6. Whether you are familiar with any laws/acts that punish honor killing?
7. Whether you believe honor killing is right or wrong?
8. What is the role of khap panchayat in honor killing?

Survey Results

QUESTION 1
Do you believe in inter-caste marriages or not?
ANSWER 1
The opinion poll along with a short survey was conducted over digital media and on-ground reports. After the survey, the poll and its analysis gave an intriguing glance at the progress of our nation and the new generation. At least, 81% of the population still does not believe that Inter Caste Marriages should be allowed, and people still treat it as a social taboo, highlighting that the caste system has been an age-old concept of elders being preached through generations. Ideally, their concepts are rooted in the ground, which makes them more regressive in the contemporary context. A major factor quoted by these respondents has been social peer pressure which still exists in rural areas and villages. Moreover, they believe that it can be a traditional progressive way for them to achieve a relationship between two people with similar caste backgrounds, statuses, and interests. For them, this can make the quality of the bond look better and that adjustment between the couple becomes much easier this way. The other 17% of people have views opposite to that of the people who favor same-caste marriages. They believe that inter-caste marriages should be an essential fundamental right for a person to choose whom to marry, pushing out the cultural and social barriers. They focus on the progressive and developing lifestyle of individuals linked with urban areas. The remaining 2% of fractional respondents believe that they can adjust to both types of circumstances and do not wish to have a difference of technical opinions.

QUESTION 2

Are you familiar with any Law/Act which punishes the doers of honor killing?

ANSWER 2

The opinion poll and the replies to the particular question in the survey have been astonishing. To our surprise, people are not even aware of the fact that what exactly can be referred to as honor killing. Usually, people from rural backgrounds do not even know that such terms exist, definitely, the majority of 95% of respondents were not even aware of the laws and actions vis-a-vis honor killing. Especially the female proportion of the area has no clue whatsoever, about the same. They said that this is something that is not widely discussed, showing a lack of active social participation. To counter the same, the remaining 5% of people had a different view. They were aware of the crimes and how it is a punishable and cognizable offense, yet they are not aware of the legal mechanism which counters the same or how effective measures can be used to report such issues when it comes to highlighting the honor killing in our nation. This also showcases how more awareness needs to be spread in the rural areas to make them more legally involved in the process of activism and voicing their rights and wrongdoing, against this crime. People need to still connect with the legal machinery that is followed in our state to counter such challenges.

QUESTION 3

Whether honor killing is right or wrong in your view?

ANSWER 3

The collective response has been that the concept of honor killing has no rationale behind the same, it is just another inhuman notion to forcefully punish a particular gender. Usually, the respondents agreed to the new modernizing changes which are being brought either by the new ways and methodologies being used by the government for raising standards of living for individuals or having better development works and initiatives in different fields across the nation with the active involvement of women. A right way to sum up they responded that it is only in India that women are given the status of goddess, according to them, and we should not only keep it for the sake of it but practice the same by giving equal respect and recognition to them.

Question 4

Role of khap panchayat in honor killing?

Answer 4

The opinion poll and the replies to the particular question in the survey have been astonishing. To gather upon 66% of the total people were with the idea of showcasing their inclination towards the decision of Khap Panchayat as the last and binding, showing their orthodox thinking and societal upbringing and the environment in which they have been living, whereas 34% people believed that there should be proper legislative work done to seek the right justice, this showed the new era thinking which is generally seen in the young minds.

Question 5
Do you believe in inter-religious marriages?
Answer 5
100 percent of people were of the opinion that there shouldn't be inter-religious marriage. They believe that it is against religious practices and social order. Personal laws and social factors play a vital role in this particular thinking. The cultural disparity is a big common ground.

Way Forward

Honor Killing has a great pessimistic impact on the society in which we live. As individuals, we can combat the age-old frame of mind and the concept of Shame Killing. It can be done by using modern-day ideal social reforms and by inculcating the values of the new and upgraded schooling. Moreover, it is also important for think tanks to disassociate the cultural prejudices linked with the name of the respect of the castes and the community. The holistic approach can be developed by following the new changes and adapting to contemporary beliefs.

Firstly, we must develop the fundamental moral essence of equality among the different genders and sects. For a society to progress, the key element that is required is a basic understanding of equal treatment. Then the aspect of respect between the two genders and different sexuality. In the majority of cases, Women are seen as inferior to men in society and are usually divided by fragmented social barriers and norms. There should be an attempt to establish a balance between the genders. The more Women are considered equal, the less their actions will be questioned in a progressive society.

The right way to put a stop to Honor killings is a collective action to define the model of a progressive society. It is high time we realize the myths in the pluralistic and male-dominated society. For us to bring a change, it is necessary to eradicate these from the minds of the people. The focus can be more on the rural and underdeveloped regions where education can play an important aspect. Local governments of a respective state and the nongovernmental organizations can further collaboratively work on taking workshops and seminars related to fostering family growth, family relationships, and right parenting which focus on living a healthy lifestyle.

Most of the developing nations like India, are showcasing and recognizing the power of women. Females are now diligently leading and governing the important roles of different sectors in various economies. This not only has led to freedom of thought for women but people in those places have started to accept and counter the atrocities that used to happen against women. Giving equal early educational rights, economic rights and social rights have proved to be an efficient factor in working on uplifting the conditions of women in these countries. Institutions and other funded initiatives should work on a progressive curriculum that can cover such topics and matters dedicated to such relationship problems. With this, ensuring a mature relationship is easier in comparison to different situations.

Multiple human rights advocates and concerned organizations do cross-examine the matter of honor killings labelling it as similar to the crimes committed in passion, which may include dowry, refusal to arrange marriage, sexual harassment, or interference with other causes. To curb the same, a collective effort can be put in the direction leading to better digital connectivity amongst the self-help groups and physical communication between them which can act as an effective coefficient. Curbing the digital divide in this global village has inspired different societies and sections to learn from each other for a comparative change. This can be further built with values of tolerance, humanism, and leadership.

When we trace multiple studies on Honor killings, it is still highlighted as a sensitive and personal global issue. This is not only prevalent in India but in the Middle East and North African region. There are a large number of cases that go unreported and unheard. With better education and awareness of women's rights, the chances of the cases being reported and matters filed will increase. Further having a strong legal mechanism to prevent honor killings and stringent actions against those who indulge in it is highly suggested. The media as a watchdog can be an important pillar in voicing up against these atrocities. Most of the tribes of low-coverage areas who have their customs get exemptions from some laws.

The distinction between the rule of law and conflicting customs should be considered moreover in favor of the law. The customs overriding the law are not only old and have no logic but also hinder the progress of those regions and make them suffer more. The investment in those regions can be impeccable in terms of bringing a positive change. Governments should also work in favour of funding schemes and initiatives that prioritize women and child healthcare as a whole. Giving legitimacy to the social regulations can lead to a different prospect which can be changed by this type of legal and economic solution by the state.

In the past decades, there has been a lack of activism related to the working of major cultural sects of society. The female atrocities and crimes against women get covered quickly, to make sure they get justice, attempts should also be made to have transparency in investigations that are conducted. There should be agencies like the Commission for Women in all provinces and states in the global areas and nations. Giving these authorities more rights than a statutory body will be more beneficial and in the favour of Women across all regions. With this, the development will be more consistent and will ensure new aspects of improvement in countries.

At last, it is important for us all to know that we should understand the main fundamental importance of women's power. Honor killings have been an old-age illogical, illegal, and abrupt way which is considered as removing shame from families. Ideally, the concept of family and bringing shame is not only a traditional myth but has false consideration over matters. Eliminating honor killing also needs a multiple-dimensional approach. This approach can highlight the first attempt to work over the factors compelling men to not change this rudimentary ideology and secondly work on the development and progressive factors for the women who wish to grow and get better with their lives.

CONCLUSION

India, with its rich cultural walls and diverse traditions, is at the intersection of progress and entrenched social problems. Two such complex phenomena, honor killings, and the caste system, continue to cast a shadow over the nation and society. This essay examines the relationship between honor killings and the Indian caste system, shedding light on their historical roots, contemporary manifestations, and the urgent need for social change. Understanding the modern landscape of honor killing and the Indian caste system. the past is necessary. Deeply rooted in the social structure, the caste system goes back thousands of years. Dating back to Vedic times, the caste system classified people based on their birth into rigid social hierarchies that determined their occupation, social status, and interactions with others. (Bethany A. Corbin, 2014) Although this hierarchical structure was formally abolished by the Indian Constitution, it continues to influence social dynamics. On the other hand, honor killings are rooted in a distorted interpretation of social norms, especially those related to sex and marriage. The idea of preserving family honor, often associated with caste purity and social expectations, has led to tragic honor killings. The intersection of caste and honor has created a deadly plot that threatens the lives of those who dare to challenge traditional norms. Despite legal frameworks and social progress, both honor killings and the caste system continue to exist in modern India. Honor killings, often linked to inter-caste or inter-religious marriages, reflect deep-seated prejudices in society. Families unable to accept the perceived loss of caste purity resort to extreme measures to restore their honor. Victims, mostly women, face violence and death if they choose a partner outside their caste or community. Although officially outlawed, the caste system continues to shape social interactions and opportunities. Discrimination, both blatant and subtle, permeates various areas of life, including education, work, and marriage. Hierarchical structure reinforces inequality and hinders people and the pursuit of social justice and equality. (Kanchan et al., 2016) The complex web of honor killings and the caste system reveal a symbiotic relationship where one reinforces the other. The caste system provides a framework for social expectations and creates a rigid structure that determines who can marry and be. Any deviation from these norms is seen as an affront to the caste hierarchy, leading to a desperate attempt to restore honor through violent means. The intersection of caste and honor is seen in the disproportionate targeting of individuals from marginalized castes and communities. Dalit, who are often at the bottom of the caste hierarchy, face increasing discrimination and violence that worsens when they challenge established norms through inter-caste marriages. (SEV'ER & YURDAKUL, 2001) The interconnections of these issues underline the need for a holistic approach to dismantling deeply entrenched social norms. Fighting honor killings and the caste system in India is a huge challenge. Although the legal framework is the basis for solving these problems, there are obstacles to its implementation. Law enforcement agencies sometimes lack the sensitivity or resources to effectively deal with honor killings, allowing criminals to escape justice. In addition, deep-rooted social and cultural norms often prevent the effective implementation of laws. The caste system, despite constitutional provisions for affirmative action and anti-discrimination initiatives, persists due to cultural inertia and resistance to change. Prejudices passed down through generations continue to shape individual attitudes and perpetuate discrimination and inequality (XAVIER, 2015). Eradicating these deeply rooted beliefs requires a concerted effort from both the government and civil society. Addressing honor killings and the caste system requires a comprehensive strategy that includes law reforms, social awareness campaigns, and educational initiatives. Legislation alone cannot bring about the desired change; it must be accompanied by efforts to challenge and change social attitudes.

REFERENCES

Bhandari, R. (2021). Honor killing as a dark side of modernity: Prevalence, common explanations, and structural factors. *Social Sciences Information. Information Sur les Sciences Sociales.*

Caffaro, F., Ferraris, F., & Schmidt, S. (2014). Gender Differences in the Perception of Honor Killing in Individualist Versus Collectivistic Cultures: Comparison Between Italy and Turkey. *Sex Roles*, 71(9–10), 296–318. DOI: 10.1007/s11199-014-0413-5

Chesler, P. (2021). *Honor Killing: A Form of Femicide. Dignity: A Journal of Analysis of Exploitation and Violence*, 6(1), 1-25.

Corbin, B. A. (2014). Between Saviors and Savages: The Effect of Turkey's Revised Penal Code on the Transformation of Honor Killings into Honor Penal Code on the Transformation of Honor Killings into Honor Suicides and Why Community Discourse Is Necessary for Honor Crime Education. *Emory International Law Review*, 29(2).

Haq, A. (2022). Honor killings in the Eastern Mediterranean region: A narrative review. *The Lancet. Psychiatry.*

Ihugba, U. (2020). *Introduction to Legal Research Method and Legal Writing.* DOI: 10.2307/jj.8155048

Jarrar. S. M. (2019). *THE DISHONORABLE HONOR CRIMES IN LITERATURE . INTERNATIONAL JOURNAL OF ENGLISH LANGUAGE, LITERATURE AND TRANSLATION STUDIES (IJELR).* Vol 6(1)

Kanchan, T., Tandon, A., & Krishan, K. (2016a). Honor Killing: Where Pride Defeats Reason. *Science and Engineering Ethics*, 22(6), 1861–1862. DOI: 10.1007/s11948-015-9694-5 PMID: 26293131

Kumar, R. K. (2023). Honor Killing: Challenges Indian Judicial System. [IJCRT]. *International Journal of Creative Research Thoughts*, 11(1), 1–8.

Ministry Of Home Affairs. (2016). Murder rate across the States: Rajya Sabha unstarred question no. 2449. Retrieved from https://sansad.in/getFile/annex/241/Au2449.docx?source=pqars

Ministry of Home Affairs. (2023). Murder rate across the states: Rajya Sabha unstarred question no. 3734. Retrieved from https://ppl-ai-file-upload.s3.amazonaws.com/web/direct-files/10919250/4686a6a3-e900-4d38-b062-93ee35b3b36a/3734-1.pdf

Mukherjee, S. (2023). *The crime of honor killing: A socio-criminal perspective.* ISBN- 9391820751

Olwan, D. M. (2013). Gendered Violence, Cultural Otherness, and Honor Crimes in Canadian National Logics. *Canadian Journal of Sociology*, 38(4), 533–556. DOI: 10.29173/cjs21196

Sev'Er, A., & Yurdakul, G.SEV'ER. (2001). Culture of Honor, Culture of Change. *Violence Against Women*, 7(9), 964–998. DOI: 10.1177/10778010122182866

Singh, D., & Bhandari, D. S. (2021). *Legacy of Honor and Violence: An Analysis of Factors Responsible for Honor Killings in Afghanistan, Canada, India, and Pakistan* as Discussed in Selected Documentaries on Real Cases. *SAGE Open*, 11(2), 215824402110223. DOI: 10.1177/21582440211022323

Tandon, A., & Kanchan, T. (2016). Honor killing: Where pride defeats reason. *Science and Engineering Ethics*, 22(6), 1861–1862. DOI: 10.1007/s11948-015-9694-5 PMID: 26293131

Vesvikar, M., & Agarwal, M. (2022). HONOR KILLING IN INDIA. *Perspectives in Social Work*, 31(1), 48–62.

XAVIER, M. S. (2015). *Honor Killings: A Global Concern*. PARIPEX - INDIAN JOURNAL OF RESEARCH, 4(3).

Chapter 18
Role of Class Conflict in Honor Killings

Deepika Pandoi
GLA University, India

Somendra Ashok Singh
https://orcid.org/0009-0007-4083-3815
GLA University, India

ABSTRACT

In India, a sizable population is frequently the victim of terrorism, famine, torture, humiliation, mutilation, and murder. Among these is the complicated phenomena known as "honor killing," which reflects a startling social crime, a moral conundrum facing the civilizations, and an obstacle across cultural boundaries. Generally speaking, intentional killing is murder, even when inadvertent killing is possible. According to this perspective, honor killing is defined as murder, typically committed by a member of the victim's own family or friends in order to exact revenge or shame for any disloyalty or other actions deemed inappropriate by the culture. In light of this, the purpose of the article is to investigate societal perspectives and attitudes about women's rights to life, equality, dignity, and self-determination in all spheres of life, as well as related theoretical issues. The theoretical implications of honor killing in connection to the accuser and victim are covered in this work.

BACKGROUND

Honor killing, a heinous practice claiming countless lives, is often attributed to cultural and religious factors. However, this chapter argues that class conflict plays a pivotal role in perpetuating honor killing, particularly in societies with entrenched social hierarchies. Through a critical lens, the Author examines how class dynamics intersect with gender, power, and social capital to create an environment conducive to honor killing. The Author contends that class conflict fuels the desire to maintain social status, control resources, and protect family honor, leading to the brutal suppression of perceived transgressions. This chapter draws on empirical evidence from various cultural contexts to illustrate the insidious ways in which class conflict perpetuates honor killing. By uncovering the complex relationships between class, power, and honor killing, we aim to inform more nuanced interventions and policy responses to eradicate this devastating practice. Ultimately, this research seeks to contribute to a deeper understanding of the structural drivers of honor killing and promote a more equitable society.

Research Methodology

The purpose of this chapter is to gain an understanding of honor killings as a result of class conflict. The information for this topic was collected in the form of checking records from libraries/Newspaper/Magazines/Sample/Internet/Research papers etc. Therefore, both qualitative and secondary research strategies had been adopted for this study in order to address its objective covering both primary and secondary sources. (Anderson & Poole, 2001) Data was collected to gain an understanding of people's perception of Honor killing, to understand whether it is a socio-political cultural issue or if it's regarded as a religious phenomenon or something else. Certain characteristics such as the participant's ethnicity, age, and gender need to be observed using qualitative methods to avoid biases.

From the primary and secondary research carried out (Tiwari, 1999), it became clear that Honor killing is not condoned by any religion but was actually motivated by cultural beliefs and that once the community thought someone had violated the cultural norms and values, they are subjected to violence and torture. After doing intensive research, it can be concluded that Honor killing is not restricted to any geographical entity but takes place across the globe; it's a phenomenon which has been around for many centuries. This problem has global ramifications, which has only recently been highlighted in the media, but there are many different organizations and state forces assigned to help tackle the problem of Honor killing. The chapter gives a clear understanding of Honor killing, even though there is not one universal definition. Further, it gives an understanding of what Honor killing is perceived to be. However, from all the information that was collected on perceptions of Honor killings, it is considered a crime and a form of physical behaviour in order to gain prestige.

Key Terms

"Honor killing" and the "role of class conflict" make up the core of the concept. The topic is contextualized by broader themes like "Theoretical Aspect" (Martin, 2013), and "Historical Background" (Goldstein, 2002). Phrases like "Caste System," "Patriarchal Mind Set," and "Khap Panchayat" (*Shri R*, 2024) relates to the in-depth meaning of the chapter. Utilizing a variety of online resources, including the Library of Congress, Research Gate, Google Books, Springer, JSTOR, Sage, IJSSHR, Scopus, Web of Science, Taylor & Francis, and Google Scholar, we chose pertinent papers using "feminist thinking" (Khan, 2006), "gender roles" (Hoskin et al., 2017) and "patriarchy" (Shetty et al., 2019) such keywords.

Literature Review

Research suggests that class conflict plays a significant role in honor killing, particularly in societies where economic and social inequality is prevalent. Bourdieu (1990) argues that honor killing is a means of maintaining social capital and defending class boundaries. Al-bona (1988) highlights how class conflict intersects with gender and patriarchy, leading to honor killing. Wikan (2003) shows how economic insecurity and class anxiety can trigger honor killing. Ahmadi (2003) explores how class conflict and economic competition contribute to honor killing in Iraqi Kurdistan. Adriss (2017) discusses how class-based honor killing is used to maintain social hierarchy and control resources.

Sen (2005) explores how class-based honor killing is used to maintain social control and reinforce patriarchal norms in India. Bishai (2011) examines the intersection of class, gender, and honor killing in the Palestinian context. Mojab (2015) discusses how class conflict and economic inequality contribute to honor killing in Kurdish communities. Gill (2014) analyses the role of class and caste in honor killing in India, highlighting the ways in which social hierarchy perpetuates violence against women. Thapar-Bjorkert (2013) explores the relationship between class, gender, and honor killing in the UK's South Asian diaspora communities.

Future Research Directions

This chapter is unique in that it sheds light on the topic 'Role of class conflict in Honor killing', broadening the conversation about the prevailing prejudices that motivate these terrible occurrences and emphasizing the need of using multidisciplinary techniques to fully understand the intricate interplay between historical (Goldstein, 2002), cultural, sacred, and fiscal factors. Few research has been done on it, but this one is distinctive since it investigates how class struggle feeds into and sustains Honor killing by interacting with other forms of oppression such as gender, caste, and ethnicity, explores the historical causes of Honor killing and class conflict and examines how education and awareness initiatives can lessen instances of Honor killing and class warfare.

In order to comprehend the part that class conflict plays an important role in Honor killing, it also applies feminist and Marxist perspectives (McGraw-Hill, 2010). Additionally, it investigates how class struggle plays a part in Honor killing in various cultural contexts. The final goals are to create and assess community-based programs that address Honor killing and class conflict, to do quantitative research to look at the relationship between Honor killing and class conflict, and to do in-depth qualitative research to look at the viewpoints and experiences of those who are impacted by Honor killing and class conflict, which are highly recommended by the author. Still there is a scope for future researchers as this chapter does cover the political and economic factors affecting the role of class conflict in Honor killings.

INTRODUCTION

It describes the violent, even murderous; acts committed by male members of the family against female relatives whom they feel have brought dishonor to the family. These acts are referred to as honor killings. For a number of reasons, such as refusing to get married in an arranged marriage, experiencing sexual assault, wanting a divorce even from an abusive husband, or even being accused of infidelity, a woman may become the target of her family.

Occasionally, men may also fall victim to honor killings committed by the families of women whose relationships they believe to be inappropriate. In the society where it is practiced, the term "Honor killing" refers to both males and women. The collaborative aspect of honor killings—many members of the extended family plot the act together, sometimes with the help of a formal family council—makes them unique from other types of crimes.

The relationship between Honor killings and the family's collective control over women's behaviour, particularly with regard to sexuality, male interaction, and marriage, is another noteworthy aspect. A further factor is the significance of the family's standing in the community and the stigma attached to status loss, especially in close-knit communities. The fact that those who commit Honor killings frequently escape social censure because their actions are viewed as acceptable is another important component of the practice.

Estimates of the frequency of honor killing are highly variable and difficult to pinpoint. The majority of nations do not routinely gather data on honor killings, and many of these killings are registered by the families as suicides or accidents.

Even so, honor killings are frequently connected to Asia, particularly to South and Middle East Asia. They happen everywhere in the world. Many techniques, including stoning, stabbing, beating, burning, beheading, hanging, slashing the throat, deadly acid attacks, shooting, and strangling, are employed in honor killing. At times, the killings are carried out in public to alert other women in the neighbourhood to the potential repercussions. Families frequently choose young girls and boys to play the role of the killer in order to maximize the perpetrator's chances of obtaining a favorable court outcome. The most common reasons for Honor killings are disobeying the community's dress code for females, refusing to arrange marriage, marrying someone outside of one's class, caste, or religion, engaging in lesbian and gay relationships, or engaging in pre-marital or extramarital sexual activity, whether consensual or non-consensual.

Even inter-caste or inter-class weddings are not permitted to be handled peacefully; rather, they must be considered as a matter of honor by the community, which is prepared to take over if the family refuses, compelling the household to put aside their daughters in the greater good of the class or caste. Thus, the concept of honor operates at the expense of individual sensibility and values. Honor killing is an issue of society that occurs in a wide range of societies around the world. It refers to the killing of a loved one for the sake of honor that is thought to be tarnished by their behaviour. This study looks at the significance of Honor killings in India, which are sometimes seen as an example of violence against women. Specifically, women play distinct roles as both male victims and perpetrators, and a major component of honor killings in India is societal compliance to Honor norms and collectivism, particularly when these norms cut across group boundaries. Last but not least, there seems to be a notable pattern of contradictions between statements made in public about regaining lost honor and private, individual rejections of violent behaviour, undermining the function of collective social institutions like *'Khap panchayat'*.

The word "Honor killing" is not defined explicitly. Honor killing refers to killings perpetrated by family members or members of the same caste or class. The *khap panchayats* execute death sentences. The explanation is that the perpetrators have brought "shame" or "dishonor" upon the family, caste, or class. Indian society is multi-ethnic and Multi traditional, with many cases, classes, creeds, and sections where people feel their class is the best overall and that each member should live up to their social and cultural norms throughout their lives, with women being seen as the family's bearer of honor. Because of how deeply ingrained this belief is, every effort by women to violate their rights is viewed as an assault on the cultural standards of the community at large and is vigorously opposed by the entire society. When a family member takes these actions out of a sense of honor, it can result in honor killing. Usually, women are the targets of these crimes, but more recently, there have been some instances where men have also been singled out for murder in the name of honor killing, despite of the fact that there are no laws specifically prohibiting family members from killing their relatives.

The murder of the family member because the executioner feels the victim has brought dishonor or shame to the family is known as honor killing or shame killing. Moreover, the victim has transgressed the rules of their community or faith, typically for different reasons such as divorcing or being separated from one spouse, declining to get married in an arranged marriage, being in a relationship that is frowned upon by their family, community, or religion, having Descriptions of Honor Killing: Honor crimes are unlawful orders issued by *'panchayats'* based on caste, class, or community that forbid or restrict marriages, social boycotts, and even the murder of couples.

The problem known as "Honor killing" has several facets, including a moral quandary within the society, an intercultural difficulty, and a startling social crime. (Deol, 2014) Murder is often defined as deliberate, hate-filled killing, even if killing can occur accidentally. This perspective holds that Honor killing constitutes murder (Welchman & Hossain, 2014). Usually, the killing of a female family member by her own friends or family as a form of punishment, humiliation, or disHonor brought on by betrayal or any other actions that are not acceptable in the culture (Nasrullah et al., 2009). Although women make up the majority of Honor killing victims, males might occasionally also be involved. The average age of a female Honor killer is 23 years old (Bruinsma & Weisburd, 2013). The victims of Honor killings also include men. The English phrases "Honor" and "perception" are key in understanding the motives behind this type of homicide. In Hindi and Urdu languages and cultures, the term *"Izzat"* is translated as "Honor" in English. *"Izzat"* is a general concept that encompasses justice, social position, Honor, reputation, decency, and respect. "Family *Izzat*," which promotes social contacts and connections, is prevalent in many cultures. It is required of all family members to preserve and improve their family *izzat*. Social mobility is the process of moving from a low status to a high-status place through marriage partnerships, career and academic achievement, The English terms "perception" and "Honor" are crucial to comprehending the motivations behind this kind of killing. The English word "Honor" is translated as *"Izzat"* in the languages and cultures of Hindi and Urdu. *"Izzat"* is a broad term that includes decency, respect, Honor, social standing, fairness, and reputation. Many cultures emphasize "Family *Izzat*," which fosters relationships and social interactions. Every family member has an obligation to maintain and enhance their family *izzat*. Advancing from a low-status to a high-status environment through marriage, professional and academic success, and other means has been referred to as social mobility. Thus, the phrase "Honor killing" exemplifies the negative aspects of *izzat*. Honor killing is thought to restore the so-called "Honor" within the family.

Definition: Human Rights Watch

Honor killings are instances of family members exacting revenge—typically by killing—on female relatives who they believe have brought disgrace upon the family. A woman may come under attack from her family for a number of reasons, such as refusing to get married with an arranged marriage, experiencing sexual assault, filing for divorce—even from an abusive spouse—or engaging in adultery. An attack on a woman's life can begin just with the belief that she has acted in something that "dishonors" her family. Men may also occasionally become victims of honor killings committed by members of a woman's family who they believe to be in a not appropriate relationship, or they may become involved in homosexual activities

Historical Account of the Honor Crimes

No culture or religion is exclusive to the ideas of honor and shame, nor is the use of these ideas to excuse acts of violence and even death. In actuality, historical occurrences and literary works from several nations reflect honor and violence motivated by honor. Honor killings date back to the time of ancient Rome, when the senior male in the family, known as the pater families, had the power to put an unmarried daughter who was involved in sexual activity to death or an unfaithful wife to death. In medieval Europe, honor-based crimes were acknowledged. In the past, Jewish law mandated that an adulterous woman and her partner be stoned to death. Honor killing has a long historical background, since ancient times, people have been killing family members, saying that this is done to protect the family's Honor. Murders have historically been a gender-based crime meant to maintain patriarchal rule over women in society. However, this does not mean that the man has been wholly unaffected by the evil. There have also been reports of males being killed, primarily for indulging in homosexual practices or for refusing to participate in an arranged marriage. However, several incidents can be witnessed when daughters, daughters-in-law, wives, etc. are slain, generally for reasons like chatting to another guy, involvement in adulterous relationships, pre-marital. Honor killings have spread throughout the world and gained significant traction over time. When it comes to India, Honor killings have primarily been documented in the northern states of the Punjab region, the state of Rajasthan, Haryana, India, and Uttar Pradesh.

In Ancient times, Historian Matthew A. Goldstein (Goldstein, 2002), who examined Honor killings in the Roman Empire, shows how men's need to make sure the children their wives bore was their own was the driving force behind these homicides as well as the idea of "Honor" in general. Because women could be more readily managed and, consequently, males could be more secure of their children's futures, this "Honor" was placed on their shoulders. Roman law did not introduce the idea of "Honor," as it was understood to be carried by women, for the first time. The Hammurabi Code, enacted in 1780 BC by the Babylonian king Hammurabi, who ruled Mesopotamia (present-day Iraq) from 1792 and 1750 BC, was particularly harsh in punishing female adulterers. They would be bound and cast into the river to perish as punishment. Men would frequently kill their wives when they suspected them of being unfaithful, and they would even kill their daughters when they decided to elope. In addition, it was not uncommon for brothers to murder their sisters if the latter refused to wed the guy their family had selected. During the Roman era, the oldest man in a household had the authority to murder a family member if she was having extramarital or premarital affairs. Blackstone asserted that murder was permitted under Roman law when it was "performed in defense of chastity either of oneself or of relations."

In ancient India, the Laws of Manu (Husseini, 2021) were composed in 200 BC. "A faithful wife must constantly worship a husband as a god, even if he is devoid of good qualities, lacking in virtue, or seeking pleasure elsewhere." However, "the king shall cause a wife to be devoured by dogs in a place frequented by many if she violates the duty which she owes to her lord, proud of the excellence of her relatives or her own excellence."

Men would often kill their wives when they suspected them of being unfaithful, and they would even kill their daughters when they decided to elope. In addition, it was not uncommon for brothers to murder their sisters if the latter declined to wed the guy their family had selected for them. While in Medieval region, the church even made an effort to shield adulterers and promiscuous women who later repented and vowed to abstain from sexual activity, but this did not stop some families from murdering their once-sexually active daughter because they were so repulsed and ashamed of their reputation. Even in Christian Rome and a large portion of medieval Europe, honor killings by husbands or grandfathers due to adultery committed by the wife were so widespread that the Church, in some cases, condoned it and local governments allowed it.

There are still killings to "clean a family's sins" as late as the Victorian era among the aristocrats and in today's era it can be seen that the cases of Honor Killing in male are less in number as being compared to women across the world.

Reasons Behind the Preponderance of Honor Killings with Special Reference to India

Patriarchal Mindset: The word "honor" is frequently connected to honor killing. Numerous definitions of honor associate it with shame. This idea is invariably associated with the women in the family, and men are seen as the ones who watch over women and stop them from misusing their position of honor. This demonstrates patriarchy. In today's world, mindset is still common. Women's rights, autonomy, and choices are viewed as oppressions that go against these cultural mores and customs. Hence, these honor killings won't stop until people grow to be tolerant of one another's choices and respect each person's right to personal liberty.

Caste System: The caste system is a curse that exists in Indian society within the entire country. In India, some cultural groups, individuals, or the *'gotras'* of the individual or their parents forbid the inter-caste marriage. Interfaith marriages also contribute to honor killing, in addition to inter-caste unions. According to a National Commission of Women study, of the 326 conflict cases surveyed, 72% were the result of marriages between different castes, and 3% were the result of marriages between different religions (Prabhune, 2024). In a Supreme Court case, Justice *'Markandey Katju'* stated that honor killings are cold-blooded murder, with no honor involved. The Supreme Court further stated that intercaste and interreligious marriages should be encouraged in order to enhance the social fabric of society.

Khap Panchayat: Known for its ability to influence social issues within a nation, *'Khap Panchayats'* are informal groups of people or community organizations that are particularly prevalent in villages and particularly on Northern India . These individuals take the law into their own hands and commit offensive acts that jeopardize the lives of those who choose to marry voluntarily.

The courts have issued a number of legal rulings in response to Khap Panchayat's actions. One such important case is *Smt. Laxmi Kachhwaha vs. State of Rajasthan* (1999). In this case (*Shri R*, 2024), a PIL was filed at the Rajasthan High Court against the illegal functioning of the *Khap Panchayat,* which violated the individual's basic rights. The court ordered state authorities to limit the operation of Khap Panchayat and arrest and punish its members. As a result, it should be removed entirely. Lack of knowledge on rights and how to assert them is a contributing factor to honor murders.

Absence of Distinct and Tight Laws: The Indian Legal System does not yet recognize Honor killings as a crime, as they are considered a custom. These crimes are becoming more common, but they are not recognized by the law, nor are the victims protected, nor are there consequences or accountability measures in place. According to Statistics provided by United Nations up to November 28, 2013, one in five cases of Honor killing every year comes from India. Of the 5000 cases reported internationally, 1000 are from India (Mr. Suresh Kumar, 2023).

The Theoretical Aspect

It is crucial to examine the theoretical framework that highlights the core ideas of the natural law and positivism in law in order to comprehend the socioeconomic marginalization, legal position, and protection afforded to runaway couples.

According to Rex Martin (Martin, 2013), fundamental human rights have their roots in natural rights. One such essential human right that dates back to the Natural Rights period is the ability to select one's life partner. According to the doctrine of natural rights, there are inherent rights within a state that are natural that are defined by the lack of government. John Locke, its principal proponent, believed that individuals were equal, self-sufficient, and free in the natural condition. According to his conception, people have inherent rights to life, freedom, wellness, and the products of their labour. These rights also come with obligations that, regardless of the state of nature, normatively direct other people's behaviour to respect these rights. Similar to this, the fundamental right to liberty is the right to marry and live a dignified life free from intimidation or fear. Every person is so required to use their rights while reciprocally respecting the inalienable rights of others. The tradition of natural rights recognized the significance of two primary categories of rights: the right to specific freedoms of behaviour and the right to be free from specific harm caused by others. The fundamental tenet of the Natural philosophy is directly at odds with how this theory is understood in light of specific Honor Killing practices that are currently causing youth to be socially excluded.

Positive Theory

John Austin's "Positive law" idea is predicated on the Legal Positivist theory, which came after the Natural Rights doctrine. In this way, the freedom to choose a spouse is more than simply a theoretical concept. The legal acknowledgment of the right to get married is granted by the idea of "positive law." According to Jane Duran (Duran, 2005), positivists propagate the idea that most people in society should be accustomed to deferring to the sovereign entity. The source of an order and the one who carries it out are recognized as the sovereign. In light of this, couples who enter into runaway marriages are entitled to appropriate legal protection and entitlements as long as their marriage is duly recognized as a legal actuality. Nonetheless, the tacitly accepted societal mandate contributes to the widespread marginalization of young people in rural and urban India through the practice of Honor killing, when they are denied the opportunity to exercise their constitutional right to choose a mate. By applying positive theory, we can develop empirical evidence-based understanding of class conflict and honor killing, identifying patterns and testing hypotheses to explain this complex phenomenon.

Theory of Symbolic Interaction

Apart from engaging in homosexual activities, men can also sometimes end up being perpetrators of honor killings carried out by family members of women who they perceive to be in inappropriate relationships (Mishra, 2001).

George Herbert Mead and Herbert Blumer developed the notion of symbolic interaction, which defines it as dialogue between people within a society. According to this perspective, society is a product of people's regular social interactions with one other. This theory describes how humans assign symbols to one another and interpret situations according to how they interact with one another. For instance, we abide by the traffic police's directives (waving hands, displaying symbols, and signaling lights) and observe the driving regulations as they have been presented to us in order to ensure road safety. People in the community via encounters determined that if we abide by the laws, we may prevent traffic jams and accidents. Green lights mean go, red lights mean stop, and yellow lights mean wait. It is via our contacts with other members of our society that we acquire this behaviour. It is crucial to understand that our interpretations are frequently arbitrary in this situation. Our actions are dictated by our perceptions of be true as opposed to what is verifiably true. For instance, a passer-by may caution you, "Don't sit under the tree; it is full of ants which might harm you," when you are seeking shade from the heat after a long walk. "I am sitting here for shade and there is no problem found here," you said in response to the other individual. Afterwards, you noticed that a large group of ants had arrived and were moving towards the tree's trunk. Then you began to interpret the passer-by's comment, realizing that every tree has ants, and you made the decision to not sit beneath it. This demonstrates how people interpret everything in their lives—including their experiences—in the same way, without fully realizing it Sydney. Given that both assertions include meaning and change. The fact that a person may sit beneath a different tree and possibly avoid ants there makes change even more significant. Similarly, Honor is seen as the most valuable quality in Indian society and is mostly observed in patriarchal households, regardless of caste, religion, or geographic identity. When women's misbehaviors, financial gain or loss, and power imbalances bring dishonor to families. Given that the family still has a significant amount of power in Indian society, the significance placed on family Honor is significant. Honor killing occurs when a family member is killed by another family member because the perpetrators believe the victim brought shame upon the family, disregarded community norms, religious or caste principles, or refused an arranged marriage in favour of a partner the family didn't approve of, had an extramarital affair, experienced sexual assault, worn an unapproved outfit, etc. This murdering tradition dates back decades, and people continue to copy it now as a symbol that they follow to uphold their Honor by understanding it in a different way, taking their community's innocent life. This results in the family's rules, beliefs, and faith being broken.

Symbolic theory's relation with Honor killing: Symbolic theory provides a nuanced understanding of class conflict and honor killing, highlighting the role of symbols, language, and social constructs in perpetuating this practice. By applying symbolic theory, we can understand honor killings as a complex phenomenon rooted in symbolic dimensions, interaction, and power dynamics, requiring a nuanced approach to challenge and transform the underlying symbolic structures. It offers a nuanced understanding of class conflict, highlighting the complex ways in which symbols, language, and social constructs shape and are shaped by class relations.

Marxists Theory

When examining the problem of runaway marriages, traditional patriarchal views as well as Marxist theories of Historical Materialism and Cultural Relativity come into play. Since they clarify the socioeconomic and cultural factors that influence human behaviour and circumstances, these theories in the discourse surrounding human rights become especially more pertinent (George Ritzer-Sociological Theory (8th Edition) -McGraw-Hill (2010). Below is a discussion of a few of them: The Historical Materialism doctrine proposed by Marx the basic tenet of Karl Marx's theory is that there is perpetual conflict in society between the bourgeoisie (haves) and proletariat (have-nots). The haves constantly put up violent resistance against the weaker group, the have-nots. This premise can be used by couples who are taking advantage of their right to tie the knot but are threatened because one of the spouses has a lower socioeconomic standing. Historical Materialism has had a significant influence on feminist thought as well. The establishment of patriarchy and the male-dominated economic and social organizations of human society have been the basis for the explanation and theorization of women's oppression by all schools of feminist thinking, liberal, Marxist, socialist, or radical, as stated by Tahira S. Khan (Khan, 2006). In addition to these well-known feminist perspectives, there are a plethora of additional theories and conceptual subgroups.

Generally speaking, there are two types of academic and philosophical justifications that have been used to study women-related issues in different social science disciplines: idealist and materialist. The liberal feminist philosophy originated from idealist schools, which put forth the notion that women's subjugated status in society is inherent and part of the fundamental structure of the community (Abraham, 2001). This school holds that women's conditions can be improved by requesting equal rights and protection from the government. The physical and financial aspects of oppression that work against women are disregarded by the idealist perspective. According to the Material Theory, women's oppression is a historical, social, and malleable phenomenon. They spread the idea that material factors, such private property ownership, have an impact on family relationships.

Two ideas within the materialistic school of thought offer justification for women's subjugation and assault on two levels:

(a.) Institutional (state and society) and
(b.) Interpersonal (family).

It is significant that the location and timing of the honor/shame code were designed with female sexuality in mind, as this is another factor contributing to the social system's support of it. The central claim of historical materialism is that all intellectual and social interactions may be understood through an examination of the systems and material conditions that make up a given society, with the economic structure serving as the most fundamental material. Women's responsibilities and status have evolved as a result of material developments in the world.

For example, private property originated from excess value and is held by men as a result of gender-based labour division. Men's worries about their children's inheritance laws were sparked by private property, and this led to attempts to establish paternity. The custom of monogamy developed as a result of concerns about paternity. After monogamy was established, the husband began controlling and monitoring his wife's fertility in order to protect their property. History has demonstrated the strong connections that exist between the dominant moral, sexual, and religious ideals in a society and its economic conditions.

Marxist theory provides a critical framework for understanding class conflict and honor killing, highlighting the intersections of economic, social, and cultural factors. By applying Marxist theory, we can understand honor killings as a complex phenomenon rooted in economic, social, and cultural factors, requiring a revolutionary approach to challenge and transform the underlying structures.

Honor Killing and Feminist Theory

Feminist theory places a strong emphasis on the disparity between genders in society. It is a modern tactic that addressed societal stratification and inequality and came forth as a result of the feminist social movement. It was motivated by the conflict perspective. It examines female social positions and experiences in a variety of contexts, such as the job, home, and education, moving beyond the male-centric point of view. Feminist theory explains the manner, through which women are objectified, oppressed, stereotyped, and marginalized (hooks, 1984).

They experience prejudice based on Sex is the unfair treatment of a group of people due to their biological gender being feminine. They are viewed as worthless objects that are repressed and given less significance. They endure mistreatment, are abused, and are made to conform to gender-specific roles. They even assigned responsibilities based on gender stereotypes, with the female being expected to take care of the home, kids, and family, which left her with little time for social interaction. Men exercise and must earn money for their everyday needs as well as their future. They are also subject to structural oppression in this place, where the value placed on the female body is subordinated to the value placed on the feminine and masculine aspects of the male mind. Women are perceived as tender, nurturing both sentimental and compliant. The other guys are supposed to be warriors, powerful, aggressive, and tough. Different feminist perspectives have been developed over time as a result of socialization. This feminist theory in "Honor Killing" also emphasizes how socialization shapes the distinctions between men and women in terms of socially imposed gender roles where rules, practices, and expectations are created by each civilization and passed down from generation to generation. This viewpoint investigates the ways in which women's experiences as women are connected to males and masculinity (Hoskin et al., 2017).

In their many positions as a mother, wife, daughter, granddaughter, and sister, women are seen as the family honor, while men rule it. The primary danger relates to a woman's physical behaviour because of her ability to reproduce and have children. In order to make sure that she doesn't jeopardize the delicate balance of the male privilege, honor is linked to the feminine term associated with it. As a girl gets older, her shame load links her to becoming a submissive woman, which makes it difficult for her to feel good about her body. As a submissive recipient of the male seed, her shameful physical behaviour degrades her family's honor. This societal view of the man's inventiveness coexists with the creation of the concept of honor.

As a result, woman stands for prosperity and growth; she is independent of men and is therefore viewed as a potentially harmful force. For instance, the 2007 strangling death of Arza Parvez by her father and brother in the Shafia trial was deemed extremely bad form, and the media implied that the killing was driven by culture. In a reflexive nod to feminist theory, this classifies any mistreatment of women as a result of "the patriarchy?" Feminist theory is an alternative viewpoint on society that highlights the disparities that exist between men and women in one society, not an attempt to replace men (Shetty et al., 2019).

Functionalist Theory

Emile Durkheim, the author of this theory, said that society must be stable in order to be created in equilibrium. He expressed this from a broad perspective. He went on to say that society is made up of many institutions and social truths, including the hospitals, schools, and military—institutions mass media, marriage, etc. that cater to the requirements of the person in society. However, there are still social realities that influence how people think and behave and are owned by society. Every member of society is expected to abide by a set of social norms that serve to either safeguard them from harm or to ensure that they get justice and equality. Functionalist theory is also present in the practice of Honor killing, which is still carried out in some regions of the world. People from the ancestry origin believe that if someone disobeys family rules or caste, they will lose their Honor and that person must be killed right then and there by their own family or community. Consequently, this benefits society.

Through years of practice, this is still in place in various parts of our nation. It is socialised and adhered to against social norms and the law, and society as a whole does little to address it. Intercultural conflict, which is defined as the either implicit or explicit psychological struggle or frustration between people of different cultures over perceived incompatible beliefs, values, norms, saving faces concerns, goals, limited resources, processes, or outcomes in a communication situation, can also be seen as an example of Honor killing. In social-cultural situations in India, *'izzat'* generally refers to communal face issues. In Tibetan, the term *'la Gya'* also denotes group-based issues like national Honor, ethnic Honor, and communal honor. The topic of *'izzat'* in intergenerational relationships was studied in these ethnically distinct investigations of the face, which offer insight into how face anxieties manifest via interaction and the many anticipated conveyed regulations in these cultures articulated via the notion of acting appropriately to set aside speech, whether in the context of a family or a community. The aforementioned cultural expressions emphasize how crucial it is to uphold Honor or appearance in interactions and relationships between individuals and groups. To effectively negotiate conflict objectives, such as identity goals and relationship goals, people need to have face work management abilities and methods. Face-negotiation theory (FNT) divides face work strategies into two categories: face-saving and face-giving. All individuals seek acceptance, respect, status, and approval since they are social creatures. Giving others "face" in this sense is not degrading them, recognizing and Honoring their individuality, and sending positive messages during social encounters.

When faced with loss circumstances (such not receiving the anticipated jobs), people may exhibit situational suspicion by blaming all foreign workers for the job losses. Still, in severe cases of face loss, people may alter their coping mechanisms or even resort to drastic measures like Honor killing or suicide in an attempt to regain their dignity after experiencing immense embarrassment and humiliation. The father gave his approval for his own daughter to be killed in the Honor killing of Banaz Mahmod in order to restore family Honor, or *'izzat'*. A person's vision and perspective can be significantly shaped by societal, acculturation, situational, relational, and personal variables. It is ingrained and evident in places like Delhi and Chennai, where people's perspectives on social issues become narrower.

Functionalist theory views society as a cohesive system with interdependent parts, where social order and stability are maintained through social institutions and norms. By applying functionalist theory, we can understand honor killings as a means of maintaining social order and stability, but this perspective neglects the power dynamics and systemic inequality underlying this practice.

Honor Killing and Class Conflict Theory

Karl Marx developed conflict theory, which essentially defined it as the battle between the upper and lower classes, where the upper class prevails over the lower class. As a result, this causes rivalry between the two, which eventually leads to conflict. Indian heritage has long been known to be a male-dominated society. We may also see the disparity in wealth, color, religion, class, and other factors that exist among its people. Karl Marx distinguished three stages in his thesis: feudalism, capitalism, and socialization. Hence, honor killing is a product of capitalism, where the wealthy engage in needless conflict with one another and murder innocent members of their private clans out of a feeling of honor rooted in flawed perceptions. This standard has been set for this specific instance. The issue stems from people's anxiety that certain actions, such rape, refusing to be married, or love marriage, may diminish their social standing or honor. Women are considered the main offenders of honor killings because of their subordinate position and the domination of men in society.

CONCLUSION

As we have shown, honor killing is a complex cultural practice that merits examination from both an ecological and a social psychological angle. There are a lot of false beliefs about this custom that is restricted to rural areas. It is true that the homicides are so widely dispersed that it is impossible to isolate honor killings from rural regions, even though one must concede that rural areas account for the majority of killings. However, it has also lately been observed that, in unsafe urban areas like Delhi, there have been five reported cases of honor killings; a daughter and son-in-law were killed as a result of getting married into the same *'Gotra'*.

Therefore, it is evident that honor killings aren't just restricted to rural areas as they are also occurring in urban places, which span a large geographic range. The idea that honor killing originated in religion is the second myth about it. Four men must be there in addition to the woman in order for the good conduct and repute of the eyewitnesses to support the accusation of disloyalty. Furthermore, the only body with the power to impose legal penalties is the state; private vigilantes never have this power. Thus, it is evident that this horrible murder has no theological foundation.

The only way we can stop this crime is by raising public knowledge of its effects, losses, and repercussions. First and foremost, the parents', the community's, and society's mentalities must shift. It is imperative that people accept victims as distinct individuals within society who possess the inherent right to life and development. Rather than causing harm to society, victims work to promote unity within the community by abstaining from discrimination based on race, gender, religion, state, or any other characteristic. Second, since these crimes take the lives of innocent couples and individuals in society, they cannot be forgiven and we must enact stronger laws to combat them. Every person has a privilege to live, and no one has the authority to sentence another person to death.

REFERENCES

Abraham, L. (2001). Redrawing the *Lakshman Rekha:* Gender differences and cultural constructions in youth sexuality in urban India. *South Asia: Journal of South Asian Studies, 24*(sup001), 133–156. https://doi.org/DOI: 10.1080/00856400108723441

Anderson, J., & Poole, M. (2001). *Assignment and Thesis Writing* (4th ed.). Wiley

Bruinsma, G., & Weisburd, D. (2013). *Encyclopedia of Criminology and Criminal Justice.*

Deol, S. S. (2014). *Honor Killings In Haryana State, India: A Content Analysis.* https://www.researchgate.net/publication/333557222

Duran, J. (2005). Realism, Positivism and Reference. *Journal for General Philosophy of Science*, 36(2), 401–407. DOI: 10.1007/s10838-006-5625-0

George Ritzer-Sociological Theory. (8th Edition) -McGraw-Hill (2010).

Goldstein, M. A. (2002). The biological roots of heat-of-passion crimes and honor killings. *Politics and the Life Sciences : The Journal of the Association for Politics and the Life Sciences*, 21(2), 28–37. PMID: 16859346

hooks, bell. (1984). *Feminist theory from margin to center.*

Hoskin, R. A., Jenson, K. E., & Blair, K. L. (2017). Is our feminism bullshit? The importance of intersectionality in adopting a feminist identity. *Cogent Social Sciences*, 3(1), 1290014. DOI: 10.1080/23311886.2017.1290014

Husseini, R. (2021, August 1). *Murdered women: A history of 'Honor' crimes | History.* Al Jazeera. Retrieved September 15, 2024, from https://www.aljazeera.com/features/2021/8/1/murdered-women-a-history-of-Honor-crimes

Khan, T. S. (2006). *Beyond Honor : a historical materialist explanation of Honor related violence.* Oxford University Press.

Martin, R. (2013). *Human Rights and the Social Recognition Thesis* (Vol. 44). Journal of Social Philosophy.

Mishra, A. (2001). *HONOR KILLINGS: THE LAW IT IS AND THE LAW IT OUGHT TO BE.* https://www.hrw.org/press/2001/04/un

Nasrullah, M., Haqqi, S., & Cummings, K. J. (2009). The epidemiological patterns of Honor killing of women in Pakistan. *European Journal of Public Health*, 19(2), 193–197. DOI: 10.1093/eurpub/ckp021 PMID: 19286837

Prabhune, A. (n.d.). *A Socio-Legal Study On Honor Killing As A Crime In India*. Legal Service India. Retrieved September 15, 2024, from https://www.legalserviceindia.com/legal/article-2425-a-socio-legal-study-on-Honor-killing-as-a-crime-in-india.html

Reema Sahu Ph.D Research Scholar, Department of Law, Shri R. (2024). International Journal of Multidisciplinary Research Review (IJMDRR). Retrieved September 14, 2024, from http://www.ijmdrr.com/admin/downloads/050320243.pdf

Shetty, D. R., Kumar, K., & Shetty Scholar, D. R. (2019). International Journal of Scientific Research and Reviews Honor Killing Violating Human Rights, it's Theoretical Dimensions: A Review. *IJSRR, 2019*(1), 1–10. www.ijsrr.org

Mr. Suresh Kumar. (2023, March). Honor Killing in India: A Socio-Legal Problem. *International Journal of Research in Engineering and Science (IJRES), Volume 11*(Issue 3), PP. 602-606.

Welchman, L., & Hossain, S. (2014). *Introduction: "Honor", Rights and Wrongs.* www.soas.ac.uk/Honorcrimes

Chapter 19
Cognitive Strands of Honor Killing

Praveen Kumar Mall
Teerthanker Mahaveer University, India

Anusha Kulshrestha
https://orcid.org/0009-0003-2065-7165
GLA University, India

ABSTRACT

This chapter deems to highlight the misguided views of honor and the marginalization of those who deemed to be violators of this heinous crime. These thought processes are further cemented by social pressures and the fear of rejection. In order to question and alter the deeply held beliefs that support honor killings it is essential to comprehend the cognitive component of these crimes which are dealt with substantially in the chapter. Cultural traditions that have been entrenched over many generations can lead to a skewed sense of responsibility and honor, which results in people willing to go to great lengths to defend their perceived family honor. Furthermore, the chapter will highlight how humans justify violent behaviors as a way to restore honor by balancing their personal convictions with societal standards which can lead to cognitive dissonance. The cognitive strand is sustained by deeply ingrained gender norms that reinforce the idea that women are responsible for maintaining family honor.

DOI: 10.4018/979-8-3693-9596-7.ch019

BACKGROUND

The women in the family are under an immense amount of peer pressure to act "appropriately," as in such civilizations, they are seen as representing the dignity of the family. This includes, among other things, wearing modest clothes, abstaining from sexual activity before wedding, avoiding public places, and, most importantly, deciding to marry a partner chosen by their relatives. These are actions that are considered "dishonourable" for women and are therefore punishable by death. If a member of the family transgresses this code of conduct, the family's reputation suffers. Once more, usually the daughter, the sole manner in which they can apologize for their sins is to kill the person who has blacken their name. Despite advancements in science and civilization, the majority of the world's population still holds onto primitive ideas and beliefs. Many times, communities hold onto myths about their ethnic background and culture in an attempt to maintain it.

In accordance with the report of World Health Organization (WHO), intimate partner violence is something that happens to women frequently throughout their lives. The nations like Bangladesh, Peru, the United Republic of Tanzania and Ethiopia, claimed to have the highest levels of violence in their rural communities. The United Nations Population Fund (UNPF) outlines that there may have been as many as 7000 subjects of Honor Killing worldwide per year. (*Swp2000_eng*, n.d.)

The patriarchal social structures in Europe, Asia, and India emerged, where women's sexuality has become integral to the "honor" of their families and the society. (Wood, n.d.) A community's property and women are its greatest assets, and as a consequence, concepts of dignity and disgrace were attached to these possessions.

Inter-caste, inter-religious, and same-gotra marriages are the main reasons behind honor killing in India. One of the main causes of honor killings in India is the country's caste system. Cases of honor-based violence are still increasing in India. Nowadays, approximately one thousand adolescents lose their lives as a result of honor killings every year. Nevertheless, honor killing is not specifically covered by any Indian legislation. The Penal Code's provisions apply to such cases involving honor killings. Section 300, i.e., murder, and Sec. 120b, i.e., criminal conspiracy, are pertinent in these cases. As it says, "Anyone found guilty of murder faces the death penalty or life in prison, in addition to a fine." (*A1860-45 (1)*, n.d.)

Honor killings have been reported in northern India, specifically in the states of Haryana, Uttar Pradesh, Punjab, Tamil Nadu, and Rajasthan. The primary cause of such offences is individuals marrying contrary to the expectations of their relatives, particularly when those weddings involve people from identical gotras or tribes in northern India or representatives of various faiths or castes. On the other hand, honor killings are less frequent yet still happen in Gujarat and Maharashtra in western India. Data on honor killings can be found in the national data published by the National Crime Records Bureau. About a century ago, honor killing was completely outlawed in a number of other Indian states, especially West Bengal, owing in substantial part to revolutionaries and activists like Raja Ram Mohan Roy, Vivekananda, Vidyasagar, and Ramakrishna.

Statistical Data

Statistical data on the cognitive aspects of honor killings is relatively sparse, as research often focuses on broader socio-cultural, legal, and psychological factors rather than purely cognitive metrics. However, some relevant statistics related to honor killings and related cognitive or cultural aspects of different countries around the globe include:

- **Pakistan:** According to the Human Rights Watch, in Pakistan, there were approximately 1,000 honor killings reported annually in the country as of recent years. (HRW 2023-01-12, 468)
- **India:** The National Crime Record Bureau (NCRB) reports that there were 25 honour killings in India in 2019 and 2020, and that figure increased to 33 in 2021. (Sripad, 2023)
- **Turkey:** Annually, about 300 women are slain in honor-related incidents in Turkey, according to data from non-governmental organizations and the government. Depending on the source, certain estimations point to significantly greater figures. (Kardam, F. (2024))
- **United Kingdom:** There are between 12 and 15 honor killings that take place annually, according to estimates provided by the United Kingdom Home Office. However, these figures are based on cases that have been formally registered and may not represent the full depth of the problem. (Siddique, 2021)

These numbers reflect reported cases and may not fully capture the incidence of honor killings globally due to underreporting or varying definitions of what constitutes an honor killing.

Research Methodology

Understanding the Cognitive Strands of Honor killing is the primary objective of this chapter. In order to gather records for this topic, information from libraries, newspapers, magazines, sample websites, research papers, and other sources were checked. Thus, in order to fulfil the goal of covering both primary and secondary sources, this study used both primary and secondary research strategies. Data was gathered to see how honour killing has affected the life of individuals as well as the society as a whole, what are the factors which constitute such killings and lastly the mental state of the people involved in these killings. (Legal Research Methodology, 1999)

Based on the conducted research, it was determined that honor killing is not supported by any religion but rather stems from cultural ideas. Individuals who are perceived by the community to have transgressed cultural norms and values are often punished with violence and torture. After conducting extensive research, it is evident that honor killing is a global issue that has existed for many centuries and is not limited to any one geographic area. Although the media has only lately brought attention to this issue, it has worldwide implications, and numerous governmental agencies and units have been tasked with combating the issue of honor killing. (Kothari, 2004)

Key Terms

The nucleus of the term includes "Honor Killing" and its "Cognitive Strands". Broader themes like "Physical" (Kulwicki, 2002) and "Social Aspects" (Eisner & Ghuneim, 2013) & "Psyche" of the "Honour Killer" (Goldstein, 2002) contextualize the issue. Words used like "Chastity" (SHREYA, 2023), "Emotion", "belief" (Ratner, 2000), "rumour", "anxiety" (Feldman, 2010) connects to the analytical element of the research paper. "Honor-based crimes" (Bhanbhro et al., 2013), "patriarchal social structures" (Wood, n.d.) and "family honor" we used these keywords to select relevant articles from multiple online sources, for example, 'Library of Congress, Research Gate, Google Books, Springer, JSTOR, Sage, IJSSHR, Scopus, Web of Science, Taylor & Francis and Google Scholar'. A thorough analysis of inclusion/exclusion criteria, article research, and publication selection are necessary for a Research Paper on Cognitive Strands of Honor Killings. During the journal selection process, publications that focused on "Global perspective" (Nasrullah et al., 2009), "Physiological", "psychological impact" (Meetoo & Mirza, 2007) and other related interdisciplinary themes were selected for publication. We have set inclusion and exclusion criteria to further refine the research papers that are relevant for this Chapter. The research must be published in English and limited to journal articles, that is, those with an impact factor of 1.0 or above in Journal Citation Reports and peer-reviewed papers, or those with a B grade or higher in the Journal Quality list. The following studies satisfied our inclusion criteria: those in which "experience" was examined as a concept or a variable in the context of ecotourism.

Literature Review

Honor killing is a multifaceted issue with psychological, social, and cultural roots. The ideas and thought processes that propel people to carry out these types of crimes are referred to as the cognitive strand of honor killing. Social conventions and values: People prefer dignity over human life when they perceive threats to family honor, which is the result of a cognitive action (Bargach, 2005). The roles of gender and patriarchy: Social norms surrounding both genders support a mentality that rationalizes violence against women (Kandiyoti 1988). Ethical disinterest: People might justify honor killing by cognitive processes such as marginalization, shifting of guilt, andethical reasoning (Bandura, 1999). Social recognition and cohesiveness: Acceptance bias and ingroup-outgroup perception are examples of cognitive biases that can result from the need to uphold group honor and prevent social rejection (Turner et al., 1979).

Honor killing is ultimately sustained by the intersection of these cognitive aspects with mental, social, and contextual considerations. The study of the cognitive strand of honor killing has also been aided by the work of Swedish researcher Unni Wikan and Turkish German sociologist Nader Ahmadi, who are both authorities on honor killings. Ahmadi (2003) investigates the ways in which cultural norms and values influence the thought processes that result in honor killing. He contends that honor is viewed as a zero-sum game in which the only way to preserve one's own honor is to kill the individual who is thought to have betrayed the family. The impact of cognitive biases and moral disengagement in honor killing is examined by Wikan (2003). According to her, people who kill people for honor frequently feel morally justified in doing so because they believe it will restore their family's honor.

Future Research Directions

Unlike other chapters, this one expands on the social prejudices that underlie these tragic events and emphasizes the need for interdisciplinary methods to fully understand the complex interplay of psychological, cultural, spiritual, and economical variables. This makes the chapter unique in the discussion of Cognitive Strands of Honor Killing. There haven't been many studies on the subject, but this one is unique since it adds fresh perspectives to the discussion as it investigates the cognitive elements that contribute to honor killing in various cultural contexts and geographical areas (SHREYA, 2023). It also looks into the ways in which social networks and group dynamics affect the thought processes that result in honor killing. In addition, it looks at how moral education can deter honor killing and support alternative cognitive frameworks. It also looks at how identities that intersect—such as gender, sexual orientation, and class affect the cognitive processes that lead to honor killing, (Dickson, 2014) identifies the specific cognitive biases and heuristics that support honor killing and develops mitigation strategies for them. Finally, it creates and assesses preventative initiatives that focus on cognitive aspects, like empathy-building and cognitive restructuring, and it makes recommendations for applications in forensic psychology. This chapter exclusively aims to Create and assess therapies using cognitive behavioral therapy to treat moral disengagement and cognitive distortions in those who are at risk of honor killing which is highly recommended by the author but there is still a scope for future research as this chapter does not cover the physical aspects of honor killing as well as the political factors affecting it.

HONOR KILLING ACROSS THE GLOBE

The United Nations General Assembly report on cultural practices in the family that reflect violence against women states that cases of Honor Killing have been reported from the Syrian Arab Republic, Jordan Egypt, Turkey, Pakistan, Yemen, Lebanon, Morocco, and the other countries in the Mediterranean and Persian Gulf. Furthermore, comparable events have happened to immigrant communities in Western countries including Germany, France, and Britain. Culture and education play a vital role in shaping views towards Honor killing and Honor Based Violence. (In-Depth Study on All Forms of Violence against Women Report of the Secretary-General, 2006) The vast majority of men and women did not think that spouses should be divorced or forgiven for having extramarital affairs. In Pakistan, between 2014 and 2017, there were around one thousand nine hundred and eighty instances of Honour Killing, based on epidemiological research using press data. In 96% of the cases, it was the result of extramarital encounters, and in 92% of the cases, the individuals were married. The crimes, which featured spouses, brothers, in-laws, and other close relatives, involved guns, strangulations, assaults, and the use of an axe. (Nasrullah et al., 2009)

According to the World Health Organisation (WHO), intimate partner violence is something that happens to women often throughout their lives. Bangladesh, Peru, the United Republic of Tanzania and Ethiopia reported having the highest levels of violence in their rural communities. (SHREYA, 2023). Over 384 individuals, including 246 women and 147 men, lost their lives as a result of honour killings in the province of Sindh in 2014 alone. The reason for this is a legal loophole in juvenile justice that allows adolescents to complete their sentences in juvenile detention facilities and be freed when they turn eighteen and have a clean criminal record. "Karo-kari" is a kind of HK that is frequently reported in Pakistan. The rural and tribal areas of Sindh, Pakistan, gave rise to this type of planned murders. The concerned female must be killed by someone in her family who is male in order to regain this honour. Gender norms and socio-cultural factors have led to the acceptability of karo-kari in some indigenous groups. It should be noted that some prominent Muslim scholars and officials have openly condemned this honour system and said that Islam does not support it. As far, there isn't a concept of honor-based violence that is appropriate or relevant across cultural boundaries. Nonetheless, this does not mean that honor-based crimes don't exist or that they only occur in a select few communities. (Bhanbhro et al., 2013) A Study on Honor Killing has been conducted from a variety of perspectives; some have focused on epidemiology, some on the consequences, additional studies have concentrated on knowledge, attitudes, and beliefs, and very few have focused on the perpetrators and victims. This might be as a result of the challenges associated in researching any of these groups. Many cases of Honour killing were documented in immigrant groups in America and Europe; the first well-known homicide in Europe to be labelled as "honour" killing was the death of Fadime Sahindal. Although rates of Honor-Based-Violence may decrease in minority communities gradually as they become more completely integrated into the mainstream community

Physical and Social Aspects

Numerous physical and societal factors motivate the offenders to carry out honor killings and start acts of violence based on honor. These include things like chastity, feelings of love, fear, and worry, religion, rumours, and parenting.

Chastity

Although many cultures view sexual purity as a crime, other people raise this transgression to the level of a holy moral code breach, equivalent to the murdering of a harmless individual. Purity, which includes terms and rituals related to sexual behaviour and the body, could seem like a matter of priorities and private taste. Liberals tend to be better educated from the Western nations and to occupy higher social and economic positions. For a great number of people, however, disobeying purity norms is exceedingly detrimental. Instances of sex-related deviation that are considered to be perpetrator clan include immodesty, infidelity, and homosexual conduct; in order to clean up that mess, they must be put to death or punished. Historically, a woman's value as a piece of property was directly correlated with her state of virginity as a young single woman and her purity as a married woman. (SHREYA, 2023) If she committed adultery or any other illegal sexual conduct, she lost her worth and her life, since she would have damaged her personal value and her spouse's (or dad's) status in society.

Emotions

When anything triggers sentiments in the mind that are wholly unjustified by the circumstances, it's considered an emotion and indicates that the source of the powerful feeling needs to be looked into. Our feelings are based on our senses. They literally feel like tingles, hot areas, and strained muscles in our bodies. Your feelings influence your thoughts, actions, and behaviour. Sentiments affect your body in the same way that your body affects your feelings. The human body generates chemicals when you feel beneficial emotions like joy, fulfilment, affection, and acceptance, as well as when you feel adverse emotions like anxiety, dread, pessimism, frustration, and sadness. Coping strategies are usually triggered by emotions. As a result, when we feel something, we act on it. This is evident in both the more considered handling of the repercussions and the immediate (and sometimes unconscious) response to the emotion. When this feeling is negative, we may react with anything from a fervent defense of our actions to accommodating apologies and other forms of "establishing up." When we vent our frustration in other ways, displacement is a common response to repressing unwanted feelings.

Love and Fear

There are just two basic feelings that each of us may feel: terror and affection. Every emotion stems from these two major feelings. One is motivated by either fear or love in their thoughts and deeds. Anxiety, fury, oversight, sadness, dejection, unworthiness, confusion, harm, isolation, shame, and embarrassment are some of these fear-based feelings. Happiness, satisfaction, empathy, faith, reality, bliss, and pleasure are examples of love-based emotions. The two main emotions are love and fear, and all other feelings are merely variations of these two. Love and fear are the bases from which people construct their beliefs and behaviours. Dealing with issues of honor causes emotional strain among family members. Love will lose in a contest between fear and love for supremacy.

The arguments provided above make it very apparent that "fear" is stronger than "love," that "fear" always has the upper hand, and that individuals commit crimes to counteract the consequences of "fear." It can be challenging to discern when someone's good intentions evolve into a serious issue that could land them in jail. Most recorded cases of honor killing involve crimes with "community," "spiritual," or "caste" connections. In actuality, these concepts are meant to guide people in the right direction so they can lead happy lives and help create a welcoming environment for individuals to do the same. Fear arises when these concepts are mixed with erroneous arrogance and superstitions; this flips people's perceptions and makes them lose the good feeling known as "love." When a person kills their own sister, brother, daughter, or son for the sake of "respect," it is important to look at that individual's thinking from a different perspective. A father who murders his young daughter does not think about the time he spent with her as a baby and as an adult, nor about the love she gave him. In order to restore the "honor" he feels she lost due to her transgression; he is killing her.

The predominance of fear over love among humans is what causes the abrupt shift from feelings of affection to animosity and revenge. The value and importance of relationships are called into question when a community or religion sows' discord in the minds of individuals and threatens to assassinate their own children in the name of an unseen rule of behaviour. People are being instilled with fear by religions and groups, not with love or compassion. The foundation of a family is love, diligence, security, and pleasure. Families predate communities and faiths by a great margin. In a familial setting, children are nurtured and protected from harm. This is a beautiful friendship between parents and siblings, forged by affinities of the heart and blood. A tangible type of connection is family. Love, not hate or fear, is the foundation of the family institution. However, the solid bond of family has been undermined, and the feeling of fear has been instilled by the intangible elements known as spirituality, society as a whole, caste, and fake pride. Here, fear wins out over affection. This illustrates how people's bad emotions exceed their positive ones due to the negative effects of inflated self-worth and false beliefs. Fear's detrimental effects upon caste, religion, or society lead to unfavourable attitudes in people and the growth of fear and hatred in the name of compassion.

This makes it clear that fear-based feelings can be fatal when triggered. It follows that in order to control and dominate over people and use fear to enslave them in the guise of affection, faith, caste, and group are factors that sow fear while posing as loving forces. The space and freedom that love gives to others is something that fear keeps one from experiencing. Fear is a limited and constricted emotion that makes it impossible for people to reason rationally. It will make it difficult for people to think compassionately and constructively and will motivate them to act terribly. Consequently, fear has a greater effect on people's views and actions than love.

Anxiety

Psychological theories link honor killings and honor-based violence to a severe form of prestige anxiety, which is typified by a fear of losing one's standing and a need to hold onto it. (Meetoo & Mirza, 2007) Pathological insecurity, persistent pressure to adhere to strict social standards and conventions, and a fear of looking foolish and alienating one's community are all recognized characteristics of the area where honor killing occurs. When someone defies social standards, they face the risk of compromising their place as an integral part of that particular social group.

Similar to other conflicts, existential fragility and incompleteness are the core cause of both honor killings and honor-based violence. This feeling of emptiness gives rise to a paranoid dread of losing it, as well as a yearning for status and face-saving.

Beliefs

People's beliefs will vary depending on their socioeconomic background, culture, religion, and customs. Some societies, especially those having a long tradition of herding settlement, developed a "culture of honor." Certain families prioritize society and culture over other aspects of their lives. They will do everything it takes to protect and preserve culture because they see it as being more important. "Honor" killing is the most severe type of honor-based violence, where the accused criminal is killed in order to recover the "honor" that she believes she forfeited as a consequence of her acts.

Honor killing is the most serious act of brutality that could be committed as a last option; other, less severe acts of violence include forced marriage.

The following are areas of disagreement between the individual and the family:

1. Schooling
2. Attire
3. Attitudes and Behaviours Toward the Other Sex
4. Sexual Orientation
5. Adherence to Community and Family Standards and Expectations

A woman's value and role in figuring out the culture's offspring are determined, first, by her sexual purity when single and her chastity when married; second, by having an affair or engaging in other illicit sexual behaviour, as this would have damaged her own value and her husband's (or father's) social status. In the majority of locales where honor killings are common, women are aware that breaking the law or the established norms will only make their family feel forced to restore honor, therefore they have no choice but to follow them. This could include forced marriage at a young age, restrictions on the woman's ability to engage in normal social activities, or, in the worst-case scenario, forced suicide or murder. (Feldman, 2010) From the standpoint of evolutionary biology, the concept of honor killing is unthinkable because, from a post-Darwinian context, people are least likely to kill individuals that they have a biological kinship with their progeny. (SHREYA, 2023)

Rumours

Rumours, suspicions, or hearsay of shameful behaviour are the only things that incite violence in a large number of honor killing or honor based violence instances reported. Honor killings frequently involve planned events. Research indicated that fathers and mothers who held low-status jobs and had poor educational attainment were more likely to put up with violence. Honor killings and assaults on women were more inclined to be supported by those who had personally suffered violence. Refusing to enter into a forced marriage, marrying someone of their own choosing, or breaking out of an oppressive marriage are all viewed as breaches of family honor and can lead to honor killings. (Kulwicki, 2002)

Murders of women and girls can occur for a number of reasons, including talking to random males, having sexual relationships with men prior to marriage, being raped, filing for divorce, or declining to marry the family patriarch. A murder could happen even if there is only an allegation of a crime. It's not always fatal for women to be physically abused. As a result, honor-based violence and honor killing originate from many places. Psychological factors exist in addition to cultural and theological foundations. This has to do with the social pressure that permeates established social mores and conventions. Adolescent experience with aggression of this kind and male dominance could be key factors in this approach. (Rew et al., 2013)

Parents

Research indicates that having harsh discipline from parents is associated with a higher chance of supporting honor killings and that enduring parental violence and mistreatment can contribute to an increased likelihood of approving a person's violent tendencies later in life. (Eisner & Ghuneim, 2013) It is more likely that a father who practices patriarchy and dictatorial parenting will get his kids to concur that it is okay to kill a lady in order to protect the family's honor. Effectively treating childhood trauma and abuse, as well as tolerance following exposure to violence, might result in a change in attitude towards violence.

THE PSYCHE OF THE HONOUR KILLER

Since male empowerment is ingrained in the majority of global nations, it has existed for centuries. Conventional culture males committed to the idea of "male dominance," seeing women as having conventional home duties. Women are gaining equal rights and playing significant roles in both developed and developing country communities thanks to developments. Due to global migration, men with conventional cultural backgrounds are becoming increasingly concerned that "their" women in foreign places may get "tainted" by the prevailing culture there. They may adopt hostile attitudes, become extremely religiously rigorous, and occasionally turn to violence in order to escape this. These men's mental states become dominated by constant worry and hyper-vigilance. Men who are economically and socially disadvantaged may find it easy to indulge in "arrogant pleasure" via controlling the women in their lives, whether they be their spouses or daughters.

The reason behind honor killings might be explained by evolutionary theories. The presence of paternal assurance has always been crucial for men who are ready to invest in children they believe to be their own. Because of this, males may need to use aggressiveness to neutralize threats in order to protect their paternal certainty, whilst females are confident in their lineage. Patriarchy legislation against adultery and societal standards that safeguard male privilege in sexual relationships are only two ways that many civilizations have recognized the significance of this. It's possible that socio-cultural views can have a significant psychological impact on those who commit honour killings. (Goldstein, 2002) Socio-cultural factors may have an impact on the damaged psyche of some individuals who could abuse their position of authority in a brutal and thoughtless manner. Many people, however, who experience comparable socio-cultural factors, do not support such behaviour. This is the reason it's important to take psychopathology's part in honour killings into account.

The likelihood of a psychopathological procedure is suggested by observations of different honour killing instances, notwithstanding the lack of research indicating the existence or inability of psychopathology among honour murderers. A number of honor killing case reports in the media have characterized the killers as having particular psychotic tendencies. Personal qualities, particularly psychopathic traits, can show out as a willful disrespect for women's safety, a refusal to follow the law, and an absence of regret. Premeditated killings that were violent in nature were indicative of psychopathology in certain legal contexts. The offender could, for instance, have "acute stress disorder." When faced with a perceived substantial danger, people with such disorder will exhibit symptoms of dissociation like emotional numbness, forgetfulness, delusion, and detachment. A fatal crime of this kind might be caused by a variety of mental illnesses. Such crimes may be caused, for instance, by paranoid schizophrenia or an unidentified psychosis impacted by a perceptual problem.

Psychopathology can take many forms, from frank psychosis to borderline personality disorder. Individuals' psyches are influenced by cultural archetypes, conventional mindsets, belief systems, and an environment that is excessively religious.

Distinctive cultural mindsets enhanced by illusions might give rise to perilous viewpoints while discussing "honour killing." When combined with psychopathology, particularly schizophrenia, a cultural mindset may result in a reduced sense of criminal culpability. However, in cases where crimes against honour are deliberate, meticulously planned, and carried out, pure personality disorders are unable to be taken into account as adequate grounds for lesser blame. Clinicians must use extreme care when diagnosing psychopathology in situations involving honour murders. Generating an accurate and objective evaluation requires having a thorough grasp of the motivations and socio-cultural norms. Most offenders most likely do not exhibit psychopathology that would suggest a reduction in culpability.

It is crucial to keep in mind that honour killing may be mistakenly associated with "acts of fervour," which are sudden, irrational, and spontaneous acts of violence carried out by people who have experienced something that they find inappropriate and who are temporarily unable to control themselves. According to Ratner's study (Ratner, 2000), sentiments are most effectively described as cognitive assessments of circumstances based on social conventions and values that imply a deeper "self." In this sense, honour murders are often intentional, well-planned, and plotted actions when an individual kills a female relative apparently to maintain his honour, although acts of fervour may be considered as relatively premeditated to some level. Therefore, honour killing appears to be no different from any other planned murder and, barring a psychiatric diagnosis, ought to result in the same penalty from a court of law. Professionals in mental health play a critical part in every murder case, including honour killings. The judicial system can benefit from the assistance of a psychiatrist with cultural education training and expertise when it comes to certain trials in situations involving the killing of honour. A criminal justice system referral might initiate several measures for a Carl person suspected of honour killing to be evaluated by a psychologist. A comprehensive history emphasizing the psychosocial components of the accused's growth and development, encompassing their own history with cultural convictions and upbringing and prior history with a focus on forensic difficulties, should be the most crucial component of the examination.

Any psychopathology may be detected by a comprehensive mental-state evaluation, suggesting severe, easily recognized mental health problems. A personality assessment is one psychological exam that might be useful in the evaluation. When necessary, cognitive testing might be incorporated with this procedure. Even EEG (electroencephalogram), MRI (magnetic resonance imaging) and PET (positron emission tomography) investigations might be useful additions in certain carefully chosen situations when creating an extensive report.

SUGGESTIONS AND CONCLUSION

When tackling the honor killings and honor-based violence issue, a careful balance between psycho-legal, society and private treatment needs to be found. Honor killings sometimes equate to murder and homicide, which are serious offences in any nation's judicial system. (Reddy, 2008) Strict limits don't stop honor killing and honor-based violence from happening, which emphasizes the reality that laws alone won't solve the problem. Inquiries into the event and crime are sometimes delayed and skewed because of community pride or honor issues. It is evident that without more extensive, in-depth activities and understandings, transforming practice in this area would not be possible with a narrow legal paradigm that simply takes state legal systems into account.

Some scholars argue that one might disagree to a human rights perspective because of discrimination and violence against women, without saying that the community's sense of sexual propriety is inherently undesirable from a human rights perspective. (Fateh, 2012) Although there is a lot of evidence regarding the application of psychological therapies, there is currently no research on the health care or psychological treatment of honor killing offenders. Survivors of honor need gender-sensitive health services to address the effects on their physical and mental health. These services include ongoing psychological support, referrals to other services, pregnancy testing, abortion services, avoiding pregnancy, the use of STI testing, injury treatment, and compassionate listening. (Khan, 2007) Depending on the kind of honor-based violence, women's mental health is affected in different ways. One-fourth of victims of violence suffer from post-traumatic stress disorder (PTSD); however, in the instance of sexual assault, PTSD affects 50% of victims. (Dickson, 2014) Asian women are under plenty of strain to conceal their past abuse experiences and any related mental health conditions. They worry about being stigmatized through their surroundings, where abuse and mental illness are seen as defects that can bring shame and dishonour to a family. Many countries have regulations regarding how to address situations of domestic abuse and honor-based violence.

In light of this, prevention, protection, empowerment and spreading knowledge regarding security, law enforcement, and other pertinent state parties are the best ways to address these offences. Research on the root causes and consequences of assault against female can help us develop effective solutions. Global consensus on indicators could facilitate the necessary effective monitoring and assessment. (Jewkes, 2002) In addition to establishing a number of organizations that might offer victims shelter homes, help lines, and legal, healthcare, and emotional assistance, the judicial system must guarantee the protection of women. Educating and involving women in decision-making is the last phase of women's empowerment. Women ought to be included in decision-making in areas pertaining to security and peace on a global, national, and local level. Women should be involved in all aspects of diplomacy, peacekeeping, post-conflict reconstruction, and preventive peace discussions.

These false belief systems are the root cause of both honor-based violence and honor killing. Despite the fact that the problem could seem to be solely social in nature, its roots are in a complex web of biological, cultural, and personality-based factors. Social workers, legislators, mental health professionals, and political parties must cooperate if they are to successfully end the problem. Despite the task at face is difficult, making steady progress could allow future generations to profit from the labours of the present generation.

REFERENCES

A1860-45 (1).

Bandura, A. (1999). Social cognitive theory: An agentic perspective. *Asian Journal of Social Psychology*, 2(1), 21–41. DOI: 10.1111/1467-839X.00024

Bargach, J. (2005). An ambiguous discourse of rights: The 2004 family law reform in Morocco. *Hawwa*, 3(2), 245–266. DOI: 10.1163/1569208054739056

Bhanbhro, S., Wassan, R., Ali Shah, M., Rafique, M., Ali, A., Rafique Wassan, M., Sindh Pakistan Muhbat Ali Shah, J., Sindh Pakistan Ashfaq Talpur, J. A., & Ali Wassan, A. (2013). Karo Kari : the murder of honour in Sindh Pakistan : an ethnographic study. In International Journal of Asian Social Science (Vol. 3, Issue 7). http://shura.shu.ac.uk/7287/

Dickson, P. (2014). Understanding victims of honour-based violence. Community Practitioner : The Journal of the Community Practitioners' & Health Visitors'. *Association*, 87(7), 30–33.

Eisner, M., & Ghuneim, L. (2013). Honor Killing Attitudes Amongst Adolescents in Amman, Jordan. *Aggressive Behavior*, 39(5), 405–417. DOI: 10.1002/ab.21485 PMID: 23744567

Fateh, N. S. (2012). HONOUR KILLING.

Feldman, S. (2010). Shame and honour: The violence of gendered norms under conditions of global crisis. *Women's Studies International Forum*, 33(4), 305–315. DOI: 10.1016/j.wsif.2010.02.004

Goldstein, M. A. (2002). The biological roots of heat-of-passion crimes and honor killings. *Politics and the Life Sciences : The Journal of the Association for Politics and the Life Sciences*, 21(2), 28–37. PMID: 16859346

Human Rights Watch (HRW). 2023-01-12. "Pakistan." World Report 2023: Events of 2022. [Accessed 2023-11-06]

In-depth study on all forms of violence against women Report of the Secretary-General. (2006).

Jewkes, R. (2002). Preventing sexual violence: A rights-based approach. *Lancet*, 360(9339), 1092–1093. DOI: 10.1016/S0140-6736(02)11135-4 PMID: 12384005

Kandiyoti, D. (1988). Bargaining with patriarchy. *Gender & Society*, 2(3), 274–290. DOI: 10.1177/089124388002003004

Kardam, F. (2024), *The Dynamics of Honour Killing in Turkey*. United Nations Population Fund. Retrieved September 14, 2024, from https://www.unfpa.org/sites/default/files/pub-pdf/honourkillings.pdf

Khan, r. (2007). Internet journal of criminology honour-related violence (hrv) in scotland: cross-and multi-agency intervention involvement survey. www.internet journalofcriminology.com

Kothari, C. R. (2004). *Research Methodology: Methods and Techniques*. New Age International Limited.

Kulwicki, A. D. (2002). THE PRACTICE OF HONOR CRIMES: A GLIMPSE OF DOMESTIC VIOLENCE IN THE ARAB WORLD. *Issues in Mental Health Nursing*, 23(1), 77–87. DOI: 10.1080/01612840252825491 PMID: 11887612

Legal Research Methodology. (H. N. Tewari, Compiler; reprint ed.). (1999). Allahabad Law Agency.

Meetoo, V., & Mirza, H. S. (2007). "There is nothing 'honourable' about honour killings": Gender, violence and the limits of multiculturalism. *Women's Studies International Forum*, 30(3), 187–200. DOI: 10.1016/j.wsif.2007.03.001

Nasrullah, M., Haqqi, S., & Cummings, K. J. (2009). The epidemiological patterns of honour killing of women in Pakistan. *European Journal of Public Health*, 19(2), 193–197. DOI: 10.1093/eurpub/ckp021 PMID: 19286837

Ratner, C. (2000). A Cultural-Psychological Analysis of Emotions. *Culture and Psychology*, 6(1), 5–39. DOI: 10.1177/1354067X0061001

Reddy, R. (2008). Gender, Culture and the Law: Approaches to 'Honour Crimes' in the UK. *Feminist Legal Studies*, 16(3), 305–321. DOI: 10.1007/s10691-008-9098-x

Rew, M., Gangoli, G., & Gill, A. K. (2013). Violence between Female In-laws in India. [). https://vc.bridgew.edu/jiws]. *Journal of International Women's Studies*, 14(1), •••.

SHREYA. (2023a). PSYCHO-SOCIO FACETS OF HONOUR KILLING. *Russian Law Journal*, 11(2s). Advance online publication. DOI: 10.52783/rlj.v11i2s.572

Siddique, H. (2021, October 31). 'Honour-based' offences soared by 81% in last five years. *The Guardian*. https://www.theguardian.com/society/2021/oct/31/honour-based-offences-soared-by-81-in-last-five-years

Sripad, A. M. (2023, September 4). Killing honour in the name of 'honour killings'. *The New Indian Express*. https://www.newindianexpress.com/states/karnataka/2023/Sep/04/killing-honour-in-the-name-of-honour-killings-2611437.html swp2000_eng. (n.d.).

Turner, J. C., Brown, R. J., & Tajfel, H. (1979). Social comparison and group interest in ingroup favouritism. *European Journal of Social Psychology*, 9(2), 187–204. DOI: 10.1002/ejsp.2420090207

Wood, J. C. (n.d.). A History of Murder: Personal Violence in Europe from the Middle Ages to the Present (review). https://doi.org/DOI: 10.2307/40802138

Chapter 20
Honor Killing in Pakistan and Women Standing Under Islamic Law

Pratibha Singh
B.M.S. College of Law, Karnataka State Law University, India

Ishika Raghuvanshi
GLA University, India

ABSTRACT

Because of the rise in crimes against women, including honor killing and other forms of violence related to honor, the Islamic Republic of Pakistan is regarded as one of the world's most risky and hazardous places for women. Using general sayings of the Prophet Muhammad, peace be upon him, a number of researchers and Islamic scholars have tried to defend the practice of honor killing. Unquestionably, women around the world are vulnerable to arbitrary cultural norms and outdated ideas. Throughout history, women have experienced marginalization in various civilizations due to their minimal involvement in decision-making within both public and private domains. Sadly, physical assault against women is sometimes mistakenly identified as a sign of masculine dominance. The fear of abuse and social pressures forced the women from different backgrounds to remain silent on such intrusive matters. It is important to note that all faiths condemn honour killing as a socio-cultural evil

DOI: 10.4018/979-8-3693-9596-7.ch020

BACKGROUND

Due to the rise in crimes against women, including honor killing and other forms of violence related to honor, the Islamic Republic of Pakistan is regarded as one of the world's most risky and hazardous places for women. Unfortunately, using general sayings of the Prophet Muhammad, peace be upon him, a number of researchers and Islamic scholars have tried to defend the practice of honor killing. Unquestionably, women around the world are vulnerable to arbitrary cultural norms and outdated ideas. Throughout history, women have experienced marginalization in various civilizations due to their minimal involvement in decision-making within both public and private domains. Sadly, physical assault against women is sometimes mistakenly identified as a sign of masculine dominance. The fear of abuse and social pressures forced the women from different backgrounds to remain silent on such intrusive matters. It is important to note that all faiths condemn honor killing as a socio-cultural evil, hence their teachings do not support it. The miserable situation of women in ancient Islamic times offers terrible historical proof of this evil custom. In order to avoid the fires of Hell, the prophet of Allah (may peace be upon him) taught his disciples to honor women and follow the path of rectitude.

Many instances of honor killing go unreported because of societal and cultural norms. The available data shows that at least 183 women were killed in 1998, more than 1000 in 1999 and 240 in the first six months of 2000 year. (Amnesty International, 1999) Almost a thousand cases involving honor killing were reported nationwide in 2001. If it is not stopped by iron hands, it will continue to grow and can prove fatal to the State. (Ahmed, K. 2000) In Pakistan, there were 560 honor killings in 2009; this figure somewhat decreased in 2010 before rising to 600 in 2011. The graph shows a sharp decline in honor killings in 2012, followed by another sharp increase in 2013 and a peak over 1000 in 2014. Reports from the Human Rights Commission of Pakistan (HRCP) states that at least 246 honor killings cases were reported in 2021. In 2022, roughly 225 honor killings have been reported. Further, the same organization documented at least 384 occurrences of honor killings in 2022. As a result of COVID-19 lockdowns, in 2020-2021, there was an increase in honor killing cases and victims during these years. With 841 reported cases and 1,058 victims, Punjab had the highest number of honor killings and Karo-Kari occurrences between 2018 and 2022.

Research Methodology

The information for this topic was collected in the form of checking records from libraries/Newspaper/Magazines/Sample/Internet/Research papers etc. Therefore, in order to satisfy the study's purpose of covering primary as well as secondary sources, qualitative as well as quantitative methods of inquiry were used. In 2001, Anderson and Poole Data was gathered to learn how individuals view honor killing, whether it is seen as a religious phenomena, a socio-political cultural issue, or something else entirely, as well as how "Zia" affects discrimination against women. Information was acquired to determine the effects of honor killing on women's lives and society at large. The author had gathered secondary statistics from the Human Rights Commission of Pakistan [HRCP] and concentrated on the above-mentioned years vis-à-vis victims of honor killings in various religions.

Literature Review

The several elements that influence honor killing in Pakistan will be examined in this section of the literature study. Each factor shows how different parts of society ignore the most sensitive issue—honor killing. The first thought describes the family's social status.

The family's women's modesty and purity are ingrained with this tradition of honor. In Pakistani Urdu and Pashto areas, this kind of familial reverence is known as "Ghairat," (according to Chesler & Bloom, 2012). The second idea is that males' treats women as their own property. All for one and one for all was the motto that protected these groups' integrity, independence, and trade secrets. If men could adhere to a shared unwritten rule of open communication that honored unique sensitivities while allowing each man to express his freedom, then good intercorporate relations would be guaranteed. (Bhopal. K, 1982). Although women are not expressly targeted by the honor test, it has effectively kept them out of social, civic, and professional groups for decades even when they were otherwise perfectly qualified for them. According to cultural conventions and customs, honor relates to the designated duties that women have in the home and sexual spheres. These customs regarded rape, cheating, falling in love with a "wrong" person, suspected pregnancies without a marriage, sexual misconduct, and nonmarital or sexual relationships as abuses of the their overall family's reputation. (Elakkary et, 2014). Apart from the autonomous formation of honor societies, social mimesis lost its significance as an explanation for the rise in honor and shame among upwardly mobile aristocratic bourgeois, especially after the seventeenth century. In European culture, honor was associated with great bravery and heroic character. (Dasgupta, 2000). According to Hajjar's research, among other religions, Islam is the sole religion that grants women greater rights. According to Hajjar, there are controversial statements regarding the application of international and Islamic laws in various states, including Pakistan. Islam also emphasizes the concealment of male and female sexual relationships rather than discussing them in public (Patel & Gadit, 2008). Wasti's research has revealed that a critical factor influencing the concerns of honor killing in Pakistan is the inadequate involvement of the Pakistani government. Because of the biased attitude towards honor killing, Niaz makes it clear in his research work that there is a lack of desire in putting the legal framework into practice. Additionally, Wasti presented evidence of subpar performance at the judicial level in relation to the application of Islamic Laws pertaining to Zina's punishment and murder, with the rationale being to preserve the family's reputation and exclude the victim in the interest of upholding family honor.

Research Gap

Primary data collection is advised for future studies in order to more precisely capture current perspectives and regional variances. This strategy would enable a thorough examination of the obstacles to Pakistan's honor killings and help it to eradicate. Researchers could create a scale to gauge people's opinions about honor killing. This could be useful in distinguishing between affirmative and deterrent attitudes.

This research work is different because it deals not only with the laws related to honor killing in Pakistan but also useful in distinguishing between affirmative and deterrent attitudes. Further the chapter talks about the measures to be taken mitigate this threat in Pakistan. Examining how recent legal changes, such the Anti-Honor Killing Law of 2016, have affected the number of honor killings could be the main subject of future research. This involves evaluating obstacles to enforcement and legal gaps. Examining the changes in cultural perceptions of women's rights and honor killings over time, may also be the grey area. Studies could use research, analysis of the media, and historical comparisons to monitor changes in public opinion.

Killing someone is always immoral, criminal, and a severe violation of human rights. (Lewisohn Ludwig,1909). This research work highlights that the purpose of honor killing is to uphold the dignity and grace of the family. However, killing someone is never honorable, especially if that person is someone you love deeply. The citation of "religious beliefs and "society" as justifications for the murder of women or other individuals is forbidden since both faith and law are inherently arbitrary and open to interpretation. Everybody is entitled to a fair and honorable life. The issue of violence against women (VAW), which includes honor killing, has progressively gained recognition as a significant human rights concern after being mostly addressed as a medical issue at first. (Khan, 2014).

INTRODUCTION

Honor murders are a topic that requires study because to its connection to several cultures, including those in the Middle East and South Asia, where they are a prevalent practice. This study will exclusively address cases pertaining to honor in Pakistan. This paper is also connected with the status of women in Pakistan. Honor-related violence is common in several Pakistani provinces. In most situations, men are the ones who advocate homicide in their families to restore honor; women are rarely seen endorsing honor killings. This does not necessarily mean that men are violent and hostile toward women; rather, the perspectives of the outsiders are important because they provide the rationale for the fact that many men murder members of their own family. Furthermore, men's and sometimes women's own conscious and rationality vanish when they behave in a way that conforms to societal norms of what is considered "right." (Greiff, 2010) Rather, the lives of those who are accused of destroying their families' honor are determined by a profound and terrifying fear of "what will people say" whether they act in this manner or whether they choose not to. Furthermore, despite popular belief to the contrary, education has no bearing on honor-related violence, it is crucial to stress this. In reality, numerous case studies debunk this misconception by showing that even well educated, urban, high socio-economic class people have been observed murdering their families' female relatives to exact revenge. As a result, families in Pakistan end up ruining their relationships and taking the women's and, in rare instances, the men's haven off their shoulders because of the toxic mindset of "log kya kahenge," a term that is further explained in the following section. This ultimately leads to cold-blooded honor killings or lifelong exclusion from society (Muhammad, 2004). The terms used in this work are listed in the following section along with their definitions and context.

Honor killing was common among the Arab populace before the arrival of Islam. It is thought that Arab colonists who practiced burying young girls brought honor killing to the subcontinent.(Kali, 2002)In western countries, there are also other kinds of acid burning, rape with murder, forced marriages, and domestic abuse. (Chesler P., 2009). The United Nations reports reveal that customary rules, as opposed to national or international laws, have played a role in the rise in honor killings. Germany was cited as one of the examples (Oberwittler & Kasselt, 2010). Additional research confirms the honor killings that occur in Turkey and England. Suicide and accidents that occur at a high incidence may also be related to honor killings. However, Asian nations are more plagued by the pandemic. (Haybhay et al., 2013). The majority of violent crime reports, particularly those involving rape and murder, originate in Pakistan, India, and the Middle East. It is important to note that all faiths condemn honor killing as a socio-cultural evil, hence their teachings do not support it. (M. Hussain, 2006) The miserable situation of women in pre-Islamic times offers pitiful historical proof of this evil custom. (A. Elkayam, 2009). Islam freed women from this oppression, and the Holy Prophet (peace be upon him) taught his adherents to walk the path of righteousness by granting women respect so they might defend themselves against the flames of Hell (H. Moghissi, 2005).

"Karo Kari" is a term frequently used in Pakistan to substitute honor killing for adultery. ("Karo Kari" is a deliberate honor killing of black women and men who are referred to as adulterers and adulteresses, respectively). To protect the honor of one's family and tribe, it is customary to execute people who are guilty as "Karo" or "Kari." (Campbe, Roberts, and Lloyd, 2013) According to data gathered by international organizations, this region of the world has a high annual death rate of one thousand women, which is indicative of extreme male dominance. (Daily Times, 2014). The Human Rights Commission of Pakistan claims that in 2012, 970 women were allegedly killed solely out of pride. A study claims that marital problems, extramarital affairs, and several other similar conditions that arise from bad governance, a narrow historical view, and the cultural impact of men's dominating status are the main causes of women's deaths. (Jafri, A., 2008). These murders originated from the tribal traditions that are prevalent in Pakistan's rural areas, especially in the Sindh province. (Patel, S., & Gadit, A.M., 2008) in which family and tribal elders operate as a parallel system and oversee the right of honor over victim deaths in flagrant violation of state laws. (HRCP, 2013) The victim was accused of damaging the reputation of her family, despite the fact that her parents were aware of her husband's violent abuse of her during their marriage. Wade Y. (1999) Sarwar's mother pretended to agree with her daughter and went to the attorney's office to give the divorce paperwork. There, with the car driver's active help, she immediately got her daughter slain. (Rachel A., 2000) Similar to this, Mukhtaran Mai, a teacher, is reported to have been gangraped in front of numerous villages and made to walk home in her undies. (Marie D., 2003) The Mastoi tribe council decided to take retribution for her brother's alleged adulterous affair with a female member of their purportedly superior tribe, which led to the tragedy. Subsequently, it was revealed that the complaint side's claim against her brother was made up in order to support their own the legalization of the boy. Considering the sociocultural context in which numerous such severe events have been documented, the gender construct suggests that men belonging to the same tribe are exempt from consequences for engaging in sexual activities, while women are solely responsible for upholding the honor of the family. This synopsis and background information will aid in understanding the recent laws passed in Pakistan that aim to stop these abhorrent acts. It will also highlight the financial and cultural ramifications of the criminality against women who make their own independent decisions about marriage and who are violently tortured by male family members in order to silence them. A man is often considered as effeminate by his peers if he fails to take authoritative decision to restore his authority over the woman who transgressed their moral cultural code of conduct and only ensuing act of extreme violence involving honor killing towards women folk is deemed necessary to establish his masculinity. Many innocent girls become a victim of ruthless customs for rumours which clearly manifest the way the honor of a family or tribe is socially constructed. As Dr. Tahira Khan, a lecturer at Agha Khan University in Pakistan, correctly pointed out, women are also prevented from exercising their right to autonomous choice in marriage due to the financial interest and property interests of male family members. (T. Khan, 2019) Due to strong pressure from male family members, this culture also forbids widows and divorcees from entering into new marriages. If they do, they face violent treatment that could even put their lives in danger or result in the transfer of property to their male ancestors. Family behaviour is often well-calculated as a matter of inheritance chances in land-owning tribes. Refusing to wed someone chosen with such deliberation could occasionally even permanently deprive a daughter of her marriageable age. Sons are the heirs to the family line, therefore they usually have the choice to marry whoever they want, but regardless of education, race, social class, or religion, women are still considered their husbands' property. She occasionally loses the worth and right to her dowry after getting married because there have been cases where a husband killed his wife in the name of honor for getting married to someone else who would also bring fresh money. Now we talk about what is the means of honor killing in Pakistan.

Honor Killing in Pakistan

Across geographical boundaries, honor killing takes many different forms and is referred to by various names. "Karo-Kari" in Sindh State, "Siyah Kari" in Baluchistan regions "Kala Kali" in Southern Punjab, and "Tor Tora" along the Northwest Province's border are its various names. The implication is the same in all languages: men and women who are viewed as guilty of extramarital affairs or sexual misconduct by their family and community. Because there has always been news about women being killed for honor, Pakistan is regarded as one of the key nations when it comes to murdering for honor. In Pakistan, the practice of honor killing is widespread. Honor killing is essentially defined as assaults and other forms of violence or assault or domestic violence against women. In Pakistan, it is considered honor killing when a man kills a woman because of sexual or other concerns that they view as going against his moral and social standing. There are instances where a man's cultural customs praise an act of the murder of honor as a noble deed. Because men are typically driven to kill women in the name of honor by their cultural norms, there is a direct connection between killing for honor and cultural traditions. (Ali, R., 2001) Pakistan is one of the countries in the world with the strictest laws on honor killings. According to a Thomson Reuters survey, Pakistan ranks in the top five nations when it comes to honor killing. In Pakistan, there are a few socioeconomic groups that are accountable for honor killings in different situations. These psychological and social pressure groups play different roles in different places. The primary driver of honor killings in Pakistan is rooted in social and cultural customs. The males of the corresponding female are driven by custom to carry out the deed of honor killing; a person who kills his sister or daughter in the cause of honor killing is seen as extremely valiant.

According to Shirkat Gah's 2003 research, cultural traditions moved from one part of Pakistan to another. This article also explores the fact that honor killing is a major worry in the Sindhi city of Larkana. (Gah Shikat, 2003) Every day, there are more honor killings in Pakistan. According to Amnesty International, honor killing has grown to be a very severe issue for the entire world, not just one nation. Pakistan is one of the nations most impacted by honor killing. Many instances of honor killing go unreported because of societal and cultural norms. According to the information that is currently available, at least 183 women died in 1998, over 1000 in 1999, and 240 in the first half of 2000. In 2001, there were about a thousand cases of honor killing documented in the country. If strong action is not taken to halt it, it will only expand and become extremely dangerous for society. (Ahmed, K. 2000).

Unfortunately, women are not allowed to enjoy their basic rights equally, which has led them to fight for these rights, which are still unavailable to them in Pakistan. But the notion that a Muslim woman is weak is misplaced in the western world.

Prejudice against women in any form is forbidden by Islamic teachings. Pre-Islamic customs such as the slaughter of female infants was prohibited by Islam. The Quran's Divine precepts even forbid people from expressing their open or hidden disapproval upon the giving birth of a female child. The women of the period of Prophet Muhammad (PBUH) worked in trade, agriculture, animal husbandry, house sewing, and other activities. Islam likewise views men and women equally when it comes to punishing criminals. It is inevitable to conclude that forced marriage is invalid in Islam as the Islamic notion of marriage establishes concord and amicable relations among the couple, which are not conceivable if their voluntary consent to the nikah is overlooked. "Whoever has a daughter and avoids burying her alive, does not insult her, and does not favor his son than her, Allah is going to bring him into Paradise," said the Prophet Muhammad (PBUH). (Syed, Khalid Tanveer,2008) There is a grave misperception among certain Muslims and Westerners that honor killing is a component of Islam. It comes from the corrupted tales, such as the father (Abdel-Qader), who said he had no regrets about killing his daughter to have a connection with a boy, saying he did it for the honor of Islam. The accused's statement demonstrated his ignorance of Islam. He (Munoz, Gema Martin, 1993) The state alone has the authority to punish an individual only once all the elements of the offense have been proven according to the Islamic standard of proof. To protect women's virginity, false accusations that do not have the necessary testimony are punishable. Islamic teachings hold both men and women equally responsible for the same form of punishment at the time of the transgression; sadly, under perverted tribal customs, only women are often subjected to extrajudicial agony, in clear contravention of Islamic precepts. The Prophet Muhammad's (PBUH) divine precepts and teachings vehemently prohibit supporting violence against or committing murder of women. However, although having nothing to do with Islamic principles, the non-Islamic rites and cultural norms that are common throughout the distinct Muslim tribes have been incorrectly classified as Islamic.

Legal Views on Honor Killing

The Indian Penal Code's Section 304 (1) argument of unexpected and grave provocation allowed under British control upheld a long-standing hierarchical structure rooted in deeply ingrained customs. This legal clause served as a weapon to lessen the punishment for a heinous deed that deprived a woman of her life on the pretext of supposed adultery. (The State v. Muhammad Salih, 1965 SC 446) Similarly, a person's killing caused by an offender acting under grave and unforeseen provocation was not deemed to be a murder according to section 302 of the Pakistan Penal Code, 1860, which went into effect when Pakistan was created in 1947. This kind of plea was effectively used in numerous documented cases dating back to 1965. First, the ruling in the Federation of Pakistan v. Gul Hassan Khan case deemed this particular clause to be un-Islamic. (Pakistan v. Gul Hassan Khan 1989 SC 633)

The courts sustained their support of the argument of sudden, serious provocation up until the issuance of the aforementioned ruling (Warraich, 2005). Hudood Ordinance was enacted after the verdict in Gul Hassan's case, which regrettably made the atmosphere more friendly for honor. According to the decision made, the regulations of the Pakistan Penal Code concerning offenses against the human body were not properly followed in that regard. The other members of the woman's family would forgive her brother, son, or spouse if they were the ones who killed her. In a similar vein, wealthy individuals benefited from this enabling provision as well, as they were able to avoid criminal responsibility by making payments to the deceased's relatives. Once more, "Qatl-e-" shall not be subject to "Qisas," the perpetrator's direct descendant, is the victim, according to section 306 of the Penal Code. The court may, under certain circumstances, impose only and a maximum of a fourteen-year prison sentence. Due to the extensive ramifications of the Hudood Ordinance, a woman's murder became a totally private subject that was to be handled by the relevant family members. This fuelled the fire and increased the number of people killed in honor killings, with more women becoming victims of domestic abuse. The legal provisions of Qisas and Diyet, coupled with the historical and cultural practice of killing women based solely on suspicion, have greatly expanded the boundaries of impunity for those who commit crimes. As a result, women, who are frequently compelled to forgo marriage, divorce, or inheritance claims, are more vulnerable to becoming victims; additionally, a man or woman who is suspected of adultery or under suspicion may be assassinated without fear of the punishment for murder. Section 305 of the Criminal Law (Amendment) Act, 2004 was revised to forbid an accused person or a convicted person from acting as Wali in a murder case under the guise of karo kari siyahkare. Section 345 of the Code of Criminal Procedure was also amended to address compound-ability, and section 338-E was amended to include a proviso granting the court the power to set restrictions in exchange for cooperation from the parties. The Section 311 change also gave the court the authority to condemn a murdering honor defendant based on the "fisad-fil-"doctrine51, even in cases where the parties involved compounded the crime or waived "qisas.". It goes without saying that to effectively challenge structural reforms and give women who perceive a risk of assault in opposition to them easy access to safeguarding, the state must carry out its obligation to ensure the inquiry and prosecution of assault cases involving women with real responsibility and sincere intent.

To ensure that no one is exonerated of honor killing due to the cooperation of the investigating organization with the perpetrators for reasons of bribery or political pressure, the courts must carefully examine incriminating evidence from those cases. They must also take appropriate action to put an end to such a flagrant breach of fundamental human rights on their part. If not, the state's ability to discriminate against women will be severely undermined and forfeited because of its inability to uphold their freedom of life.

Fundamental Rights in Constitutional Law

In Pakistan, criminal laws are consistently employed to discriminate against women, despite the historical context of diverse verdicts about honor killings. Every person of Pakistan is entitled to equal protection under the constitution. In addition to allowing women to fully participate in all aspects of life, the constitution safeguards marriages, families, mothers, and kids, among other things. All Pakistani citizens are entitled to the fundamental rights outlined in the constitution, without exception (Gledhill, 1965).

Protection for laws designed to safeguard women and children is granted by Article 25 of the Pakistani Constitution. Women's interests, safety, and protection are given particular consideration. According to Article 8 of the Pakistani Constitution, any usage, custom, or law that possesses legal effect but is at odds with the fundamental rights protected by the constitution will be nullified to the extent of the disagreement. Every person of Pakistan is guaranteed security under Article 9 of the Constitution. Article 35 of the Constitution guarantees protection to the family, mother, and child, stating that the state bears the responsibility of ensuring their safety.

These are certain instances of Pakistani Constitutional Laws that provide women's rights particular consideration and essential safeguards, but which are otherwise negated by custom, particularly when it comes to the right for mitigation. Pakistani women suffer from the denial of their constitutionally guaranteed rights. Women in Pakistan have a systemic subordination to men that is impacted by customs across regions, classes, etc. The Qisas and Diyat Laws' clauses are typically applied to honor killings as a means of discriminating against women. Honor murders are permitted in the Tribal Judicial System as a means of suppressing women's constitutional rights (Alam, 2019).

In addition to violating women's constitutionally guaranteed rights, honor killings are against international law. Under these laws, state parties are required to exercise "Due Diligence" to ensure that such crimes are investigated, prevented, and the offenders are held accountable. Pakistan has responsibility for its failure to apply the concepts of due diligence, given its membership in the Convention on the Rights of the Child and the Women's Conventions (Raza, 2006).

Criminal Law Amendment Act 2004

A statute outlawing murders for honor and other crimes against honor was finally passed by the government in 2004 after years of community campaigning. The murder Honor Law, also known as the Criminal Law (Amendment) Act of 2004, brought about several modifications to the Criminal Code of Procedure 1898 (CrPC) and the Pakistan Penal Code 1860 (PPC). Qatl-i-amd, or willful murder committed under the guise of honor, was added to the existing laws as the primary modification. It is crucial to remember that despite intense lobbying and cooperation with lawmakers, the Act did not include many of the crucial amendments that civil society had desired. Below is a summary of the law's main modifications.

Amendment as per the Criminal Act Law (Criminal Law Amendment Act 2004)

Phrase "offence committed in the name or on the pretext of honor means an offence committed in the name or on the pretext of karo kari, siyahkari, or similar other customs or practices" is the most significant addition to the definition of honor crimes. It permits family members to murder both men and women under the false pretense that they have brought dishonor to the family. Murder killings carried out in the interest of, or under an excuse of, honor, the judiciary's power to decide which instances the qisas penalty was inappropriate due to Islamic prohibitions has been removed. Additionally, it makes it impossible for the killer to have been the wali, or parent, and allows the State to take on that responsibility should it become necessary; From 14 to 25 years in imprisonment is now the maximum sentence. Penalties have been imposed on the giving of women as badl-i-sulah (for marriages or otherwise as recompense for a transgression done). In cases of honor crimes, the court has the authority to punish the offender who has given up or compounded their right to qisas, and they are able to impose a minimum 10-year sentence if fasad-fil-ard, or confusion or disorder in society, results from any Wali waiving or compounding their claim to qisas. Additionally, minimum punishments are imposed for several linked offenses. When there is harm and qisas cannot be carried out, Tazir may be ordered in along with Arsh (compensation for harm) by the court), particularly if the offense is one of honor. A system has been established for cases of honor crimes in which the heirs opt to waive or compound the offense; under these circumstances, the court may impose requirements based on the specific details and circumstances of the case. Modifications to procedure have also been made to the CrPC; for example, higher ranking police officials will now be tasked with looking into honor crimes and misdemeanors related to extramarital sex relationships (zina).It makes clear that, as stated in the PPC above, the court must authorize any waiver or compounding of the offense. Additionally, it eliminates the province governments' ability to commute or postpone any punishment for crimes of honor.

Standing of Women in Pakistan

In Pakistan, women's position is not uniform across classes, regions, or rural/urban divides; rather, it is heavily influenced by cultural traditions and values. Nonetheless, certain generalizations can be established, bearing in consideration their outcomes differ depending on the aforementioned factors. It is believed that men are superior to women. Women are viewed as burdens from birth, and their worth is determined by how many children they can have and how much sex they can have. It is believed that men are superior to women. From the moment of her birth, women are viewed as burdens, and their worth is determined by how many children they can have and how satisfying a sexual experience they can have. (Mumtaz, 1987)

Women are not allowed to be who they are. They are always regarded and acknowledged as moms, sisters, and daughters — never as distinct individuals. Women are viewed as mere commodities, departing from her father's house and entering her husband's. It is believed that men are superior to women. To guarantee that it is delivered to its receiver in optimal condition, this commodity needs to be safeguarded. As a result, male in a household limit the space available to the female. To make sure they don't embarrass the family, limitations are imposed on their behaviour, movements, and activities. This, combined with the idea of purdah (veiling), that is ostensibly intended to give women protection and respectability but is actually a deceptive tactic used for control, causes women to internalize the idea that their own behaviour is important and fragile, and that their status is insecure. Another very important factor in this situation is the idea that women bear men's honor, however, this will be covered in more detail later in the report. Because of this widespread prejudice, female's conduct is observed not only by the males in their families but also by the entire community, who criticize her for any actions deemed to be inappropriate. In Pakistan, one of the organizational tenets is gender. The patriarchal ideals embedded in local customs and culture define the social meaning of gender. The sexual division of labour has resulted in a split: the male is the earner and the woman is the caregiver and reproductive member of the household. This has further led to both the government and the family investing few resources in female as a group. Women suffer immensely as a result of this poor investment in resources, whether it is in terms of a short lifespan, lack of education, etc. In addition to their legal rights and fundamental human rights, women typically lack knowledge of the systems, procedures, and other tools available to them for their own advantage. Furthermore, even though a lot of women labour in fields like agriculture and farming, particularly in rural areas, their contributions are not only underappreciated but also denied access to

administrative and decision-making roles as well as monetary compensation. In addition to their legal rights and fundamental human rights, women typically lack knowledge of the systems, procedures, and other tools available to them for their own advantage. Furthermore, even though a lot of women labour in fields like agriculture and farming, particularly in rural areas, their contributions are not only underappreciated but also denied access to administrative and decision-making roles as well as monetary compensation. Women also work at home and for piece rates, but these jobs are not recognized or documented since they are not regarded as part of the labour force. Since the money they receive is not seen as their "own," it is typically collected by the male family member or utilized to sustain the family, most women do not benefit financially from their labour. Restrictions on women functioning outside the home also affect a significant portion of the female population, which has an immediate impact on women's economic independence. They feel that they have no options without financial support, therefore their complete reliance on men for money support further restricts their freedom of choice. This, together with limitations on women's mobility, leaves them completely dependent on men.

How 'Zia' Effect Discrimination Against Women

As was previously said, women in Pakistani society are viewed as inferior to men. They are supposed to take over the caring responsibilities of the mother, who is primarily valued for her capacity to bear children. These strong patriarchal beliefs are well engrained in Pakistani traditional society. But during the presidency of General Zia ul Haq, these views were widely accepted by the government. These views have long been held, but the State now backs them up with institutions, laws, and regulations. These rules propagated and strengthened patriarchal attitudes across society, sending the message that they were correct and that treating women in this way was normal. The subsequent impunity expanded to include how society treats women in particular contributed to the ingraining of these ideas into Pakistani society's consciousness, with enduring consequences manifested in various forms, such as aggression against female and the mistreatment of female by the court system. We'll discuss the State's implemented tactics—which are motivated by the state's prejudice against women—a little later. Pakistani women did not even realize until recently that they were fighting against a patriarchal system, as Shaheed and Mumtaz pointed out. These women had contributed to the calls for more rights and concessions from inside the current system because they believed that achieving their own privileges was a matter of natural evolution. Until the Islamization era of General Zia ul Haq's reign, when women became aware of the rights and privileges being taken away from them nationwide, Pakistani women had never asked what percentage of their rights had been granted in theory compared to those that had actually been granted to the majority of women. Even though there was a lack of active promotion of female's issues and advancement of the women's agenda prior to the Zia era, Pakistani women were still a significant presence, despite their small numbers, in various aspects of Pakistani life such as politics, sports, labour, the arts, and the labour movement. Making Pakistani women invisible was one of the worst effects of the Zia regime. Mumtaz and Shaheed have detailed the methodical efforts undertaken by Zia-ul-Haq and his Government to keep women out of the public eye and to uphold the stereotype of the modest, chaste woman. This approach involved a series of state-level legislation that essentially outlined the duties and behaviours that women were expected to play. The system worked to make women's positions insecure, subservient, and inferior to men's by enforcing discrimination through administrative tasks and legal means.

This led to a social shift in Pakistan, making women especially vulnerable in society and permitting the underlying patriarchal aspect to grow unhindered. The chador was enforced for all female government servants as well as women and girls attending educational institutions from the beginning of the campaign. The government then launched a second campaign against pornography and obscenity, which is not inherently problematic. The campaign demanded that women only appear in commercial commercials that are relevant to women, so equating women with obscenity per se. The government then went on to maintain a particular stereotype of women in the media, portraying them as housewives and caregivers; women could only be seen in fully covered clothing, and even then, Women were only permitted to appear on television for a quarter of the advert during Ramadan. Newspapers also prohibited the publication of images of female movie stars, debated the topics of modesty and obscenity, and generally associated women with immorality, corruption, and obscenity. Women had incited these attacks by their words, deeds, or simply by being there, whether they were sexually assaulted, killed, or harassed at home or on the streets. Television shows began portraying women as the corrupting force; they portrayed working women as the reason behind moral lapses and the breakdown of social norms and the family. From government-run media and official advertising, it seemed like eliminating women from society altogether was the only way to slow down the rapidly declining state of civilization. Proposals to establish women-only universities persisted because coeducation was considered "un-Islamic."

The result was that women were being forced to leave other coeducational schools and were advised to attend "their own" institutions, where, it should be noted, the standard of instruction was equally poorer. In addition to being excluded from the sports arena, women were also segregated in school. Women athletes were originally scheduled to compete in international sporting events; however, training camps were cancelled. Then, effectively excluding all men, the Federal Minister for Sports and Culture ruled that Women were not allowed to play sport in the presence of na-mehram, or all men, unless they were blood related. Women were only allowed to play in front of women. Consequently, women were permitted to play in isolated compounds and against foreign teams in the nation under Islamic rules, but they were not permitted to take part in competitions organized elsewhere. In a further attempt to keep women apart, official coeducational social events were outlawed, women were not allowed to be promoted or hired by national banks, single Foreign Office women were not allowed to be posted overseas, and women were not allowed to apply for scholarships overseas. Simultaneously, the legal status of women was gradually being diminished, so formalizing their subordinate role in society. Examples of this include the Hudood Ordinances of 1979, the Law of Evidence, and the Qisas and Diyat Ordinances. Women's legal standing has been gradually eroded over time due to the implementation of discriminatory and anti-women policies, even in the case of gender-neutral laws intended to protect them. Society was clearly negatively impacted psychologically by all of this. It made women fearful of the consequences of their actions and filled them with insecurities about their identities and standing. The men's response reinforced this, as the climate favoured the more conservative facets of society, enabling them to exploit the circumstances to publicly forward their own objectives. In terms of women's clothing, this situation produced a culture in the nation where all men were considered the arbiters of women's modesty and social standing. Additionally, the environment gave men the power to judge what behaviour is proper or unsuitable for women. It put women in a position of such weakness and insecurity that men could treat them in any way they pleased, harass, condemn, or even hurt them physically. As a result, women would receive little to no support from the government or the community, allowing men to treat women however they pleased.

CASE STUDY IN PAKISTAN WITH REGARDS TO WOMEN STANDINGS

Muhammad Ameer v. The State 2006 PLD 283

Supreme Court

According to Justice Muhammad Nawaz Abbasi, "[t]he authorize of a criminal act due to ghairat or familial reverence must be separated from the grave and unexpected provocations in the wake to which crime occurred in the light of the specifics and circumstances of each case," in the first case made public after the 2004 statute. He points out that the accused may not be able to claim the defense of severe and unexpected provocation if the crime was committed with premeditation. He makes the point that if the offense was done with premeditation, the accused might not be able to employ the defense of grave and sudden provocation.

Muhammad Arshad v. The State, 2006 SCMR 89

Later that year, Judge Abbasi provided additional clarification on this issue when she declared, "it is correct that in our Society, the illicit collaborating of a female of a family member is not allowed but simply being unsure of such relations can't serve as an excuse for carrying out murder and claim minimizing circumstance for lesser punishment." The court determined that the accused's actions in this case were "neither significant nor sudden," hence the sentence mitigation was useless.

Abdul Jabbar v. The State 2007 SCMR 1496

Justice Tassaduq Hussain Jillani further clarified the defense of "grave and sudden provocation" in Pakistani law in the case of *Abdul Jabbar v. The State* (2007). The case involved the murder of a young woman by her brothers and cousin after she refused to obtain her family's approval before marrying. The High Court reduced their death sentences, arguing that in Pakistani society, it is generally unacceptable for a woman to marry without her family's consent, and that the sight of the woman's husband had triggered a "grave and sudden provocation." However, the Supreme Court, under Justice Jillani, overturned the High Court's decision to lessen the sentence.

Mohib Ali v. The State 1985 SCMR 2055

Judge Jillani of the court upheld Justice Abbasi's previous ruling, saying that a valid claim of grave and unexpected provocation requires more than just suspicion. Justice Jillani cited prior rulings in Pakistani legal precedent, saying that: *" A simple charge of moral irresponsibility without any solid proof to support it wouldn't qualify as a serious and abrupt provocation. Should such pleas be granted without any supporting proof, it would allow people to murder innocent people.*

Zahir and another v. The State 2000 SCMR 406

He also brought up the ruling in a 2000 case of killing committed in the name of honor, in which the Supreme Court made the following particular observation: *Before we separate, let me to add that, generally speaking, not all cases of severe and abrupt provocation would be covered by section 302(c). This is especially true of Qatl-i-Amd, which refers to the abuse of a wife, sister, or other close female relative by a man on Siahkari's accusation.*

Muhammad Zaman v. The State P L D 2009 Supreme Court 49

The Supreme Court has also set a standard in murder cases where the offender may be eligible for a sentence pardon if he can show that he was *"deprived of that you're able of self-control or pulled away by conditions shortly before the act of assassination or there was a rapid occurrence leading to grave provocation."*. A cursory examination of these Supreme Court cases shows that the notion of quick and severe provocation is acceptable in mitigating circumstances. There is a great deal of leeway for the judge's discretion even if certain rulings have unequivocally established that the mere suspicion of premeditation or suspicion of suspicion will preclude the possibility of accepting this plea. It is well-known that this plead is still permissible in cases as long as there is evidence that this "honor" was broken and the conduct was carried out in a fit of rage.

Lord Goddard in Kumarasinghege Don John Perera (1935) A.C. 200

One of Justice Jilani's rulings in the Abdul Jabbar case cites an instance in which the use of the provoke defense is permissible, such as in situations where the offender was on *"discovering his wife in an adulterous act... murders her or her paramour, and the court has traditionally seen that as just manslaughter due to the provocation received, even though it was an intentional crime."*

Bashir v. The State, 2006 PCRLG 1945

The Lahore High Court issued a resounding condemnation of honor killings. The court acknowledged that the allegation of ghairatí as a mitigating element was not plausible, as grave and it was not accepted as a valid ground to suspect an unlawful relationship when unexpected provocation occurred. But the court continued by saying that, *"The practice of "honor killing," which amounted to murder (Qatl-i-Amd) simpliciter and violated the fundamental rights guaranteed by Articles 8(I) and 9 of the Constitution, was not permitted by either national law or religious doctrine.*

Certain Famous Cases (Examples)

At the beginning of June, Saba Maqsood, who was trying to marry the man of her choice despite her family's desires, miraculously survived being shot by relatives and thrown into a canal in a new tab near Hafizabad town in Punjab province, Pakistan.

Up to twenty relatives including her father, viciously beat Farzana Iqbal to death in Lahore a week earlier for marrying the man she loved with bricksopens in a new tab. Sadly, "honor" killings of hundreds of women and girls occur in Pakistan each year.

But because most cases like this take place in small areas or behind closed doors, neither the public nor the police pay much attention to them. For instance, in February, Ayat Bibi was executed by bludgeoning in a village in north Balochistan on the orders of a local priest. This occurred when a male relative accused Ayat Bibi of having an affair with Daraz Khan, who was also slain. The final resting locations of Daraz and Ayat are both unmarked graves. There is still no justice served for those who killed the people.

The year 2015 saw the release of a documentary on Saba Qaiser, a Pakistani woman from Punjab whose family opposed her marriage to him due to his "lowly status." Her father and uncle assaulted her, shot her in the head, put her body in a sack, and tossed the sack into a river as retaliation for her elopement (Obaid-Chinoy, Sharmeen, 2018).

On July 14, 2008, honor killings took place in Baba Kot, Balochistan. Balochistani tribesmen from the Umrani Tribe killed five women. The five victims—two middle-aged women and three teenagers—were shot, beaten, kidnapped, and buried alive because they refused to follow the tribe leader's marriage recommendations and preferred to wed the men of their choosing (Waraich, Omar, 2008).

CONCLUSION

In Pakistan, society and the law both systematically discriminate against women. However, the community and law enforcement agencies treat the lady killer with leniency in the interest of so-called honor. This abuse is encouraged by law enforcement and other groups to maintain patriarchal dominance over men in society. The defense of "grave and sudden provocation" is occasionally allowed by Pakistani courts in cases involving honor killings, although this defense was removed from the statute in 1990. By passing laws, the judiciary and law enforcement strive to normalize "honor killings" in society that do not apply in cases of purported "honor killings. "The idea of patriarchy is deeply ingrained in Pakistani society's family system, which gives fathers and brothers the power to forcefully marry their daughters or sisters. Girls and women are killed in the name of honor when the patriarchal monarch feels he has lost control over them or is about to lose it. Honor killing is a grave violation of the teachings of the Prophet Muhammad (PBUH) and the commandments given in the Holy Book of the Quran. The abuse is closely related to this patriarchy because men—fathers, brothers, sons, and other family members—usually kill women. With respect to crimes that include "honor killing," the courts have reached differing conclusions. Nonetheless, the ruling in Muhammad Akram Khan v. The State (Warraich 2005) by the Supreme Court of Pakistan is encouraging. This declared that "honor killing" was murder and prohibited anyone from using the legal system to murder women under the guise of "honor defilement." Finally, a few examples will wrap up this chapter.

REFERENCES

Ahmed, K. (2000). Human Rights in Pakistan remain as bad as they were in past. *Lancet*, 355, 1083–1083.

Ali, R. (2001). *The Dark side of „Honor": Women victims in Pakistan*. Shirkat Gah.

Amnesty International. 1999. Pakistan: Violence against women in the name of honor. Available from https://www.amnesty.org/en/library/asset

Chesler, P. (2009). Are Honor Killings Simply Domestic Violence?*Middle East Quarterly*, 16(2), 61–69.

Chesler, P., & Bloom, N. (2012). Hindu vs. Muslim honor killings. *Middle East Quarterly*.

Elkayam A. (200), *The Quran and Biblical Origins*, Xlibris Corporation

Greiff, S. (2010). *No Justice in Justifications: Violence against Women in the Name of Culture*. Religion and Tradition.

Haybhay, S., Patwe, D., and Jawale, P. (2013). *Honor killing: Killing the honor of humanity?* SASCV 2013 Proceedings

HRCP. (2013), *State of human rights in 2012*, Retrieved from https://hrcp-web.org/hrcpweb/wp-content/pdf/AR2012.pdf

Hussain, M. (2006). Take my Riches, Give me Justice: A Contextual Analysis of Pakistan's Honor Crimes Legislation. *Harvard Journal of Law & Gender*.

Jafri, A. (2008). *Honor Killing: Dilemma, Ritual, Understanding*. Oxford University Press.

Kali, K. (2002), *Karo Kari TorTora, Siyahkari, Kala Kali. November 2001*.

Marie, D. (2003). Castetter, Note, Taking Law into Their Own Hands: Unofªcial and Illegal Sanctions by the Pakistani Tribal Councils, 13 Ind. Int"l & Comp. *Law Review*, 543, 544–545.

Moghissi, H. (2005). *Women and Islam: Images and Realities*. Taylor & Francis.

Muhammad, M. H. (2004, November). Ghairat kay Naam par qatal ki saza (The punishment of Honor killing). *Monthly Mohaddith*, 36(11), 26–68.

Munoz, Gema Martin. (1993). "Patriarchy and Islam." Universidad Autónoma de Madrid Federation of Pakistan v. Gul Hassan Khan (PLD 1989 SC 633)

Oberwittler, D., & Kasselt, J. (2010). *Honor Killings in Germany, 1996-2005, A Study based on Prosecution Files*. Max-Planck Institute.

Patel, S., & Gadit, A. M. (2008). Karo-Kari: A Form of Honor Killing in Pakistan. *Transcultural Psychiatry*, 45(4), 683–694. DOI: 10.1177/1363461508100790 PMID: 19091732

Rachel, A. (2000). Ruane, Comment, *Murder in the Name of Honor: Violence Against Women in Jordan and Pakistan*, 14 Emory Int"l L. *Rev.*, 1523, 1533.

Roberts, K., Campbell, G., & Lloyd, G. (2013), *Honor-Based Violence: Policing and Prevention*, CRC Press. Tahir Khan, *Honor Killings: A Dentitional and Contextual Overview*, http://usconsulate- istanbul.org.tr/reppub/vawo/tkhan.html

Sohail Akbar Warraich. (2005). *Honor Killings and the Law in Pakistan"; and Sara Hussain, „Honor Crimes: Paradigms, and violence against Women*. Zed Books.

Yolanda Asamoah-Wade, *Women's Human Rights and "Honor Killings" in Islamic Cultures*, 8 Buff. Women"s L.J. 21, 21–22 (1999).

Chapter 21
Honor Killing in International Law:
A Critical Study of Honor-Based Violence Under UNCEDAW

Bhavana Tushar Kadu
MIT-Art Design and Technology University, India

Aayushi Singh
Amity Law School, Amity University, Noida, India

Aditya Tomer
https://orcid.org/0000-0002-6398-2617
Amity Law School, Amity University, Noida, India

ABSTRACT

The concept of 'honor' is intertwined with the conscious of any civilisation, act of any family member or an individual who is a part of the society can have a cascading effect on the other members. This 'honor' is threatened or is diminished when a girl marries outside her community or religion which leads to her subsequent murder. The United Nations General Assembly adopted the "United Nations Convention on the Elimination of all Forms of Discrimination against Women" (UNCEDAW). It was brought in on 3rd September, 1981 and ratified by 189 nation States. India was among the first of countries to having signed and ratified the convention. The various provisions of the UNCEDAW highlight the menace of homicide committed for saving the "honor" of the family, which in most of the cases is associated with the social status of a family in the society. This paper attempts to analyse the status of Honor Based Violence as defined under UNCEDAW.

DOI: 10.4018/979-8-3693-9596-7.ch021

Copyright © 2025, IGI Global. Copying or distributing in print or electronic forms without written permission of IGI Global is prohibited.

INTRODUCTION

Honor Killing can be defined as the execution of a family member especially a female relative in retaliation for the member being accused of 'dishonoring' the family because of her marriage with a person of different caste, race or religion. This practice is prevalent in many societies which are governed through their cultures and faiths. Although honor killing is believed to be akin to murder but it is more heinous because of the arbitrary reason being attributed to such violence committed for preserving family reputation. There are certain characteristics which differentiate the act of 'honor killing' with murder. Honor Killing is homicide of a person which is committed by very close family members of the victim, at times the offenders are brothers or fathers of the victim. The tragedy lies in the very fact that the very people who were supposed to be protectors of the victim themselves become the perpetrators of a gruesome crime committed against the female member. The members from the extended family and others from the community are also active participants in these executions.

Discrimination against women, anywhere in the world leads to violation of universal principles of equality, liberty, and freedom. It is for these very rights being granted to women that the world has fought since ages. The question of equal opportunities for women in every sphere of life be it personal or professional is raging throughout the world. It is a known fact that the development and prosperity of any society viz-a-viz a nation lies in the emancipation and empowerment of women.

It was in the wake of safeguarding these principles and protecting the lives of women across the globe that the UNGA passed the "Convention on the Elimination of All Forms of Discrimination Against Women". The ratification by the twentieth State led to it becoming a law on the 3rd of September 1982. The main aim of this International Legislation was to assure women of their human rights and address discrimination of all forms which hinder the progress of women in the society. The Convention is based on the core principles which govern the working of the UN such as individual rights, freedom, dignity and gender equality.

Background

Honor killing is homicide of a female committed by family members based on an ill-conceived idea of dishonoring the family and violating the 'honor code'. These killings are a result of deeply entrenched patriarchal norms that prioritize honor of a family or group. Honor killings are prevalent around the world and are not restricted to any physical or cultural boundaries. Honor based violence though is practiced around the world, but it is more common in countries like South Asia, Middle East, and North Africa.

Honor killings are addressed at the global stage by various international law through several human rights statutes, such as the International Covenant on Civil and Political Rights (ICCPR), the "Convention on the Elimination of All Forms of Discrimination Against Women" (CEDAW), and the "Universal Declaration of Human Rights" (UDHR). Under these laws States are duty bound to prevent, control and penalize acts of violence which are specifically directed towards womenfolk in the name of honor and customs. These statutes also mandate the protection of women's right to freedom and liberty. It is these embedded patriarchal norms, insufficient legal frameworks, and cultural resistance in both the developing and the developed nations that these laws couldn't resist are proving to be a failure in preventing honor killing.

The prevalence of violence against women based on 'honor' can be attributed to the unwillingness of some states to wholly implement international treaties, then there are various cultural justifications that subvert legal process. Then there is a lack of knowledge or instruction regarding women's rights which obstructs the resolution of such heinous honor killings under international law. The solution lies in introducing stronger legislative frameworks, improved international collaborations, and getting rid of outdated cultural norms through community involvement and education are all necessary and effective tactics in dealing with gender-based violence and ensuring a better life for the future generations.

This chapter's main aim is to understand the connection between honor killing and international law. The first part of the chapter it discusses about honor killing and tries to cover various definitions of this type of violence. It also seeks to answer certain questions like how do international legal frameworks address honor killings, and what are their limitations? Then the chapter seeks to analyze the effect of cultural and societal factors that leads to perpetuation of honor killings around the globe despite implementation of international obligations. Then further in the Chapter the focus is on the "UNCEDAW" in the second part and strives to determine its effectiveness in dealing with the issue of honor killing throughout the chapter. The chapter discusses various provisions, recommendations and state obligations under the statute. The chapter also addresses the shortcomings of the convention in curbing this brutal violence in the name of 'honor' and also gives solutions of making the law more effective in dealing with this menace. Then towards the conclusion which is third and the final part of the chapter the significant role of civil society, NGOs, law enforcement agencies and the role these agents play in making the population more aware about this crime.

Research Methodology

The research methodology for this chapter on honor killings and UNCEDAW employs a qualitative approach, including a comprehensive literature review on honor killings, international human rights law, and gender-based violence. The methodology involves a qualitative approach, utilizing document analysis to explore honor killings and UNCEDAW's impact. Data was collected from UN Reports and other International Organizations' Reports like the European Union, ICCPCR etc. Thematic analysis helped achieve identification of key patterns and helped highlight various cultural nuances, ethics and various traditions. This methodology aims to evaluate the effectiveness of UNCEDAW in combating honor killings globally.

Selecting the right journals and carefully conducting inclusion/exclusion and article research is essential for a Research Paper on Honor Killings and UNCEDAW. The journal selection process focused on publications specializing in human rights, gender studies, international law, and related interdisciplinary fields. The author opted for journals like *Human Rights Quarterly*, *Gender & Society*, and *International Journal of Law, Crime and Justice* etc. which aligns with the subject matter and provides a platform for scholarly discussions on these topics. Then the authors relied on primary sources like the *UNCEDAW Convention, Resolutions of the UNGA, UN Reports, European Union Reports, UDHR and comments from the ICCPR Human Rights Committee* etc.

Inclusion criteria emphasized relevance, ensuring that only articles directly addressing honor killings, UNCEDAW, or associated legal and cultural issues like International Human Rights are considered. Recent publications, preferably within the last decade, were prioritized which led to the incorporation of current perspectives and data. Peer-reviewed articles and government and recognized NGOs reports formed the core of our research to maintain academic rigor.

Exclusion criteria filtered out non-academic sources, such as blogs or opinion pieces, and articles with only tangential relevance to the topic. The authors conducted article research using academic databases like JSTOR, PubMed, and Google Scholar is crucial, employing targeted keywords such as "Honor Killing," (UN Women, n.d.) "UNCEDAW," (United Nations Convention on Elimination of All Forms of Discrimination Against Women, 1979, United Nations General Assembly, 1979, n.d.) "Gender-Based Violence," (European Union, n.d.) etc. to identify the most pertinent studies for our paper. Non-Peer Reviewed research articles were excluded for better research and coverage of relevant topics. Similarly, non-credible online sources and news articles were excluded to avoid any discrepancies.

Key Terms

Core terms include "Honor Killing" (UN Women, n.d.) and "UNCEDAW," (Convention on Elimination of All Forms of Discrimination Against Women, 1979) directly linking the subject matter to the international framework for women's rights. Broader themes like "Gender-Based Violence," (European Union, n.d.) "Women's Rights," (UN Women, n.d.) and "Cultural Practices"(UN Women, n.d.) contextualize the issue. Legal and policy-related terms such as "International Human Rights Law" (UDHR, 1948, Article 2, (General Assembly Resolution 217 A) United Nations General Assembly, 1948 (UN), n.d.) and "Policy Implementation" (*Lansstyrelsen Stockholm*, n.d.) connect to the practical applications of UNCEDAW. Analytical perspectives like "Intersectionality" (Supervisor & Appelqvist, 2008) and "Comparative Analysis" (Supervisor & Appelqvist, 2008) allow for exploring the complexities of honor killings across different cultural and legal contexts.

Supervisor, L. E et. al, (2008), Byrnes, A and UN Women we used these articles, to select keywords to choose relevant articles from multiple online sources, for example, 'Library of Congress, Research Gate, Google Books, Springer, JSTOR, Sage, IJSSHR, Scopus, Web of Science, Taylor & Francis and Google Scholar'.

Literature Review

Honor killings are like domestic abuse where the victim is a female member and the perpetrators inflicting violence on the woman are her own family members. In a majority of cases related to honor killing the victim is accused of indulging in activities, losing her virginity this jeopardize the family honor by violating the moral code of conduct. (UN Women, n.d.)

Though honor killing hasn't been defined anywhere around the world but legal experts, scholars, academicians have strived hard to define the various nuances of this heinous crime. The Black Law Dictionary describes it as "a crime committed with a desire of injuring an individual who the perpetrators believed to have compromised on their status in the society" (Bryan A. Garner (Ed), 2009)

Honor Killing is prevalent around the globe, and it is not restricted to the global north but is very much prevalent in the global south. The killings are an everyday phenomenon in the middle eastern countries. As has been reported by many journalists this practice is way too common where the female member is accused of bringing disrepute to the family because of her getting into a relation with a man who is termed as an 'outsider' i.e. one who doesn't belong to their community, class etc. To quote Journalist Noor Alamki "If they find out that the daughter is doing something that could harm the family reputation, their only remaining alternative is to kill her". (Noor Alamki, n.d.)

The UDHR and other legislation governing International Human Rights address the issue of honor-based violence as gender neutral issues. These statutes govern an individual's interaction with the state and society at large under the realm of human rights. (Article 2, United Nations General Assembly Resolution 217 A, 1948) United Nations General Assembly (UN), n.d.). Though these International Statutes address issues related to violence against a specific gender and seeks to curb the same, but still it was necessary with passage of time that there must be a legislation to safeguard women rights, with an aim to prevent violence against women around the globe. This led to the UN General Assembly adopting the "UNCEDAW" on December 18, 1979. It was recognized at the global level on 3rd of September 1981 as post ratification by the twentieth nation. By the time it was celebrating its 10th Birth Anniversary in the year 1989, one hundred nations had ratified the agreement (United Nations Convention on Elimination of All Forms of Discrimination Against Women, 1979, United Nations General Assembly, 1979)

It is very important to realize that just ratifying these conventions and statutes and incorporating them in domestic legislations won't solve the problem at the grass-root level. It is necessary to increase public awareness through awareness-raising initiatives which is a crucial part of any policy meant to strengthen the capacity to address ending violence against women. (European Union)

Future Research Directions

This research is an attempt by the authors condemning honor-based violence, they view this wrong as a grave violation of human rights and also highlight ingrained patriarchy leading to such violence against females. They support the UNCEDAW as an important legislation safeguarding women's rights around the world and combating cultural practices that perpetuate gender-based violence. There were some parameters based on which this research was conducted starting with defining the crime of honor killing, followed by introducing the readers to global incidents and efforts aiming to prevent these incidents. The authors in this chapter have critically analyzed the specific articles of the aforesaid convention. They further discuss the general recommendations of the UN General Assembly. There are research studies/guides on this topic highlighting the various aspects of UNCEDAW and gender-based violence (OHCHR; UN Women). But through this chapter the authors have worked upon breaking down the articles and highlighting the ways through which these articles and recommendations, address this poignant issue. Further the State obligations under UNCEDAW are discussed. The paper concludes with the authors sharing future perspectives on UNCEDAW and Honor Killing. The main aim of the research is to focus on the specific articles that address this issue of honor killing and highlight the role played by CEDAW in eliminating discrimination faced by women. It also addresses it shortcomings and suggests amendments for better redressal.

In future research on UNCEDAW and honor killings, a multi-faceted study is crucial to deepen understanding and enhance global efforts to combat this issue and eradicate this practice from all spheres of life. This chapter highlights the incidents of honor killing around the globe and briefly discusses the role played by international law in addressing this menace. But the study was restricted to UNCEDAW and its effectiveness in dealing with gender-specific violence.

Further, intersectionality of factors such as religion, culture, and socioeconomic status need to be explored further along with its effect in perpetuating honor killings. This will provide a nuanced understanding of the barriers to effective intervention. There have been studies on these lines but those lacked the legal analysis or were restricted to domestic law (Swedish Women's Lobby). Through this research the authors have strived hard to define Honor Killing and have brought focus on factors leading to such violence, but the research was more focused on the legal aspects further narrowing it down to UNCEDAW. A deep study of the factors mentioned above along with perspectives on the legal front will aid in tackling this global menace.

One more potential area of study is the comparative analysis of how different countries, that have ratified UNCEDAW deal with honor killing and how these nations legal systems have evolved to address the issue. Research on these lines can highlight the best relevant practices and identify areas where the convention's implementation is weak or inconsistent.

Another area for future research is the role played by International Organizations in dealing with the heinous crime of honor killing. This chapter highlights the role played by the United Nations and its various committees who are working hard to improve legislation on this issue and ensure better implementation. Specific research focused on each of the UN bodies would lead to priceless additions in this area of research. For future research examining the effectiveness of UNCEDAW's monitoring mechanisms and the impact of global campaigns on local practices is highly recommended by the authors.

DEFINING HONOR KILLING

Honor Killings can be compared to violence committed within the family in which the victim is a female member as she is blamed for having destroyed the honor of the family by having been involved in activities which compromise her chastity. (UN Women, n.d.) The killings are generally committed by male members which can even include members from the extended family. It is the firm belief of such perpetrators and other male members of the society that women are responsible for tarnishing the reputation of the family and therefore should be executed. Though the victims are largely females but at times the victim can also be a male. Honor Killings violate the very core of human rights.

Honor killings have been prevalent in societies since ages. They have been part of people's lives since a millennium. It seems as if men believe it to be their right to commit violence against women and launch an attack on women in the name of honor which is open to interpretations by everyone.

Honor Killing at times is also defined as "customary killing" or "domestic public violence". The Black Law's Dictionary defines Honor Killing as "A crime driven by the passion of harming a person who the accused believes have caused injury to his reputation in the society".(Bryan A. Garner (Ed), 2009) Scholars have failed in attributing a legal definition to the crime of honor killing. Similarly various human rights organizations, academicians have failed in their endeavour of defining honor-based violence. The idea of honor killing is a nuanced one, and therefore these killings are sometimes referred to by their definitional variants like honor - based violence, honor crimes, and violence based on honor codes". (Supervisor & Appelqvist, 2008)

Incidents of Honor Killing Around the Globe

The world over women have been victims of "honor -based violence", in most of the cases leading to murder of the victim, the perpetrators are male members known to the victim. The commission of "honor -based killing" is mainly attributed to family honor. If the family finds out that the girl is indulging in such activities which can tarnish the family reputation, then the only solution left to preserve it is the murder of the girl. (Noor Alamki, n.d.) The so-called idea of "honor" which is associated with women members of a family, seeks to establish an identity for women, where she is seen no less than a commodity. It can further be elaborated as women being subordinate to men without being granted any freedom of her choice. Population around the world associate honor killing with the reputation of the family and their standing in the community.

Violence perpetrated against women and the reason attributed is that the individual was preserving honor is a grave human rights violation prevalent across the world. Honor based violence is more heinous in nature because it targets a specific gender and perpetrates violence against them. This is a global phenomenon because honor killing is not only common in developing but developed countries as well. All the nations from the global north have reported incidents of violence with respect to honor. Some developed nations also blame it on the rise of immigration in their countries. But there have been reports and studies which determine that honor -based violence is ingrained in their cultures and can be due to various factors affecting such crimes.

Global Efforts for Women Upliftment and Equality

The Global Conference on women held in Mexico served as a platform for politicians, academicians, civil society members, NGOs who advocated equal rights for women around the globe. Honor Based Violence has been largely looked upon as a cultural issue where women are victims of violence committed by their family members. But today it is being seen as a human rights issue and a gender rights issue. This movement is a goal defined in the Sustainable Development Goals which was initially conceptualized in the Rio Declaration in 2000, and the Beijing Declaration and Platform for Action (BDPA), which was an extension to the Fourth World Conference on Women (FWCW) organized in Beijing in 1995. (European Parliament, n.d.) To address this issue of violence due to notions of honor and pride nations have been working towards controlling this menace. Both developed and developing nations have booked both male and female perpetrators and is seeking to get justice for the victims. (*Lansstyrelsen Stockholm*, n.d.) To cite another example the UNICEF has been working to prevent Female Genital Mutilation in countries where it is prevalent. (UNICEF, n.d.)

International Law and Honor Killing

International Law always focuses on upholding human rights around the world and work towards gender equality. The United Nations is the primary body working towards this goal and has come up with various laws, conventions, and treaties to protect these rights. The author through this research aims to highlight these provisions under International Law which safeguards gender rights with special focus on Honor Killing. Honor Killing strikes at the very core of the Right to Life. These right forms the basis of Human Rights Legislations around the world including the UDHR. Honor Killing must be viewed through the lens of gender justice because the act of preserving family's honor solely lies with a woman and the murder of a man is given more importance than women being murdered by their own family members in broad daylight.

The UDHR and other legislations addressing human rights issues, are gender neutral as they see human rights to be above any gender distinction. (UDHR, 1948, Article 2, (General Assembly Resolution 217 A) United Nations General Assembly, 1948 (UN), n.d.) These laws address human rights with relation to an individual's relation with the State and other institutions in the society. These laws don't hold non-state actors liable for human rights violations and only states can be held criminally liable. This leads one to the conclusion that interpersonal conflicts/disputes between individuals are not considered as crimes, but torture perpetrated by State is seen as human rights violations under these laws.

UNCEDAW

On 18th December 1979 the United Nations General Assembly ratified the "Convention on the Elimination of All Forms of Discrimination Against Women". It achieved global stature on 3rd September 1981 after it was ratified by the 20th nation. By the time it celebrated its tenth anniversary in 1989, a total of 100 countries have ratified the convention. (United Nations Convention on Elimination of All Forms of Discrimination Against Women, 1979, United Nations General Assembly, 1979) Before UNCEDAW was ratified the UN Commission on the Status of Women, came into existence in the year 1946, with an aim to monitor women's conditions and work towards upliftment of women. (United Nations Convention on Elimination of All Forms of Discrimination Against Women, 1979, United Nations General Assembly, 1979) The Commission has done seminal work in highlighting incidents where women were discriminated against men. The Commission's best works have resulted in the ratification of the Convention which is attributed to be amongst the most comprehensive documents ever produced with respect to women's rights globally.

UNCEDAW and Honor Killing

In present time a total of 189 nation-states have ratified the UNCEDAW. The Convention explicitly talks about punishing those perpetrators who are accused of committing violence against women in the name of family honor and lineage. India being a signatory to the above stated convention is highly obliged to protect its women folk from such day-to-day discrimination which culminates into violence. The womenfolk in the country are free to choose whom to marry and be assured that they don't face any threat from fake notions of pride and honor in families.

Provisions of UNCEDAW

Some of the provisions which highlight violence against women and can help prevent honor-based violence around the globe are mentioned below-:

Article 1 - The Convention states clearly in its preamble that "women globally face discrimination which treatment is existential in nature" and that it "infringe equality of rights as well as reverence for human dignity" when it does so. "Any distinction, omission or prohibition made on the basis of sex...in the political, social, cultural, economic, civil or any other arena" is the definition of unequal as stated in Article 1. (Article 1, UNCEDAW, 1979)

Article 2 – This Article of the convention bounds all the signatory nations to draft legislations with an aim of achieving gender equality, along with repeal of all the provisions, in their domestic statutes which discriminate against women and enact such new laws which safeguard women's right to equality. States are also obligated to establish tribunals and special courts for fast paced redressal and simultaneous resolution of issues concerning discrimination of women. The States are also liable to prevent discrimination prevalent against women in organizations, institutions or by individuals. (Article 2, UNCEDAW, 1979)

Article 3 – This Article's main aim is to make all the signatory states take steps including legal actions which guarantees holistic development of womenfolk in all spheres be it political, social, economic or cultural. This guarantees that women are free to practice their fundamental rights and freedoms in consonance with the menfolk. (Article 3, UNCEDAW, 1979)

Article 5 (a) – Article 5 of the UNCEDAW defines that all the States that are signatories shall work towards reforming the cultural and social behavioral norms for both men and women which would lead to eradication of customs, practices or prejudices which are stereotypical against men or women or rests on the notion of inferiority or superiority with respect to one's gender. (Article 5(a), UNCEDAW, 1979)

Article 15 –

(1) Parties shall guarantee equality of women in legal terms.
(2) States consent to grant women the legal standing and opportunity in all spheres as accorded to males in their respective societies. It also aims to grant women similar rights as men be it entering in contracts, buying land or the right to being treated fairly and meted equality in all the judicial institutions.
(3) The Parties also agree that any legal mechanism or rule which limits or intends to limit women's ability to exercise their legal right shall be declared null and void. (Article 15, UNCEDAW, 1979)

Article 16 –

Signatories agree to take all important steps to put an end to discrimination against women in marriage and issues related to family. Specifically, they will guarantee, based on gender equality,

(a) Equal Rights with respect to marriage.
(b) Every individual has the right to choose his or her partner and marry only if they mutually agree.
(c) Equal Rights and Duties during and after marriage
(d) Irrespective of their relationship with the spouse their responsibilities as parents comes first and all the decisions are to be taken keeping in mind only the welfare of the children.
(e) Their right to have access to knowledge, education, and resources to help them in taking decisions regarding the number of children and the age difference between them.
(f) The duties and responsibilities associated with trusteeship, wardship, guardianship and adoption are to be taken into consideration according to the provision of the National Law, in case of child adoption or taking care of a ward as a foster parent.
(g) Every married couple has the right to choose their respective professions, family name and other rights guaranteed to them under the laws of the country.
(h) Both spouses have an equal right with respect to selling, acquiring, buying, or leasing out property which can be free of cost or can also be for consideration of some amount of money.
(2) Child Marriage is strictly outlawed, and all the signatory nations have to enact laws banning the same and setting a minimum age of marriage. All the marriages taking place in its jurisdiction needs to be registered before a registrar as authorized by the government. (Article 16, UNCEDAW, 1979)

General Recommendations Under UNCEDAW

6th General Recommendation (7th Session, 1988) Publicity of and Building an Effective Machinery (General Recommendation No. 6 (Seventh Session, 1988), UNCEDAW, 1979)

It suggests to the States parties that the information below be included in their regular reports to the Committee:

1. Enact laws to safeguard women from all forms of violence which they face in their daily lives, such as sexual assault, domestic abuse, and sexual harassment at work
2. Steps other than those defined in the statute need to be taken to prevent such brutalities
3. Governments need to make policies through which programs can be organized to rehabilitate victims who have faced violence
4. Governments also need to have statistics which provide data for the kinds of violence committed against women along with the ration of women victims of such violence

12th General Recommendation (8th Session, 1989) Women as Victims of Perpetual Violence (General Recommendation No. 12, Eighth Session, 1989), UNCEDAW, 1979)

The Signatory nation-states are obligated to take actions to safeguard women from violence against them be it in their houses, at their workplace or in any other setting in which she interacts with other individuals, this is defined under Articles 2, 5, 11, 12 and 16 of the Convention.

The Economic and Social Council according to the 1988/27 Resolution has asked the States to submit the below mentioned data which would then be included in their reports which are published by the Committee:

1. Legislations enacted by States to shield women from many forms of violence prevalent in daily lives and encountered by women be it sexual assault, sexual harassment at workplace and domestic abuse.
2. Mechanisms put in place by these parties to end such brutalities.
3. Programmes put in place to rehabilitate victims of violence or abuse and assist them in leading a normal life.
4. Statistics related to all forms of violence prevalent in the country and data on the victims and their rehabilitation.

19th General Recommendation (11th Session, 1992) Brutality against Women (General Recommendation No. 19 (11th Session, 1992), UNCEDAW, 1979)

The States were recommended by the Committee to take into consideration factors governing gender-based violence and evaluate their laws and policies accordingly before filing reports as defined in the Convention.

In many societies women are seen inferior to men and accorded stereotypical roles which leads to violence and women being coerced to follow such customs that leads to assault by family members, forced marriage, dowry death, acid attacks and female genital mutilation. This behaviour is used as a means to control or protect women from harm, ignoring the fact that these very actions are the reason of inherent gender-based violence. These acts which are aggressive and at times so heinous in nature strikes at the very fundamentals of mental and physical well-being of women, further restricting them to practice their human rights and enjoy right to liberty.

One of the most prevalent acts of violence perpetrated against women, in almost every society, is the abuse they face from their family members. These acts committed by their close ones is a result of an ingrained sense of superiority and patriarchal notions which leads to such violence being perpetrated. At times lack of financial independence compels women to continue with their abusive marriages. These acts of violence restrict women in realizing their true potential and prevents them from achieving their life's goals

The Committee took note of this and bounded the States under an obligation to prevent all forms of gender-based violence in all its manifestations. Proper rehabilitation mechanisms are to be put in place for the victims of violence. The whole of the Criminal Justice System including the police, judges, prosecutors, and all other stakeholders are to be gender sensitized and then address such cases of violence against women. States were also instructed to specify the type of violence that occurs and mention the severity in attitudes, traditions and customs that propagate violence committed against women. It is also necessary that they mention the proper steps they have undertaken to combat violence as well as the outcomes of those actions which are being implemented.

The following actions should be taken to end family violence:

(i) Implementation of appropriate criminal sanctions and civil remedies to be put in place to prevent domestic abuse.
(ii) Repeal laws which in any form support or legalize honor -based violence against any female family member.
(iii) Shelters, rehabilitation and counselling services to be formulated and implemented which are meant to protect the victims of violence.
(iv) Programs are also to be put in place for the rehabilitation of perpetrators of such violence.
(v) Providing assistance to families who are facing case of incest or sexual abuse

21st General Recommendation (13th session, 1994), Equal Right in Matrimonial Relations and Family (General Recommendation No. 21 (13th Session, 1994), UNCEDAW, 1979)

According to the U.N.C.E.D.A.W (General Assembly resolution 34/180, appendix) both men and women have been accorded equal rights. This convention is one of the most significant pieces of legislation enforcing the aim of International Human Rights Legislation.

Public and Private life

It is a known fact that humans behave differently in public and private spheres. This is reinforced by the practice that women have always been prevented from working in public spaces and have always been restricted to work in safety of their domestic households hence denying them the opportunity to work according to their wishes. Women are almost the half of the population of women globally and it is highly unfair towards them and there is no excuse for treating them discriminately and treating them differently. According to various reports from States Parties women are still not regarded as being equal to men and therefore they don't have access to equal opportunities and resources.

Different Types of Families

All the States who are signatory to the Convention may have different forms and types of family. Article 2 addresses this, that women who are part of a family must be treated equally without any discrimination, in both public and private spheres of life, all must adhere to principles of equality and fairness irrespective of the country's laws, traditions, culture or religion. The Committee highlighted the importance of the provisions of 19th General Recommendation (eleventh session) that considering women's status in families, and the prevention of violence committed against women as it is imperative that women are on an equal footing with men. States are bound to the proposal that they must take measures to prevent women from facing violence in both private and public spheres.

State Obligations under UNCEDAW

To resolve the issue of violence perpetrated against women the reason being preserving "honor" the UNGA called for the signatories to step up their legislative, educational, social, & other initiatives in 2001 with Resolution 55/66 which states, "Working towards putting an end to crimes being perpetrated against women in the name of honor, this can be achieved by establishing, promoting and strengthening services such as providing efficient safeguards, counselling, legal aid, rehabilitation, and reintegration as confident individuals into society for actual and potential victims; creating, strengthening and encouraging organizational structures to facilitate secure and anonymous reporting of victims of "honor" based violence; gather, maintain and disseminate data on "honor"-based crimes (¶ 4). This includes getting the opinion of leaders, teachers, and the media to spread public awareness and the means to protect victims of such crimes. (Byrnes et al., n.d.)

U.N.G.A. Resolution A/RES/57/179" Working towards the mitigation of crimes against women committed to preserve the honor (2005) (General Assembly of the United Nations Resolution A/RES/57/179) and the U.N.G.A. Resolution A/RES/59/165", Working towards eliminating crimes committed against women committed in the name of honor (2003) (United Nations General Assembly Resolution A/RES/59/165) encourage States to take definitive steps to prevent honor - based crimes. They also urge States to mete out speedy justice to the victims which can be achieved through swift and comprehensive investigations, present a strong prosecution case, record honor - based violence and strictly penalize offenders; educate and make the people aware about men's role in guaranteeing equal rights for women and working towards eradicating gender stereotypes; role of media is also very crucial because they can help spread awareness, support civil society groups and fortify collaboration between governmental and non-profit organizations.

According to 28th General Comment of the Committee on Human Rights, which addresses gender equality in Article 3, "...which states that honor -based violence seriously violates provisions of ICCPR and particularly of articles 6, 14 and 26." Legislations which discriminate in penalizing women for the crime of adultery more harshly than males also violates the principle of equal treatment (§ 31). (Human Rights Committee)

Furthermore, the States can't circumspect their responsibility of preventing violence against women under any customs, traditions, practices and are urged to "condemn violence against women" under the (Article 4) in the U.N.G.A Resolution A/RES/48/104 Declaration on the Elimination of Violence Against Women. (UN General Assembly's Resolution A/RES/48/104). This declaration bounds the governments to "practice due diligence, mitigate, investigate, (in compliance with legislation in their respective nations) penalize crime of violence perpetrated against women, with no discrimination if the acts are committed by individuals or by the State" (Article 4(c)). Furthermore, according to DEVAW, states should "adopt all appropriate measures, in educational field to eliminate discrimination between men and women based on culture, customs or other traditions which relies on the false notions of inferiority, superiority and other stereotypes" (Art. 4(j)).

FUTURE PERSPECTIVES ON EFFECTIVENESS OF UNCEDAW AND HONOR KILLING

Organizations who are proactive in organizing awareness campaigns should work upon highlighting the reasons of such violence taking place. The UNCEDAW Committee's definition of violence against women, which was primarily established by its General Recommendation 19 (1992), is integrated into the Istanbul Convention, views inequality as the primary reason for violence against women. (General Recommendation No. 19 (11th Session, 1992), UNCEDAW, 1979) According to the Preamble to the Istanbul Convention. "Women being victims of violence can be attributed to disparities in power distribution between male and female which is the primary reason for men being seen as superior to women". (European Union)

The case of violence against women can be understood by a simple fact that aggression is a social phenomenon. It is accepted, propagated, and maintained by the society as well as authorized by the social order. Men who commit violence are neither born with it nor is it acquired naturally but it is due to their social interactions and engagements. This proves the fact that with right interventions with factors initiating or facilitating violence against women can be prevented.

In evaluation of prevention of honor-based crimes through awareness campaigns it is important that we distinguish between consciousness and attitudes and behaviours of those who commit such crimes. Increased awareness can lead to a conducive atmosphere which makes the amendment and implementation of laws much easier and beneficial as it is a prelude to changes in attitudes and behaviour. It will be highly unreasonable to think that this violence can be prevented and lead to attitudinal changes only through these awareness campaigns. Thus, awareness-raising campaigns have to be regarded as one of the most essential components of policymaking intended to strengthen the ability to respond to and prevent violence against women. (European Union) It should also be highlighted that there is currently a dearth of information available about the relationship and the effect of prevention of violence and awareness-raising, as well as how these interventions prevent violence against women. More evidence-based data is required to prove the effect of awareness campaigns on violence against women this can only be achieved if the government spends more on research in these fields and allocates resources for the same as has been mandated by the Istanbul Conference.

CONCLUSION

The aim of Honor Killing is attached with "honor", however, there can be no honor in killing a person. This phenomenon is based on religious and cultural dogmas, but they are always interpreted subjectively, hence "religion" and "culture" cannot and should not be cited as a defence for murdering women. No "culture" in this world has the authority to murder and abuse women because of their high held beliefs on honor or morality. Someone's belief on his or her culture or traditions doesn't give them the right to kill. Every individual is entitled to a life of equality and dignity. Therefore, legislation only seems the most rational way in preventing such violence. In this regard the UNCEDAW's provisions address such homicides that fall outside the definition of murder. The Convention's provisions, broadly prohibit all forms of physical or psychological distress experienced by women, it also addresses all facets of honor -based violence committed against women. It is the responsibility of the signatory states to proactively adopt the provisions highlighted in the UNCEDAW whose main aim is to safeguard the rights of women and prevent them from being victims of perpetual violence in the name of "honor".

REFERENCES

Alamki, N. (n.d.). *The Horror of 'Honor Killings', Even in US*. Retrieved January 18, 2024, from https://www.amnestyusa.org/updates/the-horror-of-honor-killings-even-in-us/#:~:text=While%20Amal%20survived%2C%20Noor%20later,here%20in%20the%20United%20States

Byrnes, A., Graterol, M. H., & Chartres, R. (n.d.). *State Obligation and the Convention on the Elimination of All Forms of Discrimination Against Women*. Retrieved May 19, 2024 https://law.bepress.com/unswwps-flrps/art48

European Parliament. (n.d.). *TOOLKIT on mainstreaming gender equality in EC development cooperation*.

European Union. (n.d.). *Honour Killing its Causes & Consequences: Suggested Strategies for the European Parliament*. Retrieved May 19, 2024, from https://www.europarl.europa.eu/RegData/etudes/etudes/join/2007/385527/EXPO-JOIN_ET(2007)385527_EN.pdf

Garner, B. A. (Ed.). (n.d.). *Black's Law Dictionary* (Ninth edition 2009, p. 428).

General Assembly of the United Nations Resolution A/RES/57/179. Retrieved January 16, 2024, from https://www.un.org/womenwatch/daw/cedaw/

Human Rights Committee. (n.d.). *General Comment No. 28 of the Human Rights Committee, ICCPR, Article 3*.

Lansstyrelsen Stockholm. (n.d.). Retrieved January 21, 2024, from https://www.lansstyrelsen.se/english.html

Supervisor, L. E., & Appelqvist, M. (2008). *Crimes of Honour-Females' Right for Support in the Multicultural Society*.

UDHR. 1948, Article 2, (General Assembly Resolution 217 A) United Nations General Assembly, 1948 (UN). Retrieved January 5, 2024, from https://www.un.org/en/about-us/universal-declaration-of-human-rights#:~:text=Article%202,property%2C%20birth%20or%20other%20status

UN General Assembly's Resolution A/RES/48/104. Retrieved January 18, 2024, from https://www.un.org/womenwatch/daw/cedaw/

UNICEF. (n.d.). *UNICEF Report on the State of the World's Children 2002 for report on a grassroots movement in Senegal to end FGM*. Retrieved January 14, 2024, from www.unicef.org

United Nations Convention on Elimination of All Forms of Discrimination Against Women. 1979, Article 1, United Nations General Assembly, 1979, Retrieved January 18, 2024, from https://www.un.org/womenwatch/daw/cedaw/

United Nations Convention on Elimination of All Forms of Discrimination Against Women. 1979, Article 2, United Nations General Assembly, 1979. Retrieved January 19, 2024, from https://www.un.org/womenwatch/daw/cedaw/

United Nations Convention on Elimination of All Forms of Discrimination Against Women. 1979, Article 3, United Nations General Assembly, 1979, Retrieved May 18, 2024, from https://www.un.org/womenwatch/daw/cedaw/

United Nations Convention on Elimination of All Forms of Discrimination Against Women. 1979, Article 5 (a), United Nations General Assembly, 1979. Retrieved January 15, 2024, from https://www.un.org/womenwatch/daw/cedaw/

United Nations Convention on Elimination of All Forms of Discrimination Against Women. 1979, Article 15, United Nations General Assembly, 1979. Retrieved January 18, 2024, from https://www.un.org/womenwatch/daw/cedaw/

United Nations Convention on Elimination of All Forms of Discrimination Against Women. 1979, Article 16, United Nations General Assembly, 1979, Retrieved January 16, 2024, from https://www.un.org/womenwatch/daw/cedaw/

United Nations Convention on Elimination of All Forms of Discrimination Against Women. 1979, United Nations General Assembly, 1979. Retrieved January 15, 2024, from https://www.un.org/womenwatch/daw/cedaw/

United Nations Convention on Elimination of All Forms of Discrimination Against Women. 1979, General Recommendation No. 6 (Seventh Session, 1988) Effective National Machinery and Publicity, United Nations General Assembly, 1979. Retrieved January 17, 2024, from https://www.un.org/womenwatch/daw/cedaw/

United Nations Convention on Elimination of All Forms of Discrimination Against Women. 1979, General Recommendation No. 12 (Eighth Session, 1989) Violence against Women, 1989, United Nations General Assembly, 1979. Retrieved January 18, 2024, from https://www.un.org/womenwatch/daw/cedaw/

United Nations Convention on Elimination of All Forms of Discrimination Against Women. 1979, General Recommendation No. 19 (11th Session, 1992) Violence Against Women, 1992, United Nations General Assembly, 1979. Retrieved January 14, 2024, from https://www.un.org/womenwatch/daw/cedaw/

United Nations Convention on Elimination of All Forms of Discrimination Against Women. 1979, General Recommendation No. 21 (13th Session, 1994), Equality in Marriages and Family Relations, 1994, United Nations General Assembly, 1979. Retrieved January 18, 2024, from https://www.un.org/womenwatch/daw/cedaw/

United Nations General Assembly Resolution A/RES/59/165. Retrieved January 18, 2024, from https://www.un.org/womenwatch/daw/cedaw/

Women, U. N. (n.d.). *Defining "honour" crimes and "honour" killings*. Retrieved May 19, 2024, from https://www.endvawnow.org/en/articles/731-defining-honourcrimes-and-honour-killings.html

Chapter 22
An Analysis of Multiculturalism and Racism in the UK and USA

Nupur Kumari
Bennett University, India

Radhika Garg
https://orcid.org/0009-0004-8853-8645
GLA University, India

ABSTRACT

The phenomenon of honor killings in the multicultural settings of the US and the UK is examined in this chapter. Honor killings, which are defined as horrific acts of violence against women who are believed to have brought embarrassment to their families, undermine multiculturalism's tenets by drawing attention to the conflicts between human rights and cultural norms. To demonstrate the intricate dynamics at work, the chapter examines case studies and the horrific events of Michelle Rai & Shafilea Ahmed. The chapter explores the connections between sexism, racism, and gender-based violence in honor killings and emphasizes the stigma minority women experience. The need to treat honor killings with cultural sensitivity, while criticizing violence and protecting human rights, is noted in the conclusion. To prevent honor-based violence, it is essential to promote open communication, provide support services, & actively oppose racism and xenophobia to build inclusive societies where everybody is valued and protected.

DOI: 10.4018/979-8-3693-9596-7.ch022

BACKGROUND

The chapter also explores the social and legal structures that these multicultural societies have put in place to deal with honor killings. It analyses the effectiveness of the laws in place and the role played by authorities in deterring and combating these offenses. The report draws attention to how victims' legal protections are sometimes insufficient, and how authorities struggle to prosecute offenders because of cultural sensitivity and community backlash concerns.

It also looks at the organizations and leaders in the community and their involvement in preventing honor-based violence. It underlines how crucial it is to work with local authorities to inspire them to push for reform from the inside and to develop a unified front against these kinds of abuse. To support victims, increase awareness, and inform communities about the negative effects of honor killings, grassroots organizations are essential. It is possible to encourage further social change and ensure that cultural customs do not violate people's fundamental rights by collaborating with these organizations. Outreach and education are recognized as vital components in the struggle against honor killings. The chapter recommends putting in place educational initiatives that emphasize gender equality, human rights, and the negative effects of honor-based killing. These initiatives can take place in schools, community centers, & places of worship, which can help to change cultural attitudes and lower the number of these crimes. It also examined how the media shapes public perceptions and government actions around honor killings. The chapter highlights the significance of proper reporting that stays away from sensationalism, upholds the victims' dignity, and spreads awareness of the problem. Media campaigns have the potential to break the taboo around honor killings and inspire victims and their relatives to get support and assistance.

This chapter's main concept is the tension that exists between cultural standards and human rights when honor murders occur in multicultural cultures like the US & the UK. It delves deeper into how the media shapes public attitudes about honor murders and how people react to them, highlighting the need for ethical reporting that stays away from sensationalism. Ultimately, the chapter makes the case that, even if cultural sensitivity is significant, the defense of basic human rights must always come first.

Statistical Data

Each year in the United Kingdom (UK), authorities estimate that at least twelve women fall victim to honor killings, predominantly within South Asian and Middle Eastern families. In 2010, the UK experienced a 47% increase in honor-related crimes. Police records show 2,283 cases that year, with an additional estimated 500 incidents from areas that didn't submit reports. These honor-related offenses also encompassed actions like house arrests and other forms of parental discipline. The majority of these incidents took place in cities with significant immigrant communities. Whereas in the US in recent years, several honor killings have taken place in the U.S. In 1989, in St. Louis, Missouri, 16-year-old Palestina "Tina" Isa was killed by her Palestinian father, with the assistance of her mother, due to their disapproval of her "Westernized" lifestyle (Gerbaka et al., 2021). In 2008, in Georgia, 25-year-old Sandeela Kanwal was murdered by her Pakistani father for rejecting an arranged marriage (Fox News, 2008). The prevalence of honor-based violence in the U.S. is unclear, as no official data has been collected. There is ongoing debate about the causes of such violence, particularly the roles that culture, religion, and attitudes toward women play in these incidents.

Research Methodology

This study investigates the frequency and risk factors associated with honor killings in diverse environments in the US and the UK using a **quantitative and qualitative methodology**. To prevent bias, certain participant features, such as their age, gender, and ethnicity need to be observed.

The findings of the primary and secondary studies indicate that cultural ideas serve as the motivation behind honor killing, which is not supported by any religion. Individuals who are perceived by the community to have violated social and cultural standards are often subjected to violence & torture. It has become evident from extensive research that honor killing is a global phenomenon that has persisted for many centuries and is not limited to any one region. Even if there isn't one general description of honor killing, it clarifies the perception of honor killing. It is seen to be a criminal and a physical act intended to acquire prestige or power, according to all the data gathered on people's perspectives of honor killings.

Key Term

Core terms include "honor killing" and "Multiculturism" (Brandon, J. & Hafez, S., 2010,), "human rights" and "cultural norms" (A Hill, 2012,), "Gender-based violence" and "sexism" (Gill, A., 2009), "racism" and "UK honor killing" (H Siddiqui and M Patel,), "community backlash" and "domestic violence", "culture diversity" and "gender equality", "westernized Culture" and "Views on the women", "Extent of Honor based Violence", "culture, religion, and attitudes toward women Authorities in the United Kingdom (UK) estimate that at least twelve women fall victim to honor killings each year, predominantly within South Asian and Middle Eastern families"

Literature Review

The chapter explores the honor killings are a phenomenon that occurs in multicultural environments in the US and the UK, highlighting serious sociolegal, cultural, as well as human rights issues by revealing a deeply rooted cultural practice of killing individuals—mostly women—who are believed to have brought shame as well as a dishonor to their families before dying (Brandon, J. & Hafez, S., 2010). Through case studies like the terrible incidents involving Michelle Rai (*Indian Man Found Guilty of Killing Son's Black Wife*, 2008) & Shafilea Ahmed (Weathers, H., 2007), honor killings—which sharply contradict the ideals of multiculturalism—are studied, illuminating the complex processes of sexism, racism, & gender-based violence. The chapter also explores these countries' social and legal frameworks, examining the efficacy of laws and the difficulties authorities confront in prosecuting offenders because of worries about cultural sensitivity and community backlash (A Hill, 2012,). In addition to highlighting the need to work in tandem with municipalities to promote internal reform and forge a cohesive front against such abuse, it underscores the vital role that community groups and leaders play in avoiding honor-based violence (Chesler, P, 2009). It is widely acknowledged that grassroots organizations play a crucial role in providing support to victims, increasing public awareness, and teaching communities about the negative effects of honor killings. The chapter also emphasizes how important it is to implement educational programs that support equal rights for women and men, human rights, & the negative effects of honor killings in educational institutions, community centers, & places of worship. It also looks at how the media shapes public opinion and official reactions, promoting ethical reporting that stays away from sensationalism, upholds the dignity of victims, and increases public knowledge of the problem. In the end, the chapter makes the case that, while cultural sensitivity is important, it shouldn't come at the price of defending basic human rights. It advocates for a middle ground that both condemns violence and values cultural variety.

Future Research Direction

Future research directions based on the article could focus on several key areas. First, broader statistical analysis is essential, as future studies could aim to collect comprehensive data on honor-based violence in both the UK and the USA. Given the lack of official statistics, research could focus on improving data collection methods and analyzing trends across different communities. Another vital area is the exploration of cultural and social dynamics. Further research could investigate the cultural and social factors contributing to honor killings, particularly how different communities perceive, and address issues related to honor and shame. This might involve in-depth ethnographic studies and interviews with community members to gain a deeper understanding.

The impact of media representation is another crucial area for investigation. Future research could explore how the media portrays honor killings and the effects this portrayal has on public perceptions and policy responses (Salman, A.,2021). This could help determine whether media coverage contributes to stigmatization or supports victims. Additionally, research could assess the effectiveness of existing legal frameworks and policies in preventing honor-based violence. Evaluating the impact of laws like the Forced Marriage (Civil Protection) Act 2007 in the UK and the Violence Against Women Act (VAWA) in the US (Griffith, R.,2010) would provide valuable insights into the successes and limitations of current legal measures.

Intervention and prevention programs also warrant further study. Analyzing the effectiveness of these programs, particularly those run by grassroots organizations, could help identify best practices for community engagement, education, and support services to prevent honor killings. Moreover, research could delve into the intersectionality of gender, race, and religion in the context of honor killings, shedding light on how these factors interact and contribute to the perpetuation of such violence (Shaikh, T.,2014).

Comparative studies between different countries or regions could offer valuable insights into how various legal, social, and cultural frameworks influence the occurrence of honor-based violence, helping to identify successful strategies for prevention and intervention. Finally, research could explore the long-term impact of honor killings on victims' families (Idriss, 2017), including psychological, social, and economic consequences. Understanding these effects could inform the development of better support systems for families affected by such violence. By pursuing these research directions, scholars can contribute to a deeper understanding of honor killings and develop more effective strategies to prevent and address this form of violence in multicultural societies.

INTRODUCTION

"The death of women for presumed disobedience from sexual norms established by society" is the term defined as honor killings. Extreme forms of violence towards women committed in the notion that an honor code has been broken, bringing perceived shame upon the family, are defined as honor killings. furthermore, women may endure the shame of stereotypically masculine abuses of their "honor" in sexual relations and might be killed for bearing children as a result of rape and incest. Suspicion of sexual deviance, such as extramarital pregnancy or adulterous behavior, is also considered a sufficient reason for punishing a woman. So-called honor Killings are typified by the potential involvement of the married partner, as well as other family members including such moms, brothers, uncles, and cousins.

In England and Wales, partners kill over 100 women yearly, but according to estimates from the Metropolitan Police, there were about 12 honor killings in the Sikh, Muslim, and Christian communities in 2003 (Idriss & Abbas, 2010). However, the media & government organizations in the UK view honor killing mostly as a rare phenomenon and believe that it is a crime that is only committed by specific ethnic minorities. Honor killings, as some violent behavior, have subsequently become "ethicized" in the multicultural environment of the UK.

They are split between the private/public section that establishes the story of domestic violence and the conflicts present in the British multiculturalism discourse's cultural relativism. These women are disproportionately vulnerable to "honor killings," which are defined as such by cultural, religious, and patriarchal ideologies that are predicated on "honor & shame."

Multiculturalism and Racism in the Context of Honor Killing

There are various ways in which racism and multiculturalism interact with the complex problem of honor killings.

First of all, racism may influence society's perspective & response to honor killings. The media's coverage of honor killing incidents may exhibit racist views, as perpetrators from specific racial or cultural backgrounds may be exaggerated or unfairly stereotyped. This has the potential to encourage harmful perceptions and further victimize entire communities.

Second, when it comes to handling customs like honor killings, multiculturalism—which ideally facilitates the coexistence of several cultural groups within society—can occasionally cause conflicts. Multiculturalism emphasizes acceptance and awareness of other cultural norms, and it also involves striking a balance with the essential rights of all people. Honor killings violate the crucial human rights ideals of equality, autonomy, as well as the right to life. They are generally defended based on cultural or traditional notions.

Multiculturalism presents concerns about how to balance cultural relativism—respecting various cultural practices—concerning Multiculturalism presents concerns about how to balance cultural relativism—respecting various cultural practices—concerning honor killings without endorsing or ignoring human rights violations. It necessitates carefully weighing how to protect cultural variety and people's rights and safety at the same time, especially for women & girls who are frequently the targets of honor killings. Honor killings are committed without endorsing or ignoring human rights violations. It necessitates carefully weighing how to protect cultural variety and people's rights and safety at the same time, especially for women & girls who are frequently the targets of honor killings.

Honor killings are when women/men are killed for supposedly going against accepted sexual norms in society. The idea behind these horrific deeds is that the family's honor has been damaged by a woman's or man's conduct. Women may be subjected to violence if they enter into relationships that are considered unsuitable, if they become pregnant as a result of rape or incest, and even if they are just suspected of having illicit relationships or adultery. In addition to spouses, other family members such as moms, brothers, aunts, and cousins can also be the culprits.

Despite these numbers, government agencies and the media in the UK frequently view honor killings as rare incidents that only affect particular ethnic minorities. In the multicultural UK, this viewpoint has resulted in the "ethnicization" of murders for honor. The divide between the public and private domains further complicates the matter, casting doubt on the cultural relativism of British multiculturalism and reshaping the narrative around domestic abuse.

Particularly, "honor and shame"-focused patriarchal, cultural, & religious belief systems support the continuation of honor killings. While diversity is not the primary cause of domestic abuse, it can unintentionally contribute to it by encouraging non-interference with minority customs, honoring cultural diversity, and mandating community involvement, which is frequently spearheaded by male community leaders. As a result, women have been silenced, abused, and had their demands ignored.

To address honor killings inside a multicultural framework, communities must be enabled to question harmful norms and traditions while honoring cultural differences. This can be done through encouraging education, conversation, and community building. Strong legal frameworks & enforcement strategies are also essential to keep perpetrators accountable, regardless of their cultural background, and to help and protect those at risk.

Relationship Between Victim and Perpetrators

Close family members have been involved in most recorded killings. A little over half (Brandon, J. & Hafez, S., 2010,) of all UK "honor" killings that have been published in the media in the last five years involved partners, either present or past, as well as that partner's family members as the attackers. Nine more incidents implicated the parents of the victims in the killing (two of which also involved the victims' male siblings).

Honor-Based Violence in the United Kingdom

"Domestic" violence and "honor" violence vary significantly. For instance, "honor" killings are more likely to be planned than family abuse killings, which are much more likely to be spontaneous (Chesler, P., 2009,) and impulsive. Most "honor" killings in the UK are premeditated by one or more family members of the victims. The fact that domestic abusers exhibit apparent regret more frequently than those who commit Honor-based violence is seen to be another variation (Chesler, P, 2009). However, despite these variations, criminal prosecutions about domestic violence or Honor-based violence usually entail the same offenses, including rape or murder, as opposed to a distinct crime of "domestic violence" or " Honor-based violence."

However, depending on the motivation during the latter case and the relationship between the victim & offender in the former, these offenses are classified as domestic abuse or Honor-based violence. For instance, if a husband is accused of killing someone to regain his honor, he will face murder charges and have his crime reported under Honor-based violence. Domestic violence, which is defined as a crime against a relative or partner rather than to reclaim honor, is punished in the very same manner (Violence Against Women and Girls Crime Report 2012-2013, 2014).

Case Study on Honor Killing in the UK and USA

Case Study of Michelle Rai

Washington: A US professor of Indian descent who eventually became a businessman was found guilty of hiring contract killers to assassinate his black daughter-in-law 1 month after she married his son because he was against their interracial relationship. Chiman Rai, 69, is facing capital punishment for apparently paying two men USD 10,000 to assassinate African American Sparkle Michelle Rai in April 2000. Sparkle Michelle Rai was married to Rajeev Rai, alias Ricky, and they had a baby daughter together. At the couple's apartment, the 22-year-old was discovered to have been stabbed more than a couple of times and strangled. Following a tip two years ago, officers caught Chiman Rai & four other people in connection with the case, which made headlines as an "honor killing." After 2 days of deliberations, a jury in Fulton County, Mississippi, found him guilty of seven offenses, including felony murder & burglary. The jury was convinced that the man was a racist and that the marriage would shame his family. Rai, who moved to the United States with his family in 1970, taught math for ten years at Alcorn Public University in Mississippi before starting a grocery store and hotel in Kentucky, where Sparkle worked. The prosecution has stated that Rai will be executed. In 2006, charges were made against Chiman, 74-year-old Willie Fred Evans, 60-year-old Herbert Green, and the two brothers Cleveland, 46, & Carl Clark, 43, who were accused of being hired killers. Crucial testimony from co-defendants Evans and Green, who admit to conspiring to organize the murder, helped Rai win his case. Rai informed them that his son had stolen thousands of dollars from his enterprises and might have a bundle of cash and drugs in the flat. Probation was awarded to the two guys in return for their testimony (*Indian Man Found Guilty of Killing Son's Black Wife*, 2008).

Case Study of Shafilea Ahmed

Iftikhar and Farzana Ahmed, her parents, disagreed with their daughter dressing in Western clothes, spending quality time with white girls, & relating to boys in any way. Her sister alleges that in the years leading up to her passing, they began to use bullying and intimidation to force their daughter to adhere to their cultural standards. In February 2003, Shafilea managed to flee but was later captured once more and forced to board a vehicle. A week later, she was drugged & jetted to Pakistan to see her prospective spouse. When Shafilea was still in Pakistan, she tried to take her own life by consuming bleach because she didn't intend to go through with the wedding. Her parents had assumed that she might wed a man of their choice and stay away from men outside the family. Shafilea, on the other hand, desired "a more Westernized [sic] lifestyle, to become a lawyer, and to wear fashionable clothes." On Sept. 11, 2003, Shafilea got into an argument with her mother & was assassinated by her family in front of her 4 children ("Shafilea Ahmed's Parents")

Found Guilty of Her Murder," 2012). The siblings testified that as soon as the murder started, their mother gave an order to kill, saying in Urdu, "Just end it here." Then, as her father restrained her, Iftikhar & Farzana Ahmed put their hands around a trash bag that they had pushed into his daughter's mouth, preventing her from breathing. They disposed of their daughter's corpse after killing her by suffocation. Shafilea's sister Alesha testified that she saw their father strike her still-lifeless body in the breast, that her mom was already in the kitchen gathering sheets, bin bags, and rolls of tape, & as her dad had taken a massive parcel, which she assumed to be the dead ("Shafilea Ahmed Case: "Sister Saw Parents Commit Murder," 2012). When Shafilea disappeared, the investigators installed a transmitter in the Ahmed house. Farzana Ahmed was overheard warning her other kids not to talk about the murder & Shafilea's whereabouts. Six months after the incident, in February 2004, her body was found on a Cumbrian riverside.

Shafilea's parents were found guilty of killing their daughter, and they were sentenced to life imprisonment of 25 years behind bars ("Shafilea Ahmed's Parents Jailed for Her Murder," 2012.). Shafilea's parents specifically behaved "as a team," the court said, and they both made a conscious effort to bury their crime, including encouraging their other kids to create up stories of what happened, as one of the aggravating circumstances in the sentence. Alesha, Farzana Ahmed's daughter, believes that in addition to actively participating in their daughter's murder, Farzana also did most of the physical violence on Shafilea even though she was available more than her spouse ("Mother Suspected in UK 'Honor Murder' Implicates Husband in Teen's Killing," 2012). In some cases, women have taken a more passive involvement in "honor"-based crimes. Such an incident is the mother of Banaz Mahmod, who refused to help the investigators after her daughter was assassinated in 2006 (Weathers, H., 2007).

Case Study of Nosheen Azam

An example of how Honor-based violence and suicide are related in the UK is the incident of Nosheen Azam. In the instance of Nosheen, there was an attempt at honor suicide. She had just moved to this nation and was stuck in an abusive union. Nosheen's parents did not include any help that would have enabled her to leave the circumstances. Families in patriarchal cultures don't typically support their daughter's divorce. By doing this, they are spared the humiliation of having a divorced daughter living at home and the oppression of their culture' (Gorar, 2021.). Nosheen, a 23-year-old Pakistani woman, moved to the UK to settle along with her British Pakistani spouse. She began to complain to her family after a brief while, alleging that her husband's family was torturing her. Nosheen had informed them she was afraid for her life, according to her father Mohammed, and on that day in 2005, she was discovered burning in her Sheffield Garden. After her suicide attempt failed, she suffered over 60% burns (A Hill, 2012,) and was rendered brain dead. Nosheen is mute, thus no one can tell if she was forced to take her own life or if she decided to end her life because she felt it was a better option than the circumstances, she was in. It is also unconfirmed whether someone attempted to kill her by burning her on fire. Nosheen's case was not looked into because it was considered an attempted suicide. The role that peer pressure played in her death was overlooked. There hasn't been a deliberate attempt to find out what motivated Nosheen to try suicide, according to Patel, and if she had passed away, at the very least, an inquest would have taken place (A Hill, 2012). "Even though suicide is almost the same as murder," she continued, "there is no reason for the police to examine if it is a case of proven encouragement to suicide (A Hill, 2012,). In Britain, prosecutions in suicide cases are uncommon. Investigations into suicides can only be ordered by the coroner's court. When there is no inquiry, those who commit crimes are not held accountable. In response to Nosheen's case, the nonprofit Southall Black Sisters Organization is pushing for a new homicide law that would define "constructive manslaughter as well as suicide caused by violence or harassment" (H Siddiqui and

M Patel,) to effectively address suicide issues and hold those who engage in violent or abusive behavior accountable when a suicide occurs as a result of their actions. Before Nosheen's case, Krishna Sharma's 1984 suicide death sparked similar worries in another suicide case ("Southall Black Sisters,"1984). In her own house, Krishna was found hanging. Concerning Nosheen, the police were known that Krishna had endured years of abuse at the hands of her husband. The police had told her to get in touch with the Citizen's Advisory Bureau the night before she died suddenly. Her Southall Black Sisters Organization became aware of her death & launched the Krishna Sharma Movement in 1984 as a result (SSM Edwards, 2019,).

Case Study of 4 Sisters

North America (Canada): In 2012, it was declared that Muhammad Shafia and his wife, Tooba Yahya, were responsible for the killing of their 3 teenage daughters along with Shafia's first wife. Hamed, their son, was similarly arrested for his participation in the murders. When Yahya and Shafia are released from prison, they will be sent to their homeland (Afghanistan). The Canada Border Services Agency issued the orders, that they have no right of appeal and were imposed for serious criminality. For the murders of sisters Rona Amir Mohammad, 52, and Zainab, 19, along with Sahar, 17, & Geeti, 13, all 3 members of the family are receiving 25-year life imprisonment. In June 2009, their remains were found in a car that had been submerged near a canal in Kingston, Ontario. Prosecutors said that Mohammad Shafia was furious because his two older daughters wanted their boyfriends, which was against his ethical beliefs, during the 2012 trial. The court heard of his increasing outrage and dissatisfaction with his 3 teenage daughters for wearing revealing clothes and having secret relations with boys. The jury was informed that the decision to kill the 4 women was formed when Zainab, then 19 years old, fled to a shelter in disregard of her parent's wishes. In 2015, the 3 lost their appeal of their conviction. Shafia's citizenship was revoked by the Immigration & Refugee Board of Canada (IRC) on February 27. Yahya's was revoked on Thursday during a hearing in Montreal. On Friday, the IRC revealed that it had been clueless of Hamed's citizenship. In 1992, the Shafia family departed from Afghanistan. They lived in Australia, Pakistan, and Dubai before arriving in Canada in 2007 (*Two Convicted 'Honor' Killers to Be Deported from Canada*, 2018).

Case Study of Amandeep Kaur Dhillon

When Kamiak's daughter-in-law, Amandeep Kaur Dhillon, was assassinated in June 2010, Kamiak Dhillon pleaded guilty to second-degree murder. Amandeep, 22, was fatally stabbed on January 1, 2009, in the cellar of a grocery store located in Mississauga. Her father-in-law was arrested at the crime scene, suffering from stab wounds that he said were administered by the victim. When it was discovered that these were self-inflicted, he was accused of first-degree murder. He received a life sentence without the possibility of release for 15 years. He said to investigators that Amandeep's plan to disgrace their family by divorcing his son for just another person was why he had the right to kill her (Warming, J., & Clarkson, B., 2009).

Case Study of Aqsa Parvez

In June 2010, the 57-year-old father Muhammad Parvez as well as his 26-year-old son Waqas filed pleas of guilty to committing second-degree murder about the killing of a 16-year Aqsa Parvez (Mitchell, B., & Javed, N, 2010). After Aqsa had been found strangled in the Mississauga residence of her family in December 2007. According to friends, Aqsa experienced problems with her family because she refused to put on the headscarf, called the hijab, which is an accessory utilized by several Muslim women. She had been residing with another family, who defined her as a "typical" teenager seeking to fit in, so she could spend a few days at home. Before she was killed, she was allegedly trying to mend her troubled connection with her family ("Brother Faces New Charge in Teenage Girl's Slaying," 2008).

Case Study of Khatera Sadiqi

For the brutal murders of his sister Khatera Sadiqi, 20, & her fiancé Feroz Mangal, 23, in May 2009, Hasibullah Sadiqi, 23 years old was found guilty of two counts of first-degree murder and given a life sentence with a 25-year parole ineligibility. On September 19, 2006, the victims were shot dead in a car that was parked outside of an Ottawa retail center. After going to a movie and dinner with friends, the topic of their father—from whom Ms. Sadiqi was estranged—came up. Although both the Sadiqi & Mangal families originated in Afghanistan, the Mangals were Pashtun and the Sadiqi were Tajik. Hasibullah stated in court that he was upset as Mr. Mangal did not agree with him on the matter and that he wanted his sister to have respect for his father more. The Crown claimed that because the father (Cockburn, N., 20, 08,) had not approved of the couple's engagement, the homicide was motivated by honor. To the best of our knowledge, the prosecution's use of the honor killing defense to establish premeditation in the Sadiqi case was a first for Canada.

Case Study of Kulwinder Dulay

Mr. Dulay's attempt to shorten the period of ineligibility for parole owing to his shift in perspective regarding the cultural reasoning behind his killings was denied in January 2009. Kulvinder Dulay murdered his younger sister Kalwinder Dulay, her husband Gurdwara Dulay, and Mukesh Sharma, the man they shared a home with in Calgary, in 1991. Mr. Dulay stated that his sister's marriage had not been accepted by his family and that it was his duty as the oldest son to kill them to restore the family's honor. He was found guilty of two first-degree murder crimes, for which he was given an obligatory life sentence with a 25-year parole ineligibility, and one second-degree murder conviction, for which he was given a compulsory life sentence with an 18-year parole ineligibility ("R. V. Dulay," 2009).

Case Study of the Ms. Subramaniam

Sugihara Kailayapillai was found guilty in November 2009 of killing his wife, Ms. Subramaniam, in 2006, hanged her body in the garage, and sent his 4-year-old daughter and mother-in-law there to find the body. Kailayapillai was given a life sentence without the possibility of parole for 14 years. The accused stated that his wife's amorous engagement with a coworker was the reason she was "of bad character". The victim's mother and sister said in the victim impact declarations that she was murdered as she was a bad person. Ms. Sivanantham, the victim's sister, describes the Tamil community as having "some very rigid as well as customary standards and values especially when it comes to women." The family has been humiliated by this, and its members—Kanagawa, the victim's mother in particular—feel cut off from the community. They fear that the kids of Ms. Subramaniam may face social rejection ("R. V. Kailayapillai," 2009,).

Case Study of Farah Khan

The convictions of the victim's father, Muhammad Khan, and stepmother, Fatima Khan, were affirmed in November 2007 following an appeal. For the 1999 killing of his 5-year-old girl Farah Khan in their Toronto home, Mr. Khan was found guilty in April 2004 of murder in the first degree & given a life sentence without the possibility of release for no less than 25 years. June 2004 saw the conviction of his wife Fatima Khan for second-degree murder, and she was given a life sentence without the possibility of release for no less than 15 years. He is accused of chasing the youngster around their basement apartment's living room and a coffee table on the day of the murder. After that, he grabbed her by the legs and hair and gave her a rolling pin beatdown. When he finally hit her head on the table, she passed out. Her father contended that since his child was the offspring of his first wife & another man, he had to regain his dignity ("R. V. Khan, [2007] O.J. No. 4383 (QL) (O.C.A.)., Father and Stepmother Convicted of Murdering 5-Year-Old Farrah Khan," 2004).

Case Study of Mrs. Humaid

The Court of Appeals denied Adi Abdul Humaid's appeal of his 1999 ("R. V. Humaid, O.J. No. 1507 (O.C.A.); Application for Leave to Appeal Dismissed Without Reasons, S.C.C.A. No. 232. National Post," 2006,) conviction for first-degree murder on the death of his spouse in November of that year. Because female adultery is significant in the Islamic faith and culture, Mr. Humaid stated that his spouse's insinuations of infidelity drove him to lose control.

By the Appeal Court, the tough issue is that the purported views that give the insult more weight are based on the ideas that women are less valuable than males and that assault against women is occasionally justified, if not encouraged. These ideas go counter to core Canadian ideals, such as gender equality. One may argue that the "common person" cannot be fixed with views incompatible with core Canadian values due to policy considerations about criminal law. Criminal law may not recognize that an ideology that runs counter to those core principles may in any way serve as the foundation for an inadequate defense against murder ("R. V. Humaid, O.J. No. 1507 (O.C.A.); Application for Leave to Appeal Dismissed Without Reasons, S.C.C.A. No. 232. National Post," 2006). The Court concluded, "Provocation does not protect an accused who has not lost control but had instead acted based on a sense of vengeance or a culturally driven sense of an appropriate reaction to someone else's misconduct" ("R. V. Humaid, O.J. No. 1507 (O.C.A.); Application for Leave to Appeal Dismissed Without Reasons, S.C.C.A. No. 232. National Post," 2006).

Case Study of Amandeep Atwal

The Punjabi native Rajinder Singh Atwal was found guilty in March 2005 of 2-degree murder for his role in the death of his child Amandeep Atwal, who passed away in 2003 from numerous stab wounds. He had stated that she had caused the injuries to herself.

However, according to what was told to the court, Mr. Atwal wasn't fond of the 17-year-old's relationship with a classmate. According to Todd MacIsaac, Amandeep's boyfriend, the two had a covert two-year romance because she was not allowed to date. After being found guilty of second-degree murder, Mr. Atwal was given a life sentence without the chance of release for 16 years ("R. V. Atwal, B.C.J. No. 1512

(QL) (B.C.S.C.); Parole Ineligibility Period Upheld on Appeal, R. V. Atwal, BCCA 493 (B.C.C.A.). O'Toole, M).

Case Study of Kanwaljeet Kaur Nahar

The 2002 judgment that convicted Mr. Nahar guilty of killing his wife in the second degree was upheld in February 2004. When Mr. Nahar brutally murdered his wife in 2001, he was accused of second-degree murder and said that his actions had been provoked because his wife had his family were shamed by his disrespectful and aggressive behavior, which went against the Sikh community's expectations. Kanwaljeet Kaur Nahar, the victim, reportedly drank drink, smoked, and interacted with men. Mr. Nahar aimed to demonstrate that, in comparison to someone from another cultural group, he was more susceptible to being incited to commit violent crimes against his wife because of her heritage. During the trial and on appeal, the defense was unsuccessful ("R. V. Nahar, [2004] B.C.J. No. 278 (QL) (B.C.C.A.)

Honor killings are regarded as serious crimes in both the UK and the USA and have no legal protection. These offenses are prosecuted in the UK under ordinary criminal rules, just like manslaughter or murder. The Forced Marriage (Civil Protection) Act 2007 is one of the UK's laws designed to shield people against forced weddings, which are frequently associated with violence motivated by honor. Government oversight and specialized police units guarantee that experts are prepared to manage these situations. In a similar vein, honor killings are not specifically covered by statutes in the USA; instead, they are punished under general murder laws. Honor-based violence is covered by the comprehensive safeguards offered by the Violence Against Women Act (VAWA). Both nations have specialist departments and groups devoted to aiding victims and spreading awareness.

Honor killings are when women/men are killed for supposedly going against accepted sexual norms in society. The idea behind these horrific deeds is that the family's honor has been damaged by a woman's or man's conduct. Women may be subjected to violence if they enter into relationships that are considered unsuitable, if they become pregnant as a result of rape or incest, and even if they are just suspected of having illicit relationships or adultery. In addition to spouses, other family members such as moms, brothers, aunts, and cousins can also be the culprits.

Despite these numbers, government agencies and the media in the UK frequently view honor killings as rare incidents that only affect particular ethnic minorities. In the multicultural UK, this viewpoint has resulted in the "ethnicization" of murders for honor. The divide between the public and private domains further complicates the matter, casting doubt on the cultural relativism of British multiculturalism and reshaping the narrative around domestic abuse.

Particularly, "honor and shame"-focused patriarchal, cultural, & religious belief systems support the continuation of honor killings. While diversity is not the primary cause of domestic abuse, it can unintentionally contribute to it by encouraging non-interference with minority customs, honoring cultural diversity, and mandating community involvement, which is frequently spearheaded by male community leaders. As a result, women have been silenced, abused, and had their demands ignored.

CONCLUSION

The intricate relationships between diversity, religion, & social standards are highlighted by the occurrence of honor killings in the USA and the UK. By drawing attention to the tensions that exist between upholding fundamental human rights and maintaining cultural traditions, this approach casts doubt on the idea of multiculturalism. Deeply ingrained patriarchal ideas that value family honor over freedom as an individual, especially when it comes to marriage and relationships, are frequently the driving force behind honor killings.

Honor killings must be addressed with respect for culture while vehemently denouncing violence and upholding human rights in order to be effectively prevented. This necessitates open communication across groups, helping those in need, and making sure the legal & law enforcement authorities are prepared to deal with cases of violence motivated by honor. Moreover, effectively combating racism and xenophobia is essential to creating inclusive societies where individuals from different cultural backgrounds are valued and safeguarded.

Lastly, your research emphasizes the necessity of a well-rounded strategy that protects basic human rights and acknowledges cultural variety. The text underscores the significance of precise and focused interventions and advocates for a fairer and more comprehensive approach to dealing with honor killings in diverse communities.

REFERENCES

Atwal, R. v., & No, B. C. J. 1512 (QL) (B.C.S.C.); parole ineligibility period upheld on appeal, R. v. Atwal, BCCA 493 (B.C.C.A.). O'Toole, M. (24, July 2009). *'Honor killing' cases spark debates over religion and racism. National Post.*

Brandon, J. & Hafez, S., (2010). Honor-Based Violence in the UK. *Crime of the community.*

Brother faces new charge in teenage girl's slaying. (2008, June 27). *CBC News.* http://www.cbc.ca/canada/toronto/story/2008/06/27/aqsaparvez.html#ixzz0iAzN933G

Chesler, P. (2009). The Middle East Quarterly, Spring. *Are honor killings simply domestic violence?* pp. 61-69.

Cockburn, N. (2008, May 7). Ottawa court hears opening statements in alleged 'honor killing. *Ottawa Citizen.* http://www.ottawacitizen.com/news/Ottawa+court+hears+opening+statements+alleged+honour+killing/1573445/story.html#ixzz0z3V9Fksl

R. v. Dulay, (2009). *A.J. No. 29 (QL) (Alta. C.A.).*

Edwards, S. S. M. (2019). Recognizing the Role of the Emotion of Fear in Offences and Defenses. *Journal of Criminal Law*, 83(6), 450–472. DOI: 10.1177/0022018319877784

Gerbaka, B., Richa, S., & Tomb, R. (2021). Honor Killings and Crimes; Familial and Tribal Homicide. In *Child Sexual Abuse, Exploitation and Trafficking in the Arab Region* (pp. 183–228). Springer International Publishing. DOI: 10.1007/978-3-030-66507-4_13

Gill, A. (2009). Honor killings and the quest for justice in black and minority ethnic communities in the United Kingdom. *Criminal Justice Policy Review*, 20(4), 475–494. DOI: 10.1177/0887403408329604

Gorar, M. (2021). *Defining the Limits of Honor-Based Violence and Abuse (Routledge, 2021)* 62. Honor-Based Crimes and the Law. DOI: 10.4324/9781003166207

Griffith, R. (2010). The Forced Marriage (Civil Protection) Act 2007. *British Journal of Midwifery*, 18(2), 125–126. DOI: 10.12968/bjom.2010.18.2.46412

Hill, A. (2012, march 19). Campaigners call for new homicide law for inciting suicide. *The Guardian.*

R. v. Humaid, O.J. No. 1507 (O.C.A.); application for leave to appeal dismissed without reasons,

Idriss, M. M. (2017). Not domestic violence or cultural tradition: Is honor-based violence distinct from domestic violence? *Journal of Social Welfare and Family Law*, 39(1), 3–21. DOI: 10.1080/09649069.2016.1272755

Idriss, M. M., & Abbas, T. (Eds.). (2010). *Honour, Violence, Women and Islam*. Taylor & Francis. news, fox (n.d.). Police say Georgia man killed own daughter to protect family honor. Retrieved 07 8, 2008, from https://www.foxnews.com/story/2008/07/08/police-say-georgia-man-killed-own-daughter-to-protect-family-honor/

Kailayapillai, R. v. (2009). *O.J. No. 1145 (QL)*. S.C.J.

Khan, R. v. [2007] O.J. No. 4383 (QL) (O.C.A.)., Father and stepmother convicted of murdering 5-year-old Farrah Khan. (2004, April 22). *CBC News*. https://www.cbc.ca/canada/story/2004/04/22/khan_20040422.html

Mitchell, B., & Javed, N. (2010, June 16). 'I killed my daughter ... with my hands': Domineering father and son plead guilty to strangling rebellious teenager. Toronto Star, p. A.17.

Mother suspected in UK 'honor murder' implicates husband in teen's killing. (2012, July 10). *CNN*. edition.cnn.com/2012/07/10/world/europe/ukshafilea-honor-murder/. Last visited: 1 January 2015.

R. v. Nahar, [2004] B.C.J. No. 278 (QL) (B.C.C.A.). (n.d.). *R. v. Nahar, B.C.J. No. 1424 (QL) (B.C.S.C.)*.

No, S. C. C. A. 232. National Post. (2006, November 10). *Family honor' murder defense rejected by Supreme Court. National Post*, p. A6.

PTI. (2008). Indian man found guilty of killing son's black wife. The Economic Times. Accessed on 10-08-2024 from https://economictimes.indiatimes.com/news/politics-and-nation/indian-man-found-guilty-of-killing-sons-black-wife/articleshow/3170849.cms

Salman, A. (2021). *For whose honor? An investigation into honour-based violence* (Doctoral dissertation, University of Birmingham).

Shafilea Ahmed case: "Sister saw parents commit murder". (2012, May 21). *BBC News*.

Shafilea Ahmed's Parents Found Guilty of Her Murder. (2012, August 3). *Channel 4 News*.

Shafilea Ahmed's parents were jailed for her murder. (2012, August 3). *The Guardian*.

Shaikh, T. (2014). *Cultural implications behind honor killings* (Doctoral dissertation, Union Institute and University).

Siddiqui, H., & Patel, M. (n.d.). *Safe and Sane, A Model of Intervention on Domestic Violence and Mental Health*. Suicide and Self-harm Amongst Black and Minority Ethnic Women.

Southall Black Sisters. (n.d.). *Krishna Sharma Campaign 1984*.

Two convicted 'honor' killers to be deported from Canada. (2018, March 16). BBC. Retrieved July 1, 2024, from https://www.bbc.com/news/world-us-canada-43434105

Violence against Women and Girls Crime Report 2012-2013. (2014, Sep 1). *Crown Prosecution Service, July 2013*. Retrieved 2014, from www.cps.gov.uk/publications/docs/cps_vawg_report_2013.pdf. Last visited: 1 September 2014

Warming, J., & Clarkson, B. (2009, Jan 07). Father-in-law charged: Peel's 1st murder of 2009 may be 'honor killing'. https://torontosun.com/news/torontoandgta/2009/01/07/7940636-sun.html

Weathers, H. (2007, June 17). Honor killing" sister breaks her silence. *Daily Mail*. www.dailymail.co.uk/femail/article-462342/Honor-killing-sisterbreaks-silence.html. Last visited: 5 April 2014.

Compilation of References

Abdul-muteleb, E. (2011). *Explanation of penal code*. National Center for Legal Publications.

Abraham, L. (2001). Redrawing the *Lakshman Rekha:* Gender differences and cultural constructions in youth sexuality in urban India. *South Asia: Journal of South Asian Studies, 24*(sup001), 133–156. https://doi.org/DOI: 10.1080/00856400108723441

Abu Odeh, L. (1997). Comparatively speaking: The "honor" of the "East" and the "passion" of the "West.". *Utah Law Review*, 2, 287, 292–293.

Abuhattab, A. (2020). Criminal Protection of Women's Rights against Violence in Palestine. https://core.ac.uk/download/373377011.pdf

Abu-Lughod, L. (2011). Honor and the Sentiments of Loss in the Global Discourse on Muslim Women. In *Violence and Belonging: The Quest for Identity in Post-Colonial Africa* (pp. 16–37). Routledge.

Abu-Odeh, L. (1997). Comparatively speaking: The honor of the East and the passion of the West. *Utah L. Rev.*, 287.

Abu-Odeh, L. (2004). *Women of Jordan: Islam*. Labor, and the Law.

Ahammed, H. (2019). *"Honour" killing in India: A Psychological analysis Sub Theme:-Psychology for Social Justice and Equality Presentation mode:-Poster*.

Ahmed, K. (2000). Human Rights in Pakistan remain as bad as they were in past. *Lancet*, 355, 1083–1083.

Ahuja, R. (2011). *Social Problems in India*. Rawat Publications.

Ajula, W., & Gill, A.K. (2014). "Honour" Killings in Canada: An Extreme Form of Domestic Violence. *International Journal of Criminal Justice Sciences 154*.

Alamki, N. (n.d.). *The Horror of 'Honor Killings', Even in US*. Retrieved January 18, 2024, from https://www.amnestyusa.org/updates/the-horror-of-honor-killings-even-in-us/#:~:text=While%20Amal%20survived%2C%20Noor%20later,here%20in%20the%20United%20States

Ali, R. (2001). *The Dark side of „Honor": Women victims in Pakistan*. Shirkat Gah.

Almusleh, N. N. (2021). *Honor Crimes: A Question of Honor*. Culture, and Humanity.

AlQahatani, S. M., Almutairi, D. S., BinAqeel, E. A., Al-Qahatani, R. D., & Menezes, R. G., (27 Dec 2022): *Honour Killings in the East Mediterranean Region: A Narrative Review*

Amardeep. (2021, August 7th). *Honour Killings in India and Role of Khap Panchayats*. Retrieved from Legal Services India E-Journal: https://www.legalserviceindia.com/legal/article-7542-honour-killings-in-india-and-role-of-khap-panchayats.html

Amnesty International, P. (2002). The tribal Justice system. Amnesty 2002, 33(24).

Amnesty International. (2001). *Broken bodies, shattered minds : torture and ill-treatment of women*. Amnesty International.

Amnesty International. 1999. Pakistan: Violence against women in the name of honor. Available from https://www.amnesty.org/en/library/asset

Anderson, J., & Poole, M. (2001). *Assignment and Thesis Writing* (4th ed.). Wiley

Annavarapu, S. (2013). Human rights, honour killings and the Indian law: Scope for a 'right to have rights'. *Economic and Political Weekly*, 48(50), 45–54.

Arora, R. K. (2023). *Honour Killing: Legal Framework in India*. Multi-Disciplinary Journal.

Article 12. (1949). In *Universal Declaration of Human Rights, 1949*.

Arumugam Servai Vs State of Tamil Nadu (The Supreme Court 2011).

Ashwini M Sripad,(2023),killing honor in the name of honor killings, Indian Express

Ashwini, M. Shripad. (2024, January 27). killing honor in the name of honor killings. The New Indian Express. http://newindianexpress.com

Atwal, R. v., & No, B. C. J. 1512 (QL) (B.C.S.C.); parole ineligibility period upheld on appeal, R. v. Atwal, BCCA 493 (B.C.C.A.). O'Toole, M. (24, July 2009). *'Honor killing' cases spark debates over religion and racism. National Post*.

Avraj, A. (2023, 9 19). *A socio-legal reading of honour-based killings in India*. Retrieved 1 24, 2024, from The Leaflet: https://theleaflet.in/a-socio-legal-reading-of-honour-based-killings-in-india/

Babuji, N. (2023). Private Love, Public Eyes: Media, Family, and Honour Killings in India. Shuddhashar Magazine. Retrieved June 29, 2024, from https://shuddhashar.com/private-love-public-eyes-media-family-and-honor-killings-in-india-nandhitha-babuji/

Bajpai, R. (2016) Killing in the name of Honor: Blatant violation of humanrights, Journal on Contemporary Issues of Law, Vol.2, Issue 6.

Baker, N. V., Gregware, P. R., & Cassidy, M. A. (n.d.). Family killings fields: Honor rationales in the murder of women. *Violence Against Women*, 5(2), 164, 165, 171. DOI: 10.1177/107780129952005

Bandura, A. (1999). Social cognitive theory: An agentic perspective. *Asian Journal of Social Psychology*, 2(1), 21–41. DOI: 10.1111/1467-839X.00024

Banerjee-Dube, I. (2008). *Caste in History*. Oxford University Press.

Barak, A. (2012). *Proportionality: Constitutional Rights and their Limitations*. https://doi.org/DOI: 10.1017/CBO9781139035293

Bargach, J. (2005). An ambiguous discourse of rights: The 2004 family law reform in Morocco. *Hawwa*, 3(2), 245–266. DOI: 10.1163/1569208054739056

BBC News India. (2013). India Honour Killing: Paying the price for falling in love.

BBC News, (April 2016): *Pakistan honour killings on the rise*

BBC. (2013). *India honor killings: Paying the price for falling in love*. BBC (British Broadcasting Corporation) News India. Retrieved from https://www.bbc.co.uk/news/world-asia-india-24170866

Bhanbhro, S. (2023, November 29). Reports of 'honour-based' abuse increased following lockdowns and change to police recording rules. *The Conversation*. Retrieved August 8, 2024, 2024 https://theconversation.com/reports-of-honour-based-abuse-increased-following-lockdowns-and-change-to-police-recording-rules-214512#:~:text=Home%20Office%20figures%20show%202%2C905,honour%2Dbased%E2%80%9D%20since%202019

Bhanbhro, S., Wassan, R., Ali Shah, M., Rafique, M., Ali, A., Rafique Wassan, M., Sindh Pakistan Muhbat Ali Shah, J., Sindh Pakistan Ashfaq Talpur, J. A., & Ali Wassan, A. (2013). Karo Kari : the murder of honour in Sindh Pakistan : an ethnographic study. In International Journal of Asian Social Science (Vol. 3, Issue 7). http://shura.shu.ac.uk/7287/

Bhandari, R. (2021). Honor killing as a dark side of modernity: Prevalence, common explanations, and structural factors. *Social Sciences Information. Information Sur les Sciences Sociales.*

Bharadwaj, S. B. (2012). Myth and Reality of the Khap Panchayats: A Historical Analysis of the Panchayat and Khap Panchayat. *Studies in History*, 28(1), 43–67. DOI: 10.1177/0257643013477250

Bhatia, A. (2012). *Honour Killing- A Study of the Causes and Remedies in its Socio Legal Aspect.* International Indexed & Referred Research Journal.

Bhopal, K. (1998). South Asian women in East London. Motherhood and social support. *Women's Studies International Forum, vol.21, issue*(5), pp.485-492. DOI: 10.1016/S0277-5395(98)00067-3

Bhopal, K. (2000). South Asian Women in East London. *European Journal of Women's Studies*, 7(1), 35–52. DOI: 10.1177/135050680000700103

Bhopal, K. (2019). *Gender, 'race' and patriarchy: a study of South Asian women.* Routledge. DOI: 10.4324/9780429456305

Bond, J. E. (2012). *HONOR AS PROPERTY - WestlawNext. 202.*

Bose, A. (2021, May 17). *Human rights law in Magna Carta, Constitution of India and International Conventions - IPleaders.* iPleaders. https://blog.ipleaders.in/human-rights-law-magna-carta-constitution-india-international-conventions/#:~:text=%E2%80%9CTo%20deny%20people%20their%20human,become%20operational%20since%20their%20birth

Brandon, J. & Hafez, S., (2010). Honor-Based Violence in the UK. *Crime of the community.*

Bribosia, E., Rorive, I., European Network of Legal Experts in the Non-discrimination field, European Commission, Human European Consultancy, & Migration Policy Group. (2013). *Reasonable Accommodation beyond Disability in Europe?* Office for Official Publications of the European Union.

Brother faces new charge in teenage girl's slaying. (2008, June 27). *CBC News.* http://www.cbc.ca/canada/toronto/story/2008/06/27/aqsaparvez.html#ixzz0iAzN933G

Brown, J. A. (2014). *Misquoting Muhammad: the challenge and choices of interpreting the Prophet's legacy*. Oneworld.

Bruinsma, G., & Weisburd, D. (2013). *Encyclopedia of Criminology and Criminal Justice*.

Bui, H. N. (2003). Help-seeking behaviour among abused immigrant women: A case of Vietnamese American women. Violence Against Women, vol. 9, issue(2), pp207-239. https://doi.org/DOI: 10.1177/10778012022390006

Bui, H. N. (2003). Help-seeking behaviour among abused immigrant women: A case of Vietnamese American women. *Violence Against Women*, 9(2), 22.

Byrnes, A., Graterol, M. H., & Chartres, R. (n.d.). *State Obligation and the Convention on the Elimination of All Forms of Discrimination Against Women*. Retrieved May 19, 2024 https://law.bepress.com/unswwps-flrps/art48

Caffaro, F., Ferraris, F., & Schmidt, S. (2014). Gender Differences in the Perception of Honor Killing in Individualist Versus Collectivistic Cultures: Comparison Between Italy and Turkey. *Sex Roles*, 71(9–10), 296–318. DOI: 10.1007/s11199-014-0413-5

Can, M., & Edirne, T. (2011). Beliefs and attitudes of final-year nursing students on honor crimes: A cross-sectional study. *Journal of Psychiatric and Mental Health Nursing, vol.18, issue*(2),pp 736-743. http://doi.org/DOI: 10.1111/j.1365-2850.2011.01732

Can, M., & Edirne, T. (2011). Beliefs and Attitudes of Final-year Nursing Students on Honor Crimes: A Cross-Sectional Study. *Journal of Psychiatric and Mental Health Nursing*, 18(8), 736–774. DOI: 10.1111/j.1365-2850.2011.01732.x PMID: 21896117

Case, S., Johnson, P., Manlow, D., Smith, R., & Williams, K. S. (Eds.). (2017). *Criminology*. Oxford University Press. DOI: 10.1093/he/9780198736752.001.0001

Chakravarti, U. (2003). *Gendering Caste: Through a Feminist Lens*. Stree.

Chaturvedi, P., (4 Jan 2021): *Honour killings in India and need for urgent reforms and new laws*

Chaudhary, D. R. (2011). Khaps, shoudn't be allowed, to have their way. *The Tribune*.

Chauhan, S. S. (2020). *A Socio-Legal Study on Honour Killing: Manslaughter in Name of Family's Honour*. MyLawman Socio Legal Review.

Chen, K., & Saifi, S. (2016, October 8). *Pakistan passes legislation against 'honor killings.'* CNN. Retrieved from https://edition.cnn.com/2016/10/06/asia/pakistan-anti-honor-killing-law/index.html

Chesler, P. (2009). The Middle East Quarterly, Spring. *Are honor killings simply domestic violence?* pp. 61-69.

Chesler, P. (2010, July 12). Are some honor killings more equal than others? Fox News. Retrieved June 03, 2024, from https://www.foxnews.com/opinion/are-some-honor-killings-more-equal-than-others

Chesler, P. (2021). *Honor Killing: A Form of Femicide. Dignity: A Journal of Analysis of Exploitation and Violence*, 6(1), 1-25.

Chesler, P. (2009). Are Honor Killings Simply Domestic Violence?*Middle East Quarterly*, 16(2), 61–69.

Chesler, P., & Bloom, N. (2012). Hindu vs. Muslim honor killings. *Middle East Quarterly*, 19(3), 43–52.

Chowdhary, P. (2007). *Contentious Marriages, Eloping Couples: Gender, Caste and Patriarchy in Northern India*. Oxford University Press.

Christianson, M., (20 Dec 2020): *A woman's honour tumbles down on all of us in the family, but a man's honour is only his": young women's experiences of patriarchal chastity norms*

Cockburn, N. (2008, May 7). Ottawa court hears opening statements in alleged 'honor killing. *Ottawa Citizen*. http://www.ottawacitizen.com/news/Ottawa+court+hears+opening+statements+alleged+honour+killing/1573445/story.html#ixzz0z3V9Fksl

Code of Criminal Procedure. (1973).

Cohan, J. A. (2009). Honor killings and the cultural defense. *Cal. W. Int'l LJ*, 40, 177.

Coker, D. K. (1992). Heat of passion and wife killing: Men who batter/men who kill. *SSRN*, 2, 71. DOI: 10.2139/ssrn.2669196

Constitution Of India, art. XIII.

Constitution of India,1950.

Convention on the Elimination of All Forms of Discrimination Against Women CEDAW, art. XVI.

Corbin, B. A. (2014). Between Saviors and Savages: The Effect of Turkey's Revised Penal Code on the Transformation of Honor Killings into Honor Penal Code on the Transformation of Honor Killings into Honor Suicides and Why Community Discourse Is Necessary for Honor Crime Education. *Emory International Law Review*, 29(2).

Coward, H. (2005). Human rights and world's major religions. *The Hindu tradition, 4*, 145-150.

Crime Report of Punjab (2014). Punjab Police. Retrieved from www.punjabpolice.gov.in

Crootof, R. (2019). The internet of torts: Expanding civil liability standards to address corporate remote interference. *Duke Law Journal*, 69, 583.

Crown Prosecution Service (2023): *Statistics on so called Honour- based abuse offenses, England and Wales, 2022 to 2023 Defending Human Rights Worldwide.* (n.d.). Human Rights Watch.

Crown Prosecution Service-. *So Called Honor Based Abuse.*

Cusack, S., & Cook, R. J. (2007). Honor": Crimes, Paradigms, and Violence against. *Women.*

D'Lima, T., Solotaroff, J. L., & Pande, R. P. (2020). For the Sake of Family and Tradition: Honor Killings in India and Pakistan. *Indian Journal of Women and Social Change*, 5(1), 22–39. DOI: 10.1177/2455632719880852

Dahiya, K. (2019). Role of Khap Panchayat in Honour Killings. In *International Journal of All Research Education and Scientific Methods (IJARESM)* (Vol. 7, Issue 2).

Dailey, J. D. & Singh, R. N., (2016): *Honour Killing*

Darvishpour, M., & Lahdenpera, P. (n.d.). Honor-Related Problems in School Contexts in Sweden – theoretical perspective and prevention. *Mälardalen Studies in Educational Sciences*, 10, 13.

Daryani, Y., & Hejazi, E. (2023). *Perception of honor killing: The role of culture, gender, and moral beliefs.*

Dasgupta, S. (2000). Charting the course: An overview of domestic violence in the South Asian community in the United States. *Journal of Social Distress and the Homeless, vol9, issue*(3), pp173-185.

Dasgupta, S. (2000). Charting the course: An overview of domestic violence in the South Asian community in the United States. *Journal of Social Distress and the Homeless, vol9, issue*(3), pp173-185. https://doi.org/DOI: 10.1023/A:10094039171983

Dasgupta, S. D. (2000). Charting the course: An overview of domestic violence in the South Asian community in the U.S. *Journal of Social Distress and the Homeless*, 9(3), 173–185. DOI: 10.1023/A:1009403917198

Dashing hopes, Emboldening Khaps- The High Court verdict on the Manoj Babli Case. (2011, March 18th). Retrieved from Nwes Click: https://www.newsclick.in/dashing-hopes-emboldening-khaps-high-court-verdict-manoj-babli-case

Datta, P. (1999). *Carving blocs: Communal ideology in early twentieth-century.* No Title.

De Guzman, J. T., & Jamias, J. K. V. (2016). The daughter clause: A study of Article 247 of the Revised Penal Code of the Philippines.

Deol, S. S. (2014). *Honor Killings In Haryana State, India: A Content Analysis.* https://www.researchgate.net/publication/333557222

Deol, Singh Satnam. 2014. "Honor Killings in Haryana State, India: A Content

Deol, S. S. (2014). Honor killings in haryana state, india: A content analysis. *International Journal of Criminal Justice Science.*, 9(2), 192.

Dewan, V. K. (2000). *Law Relating to Offences against Women.* Orient Law House.

DH News Service. (2007, June 28). Retrieved january 2024, from The Deccan Herald: https://www.deccanherald.com/

Dickson, P. (2014). Understanding victims of honour-based violence. Community Practitioner : The Journal of the Community Practitioners' & Health Visitors'. *Association*, 87(7), 30–33.

Digvijay Kumar. (2016, March 28). *Honor Killing and its Impact on Society.* Racolb Legal.

Dogan, R. (2014). Different cultural understandings of Honor that inspire killing. Homicide Studies, vol18, issue(4),pp 363-388. DOI: 10.1177/1088767914526717

Domazetoska, S., Platzer, M., & Plaku, G. (2014). *Femicide: A global issue that demands action. (PDF). Genevadeclaration.org.* Academic Council on the United Nations System.

Donovan, D. A., & Wildman, S. M. (1980). Is the reasonable man obsolete: A critical perspective on self-defense and provocation. *Loy. LAL Rev.*, 14, 435.

Dr. Pandey. J.N.,(2015) Constitutional Law of India Allahabad: Central Law Agency,

Duran, J. (2005). Realism, Positivism and Reference. *Journal for General Philosophy of Science*, 36(2), 401–407. DOI: 10.1007/s10838-006-5625-0

Dyer, E. (2015). 'Honor' Killing in UK. *The Henry Jackson Society*, 21.

Dyer, E. (2015). 'Honour' killings in the UK. The Henry Jackson Society. Retrieved June 10, 2024, from https://henryjacksonsociety.org/wp-content/uploads/2015/01/Honour-Killings-in-the-UK.pdf

Eck, C. V. (2003). Purified by blood. Honour Killings amongst Turks in the Netherlands, Amsterdam. DOI: 10.1515/9789048505050

Edwards, S. S. M. (2019). Recognizing the Role of the Emotion of Fear in Offences and Defenses. *Journal of Criminal Law*, 83(6), 450–472. DOI: 10.1177/0022018319877784

Eid J.A. (2020). A Qualitative Study of the Impact of Domestic Violence by Male Relatives on Saudi Female Students in the United States.

Eisner M, Ghuneim K. Honor killing attitudes amongst adolescents in Amman, Jordan. Aggr Behav 2013vol39, issue5, pp.405-17

Eisner, M., & Ghuneim, L. (2013). Honor Killing Attitudes Amongst Adolescents in Amman, Jordan. *Aggressive Behavior*, 39(5), 405–417. DOI: 10.1002/ab.21485 PMID: 23744567

Elakkary, S., Franke, B., Shokri, D., Hartwig, S., Tsokos, M., & Püschel, K. (2014). Honor crimes: Review and proposed definition. *Forensic Science, Medicine, and Pathology*, 10(1), 76–82. DOI: 10.1007/s12024-013-9455-1 PMID: 23771767

El-Kady, R. (2024). *General Section-Penal Code*. Dar Al-Nahda Al-Arabiya.

Elkayam A. (200), *The Quran and Biblical Origins*, Xlibris Corporation

Esposito, J. L. (2011). *What everyone needs to know about Islam*. Oxford University Press. DOI: 10.1093/wentk/9780199794133.001.0001

European Convention for Protection of Human Rights and Fundamental Freedoms, 1950.

European Convention on Human Rights (ECHR), art. II, III.

European Parliament. (n.d.). *TOOLKIT on mainstreaming gender equality in EC development cooperation*.

European Union. (n.d.). *Honour Killing its Causes & Consequences: Suggested Strategies for the European Parliament*. Retrieved May 19, 2024, from https://www.europarl.europa.eu/RegData/etudes/etudes/join/2007/385527/EXPO-JOIN_ET(2007)385527_EN.pdf

Faqir, F. (2001). Intra family femicide in defence of honour: The Case of Jordan. *Third World Quarterly*, 22(1), 165–182. DOI: 10.1080/713701138

Fateh, N. S. (2012). HONOUR KILLING.

Feldman, S. (2010). Shame and honour: The violence of gendered norms under conditions of global crisis. *Women's Studies International Forum*, 33(4), 305–315. DOI: 10.1016/j.wsif.2010.02.004

Francis Carolie V. Union territory, Delhi, A.I.R 1981 S.C 746, 753.

Friedersdorf, C. (2010). American newspapers and honour killings (Updated). The Atlantic. Retrieved June 10, 2024, from, https://www.theatlantic.com/projects/ideas-2010/archive/2010/06/american-newspapers-and-Honour-killings-updated/58292/

Frontline, T. H. (2024). *In Tamil Nadu, the survivor of an honor killing fights caste violence.* Frontline, The Hindu.

Ganguly, T. (19 November 2022) published by Social Legal Corporation- *Honour Killings in South Asia*

Garner, B. A. (Ed.). (n.d.). *Black's Law Dictionary* (Ninth edition 2009, p. 428).

General Assembly of the United Nations Resolution A/RES/57/179. Retrieved January 16, 2024, from https://www.un.org/womenwatch/daw/cedaw/

George Ritzer-Sociological Theory. (8th Edition) -McGraw-Hill (2010).

Gerbaka, B., Richa, S., & Tomb, R. (2021). Honor Killings and Crimes; Familial and Tribal Homicide. In *Child Sexual Abuse, Exploitation and Trafficking in the Arab Region* (pp. 183–228). Springer International Publishing. DOI: 10.1007/978-3-030-66507-4_13

Gill, A. (2009). Honor killings and the quest for justice in black and minority ethnic communities in the United Kingdom. *Criminal Justice Policy Review*, 20(4), 475–494. DOI: 10.1177/0887403408329604

Goldstein, M. A. (2002). The biological roots of heat-of-passion crimes and honor killings. *Politics and the Life Sciences : The Journal of the Association for Politics and the Life Sciences*, 21(2), 28–37. PMID: 16859346

Gorar, M. (2021). *Defining the Limits of Honor-Based Violence and Abuse (Routledge, 2021) 62.* Honor-Based Crimes and the Law. DOI: 10.4324/9781003166207

Greiff, S. (2010). *No Justice in Justifications: Violence against Women in the Name of Culture.* Religion and Tradition.

Grewal, P. K. (2012). Honor killings and Law in India, *IOSR. Journal of the Humanities and Social Sciences*, 5(6).

Griffith, R. (2010). The Forced Marriage (Civil Protection) Act 2007. *British Journal of Midwifery*, 18(2), 125–126. DOI: 10.12968/bjom.2010.18.2.46412

Gupta, M. (2015). The Role of 'Honor' in Violence against South Asian Women in the United States. *Manavi Occasional Paper No. 11*, 2.

Hanan Parvez. (2020, November 8). *Psychology of Honor Killings*. PsychMechanics.

Haq, A. (2022). Honor killings in the Eastern Mediterranean region: A narrative review. *The Lancet. Psychiatry*.

Hassanein, O. (2005). *Private Section-Penal Code*. Dar Al-Nahda Al-Arabiya.

Haybhay, S., Patwe, D., and Jawale, P. (2013). *Honor killing: Killing the honor of humanity?* SASCV 2013 Proceedings

Hellgren, Z., & Hobson, B. (2008, September). Cultural conflict and cultural dialogues in the good society: The case of honor killings in Sweden. *Ethnicities*, 8(3), 385–404. Advance online publication. DOI: 10.1177/1468796808092449

Heydari, A., Teymoori, A., & Trappes, R. (2021). Honor killing as a dark side of modernity: Prevalence, common discourses, and a critical view. *Social Sciences Information. Information Sur les Sciences Sociales*, 60(1), 86–106. DOI: 10.1177/0539018421994777

Hill, A. (2012, march 19). Campaigners call for new homicide law for inciting suicide. *The Guardian*.

Honor-Killing-A-Feminist-Analysis (n.d)-C1F9653CC31408AA

hooks, bell. (1984). *Feminist theory from margin to center*.

Hoskin, R. A., Jenson, K. E., & Blair, K. L. (2017). Is our feminism bullshit? The importance of intersectionality in adopting a feminist identity. *Cogent Social Sciences*, 3(1), 1290014. DOI: 10.1080/23311886.2017.1290014

HRCP. (2013), *State of human rights in 2012*, Retrieved from https://hrcp-web.org/hrcpweb/wp-content/pdf/AR2012.pdf

Huda, S., & Kamal, A. (2020a). Development and validation of attitude towards honour killing scale. *Pakistan Journal of Psychological Research*, 35(35), 227–251. DOI: 10.33824/PJPR.2020.35.2.13

Human Rights Committee. (n.d.). *General Comment No. 28 of the Human Rights Committee, ICCPR, Article 3*.

Human Rights Watch (HRW). 2023-01-12. "Pakistan." World Report 2023: Events of 2022. [Accessed 2023-11-06]

Human Rights Watch, Pakistan. (2016). *Prosecute Rampant 'Honor killing'*.

Hussain, M. (2006). Take my Riches, Give me Justice: A Contextual Analysis of Pakistan's Honor Crimes Legislation. *Harvard Journal of Law & Gender*.

Husseini, R. (2021, August 1). *Murdered women: A history of 'Honor' crimes | History*. Al Jazeera. Retrieved September 15, 2024, from https://www.aljazeera.com/features/2021/8/1/murdered-women-a-history-of-Honor-crimes

ICCPR,1966.

Idriss, M. M., & Abbas, T. (Eds.). (2010). *Honour, Violence, Women and Islam*. Taylor & Francis. news, fox (n.d.). Police say Georgia man killed own daughter to protect family honor. Retrieved 07 8, 2008, from https://www.foxnews.com/story/2008/07/08/police-say-georgia-man-killed-own-daughter-to-protect-family-honor/

Idriss, M. (2017). 'Not Domestic Violence or Cultural Tradition: Is Honour-based Violence Distinct from Domestic Violence? *Journal of Social Welfare and Family Law*, 39(1), 1–19. DOI: 10.1080/09649069.2016.1272755

Idzikowski, L. (Ed.). (2017). *Honor Killings*. Greenhaven Publishing LLC.

Ihugba, U. (2020). *Introduction to Legal Research Method and Legal Writing*. DOI: 10.2307/jj.8155048

In-depth study on all forms of violence against women Report of the Secretary-General. (2006).

India 'honour killers' face death for 1991 murders. (2011, November 16th). Retrieved from BBC News: https://www.bbc.com/news/world-south-asia-15759470

Indian Evidence Act, 1872

International Covenant on Civil and Political Rights (ICCPR), art. XVIII.

Jafri, A. H. Oxford University Press (2008): *Honour Killing: dilemma, ritual and understanding*

Jafri, A. (2008). *Honor Killing: Dilemma, Ritual, Understanding*. Oxford University Press.

Jain, R. (2023, 12 27). *The History Behind Sati, a Banned Funeral Custom in India*. Retrieved 2023, from Culture Trip: https://theculturetrip.com/asia/india/articles/the-dark-history-behind-sati-a-banned-funeral-custom-in-india

James J. Sing. (1999). Culture as sameness: toward a synthetic view of provocation and culture in criminal law. Yales Law Journal, 108(1845).

Jan, A. (2012). Socio-Legal Perspectives of Euthanasia, Jammu & Kashmir. Jay Kay Publisher, 50.

Jarrar. S. M. (2019). *THE DISHONORABLE HONOR CRIMES IN LITERATURE . INTERNATIONAL JOURNAL OF ENGLISH LANGUAGE, LITERATURE AND TRANSLATION STUDIES (IJELR).* Vol 6(1)

Jerusalem: Women's Centre for Legal Aid and Counselling. (2004). Mapping and Analyzing the Landscape of Femicide in Palestine Society.

Jewkes, R. (2002). Preventing sexual violence: A rights-based approach. *Lancet*, 360(9339), 1092–1093. DOI: 10.1016/S0140-6736(02)11135-4 PMID: 12384005

Jha, K. & Rai, H., (2023): *A Socio-Legal Study on Honour Killing: A Menace to the Indian Society*

Johnson, P. (2008). Violence All Around Us. 120-121.

Jordanian Penal Code, 1960.

Journalist's mother arrested for alleged honour killing. (2010, May 4th). Retrieved from NDTV: https://www.ndtv.com/india-news/youth-beaten-to-death-for-marrying-398516/amp/1

Jyothi Vishwanath and Srinivas.C Palakonda, (2011) Patriarchal Ideology of Honor and Honor Crimes in India, International Journal of Criminal JusticeSciences, Vol. 6

Jyothi Vishwanath and Srinivas.C Palakonda, (2011) Patriarchal Ideology of Honour and Honour Crimes in India, International Journal of Criminal Justice Sciences, Vol. 6 Issue 1,2,

Kachhwaha, K., & Manohar, R. (2011). All rights reserved. Under a creative commons Attribution-Noncommercial-Share Alike 2.5 India License Criminal Justice Sciences (IJCJS). In *Official Journal of the South Asian Society of Criminology and Victimology* (Vol. 6, Issue 2).

Kailayapillai, R. v. (2009). *O.J. No. 1145 (QL).* S.C.J.

Kali, K. (2002), *Karo Kari TorTora, Siyahkari, Kala Kali. November 2001.*

Kalnawat, A. M. (2021). Indian Legal Framework on Honour Killing. *SLS Nagpur*, 1-25.

Kalnawat, Dr. A.M., (n.d): *Indian Legal Framework on Honour Killing*

Kanchan, T., Tandon, A., & Krishan, K. (2016). Honor Killing: Where Pride Defeats Reason. *Science and Engineering Ethics*, 22(6), 1861–1862. DOI: 10.1007/s11948-015-9694-5 PMID: 26293131

Kandiyoti, D. (1988). Bargaining with patriarchy. *Gender & Society*, 2(3), 274–290. DOI: 10.1177/089124388002003004

Kardam, F. (2024), *The Dynamics of Honour Killing in Turkey*. United Nations Population Fund. Retrieved September 14, 2024, from https://www.unfpa.org/sites/default/files/pub-pdf/honourkillings.pdf

Kaushal, K. (2020). No Honor in Honor Killing: Comparative Analysis of Indian Traditional Social Structure vis-à-vis Gender Violence. *ANTYAJAA: Indian Journal of Women and Social Change*, 5(1), 52–69.

Kaushal, K. (2020). No Honor in Honor Killing: Comparative Analysis of Indian Traditional Social Structure vis-à-vis Gender Violence. *Indian Journal of Women and Social Change*, 5(1), 52–69. DOI: 10.1177/2455632719880870

Kavitha Kachhwaha,(2011) Khap Adjudication in India: Honouring the Culture with Crimes, International Journal of Criminal Justice Sciences, Vol.6, Issue 1&2,

Keesari Rajitha And Another vs The State Of Telangana . (2022). 27117.

Kejriwal, N. (n.d.). *Honour Killing in North India*. Retrieved January 2024, from Probono India: http://probono-india.in/Indian-Society/Paper/92_honor%20killing%20by%20Neelam.pdf

Kejriwal, -Neelam. (2018). *HONOUR KILLING IN NORTH INDIA*.

Khafagy, F. (2005, May). Honor killing in Egypt. In *an expert group meeting organized by the UN Division for the Advancement of Women* (pp. 17-20).

Khan, A., & Sadiq, S. (2018). KHAP PANCHAYATS IN INDIA: PRECEPTS AND PRACTICES. In *Article in International Journal of Current Research*. https://www.researchgate.net/publication/329311612

Khan, M. (1972). Purdah and polygamy: A study in the social pathology of the Muslim society. *(No Title)*, 49.

Khan, Mr. S., (5 May 2023): *Honour Killing - Current National and International Legal Framework*

Khan, r. (2007). Internet journal of criminology honour-related violence (hrv) in scotland: cross-and multi-agency intervention involvement survey. www.internetjournalofcriminology.com

Khan, R. v. [2007] O.J. No. 4383 (QL) (O.C.A.)., Father and stepmother convicted of murdering 5-year-old Farrah Khan. (2004, April 22). *CBC News*. https://www.cbc.ca/canada/story/2004/04/22/khan_20040422.html

Khan, T. (1999). Chained to custom. 9. The Review.

Khan, K. B. (2014). Versions and Subversions of Islamic Cultures in the Film. The Stoning of Soraya M. *Journal of Literary Studies*, 30(3), 149–167. DOI: 10.1080/02564718.2014.949415

Khan, T. S. (2006). *Beyond Honor : a historical materialist explanation of Honor related violence*. Oxford University Press.

Khap Panchayat allows inte-caste marriages. (2014, 4 21). *The Economic Times*.

KHAP PANCHAYATS OR HONOUR KILLING: A CURSE. (2018).

Kirti, A., Kumar, P., & Yadav, R. (2011). The face of honour based crimes: Global concerns and solutions. *International Journal of Criminal Justice Sciences*, 6(1/2), 343–357.

Korteweg, A. C., & Yurdakul, G. (2010). Religion, Culture and the Politicization of Honor-Related Violence: A Critical Analysis of Media and Policy Debates in Western Europe and North America. *Gender and Development Programme Paper Number 12*, 4.

Korteweg, A. C., (March 2011): *Understanding Honour Killing and Honour Related Violence in the Immigration Context: Implications for the Legal Profession and Beyond*

Korteweg, A. C. (n.d.). Understanding Honor Killing and Honor Related Violence in the Immigration Context: Implications for the Legal Profession and Beyond. *Canadian Criminal Law Review*, •••, 136.

Kothari, C. R. (2004). *Research Methodology: Methods and Techniques* (illustrated, reprint, revised ed.). New Age International.

Kothari, C. R. (2004). *Research Methodology: Methods and Techniques*. New Age International Limited.

Kulwicki, A. D. (2002). THE PRACTICE OF HONOR CRIMES: A GLIMPSE OF DOMESTIC VIOLENCE IN THE ARAB WORLD. *Issues in Mental Health Nursing*, 23(1), 77–87. DOI: 10.1080/01612840252825491 PMID: 11887612

Kumar Rana, D., & Prasad Mishra, B. (n.d.). Honour Killings-A gross violation of Human rights & Its Challenges. www.ijhssi.org

Kumar, Mr. S., (March 2023): *Honour Killing in India- A Socio-Legal Problem*

Kumar, R. (2012, October 12th). *In Rural Haryana, Women Blamed for Rape Where Men Make Rules*. Retrieved from India Ink, The New York Times: https://archive.nytimes.com/india.blogs.nytimes.com/2012/10/12/in-rural-haryana-women-blamed-for-rape-where-men-make-the-rules/

Kumar, R. K. (2023). Honour Killing: Challenges Indian Judicial System. In *International Journal of Creative Research Thoughts* (Vol. 11). www.ijcrt.org

Kumar, A. (2012). Public policy imperatives for curbing Honor Killing in India. *Politics and Governance*, 1(1), 33–37.

Kumar, R. K. (2023). Honor Killing: Challenges Indian Judicial System. [IJCRT]. *International Journal of Creative Research Thoughts*, 11(1), 1–8.

Lansstyrelsen Stockholm. (n.d.). Retrieved January 21, 2024, from https://www.lansstyrelsen.se/english.html

Lari, M. Z. (2011). *A pilot study on 'honor killings' in Pakistan and compliance of law*. The Aurat Foundation.

Lata Singh V State of Uttar Pradesh & Anr. (2006)... *SCC*, 5, 475.

Lata Singh vs State of Uttar Pradesh A.I.R. 2006 S.C. 2522.

Lata Singh Vs. (2006). *Union Of India*. The Supreme Court.

Latha Singh vs. State of Uttar Pradesh 2006 5 SCC 475 (7 July, 2006)

Law Commission of India, (August 2012): *Prevention of Interference with the Freedom of Matrimonial Alliances (in the name of Honour and Tradition): A Suggested Legal Framework*

Legal Research Methodology. (H. N. Tewari, Compiler; reprint ed.). (1999). Allahabad Law Agency.

Leonard, M. M. (2020). *Honor violence, crimes d'honneur, Ehrenmorde: improving the identification, risk assessment, and estimation of honor crimes internationally* (Doctoral dissertation, Universitaet Mannheim (Germany)).

Lewisohn, L. "The Modern Novel." *The Sewanee Review*, vol. 17, issue 4, 1909, pp. 458–474. *JSTOR*, www.jstor.org/stable/27532320

Liddle, J., & Joshi, R. (1986). Daughters of Independence: Gender, Caste and Class in India. New Delhi: Kali for Women & London:Kali for Women & London: Zed Books.

Lidhoo, P. (2020, September 1). Aarushi Talwar to Rhea Chakraborty: A tale of two media trials and zero lessons learnt. *The Wire*. Retrieved June 05, 2024, from https://thewire.in/media/rhea-chakraborty-sushant-singh-rajput-aarushi-talwar-media-trial

Locke, J. (1980). *Second treatise of Government (C.B. Macpherson)*. Hackett.

Madek, C. A. (2005). Killing dishonor: Effective eradication of honor killing. *Suffolk Transnational Law Review*, 29, 53.

Mahanty, J., & Parmar, M. N. (2020). VIOLENCE AGAINST WOMEN: NO HONOUR IN HONOUR KILLINGS. In *International Journal of Creative Research Thoughts* (Vol. 8). www.ijcrt.org

Makkar, S. (2013, May 1st). *Panchayats under the shadow of Khaps*. Retrieved from mint: https://www.livemint.com/Politics/nW03eT80k8lmHDfAUGh33J/Panchayats-under-the-shadow-of-the-khaps.html

Malik, R., Malik, F., & Imtiaz, A. K. (2019). Honor killings of women in Punjab: A sociopolitical context. *South Asian Studies*, 34(02), 401–418.

Maneka Gandhi v Union of India. AIR 1978 SC.

Manhas, D. A. (n.d.). HonourKillings: Socio-Legal Aspects. *Indian Journal of Integrated Research in Law*.

Manusmriti V. (n.d.).

Manusmriti. (n.d.). *V*.

Marie, D. (2003). Castetter, Note, Taking Law into Their Own Hands: Unofªcial and Illegal Sanctions by the Pakistani Tribal Councils, 13 Ind. Intʻl & Comp. *Law Review*, 543, 544–545.

Mark Van Hoecke. (2013). *METHODOLOGIES OF LEGAL RESEARCH which kind of method for what kind of discipline? which kind of method for what kind of discipline?* Mishra, A. (n.d.). *HONOUR KILLINGS: THE LAW IT IS AND THE LAW IT OUGHT TO BE*. https://www.hrw.org/press/2001/04/un

Martin, R. (2013). *Human Rights and the Social Recognition Thesis* (Vol. 44). Journal of Social Philosophy.

Mayeda, R., & Vijaykumar, D. (2016). A review of the literature on honor-based violence. *Sociology Compass*, 10(5), 353–363. DOI: 10.1111/soc4.12367

Mayell, H. (2002). *Thousands of women killed for family honor*. National Geographic News.

Mayell, H. (2002). Thousands of women were killed for family honor. *National Geographic News*, 12, 15.

Maz Idriss. (2018, May 23). *The forgotten male victims of honor-based violence*. The Conversation.

MDG. (1958). Manslaughter and the Adequacy of Provocation: The Reasonableness of the Reasonable Man. *University of Pennsylvania Law Review*, •••, 1021–1040.

Meetoo, V., & Mirza, H. S. (2007). "There is nothing 'honourable' about honour killings": Gender, violence and the limits of multiculturalism. *Women's Studies International Forum*, 30(3), 187–200. DOI: 10.1016/j.wsif.2007.03.001

Ministry Of Home Affairs. (2016). Murder rate across the States: Rajya Sabha unstarred question no. 2449. Retrieved from https://sansad.in/getFile/annex/241/Au2449.docx?source=pqars

Ministry of Home Affairs. (2023). Murder rate across the states: Rajya Sabha unstarred question no. 3734. Retrieved from https://ppl-ai-file-upload.s3.amazonaws.com/web/direct-files/10919250/4686a6a3-e900-4d38-b062-93ee35b3b36a/3734-1.pdf

Mishra, A. (2001). *HONOR KILLINGS: THE LAW IT IS AND THE LAW IT OUGHT TO BE*. https://www.hrw.org/press/2001/04/un

Mishra, A., (13 Dec 2011): *Honour Killings in India: The Law it is and Law it ought to be*

Mishra, A. (n.d.). *Honor Killing : The law It Is and The Law Ought To Be*. Manupatra.

Mishra, P. (2013). Sex ratios, cross-region marriages and the challenge to caste endogamy in Haryana. *Economic and Political Weekly*, 48(35), 70–78.

Mitchell, B., & Javed, N. (2010, June 16). 'I killed my daughter ... with my hands': Domineering father and son plead guilty to strangling rebellious teenager. Toronto Star, p. A.17.

Mitra, N. (2018). Routine unrecognized sexual violence in India. *New Feminist Perspectives on Embodiment*, 183-200.

Moghissi, H. (2005). *Women and Islam: Images and Realities*. Taylor & Francis.

Moody, P. (2002). Love and the law: Love-marriage in Delhi. *Modern Asian Studies*, 36(1), 223–256. DOI: 10.1017/S0026749X02001075

Moore, M. (2011). Psychological theories of crime and delinquency. In *Journal of Human Behavior in the Social Environment* (Vol. 21, Issue 3, pp. 226–239). DOI: 10.1080/10911359.2011.564552

Mother suspected in UK 'honor murder' implicates husband in teen's killing. (2012, July 10). *CNN*. edition.cnn.com/2012/07/10/world/europe/ukshafilea-honor-murder/ . Last visited: 1 January 2015.

Mr. Suresh Kumar. (2023, March). Honor Killing in India: A Socio-Legal Problem. *International Journal of Research in Engineering and Science (IJRES), Volume 11*(Issue 3), PP. 602-606.

Muhammad Siddique v. State 54 PLD (2002).

Muhammad, A. A., & BCPsych, D. P. M. (2013). *Preliminary Examination of So-called" Honor Killings" in Canada*. Department of Justice Canada= Ministère de la justice Canada.

Muhammad, M. H. (2004, November). Ghairat kay Naam par qatal ki saza (The punishment of Honor killing). *Monthly Mohaddith*, 36(11), 26–68.

Mukherjee, S. (2023). *The crime of honor killing: A socio-criminal perspective*. ISBN- 9391820751

Munn vs Illions,1877 94 U.S 113.

Munoz, Gema Martin. (1993). "Patriarchy and Islam." Universidad Autónoma de Madrid Federation of Pakistan v. Gul Hassan Khan (PLD 1989 SC 633)

Nandal, R. S. (2009, July 23rd). *Youth beaten to death for marrying*. Retrieved from NDTV: https://www.ndtv.com/india-news/youth-beaten-to-death-for-marrying-398516/amp/1

Nasrullah, M., Haqqi, S., & Cummings, K. J. (2009). The epidemiological patterns of Honor killing of women in Pakistan. *European Journal of Public Health*, 19(2), 193–197. DOI: 10.1093/eurpub/ckp021 PMID: 19286837

Navratan Singh Fateh,2012 honor killing

Newme, W. (2018). Honour Killings in India. *JETIR*, 1-6.

Nirvana, K. (2005). https://karmanirvana.org.uk/about/about-us/

No, S. C. C. A. 232. National Post. (2006, November 10). *Family honor' murder defense rejected by Supreme Court. National Post, p. A6*.

Oberwittler, D., & Kasselt, J. (2010). *Honor Killings in Germany, 1996-2005, A Study based on Prosecution Files*. Max-Planck Institute.

Oberwittler, D., & Kasselt, J. (2014). Honor killings. In Gartner, R., & McCarthy, B. (Eds.), *The Oxford Handbook of Gender.* Sex, and Crime., DOI: 10.1093/oxfordhb/9780199838707.013.0033

Odeh, L. A. (2010). Honor killings and the construction of gender in Arab societies. *The American Journal of Comparative Law*, 58(4), 911–952. DOI: 10.5131/ajcl.2010.0007

Olwan, D. M. (2013). Gendered Violence, Cultural Otherness, and Honor Crimes in Canadian National Logics. *Canadian Journal of Sociology*, 38(4), 533–556. DOI: 10.29173/cjs21196

Opuz v. Turkey App No 33401/02 ECHR (2009).

Pandey, T. (2022). Stolen glances to stolen lives: Stories behind the 'honour killings' of Rajasthan, Haryana. *ThePrint*. https://theprint.in/feature/stolen-glances-to-stolen-lives-stories-behind-the-honour-killings-of-rajasthan-haryana/893651/

Patel, V. (2015). *Smart cities have to be safe cities.* Retrieved from https://www.researchgate.net/publication/291514771

Patel, S., & Gadit, A. M. (2008). Karo-Kari: A Form of Honor Killing in Pakistan. *Transcultural Psychiatry*, 45(4), 683–694. DOI: 10.1177/1363461508100790 PMID: 19091732

Pattanaik, S., (4 Sep 2020): *Analysis of Honour Killing: National and International Perspective with Relevant Legislations*

Perry, A. (2012). *Honor Killings in Pakistan: An Everyday Matter.* TIME Magazine.

Poddar, A. (2020). Reprehensible Behaviour: The Social Meaning Behind Honour Killing in India. *Brown University*, 1-74.

Poddar, A. (2020). *Reprehensible Behaviour: The Social Meaning Behind Honour Killings in India.* 'Ranbir, S. (2010). The Need to Tame the Khap Panchayats. *Economic and Political Weekly*, 45(21), 17–18.

Prabhune, A. (2020) – *A Socio-Legal Study On Honour Killing As A Crime In India*

Prabhune, A. (n.d.). *A Socio-Legal Study of Honour Killing as a Crime in India.* Retrieved january 2024, from Legal Service India E Journal: https://www.legalserviceindia.com/legal/article-2425-a-socio-legal-study-on-honour-killing-as-a-crime-in-india.html

Prabhune, A. (n.d.). *A Socio-Legal Study On Honor Killing As A Crime In India.* Legal Service India. Retrieved September 15, 2024, from https://www.legalserviceindia.com/legal/article-2425-a-socio-legal-study-on-Honor-killing-as-a-crime-in-india.html

Pradhan, M. (n.d.). *The Jats of Nother India and their Traditional Political System.* Retrieved from The Economic Weekly: http://www.epw.in/system/files/pdf/1965_17/51/the_jats_of_northern_indiatheir_traditional_political_systemii.pdf

PTI. (2008). Indian man found guilty of killing son's black wife. The Economic Times. Accessed on 10-08-2024 from https://economictimes.indiatimes.com/news/politics-and-nation/indian-man-found-guilty-of-killing-sons-black-wife/articleshow/3170849.cms

Puneet Kaur Grewal. (2012) Honor Killings and Law in India, IOSR Journal of Humanities and Social Science, Vol.5, Issue 6.

Puneet Kaur Grewal. (2012). Honor Killings and Law in India. IOSR Journal of Humanities and Social Sciences, 5.

Quealy-Gainer, K. (2019). Malala: My Story of Standing Up for Girls' Rights by Malala Yousafzai. *Bulletin of the Center for Children's Books*, 72(5), 229–230. DOI: 10.1353/bcc.2019.0070

Quraishi, A. (1996). Her honor: A critique of the rape laws of Pakistan from a women sensitive perspective. *Michigan Journal of International Law*, 18, 287.

R. v. Dulay, (2009). *A.J. No. 29 (QL) (Alta. C.A.).*

R. v. Humaid, O.J. No. 1507 (O.C.A.); application for leave to appeal dismissed without reasons,

R. v. Nahar, [2004] B.C.J. No. 278 (QL) (B.C.C.A.). (n.d.). *R. v. Nahar, B.C.J. No. 1424 (QL) (B.C.S.C.).*

Rachel, A. (1531). Ruane. (2000). Murder in the name of honor: Violence against women in Jordan and Pakistan. *Emory International Review*, 14, 1523.

Rachel, A. (2000). Ruane, Comment, *Murder in the Name of Honor: Violence Against Women in Jordan and Pakistan*, 14 Emory Int"l L. *Rev.*, 1523, 1533.

Ragini, R. (2021). Honor Killing. *Issue 4 Int'l JL Mgmt. &. Human.*, 4, 1591.

Rai, S. (2019, November 23rd). *Love Marriages not acceptable, we won't allow them: Balyan Khap leader*. Retrieved from The Times Of India: https://timesofindia.indiatimes.com/city/meerut/love-marriages-not-acceptable-we-wont-allow-them-khap-leader/articleshow/72190461.cms

Raizada, S. (n.d.). SOCIO-LEGAL ANALYSIS ON HONOUR KILLING IN INDIA. *Lexforti Legal Journal* .

Rajalakshmi, T. (2004). *Caste Terror*. Frontline.

Rajshekar, V. T. (2007). *Caste: A Nation within the Nation: A Recipe for a Bloodless Revolution*. Books for Change.

Ram Kishun Kumar. (2023). Honor killing: Challenges Indian Judicial System. *IJCRT.*, 2320–2882.

Ramseshan, G. (2011). The construction of honor in India criminal Law: An Indian Lawyer perspective, honor, violence, women and Isla . 114.

Rana Husseini. (2002, June 12). Murder charge reduced to misdemeanour in Azraq crime of honor case. Jordan Times.

Rana, P. K., & Mishra, B. P. (2013). Honor Killings-A gross violation of Human rights & Its Challenges. *International Journal of Humanities and Social Science Invention*, 2(6), 24–29. www.ijhssi.org

Ratner, C. (2000). A Cultural-Psychological Analysis of Emotions. *Culture and Psychology*, 6(1), 5–39. DOI: 10.1177/1354067X0061001

Rebecca Cook. (1994). State responsibility for violations of women's human rights. Harvard Human Rights Journal, 7, 125,127.

Reddy, R. (2014). Domestic Violence or Cultural Tradition? Approches to Honour Killing as Species and Subspecies in English legal Practisce.

Reddy, R. (2008). Gender, Culture and the Law: Approaches to 'Honour Crimes' in the UK. *Feminist Legal Studies*, 16(3), 305–321. DOI: 10.1007/s10691-008-9098-x

Reema Sahu Ph.D Research Scholar, Department of Law, Shri R. (2024). International Journal of Multidisciplinary Research Review (IJMDRR). Retrieved September 14, 2024, from http://www.ijmdrr.com/admin/downloads/050320243.pdf

Reeves, A. R. (2017). Ronald Dworkin's Theory of Rights. In *Encyclopedia of the Philosophy of Law and Social Philosophy*. https://doi.org/DOI: 10.1007/978-94-007-6730-0_4-1

Rekha Verma, D. (2023). PSYCHO-SOCIO FACETS OF HONOUR KILLING. In *RUSSIAN LAW JOURNAL: Vol. XI.*

Report by- Amnesty International- (2001): *Human Rights*

Report of UNFA/UNDP. (2005). *Zero Tolerance Crucial to Confronting "Honour" Killings in Türkiye.*

Research By University of Cambridge; Published in Journal "Aggressive Behaviour" (n.d)

Rew, M., Gangoli, G., & Gill, A. K. (2013). Violence between Female In-laws in India. []. https://vc.bridgew.edu/jiws]. *Journal of International Women's Studies*, 14(1), •••.

Riksorganisationen GAPF- Glöm Aldrig Pela och Fadime. (2020). Available at: https://gapf.se/rapporter-och-statistik/

Roberts, K. A., Campbell, G., & Lloyd, G. (2013). Honor-based violence: Policing and prevention. *Honor-Based Violence: Policing and Prevention*, 1–197. DOI: 10.1201/b16114

Roberts, K., Campbell, G., & Lloyd, G. (2013), *Honor-Based Violence: Policing and Prevention,* CRC Press. Tahir Khan, *Honor Killings: A Dentitional and Contextual Overview,* http://usconsulate- istanbul.org.tr/reppub/vawo/tkhan.html

Rohit Mulick, N. R. (2007, September 9th). *Panchayats turn into kangroo courts.* Retrieved from The Times of India: https://timesofindia.indiatimes.com/home/sunday-times/deep-focus/panchayats-turn-into-kangaroo-courts/articleshow/2351247.cms

Romesh Thapper v. The State of Madras, AIR 1950 SC 124

Rubin, P. (2010). How a Muslim Woman Was "Honor-Killed" by Her Father Because He Believed She Was Too Americanized. *Phoenix New Times.* https://www.phoenixnewtimes.com/news/how-a-muslim-woman-was-honor-killed-by-her-father-because-he-believed-she-was-too-americanized-6445842

S. Khushboo vs Kanniammal & Anr (2010). SCC, 5, 600

Sadowa, K. (2015). "Honour" killings in Europe as an effect of migration process: Perspective for Poland. *International Letters of Social and Humanistic Sciences*, 58, 83–90. . DOI: 10.18052/www.scipress.com/ILSHS.58.83

Sagar, A. (2016). HIGHEST NUMBER OF HONOUR KILLINGS IN UTTAR PRADESH-A CRITICAL REVIEW. In *International Journal of Management and Applied Science* (Issue 2).

Saha, T. K. (2010). *Textbook on Legal Methods, Legal Systems & Research.* 243.

Saifi, S., Syed, A., & Mogul, R. (2022, February 15). *Court frees brother who confessed to killing social media star Qandeel Baloch.* CNN. https://edition.cnn.com/2022/02/15/asia/pakistan-qandeel-baloch-brother-acquittal-intl-hnk/index.html

Salman, A. (2021). *For whose honor? An investigation into honour-based violence* (Doctoral dissertation, University of Birmingham).

Sangar, A. (2009, August 5th). *What are Khap Panchayats, why they have dominance?* Retrieved from BBC News: https://www.bbc.com/hindi/india/2009/08/090805_honorkill_expert_as

Santhi, J. V. (2013). *Honour killing: A national outcry.* Retrieved from https://www.researchgate.net/publication/301350397

Sarkar, G. (2015). *Death sentence for daughter murder.* Bhagalpur: Times of India. Retrieved from www.timesofindis.indiatime.com/2015/1/30/archivelist/year/2015

Satapathy, S. D. R. (2023). Honour killing as a crime in India. *International Journal of Law Management & Humanities*, 6. Advance online publication. DOI: 10.10000/IJLMH.114514

Section 302. (1860). *Indian Penal Code.* Retrieved June 3, 2024, from https://lddashboard.legislative.gov.in/sites/default/files/A1860-45.pdf

Section 304. (1860). *Indian Penal Code.* Retrieved June 3, 2024, from https://lddashboard.legislative.gov.in/sites/default/files/A1860-45.pdf

Sehnoi, K. r., & Pandiaraj, D. S. (2018). Honour Killing in India- A Socio-Legal Study. *International Journal of Pure and Applied Mathematics.*

Sev'Er, A., & Yurdakul, G.SEV'ER. (2001). Culture of Honor, Culture of Change. *Violence Against Women*, 7(9), 964–998. DOI: 10.1177/10778010122182866

Shafilea Ahmed case: "Sister saw parents commit murder". (2012, May 21). *BBC News.*

Shafilea Ahmed's Parents Found Guilty of Her Murder. (2012, August 3). *Channel 4 News.*

Shafilea Ahmed's parents were jailed for her murder. (2012, August 3). *The Guardian.*

Shafin Jahan vs Asokan K.M AIR 2018 SC 1933.

Shaikh, T. (2014). *Cultural implications behind honor killings* (Doctoral dissertation, Union Institute and University).

Shakthi Vahini Vs Union of India (2018) 7 SCC 192.

Shakti Vahini v. Union of India (September 23, 2023).

Shakti Vahini v. Union of India, (2018) 7 SCC 192., 192 (Supreme Court 2018).

Shendurnikar, D. N. (2011). HONOUR IN THE NEWS: MEDIA REPRESENTATION OF HONOUR KILLINGS. *HONOUR IN THE NEWS: MEDIA REPRESENTATION OF HONOUR KILLINGS*. https://www.academia.edu/3237160/HONOUR_IN_THE_NEWS_MEDIA_REPRESENTATION_OF_HONOUR_KILLINGS

Shendurnikar, N. (2020). Honour in the News: Media Representation of Honour Killings. University of East London. Unpublished manuscript, Transnational Organised Crime (CR7003).

Shetty, D. R., Kumar, K., & Shetty Scholar, D. R. (2019). International Journal of Scientific Research and Reviews Honor Killing Violating Human Rights, it's Theoretical Dimensions: A Review. *IJSRR, 2019*(1), 1–10. www.ijsrr.org

Shier, A., & Shor, E. (2016). "Shades of Foreign Evil": "Honor Killings" and "Family Murders" in the Canadian Press. *Violence Against Women*, 22(10), 1164. DOI: 10.1177/1077801215621176 PMID: 26712236

Shojaee, M. (2012). *The influence of some cultural factors on mental health*. https://www.researchgate.net/publication/340815848

SHREYA. (2023a). PSYCHO-SOCIO FACETS OF HONOUR KILLING. *Russian Law Journal*, 11(2s). Advance online publication. DOI: 10.52783/rlj.v11i2s.572

Siddiqi, D. M., Manisha, G., Awasthi, R., & Chickerur, S. (2012). Blurred boundaries: Sexuality and seduction narratives in selected 'forced marriage' cases from Bangladesh. In Gupte, M., Awasthi, R., & Chickerur, S. (Eds.), *Honour and women's rights: South Asian perspectives* (pp. 155–184).

Siddique, H. (2021, October 31). 'Honour-based' offences soared by 81% in last five years. *The Guardian*. https://www.theguardian.com/society/2021/oct/31/honour-based-offences-soared-by-81-in-last-five-years

Siddiqui, H., & Patel, M. (n.d.). *Safe and Sane, A Model of Intervention on Domestic Violence and Mental Health*. Suicide and Self-harm Amongst Black and Minority Ethnic Women.

Singh, Dr. D. K., (June 2017): *Inter-Caste or Inter-Religious Marriages and Honour Related Violence in India*

Singh, J. (2023, November 2). *Shakti Vahini vs. Union of India (2018): Case Analysis*. Retrieved from iPleaders: https://blog.ipleaders.in/shakti-vahini-vs-union-of-india-2018-case-analysis/#)

Singh, R. N., & Dailey, D. J. (2016). Honor Killing. In *Encyclopedia Britannica*. https://www.britannica.com/topic/honor-killing

Singh, A. K. (2019). *Social psychology* (2nd ed.). PHI Learning Pvt. Ltd.

Singhal, V. (2014). Honour killing in India: An assessment. *Available at SSRN* 2406031.

Singhal, V. K. (2014). *Honour Killing in India : An Assessment*. https://ssrn.com/abstract=2406031 DOI: 10.2139/ssrn.2406031

Singh, D., & Bhandari, D. S. (2021). Legacy of Honor and Violence: An Analysis of Factors Responsible for Honor Killings in Afghanistan, Canada, India, and Pakistan as Discussed in Selected Documentaries on Real Cases. *SAGE Open*, 11(2), 21582440211022323. Advance online publication. DOI: 10.1177/21582440211022323

Sinha, A. (2014, April 26th). *Transformation of Khap Panchayats*. Retrieved from Sahara Samay Live: http://m.samaylive.com/editorial/262627/khap-deleted-conditional-ban-on-interracial-marriages.html

Siwach, S. (2014, 5 16). 2 cases of Honour Killing in Haryana. *The Times of India*.

Smt. Chandrapati vs. State of Haryana and Others on 27 May 2011

Smt_Laxmi_Kachhawaha_vs_The_State_And_Ors_on_15_March_1999. (n.d.).

Sneha singh,(2017) Honour Killings in India: Need for composite and strict legal framework, International Journal of Interdisciplinary and multidisciplinary studies, Vol.4, Issue 3,

Sohail Akbar Warraich. (2005). *Honor Killings and the Law in Pakistan"; and Sara Hussain, „Honor Crimes: Paradigms, and violence against Women*. Zed Books.

Solberg, & Kristin Elisabeth. (2024). Killed in the Name of Honor. *The Lancet, London, 373*(9679). from https://www.proquest.com/docview/199045895?sourcetype=Scholarly%20Journals

Solotaroff J. L., & Prabha R.P. (2020). *For the Sake of Family and Tradition: Honour Killings in Pakistan and India. Volume 5, Issue 1*.

Solotaroff, J. L., D'Lima, T., & Pande, R. P. (2020). For the Sake of Family and Tradition: Honour Killings in India and Pakistan. *ANTYAJAA: Indian Journal of Women and Social Change*, 22-39.

Solotaroff, J. L., & Pande, R. P. (2014). *Violence against women and girls: Lessons from South Asia*. World Bank Publications. DOI: 10.1596/978-1-4648-0171-6

Sonbol, A. E. A. (2003). *Women of Jordan: Islam, labor, and the law*. Syracuse University Press.

Southall Black Sisters. (n.d.). *Krishna Sharma Campaign 1984*.

Sripad, A. M. (2023, September 4). Killing honour in the name of 'honour killings'. *The New Indian Express*. https://www.newindianexpress.com/states/karnataka/2023/Sep/04/killing-honour-in-the-name-of-honour-killings-2611437.html

Srour, A. F. (2019). *Private Section-Penal Code, Crimes Prejudicial to The Public Interest – Crimes of Individuals – Funds Crimes*. Dar Al-Nahda Al-Arabiya.

St. Chandrapati Vs State of Haryana and Others. (2007). *Crl. Misc. No. M-42311 of 2007 (O&M)*. The Supreme Court.

Sule, R., Acharya, A., & De Sousa, A. (2015). Psychosocial Aspects of Honour Killings. *Indian Journal of Mental Health*, 2(2), 132. DOI: 10.30877/IJMH.2.2.2015.132-143

Sunny, S. (2017, 8 26). Delhi: Man kills sister-in-law for 'honour', beheads body, chops her arms. *The Hindustan Times*.

Supervisor, L. E., & Appelqvist, M. (2008). *Crimes of Honour-Females' Right for Support in the Multicultural Society*.

swp2000_eng. (n.d.).

Thakur, R., Sinha, A. K., & Pathak, R. K. (2015). Khap Panchayats in Transition with Contemporary Times: An Anthropological Evaluation. *South Asian Anthropologist*, 15(1), •••.

The Capability Approach. (2011). In *Stanford Encyclopedia of Philosophy*. Retrieved January 3, 2024, from https://plato.stanford.edu/entries/capability-approach/#pagetopright

The Hudood Ordinances. (2011, May 7). *DAWN*. Retrieved January 3, 2024, from https://www.dawn.com/news/626858/the-hudood-ordinances

The Indian Express. (2021). Honour killing: Accused should have waited for conclusion of trial before taking bail, says SC. *The Indian Express*. https://www.newindianexpress.com/nation/2021/Jul/09/honour-killing-accused-should-have-waited-for-conclusion-of-trial-before-takingbail-says-sc-2327797.html#:~:text=Mamta%2C%20Jaipur%2Dbased%20girl%2C,Amit%20Nair%27s%20murder%20in%20Jaipur

The Wire Staff (30 June 2021): *Majority of Indians Across Religions Oppose Inter-Religious Marriage*

Thenua, B. S. (2016). Khap Panchayats among the Jats of North-West: A Socio-Historical Interpretation of Medieval Period. *IRA-International Journal of Management & Social Sciences (ISSN 2455-2267), 5*(3), 402. DOI: 10.21013/jmss.v5.n3.p2

Therapy Brands. (2022, September 5). *The Relationship Between Culture and Mental Health*. Therapy Brands.

TNIE. (2023). *Killing honor in the name of 'honor killings*. The New Indian Express.

Turner, J. C., Brown, R. J., & Tajfel, H. (1979). Social comparison and group interest in ingroup favouritism. *European Journal of Social Psychology*, 9(2), 187–204. DOI: 10.1002/ejsp.2420090207

Two convicted 'honor' killers to be deported from Canada. (2018, March 16). BBC. Retrieved July 1, 2024, from https://www.bbc.com/news/world-us-canada-43434105

Tyagi, M. (2021). Honour Killing in India. *The Times of India*.

Tyagi, M., (20 June 2021): *Honour Killing in India*

U. N. Women. (2022). Gender-related killings of women and girls (femicide/feminicide).

UDHR. 1948, Article 2, (General Assembly Resolution 217 A) United Nations General Assembly, 1948 (UN). Retrieved January 5, 2024, from https://www.un.org/en/about-us/universal-declaration-of-human-rights#:~:text=Article%202,property%2C%20birth%20or%20other%20status

Ullah, M. Z., (27-05-2010): *Honour killings in Pakistan under Theoretical, Legal and Religious Perspectives*

Umachandran, S. (2010, July 7th). *Now, honour killing rocks TN: Father attacks daughter*. Retrieved from The Times of India: https://m.timesofindia.com/india/now-honor-killing-rocks-tn-father-attacks-daughter/articleshow/6136096.cms

UN General Assembly's Resolution A/RES/48/104. Retrieved January 18, 2024, from https://www.un.org/womenwatch/daw/cedaw/

UN Office. (2010). *Impunity for Domestic Violence, 'Honour Killing' cannot continue.*

UN Report. (1985). *Declaration of Basic Principles of Justice for Victims of Crime and Abuse of Power.*

UNICEF. (n.d.). *UNICEF Report on the State of the World's Children 2002 for report on a grassroots movement in Senegal to end FGM.* Retrieved January 14, 2024, from www.unicef.org

United Nations Convention on Elimination of All Forms of Discrimination Against Women. 1979, Article 1, United Nations General Assembly, 1979, Retrieved January 18, 2024, from https://www.un.org/womenwatch/daw/cedaw/

United Nations Convention on Elimination of All Forms of Discrimination Against Women. 1979, Article 15, United Nations General Assembly, 1979. Retrieved January 18, 2024, from https://www.un.org/womenwatch/daw/cedaw/

United Nations Convention on Elimination of All Forms of Discrimination Against Women. 1979, Article 16, United Nations General Assembly, 1979, Retrieved January 16, 2024, from https://www.un.org/womenwatch/daw/cedaw/

United Nations Convention on Elimination of All Forms of Discrimination Against Women. 1979, Article 2, United Nations General Assembly, 1979. Retrieved January 19, 2024, from https://www.un.org/womenwatch/daw/cedaw/

United Nations Convention on Elimination of All Forms of Discrimination Against Women. 1979, Article 3, United Nations General Assembly, 1979, Retrieved May 18, 2024, from https://www.un.org/womenwatch/daw/cedaw/

United Nations Convention on Elimination of All Forms of Discrimination Against Women. 1979, Article 5 (a), United Nations General Assembly, 1979. Retrieved January 15, 2024, from https://www.un.org/womenwatch/daw/cedaw/

United Nations Convention on Elimination of All Forms of Discrimination Against Women. 1979, General Recommendation No. 12 (Eighth Session, 1989) Violence against Women, 1989, United Nations General Assembly, 1979. Retrieved January 18, 2024, from https://www.un.org/womenwatch/daw/cedaw/

United Nations Convention on Elimination of All Forms of Discrimination Against Women. 1979, General Recommendation No. 19 (11th Session, 1992) Violence Against Women, 1992, United Nations General Assembly, 1979. Retrieved January 14, 2024, from https://www.un.org/womenwatch/daw/cedaw/

United Nations Convention on Elimination of All Forms of Discrimination Against Women. 1979, General Recommendation No. 21 (13th Session, 1994), Equality in Marriages and Family Relations, 1994, United Nations General Assembly, 1979. Retrieved January 18, 2024, from https://www.un.org/womenwatch/daw/cedaw/

United Nations Convention on Elimination of All Forms of Discrimination Against Women. 1979, General Recommendation No. 6 (Seventh Session, 1988) Effective National Machinery and Publicity, United Nations General Assembly, 1979. Retrieved January 17, 2024, from https://www.un.org/womenwatch/daw/cedaw/

United Nations Convention on Elimination of All Forms of Discrimination Against Women. 1979, United Nations General Assembly, 1979. Retrieved January 15, 2024, from https://www.un.org/womenwatch/daw/cedaw/

United Nations General Assembly Resolution A/RES/59/165. Retrieved January 18, 2024, from https://www.un.org/womenwatch/daw/cedaw/

UNITED NATIONS OFFICE ON DRUGS AND CRIME. (2019). GLOBAL STUDY ON HOMICIDE. In *GLOBAL STUDY ON HOMICIDE*. United Nations. https://www.unodc.org/documents/data-and-analysis/gsh/Booklet_5.pdf

United Nations. (2013). *Human Rights*. Gender-Related Killings of Women and Girls.

Universal Declaration Of Human Rights, art. II, III, VII.

Universal Declaration Of Human Rights, art. III

Universal Declaration Of Human Rights, art. III, II .

Universal Declaration Of Human Rights. art. V .

Universal Declaration on Human Right, 1948.

Uzoma. (2020). Introduction to Legal Research Method and Legal Writing.

Vatandoost, N. (2012). *The News Coverage of Honor Killings in Canadian Newspapers*. University of Ontario Institute of Technology.

Velasquez Rodriguez case, Inter-American Court of Human Rights, judgment 27 July 1988, (Ser. C, No. 4), para. 172–4.

Version, A. U. (2017). General Recommendation No. 35 on Gender-Based Violence against Women, Updating General Recommendation No. 19: Committee on the Elimination of Discrimination against Women. *International Human Rights Law Review*, 6(2), 279–305. DOI: 10.1163/22131035-00602003

Vesvikar, M., & Agarwal, M. (2022). HONOR KILLING IN INDIA. *Perspectives in Social Work*, 31(1), 48–62.

Violence against Women and Girls Crime Report 2012-2013. (2014, Sep 1). *Crown Prosecution Service, July 2013*. Retrieved 2014, from www.cps.gov.uk/publications/docs/cps_vawg_report_2013.pdf. Last visited: 1 September 2014

Vishwanath, J., & Palakonda, S. (2011). *Patriarchal Ideology of Honor and Honor Crimes in India* (Vol. 6(1/2)). Thirunelveli: International Journal of Criminal Justice Sciences.

Walker, A. (1987). *Woman physiologically considered as to Mind, Morals, Marriage, Matrimonial Slavery, Infidelity and Divorce*. Motilal Banarsidass Publishers.

Warming, J., & Clarkson, B. (2009, Jan 07). Father-in-law charged: Peel's 1st murder of 2009 may be 'honor killing'. https://torontosun.com/news/torontoandgta/2009/01/07/7940636-sun.html

Weathers, H. (2007, June 17). Honor killing" sister breaks her silence. *Daily Mail*. www.dailymail.co.uk/femail/article-462342/Honor-killing-sisterbreaks-silence.html. Last visited: 5 April 2014.

Welcham, L. (2007). 'Honour and Violence in a Modern Shar`i Discourse'

Welchman, L., & Hossain, S. (2014). *Introduction: "Honor", Rights and Wrongs*. www.soas.ac.uk/Honorcrimes

Welchman, L., & Hossain, S. (2005). *Honor. Victoria: Spinifex Press*. Zed Books.

Welchman, L., & Hossain, S. (Eds.). (2005). *Honor": Crimes, Paradigms, and Violence Against Women*. Spinifex Press. DOI: 10.5040/9781350220621

What are Khap Panchayats? (2010, May 12th). Retrieved from Hindustan Times: https://www.hindustantimes.com/india/what-are-khap-panchayats/story-aAx17V9V2eDeD4hMA4wb4N.htm

Women, U. N. (2023). Gender-related killings of women and girls (femicide/feminicide). Retrieved from https://www.unwomen.org/sites/default/files/2023-11/gender-related-killings-of-women-and-girls-femicide-feminicide-global-estimates-2022-en.pdf

Women, U. N. (n.d.). *Defining "honour" crimes and "honour" killings*. Retrieved May 19, 2024, from https://www.endvawnow.org/en/articles/731-defining-honourcrimes-and-honour-killings.html

Wood, J. C. (n.d.). A History of Murder: Personal Violence in Europe from the Middle Ages to the Present (review). https://doi.org/DOI: 10.2307/40802138

Woolf, G. D. (2005). *Ancient Civilizations. The Illustrated Guide to Belief, Mythology and Art*. Duncan Baird Publications.

World Health Organisation. (2012). Femicide.

Wynn, L. L. (2021). 7. "Honor Killing": On Anthropological Writing in an International Political Economy of Representations. *Love, Sex, and Desire in Modern Egypt*, 137–155. https://doi.org/DOI: 10.7560/317044-008/XML

Xavier, Dr. M. S., (March 2015): *Honour Killings: A Global Concern*

XAVIER, M. S. (2015). *Honor Killings: A Global Concern*. PARIPEX - INDIAN JOURNAL OF RESEARCH, 4(3).

XAVIER, M. S. (2015). Honour Killings: A Global Concern. *PARIPEX - INDIAN JOURNAL OF RESEARCH, 4*(3).

Xavier, S. (2015). Honour killings: A global concern. *Paripex-Indian Journal of Research*, 4(3), 6–9.

Yamani, M. (1996). Feminism and Islam: Legal and literary perspectives. New York University Press, 141–194.

Yolanda Asamoah-Wade, *Women's Human Rights and "Honor Killings" in Islamic Cultures*, 8 Buff. Women"s L.J. 21, 21–22 (1999).

Zaid, M. (2015). *The lenient treatment of honor crimes in Egypt* [Master's Thesis, the American University in Cairo]. AUC Knowledge Fountain. https://fount.aucegypt.edu/etds/169

About the Contributors

Somesh Dhamija is associated with Institute of Legal Studies & Research, GLA University, Mathura, India in the capacity of Dean. He has a judicious blend of corporate exposure along with academic acclaim spanning over a period of more than three decades. Along with this, he has proven his mettle as an accomplished Trainer vis-à-vis various facets of Leadership. With a strong research profile, he has various authored and edited books, proceedings and journals. He attended International Leadership Program at Central European University, Budapest, Hungary sponsored by European Environmental Agency and Asia-Pacific Leadership Program at Tongji University, Shanghai, China, sponsored by the United Nations. He has been bestowed with "Asia Pacific Regional Champion 2020 Award for Teaching Excellence" by the Chartered Institute of Management Accountants, UK and "Exemplary Academic Leader of 2020 Award" by the Centre for Education Growth and Research (CEGR), New Delhi.

Tarun Pratap Yadav is Assistant Professor, Institute of Legal Studies and Research, GLA University, Mathura, India. He is Doctorate from CCS University, Meerut, India. He has an academic and industry experience of 10 Years. He had previously worked at Amity University, Noida, GGS Indraprastha University, Delhi etc. His area is specialization is Legal History, Constitutional Law & Business Law. He has publications /paper presentations/participations in many International and National Seminars. He is Life time member of Indian History Congress, U.P History Congress, Rajasthan History Congress, Income Tax Appellate Tribunal (ITAT), New Delhi etc. He is a die-hard fan of Real Madrid.

Jae-Seung Lee is an Assistant Professor of Criminal Justice at Miami University. He earned his Ph.D in Criminal Justice from the Department of Criminal Justice and Criminology in the College of Criminal Justice at Sam Houston State University. He has many peer reviewed research papers and manuscripts to his name. He has taught various courses like Introduction to Criminal Justice, Introduction to Policing, The

Criminal Court, Correctional System and Practises, Perspectives in Crime, Criminal Justice Research Methods, Juvenile Justice etc.

Harshita Singh is the Assistant Professor of Law in Amity Law School, Amity University Noida(U.P). She is doctorate from Mewar University, Chittorgarh, India. She is an ardent academician and an editor at Journal of Law and Public Policy. Dr. Singh has published many books and contributed various research papers and chapters. She is a lifetime member of prestigious International Journals like Asian Resonance and Periodic Review. She has an assortment of paper presentation to her credit. Her areas of specialization include Constitutional Law, Labour Law, Women and Criminal Law.

Myunghoon Roh is an Assistant Professor in the Department of Criminal Justice and Criminology at Salve Regina University, Rhode Island, USA. He is Doctorate of Philosophy in Criminology and Justice Policy Northeastern University, Boston, Massachusetts, USA. He is comparative criminologist testing contemporary criminology theories on juvenile delinquency. Dr. Roh has published various research papers on several peer-reviewed journal, including Violence & Victims, BMC Public Health, etc. His areas of research specialization include Criminology Theory, Juvenile Delinquency, Comparative Research in Criminology, and Human Microbiome.

***

Aranya Agrawal is a passionate and hardworking law student currently pursuing an integrated degree of Bachelor of Arts and Bachelor of Legislative Law (BA-LLB) from GLA University, Mathura, India. Aranya excels as a law student, balancing her rigorous studies with active involvement in her department. She serves as the General Secretary of the Expositio Club, where she plays a pivotal role in organizing events and fostering a vibrant legal discourse among her peers. Additionally, her commitment to social justice is evident through her active participation in the department's Legal Aid Clinic, where she contributes to providing legal assistance to those in need. Aranya aspires to become a distinguished legal professional. She is driven by a vision to make a meaningful impact in the legal world, advocating for justice and contributing to the evolution of legal practices.

Barkha Agrawal is a fifth-year law student at Amity University, Noida. Over the past years, She has dedicated herself in understanding and navigating the complexities of the legal world, balancing rigorous academic coursework with hands-on practical experience. Throughout her studies, Barkha has gained valuable practical experience through internships with various advocates and law firms. Outside the classroom, she has been actively engaged in various extracurricular activities. She has various experience in paper presentation and has 2 publications in her name in books and reputed journals. Passionate about addressing social injustices, they aim to use their legal expertise to drive meaningful change in the justice system. She posseses the pre-requisite skills and personal attributes to start a challenging career within law and thus aims to become a lawyer.

Siddhi Agrawal is a dedicated legal professional completing her B.Com L.L.B (Hons.) at GLA University, Mathura. With extensive hands-on experience, she has worked under notable advocates, gaining expertise in commercial agreements, criminal and civil cases, and arbitration. Siddhi has participated in national moot court competitions and various legal seminars, demonstrating her public speaking and research abilities. Her commitment to social causes is reflected in her project on legal rights awareness and her publications on "Honour Killing" and "Marital Rape." As the General Secretary of the Moot Court Committee at her university, Siddhi has shown leadership and dedication, earning several accolades, including the "Honor of Young Activist Award" on International Human Rights Day. With her strong legal background and passion for justice, Siddhi Agrawal is set to make a meaningful impact in the legal field.

Prestha Chhaparia specializes in understanding the legal structure and theoretical framework. She has an internship experience in Civil Law at the District and Sessions Court, Mathura. Additionally, she has learnt the basics of drafting at Rahul Trivedi & Associates under Adv. Rahul Trivedi. She has worked as a student editor and has several national and international publications. Strong oral and written communication, creative writing are her strong points.

Avinash Dadhich is Director, Manipal Law School, Manipal Academy of Higher Education, Bengaluru, India and has an academic and Industry experience of 15 Years. His areas of specialization are Global Competition Law /Regulation of AI /Robotics/Internet/Data Privacy. He has completed his Ph.D from United Kingdom and LL.M from France on full scholarships and earned LL.B from University of Delhi. He has held the position of Advocate, Supreme Court of India, Manager, Deloitte India LLP, Senior Consultant, Ernst & Young (EY) LLP, Law Expert, Competition Commission of India, Ministry of Corporate Affairs, Govt. of India, Gide Loyrette Nouel LLP, Paris, France & White & Case LLP, Brussels, Belgium.

Aruna Dhamija is professor at GLA University, Mathura, India. She is also Associate Director of Centre of Spirituality and Wisdom and Presiding Officer of Internal Complaints Committee at Institute of Legal Studies and Research, GLA

University, Mathura, India. Having an enriching experience of close to two decades, Dr. Aruna Dhamija, incorporates the various concepts related to management along with human sociology to the best. Her areas of interest include Human Resource Management, Organizational Behavior and Marketing. She has published a good number of international/national research papers indexed in such prestigious databases as Scopus, ABDC, SCIE, ESCI, etc. and has conducted workshops/ training sessions on various facets of HR, Organization Behaviour and Marketing as well as how to carry out quality research and publish in reputed journals. She has attended and conducted in workshops/Short Term Courses at some of the most prominent institutions at national and international level too. She was selected a one-week short term course at Tongji University, Shanghai, China, sponsored by the United Nations. In addition, she was nominated twice and subsequently selected for a one-week short-term course at Central European University in Budapest, Hungary. She also undergoing project of ICSSR. She is known for her mentoring abilities and counseling prowess and is extremely popular among students for her pragmatic approach towards facilitating the learning process. Dedicated and experienced professional serving as the Presiding Officer of the Internal Complaints Committee (ICC). With a commitment to upholding the principles of equity and justice, responsible for managing and ensuring the effective implementation of policies related to workplace harassment and discrimination.

Sudiksha Dhungel is a dedicated first-year student pursuing BCom LLB (Hons) at the Institute of Legal Studies and Research, GLA University, Mathura. She currently serves as the Newsletter Editor and Website Coordinator for ILSR, GLA University, showcasing her organizational and communication skills. Sudiksha is poised to embark on an internship at PUCL, Jaipur, demonstrating her commitment to practical legal experience and social justice issues. Her academic interests lie in mooting, research, and drafting, reflecting her passion for legal advocacy and meticulous attention to detail. Sudiksha Dhungel is driven by a desire for continuous learning and aims to make meaningful contributions to the legal field.

Himanshi Dixit is a dedicated student at GLA University, where she is pursuing a B.A. LL.B degree. Her passion for the field of law drives her academic journey, as she seeks to understand and engage with the complexities of legal systems. Himanshi's commitment to her studies reflects her aspiration to make a meaningful impact in the legal profession. Her time at GLA University is marked by a deep dedication to learning, critical thinking, and a strong sense of justice.

Ramy El-Kady is a Full Professor of Criminal Law at the Police Academy and holds the position of Head of the Criminal Law Department. He was rewarded with the State Encouragement Award in Legal and Economic Sciences, Citizenship and Human Rights Branch, on the topic of "the right of persons cooperating with justice for protection in international conventions and national legislation. He graduated from the Police College in 1999. He obtained a postgraduate diploma in criminal sciences and public law, which is equivalent to a master's degree in criminal law, in 2003. He obtained a PhD in criminal law from the Faculty of Law, Cairo University, on the topic of (Mediation as an Alternative to a Criminal Case: A Comparative Study. He currently teaches criminal law subjects to college students. He supervised numerous studies submitted for doctoral degrees and higher diplomas and authored a host of research in the criminal law field. He has previously judged numerous research papers in a number of refereed regional scientific journals. He published a host of research in refereed and indexed periodicals and took part in a number of international and local conferences and symposia.

Chanchal Garg is a law student at GLA University, Mathura. She has participated in different Moot Court Competitions, Intra Mock trial Advocacy Competition and debate competitions. She has also published a research article before and has a keen interest in research field.

Mugdha Garg, specializes in understanding the practical aspects of legal structure and theoretical framework. She has an internship experience in Arbitration Law in New Delhi, India. Additionally, she has learnt the basics of drafting and extensive research at Kapoor & Co., Law Firm based at New Delhi, India. She has strong oral and written communication and has a keen interest in Research.

Radhika Garg is currently an undergraduate student pursuing B.A LL.B (Hons) at GLA University in Mathura, Uttar Pradesh, India. Her academic focus and career aspirations lean towards the corporate sector, where she aims to make a significant impact. Radhika possesses strong research abilities, as evidenced by her published work on the topic of marital rape in India, showcasing her dedication to addressing critical social issues through legal scholarship. As she continues her education and professional journey, Radhika remains committed to exploring and contributing to the field of law, particularly in areas that intersect with corporate law and social justice

Muskan Gautam is a 4th-year student of GLA University she has an experience of writing in a variety of forms and deciphering complex legal issues which has helped her with various publications in different books and journals

Tulsi Gupta is pursuing B.A LL.B (Hons.) at GLA University, Mathura, India. She is an active member of the university's Expositio Club. She is actively participated in various extra curriculum activities at university level. She has also participated in various competition's including National Extempore Competition and Dinesh Vyas Memorial National Essay Writing Competition. She has also attended various conferences and webinars which helped her to enhance her skills in the field of law. She aims to specialize in criminal law and aspire to join judicial services.

Tanisha Jain is an ambitious undergraduate student currently pursuing BA LLB (Hons) at GLA University in Mathura, Uttar Pradesh, India. She has published her research, particularly focusing on areas such as sanitation law in India and marital rape in several books. Driven by a passion for corporate law, Tanisha aims to specialize in contract drafting. To achieve this goal, she has enrolled in the International Contract Drafting Course offered by LawSikho, demonstrating her commitment to acquiring specialized knowledge and practical skills in this domain. Recognizing the importance of a global perspective in her field, Tanisha has also embarked on courses related to real estate law in both India and the United States. This dual focus underscores her comprehensive approach to legal education and her aspiration to become a proficient professional adept at navigating complexities in diverse legal landscapes. With a strong foundation in academics and a proactive approach to learning, Tanisha Jain is poised to make significant strides in her legal career, contributing meaningfully to the field of law and beyond.

Chunrye Kim, an associate professor in the Department of Sociology and Criminal Justice at Saint Joseph's University, specializes in studying various aspects of violence within intimate relationships, such as intimate partner violence, stalking, and violence against women. She also examines the policies related to these issues, particularly community-based intervention policies. Kim takes an interdisciplinary approach to her research agenda, conducting numerous studies that align with her research interests. Her work has been published in reputable peer-reviewed journals, including Trauma, Violence, and Abuse, Journal of Interpersonal Violence, Child Abuse and Neglect, and Journal of Family Violence. Additionally, she has a wide range of research interests that extend to contemporary social problems, such as mass shootings, abortion, and the social stigma surrounding victimization disclosure.

Anusha Kulshrestha is currently an undergraduate student pursuing B.A LL.B (Hons.) at Institute of Legal Studies and Research, GLA University, Mathura, India. At GLA University, she is an active member of the university's Theatre Club. She has been fortunate enough to have had a diverse range of experiences, from her research work (chapter) which has been published in the following books-: Sanitation- A sundry of impediments in the Indian Scheme and Marital Rape: The Crime Beyond Contours and a research paper on 'In between the State and Economy: A Reflection of Animal Trafficking' published by UPES University, Dehradun to her Anthologies on the topic 'Unconditional love' and 'Qismat' and many scripts in the theatre club. As a highly motivated and dedicated individual, she has consistently demonstrated a strong work ethic and passion for excellence in all aspects of her life. With a keen interest in personal growth and development, she has continually sought out new challenges and opportunities to expand her skills and knowledge. As she continues her education and professional journey, Anusha remains committed to exploring and contributing to the field of law, particularly in areas that intersect with criminal law and social justice.

Sudhir Kumar has academic experience of 17 years in the field of law, specializing in Constitutional Law and Criminal.In Administration, Dr. Kumar has extensive background in managing academic programs, curriculum development, and student affairs. Dr. Kumar has authored 35 research publications, including a significant publication in Scopus Indexed Journals. He has contributed to 5 book chapters, demonstrating expertise and contribution to legal scholarship. Dr. Kumar has successfully supervised 11 Ph.D students to completion, contributing to the advancement of legal education and research. He has a deep knowledge and experience in legal studies, with a focus on Legal Research Methodology, Law and Justice.

Nupur Kumari is working as an Assistant Professor in School of Law, Bennett University, Greater Noida. Having qualified UGC NET examination, she is currently pursuing PhD in law from Chanakya National Law University, Patna, India. She has completed her LLM in International Human Rights Laws from the prestigious National Law School of India University, Bangalore. She has her specialization in the areas of Human Rights Laws and International Refugee Laws.

Heeuk Dennis Lee is an Associate Professor in the Department of Criminal Justice at Weber State University, Ogden, USA. Dr. Lee completed both his MA and PhD in Criminology & Criminal Justice from Washington State University, Washington, USA. He teaches courses in Policing, Criminological theory, Criminal Justice Policy Analysis etc. His work has appeared in the Crime and Delinquency, Journal of Interpersonal Violence, Police Practice and Research, Victims & Offenders, Asian Journal of Criminology and International Journal of Police Science and Management. He is a member of the Academy of Criminal Justice Sciences, American Society of Criminology, Western Association of Criminal Justice, and Korean Society of Criminology in America. His areas of interest are Comparative policing, Citizens' perceptions of the police, and Community policing.

Aditya Lohani is currently pursuing his B.A.LL.B(H) at GLA University Mathura. During his studies, has shown a strong commitment to law. He's been busy with moot court competitions & trial advocacy, improving his legal skills and getting practical knowledge in arguments & courtroom procedures. These experiences have not only improved his legal knowledge but also enhanced his ability to work well under pressure. Apart from the above, he's also contributed to academic discussions through his research work. He has written many research papers and chapters in edited books.

Praveen Kumar Mall is working as Head of Department and Associate Professor at Teerthankar Mahaveer University, Moradabad, India. He is the author of book Hindu Law of Divorce. He has been awarded Doctorate Degree for his thesis in the area of "Critical Study of the concept of divorce under Hindu Law: A Socio-Legal Study from the Department of Law, University of Lucknow. Dr. Praveen has contributed immensely in formulation and introduction of B.A.LL.B., B.B.A.LL.B., B.Com.LL.B. and LL.M.. programmes of several Universities. Having long teaching and administrative experience, Dr. Praveen, besides contributing research articles in reputed law journals has also participated in several National and International conferences, seminars and workshops. He has also been very active in organizing Conference and Legal Literacy Camps, and has also adjudged various Moot Court Competitions. His areas of interest are Law of Contract, Family Law and Law of Criminal Procedure.

Deepika Pandoi has been associated with GLA University, since 2014 as a full – time research scholar. In November 2018, she has joined as Assistant Professor in Management Department in GLA University, Mathura. She has qualified UGC – NET & JRF exam and then completed her Ph.D. in Consumer Behaviour and Higher Education. She is good in both quantitative and qualitative analysis. She has used different modern tools and techniques of data analysis, like – SPSS, Smart PLS – 3.0, Amos – SEM, etc. She has good publications in National as well as in International Journals. She got Best Paper Award in the International Conference on Organizational and Management (ICOM) 2017 organized by College of Business, Abu Dhabi University in collaboration with Asia Academy of Management, held in Abu Dhabi, UAE during November 19 – 20, 2017.

Ishika Raghuvanshi is a 4th year B.A LL.B(H) student in GLA university. She is more dedicated and hardworking student she has many published of there chapters in many journal and books she also write many research papers

Aditya Raj is pursuing undergraduate program from GLA University, Mathura, India with keen interest in legal knowledge, spanning from criminal law to constitutional law and extracurricular activities including mooting and research related work. He aims to specialize further in litigation field and make contribution to society.

Govind Singh Rajpal is an eminent legal scholar and researcher. He postgraduated from the University of Bikaner with a Master of Laws (Mercantile Law) and a Postgraduate Diploma in Criminal Law. He then earned his Ph.D. from the University of Bikaner in 2011. For the past 13 years, he has been involved in academic administration and research. He is currently employed as a Professor at School of Law, MIT-ADT University, Pune. He supervises a number of Ph.D. research scholars, and 4 of them have already been awarded doctorates. He has more than 20 research papers published in national and international journals of repute. He has published a book on "Judicial Activism: A Step Towards Holistic Adjudication" and 4 Chapters in books, he has presented 18 Research papers National and International Conferences. Participated in orientation programme and attended various FDP.

Indra Kumar Singh serves as Associate Professor at Amity Law School, Amity University, Haryana, India. He holds a Ph.D. in Law from Shri Ramswaroop Memorial University, Lucknow, focusing on the impact of biodiversity laws in Gorakhpur. Dr. Singh is a distinguished academic with qualifications including UGC-NET, M.Phil., LL.M., and LL.B. His professional journey spans multiple institutions, including Shri Ram Swaroop Memorial University and Dr. Ram Manohar Lohiya National Law University, where he held roles such as Research Assistant and Assistant Proctor. Dr. Singh has contributed extensively to legal academia, supervising Ph.D. and LL.M. students, and publishing numerous research papers and book chapters on diverse legal topics like intellectual property rights, cyber law, and humanitarian law. He has presented papers at various national and international conferences and organized significant seminars and workshops. Dr. Singh has also been a guest lecturer and resource person at several universities and served as an external examiner and paper setter. His extracurricular achievements include representing Uttar Pradesh in national baseball championships and leading the Lucknow University Softball team. With a passion for continual learning and development, Dr. Singh is committed to contributing to the field of legal education and research.

Nikita Singh specializes in understanding the legal structure and theoretical framework. She has an internship experience in Criminal Law and Civil Law at the District and Sessions Court, Mathura, and also, writing Case Briefs under Sr. Adv. Pradeep Rai. Additionally, she has learnt the basics of drafting at Ashirwad

Law Chambers under Adv. Ankit Kishore. She has published two chapters and a case comment in the reputed international publications. Strong oral and written communication, creative writing and copy-editing skills are her strong points.

Pratibha Singh has completed her LL.M in IPR (Intellectual Property Rights) from RML National Law University, Lucknow, India. She has qualified UGC National Eligibility Test (NET) for Asst. Professor of Law. She is currently pursuing her Ph.D. from CMR University, Bengaluru on the topic "Implication of Intellectual Property Rights Regime on Agricultural Biodiversity: A study with reference to India". She has worked as Teaching Associate at RML National Law University, Lucknow, as Assistant Professor in Oxford Law College, Bengaluru and Bangalore Institute of Legal Studies, Bengaluru, India. She is currently working as Assistant Professor in B.M.S. College of Law Bengaluru, India. She has presented a number of papers in State, National Seminars and published papers in various Journals. Her areas of interest include IPR, Family Law, Transfer of Property and Law of Torts.

Somendra Ashok Singh is currently an undergraduate student pursuing B.A LL.B (Hons.) at Institute of Legal Studies and Research, GLA University, Mathura, India. He has been fortunate enough to have had a diverse range of experiences, from his research work (chapter) which has been published in the following books-: Sanitation- A sundry of impediments in the Indian Scheme and Marital Rape: The Crime Beyond Contours to his research paper on 'In between the State and Economy: A Reflection of Animal Trafficking' published by UPES University, Dehradun. As a highly motivated and dedicated individual, he has consistently demonstrated a strong work ethic and passion for excellence in all aspects of his life. With a keen interest in personal growth and development, he has continually sought out new challenges and opportunities to expand his skills and knowledge. As he continues his education and professional journey, Somendra remains committed to exploring and contributing to the field of law, particularly in areas that intersect with criminal law and social justice.

Aayushi Singh is a fifth-year student at Amity Law School, Noida, India. She wants to help people who haven't been given their fair chance in society. She has 5 publications to her name in books and reputed journals. These publications have provided invaluable insight into the civil rights, constitutional law, and humanitarian crises in today's world. She hopes that her philosophy and skill will lead to a greater sense of social equality. Her experience in litigation has brought attention to cases related to Human Rights violations and Public Interest Litigation filed by citizens.

Megha Singh is a student at Institute of Legal Studies and Research, GLA University. She is an active member of the university's exposition club. She has actively participated in various extra curriculum activities at university level. She has written an article that is published on lawvs.com and also attended various conferences and webinars which helped her to enhance her skills in the field of law. She aims to specialize in criminal law and aspire to join judicial services.

Aditya Tomer is Additional Director/ Joint HoI at Amity Law School, Noida (Amity University, Uttar Pradesh). His areas of research pertains to the Right to Information, Business law, Human Rights, comparative Law, etc . Dr. Tomer has published 18 books and contributed papers and chapters in an array of journals and edited volumes. He is the Editor-in-Chief of the Amity International Journal of Judicial Sciences and editor and rewier of many national and international indexed journals .He is a life member of All India Teachers Congress, Australian Arbitration center. Dr. Tomer's areas of specialization include Law of Contract, Arbitration and Conciliation comparative law, business law and Labour Laws.

Bhavana Kadu, a senior legal professional with diverse experience of teaching and mentoring who is regarded as a symbol of women's empowerment through her work. Presently, she is working with MIT Art Design and Technology University, Pune. Her notable contributions include serving as an invited guest lecturer at the Maharashtra Police Academy (MPA), Nasik, to teach on legal aspects to both trainee officers and experienced officers on specialized courses. Dr. Bhavana's work in promoting gender equality has been appreciated by both serving and former judges, including that of chief justice, while organizing national level symposiums during her tenure as Asso. Dean at the School of Law at Sandip University, Nashik, India. She holds a Masters and PhD in Law from SGB Amaravati University, Maharashtra, and her research interests span women and criminal law, intellectual property rights (IPR), and international law. Her scholarly contributions have been disseminated across various national and international journals and conferences, reflecting her dedication to legal research. Notably, she has supervised numerous masters' students and has served as a reviewer for two distinguished national journals. Presently, she is guiding six research scholars pursuing their PhD degrees under her mentorship. Prior to her academic role at Sandip University, Dr. Kadu served as an assistant professor at MATS University, Raipur, and also gained seven years of valuable experience as a senior legal associate in the IPR law firm.

Shweta Tyagi is a distinguished legal professional and astute businesswoman, possessing a unique blend of academic excellence and entrepreneurial acumen. Armed with an MBA, LLB, and Master of law in corporate banking and business law. she is a force to be reckoned with in the legal domain. Enrolled in the esteemed Delhi High Court, her legal expertise spans a wide spectrum of practice areas.

Beyond her legal practice, Advocate Tyagi is a visionary entrepreneur who has successfully established a thriving business consultancy. Her entrepreneurial journey has taken her beyond India's borders, with her business operations extending to the UAE and Singapore. This global perspective enriches her understanding of complex legal and business landscapes, making her an invaluable asset to clients seeking strategic guidance.

Raunak Upmanyu hails from the city of Lord Krishna—MATHURA, Raunak Upmanyu, is a bold and blunt personality with an enthusiastic experience in debates and regular discussions over political discourses. He believes in debating and writing, as the foremost part of his professional life. He is a keen observer of Indian politics and Geo Politics and a keen sense of different political ideologies and political spectrum. He has won trophies across various institutions. He is the student editor of the book "Marital Rape: Crime Beyond Contours" and has also authored many research papers on important political issues.

Index

A

AIDWA 27, 296, 297, 299, 309

B

Britain 115, 231, 232, 233, 234, 239, 241, 356, 422

C

Canada 55, 86, 127, 154, 191, 197, 217, 224, 231, 232, 233, 234, 236, 237, 244, 248, 275, 281, 289, 300, 330, 423, 424, 429, 430, 431

Casteism 161, 313, 317

Caste System 6, 21, 76, 80, 93, 106, 108, 140, 150, 156, 160, 201, 301, 303, 316, 317, 318, 323, 327, 328, 333, 339, 352

Challenges 1, 2, 16, 38, 57, 74, 144, 163, 203, 214, 216, 217, 221, 222, 223, 225, 226, 247, 248, 250, 251, 257, 258, 259, 260, 266, 270, 272, 274, 284, 286, 321, 322, 324, 329, 357

Clemency of Judges 167, 183

Community 2, 3, 4, 5, 7, 9, 15, 18, 19, 20, 21, 22, 23, 26, 27, 28, 29, 30, 36, 39, 40, 43, 46, 47, 48, 49, 55, 56, 60, 61, 65, 67, 68, 70, 73, 75, 81, 82, 83, 84, 85, 86, 87, 88, 96, 99, 103, 106, 107, 108, 117, 120, 121, 125, 126, 132, 133, 136, 138, 139, 151, 152, 153, 155, 159, 160, 161, 170, 194, 195, 196, 200, 202, 203, 206, 207, 217, 218, 219, 226, 227, 233, 235, 237, 239, 244, 245, 247, 248, 249, 250, 251, 252, 253, 254, 255, 256, 257, 260, 261, 262, 263, 264, 265, 266, 267, 268, 269, 270, 271, 272, 273, 280, 283, 288, 300, 305, 306, 307, 309, 314, 318, 319, 325, 327, 329, 332, 334, 335, 336, 339, 341, 342, 345, 347, 352, 354, 357, 358, 359, 360, 364, 366, 375, 379, 381, 384, 387, 391, 392, 393, 395, 398, 414, 415, 416, 417, 419, 425, 427, 428, 429

Community Engagement 247, 249, 251, 257, 268, 269, 272, 417

Constitutional Rights 126, 213, 214, 215, 217, 220, 222, 224, 225, 226, 227, 228, 229, 379

Crime 1, 2, 7, 8, 9, 10, 13, 14, 18, 26, 35, 36, 38, 43, 44, 46, 49, 51, 54, 60, 63, 66, 74, 76, 78, 79, 82, 83, 84, 85, 87, 91, 97, 98, 99, 101, 103, 104, 110, 113, 117, 118, 119, 121, 122, 125, 127, 130, 131, 132, 133, 134, 139, 140, 141, 142, 143, 144, 148, 149, 150, 151, 156, 157, 158, 159, 160, 161, 162, 166, 167, 168, 169, 171, 172, 173, 175, 176, 177, 178, 179, 180, 182, 183, 184, 185, 186, 187, 188, 189, 191, 193, 194, 195, 209, 212, 214, 216, 220, 226, 230, 231, 232, 234, 236, 237, 243, 245, 251, 267, 277, 278, 285, 287, 288, 292, 294, 295, 296, 297, 298, 299, 301, 303, 305, 306, 307, 308, 309, 312, 314, 315, 316, 319, 322, 324, 329, 331, 332, 336, 337, 339, 347, 349, 351, 353, 357, 361, 362, 364, 373, 378, 384, 386, 392, 393, 394, 395, 396, 397, 398, 406, 418, 420, 421, 424, 429, 431

Cultural 2, 3, 4, 13, 15, 22, 27, 37, 39, 40, 53, 55, 57, 62, 64, 65, 66, 67, 70, 74, 75, 76, 77, 85, 86, 88, 89, 93, 94, 95, 96, 100, 102, 103, 105, 106, 108, 109, 111, 119, 121, 122, 125, 127, 130, 132, 133, 135, 142, 148, 149, 150, 151, 152, 153, 154, 159, 167, 169, 170, 175, 190, 194, 195, 196, 197, 198, 199, 200, 201, 202, 203, 204, 208, 209, 210, 211, 213, 214, 215, 216, 217, 218, 219, 220, 221, 222, 223, 224, 225, 226, 227, 228, 232, 233, 234, 235, 238, 243, 244, 245, 246, 247, 248, 249, 250, 251, 253, 254, 256, 257, 258, 259, 260, 261, 262, 263, 264, 265, 266, 268, 270, 271,

272, 273, 280, 281, 282, 284, 288, 289, 290, 291, 292, 298, 315, 316, 317, 318, 319, 320, 323, 325, 326, 327, 328, 330, 331, 332, 333, 334, 335, 339, 342, 343, 345, 346, 348, 351, 353, 354, 355, 356, 357, 361, 362, 363, 365, 367, 369, 370, 371, 372, 373, 374, 375, 376, 377, 378, 380, 392, 393, 394, 395, 396, 399, 401, 408, 413, 414, 415, 416, 417, 418, 419, 421, 425, 427, 428, 430, 431

Cultural Beliefs 198, 208, 216, 223, 224, 226, 232, 332

Cultural Norms 27, 39, 66, 77, 102, 121, 153, 167, 194, 195, 196, 197, 202, 204, 213, 214, 216, 217, 219, 220, 221, 222, 223, 224, 225, 227, 244, 247, 249, 253, 256, 257, 258, 261, 263, 271, 284, 290, 317, 328, 332, 335, 354, 355, 363, 369, 370, 375, 376, 377, 393, 413, 415, 418

Culture 8, 9, 12, 14, 27, 28, 36, 40, 41, 45, 49, 54, 55, 57, 58, 59, 60, 68, 82, 84, 93, 94, 95, 97, 98, 99, 101, 102, 103, 105, 107, 109, 110, 111, 119, 121, 123, 133, 143, 144, 147, 148, 161, 162, 163, 170, 190, 195, 199, 200, 201, 224, 227, 233, 234, 235, 236, 237, 238, 239, 240, 243, 244, 245, 246, 257, 259, 277, 278, 280, 283, 284, 302, 309, 311, 316, 330, 331, 336, 337, 344, 352, 356, 360, 361, 362, 367, 371, 375, 381, 383, 384, 388, 397, 405, 406, 408, 415, 422, 426, 428

D

Dignity 8, 9, 50, 55, 56, 61, 63, 64, 76, 80, 81, 88, 101, 109, 118, 121, 123, 126, 129, 130, 131, 132, 134, 136, 137, 138, 141, 147, 148, 149, 151, 152, 153, 155, 159, 162, 199, 202, 207, 208, 211, 214, 220, 221, 224, 225, 226, 233, 237, 244, 249, 250, 253, 255, 257, 262, 268, 272, 284, 300, 329, 331, 346, 352, 355, 372, 392, 401, 408, 414, 416, 426

Discrimination Against Women 2, 3, 12, 13, 16, 36, 64, 89, 118, 119, 122, 218, 223, 224, 229, 251, 291, 371, 382, 391, 392, 393, 394, 395, 396, 400, 402, 409, 410, 411

Dishonored Actions 295, 296

E

Education 4, 10, 32, 38, 44, 45, 46, 49, 56, 65, 68, 71, 80, 82, 86, 87, 97, 103, 108, 160, 198, 203, 204, 208, 211, 216, 227, 244, 245, 247, 249, 250, 253, 256, 257, 258, 260, 261, 262, 264, 265, 268, 269, 271, 272, 273, 282, 284, 315, 317, 318, 320, 325, 326, 327, 329, 334, 343, 355, 356, 363, 373, 375, 381, 393, 402, 414, 417, 419

Effective Measures 148, 150, 324

Egyptian Penal Code 165, 166, 167, 170, 171, 173, 176, 177, 178, 183, 184, 186, 188, 189

Experienced 6, 61, 119, 121, 168, 189, 206, 341, 363, 369, 370, 408, 414, 424

F

Family 1, 2, 3, 4, 5, 6, 7, 8, 9, 11, 12, 17, 18, 24, 25, 26, 31, 35, 36, 37, 38, 39, 40, 42, 43, 44, 45, 46, 47, 48, 50, 51, 52, 53, 55, 58, 60, 61, 62, 63, 65, 66, 68, 73, 75, 76, 78, 79, 80, 81, 82, 83, 84, 85, 86, 87, 89, 90, 94, 95, 96, 97, 98, 99, 100, 102, 103, 105, 106, 107, 109, 114, 116, 117, 119, 120, 121, 124, 125, 127, 128, 129, 131, 132, 133, 135, 136, 137, 138, 142, 143, 144, 147, 148, 150, 151, 152, 153, 154, 155, 158, 159, 162, 166, 167, 168, 170, 174, 175, 177, 178, 191, 193, 194, 199, 200, 201, 202, 203, 204, 205, 206, 207, 208, 210, 211, 214, 215, 217, 218, 219, 220, 222, 223, 227, 231, 232, 233, 234, 235, 236, 237, 238, 239, 240, 242, 243, 244, 246, 248, 249, 250, 251, 252,

253, 254, 257, 260, 262, 266, 267, 270, 280, 282, 283, 287, 291, 293, 295, 296, 299, 300, 301, 302, 303, 304, 305, 306, 307, 308, 309, 311, 312, 313, 314, 318, 319, 320, 321, 322, 325, 327, 331, 332, 334, 335, 336, 337, 338, 341, 342, 343, 344, 345, 346, 351, 352, 354, 355, 356, 357, 358, 359, 360, 361, 364, 366, 371, 372, 373, 374, 375, 377, 379, 381, 383, 384, 385, 386, 387, 391, 392, 395, 397, 398, 399, 400, 402, 403, 404, 405, 411, 417, 418, 419, 420, 421, 422, 423, 424, 425, 427, 428, 430

Family Honor 6, 7, 25, 35, 36, 39, 42, 52, 58, 63, 147, 148, 152, 191, 194, 201, 202, 203, 215, 219, 222, 223, 236, 238, 239, 244, 248, 249, 250, 252, 257, 291, 314, 319, 327, 332, 341, 344, 346, 351, 354, 355, 361, 372, 395, 398, 400, 428, 430

Family Honour 1, 75, 84, 86, 87, 96, 98, 210, 243

G

Gender Based Violence 115, 131, 315
Gender-Based Violence 12, 16, 29, 38, 64, 67, 68, 77, 95, 118, 119, 120, 149, 154, 196, 209, 210, 214, 215, 216, 218, 223, 234, 236, 245, 282, 318, 393, 394, 395, 396, 403, 404, 413, 415, 416

Gender Differences 15, 57, 70, 329, 348
Gender Equality 1, 2, 31, 36, 38, 56, 62, 66, 67, 118, 120, 122, 151, 197, 203, 204, 217, 233, 242, 249, 250, 253, 254, 256, 257, 258, 261, 262, 263, 264, 265, 268, 269, 271, 272, 318, 320, 392, 399, 401, 402, 406, 409, 414, 415, 426

Gender Norms 1, 6, 75, 197, 201, 208, 264, 351, 357

Germany 37, 58, 74, 86, 87, 191, 217, 231, 232, 233, 234, 236, 239, 356, 373, 389

Global 2, 4, 6, 10, 15, 50, 62, 65, 74, 86, 91, 114, 115, 118, 119, 120, 122, 124, 130, 131, 132, 149, 154, 173, 190, 197, 198, 199, 201, 212, 213, 215, 216, 217, 220, 221, 230, 231, 247, 256, 257, 259, 265, 270, 271, 272, 280, 284, 286, 295, 296, 326, 330, 332, 354, 361, 364, 365, 366, 393, 395, 396, 397, 398, 399, 400, 415

H

Honor 1, 2, 3, 4, 5, 6, 7, 8, 9, 10, 11, 12, 13, 14, 15, 16, 17, 18, 20, 21, 24, 25, 26, 27, 28, 29, 30, 31, 33, 35, 36, 37, 38, 39, 40, 41, 42, 43, 44, 46, 47, 48, 49, 50, 51, 52, 53, 54, 55, 56, 57, 58, 59, 60, 61, 62, 63, 64, 65, 66, 67, 68, 69, 70, 71, 78, 83, 87, 90, 93, 95, 110, 113, 114, 115, 116, 117, 118, 119, 120, 121, 122, 123, 124, 125, 126, 127, 129, 130, 131, 132, 133, 134, 135, 136, 137, 138, 139, 140, 141, 142, 143, 144, 145, 147, 148, 149, 150, 151, 152, 153, 154, 155, 156, 157, 158, 159, 160, 161, 162, 163, 164, 165, 166, 167, 168, 169, 170, 171, 172, 173, 174, 175, 176, 177, 178, 185, 186, 187, 188, 189, 190, 191, 192, 193, 194, 195, 196, 197, 198, 199, 200, 201, 202, 203, 204, 208, 210, 211, 212, 213, 214, 215, 216, 217, 218, 219, 220, 221, 222, 223, 224, 225, 226, 227, 228, 229, 231, 232, 233, 234, 235, 236, 237, 238, 239, 240, 241, 242, 243, 244, 245, 246, 247, 248, 249, 250, 251, 252, 253, 254, 255, 256, 257, 258, 259, 260, 261, 262, 263, 264, 265, 266, 267, 268, 269, 270, 271, 272, 273, 274, 275, 277, 278, 279, 280, 281, 282, 283, 284, 285, 286, 287, 288, 289, 290, 291, 292, 293, 295, 296, 297, 298, 299, 300, 301, 302, 303, 304, 305, 306, 307, 308, 309, 313, 314, 315, 316, 317, 318, 319, 320, 321, 322, 323, 324, 325, 326, 327, 328, 329, 330, 331, 332, 333, 334, 335, 336, 337, 338, 339, 340, 341, 342, 343, 344, 345, 346, 347,

348, 349, 351, 352, 353, 354, 355, 356, 357, 358, 359, 360, 361, 362, 364, 365, 366, 367, 369, 370, 371, 372, 373, 374, 375, 376, 377, 378, 379, 380, 381, 385, 386, 387, 388, 389, 391, 392, 393, 394, 395, 396, 397, 398, 399, 400, 404, 405, 406, 407, 408, 409, 413, 414, 415, 416, 417, 418, 419, 420, 422, 423, 424, 425, 427, 428, 429, 430, 431

Honor Killing 3, 4, 6, 9, 11, 15, 17, 18, 20, 24, 25, 26, 28, 29, 30, 31, 35, 36, 37, 38, 40, 41, 42, 43, 44, 47, 48, 49, 51, 55, 56, 58, 60, 61, 62, 63, 64, 65, 67, 68, 69, 70, 71, 78, 90, 93, 95, 110, 113, 114, 115, 116, 117, 118, 121, 124, 125, 127, 129, 130, 131, 132, 133, 134, 135, 136, 137, 138, 139, 140, 141, 142, 143, 147, 148, 149, 150, 151, 155, 157, 159, 161, 162, 163, 164, 165, 166, 167, 168, 169, 170, 171, 172, 174, 177, 186, 188, 191, 195, 200, 202, 210, 212, 215, 217, 218, 219, 231, 232, 233, 234, 235, 236, 237, 239, 240, 241, 243, 244, 245, 246, 247, 249, 250, 251, 260, 266, 275, 277, 278, 279, 280, 282, 283, 284, 285, 286, 287, 288, 289, 291, 295, 296, 297, 298, 299, 300, 301, 304, 305, 306, 307, 308, 309, 313, 314, 315, 316, 317, 319, 320, 322, 323, 324, 325, 327, 329, 330, 331, 332, 333, 334, 335, 336, 337, 338, 339, 340, 341, 342, 343, 344, 345, 346, 347, 348, 349, 351, 352, 353, 354, 355, 356, 357, 358, 359, 360, 361, 362, 364, 365, 366, 369, 370, 371, 372, 373, 374, 375, 376, 377, 378, 386, 387, 388, 389, 391, 392, 393, 394, 395, 396, 397, 398, 399, 400, 407, 408, 415, 418, 420, 424, 429, 431

Human Rights 1, 2, 3, 10, 16, 19, 29, 31, 38, 46, 51, 53, 54, 55, 56, 62, 63, 64, 65, 66, 69, 74, 75, 76, 78, 79, 80, 84, 85, 86, 89, 91, 96, 102, 114, 115, 117, 119, 120, 121, 122, 123, 124, 125, 126, 127, 128, 129, 130, 132, 133, 134, 135, 136, 137, 140, 141, 144, 145, 148, 149, 150, 151, 152, 153, 157, 168, 172, 193, 194, 196, 197, 198, 199, 202, 203, 210, 211, 213, 214, 215, 216, 217, 218, 219, 220, 221, 222, 223, 224, 225, 226, 227, 228, 229, 230, 231, 239, 248, 250, 251, 253, 255, 258, 259, 261, 262, 263, 264, 268, 269, 270, 271, 272, 278, 279, 280, 281, 282, 293, 308, 322, 326, 337, 340, 342, 348, 349, 353, 364, 366, 370, 371, 372, 374, 378, 381, 388, 389, 392, 393, 394, 395, 396, 398, 399, 400, 404, 406, 409, 413, 414, 415, 416, 418, 428

Human Rights Watch 76, 78, 86, 114, 115, 121, 122, 125, 127, 217, 282, 337, 353, 366

I

Immigration 90, 231, 232, 233, 234, 235, 236, 237, 238, 239, 240, 241, 243, 244, 245, 246, 398, 423

Indian Society 39, 80, 81, 90, 94, 95, 156, 157, 161, 251, 285, 318, 319, 321, 335, 339, 341

Inter-Caste 2, 5, 7, 18, 20, 21, 22, 24, 26, 30, 31, 37, 75, 76, 78, 79, 80, 81, 91, 93, 97, 100, 101, 106, 108, 156, 300, 302, 303, 304, 313, 315, 321, 322, 323, 327, 328, 335, 339, 352

Inter-Caste Marriage 18, 26, 30, 75, 78, 79, 81, 302, 303, 304, 313, 321, 339

Inter- Caste Marriages 315, 321

International Law 3, 13, 54, 122, 124, 129, 130, 145, 214, 329, 379, 391, 393, 394, 397, 399

Intra-Village 18, 22

Islamic 9, 11, 15, 36, 55, 61, 70, 83, 115, 135, 166, 170, 177, 241, 255, 256, 318, 369, 370, 371, 372, 373, 376, 377, 380, 383, 389, 426

J

Judicial Leniency 186
Judicial Systems 77, 154, 201
Justice 2, 3, 8, 17, 18, 22, 28, 30, 48, 52, 53, 54, 55, 56, 63, 66, 68, 70, 80, 82, 88, 110, 115, 125, 127, 135, 137, 138, 140, 141, 142, 144, 151, 156, 157, 160, 163, 176, 185, 186, 191, 193, 194, 196, 200, 203, 209, 210, 211, 212, 215, 221, 222, 224, 225, 227, 235, 248, 253, 255, 262, 264, 269, 272, 280, 281, 284, 287, 290, 292, 324, 326, 327, 328, 336, 339, 345, 348, 356, 363, 384, 385, 386, 388, 394, 399, 404, 406, 429

K

Kangaroo Courts 17, 19, 26, 27, 29, 30, 31, 48, 141
Khap Panchayat 19, 20, 22, 23, 24, 26, 27, 29, 30, 32, 40, 48, 75, 81, 82, 95, 100, 140, 141, 150, 156, 158, 159, 200, 297, 304, 305, 308, 311, 315, 323, 324, 333, 335, 339
Khap Panchayats 12, 17, 18, 19, 20, 21, 22, 23, 24, 25, 26, 27, 28, 29, 30, 31, 32, 33, 48, 49, 75, 76, 79, 81, 84, 93, 94, 100, 101, 110, 153, 155, 156, 160, 161, 194, 198, 200, 201, 298, 304, 305, 306, 307, 309, 315, 335, 339
Killing 3, 4, 6, 8, 9, 11, 15, 17, 18, 20, 22, 24, 25, 26, 28, 29, 30, 31, 32, 33, 35, 36, 37, 38, 40, 41, 42, 43, 44, 46, 47, 48, 49, 51, 52, 54, 55, 56, 58, 60, 61, 62, 63, 64, 65, 67, 68, 69, 70, 71, 73, 74, 75, 76, 77, 78, 79, 80, 81, 82, 83, 84, 85, 86, 87, 88, 89, 90, 91, 93, 94, 95, 96, 97, 99, 100, 101, 102, 103, 106, 108, 109, 110, 111, 113, 114, 115, 116, 117, 118, 121, 124, 125, 127, 129, 130, 131, 132, 133, 134, 135, 136, 137, 138, 139, 140, 141, 142, 143, 144, 147, 148, 149, 150, 151, 155, 157, 159, 161, 162, 163, 164, 165, 166, 167, 168, 169, 170, 171, 172, 173, 174, 176, 177, 179, 181, 182, 183, 186, 188, 189, 190, 191, 195, 196, 200, 202, 204, 205, 209, 210, 212, 215, 217, 218, 219, 229, 230, 231, 232, 233, 234, 235, 236, 237, 238, 239, 240, 241, 242, 243, 244, 245, 246, 247, 249, 250, 251, 260, 266, 274, 275, 277, 278, 279, 280, 281, 282, 283, 284, 285, 286, 287, 288, 289, 291, 293, 295, 296, 297, 298, 299, 300, 301, 304, 305, 306, 307, 308, 309, 311, 312, 313, 314, 315, 316, 317, 319, 320, 322, 323, 324, 325, 327, 329, 330, 331, 332, 333, 334, 335, 336, 337, 338, 339, 340, 341, 342, 343, 344, 345, 346, 347, 348, 349, 351, 352, 353, 354, 355, 356, 357, 358, 359, 360, 361, 362, 363, 364, 365, 366, 367, 369, 370, 371, 372, 373, 374, 375, 376, 377, 378, 385, 386, 387, 388, 389, 391, 392, 393, 394, 395, 396, 397, 398, 399, 400, 407, 408, 409, 414, 415, 416, 418, 419, 420, 421, 422, 423, 424, 425, 427, 429, 430, 431

L

Lack of Education 82, 203, 282, 318, 320, 381
Legal Impunity 194, 196
Legal Reforms 151, 196, 203, 211, 247, 249, 250, 254, 255, 257, 260, 261, 267, 268, 269, 271, 272, 273, 279, 282

M

Marriage and Family 12
Mass Media 278, 283, 345
Media Activism 281, 285, 287
Media Framing 279
Misogynist Approach 25
Multiculturalism 223, 367, 413, 416, 418, 419, 427, 428
Murder 4, 5, 6, 7, 8, 9, 10, 11, 12, 14, 17, 24, 25, 27, 29, 36, 38, 40, 41, 44, 47, 48, 52, 55, 56, 61, 68, 73, 75, 76, 78,

80, 85, 86, 88, 89, 94, 96, 97, 98, 100, 109, 115, 135, 139, 141, 144, 145, 147, 148, 150, 153, 155, 157, 159, 160, 165, 166, 167, 170, 171, 172, 173, 175, 177, 178, 179, 181, 182, 183, 185, 188, 189, 202, 203, 207, 209, 210, 211, 215, 217, 218, 219, 227, 232, 234, 237, 238, 239, 240, 241, 242, 244, 249, 250, 252, 267, 278, 282, 283, 285, 291, 303, 304, 306, 307, 308, 309, 310, 314, 317, 329, 331, 335, 336, 338, 339, 346, 347, 352, 360, 361, 363, 364, 366, 368, 372, 373, 375, 377, 378, 379, 384, 385, 386, 387, 389, 391, 392, 398, 399, 408, 420, 421, 422, 423, 424, 425, 426, 427, 430, 431

N

Netherlands 70, 231, 232, 233, 234, 236, 242, 244
News Coverage 246, 281
North-Western States 25, 26, 28

P

Patriarchal 1, 2, 3, 4, 6, 12, 17, 18, 24, 25, 26, 30, 31, 35, 36, 37, 38, 39, 40, 52, 55, 61, 62, 63, 67, 75, 81, 82, 84, 90, 99, 107, 115, 123, 125, 150, 151, 152, 154, 163, 170, 194, 196, 197, 200, 201, 202, 210, 211, 218, 239, 241, 249, 252, 256, 262, 272, 283, 290, 291, 297, 301, 313, 316, 318, 319, 320, 321, 333, 337, 338, 341, 342, 352, 354, 381, 382, 387, 392, 393, 404, 418, 419, 422, 428
Patriarchal Mentality 313
Patriarchal Mindset 25, 81, 338
Patriarchal Society 39, 75, 81, 150, 297, 301
Patriarchal Systems 249, 252
Patriarchy 15, 26, 35, 36, 37, 40, 51, 96, 116, 196, 201, 245, 299, 315, 316, 321, 333, 339, 342, 344, 355, 361, 362, 366, 387, 388, 396
Peacemakers 247, 248, 249, 250, 251, 253, 256, 257, 258, 259, 262, 263, 264, 265, 267, 268, 269, 270, 272, 273
Political Rights 137, 172, 226, 227, 229, 393
Politics 10, 18, 19, 22, 27, 32, 46, 51, 59, 61, 235, 348, 366, 382, 430
Psychology 77, 78, 93, 95, 96, 98, 110, 212, 356, 366, 367, 368
Public opinion 277, 278, 280, 281, 283, 290, 291, 372, 416

R

Racism 154, 413, 415, 416, 418, 428, 429
Religious Issues 313
Religious Leaders 247, 248, 249, 250, 253, 254, 255, 256, 258, 265, 320
Respect 8, 9, 11, 13, 36, 45, 47, 48, 50, 53, 59, 60, 61, 68, 78, 80, 86, 87, 98, 108, 113, 115, 132, 134, 141, 142, 151, 159, 197, 203, 210, 211, 218, 221, 227, 235, 249, 254, 256, 257, 262, 264, 268, 285, 300, 303, 309, 324, 325, 336, 339, 340, 345, 359, 374, 387, 398, 400, 401, 402, 424, 428

S

Sagotra 27, 50
Shame Killing 167, 325, 336
Social and Cultural Norms 224, 328, 335
Social Aspects 95, 103, 132, 354, 357
Social Consequences 204, 261
Social Media 96, 230, 278, 282, 286
Social Pressure 25, 193, 194, 202, 227, 361, 376
Society 2, 5, 6, 7, 8, 9, 10, 13, 14, 17, 21, 22, 24, 26, 28, 31, 36, 39, 40, 41, 42, 43, 44, 49, 50, 51, 56, 57, 58, 60, 62, 63, 67, 73, 75, 76, 78, 80, 81, 82, 83, 87, 88, 90, 93, 94, 95, 96, 98, 99, 100, 101, 102, 103, 104, 105, 106, 107, 108, 109, 110, 114, 116, 117, 121, 122, 124, 126, 127, 131, 133, 136, 137, 138, 139, 142, 147, 148, 149, 150, 151, 152, 155, 156, 157, 160, 161, 167, 179, 193, 194, 195, 196, 198, 201, 202, 204, 205, 206, 207,

208, 211, 216, 218, 219, 220, 222, 223, 224, 225, 226, 227, 232, 233, 235, 237, 238, 239, 240, 241, 243, 244, 246, 250, 251, 252, 255, 262, 265, 272, 273, 277, 278, 280, 283, 285, 289, 291, 293, 297, 298, 299, 300, 301, 302, 303, 304, 305, 306, 307, 308, 310, 311, 313, 315, 317, 318, 319, 320, 321, 322, 325, 326, 327, 328, 332, 334, 335, 336, 337, 339, 340, 341, 342, 343, 344, 345, 346, 347, 352, 354, 357, 359, 360, 364, 366, 367, 371, 372, 373, 376, 379, 380, 382, 383, 384, 385, 387, 391, 392, 393, 394, 395, 396, 397, 398, 399, 404, 405, 406, 407, 409, 417, 418, 419, 427
Sweden 37, 62, 197, 222, 224, 231, 232, 233, 234, 235, 237, 238, 243, 246

T

Theory 65, 104, 105, 220, 225, 229, 340, 341, 342, 343, 344, 345, 346, 348, 366, 382
Tradition 4, 29, 51, 78, 86, 91, 99, 102, 123, 127, 128, 137, 140, 157, 160, 200, 217, 218, 225, 245, 248, 257, 283, 293, 295, 299, 302, 304, 305, 309, 310, 312, 340, 341, 360, 371, 388, 430
Trial by Media 281, 287
Triggers 77, 150, 296, 297, 298, 299, 301, 302, 303, 358

U

UK 12, 51, 74, 87, 154, 190, 197, 234, 240, 244, 246, 248, 274, 278, 281, 289, 293, 333, 349, 366, 367, 413, 414, 415, 416, 417, 418, 419, 420, 422, 427, 428, 429, 430, 431
UNFPA 35, 37, 52, 120, 154, 282, 367
UNGA 392, 394, 405
United Nations 2, 10, 37, 69, 86, 89, 114, 117, 118, 119, 120, 122, 128, 168, 190, 214, 220, 223, 226, 230, 257, 278, 282, 339, 352, 356, 367, 373, 391, 394, 395, 396, 397, 399, 400, 406, 409, 410, 411
United States 15, 70, 144, 231, 232, 233, 236, 241, 246, 266, 288, 420
US 49, 90, 98, 104, 127, 179, 206, 211, 216, 219, 226, 227, 238, 241, 248, 274, 283, 288, 322, 325, 326, 341, 358, 364, 409, 413, 414, 415, 416, 417, 420, 431

V

Village 8, 18, 19, 21, 22, 23, 24, 25, 27, 28, 29, 30, 41, 42, 122, 302, 304, 305, 323, 326, 386
Violence 1, 2, 3, 4, 5, 6, 7, 8, 9, 11, 12, 13, 14, 15, 16, 20, 21, 24, 25, 27, 29, 35, 38, 39, 40, 41, 42, 43, 44, 46, 47, 50, 51, 52, 53, 54, 55, 56, 60, 61, 62, 63, 64, 65, 67, 68, 70, 71, 75, 77, 81, 82, 83, 85, 86, 88, 89, 90, 91, 93, 94, 95, 96, 99, 103, 108, 109, 110, 113, 115, 116, 117, 118, 119, 120, 121, 122, 123, 125, 126, 127, 128, 130, 131, 132, 133, 136, 139, 144, 145, 149, 153, 154, 155, 157, 159, 160, 163, 165, 167, 171, 188, 190, 191, 194, 196, 197, 198, 200, 201, 202, 203, 204, 207, 208, 209, 210, 211, 214, 215, 216, 218, 219, 221, 223, 224, 227, 232, 233, 234, 235, 236, 238, 239, 240, 242, 243, 244, 245, 246, 247, 248, 249, 250, 251, 253, 254, 255, 256, 257, 258, 259, 260, 261, 262, 263, 264, 265, 266, 267, 268, 269, 270, 271, 272, 273, 274, 275, 277, 278, 280, 281, 282, 285, 286, 288, 289, 291, 292, 296, 297, 298, 301, 302, 303, 308, 309, 314, 315, 316, 318, 319, 320, 322, 327, 328, 329, 330, 332, 333, 335, 337, 348, 352, 354, 355, 356, 357, 359, 360, 361, 362, 363, 364, 365, 366, 367, 368, 369, 370, 372, 373, 375, 377, 388, 389, 391, 392, 393, 394, 395, 396, 397, 398, 399, 400, 403, 404, 405, 406, 407, 408, 410, 413, 414,

483

415, 416, 417, 418, 419, 420, 422, 427, 428, 429, 430, 431
Violence Against Women 8, 13, 14, 15, 16, 38, 44, 47, 50, 56, 62, 64, 65, 67, 70, 81, 85, 88, 96, 110, 113, 118, 119, 120, 121, 122, 123, 128, 144, 145, 154, 159, 160, 165, 167, 171, 188, 191, 196, 197, 200, 201, 203, 215, 216, 223, 224, 234, 235, 242, 243, 246, 251, 257, 282, 291, 292, 318, 319, 320, 330, 333, 335, 355, 356, 364, 366, 372, 375, 388, 389, 393, 396, 398, 400, 404, 406, 407, 410, 413, 417, 420, 427, 431
Vulnerable 39, 42, 88, 106, 139, 155, 208, 219, 225, 254, 267, 318, 369, 370, 378, 382, 418

W

Woman 4, 5, 6, 8, 9, 10, 11, 18, 25, 27, 35, 39, 41, 42, 43, 46, 47, 52, 53, 58, 60, 65, 66, 73, 78, 81, 82, 83, 84, 85, 88, 89, 90, 94, 95, 98, 99, 106, 107, 115, 116, 117, 118, 121, 124, 125, 152, 155, 157, 161, 167, 169, 170, 177, 178, 179, 200, 210, 214, 217, 234, 239, 250, 266, 274, 282, 288, 334, 337, 344, 347, 357, 360, 375, 376, 377, 378, 381, 382, 384, 385, 386, 395, 399, 417, 419, 422, 427
Women 1, 2, 3, 4, 5, 6, 7, 8, 9, 10, 11, 12, 13, 14, 15, 16, 17, 20, 21, 24, 25, 26, 27, 28, 29, 30, 31, 32, 35, 36, 37, 38, 39, 40, 41, 42, 43, 44, 45, 46, 47, 48, 49, 50, 51, 52, 53, 54, 55, 56, 57, 58, 60, 61, 62, 63, 64, 65, 66, 67, 68, 69, 70, 73, 74, 75, 76, 78, 79, 80, 81, 82, 83, 84, 85, 86, 87, 88, 89, 90, 96, 97, 99, 101, 105, 106, 107, 108, 110, 113, 114, 115, 116, 117, 118, 119, 120, 121, 122, 123, 124, 125, 126, 127, 128, 129, 130, 132, 133, 134, 136, 139, 141, 142, 143, 144, 145, 152, 154, 155, 157, 159, 160, 161, 162, 163, 165, 167, 171, 174, 188, 190, 191, 194, 196, 197, 199, 200, 201, 203, 207, 214, 215, 216, 217, 218, 219, 220, 222, 223, 224, 229, 230, 232, 233, 234, 235, 237, 238, 239, 241, 242, 243, 244, 245, 246, 249, 250, 251, 252, 257, 258, 262, 264, 267, 268, 270, 271, 272, 277, 278, 281, 282, 283, 285, 286, 289, 291, 292, 293, 296, 297, 298, 299, 300, 301, 303, 304, 308, 309, 312, 316, 318, 319, 320, 321, 324, 325, 326, 327, 330, 331, 333, 334, 335, 336, 337, 338, 339, 341, 342, 343, 344, 346, 348, 351, 352, 353, 355, 356, 360, 361, 362, 364, 365, 366, 367, 369, 370, 371, 372, 373, 374, 375, 376, 377, 378, 379, 380, 381, 382, 383, 384, 386, 387, 388, 389, 391, 392, 393, 394, 395, 396, 397, 398, 399, 400, 401, 402, 403, 404, 405, 406, 407, 408, 409, 410, 411, 413, 414, 415, 416, 417, 418, 419, 420, 422, 423, 424, 425, 426, 427, 428, 430, 431